The Act of Teaching

Second Edition

DONALD R. CRUICKSHANK

The Ohio State University

DEBORAH L. BAINER

The Ohio State University

KIM K. METCALF

Indiana University

 McGraw-Hill College

Boston   Burr Ridge, IL   Dubuque, IA   Madison, WI   New York   San Francisco   St. Louis
Bangkok   Bogotá   Caracas   Lisbon   London   Madrid
Mexico City   Milan   New Delhi   Seoul   Singapore   Sydney   Taipei   Toronto

McGraw-Hill College

A Division of The McGraw·Hill Companies

THE ACT OF TEACHING, SECOND EDITION

 This book is printed on recylced, acid-free paper containing 10% postconsumer waste.

3 4 5 6 7 8 9 0 QPD/QPD 3 2 1 0

ISBN 0–07–000789–6

Editorial director: *Jane E. Vaicunas*
Sponsoring editor: *Beth Kaufman*
Marketing manager: *Daniel M. Loch*
Project manager: *Susan J. Brusch*
Senior production supervisor: *Mary E. Haas*
Coordinator of freelance design: *Michelle D. Whitaker*
Senior photo research coordinator: *Carrie K. Burger*
Art editor: *Joyce Watters*
Supplement coordinator: *Tammy Juran*
Compositor: *Shepherd, Inc.*
Typeface: *10/12 New Baskerville*
Printer: *Quebecor Printing Book Group/Dubuque, IA*

Freelance interior/cover designer: *Maureen McCutcheon*
Cover images: *Top: © Tom & DeeAnn McCarthy/The Stock Market:*
Bottom: © Jeff Heger Photography

The credits section for this book begins on page 467 and is considered an extension of the copyright page.

Library of Congress Cataloging-in-Publication Data

Cruickshank, Donald R.
    The act of teaching / Donald R. Cruickshank, Deborah L. Bainer,
Kim K. Metcalf. — 2nd ed.
      p.   cm.
    Includes bibliographical references and indexes.
    ISBN 0–07–000789–6
    1. Teaching. 2. Lesson planning.   I. Bainer, Deborah L.
II. Metcalf, Kim K.   III. Title.
LB1025.3.C78   1999
371.102—dc21
                                                    98–6768
                                                    CIP

www.mhhe.com

About the Authors

Donald R. Cruickshank

Donald R. Cruickshank received his degrees from the State University College at Buffalo, N.Y., and the University of Rochester. After stints as a teacher, supervisor, and principal in the Rochester schools, he began a college teaching and administrative career that took him to SUNY Brockport, the University of Tennessee, Wheelock College, and The Ohio State University. Professor Cruickshank has been the recipient of Fulbright-Hayes senior scholar awards to Australia and Brazil and has taught and lectured in Australia, Brazil, Canada, England, Scotland, Thailand, and Wales as well as throughout the United States and Puerto Rico. He has authored over 100 chapters, articles, and encyclopedia entries, and this is his eighth book. He is best known for his pioneering efforts in developing simulations and reflective teaching and his research on teacher clarity. His graduate students have won seven outstanding dissertation awards and have fashioned accomplished careers in teaching, scholarship, service, and administration.

Deborah L. Bainer

Deborah L. Bainer is an associate professor of education at The Ohio State University, Mansfield campus, where she coordinates the teacher preparation programs. She received her B.S. in biology from Geneva College and her M.S. in environmental education and Ph.D. in Teacher Education from The Ohio State University. She taught middle school and high school science in the United States and in Asia and formerly chaired the education department at Biola University. Currently, her teaching responsibilities involve general pedagogy, supervision, and science and social studies methods. Dr. Bainer works extensively with school-based partnership programs aimed at enhancing science instruction. She has authored numerous articles and book chapters reflecting her research in teachers' professional development through partnerships, and effective multicultural instruction. She was awarded the distinguished teaching award from The Ohio State University and has received community service awards for her work with teachers.

Kim K. Metcalf

Kim K. Metcalf is director of the Teacher Education Laboratory at Indiana University, Bloomington, and an associate professor of curriculum and instruction. He was awarded his M.A. and Ph.D. in teacher education and educational research and evaluation from The Ohio State University. Dr. Metcalf is a former music teacher who worked with students in grades K–12, primarily in instrumental music. His major responsibilities now focus on designing, providing, and evaluating preservice teacher education. He is coauthor with Cruickshank of the chapter "Training within Teacher Preparation" in the *Handbook of Research on Teacher Education* and is a contributor to the *International Encyclopedia of Education*. He has been recognized for outstanding research and scholarship on teaching and teacher education by the Association of Teacher Educators, the Association of Colleges and Schools of Education in State Universities and Land Grant Colleges, and the Association of Psychological Type. His current research emphasizes alternative methods of providing clinical experience in teacher education.

Contents in Brief

Contents in Detail

CHAPTER 6

Three Instructional Alternatives: Presentation, Discussion, and Independent Study

CHAPTER 7

Four More Instructional Alternatives: Cooperative Learning, Discovery Learning, Direct Instruction, and Individualized Instruction

CHAPTER 8

Evaluating Students' Learning 252

CHAPTER 9

Reflecting on Teaching 292

PART THREE

The Effective Teacher 305

CHAPTER 10

Effective Teachers: Personal Attributes and Characteristics 306

CHAPTER 11

Effective Teachers: Professional Skills and Abilities

CHAPTER 12

How the Effective Teacher Manages the Classroom

CHAPTER 13

Problems Teachers Face

Preface

What is a competent beginning teacher? Reynolds (1992),* a researcher at Educational Testing Services, sought to find out. After reviewing the research literature on learning to teach and on the act of teaching itself, she concludes that beginning teachers must enter the first year of teaching with a thorough knowledge of the subject matter they will teach, a desire to find out about their students and their school, a solid grasp of instructional methods, and a firm intention to reflect on their own actions and those of their students. Later, by the middle of that first year, novice teachers should be able to plan and teach lessons that help students relate new learning to prior understanding and experience, develop rapport with students, arrange the physical and social conditions of the classroom in ways conducive to learning, assess students' learning using a variety of measurement tools and then adapt instruction accordingly, and show improvement in their ability to reflect on teaching.

Because this text is intended to help persons such as you enter classrooms as competent beginning teachers, we have heeded Reynolds' observations. Additionally, we have taken the advice of approximately thirty teacher educators from across the country who shared course outlines with us. The outlines were obtained from universities offering courses such as "Principles and Methods of Teaching" and "The Teaching Process." Whatever the wording of the titles, all the courses focus primarily on preparing teachers to facilitate learning. Our analysis of the course outlines indicates that teacher educators who are trying to get novice teachers "up and running" largely agree on what you need to know and to be able to do. You need to enter classrooms with knowledge of and/or skill in instructional planning, instructional alternatives, effective teaching, learning theories, classroom management, student diversity, and problem solving.

In preparing this book, we have also been influenced by the personal and professional wisdom gathered while we served as K–12 teachers, school administrators, teacher educators, and researchers. For the most part, our conclusions parallel those of Reynolds and our colleagues in teacher preparation across the country. However, we would add one further ingredient to the formula for preparing competent teachers. You should know the factors influencing how you will teach. Thus, the contents of *The Act of Teaching* take into account Reynolds' conclusions, the observations and wishes of teacher educators from across the country, and our own experience.

A great many people made it possible for us to prepare this book and we wish to thank a few of them. First, we are indebted to numerous colleagues cited in the author index who have generated the knowledge about teaching and learning. Without an enormous body of professional knowledge, such a text could not be crafted. Second, we are grateful to Lane Akers, who waited patiently until time was available for this work and who then facilitated our initial effort. Relatedly, we thank Beth Kaufman and her colleagues at McGraw-Hill for their editorial guidance. Third, we appreciate the several cartoonists who permitted us to add a bit of humor, and Kathy Cruickshank Grossart, who provided illustrations. Finally, we would like to thank the following reviewers for their many helpful comments and suggestions: Kay Alderman, University of Akron; Leo Anglin, Berry College; Leigh Chiarelot, Bowling Green State University; Gerald R. Dotson, Front Range Community College; Philip McKnight, University of Kansas; Robert McNaughton, Cleveland State University; Robert McNergney, University of Virginia; Gary Stuck, University of North Carolina; Barbara Tea, Wright State University; and Kinnard White, University of North Carolina.

We are indebted to them all for their insightful suggestions.

Donald R. Cruickshank
Deborah L. Bainer
Kim K. Metcalf

*Reynolds, A. (1992, Spring). What is a competent beginning teacher? *Review of Educational Research, 62*(1), 1–35.

How to Use This Text Well

Please take sufficient time to become acquainted with this book. The following approach may be helpful:

1. Turn to the **Contents in Brief** on page vii. Note that the text contains four parts. **Part One, The Backdrop of Teaching,** permits you to better know yourself and to find out what is known about human learning. **Part Two, The Act of Teaching,** focuses on functions competent teachers must perform: instructional planning, instruction, assessment, and reflection. **Part Three, The Effective Teacher,** looks at the personal attributes and professional abilities that competent teachers need, including classroom management skills. Finally, **Part Four,** the **Practice Teaching Manual,** contains activities intended to increase selected classroom skills, your ability to reflect and learn from your teaching experiences, and your ability to be a better classroom problem solver. The text also contains a **glossary** beginning on page 459 and **indexes** (both subject and author) starting on page 469.

2. Turn to the next page, **Contents in Detail.** Now you can see precisely what content is found in each chapter and in the Practice Teaching Manual.

3. Select and turn to any of the first several chapters to see how one is set up.

Note that in the side margins there are questions we refer to as **reflective questions.** These questions are intended mostly to prompt you to consider your personal experiences and knowledge. There are no "correct" answers to them. You and your peers should find them provocative, and they should generate considerable class discussion of that section of the chapter, if time permits.

Next, note the figures, tables, cases, and "Spotlight on Research" sections. They serve to reinforce, summarize, or add new information. Occasionally you will see a cartoon that we think illustrates something text-related.

At the end of each chapter is a **Chapter Summary** followed by **Issues and Problems for Discussion, Theory into Action Activities** and **References.**

Issues and Problems for Discussion contains questions for class debate or classroom problems that classroom teachers supplied. You should find many of these issues and problems challenging and thought-provoking.

Theory into Action Activities will help you to put what you have just learned into practice.

We suggest that before reading each chapter you go through it, reviewing all these elements, *but this time read the reflective questions, the chapter summary, issues and problems, and theory into action activities.* Doing these things will prepare you for the material ahead.

The Backdrop of Teaching
PART ONE

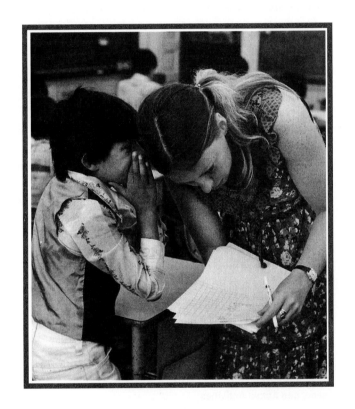

The four chapters in Part One will help you better understand yourself, your students, and the way you and they learn. In Chapter 1, Factors That Influence How We Teach, you will learn how your personal characteristics, previous experiences in schools, and the setting you will work in influence how you will teach. In Chapter 2, Teaching Diverse Children in a Diverse Society, you will find out how societal changes are affecting America's population, families, children and youth, and schools. You also will come to understand the many ways students differ from one another. Chapter 3, Three Schools of Thought about Learning and Teaching, enables you to understand several prominent theories about the way humans learn and about the values and uses these theories have for teachers. Finally, Chapter 4, Getting to Know Your Students, tells you how to find out about your students so that you can better meet their needs and help them learn.

Factors That Influence How We Teach

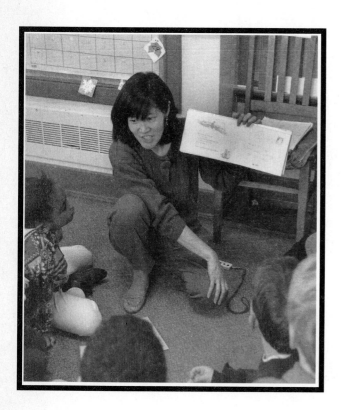

Contents

Would you believe you have been a student in elementary, secondary, and university classrooms for over fifteen thousand hours? During that time, you have observed all kinds of teachers. Have you ever wondered how they became the way they are? Have you questioned why they teach the way they do? Have you thought about what kind of teacher you will be? In this chapter we will consider three sets of factors that have influenced your teachers and likely will affect your teaching as well (see Figure 1.1).

One set consists of your *personal characteristics,* such as gender, age, experience, and personality. A second set consists of your *experience in education.* This set includes how you have been taught, how you prefer to be taught, how you prefer to teach, your knowledge of subject matter, and your teaching or pedagogical preparation. A final set of factors affecting teaching derives from the *context,* or setting, in which you teach. Context is determined by the kinds of pupils you have, class personality and size, availability of instructional equipment and material, time available for instruction, the nature of your lesson, and the dominant or prevailing views about the best way to teach.

Personal Characteristics

To a large extent, your personal characteristics dictate what you will be like as a teacher. These characteristics, mentioned in the previous paragraph and illustrated in Figure 1.2, include gender, age, experience, and personality.

FIGURE 1.1   Factors That Influence How We Teach

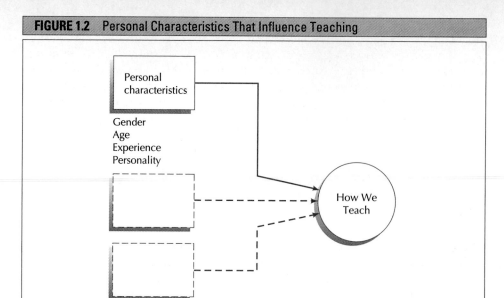

FIGURE 1.2 Personal Characteristics That Influence Teaching

HOW GENDER INFLUENCES OUR TEACHING

A number of studies have been conducted to determine whether male and female teachers differ in terms of their classroom styles (Dunkin, 1987). Although the results are inconclusive, male teachers appear to be more dominant and authoritarian than female teachers. Relatedly, their classrooms are more organized and teacher-controlled. Conversely, female teachers more often appear to maintain "warmer" classrooms and they seem to be more tolerant of misbehavior. Furthermore, some investigators have reported that in classrooms with female teachers, students are more likely to initiate a question or statement, give more incorrect answers, and take risks by guessing answers. Female teachers more than males, also seem to use praise more frequently and are more likely to provide the correct answer when students can't or don't.

Dunkin concludes that, on balance, female teachers' classrooms more often are warmer and more nurturing, while male teachers' classrooms are better organized and more task-oriented. Coulter (1987) reports similarly on gender differences. He finds that female student teachers are more "tender-minded and pupil supportive and less authoritative than males." Moreover, he notes that these gender differences are more prominent among secondary than elementary student teachers (p. 591).

Kalaian and Freeman (1994) find female secondary education majors are: more optimistic that their professional preparation will make them better teachers, more likely to use student-centered instruction, more likely to accept responsibility for teaching exceptional students, and more likely to have realistic expectations regarding teaching. Conversely, they are less confident in themselves as teachers, which may account for their more realistic expectations. Gender differences likely exist among your university professors too.

HOW AGE AND EXPERIENCE INFLUENCE OUR TEACHING

Barnes (1987) reports on studies comparing age and years of teaching experience to teaching style and effectiveness. The studies indicate that teachers are perceived as becoming better at teaching during the first few years, leveling off, and then probably declining somewhat. There also seems to be a tendency for newer teachers to accept innovation and change more easily. However, Barnes reminds us that ready acceptance of innovation may simply be a signal that newer teachers are less discriminating. Everything looks good until you have tried it.

1.1 Have your teachers shown any of the gender-related behaviors reported in research?

Beginning teachers may also be more controlling and authoritarian (Fuller & Brown, 1975). In part, this kind of teacher behavior may result from cautious advice education professors and cooperating or mentor teachers offer; for example, "Don't smile until after the winter break." In other words, when you begin student teaching or begin the first year of teaching, maintain a certain decorum and distance from your students and behave in a stern, no-nonsense manner to frighten students into paying attention and learning. However, by about midyear, you can begin to smile and be yourself. Such authoritarian novice behavior may also occur because, unfortunately, new teachers frequently receive difficult teaching assignments and are likely to "confront pupils who have less academic interest and a tendency to misbehave. Quickly disillusioned, novice teachers tend to grow increasingly authoritarian and custodial" (Kagan, 1992, p. 145).

Furthermore, younger, less experienced teachers have been found to have particular personal needs and characteristics. For example, reseachers (Artiles and others, 1994; Housner and Griffey, 1985; and Szpiczka, 1990) tell us that inexperienced teachers, including student teachers, work hard to develop a unique teacher identity, pay more heed to pupil interests than to involving pupils in instruction or monitoring their academic performance, and generally are more concerned with personal and social dimensions of teaching than with their instructional prowess.

Finally, Coulter (1987) and Cruickshank (1990) report that many confident student teachers lose a measure of self-assurance when they confront classroom life. This is to be expected when the idealism of the novice confronts the reality of the schools.

HOW PERSONALITY AFFECTS OUR TEACHING

We use the term *personality* to mean the totality of character and behavioral traits peculiar to an individual. No two persons are alike in this respect, not even identical twins. Naturally, what we are like, our personality, affects everything we do, including our teaching.

Murray (1963) is perhaps the most influential psychologist interested in personality. He notes that humans have a number of personality needs, including *achievement* (the need to do difficult tasks well), *affiliation* (the need to get along and to form friendships), and *dominance* (the need to influence and control). Each of us approaches teaching driven by urges to meet our personality needs. Therefore, each of us consciously and unconsciously does things that are likely to satisfy our needs. For example, if I need to dominate, my classroom probably will be very teacher-centered and strictly controlled. On the other hand, if I am more concerned with affiliation, my classroom may be more student-centered and somewhat warmer emotionally.

Our personality needs may be particularly influential when it comes to deciding how we will teach a particular lesson or lessons. For example, if we feel the need to dominate, we may choose ways of teaching that put us front-and-center, such as presenting or lecturing. If affiliation is our goal, then we may be prone to use discussions or discovery learning. In Chapters 7 and 8, you will learn much more about Murray's personality needs theory and about seven ways of teaching which may appeal to you based upon your unique needs.

Several research findings relate to teacher personality. Coulter (1987) reports that education majors place more value on and have a stronger commitment to people and personal relationships than noneducation students do. Morrison and McIntyre (1973) report similarly that teachers are more people-oriented than persons in most other occupational groups. Both the Coulter and the Morrison and McIntyre texts note that teachers correspondingly place less value than others on economic success. As human service professionals, teachers seem to be more interested in establishing and maintaining helping relationships than in stability in their level of income (Powell, 1992).

1.2 What differences do you recall between novice and experienced teachers you have had?

"Mirror, mirror, on the wall, who's the most sensitive, open, student-centered, and innovative teacher of all?"

1.3 Are you surprised, encouraged, or disappointed by the findings regarding personality characteristics of teachers?

1.4 How do you think your personality may affect your teaching? What positive traits do you have? What negative traits must you overcome?

Coulter found that education students, when compared with experienced teachers, are more liberal, idealistic, and supportive of K–12 students. As with self-confidence, however, these personal dispositions diminish for some students as they engage in field experiences such as student teaching. Once again, the shock of actual classroom experience probably accounts for this attitudinal change. Although disconcerting, reality shock probably occurs in every profession—a fact we should keep in mind.

Pigge and Marso (1987) find several things related to the attitudes of prospective teachers. They note that elementary education majors and students who make an early commitment to become teachers seem to share generally positive attitudes toward teaching. On the downside, Pigge and Marso find that education majors are anxious about such things as finding teaching satisfying, convincing pupils to follow directions, preparing lessons, and being able to control a class. Other concerns are that they will lack sufficient instructional materials and be unable to meet the needs of different pupils, a problem we will discuss in the next chapter.

Henjum (1969) investigated which characteristics of a student teacher's personality secondary and junior high students most admire. He concludes that in order to be successful with the younger group, student teachers must be emotionally mature, willing to experiment, somewhat extroverted, and socially adjusted. To be successful at the secondary level, students expect you to be intelligent and enthusiastic.

Experience in Education

A second set of factors influencing how you will teach are your schooling experiences. Those experiences include the way you were taught, your preferred ways of learning, your preferred ways of teaching, your proficiency in your chosen teaching or academic field, and the kind and amount of teaching preparation you are receiving (see Figure 1.3).

HOW THE WAY WE WERE TAUGHT AFFECTS OUR TEACHING

If it is true that "you teach as you were taught," then your teaching will model the teaching of your mentors, most of whom you encountered in K–12 schools. A

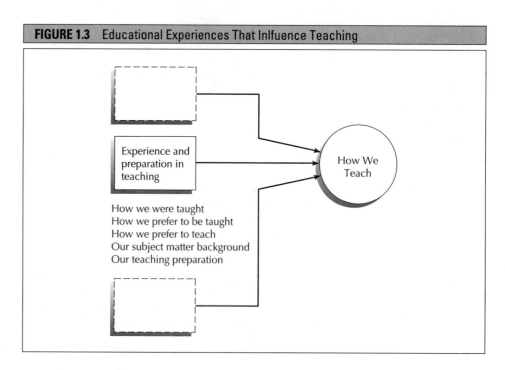

FIGURE 1.3 Educational Experiences That Inlfuence Teaching

Experience and preparation in teaching

How we were taught
How we prefer to be taught
How we prefer to teach
Our subject matter background
Our teaching preparation

How We Teach

number of investigators have observed K–12 teachers, and they have identified two dominant styles of teaching: direct and indirect. **Direct teaching,** also referred to as **expository teaching,** occurs when teachers dominate by presenting information to students, giving students directions, and using criticism (Dunkin & Biddle, 1982, p. 113). By definition, direct teaching is associated with a teacher-centered or teacher-controlled classroom in which the teacher decides what, when, and how to teach. Teachers with a direct style tend to (1) set definite academic goals, (2) use structured, sequential learning materials, (3) prescribe what students will do and how they will do it, (4) monitor and check student progress toward the goals and provide them with corrective feedback, and (5) allow sufficient time to learn the prescribed materials. Although direct teaching may sound cold and impersonal, it need not be. You may recall teachers who were direct but sometimes creative, stimulating, and humorous, too.

You have also witnessed **indirect** teaching, used by teachers who prefer to draw things out of their students. For example, these teachers may provide students with an experience or a block of information and then help them develop their own conclusions from it. By way of contrast, a teacher with a direct style might present information about the worldwide refugee problem, encourage students to discuss the information, and then evaluate the solutions currently used. On the other hand) a teacher with an indirect style might ask students to find out about the worldwide refugee problem and to present additional suggestions regarding its resolution. Teachers with an indirect style seem to be aware of and to make the most of student diversity; they also tend to be more democratic and flexible (Dunkin & Biddle, 1982, pp. 97–98). Teachers with an indirect style (1) set general rather than specific goals, (2) use more, and more varied, learning materials, (3) may set a task to be accomplished but permit students to decide how to do it, (4) serve as facilitators or mentors when students need help, and (5) provide sufficient time to accomplish the task and to consider its merit.

MacDonald (1991) has given some thought to when direct or indirect teaching might best be used. He suggests that a direct style of instruction is most effective

- when time is limited and teachers feel they must show or tell in order to cover material;
- when there are no readily available or easily understood written educational materials students can read for themselves.

On the other hand, an indirect teaching style is more advantageous

- when time is available to accomplish a learning task that requires explanation and discovery and consequently demands higher-order thinking skills such as analysis, synthesis, evaluation, or problem solving;
- when educational materials are available and understandable and a variety of materials and experiences make the concept to be learned clearer.

You will learn more about direct and indirect teaching in Chapter 3, Three Schools of Thought about Learning and Teaching.

HOW THE WAY WE PREFER TO BE TAUGHT AFFECTS OUR TEACHING

You no doubt recall some favorite teachers. You liked them for various reasons. For one thing, the way they instructed you probably made it easier for you to learn. Accidentally or purposely, they taught you in the way you preferred. For example, if you are visually oriented and like to read, they may have assigned a lot of reading. Or, if you are socially oriented and learn best by interacting with others, they may have given lots of group work. Said another way, your "best" teachers probably taught to your preferred learning style. Thus, it is likely that your future teaching will reflect both your own learning style and that of your past teachers. Of course, that could be problematic for your own students whose

1.5 Have you mostly been exposed to direct or indirect teaching? Which style do you prefer, and why?

1.6 Can you describe a teacher who taught in a way compatible with your learning style?

1.7 How do you *not* wish to be taught?

learning styles may differ from your own. Learning style is discussed further in Chapter 2, Teaching Diverse Children in a Diverse Society.

HOW THE WAY WE PREFER TO TEACH INFLUENCES OUR TEACHING

As we have mentioned, your teaching preferences are probably influenced by how you enjoy being taught. For example, those of you who learn best from direct or expository teaching may consciously or unconsciously conclude that your students share your preference. Of course, as you will learn in Chapter 2, classrooms contain students of great diversity, including diverse learning styles. The question becomes whom to please: you, the students, or both?

Zahorik (1990) believes that each education major has a preferred way of teaching and that teacher educators should help you to determine your favored style and to become more effective with it. Thus, rather than help you acquire a varied repertoire of teaching skills and strategies, we should instruct you only in the ones you like best. Zahorik feels that to determine your preference, we need to discover your beliefs about education and teaching. Then we can determine which ways of teaching most closely support these beliefs.

To discover your beliefs about education and teaching, Zahorik would have you consider the following questions: (1) What do you believe about students? (2) What do you believe is the function knowledge should serve? (3) What is the role of a teacher in the classroom? And, consequently, (4) Which way of teaching seems most compatible with your present views?

HOW OUR KNOWLEDGE OF SUBJECT MATTER AFFECTS OUR TEACHING

Your knowledge of the subject or subjects you want your students to learn should be extensive. That's why teachers specialize in a particular subject matter and grade level. The better you "know your stuff," the more potential you have for making it understood and enjoyed by others. For example, a teacher who really understands the structure of mathematics has a better chance of organizing mathematical lessons in a manner that makes sense to students. Such a teacher should be better able to stimulate interest in the subject by helping learners see what the subject entails, how to discover and use the knowledge they gain about it, and how it relates to other subjects and the students' own prior knowledge. Another sign of a good teacher is that students come to enjoy or even love a subject, and this is only possible if the teacher has enough knowledge to teach the subject enthusiastically.

To the extent that you have subject mastery, your confidence increases and you should be able to use more ways to communicate the subject to your students. Teachers confident in their knowledge of a subject can use *either* direct or indirect teaching methods. Teachers with less confidence in their knowledge of subject matter are handicapped and tend to rely heavily on other resources—mostly textbooks. If you do not know your stuff, you cannot be much of a resource yourself.

HOW OUR TEACHING PREPARATION INFLUENCES OUR TEACHING

Another contributor to the way you will teach is the quality of the teaching or **pedagogical** preparation you are receiving. Professional education for teaching includes study of both the parent disciplines of education—such as psychology, philosophy, and sociology—and their offspring, the applied fields of educational psychology and sociology, child and adolescent development, and pedagogy—(the way we plan and deliver instruction and evaluate learning). The extent and quality of the professional preparation you receive will influence both the quality and the style of your teaching. The more knowledge and skill you have in planning and delivering instruction and evaluating learning, the better your students should learn. Persons without sufficient pedagogical or teaching knowledge are forced to teach by instinct and are doomed to trial-and-error approaches. As noted earlier, Kagan

1.8 What will your preferred teaching style be like?

1.9 What do you think of Zahorik's views?

1.10 To what extent are you master of the subjects you will teach? How can you increase your mastery?

FIGURE 1.4   Contextual Factors That Influence How We Teach

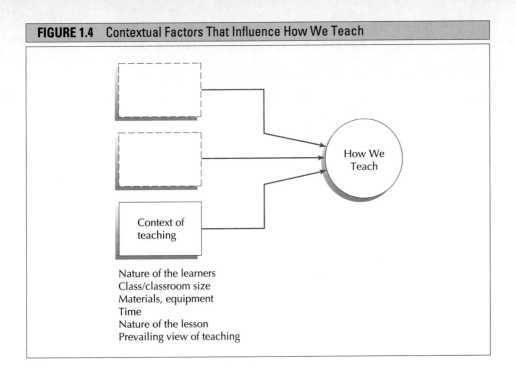

Nature of the learners
Class/classroom size
Materials, equipment
Time
Nature of the lesson
Prevailing view of teaching

(1992) finds that novice teachers, with little knowledge of pupils and teaching, "tend to grow increasingly authoritarian and custodial. Obsessed with classroom control, they may also begin to plan instruction designed not to promote learning, but to discourage children's misbehavior (p. 145).

Although knowledge of and skill in teaching are critical to success, you also need positive attitudes toward teaching, schools, and students, attitudes that university and K–12 school personnel need to foster and reinforce (Cole & Knowles, 1993).

Student teachers and graduates of colleges of education are often distinguishable as a result of the teacher preparation they have received. It is not uncommon for public and private schools to favor student teachers or graduates from a particular university because they feel these persons are better prepared and that they will have a more positive, immediate impact on students.

Context

The final set of factors influencing you as a teacher encompass the context of your workplace. Several ingredients will affect your workplace and, consequently, the way you will teach: (1) the number and kinds of learners you have, (2) class and classroom size, (3) the availability of instructional materials and equipment, (4) time, (5) the nature of the lessons you must teach, and (6) prevalent views about teaching (see Figure 1.4).

HOW STUDENT DIFFERENCES AFFECT OUR TEACHING

In the next chapter, you will be reminded that student variability is a fact of life in all schools and classrooms. You as a teacher must recognize that diversity—whether economic, cultural, gender, developmental, or other—and take it into account.

Since you will have little, if any, control over the nature of the pupils placed in your care, you are well advised to discover who they are and accept them as they

1.11   Recall effective and ineffective teachers you have had. How did they differ with respect to knowledge of child development, knowledge of how to teach, or knowledge of how we learn?

Dear Desmond,

Now that you are a young adult out in the world, you may not remember your first-grade teacher, but I remember you. I remember your blonde hair, big brown eyes, and freckles just as clearly as if you were standing here now. You were so tall and I can still see you looking down the row of heads in front of you after I'd sent you to the back of the line for something you swore you hadn't done. I remember your smiles, your tears, your fists, your heavy boots, and your angry, unhappy words.

You probably didn't know that I was a first-year teacher and that I had never experienced anyone like you before. Maybe you did know. I didn't know that working with you that year would become one of the most memorable experiences of my career. I didn't know that there were so many of you, at least one every year.

Do you remember greeting us each morning by throwing your books on the floor after finally making your way to your desk? Do you remember the range of responses that drew from me? Every day was a new challenge. I'd go home at night, often in tears, and plan my strategy for the next morning's book slam. One day, I'd be stern and take away

some privilege, and then the next day I'd try ignoring you. The day after that you might have been praised for not slamming the books as loudly as before. I'm sure it was great fun for you to try and guess what was coming next. However, I was determined to keep trying and, admittedly, I spent a lot more time trying to figure you out than I did making bulletin boards that year.

Maybe some of the other events of the year are starting to come back to you now. There were so many, and I know that I learned much, much more from them than you did. The one experience that stands out above all the rest was the day you shut yourself in the locker and you couldn't get out.

The class was coming in from recess in their usual noisy way. I remember watching the other classes walking in fairly quiet, straight lines and thinking how we really *should* work on this line stuff some. As most of the class sat down, we heard four muffled, high-pitched shrieks coming from the hall. The shrieks quickly turned into screams and by then I realized what had happened. I tried to get your locker open, but part of your coat was jammed in the door and I couldn't get the door to budge. I yelled for the custodian to

please help me and possibly remove the door. I noticed his sense of urgency subsided when he heard it was you in the locker. Remember how mad he was when you started the "How High Can You Shoot?" contest in the boys' restroom? Then, after a few long moments, you were out. When the door finally opened, you ran out and came straight for me and I hugged you easily. I felt you shaking, and for the first time I saw you as a child and not as the reason I was having doubts about my being a teacher.

So every year as I deal with others like you, I remember the locker. I remember learning that no matter how tough we act, we are *all* afraid of something. I also learned that this awareness of fear doesn't give me the right to hold it over your head but, rather, to keep your actions in perspective. I have since tried harder to find out why children do what they do instead of just dealing with their behavior afterward.

I hope you were lucky enough to have some teachers along the way that had learned these things before you came along. Thank you for teaching me.

Source: Kathy Tatham, Searforce Elementary School, Johnstown, Ohio

1.12 What do you suppose it would be like to teach: children of lower as opposed to higher socioeconomic status (SES); girls as opposed to boys; a child with a hearing-impairment; a child with learning disabilities; Desmond from Case 1.1?

are. Unhappily, newer teachers are more likely to have difficulty recognizing and responding to student variability. They are more apt to see or to want to see the class as an entity, a whole—to view it as more homogeneous than it actually is (Cruickshank & Callahan, 1983). To novice teachers the class seems to have a single face rather than many faces. However, as you study child development and gain teaching experience, you are more likely to see, accept, and provide for differences among learners. At that point, individual learners will clearly have an impact on your instructional planning and on how you will teach.

Case 1.1, written by a first-year teacher, demonstrates that many teachers do accept students as they are and can learn from them.

HOW CLASS AND CLASSROOM SIZE AFFECT OUR TEACHING

Imagine yourself teaching a large number of students, perhaps forty or more, as is normal in many classrooms throughout the world. Class size, to some extent, dictates how you will teach. In such a crowded, complex environment it is more likely, all things being equal, that you will choose to teach the class as a whole and that you will use direct or expository teaching. Conversely, having fewer learners and teaching in a less complex environment permit more teacher-student interaction. Smaller classes, therefore, are more likely to be characterized by individual and small-group instruction. (However, the nature of learners within a class, regardless of size, also weighs on how you will teach. For example, a large or small class of achievement-oriented learners allows you multiple teaching options. Conversely, a large or small class of disengaged students limits your teaching options.)

Class size also seems to have a bearing on how well students learn. Generally, research on class size supports smaller classes. Glass (1987) notes that "the relationship of class size to pupil achievement is remarkably strong. Large reductions in class size [by a third to a half] promise learning benefits of a magnitude commonly believed not to be within the power of teachers to achieve" (p. 544).

According to Robinson and Wittebols (1986), Finn and Voekl (1995), and Wenglinsky (1997), you are particularly likely to be successful when teaching reading and arithmetic in the early grades if class size is small; Finn and Voekl suggest thirteen to seventeen pupils. Robinson and Wittebols also report small class size works well with students of lower academic ability.

The physical size of your classroom also has an impact on your teaching. The availability of space in a room permits you many more instructional options than does a crowded environment. A larger room also provides everyone more private space.

1.13 How has class size affected teaching and learning in your experience? Has it impacted your learning?

HOW AVAILABILITY OF MATERIAL AND EQUIPMENT AFFECT OUR TEACHING

Teachers are limited when there are insufficient resources. A well-stocked "larder," in your case the classroom, provides great potential for instruction. A visit to so-called developing countries reveals that teachers without adequate educational materials, even textbooks, are severely limited in how or what they can teach. For example, Masai children of eastern Africa are mostly taught by educated tribesmen who have few if any resources to draw upon. In such countries and in poorer areas in America, students share desks and books, and have little paper and no audiovisual equipment. Compare this to other American classrooms where nearly every educational resource is available—multiple textbooks, reference materials, television, and computers. Thus, teachers in a poorer school often lecture out of necessity. By contrast, teachers in a wealthy school may choose to lecture but can normally employ other instructional alternatives.

1.14 What educational resources will you likely need to be the best you can be?

HOW AVAILABLE TIME AFFECTS OUR TEACHING

There are limits to the amount of instructional time available to teachers. Therefore, time, or lack of it, has a real impact on how you will teach. If you have more time, you can employ more indirect learning strategies such as experimentation and discussion. When time is short, you may have to be more direct, telling learners what they need to know through lecture, since that is a reasonably efficient way of presenting large amounts of information in a short amount of time. Of course, the burden often is on the learner to process, understand, and remember it.

You must never forget that *how* you use instructional time is extremely important. An hour of instruction can be either beneficial or wasteful. If, in that hour, you can keep your students involved and engaged, they will learn (Smyth, 1987). Chapters 3, 10, and 13 provide an important perspective on time considerations.

1.15 How will you maximize the amount of time available for instruction?

HOW THE NATURE OF LESSON OBJECTIVES AFFECTS OUR TEACHING

In Chapter 5, Planning Instruction, you will discover that there are three kinds of learning outcomes: cognitive, psychomotor, and affective. Here is an example of each:

1. *Students can recite that 6 sevens are 42 (6 × 7 = 42).* This is a cognitive objective that mostly requires the use of mental processes.
2. *Students can hold a paint brush in order to create a particular brushstroke.* This is a psychomotor objective that mostly requires physical dexterity.
3. *Students enjoy listening to orchestral music.* This objective requires the learner to "feel" something. It is affective.

1.16 Do your instructors seem to vary their teaching according to the learning objectives they have in mind?

The nature of objectives will also influence the way you teach. Can you see that each kind of objective probably requires you to teach somewhat differently? For example, suppose your objective is to help students *understand* why 6 sevens are 42; you will need to use some kind of discovery or constructive experience. When you teach students how to hold and use a paint brush, demonstration seems appropriate. If you want students to enjoy orchestral music, you might rely more on listening and valuing experiences.

HOW PREVALENT VIEWS OF GOOD TEACHING AFFECT OUR TEACHING

During different periods of history, educators have championed different ways of teaching. Such preferences can be the result of naturally occurring events. For example, when in 1957 the former USSR launched the first spacecraft, the world in general and the United States in particular saw the need to increase student understanding in mathematics and science. So, during the late 1950s and early 1960s, "new" math and science programs emerged. These programs, emphasizing problem solving and discovery, replaced older models that emphasized rote learning and memorization. The newer view of good teaching aimed to actively involve students in learning by encouraging them to ask questions, hypothesize, experiment, observe, and conclude.

In the 1960s, this preference for problem solving and discovery or inquiry teaching was pushed aside somewhat by the new national imperative to improve race relations in particular and human relations in general. To accomplish this, schools were (and still are) asked to promote and celebrate diversity: cultural, gender, and various forms of learning and developmental differences. These goals prod teachers to utilize other ways of teaching intended to help students become aware of their feelings, attitudes, and values and to help them accept those of others. Consequently, teachers are expected to foster successful group activities through discussion, teamwork, and cooperative learning (see Chapter 7).

Since the 1970s and into the present, increased international economic and political tensions have made the nation look for ways that schools can help it become more productive and efficient. Accountability became the watchword. To make schools more accountable and students more competent, educators needed to very clearly state their goals and define what their students should know and be able to do. Relatedly, teachers were expected to utilize learning incentives or rewards tied to accomplishment of precise achievements. Such goal-directed learning rekindled educators' interest in behavioral learning theory, described in Chapter 3. Consequently, good teachers were expected to use reinforcers (rewards and punishments), shape learner behavior (that is, reward learners for doing anything that demonstrates improvement), and model or get students to model how to do something correctly.

1.17 Which view of teaching appeals to you? Why?

Another strong approach to teaching and learning emerged in the 1980s, one not unlike the prevalent view held during the late 1950s and early 1960s. Known as **cognitive learning theory,** this view is built around the natural human instinct to explore the environment using prior knowledge as a guide. It has led to renewed interest in discovery learning and problem solving presented in Chapter 7. How long any of these currently prevailing views of teaching and learning will last, or to what extent that interest will permeate most schools and classrooms, remains to be seen. In any case, views of good teaching wax and wane. As a teacher who tries to stay up-to-date, you will probably pay close attention to current best teaching trends.

Some Final Thoughts

Yes, the context in which you will work, your prior experiences in education, and your personal characteristics, will influence your teaching. To the extent that you understand this, your insight into yourself and your teaching will grow. You will become more aware of who you are as a person and as a teacher and why you teach the way you do. As a consequence, your wisdom will grow, enabling you to address penetrating questions about yourself: How might my personal characteristics affect my teaching for better or worse? How might my prior experiences in education help or hinder me and my learners? How can I make the very most of my teaching situation? If you can answer these questions, you are well on your way toward becoming a reflective practitioner. Your teaching will be guided by insight rather than history, tradition, or compulsion.

Try Activities 1.1 and 1.2

CHAPTER SUMMARY

- Your personal characteristics, your experience in education, and the context in which you work influence your teaching.

- Personal characteristics that affect teaching include gender, age, experience, and personality. Although men and women are not unlike in the way they teach, men's classrooms seem to be more task-oriented, businesslike, and organized, while women's seem to be more nurturing and accepting.

- Some teacher differences are related to age and experience. Many teachers appear to be at their zenith after a few years in classrooms. Novice teachers seem more controlling and authoritarian, perhaps because of admonitions from their university professors and teaching colleagues or perhaps because their insecurity makes students seem unruly.

- Your unique personality needs or traits affect your teaching. Because you have certain dispositions, you will teach in particular ways. At the same time, many teachers share common traits such as a commitment to others, a desire to have good relationships, and certain anxieties related to teaching success. In all cases, your traits and needs spill over into your classroom, making it unique.

- Your past experiences in education affect your teaching. The way you were taught is very important since beginning teachers often model or imitate their former teachers. Most of your teachers probably used a "direct style," so, for good or bad, you probably will tend to do so.

- Your personal learning preferences likely will cause you to presume that your students want to learn in the same way as you.

- As your knowledge of subject matter increases, so too, does your confidence and competence in teaching and the likelihood that your students will learn and appreciate the subject matter you teach.

- Both the extent and quality of your professional preparation will affect your teaching. Professional knowledge and skill enable you to be wiser and more resourceful and less authoritarian and custodial.

- The context or setting in which you work will also affect your teaching. The ability to recognize and accept learner diversity and to adapt your teaching accordingly is becoming increasingly important.
- As class size increases it becomes more difficult to deal with individual students and overall class variability. Likewise, the physical size of classrooms, the availability of materials and equipment, and the instructional time available all affect the richness of any learning environment.
- Different kinds of learning objectives call for different ways of teaching and, often, for different teaching environments.
- Over the past several decades, many events have influenced prevailing approaches to teaching. During the late 1950s and early 1960s, teachers began using discovery and problem solving as instructional alternatives. During the 1960s, the emphasis shifted to teaching in ways that increased positive human interactions and tolerance, and multicultural education was born. In the 1970s teachers were expected to state teaching goals more clearly, to teach to them, and to be more accountable for pupil mastery. More recently, as a result of recent advances in cognitive learning theory, a renewed interest has arisen in discovery learning and problem solving.

ISSUES AND PROBLEMS FOR DISCUSSION

1. Which factors influencing how we teach have a beneficial impact? Which have a negative impact?
2. How do you believe any of these factors will affect you?

THEORY INTO ACTION ACTIVITIES

ACTIVITY 1.1: A Teaching Self-Portrait and Analysis   Describe what you think you will be like as a teacher. As a teacher, I think I will be:

_____

_____

_____

Now describe how you believe some of the factors mentioned in this chapter or in other chapters may shape your teaching behavior.

ACTIVITY 1.2: Your Cooperating or Mentor Teacher's Self-Portrait   If you are in a field experience, share your self-portrait with the cooperating or mentor teacher. Ask him or her to react. Perhaps your mentor would then be willing to talk about what he or she is like and the factors that seem to be influential in his or her teaching. Can you discover other factors that impact a teacher's classroom behavior?

REFERENCES

Artiles, A. J., Mostert, M. P., & Tankersley, M. (1994). Assessing the link between teacher cognitions, teacher behaviors, and pupil responses to lessons. *Teaching and Teacher Education, 10*(5),465–481.

Barnes, J. (1987). Teaching experience. In M. J. Dunkin (Ed.), *International encyclopedia of teaching and teacher education* (pp. 608–612). Oxford: Pergamon Press.

Cole, A., & Knowles, J. (1993). Shattered images. *Teaching and Teacher Education, 9,* 457–471. Vol 9, No 516

Coulter, F. (1987). Affective characteristics of student teachers. In M. J. Dunkin (Ed.), *International encyclopedia of teaching and teacher education* (pp. 589–597). Oxford: Pergamon Press.

Cruickshank, D. (1990). *Research that informs teachers and teacher educators*. Bloomington, IN: Phi Delta Kappa.

Cruickshank, D., & Callahan, R. (1983). The other side of the desk: Stages and problems of teacher development. *The Elementary School Journal, 83*(3), 251–258.

Dunkin, M. J. (1987). Teacher's sex. In M. J. Dunkin (Ed.), *International encyclopedia of teaching and teacher education* (pp. 606–608). Oxford: Pergamon Press.

Dunkin, M. J., & Biddle, B. J. (1982). *The study of teaching*. Washington, DC: University Press of America.

Finn, J. D., & Voekl, K. E. (1995). Class size. In L. Anderson (Ed.), *International encyclopedia of teaching and teacher education*. Second Edition. (pp. 310–315). Tarrytown, NY: Elsevier Science, Inc.

Fuller, F. F., & Bown, O. H. (1975). Becoming a teacher. In K. Ryan (Ed.), *Teacher education* (74th Yearbook of the National Society for the Study of Education, Part II, pp. 25–52). Chicago: University of Chicago Press.

Glass, G. V. (1987). Class size. In M. J. Dunkin (Ed.), *International encyclopedia of teaching and teacher education* (pp. 540–545). Oxford: Pergamon Press.

Henjum, J. (1969). A study of the significance of student teacher personality characteristics. *Journal of Teacher Education, 20*(2), 143–147.

Housner, L. & Griffey, D. (1985). Teacher cognition. *Research Quarterly for Exercise and Sport, 56*, 45–53.

Kagan, D. M. (1992, Summer). Professional growth among preservice and beginning teachers. *Review of Educational Research, 62*(2), 129–169.

Kalaian, H. & Freeman, D. (1994). Gender differences in self-confidence and educational beliefs. *Teaching and Teacher Education, 10*(6), 647–658.

MacDonald, R. E. (1991). *A handbook of basic skills and strategies for beginning teachers*. New York: Longman.

Morrison, A., & McIntyre, D. (1973). *Teachers and teaching*. Harmondsworth, Middlesex, England: Penguin Education, division of Penguin Books Ltd.

Murray, H. (1963). *Explorations in personality*. New York: Oxford University Press.

Pigge, F., & Marso, R. (1987). Relationships between student characteristics and changes in attitudes, concerns, anxieties, and confidence about teaching during teacher preparation. *Journal of Educational Research, 81*(2), 109–115.

Powell, R. R. (1992, June). The influence of prior experiences on pedagogical constructs of traditional and nontraditional preservice teachers. *Teaching and Teacher Education, 8*(3), 225–238.

Robinson, G. E., & Wittebols, J. H. (1986). *Class size research*. Arlington, VA: Educational Research Service.

Smyth, W. J. (1987). Time. In M. J. Dunkin (Ed.), *International encyclopedia of teaching and teacher education* (pp. 372–379). Oxford: Pergamon Press.

Szpiczka, N. A. (1990). Display of self. Unpublished doctoral dissertation, Syracuse University, Syracuse, NY.

Wenglinsky, H. (1997). *When Money Matters*. Princeton, NJ.: Educational Testing Service.

Zahorik, J. A. (1990). Stability and flexibility in teaching. *Teaching and Teacher Education, 6*(1), 69–90.

Teaching Diverse Children in a Diverse Society

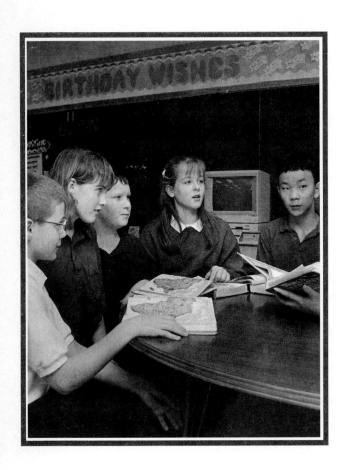

Contents

Try Activity 2.1

Chapter 1 introduced you to several factors that will influence the way you will teach. One of them is the place, or context, in which you work. Today's contexts are very dynamic due to remarkable changes in America's population and family styles, the nature of childhood, schools, and especially the diversity of students. The purpose of this chapter is to make you more knowledgeable concerning these changes. As you reflect on them, you should become more aware of your feelings about teaching diverse children in this increasingly changing society.

The Changing American Population

The 1990 census of 250 million Americans revealed the following: (1) the American population is increasing and shifting geographically, (2) Americans are living longer, (3) the percentage of youth is declining, and (4) the population is becoming increasingly diverse (Waldrop & Exter, 1990).

POPULATION GROWTH AND GEOGRAPHICAL DISTRIBUTION

During the 1980s, the U.S. population grew 10 percent, or by over 22 million people. This growth equals the entire population of Canada. However, the population growth was not evenly distributed geographically. The fastest-growing regions during the past decade were the West (up 20 percent), the South (15 percent), the Northeast (4 percent), and the Midwest (2 percent). States with the largest population gains were California, Texas, Florida, and Georgia; states with the largest percentage increases in growth were Alaska, Arizona, and Nevada. Also worthy of mention is a metropolitan revival, with cities growing at nearly double the rate of nonmetropolitan areas.

AGE DISTRIBUTION

Population growth in the 1980s was also unequally distributed by age. The fastest-growing segment consisted of older Americans. Due to increased life span, their number nearly doubled. Conversely, the same decade saw the number of youth ages 10 to 24 decline, although the under-10-year-old population grew slightly. Overall, the median population age increased from 30 to over 33.

POPULATION DIVERSITY

While population growth has occurred unevenly across geographic regions and age groups, racial and ethnic subpopulations are expanding at different rates. Leading the way are Asians, whose unprecedented immigration has led to an overall population increase of 108 percent. Much of this growth resulted from the influx of Pacific Rim people: Chinese, Koreans, and Vietnamese. Hispanic populations have increased by 53 percent, mostly due to newcomers from Central

America and Mexico. Native American populations also grew by a conspicuous 40 percent. African Americans recorded only a slightly-above-average 13 percent gain, while whites managed a below-average 6 percent increase.

The U.S. population is now approximately 80 percent white, 12 percent black, 3 percent Asian, and 1 percent Native American. Eight percent of Americans are of Hispanic origin, but they are racially mixed. It is expected that by 2010, Hispanics will outnumber blacks. Projections also suggest that after the year 2000, one-third of Americans will be members of some minority (American Council on Education, 1989).

IMPLICATIONS FOR TEACHERS

The aforementioned facts have important implications for schools and teachers. For example, as America becomes more diverse, teachers will have more minority children to teach. Consequently, we can expect a greater need for minority teachers, bilingual teachers, and teachers who are able to work effectively with minority children. In 1991, 39 percent of students but only 13 percent of all teachers were members of minority groups (*Education Week*, 1992). If you belong to one or more minority groups, our schools need you badly.

Also, as America becomes more urban, we will need teachers able and willing to work in our cities. Many large cities are unable to hire enough quality teachers. The reasons are several, but one is that most novice teachers simply do not apply to city school systems. Recently, special teacher preparation programs have been instituted to obtain necessary urban teaching staff.

As our population shifts west and southward, more teaching positions will be available in those regions and fewer in areas losing population. As school-age population holds or dwindles due to smaller families, teaching positions will be eagerly sought after. Therefore, each of you needs to ensure that you gain all you can from your teacher preparation program.

Finally, as our population is increasingly composed of older persons whose children have finished school, it will be more difficult to get support for education. A growing number of retired persons live on fixed incomes, and these people feel particularly beset by mounting property and school taxes. Clode and Jacobson (1989) bear out these implications and others.

2.1 How able and willing are you to teach minority children? to teach in the West or South? to teach in a large city?

The Changing Family

From time immemorial, the family has been the fundamental unit responsible for the health, education, and general well-being of children: indeed, the family has been the central organizing principle of societies everywhere. But in the United States, the structure and function of families have undergone profound changes in the last 30 years (Hamburg, 1995).

FAMILY TRENDS

"Traditional Family Structure Still Evaporating"; "American Family Desperately Needs Help"; "26 Percent Are Single-Parent Families"; "Working Moms Hit Milestone"; "More U.S. Kids Live in Poverty." Newspaper and magazine headlines such as these regularly remind us that the American family is changing.

Hofferth (1987) provides some specifics about changes in American families. They are smaller, since women are bearing fewer children, and this means children have fewer siblings. More marriages occur later in life, and more first marriages (about 50 percent) end in divorce. Thirty to 40 percent of all marriages are remarriages, which often create blended families ("his, hers, and theirs"). Two-fifths of white and three-fifths of African-American children will experience yet a second divorce, and, unhappily, divorce has been associated with reduced

"Kim, this is Eddie. He only has one set of parents!"

school achievement and school completion. It has also been associated with an increase in early sexual activity, childbearing, and marriage. The percentage of children living with two parents has declined to the point that one-fourth of American families are now headed by a single parent, usually female. Relatedly, Hofferth reports that families headed by women, especially African-American women, are more likely to be poor. Over half of America's children who live in female-headed families live below the poverty level.

Andrew Hacker (1982) asks, whether we are bidding "farewell to the family." He attributes the changing attitude (usually less respect) toward the traditional family to our unwillingness to accept its obligations and constraints. Telltale signs supporting this contention, says Hacker, include our reluctance (1) to remain in a less-than-ideal marriage, (2) to ensure population stability by having at least two children, and (3) to care for aging parents. In conclusion, he notes, "What we call a strong family requires a degree of dedication that most of today's adults and youth can no longer give" (p. 45). However, others maintain that the movement toward alternative family styles merely shows our acceptance of varying lifestyles (Suransky, 1982).

In any case, as a consequence of the changes, notes Hofferth (1987), there are fewer traditional *Leave It to Beaver* families consisting of a working father, homemaker mother, and children. According to 1990 census data, only 26 percent of America's children live in a two-parent family with one breadwinner and one homemaker (Center for the Study of Social Policy, 1992). Traditional families, for the first time, are not dominant. Instead, they are outnumbered by married couples who are childless or whose children do not live in the home. Other family styles, such as remarried, blended, and single-adoptive, are growing in number. (The latter refers to a single person adopting one or more children.) Another growing phenomenon is grandparents raising grandchildren.

Ultimately, the question becomes how well does each alternative family type fulfill the traditional family functions of reproduction; nurturance, caring, and intimacy; cultural transmission; and economic support? It is on this basis that alternative families and family styles will be judged. Some, including Hamburg (1992), conclude that the transformed American family is largely unprepared to meet the challenges of raising a child and therefore calls upon government health care institutions, *schools* (emphasis ours), and voluntary organizations to help.

2.2 What kind of family is "best?"

FIGURE 2.1 The American Family: An Endangered Species?

The National Broadcasting Company (NBC) has produced a ten-part film series with this thought-provoking title. Several of the portrayals follow. If the series is available, you might find it informative.

The Edholms: Blended Family (9 minutes, 16 mm, color)
Visits the home of Marg Van Horn and Chuck Edholm, who were both divorced and later married each other. Depicts the Edholms' new blended family, with five children from their previous marriages. Reviews the problems those children perceive and the problems of the stepparents. Family members discuss feelings of resentment, sibling rivalry, and jealousy but overall willingness to make their new family work.

The Hartmans: Mother Returns to Work (8 minutes, 16 mm, color)
Maria Hartman returns to work because her husband Bill's pay doesn't cover the expenses for their seven children. The family discusses the situation and the adjustments to the mother's new job. Maria would rather be at home and does not like working. The children would prefer their mother be at home, although they feel they are learning to be more independent.

The Kreinik and Bosworth Families: Single Adoptive Parents (8 minutes, 16 mm, color)
Views two separate families in which single persons have adopted children. Ms. Kreinik and Mr. Bosworth discuss their unique situations, their yearning for children, and their fulfillment through adoption. Kreink adopted two and Bosworth three—one handicapped and two from the Saigon baby lift at the close of the Vietnam War.

The Marinos: Divorcing Parents (9 minutes, 16 mm, color)
Rick, a policeman, and wife Dianne are in a bitter custody battle for their three young children. Focuses on the anger and pain as both parents make charges and countercharges. Both insist they are seeking custody as the best solution for their children.

Peggy Collins: Single Mother (9 minutes, 16 mm, color)
Peggy, who married at 16, divorced after fifteen years. Her two sons live with their father and her daughter lives with her. She works hard for minimum pay as a waitress. Peggy and Linda, her daughter, reveal emotional problems the divorce has wrought.

Other films include:
- *Sean's Story: Divided Custody* (12 minutes)
- *Shuster/Issacson: Lesbian Mothers* (9 minutes)
- *The Sorianos: Extended Family* (9 minutes)

FAMILY INFLUENCE ON SCHOOLING

Most families have a substantial influence on their offspring. For example, an analysis of data collected from over 12,000 seventh through twelfth graders reveals the following:

2.3 How did your family and community affect your education and schooling?

- The more teenagers feel their parents pay attention to them, understand them, and love them, the less likely they are to have early sex, smoke, or abuse alcohol or drugs.
- The presence of parents at key times—before school, after school, and at dinner—is associated with less negative adolescent behavior of all kinds.
- Parents' expectations that teenagers get good grades and refrain from sexual activity have a powerful influence on youth regardless of family income, family type, or race (Resnick, 1997).

Other studies also report a strong relationship between family characteristics, children's behavior, and school achievement. The relationship between the **socioeconomic status (SES)** of parents and their children's school achievement seems very strong. Children from higher SES families are much more likely to do better in school. They are more likely to be "advantaged" by their parents' positive experiences with and dispositions toward school and learning and also by the family's ability to provide educationally enriching opportunities and accoutrements such as computers, reading materials, and a place to study (Bracey, 1995; Jencks et al., 1972; U.S. DHEW, 1966; Walberg and Fowler, 1987). Additionally, it has been substantiated that parental involvement in schooling is related to better grades and greater enjoyment of school. A father's involvement seems particularly helpful while children are in grades 6 through 12 (National Center for Educational Statistics, 1997).

Whether a student is from a single- or a two-parent family also is associated with the child's achievement and behavior in school. Brown (1980) studied data comparing school achievement and school problems of over 8,000 low-income elementary and high school children of two-parent and one-parent families. He found, respectively, that 76 percent, 21 percent, and 3 percent of children lived in two-parent, one-parent, and other families. He reports that a substantially higher proportion of high achievers came from two-parent families and, conversely, that an inordinate proportion of children from one-parent families were low achievers. Further, Brown notes:

- A disproportionate number of elementary school students from one-parent homes were excessively tardy.
- Students living with one parent or a relative and students living in foster homes created a disproportionate share of elementary and secondary school discipline problems.
- Although K–12 students from one-parent and other category homes made up one-fourth of school populations, they were suspended at about twice the rate of students from two-parent homes.
- Students from one-parent homes and those living with no natural parents accounted for over half of school truancy.
- All students expelled were from one-parent families.
- One-parent and other category secondary students constituted 40 percent of the school dropouts.

Bradley (1990) discusses a study by Werner and Smith, later published in 1992, in which the researchers traced 200 high-risk Hawaiian children into adulthood. These born-into-poverty children were exposed to three risk factors: health problems at birth, parents without secondary education, and family histories of alcoholism or mental illness. Werner and Smith (1992) found that about two-thirds of these high-risk children had serious learning or behavioral problems by age 10, or delinquency records, mental health problems, or an unplanned pregnancy by their 18th birthday. However, they found delinquent children living with both parents were significantly less likely to become adult criminals. Relatedly, they discovered that those who recovered from mental health problems were twice as likely to have had two parents at home during their adolescent years. Although circumstances alter individual cases, it appears that family economic well-being and intactness are two factors having a considerable impact on K–12 student learning and social adjustment.

Another factor of considerable importance, according to Caplan, Choy, and Whitmore (1991), is family culture. For example, very poor immigrants to America with strong cultural and family traditions seem to engender in their children the attitude that success in education and life comes from hard work, rather than from luck or circumstances of birth. Caplan et al. cite the phenomenal school success of children from recently immigrated Vietnamese, Laotian, and Chinese families. These children have done remarkably well in our schools despite their attendance in low SES community schools and their limited English proficiency.

The lives of children and teachers are inextricably bound to families, parents, and other caregivers. Establishing and maintaining good relationships with such significant others is a prime concern of most teachers, as you will see in Chapter 13. Teachers are well aware of the impact parents and community have on student

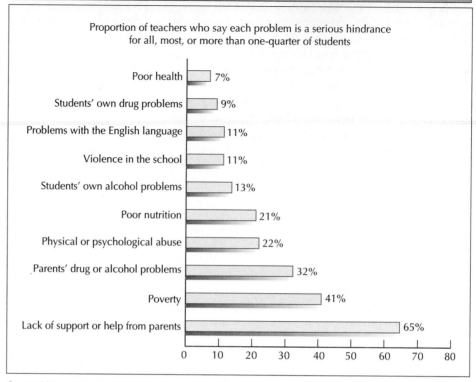

FIGURE 2.2 Lack of Parental Support—The Most Serious Hindrance to Students' Ability to Learn

Proportion of teachers who say each problem is a serious hindrance for all, most, or more than one-quarter of students

Problem	Percent
Poor health	7%
Students' own drug problems	9%
Problems with the English language	11%
Violence in the school	11%
Students' own alcohol problems	13%
Poor nutrition	21%
Physical or psychological abuse	22%
Parents' drug or alcohol problems	32%
Poverty	41%
Lack of support or help from parents	65%

Source: Metropolitan Life, (1992). *Ready or not: Grade level preparedness: Teachers' views on current issues in education.* New York: Metropolitian Life Insurance Company.

academic success and classroom behavior. A Metropolitan Life (1992) survey of the American teacher revealed that 65 percent of teachers say that lack of support or help from parents presents a problem (see Figure 2.2). In a similar 1993 survey, 80 percent of teachers polled said that promoting parental involvement in education should be the first or second priority on the national education agenda (Richardson, 1993).

To overcome lack of parental interest in and support for their children's education, syndicated columnist William Raspberry writes, "I have urged repeatedly that every community ought to have regular sessions where parents of young children can learn tricks and techniques for getting their children ready for school" (Raspberry, 1993). Specifically, Raspberry says parents should instill in their children attitudes and habits that make school learning possible; such qualities as patience, persistence, self-esteem, reading for fun, and the love of learning are particularly beneficial.

Why does Raspberry believe parents need to instill such attitudes and habits? Because "these are the things that used to be taught in religious institutions and only reinforced in schools. Now . . . they are hardly taught at all, and the resulting lack of discipline, order, and civility show up as school problems." Thus, what we know about families in general, and about the families of school-age children in particular, provides insight that can assist us in more successfully fulfilling our roles as teachers.

2.4 What might you do to increase parental interest?

IMPLICATIONS FOR TEACHERS

We can draw a few implications for teachers from the data concerning family influence on schooling. As women continue entering the workforce and delaying marriage, more and more children have somewhat older parents who have less time and energy to give to child rearing. Many of these working parents will likely maintain busy schedules, spend less time than they would like with their children, and find it difficult to schedule time for themselves. Teachers need to understand such circumstances and do their best to facilitate family needs without negatively affecting a child's school success. Also, since more students will come to your classrooms having experienced parental separation, divorce, or remarriage, you must be sensitive to their need for emotional support and for help in thinking through related concerns. Finally, inasmuch as a large number of children now live in single-parent and blended families, you need to accept alternative family styles and to include them when referring to families in class. Sensitivity is especially important here.

Because a larger number of children live in single-parent families, you should take into account that they may have fewer financial resources and may also be less supervised. Such conditions usually result in less access to educational materials in the home and poorer homework performance. Those children who are most at risk with regard to school achievement and behavior are those who live in a single-parent family and are born into poverty, who have health problems at birth, whose parents lack a secondary education, and whose families have a history of mental illness or alcoholism. Also, because we know that parents and caregivers have a positive impact on schooling, you may need to show family members how to help their children succeed. Finally, since children represent a decreasing population, you need to be a child advocate in your community and argue for improved services for all children.

2.5 To what extent would you be willing and able to take on family functions such as nurturing and caring?

The Changing Nature of Childhood and Youth

Yes, America is changing, and so also is the process of growing up in our nation. The following headlines portray a bleak picture of being raised in America today: "More U.S. Kids Live in Poverty," "Study of 8th Graders Finds 20% at High Risk of Failure," "Latchkey Kids Are More Likely to Smoke, Drink," "Students Studying TV More than Books," "Fifth Graders Organize Rebellion," "Rapes by Children Expected to Rise," "Teens Juggle Jobs, Homework to Boost Their Buying Power," "Teen Moms Know What They Are Doing."

You may feel that such headlines are sensational and exaggerated. However, in most cases the news stories are based upon governmental and scientific reports (Fuchs & Reklis, 1992). As you might suspect, the scenarios are worse for minorities and the poor, which are the most rapidly growing segments of a declining youth population. However, majority and more affluent youth, while less affected by these concerns, are more affected by others. Let's look briefly at some of the problems that affect childhood today.

GROWING UP IN POVERTY

Three reports by the Poverty and Wealth Statistics Branch of the U.S. Bureau of the Census (1991) and one from the Children's Defense Fund (1992) testify that unemployment, lower wages, and an increase in single-parent families are related

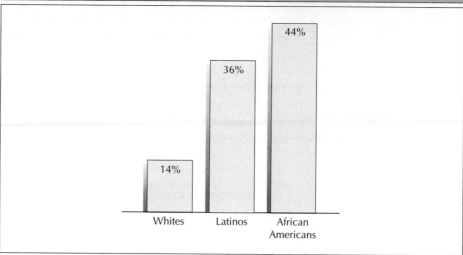

FIGURE 2.3 Percentage of White, Latino, and African-American Youth Living below the Poverty Line

2.6 Are you willing and able to teach children living in poverty? What pluses and minuses would you bring to this task?

to the rise in America's rate of poverty. Moreover, the reports point out that children of the poor suffer most gravely. Of the 63 million youth under age 18 in America, 13 million, or more than one in five, live in families whose incomes fall below the government's poverty line. Relatedly, 8.4 million youth have no medical insurance. In fact, the percentage of children living in poverty in this country is more than double that of other major industrialized nations (Dimensions, 1993).

Poverty hits hardest at America's underclass and the very young. A report by the Children's Defense Fund (1991) notes that Latino children are slipping into poverty at the fastest *rate*. This slippage is attributed mostly to lower wages rather than marital instability, since Latinos have a large proportion of both married and working parents. Figure 2.3 compares the percentages of poverty among Latino, white, and African-American youth.

Among children under 6 years of age, 23 percent live in poverty (National Center for Children in Poverty, 1990). Analysts believe this age-related vulnerability may be the result of the growing number of single, teenage mothers; insufficient welfare benefits; lack of affordable day care; and the inability of many young, two-parent families to earn necessary income. Biddle (1997) notes that growing up in poverty often means living in substandard housing, having an inadequate diet, wearing cast-off and torn clothing, and going without dental care.

CHILDREN WITH INADEQUATE SUPERVISION

About three-fourths of America's children live in two-parent families, mostly with their biological parents. However, many of these children, like those in single-parent families, are dependent upon self-care or day care. A number of factors seem to contribute to this situation. More than ever before, parents believe that both spouses must work to enjoy an adequate lifestyle. Additionally, women are looking for self-fulfillment outside the home, so that well over half of working-age women are now in the workplace. Of course, the increased number of single-parent families also contributes to the self-care/day care phenomenon.

For whatever reason, 64 percent of children do not have a parent at home full time (Center for the Study of Social Policy, 1992). This means that parents and guardians seek child care help from a variety of sources including relatives, friends, and day care providers. Many expect their children between the ages of about 7 and 13 to look after themselves. When children are regularly home alone, they are referred to as **latchkey children.** In fact, the frequency of day and self-care has become so great that today's children are often referred to as the "day care generation." Some even go so far as to argue that children today experience near abandonment (Louv, 1990).

At times, latchkey children seek refuge in libraries. A study of 125 librarians (Dowd, 1990) reports that 76 percent see significant numbers of unattended children in the library after school. On weekends, 50 percent report seeing unsupervised children. The librarians report that the 10- to 12-year-old age group seems to be using libraries most regularly as havens.

What are the effects of being supervised by someone other than a parent, or of not being supervised at all? While there is little conclusive data about the effects of day care, some express concerns: Babies or infants in day care seem to be at greater risk of developing insecure relationships with their mothers, the high rate of turnover among day care providers results in inconsistent supervision for developing children, and children cared for outside the home are at greater risk of sickness due to increased exposure to both adults and children (Wingert & Kantrowitz, 1990).

Likewise, there is little conclusive knowledge about the effects of self-care. However, a study of almost 5,000 eighth graders (Richardson et al, 1990) raises concerns. Richardson et al report that 68 percent of these children cared for themselves at least part of the time after school. When these latchkey children are compared with their supervised peers, they were twice as likely to be under stress, to feel conflict with their families, to indicate that their parents are gone too much, and to call themselves risk-takers. Additionally, they are angrier, skip school more, are more afraid when alone, and go to more parties. They were also twice as likely to drink alcohol, smoke, and use marijuana. Some of these findings might suggest that such children are better adjusted and more independent. Eighth graders who become latchkey children in elementary school are more likely to take risks (be independent) and go to parties (be social). However, there is a dark side even to this interpretation. Such children were also three times more likely to abuse substances than are their supervised peers. Children beginning self-care later, in junior high, are twice as likely to engage in substance abuse (Weisman, 1990).

Of course, children with a parent or parents at home are not necessarily adequately supervised. Furthermore, children differ in their need for supervision.

ABUSED AND NEGLECTED CHILDREN

When we read newspapers or magazines or watch television, we are well aware that child abuse is all too common. It is estimated that almost 2 million children are either abused or neglected *each year.* Abuse and neglect are defined in Public Law 93-246 as "physical or mental injury, sexual abuse, negligent treatment, or maltreatment of a child under 18 by a person who is responsible for the child's welfare under circumstances which indicate that the child's health or welfare is harmed or threatened thereby" (Child Abuse Prevention and Treatment Act of 1974). Generally, abuse and neglect are associated with parents who were themselves abused as children; stress brought about by poverty, unemployment, marital problems, or isolation; low level of parental education; poor information concerning child rearing; and a violent environment (Kauffman, 1985; Gelardo & Sanford, 1987).

 2.7 What degree of responsibility do you think parents have for child supervision?

 2.8 What do child abuse and neglect mean to you? How do you feel about persons who abuse or neglect children? How do you feel about children who are abused or neglected?

FIGURE 2.4 Some Indicators of Possible Child Abuse or Neglect

Abuse

- Repeated injuries
- Repeated complaints about stomach pain
- Repeated bruises, welts, cuts, burns, or frostbite
- Difficulty sitting or walking
- Torn, stained, or bloody clothing
- Pain or itching in genital area
- Unusual behavior for the child (disruptive or withdrawn)
- Poor peer relationships
- Undue fearfulness

Neglect

- Inappropriate or unwashed clothing
- Poor hygiene
- Poor nourishment
- Chronic sleepiness or tiredness
- Unusual need for attention

The problems of abuse and neglect are of such epidemic proportions that all fifty states have laws requiring teachers to report all suspected cases. Indicators of physical and sexual abuse and neglect appear in Figure 2.4.

"AT-RISK" CHILDREN

If students in your classroom are affected by circumstances that can torment childhood, they are at substantial risk of school failure and dropping out. Some of these circumstances we already know, are poverty, lack of supervision, and abuse and neglect. Common characteristics of children at-risk include:

- They live in a single-parent home.
- They are at home unsupervised for long periods of time.
- Their parent(s) have a low income.
- Their parent(s) have a low level of education.
- They have limited proficiency in English.
- They have siblings who have dropped out of school.
- They perform poorly in school.
- They have repeated a grade.
- They do not expect to graduate.

Case 2.1 describes a study of Aaron, a child at risk. What are some of the factors placing him at risk?

A national study of almost 25,000 eighth graders provides a snapshot of at-risk adolescents (*A Profile of American 8th Graders*, 1990). It reveals that nearly one of every two students is affected by at least one of the listed at-risk factors! One in five students has two or more risk factors, and, the study notes, these youth are especially at risk. Of course, as the number of risk factors increases, the risk of failure and of dropping out increases.

Minorities are more often affected by one or more risk factors. For example, African Americans are twice as likely as whites to come from low-income and single-parent families. Hispanics are much more likely than whites to have limited English proficiency (LEP) and to have parents who did not complete secondary school.

CASE 2.1
Aaron, A Child at Risk

Aaron Allen is an 11-year-old boy in the sixth grade. He has a small and slender build for this grade level. He comes to school well groomed and usually well dressed.

Aaron lives with his mother in a low-income area. They live in a little three-room house and receive public assistance. Aaron is an only child, and his parents are divorced. Mrs. Allen is willing to talk about Aaron. She appears to care very much about him, but admits she is losing control over him. She took a babysitting job this last summer for extra money, but money does not seem to be a big concern for Aaron.

Mr. Allen is in prison and has been out of the home since Aaron was 6 years old. This means that Aaron has been without a male figure in the home. As a result, he became very close to a 24-year-old uncle. This uncle did not work; he lived with his mother and received whatever he wanted. Constantly in trouble, the uncle was a very bad influence on the boy. Aaron's uncle was killed in a bar shooting last year. The tragedy left Aaron with no male figure to relate to at all.

Aaron gets whatever he wants at home and goes wherever he pleases. He rides his bicycle most places, but if his destination is too far, he takes a bus. He associates with older children and most of his close friends attend the junior high school, which is two blocks from the elementary school and one block from his house. Aaron is fairly well accepted by his peers. He has no juvenile record, but the police have talked to him and warned him for various actions. Mrs. Allen explained that he was caught stealing several times and was reported at the scene of a fire. When there is a problem, Mrs. Allen says she gets her son out of trouble, talks to him, and hopes he won't do it again. She explains that she threatens him, saying if he doesn't behave, "he will be taken away to a detention home in hopes that it will scare him and he will straighten up."

The information in Aaron's cumulative school folder states that he has an average IQ, but his performance is very much below the grade-level standards. He reads at a third-grade level. Aaron seems disinterested in school, with a definite "I don't care about school" attitude. He has stated many times that he does not like school and that he would not come if he did not have to. His record shows increasingly poor attendance. When he loses interest, he becomes a problem for the teacher. He continually disrupts the class and is often sent to the office. So far, this does not seem to have improved his behavior.

Recently Aaron's behavior has gotten worse. He could not care less about school or what happens to him. When his mother was contacted, she said she felt helpless and had more or less given up. For the past five to six weeks, the regular teacher has been ill, and the room has had six different substitutes. This has affected all the students in the room, but Aaron is in trouble more than usual because the substitutes will not tolerate any behavior problems. School, with the room in such turmoil, presents a real problem for Aaron.

Source: Barbara Dahmke, Grandview Heights Middle School, Columbus, Ohio.

Of course, some children are at risk even though they seem not to be afflicted by poverty, single parenthood, lack of supervision, and so forth. It is often difficult to understand why seemingly advantaged children do not achieve, or underachieve. Eighth graders interviewed in the study may provide some answers: Half said they were bored in school and go unprepared to class, and nearly half said they hardly ever discussed schoolwork with a parent.

A study of over 9,000 6- to 17-year-olds reveals an additional risk factor. Regardless of normal risk factors such as poverty, having a single parent, or lack of parental supervision, children who move often—at least six times during grades 1 to 12—are 77 percent more likely to have more behavior problems and 35 percent more likely to fail a grade (Cohen, 1993).

The National Education Association (NEA) has initiated a program to help pupils at risk. Under this program, called Operation Jump Start, as many as one-third of the nation's elementary students receive an educational "shot in the arm" by starting their school year two weeks earlier than their classmates. During that interval, teachers work with fewer than fifteen children at risk, involving their parents.

Surprisingly, a number of at-risk children turn out all right. In the earlier reported study Werner and Smith (1992) reported that one of every three such

Alderman (1990) notes that teachers must always be alert to the need to motivate students, especially when the students are at risk. She concludes that teachers of at-risk students have a particularly monumental task of helping these kids break the cycle of failure: low expectations and helplessness. After reviewing research on motivation, Alderman offers these suggestions:

• Have confidence in your ability to help these students learn.

• Hold high expectations for at-risk youth. Let them know you want and expect them to succeed.

• Assist at-risk students in establishing reachable and specific goals and in charting their own progress.

• Help children identify strategies for reaching their goals.

• Make sure children link their success to their effort.

• Let children know precisely what they did that made them successful.

Source: Alderman, M. K. (1990, September). Motivation for at-risk students. *Educational Leadership.* 48(1), 27–30.

2.9 How do you think you might feel or behave when you discover a child may be "at risk?"

students developed into competent, confident, caring adults by the time they were 18. These so-called **resilient children** tend to have a nurturing adult in their lives (not necessarily a parent), and they had easy temperaments as infants. Relatedly, Masten, Best, and Garmezy (1991) found resilient children are perceived as more appealing or attractive to adults. Moreover, they report such children have good intellectual and problem-solving skills and that, as they mature, they have a knack for finding a good environment outside the home in a church, youth, or club group, or in the family of a friend or relative that offers stability and support. Researchers at Johns Hopkins and Syracuse Universities (Winfield, 1991) report that resiliency may also be fostered when young black males participate in sports. Winfield, Wang and Gordon (1994), and Werner and Smith (1992) tell us that certain schools and teachers also are instrumental in helping at-risk students to become resilient. For example, Werner and Smith report that if schools and teachers assist at-risk children to gain good reading ability by grade four, these children will have a much better chance at later success.

How could we do a better job teaching students who are at risk of school failure? Alderman (1990) provides us with some clues in Spotlight on Research 2.1.

"HURRIED" CHILDREN

Child advocates feel that children should be allowed to be children, that they should not be hurried into school and faced with formal learning requirements at very young ages. Elkind (1981) and Postman (1983) are among those who decry the shortening and even disappearance of home-based childhood in favor of early schooling. Among the factors that contribute to rushing children through childhood are working parents, television, and growing materialism. Working parents simply have less time to spend with their offspring, and the time they do share is often marred by the stress and exhaustion of the adults' lives.

Of course, television has its good and bad aspects, and those who study child development continue to debate its impact on childhood behavior. However, it is well known that children, as well as adults, imitate what they see. And what they often see is distorted teenage and adult conduct that exaggerates violence, cruelty, and sexual behavior. It has been said that television reveals all adult secrets that young children formerly could not easily discover. As a consequence, young children, who naturally try to imitate adult behavior, may be led into re-creating acts of violence and sexual intimacy. Fortunately, there are efforts (although not well supported) to offer more television programming options that match children's normal developmental needs and interests.

Materialism is the doctrine that comfort, pleasure, and wealth are the highest goals and values one can aspire to. Society is deluged by reminders of materialistic needs, including better jobs, vacations, houses, cars, and entertainment. Parents who buy into materialism are more likely to expect their children to be achievers in all things so they, too, will obtain "the good life." Such children can be constantly on the run, participating in a variety of activities that may be undertaken more as means to an end (achieving) than as ends in themselves (fun). Thus, to some extent, children are hurried because adults are, too. However, child advocates like Elkind (1982) warn that we are so overvaluing adulthood and undervaluing childhood that adult pressures are harming children.

CHILDREN WHO ARE DISENGAGED

In a study of 20,000 high school students in California and Wisconsin, 40 percent say they are disengaged—bored and just going through the motions in school. Signs of boredom in school include reading material unrelated to class, daydreaming, doing work for other classes, and talking with peers (Plucker & Omdal, 1997). Disengaged students report that friends influence school performance and drug use more substantially than parents' positive practices at home. However, researchers find that students who come from homes where parents are firm, loving, and respectful are more likely to be engaged in school learning.

Besides taking in the potentially negative influence of friends, disengaged students are often busy with nonacademic pursuits. Two-thirds of teens work: half more than fifteen hours per week. When not working, teens spend twenty to twenty-five hours weekly with friends (Steinberg, Brown, and Dornbusch, 1996). Spotlight on Research 2.2 explores how teachers can motivate disengaged students.

2.10 How might you motivate a disengaged student to learn?

CHILDREN TODAY AND YESTERDAY

In a study conducted by Zimiles (1986), teachers and principals who had been working with K–12 children twenty or more years earlier were interviewed and asked to compare today's youth with yesterday's. In keeping with what others have pointed out in the previous sections, these long-time teachers and principals generalized that today's children are growing up more rapidly, enjoying greater freedom, and generally know more.

Zimiles' informants provided detailed explanations for these generalizations. Children today know more because of increased mobility, travel, publications, toys, and games. Unfortunately, however, that knowledge often is fragmentary, random, and not organized or integrated. Relatedly, youth are reportedly less ready to acquire new knowledge that adults and teachers introduce and are less responsive to typical school instruction. The participants in the study believe this is partly due to television and video games that are stimulating—even dazzling—and which can be turned on and turned off at will. Accordingly, children today are less willing to face the tedium of academic activities that require concentration, attention to detail, repetition, memorization, and auditory computation. Furthermore, children today are reportedly more visually and less auditorily oriented, less fond of writing, less interested in reading, less aware of language and its properties, but more poised in speech.

Zimiles' informants reported that today's children are more open, questioning, challenging, assertive, and independent. They hold school in less awe and more openly express irritation and disdain toward it. They show less respect for authority and are more aware of their rights. Moreover, today's children are perceived as more interested in immediate gratification, and less able to think about long-term goals and future usefulness of what they are learning. They enter peer groups earlier and are more dependent on them. Today's youth are more caught up in family discord, social problems, violence, and crime, and they are distracted earlier by their sexuality. Finally, they have more money and possessions.

IMPLICATIONS FOR TEACHERS

As teachers, we must know as much as possible about children collectively and about school-age children in particular if we are to deserve the label "helping profession." So many children are experiencing poverty that, on average, one of every five students is likely to be ill-nourished and in poor health, unprepared to learn, and, in some cases, homeless. Consequently, you must take your students' physical, mental, and emotional condition into account and, when necessary, be prepared to access child services supplied by the school district and community. Since poor children and their families are more poorly represented politically, teachers and schools must be visible, loud, and continuous in their support.

Unfortunately since some children have inadequate supervision, you must be prepared to have students who come to school ill, tardy, anxious, or lonely. Without unduly infringing upon family situations, you may need to keep track of children involved in self-care. Make sure they are not unnecessarily at risk due to their self-care arrangements and that they are knowledgeable about what to do in problem or emergency situations. Also, given the increased incidence of child abuse and neglect, you will need to watch for telltale signs and report suspected cases in accordance with school policy. Monitor the stressed-out children of high-pressure parents who want their children to hurry up and "make it" as well. Finally, try to find ways to engage the disengaged.

The Changing School

For the past several decades, America has been trying to cope with an ever-increasing number of scientific, economic, and educational challenges to its well-being and prosperity. Several are depicted in Figure 2.5.

While some of the challenges have come from abroad, particularly from Asia and Europe, others, such as the pursuit of equity, come from within. Whatever the challenge or its source, Americans expect their public schools to "fix whatever is broken." For the most part, America's schools have accepted these challenges and, as a consequence, have transformed themselves in a number of ways. Following is a brief description of selected challenges that our schools have accepted and how they have changed to meet them.

Challenge 1—To Foster Equity   The pursuit of equity is transforming both our society and its schools. You have matured during a period when the concept of equal treatment and opportunity has blossomed. You are probably already familiar with some of the ways this concept has affected education: for example, it has triggered the desegregation of schools and classrooms, the elimination of most same-sex

2.11 In your judgment, are youth today "better" or "worse" than in previous generations?

FIGURE 2.5 External and Internal Challenges That Have Changed Schools

Foreign Challenges

Economic competition
Educational competition → School Changes ← Domestic Challenges

Domestic Challenges
— Changing family
— Working parents
— Pursuit of equity
— Student diversity
— Poverty
— Violence, abuse
— Technology

schools, the inclusion of special-needs students in regular classrooms, the development of special programs for children with no or limited English proficiency, the fostering of multiethnic education, and so forth. This equity challenge pervades each and every day of a teacher's life. It requires that you be proactive and vigilant to ensure all students have equal opportunity and receive equal treatment.

Challenge 2—To Achieve World-Class Academic Standards   As a consequence of scientific and industrial achievements abroad, America is having a more difficult time providing its citizenry with the level of living they have become used to. America's declining position within this fierce global economic competition has been attributed in part to improved education abroad and declining education at home. Analysts frequently cite comparative student test scores which seem to show that American students are not achieving at a world-class level (Stevenson et al., 1993). Schools are attempting to answer this challenge by introducing new, more rigorous curricula, by instituting the practices of our most effective schools into those with poor track records, and by utilizing more promising teaching practices. Further, you will find that students are taking many more tests in an effort to monitor their progress better.

Challenge 3—To Support Families   Throughout history, the family was expected to support the school. More recently, the school is being asked to support the family. Both the changing family and the increasing number of women in the workforce have resulted in substantial changes at school. Increasingly, schools are asked to provide before- and after-school child care. Some schools literally begin their day before sunrise and conclude it after sunset. Relatedly, it is more difficult to communicate with working parents and fewer are available as school volunteers than before. On average, children are less likely to receive the nurturing they need, so you must be prepared to listen to them and, on occasion, to help them in nonacademic ways.

Challenge 4—To Celebrate Diversity   Given the changing demography of America, you will find students are more diverse. Since a section on the diversity of students follows, at this point it is sufficient to say that schools are responding to the diversity not only by accepting it but also by promoting its value and richness.

Challenge 5—To Utilize Technology   As society has become increasingly dependent on technology, schools are challenged to use that technology and to foster its use among students. Albeit slowly, schools have accepted the challenge. Some school

2.12   How important are the five challenges schools face? Which of these challenges might be most difficult for you?

FIGURE 2.6 Six Ways in Which Students Differ

2.13 Some would argue that schools cannot be all things to all people, that they are changing too much in order to meet such challenges. How do you feel? What do you think the role of the school should be?

districts conduct their own television broadcasts, teach broadcasting, and produce programs. Likewise, many schools have computer laboratories as well as computers in classrooms. Most schools, however, still grapple with the problem of how to help students become discriminating television consumers and sophisticated rather than game-playing computer users.

As a future teacher, you must keep abreast of these and other challenges facing schools today. Furthermore, unless you conclude that such challenges are misguided, you must work to respond appropriately to them. You can do so by getting behind school district and school building response efforts and, perhaps more importantly, by conducting your classrooms accordingly. More specifically, as you plan your curriculum and instruction, you must always be alert for opportunities to foster equity, celebrate diversity, provide for children's special needs, foster a high level of learning, utilize technology, and support your students' families and communities.

Student Diversity

> Why did I have to discover so much on the job? Have I messed up kids because I couldn't recognize some things I should have been able to see? Kids who needed attention, had poor nutrition, lacked good role models, never had a good school experience, had a messed-up family? How do I convey knowledge to these kids so they can understand it and have good feelings about themselves? So they can have success and build on it? I don't have the training to do it. I go home with these things troubling me. (Bower, 1978, p. 31)

2.14 What do you believe are the advantages of teaching diverse children? the challenges?

Student diversity is a fact of life in all our schools and classrooms. And students differ in more ways than we can count. To be effective, teachers must be aware of some of the important ways students vary and consciously take that diversity into account when planning and instructing. We cannot successfully teach subject matter without teaching the child. Let's examine some of the kinds of diversity you will find. They are illustrated in Figure 2.6.

SOCIOECONOMIC DIFFERENCES

The gulf between rich and poor American families is wider now than at any time since the 1940s, when record keeping on the gap began. Presently, the wealthiest 20 percent receive nearly half of all income, while the poorest 20 percent earn less than 4 percent (Kozol, 1990). The effects are devastating for poor children. They are more likely to be born outside of marriage; to live in one-parent, female-headed households; to live in rental housing or to be homeless; to have a working mother; to have medical and dental problems; to engage in sexual activity at an early age; and to become more involved in crime, violence, and drug abuse (Select Committee, 1989).

Low socioeconomic status (SES) children also are more educationally disadvantaged. They tend to live in communities and states that spend less on education, their teachers are often less well paid, they perform more poorly academically, they are more often identified as retarded, and they drop out of school at a higher rate. Additionally, they are more likely to enter school with experiential deficits, for example, not knowing letters, numbers, or colors (Select Committee, 1989).

Earlier, we noted that 13 million of the approximately 60 million children in America fall below the poverty line. Even more critical, 500,000 are homeless. Kozol (1990) refers to these youngsters as "the new untouchables" who grow up in environments plagued by infectious illnesses such as whooping cough and tuberculosis, come to school so tired and hungry that they cannot concentrate, and carry "the smell of destitution with them—the smell of sweat and filth and urine" (p. 52). These children of poverty are the ones hardly anyone wants to teach, and since they more likely congregate in large cities and rural areas, schools in these locations have great difficulty attracting teachers. Only 6 percent of beginning teachers plan to teach in the low-income schools where homeless children are more likely to attend (You and the System, 1990).

Fortunately, advocacy groups with particular interest in economically disadvantaged youth exist. By far the largest is the Children's Defense Fund. Others are the American Agenda and the Committee for Economic Development. Related projects directed toward such children provide special supplemental food programs, prenatal care, child immunization, early education (Head Start is a preschool program for economically disadvantaged 3- and 4-year-olds), and compensatory education (Chapter 1 makes monies available to improve skills in reading and math) (Taylor, 1989).

Teaching Low SES Youth Three things are fundamental to helping children of low socioeconomic status who live in poverty. First, early intervention by communities and schools is essential. As Joan Beck, a syndicated journalist, responding to a study reported in the *Journal of the American Medical Association,* writes:

> How can I put this strongly enough? The surest way to help children to succeed in school is to increase their fundamental ability to learn . . . using the caring and family supporting techniques of early learning during the first few years of life. (1990, p. 11A)

Second, since children of the poor often feel they have little or no control over their lives, Herculean efforts must be made to generate a sense of **efficacy** in them—that is, the sense that they can control their own destinies. All children must feel that they are worthy, they matter, they count! Third, since children of the poor often have educational deficits, you can promote the achievement of low SES students if you:

- Hold high expectations that the children can and will learn
- Respect each student's background, culture, and language style
- Help students understand what they are learning
- Teach thinking and problem-solving skills

 2.15 What experience do you have with children whose SES differs from yours? What further experience would help?

- Plan interesting and engaging learning experiences
- Set and maintain high expectations for behavior
- Maximize heterogeneous or mixed academic grouping
- Provide individual help (Cruickshank, 1990; Knapp, Turnbull, & Shields, 1990)

For the most part, this is good advice for anyone teaching children, although the issue of heterogeneous versus homogeneous grouping remains undecided.

CULTURAL DIFFERENCES

2.16 What experience do you have with children whose cultural backgrounds differ from yours? What further experience would help?

When a group of people have many things in common—for example, language, ideas, values, traditions, and behaviors—they are said to share a culture. Although there is a dominant American culture, in reality America is made up of many subcultures. These subcultures or minorities may be like the dominant culture in some ways and differ from it in others. Beyond having a common language that may not be English, these ethnic groups may also have different modes of dress, food preferences, and ways of thinking and doing.

Being somewhat different from members of the majority culture—that is, being a so-called minority student, does not make a child disadvantaged. However, in cases where ethnicity and/or race are tied to low SES, minority students often do less well in school. This reflects the fact that, regardless of subculture, low SES families usually cannot or do not provide their children with the kinds of early stimulation and academic preparation more typically afforded by middle- and upper-class families. Headden (1997) provides an example. Hispanics have a drop out rate close to 41 percent, but one-third of Hispanic children live in poverty and "start school at a substantial disadvantage: they rarely attend preschool, and their parents, often ill-educated or illiterate, don't read to them" (p. 64). Again, being disadvantaged is more a function of economics than of culture.

A major problem when minorities encounter schools is that school policy, curriculum, and instruction normally reflect the majority American culture, which may be at odds with values and behaviors children learn at home. For example, Hispanics and Native Americans are accustomed to group learning and mutual assistance, while schools often are often organized around competitive, individual learning experience.

Teaching Minority Students   Schools and teachers are making sincere efforts to respect and even encourage healthy diversity. Some of these efforts result from federal law, for example, the Bilingual Education Act (1968). As the name implies, this law sponsors programs that, in the early grades, build upon a child's native language (for example, Spanish) and then gradually introduce English in second or third grade. In this way, students learn the dominant language but maintain and value their native speech. Schools are trying a great array of programs under the rubric of multicultural education. Cushner, McClelland, and Safford (1992) describe four:

- *Teaching the culturally different.* These programs mostly try to help students "develop and maintain their own cultural identity" while also helping them develop competence in the dominant culture. Development of a positive self-concept is a central goal.
- *Human relationships.* The intention in such programs is to help "students of different backgrounds learn to communicate more effectively with others while feeling good about themselves."
- *Single-group studies.* These are mostly programs directed toward a targeted ethnic group. They celebrate that group's identity and achievements. Thus children engage in African-American studies, Native-American studies, and Hispanic-American studies.

Advocates of multicultural education feel that for too long schools have presented a narrow, Eurocentric viewpoint that focuses almost solely on the achievements of Americans of European descent. Therefore, a multicultural approach is needed. That approach, according to University of California–Riverside Professor Carlos Cortes, should focus on at least the five major American ethnic groups: Native Americans, blacks, Latinos, Asians, and Europeans. Additionally, says James Banks, professor at the University of Washington, students must learn and explore certain concepts from multiple perspectives. These concepts include immigration, intercultural interactions, and racism.

Multicultural education also must utilize multicultural teaching. Banks and others feel that teachers must use a variety of instructional alternatives since students from different cultural groups may prefer different ways of learning. For example, G. Pritchy Smith of the University of North Florida notes that Hispanic students tend to be field-sensitive learners. (This concept is presented in a later section of this chapter, Learning Style Differences.) Likewise Diane Boardly-Suber of Hampton University says that most African-American students respond well to collaborative, hands-on approaches to learning (see chapter 7).

Source: Willis, S. (1993, September). Multicultural teaching. *Curriculum Update*, 1–8.

- *Multicultural education.* In an effort to raise the consciousness of all students about various cultures and their contributions, multicultural programs have emerged. They cut across subcultures, focusing on ethnic minority music, arts, or literature, and the history of minorities in America (pp. 154–155). Spotlight on Research 2.3 explains multicultural education in more detail.

GENDER DIFFERENCES

The literature on gender differences addresses, among other things, gender roles, differences in male and female cognition, and the reactions of teachers to males as opposed to females.

Gender roles are learned early. Wynn and Fletcher (1987) report this as occurring during preschool and kindergarten. During this period, most boys begin to engage in outdoor, physical, and aggressive play, while most girls prefer art, doll play, and dancing (Carter, 1987). Although some amount of gender role learning is realistic and healthy, efforts are being made to avoid perpetuating the kind of gender role stereotyping which encourages girls to be dependent and passive and boys to be aggressive and reluctant to show emotion. Many hope that children will acquire a more balanced gender role that combines traits supposedly unique to one gender but valued by both—for example, assertiveness. Such children would supposedly possess high psychological androgyny and would be better adjusted than gender-typed persons. Evidence seems to support this position (Dusek, 1987).

Research shows that boys and girls differ in their cognitive characteristics; at issue is why and how much. Slavin (1988, pp. 528–529) cites Maccoby and Jacklin (1974), who conclude that females generally exhibit greater verbal aptitude than males, while males usually excel in visual-spatial aptitude. Biehler and Snowman (1997, pp. 105–106) note that by the elementary grades, gender differences show up in boy-girl cognitive abilities and in overall performance. Girls frequently are superior in verbal fluency, spelling, writing, reading, and mathematical computation. Boys often excel in mathematical reasoning, spatial relationships, and insight problems. It is important to note, however, that the gender differences are not great and that individual differences within each gender are large. After examining 165 studies, Hyde and Linn (1988) conclude that gender differences in verbal ability are so small as to be insignificant, and the Educational Testing Service (1997), which examined an even greater number of studies, agrees.

Tannen (1991) and others have studied why males and females differ in the way they participate in classrooms. She suggests that boys speak in class more often because they have learned to use language more publicly in play and activity groups. In such groups, language is one way that high-status boys push low-status boys around. Conversely, girls speak in class less often since they have learned to use language more privately, with best friends and for sharing secrets. Good and Brophy (1990) believe that gender differences are not genetic but acquired, and conclude, "To the extent that society begins to expect equal achievement from boys and girls in different subject matter areas, we may begin to see it" (p. 604).

Teachers and schools seem to contribute to the maintenance of gender differences. Boys receive more disapproval and blame, while girls tend to be punished more promptly for aggressive behavior such as calling out answers without first being acknowledged (Slavin, 1991, pp. 468–469). Good and Brophy (1990, p. 602) relate additional ways teachers respond differently to gender. Teachers give blander feedback to girls and more animated, detailed feedback to boys. They sometimes perform complex tasks for girls but merely coach boys to task completion. They encourage girls in grooming and manners but boys in academic striving and accomplishment. Overall, teachers tend to interact more with boys than girls.

Tannen (1991) offers the following advice to help promote gender equality in classroom interaction. Rather than ask students to "attack" an idea or a reading, sometimes ask them how they "feel" about the ideas or material being read. Rather than expect them to raise hands, encourage students to sometimes jump in at will to express themselves. Also, occasionally have students work in homogeneous, single-gender groups.

2.17 How do you think student gender will affect the way you teach?

Effective teachers are aware of gender differences and are able to establish classrooms that do not put either gender at a disadvantage. Certainly we do not want to exclude any students from participation or success in school activities because of gender. Brophy (1985) goes so far as to say that we must not only treat boys and girls the same in similar situations, but that we must overcompensate (for example, direct more math and science questions at girls) to counteract gender expectation differences.

DEVELOPMENTAL DIFFERENCES

Students differ developmentally across and within age groups. In other words, 10-year-olds not only differ from 15-year-olds, they differ from each other. These psychosocial, cognitive, and moral differences are well documented in child development and educational psychology textbooks. Biehler and Snowman (1997) present selected theories of development and then draw implications for teaching. Each theory emphasizes that children must go through predictable developmental or growth stages, and effective instruction should aim at each student's appropriate developmental level.

Psychosocial Development Erickson (1963) suggests that our adult personal and social characteristics result from passing through certain life stages. During that journey, we resolve dichotomies and conflict between positive and negative traits— for example, between trust and mistrust, autonomy and shame, initiative and guilt, industry and inferiority, identity and role confusion, generativity and stagnation, and intimacy and isolation (Biehler and Snowman, 1997, p. 43–45). A healthy personality results when we emerge with more positive than negative traits; that is, we are more trustful, more self-confident, more initiating, more productive, and clearer about our sexual and occupational roles.

One trait that educators deem crucial to healthy personality is **self-esteem,** defined as our personal judgment of our worthiness or how favorably we regard ourselves. Unfortunately, although high self-esteem may be healthy, it does not by itself translate into better school academic performance (Kohn, 1994). Thus, school programs geared to raise self-esteem do not necessarily improve student learning. Improvement in learning is more specifically related to *self-esteem as a learner,* and that seems only to result from actual improved academic performance. Said another way, if we want students to have confidence that they can succeed academically, we must ensure they are having successful academic experiences. There is no simple fix.

Biehler and Snowman suggest we can facilitate development of more positive student personalities by

- allowing young preschool children more free play and guided experimentation, and by not shaming them;
- providing preschool children with activities that foster initiative and a sense of accomplishment, while not censuring them for their questions and actions;
- presenting elementary students with tasks that are within their capacities and then rewarding accomplishment, and encouraging self-competition and cooperation; and
- assisting secondary students to consider who they are, to accept their appearance, to reflect on their sex roles, and to explore and confirm occupational choice (pp. 55–56).

Cognitive Development Piaget (1964) and his colleagues suggest that intellectual development has four stages: sensorimotor, preoperational, concrete operational, and formal operational. Furthermore, they agree that all youth proceed through all stages but at different rates. During the **sensorimotor stage** (birth to 2 years), the intellect develops primarily through using the senses and engaging in motor or physical activity. During the **preoperational, prelogical stage** (2 to 7 years), young learners develop knowledge from their personal experience, by exploring and manipulating concrete objects, and by learning the three Rs and other basic knowledge and skills. In this stage, youngsters start to use symbols such as words and numerals to represent objects.

At the **concrete operational stage** (7 to 11 years), children become capable of logical thought. Among other things, they come to understand conservation (that matter is neither created nor destroyed, but merely changes shape or form). They also can arrange or classify objects into categories, and they can place objects in order according to characteristics such as size, length, or weight.

The **formal operational stage** (11 years and up) is achieved when children more regularly are able to deal in abstractions or perform activities mentally, or "in their heads." At this stage, students are capable of understanding more abstract mathematical concepts, such as ratio. They also now are able to use complex forms of language including proverbs, metaphors, sarcasm, and satire.

In order to utilize what is known about cognitive development, Biehler and Snowman (1997), suggest that you as a teacher:

- Determine the stages of thinking of your students
- Plan learning experiences in terms of these stages
- Use lots of hands-on activities that allow children to manipulate objects
- Mix more advanced with less advanced thinkers so that children can think with and learn from each other
- Encourage students to describe the mental processes they use for reaching concepts and conclusions

Moral Development Piaget (1964) and Kohlberg (1981) have ideas about how **moral development** occurs. Piaget claims that children are capable of two types of moral reasoning: morality of constraint and morality of cooperation. Typical 6-year-olds hold to **morality of constraint.** This means that they regard rules as sacred and unchangeable: Everyone should obey rules in the same way, with no exceptions. On the other hand, typical 12-year-olds hold to **morality of cooperation.** They have reached a point where they believe that rules are flexible and that there can be exceptions to them. Typical 6-year-olds, compared with 12-year-olds, are more adamant that punishment should follow rule breaking. Conversely, 12-year-olds like to take into account the circumstances causing the rule breaking. They are also concerned that misbehavior violates some mutual social agreement.

Kohlberg (1981), too, feels that children proceed through stages of moral reasoning. He originally identified three levels of moral reasoning development, each including two stages. In the earliest of Kohlberg's levels, children 9 or younger stay out of trouble only to avoid punishment or retribution. At the second level, youth 9 to 20 years stay out of trouble because they recognize that rules have been established in order to maintain security and order. At the highest level, reached only after age 20 and only by relatively few adults, people understand, accept, and adhere to the moral principles that undergird our social rules and conventions.

As teachers, we can encourage moral development by engaging students in the discussion of moral dilemmas and moral issues (for example, capital punishment). Additionally, involving our students in the development and maintenance of classroom rules provides an excellent opportunity for children to model the thinking required to make moral decisions that govern many people.

2.18 How will you take children's developmental differences into account?

Children with Special or Exceptional Needs   What does it mean to be exceptional? **Exceptionality** is a term that is used to describe children with special physical, social, emotional, and mental qualities. Such children may be either handicapped or gifted. As Good and Brophy (1990) point out, children who are either handicapped or gifted and talented may be less than successful students unless certain adaptations are made for them (p. 631).

Individuals with **"handicaps"** or **"challenges"** are regularly categorized and labeled even though a stigma may be attached to them as a result. The intention of categorization is to spur efforts to meet their special needs, which are related to cognitive, perceptual, emotional, or behavioral problems. Special-needs categories include physical impairment (orthopedic handicaps, epilepsy, cerebral palsy); visual and hearing impairment (low vision, educationally blind); articulation disorders (stuttering, voicing problems); behavior disorders (conduct disorders, anxiety-withdrawal disorders, immaturity); hyperactivity; and learning disabilities and retardation. The term **challenged** is used increasingly to connote that these children are challenged—not handicapped.

Since learning in the early years is crucial, providing stimulating learning environments for young children is critical. The National Institute of Health argues that, in addition to your need to stimulate children, you need to identify those who need special education. Unfortunately, most children don't go into special education until about 9 years of age (Pipho, 1997).

According to the Education for All Handicapped Children Act (Public Law 94-142) and the more recent Individuals with Disabilities Education Act (Public Law 101-476), children with handicaps are to be taught in the best possible—that is, the "least restrictive," or "most inclusive"—classroom placement, and assisted by a team of specialists. A least restrictive environment is a setting that is as normal as possible. This often means that such children are placed in regular classes for all or part of the school day, a process referred to as *inclusion* or *mainstreaming*. The assisting team includes the child's teacher or teachers, the school psychologist or special education teacher, any persons providing academic or physical assistance or care, and the parents. A formal Individualized Educational Program (IEP) is developed by this team of specialists, including parents, and followed in the classroom. As teachers, you will assist in developing IEPs for children with special challenges, care for such individuals in your classrooms, and be charged with helping them succeed in reaching the goals outlined in the IEP.

Biehler and Snowman (1997), Good and Brophy (1990), Slavin (1991), and Whitmore (1980) offer many suggestions for working with students with special needs. Since these children are so numerous and their problems so varied, prospective teachers are well advised and, in some states, required, to enroll in related coursework.

The second kind of student with special educational needs is labeled gifted and talented. Gifted and talented children are blessed with some combination of above-average ability, creativity, and task commitment (Renzulli, 1979). The Gifted and Talented Act of 1978 describes such children as having intellectual, creative, academic, or leadership abilities. According to Whitmore and Maker (1985), as many as *5 percent of individuals with handicaps are gifted and talented as well.*

Unfortunately, not all children with such gifts are academically oriented or high achievers in school. Studies inform us that 42 percent of gifted high school students underachieve; 54 and 33 percent, respectively, of gifted boys and girls work below their capabilities (Alter, 1953; Gowan, 1955; see also Whitmore, 1980; Butler-Por, 1987). One study (HM Inspectors, 1978) notes that underexploitation of the gifts of children with special talents ranks as one of the most serious deficiencies in Great Britain's elementary schools. A parallel exists in America. As teachers, one of your challenges will be to meet the special needs of these students.

LEARNING STYLE DIFFERENCES

We are well aware that we harbor preferences with regard to *what* we are interested in learning and *how* we wish to learn. Some of us enjoy studying the humanities (art, music, history, philosophy, language), others the social and behavioral sciences (sociology, anthropology, psychology), natural sciences, or mathematics. Further, we prefer to obtain and process information in distinctively personal ways. Some of us prefer to work alone; others enjoy group experiences. Some learn better when information is presented visually; others learn better by hearing the information. As the saying goes, "To each his own."

Children as young as age 4 or 5 begin to display such preferences (Languis, Sanders, & Tipps, 1980). One child will enjoy solitary reading, another will enjoy group projects in social studies, while still another might relish science activities that require manipulating objects and experimenting with them.

For years, psychologists and educators have tried to better understand, describe, and measure individual learning preferences and styles. As a consequence, many different points of view have developed and a number of terms have been coined to describe these styles. Some of the terms are used quite loosely (Della-Dora & Blanchard, 1979). For example, our **learning style** can be thought of as our "learning personality." It is a consistent pattern of behavior and performance we use to approach learning experiences.

The most familiar way of measuring and describing a person's learning style is by exploring **cognitive style;** this term refers to "the consistent ways in which an individual responds to a wide range of perceptual tasks" (Dembo, 1991, p. 585). Familiarity with the following cognitive style differences should help you plan and execute your lessons in a more flexible and responsive manner.

Conceptual Tempo (Kagan et al., 1966)   We all know both impulsive and reflective people. These people differ in **conceptual tempo.** Impulsive people like to work fast, make decisions quickly, and may do things without serious forethought. Consequently, they often rush through their work in what seems to be a careless way, perhaps completing the task incorrectly because they neglect to read the directions or do not persist long enough to complete the task. Because they rush, impulsive students tend to perform more poorly in school tasks requiring analysis and attention to detail.

While impulsive students like to work quickly, reflective students are likely to take considerable time in their work and in making up their minds, usually because they consider several alternative responses before arriving at their answer. Rather than speed, they are concerned about accuracy and about ensuring that they have a good answer. Reflective learners sometimes receive poor evaluations because they are so meticulous. Although they may not finish a task, what they have completed may be nearly perfect. Reflective learners may not participate in class discussions or respond when called upon. Quite literally, they are still thinking about their answer!

Woolfolk (1990) makes clear that not everyone who works fast is impulsive. "Some people are simply very bright and quick to understand" (p. 150). Nor are slow workers necessarily reflective; they might be less bright or able to understand. She notes that some people are fast-accurate or slow-inaccurate thinkers.

As part of normal development, children become more reflective with age. However, the tendency to respond either impulsively or reflectively remains fairly stable. Children can become more reflective by learning to think before they respond or by talking themselves through each step of a complex task (Meichenbaum, 1977).

Field-Sensitive versus Field-Independent Learners (Witkin et al., 1962, 1977)   Students also differ along this continuum, which is part of one's cognitive learning style. On the one hand are students who view situations in their totality, seeing a whole pattern, or gestalt. They "see the forest" as opposed to seeing individual trees therein. Such children are called **field-sensitive,** or **field-dependent.** Persons who have difficulty reading a diagram and putting together something requiring assembly may be field-sensitive.

Field-sensitive learners seem to share certain characteristics. They tend to be more gregarious or people-oriented. Second, they are better at learning material with social content such as social studies, social sciences, and literature. Third, they have difficulty noticing or picking out details and working with material presented to them in an unstructured way. For example, field-sensitive learners may have difficulty with math word problems because they do not identify and distinguish between relevant and irrelevant information. Finally, these learners are more responsive to praise and other kinds of reinforcement and more adversely affected by criticism.

On the other hand are **field-independent** learners. They focus more easily on "the trees," or the details. Their characteristics include being more curious and self-reliant, and less conforming and obedient. Furthermore, they are more task-oriented, and they work better with unstructured tasks such as problem solving. On the downside, perhaps, field-independent students have more difficulty learning social content and working with others. Compared with field-dependent or field-sensitive students, they need less praise and are less affected by criticism.

Some studies (Fritz, 1992) indicate that boys are generally more field-independent, which may result from different child-rearing patterns. Furthermore, some believe that field sensitivity is related to one's cultural heritage. For example Mexican-American and African-American youth have been reported to be more field-sensitive than majority Americans (Ramerez & Price-Williams, 1974). Although, over time, persons may become more or less field-sensitive or -independent, each of us tends to remain one or the other and not to cross over.

Convergent/Divergent Thinking   A third aspect of cognitive style is convergence/divergence. Persons who tend to think in independent, flexible, and imaginative ways are considered more creative. Such persons are sometimes called **divergent thinkers** because they have the ability to come up with different ideas for accomplishing a task or solving a problem. Persons predisposed to think in conventional, typical ways are termed **convergent thinkers.** They search for a single, logical answer. When asked what a pencil might be used for, convergent thinkers reply that a pencil is for writing. Divergent thinkers may add that a pencil can be used for punching holes in paper, rolling clay into sheets, or as a handle for a slingshot.

Perceptual Modality Preferences/Strengths   This fourth dimension of cognitive style describes a learner's tendency to use different sensory modes to understand experiences and to learn (Keefe & Farrell, 1990). For example, some students prefer to learn visually when they see information. You may have heard a friend say, "I'm a visual person." Such persons learn most easily by reading material or seeing something demonstrated. Others are auditory learners who need to hear information in order to learn. Lectures with careful explanations or hearing a textbook on tape are effective ways for these students to learn. Kinesthetic, or tactile, learners need to be physically or even emotionally involved in order to learn. Students who need to count on their fingers to complete arithmetic computations or to manipulate objects or materials are often kinesthetic learners.

Dunn, Dunn, and Price (1987) believe we should determine the preferred learning styles of each of our students and adjust our teaching accordingly. Consequently, they have developed the Learning Style Inventory (Dunn, Dunn, and Price, 1987) for this purpose. Dunn (1984) claims that when learners are provided a context that suits them best, they will achieve more, have better attitudes toward school, and evidence fewer behavioral problems. Kolb (1985) has developed another learning style inventory.

Although the notion of learning styles is attractive to many administrators and educators, research supporting curriculum or teaching changes based solely on some aspect of learning styles is "murky at best" (O'Neil, 1990). However, research on learning styles has contributed some key understandings that can guide us as teachers. These include recognizing that people are different; that learners will respond differently to a variety of instructional methods; and that we need to respect and honor individual differences among the students who make up our classes (Brandt, 1990).

Finally and importantly, as noted in Chapter 1, we must realize that our personal learning style and teaching style generally match. Consequently, we often assume that all of our students enjoy the same kinds of learning experiences we do. Wrong! To be effective, we will have to provide many different kinds of learning activities. In the classroom, variety truly is "the spice of life."

 2.19   What are your many learning characteristics?

LEARNING ABILITY DIFFERENCES

We all know students differ in their academic performance: some are outstanding, most are average, and some have difficulty. These differences are due to four factors, namely; aptitude, attention differences, their home-community environment, and the classroom instruction they receive.

Student Aptitude   Normally, we think of students' aptitude solely as their mental ability or intelligence. We commonly accept the idea that this ability is demonstrated in how well they can perform verbal-language and/or mathematical tasks. However, some psychologists (Gardner, 1983, 1988, 1995 and Gardner & Hatch, 1989) remind us that students have multiple aptitudes. In addition to having linguistic or language ability and logical-mathematical ability, they also possess abilities (termed *intelligences*) in spatial matters, body kinesthetics, music, interpersonal relations, self-understanding, and pattern recognition (see Figure 2.7).

To understand Gardner's multiple theory of intelligence, depicted in Figure 2.7, it is necessary to understand his definition of *intelligence*. Intelligence is the ability to solve problems or make something of value. That ability must meet three conditions: brain evidence must support its existence, persons must be particularly good or bad at it, and it must be possessed and needed by animals other than humans (Checkley, 1997).

"I don't care if he does have an I.Q. of 169—I still think he's faking."

FIGURE 2.7 Eight Kinds of Intelligence

- *Linguistic intelligence* is the capacity to use language, your native language, and perhaps other languages, to express what's on your mind and to understand other people. Poets really specialize in linguistic intelligence, but any kind of writer, orator, speaker, lawyer, or a person for whom language is an important stock in trade highlights linguistic intelligence.

- People with a highly developed *logical-mathematical intelligence* understand the underlying principles of some kind of a causal system, the way a scientist or a logician does; or can manipulate numbers, quantities, and operations, the way a mathematician does.

- *Spatial intelligence* refers to the ability to represent the spatial world internally in your mind—the way a sailor or airplane pilot navigates the large spatial world, or the way a chess player or sculptor represents a more cicumscribed spatial world. Spatial intelligence can be used in the arts or in the sciences. If you are spatially intelligent and oriented toward the arts, you are more likely to become a painter or a sculptor or an architect than, say, a musician or a writer. Similarly, certain sciences like anatomy or topology emphasize spatial intelligene.

- *Bodily kinesthetic intelligence* is the capacity to use your whole body or parts of your body—your hand, your fingers, your arms—to solve a problem, make something, or put on some kind of a production. The most evident examples are people in athletics or the performing arts, particularly dance or acting.

- *Musical intelligence* is the capacity to think in music, to be able to hear patterns, recognize them, remember them, and perhaps manipulate them. People who have a strong musical intelligence don't just remember music easily—they can't get it out of their minds, it's so omnipresent. Now, some people will say, "Yes, music is important, but it's a talent, not an intelligence." And I say, "Fine, let's call it a talent." But, then we have to leave the word *intelligent* out of *all* discussions of human abilities. You know, Mozart was damned smart!

- *Interpersonal intelligence* is understanding other people. It's an ability we all need, but is at a premium if you are a teacher, clinician, salesperson, or politician. Anybody who deals with other people has to be skilled in the interpersonal sphere.

- *Intrapersonal intelligence* refers to having an understanding of yourself, of knowing who you are, what you can do, what you want to do, how you react to things, which things to avoid, and which things to gravitate toward. We are drawn to people who have a good understanding of themselves because those people tend not to screw up. They tend to know what they can do. They tend to know what they can't do. And they tend to know where to go if they need help.

- *Naturalist intelligence* designates the human ability to discriminate among living things (plants, animals) as well as sensitivity to other features of the natural world (clouds, rock configurations). This ability was clearly of value in our evolutionary past as hunters, gatherers, and farmers; it continues to be central in such roles as botanist or chef. I also speculate that much of our consumer society exploits the naturalist intelligences, which can be mobilized in the discrimination among cars, sneakers, kinds of makeup, and the like. The kind of pattern recognition valued in certain of the sciences may also draw upon naturalist intelligence.

Source: H. Gardner in Checkley, K. (1997, September). The first seven and the eighth. *Educational Leadership, 55* (1), 8–13.

Thus, Gardner and others want teachers to recognize and nurture the diversity of abilities different students have. Let's explore an example—interpersonal intelligence, or the ability to understand others.

As we know, understanding and getting along with others is an important human ability. Bell Laboratories, a high-tech think tank, reports that its most valued, productive electrical engineers excel in traits such as cooperation, empathy, rapport, and the ability to build consensus. This particular attribute is often termed **emotional intelligence,** or EQ. Gardner calls it *interpersonal intelligence* (again, see Figure 2.7).

Unfortunately, EQ is on the wane among American youth, and children with low EQ are more likely to be disobedient, to pick fights, to engage in unlawful activity, and to become pregnant (Goleman, 1995). To reverse this trend, the Yale Child Study Center is developing courses for K–12 teachers that promote student ability to control impulses, show empathy, cooperate with others, focus on a task, pursue goals, and resolve conflicts. You can learn a lot more about EQ from Elias et al. (1997) and by visiting the website **http://www.cfapress.org/casel/casel.html.**

Since Gardner recognizes at least seven kinds of intelligence, including EQ, he recommends teachers introduce and examine topics in a number of different ways (Gardner, 1995). For example, if the topic at hand is "conflict," teachers can introduce and examine it by telling a story about conflict, through formal argument about what conflict is, by engaging students in a simulation such as Starpower, or by engaging students in artistic expression—'Picture conflict'. What does it look like?" These strategies facilitate personalized, multiple ways of knowing and understanding. Gardner characterizes a good school as one that takes learning differences very seriously. In such a school, teachers develop curriculum, teach, and assess learning in ways that serve the multiple intelligences children possess.

Dusty, a Child with ADHD

Dusty Nash, an angelic-looking blond child of 7, awoke at 5:00 one recent morning in his Chicago home and proceeded to throw a fit. He wailed. He kicked. Every muscle in his body flew in furious motion. Finally, after 30 minutes, Dusty pulled himself together sufficiently to head downstairs for breakfast. While his mother bustled about the kitchen, the hyperkinetic child pulled a box of Kix cereal from the cupboard and sat on a chair.

But sitting still was not in the cards this morning. After grabbing some cereal with his hands, he began kicking the

box, scattering little round corn puffs across the room. Next, he turned his attention to the TV set—or rather, the table supporting it. The table was covered with a checkerboard Con-Tact paper, and Dusty began peeling it off. Then he became intrigued with the spilled cereal and started stomping it to bits. At this point, his mother interceded. In a firm but calm voice, she told her son to get the dust pan and broom and clean up the mess. Dusty got out the dust pan but forgot the rest of the order. Within seconds he was dismantling the dust pan, piece by piece. His

next project: grabbing three rolls of toilet paper from the bathroom and unraveling them around the house.

It was only 7:30, and his mother, who teaches a medical school course on death and dying, was already feeling half-dead from exhaustion. Dusty was to see his doctors that day at 4:00, and they had asked her not to give the boy the drug he usually takes to control his hyperactivity and attention problems. . . . It was going to be a very long day without it.

Source: Wallis, C. (1994, July 18). Life in overdrive. *Time, 144*(3), 50.

Student Attention Differences Students also vary in their ability to pay attention. Some, are so adversely affected that they are referred to as having **attention deficit disorder,** or ADD. Persons with ADD may be hyperactive inattentive, hyperactive impulsive, or impulsive but not hyperactive (*Diagnostic and Statistical Manual of Mental Disorders,* 1980). The hyperactive variety of ADD, attention deficit hyperactivity disorder (ADHD), is portrayed in Case 2.2.

Although the term ADHD was not well known two decades ago (such children were merely referred to as obstreporous), some say that up to 35 million children, mostly boys under 18 (about 4 percent) display its symptoms, which include extreme distractibility, almost reckless impulsiveness, and general difficulty in sitting or being still. In the Rochester, New York, area, 13 percent of boys ages 6 to 12 are medicated for ADHD. Some fear that adults are too willing to medicate children in order to make adult lives easier (French, 1996).

Children with such characteristics may not function well in traditional schools unless schools make accommodations. Without special care, such children have an extremely high risk of school failure, substance abuse, and lawbreaking. Additionally, they often have few friends and their parents or caregivers frequently are blamed for failure to control them. Over time, such children may lose their sense of self-worth and may fall far behind academically.

Within the classroom, teachers are urged to consider giving such children stand-up desks, seating them near the teacher, and letting them take tests in a quiet area. Other ways you can assist such children include helping them to be organized, establishing a predictable schedule of activities, assigning them a location for school possessions, and using principles of behavior modification that are presented in the next chapter. (Additional suggestions are found in Armstrong, 1996a, and Pellegrini and Horvat, 1995.) Furthermore, you are warned not to automatically label such kids as ADD or ADHD since their symptoms, if new, may be the result of some other problem such as anxiety, depression, or neurological dysfunction (Armstrong, 1996b). Figure 2.8 lists some of the symptoms of the disorder.

Finally, students differ in their interest and self-concept. Those who are interested, who have a sense that they are in control and are "OK," are better able and more likely to learn. Thus, key factors contributing to student aptitude, or ability to learn, are intelligence, emotional maturity, interest, and self-concept.

If eight or more of the following statements seem to characterize a child you know, he or she has traits common to ADHD. A medical diagnosis may be useful.

1. Often fidgets or squirms when sitting
2. Has difficulty remaining seated
3. Is easily distracted
4. Has difficulty awaiting turns
5. Often blurts things out
6. Has difficulty following directions
7. Has difficulty paying attention
8. Often shifts from one incomplete activity to another
9. Has difficulty playing quietly
10. Often interrupts or intrudes
11. Often doesn't seem to listen
12. Talks excessively
13. Often engages in dangerous play without considering consequences

Source: Adapted from Wallis, C. (1994, July 18). Life in overdrive. *Time, 144* (3), 50.

Student Environment   A student's environment includes his or her home and family, school and classroom, peer group and out-of-school life. As we have learned, home and family usually have the greatest impact on a student's school performance. However, all these factors weigh heavily.

Classroom Instruction   Walberg (1984) and others maintain that teachers can do very little to affect a student's environment or his ability to learn, but *we can provide effective instruction.* Both the quality of the learning experiences we provide and the amount of time our students engage in learning are critical to school performance.

Some of our students are fortunate. They have been blessed with high aptitude for learning a number of things, they live in a rich environment, they are enrolled in excellent schools, and they have experienced effective teaching. Most such students probably could do well in almost any school and any classroom. Other students are less fortunate. They do not have high multiple intelligences, they may be developmentally slower, they are less interested in education, and they see little good or value in themselves. These students cannot succeed in just any school or classroom; they require thoughtful, high-quality teaching and teachers. You can live up to that challenge. Chapters 10 and 11 provide many clues that will help you to be a better teacher.

2.20   Are you up to the challenge of teaching students who have difficulty learning?

Try Activity 2.2

IMPLICATIONS FOR TEACHERS

Teachers are effective in large part because they care about children enough to accommodate their seemingly endless diversity. Less effective teachers often have a difficult time either noticing or attending to the variability of students in their classes. They want and tend to see the class more as a homogeneous group. While this makes instruction less complicated, if you are to advance from a novice to a more expert teacher, you must learn to teach children who are socioeconomically, culturally, and developmentally diverse and diverse in terms of gender, exceptionality, learning style, and learning ability. To summarize, our schools need teachers who will:

- Care about economically disadvantaged youth and be willing to work with them (this implies willingness to teach in rural and urban schools)
- Help students gain a feeling of efficacy or control over their destinies

- Accept, appreciate, and promote culturally specific characteristics
- Promote the best attributes of both genders in all children
- Provide students with experiences that may help them develop positive personalities
- Take into account students' varying levels of cognitive development when teaching
- Encourage growth in moral development
- Show concern for and work with exceptional students
- Allow for students' learning, thinking, and cognitive styles and their multiple intelligences

Try Activity 2.3

Some Final Thoughts

This chapter introduced you to societal and child diversity and the challenges they present. But was it really an introduction for you? Much of what you read is not really new. How could it be? You have lived twenty years or more. You read newspapers and periodicals, listen to the radio, watch television, surf the Internet, and partake of life. You already knew that America is changing, families are changing, childhood is changing. Perhaps you have even had up-close, personal experiences related to diversity.

However, things are different now. You are going to be a teacher. You are going to be a great teacher. So you must begin not only to be aware of diversity and its challenges, but you must have or develop a positive mindset toward them. That mindset must include optimism, a sense of adventure and daring, and a desire to be a part of the solution. Your glass is half-full. Go for it!

Try Activity 2.4

CHAPTER SUMMARY

- To be an effective teacher, you must be aware of the larger social context in which we work. This includes a population that is growing in size, shifting geographically south and west and toward cities, becoming older on average, and becoming more culturally diverse.
- America's families are also changing. Parents start families later in life, and families are smaller, less stable, and increasingly likely to be headed by one parent (usually female). A strong relationship exists among family background, income, educational levels of parents, and how well children do in school. Children from low-income, single-parent homes, among other factors, are more likely to be low achievers and to develop school problems. Children with three risk factors (health problems at birth, parents without secondary education, families with histories of alcoholism and mental illness) may have serious learning or behavioral problems. Additionally, if they live in single-parent homes, they are more likely to become involved in crime and less likely to recover from mental health problems.
- The nature of childhood is changing. More children, particularly minority youth, are growing up in poverty; more lack parental supervision and must depend on self-care and day care; more are reported as abused and neglected; and more are being hurried to grow up. Children today are perceived to have increased knowledge and autonomy, but they seem less ready to respond or learn in school, and they are often perceived as less respectful.
- America's schools are changing. We are pursuing greater equity by desegregating schools, eliminating same-gender schools, educating special-needs students in regular classes, improving the way we teach low-English-proficiency students,

and offering multiethnic education. We are seeking to improve academic achievement by establishing more rigorous curricula, performing more frequent and better testing, and implementing what we've learned about effective schooling and teaching. We are providing better support for families by offering before- and after-school child care. We increasingly foster and celebrate cultural differences in schools, and we not only use but teach technology.

- Great socioeconomic disparity exists in America, and it affects childhood. Being a child in a low SES household is more often associated with being born outside marriage; living with a working mother who is single; living in rental property or being homeless; having health and dental problems; engaging in early sexual activity; becoming more involved in crime, violence, and substance abuse; attending poorer schools with lower-paid teachers; doing more poorly in school; being more often identified as retarded; and dropping out.

- Great cultural differences also characterize America today. Minorities are growing at a faster rate than the majority white population, and schools are taking this cultural diversity into account by offering a variety of programs aimed at respecting and encouraging healthy differences. Schools are also working toward eliminating gender stereotyping and providing equal educational opportunities to both boys and girls.

- Students differ developmentally, that is, psychosocially, cognitively, and morally. Teachers can facilitate children's development by assisting them in building healthy personalities, providing educational experiences suitable to each child's cognitive level, and helping them think through moral issues and dilemmas.

- Students differ according to their physical, social, emotional, and mental needs. Some have exceptional abilities and talents, while others have exceptional needs. Some also seem to have preferences regarding how they like to learn. Teachers need to recognize these exceptionalities and learning preferences and adjust their teaching accordingly.

- Students differ in how well they do in school. Some have a high aptitude for school learning, live in a stimulating environment, and attend excellent schools. Others do not. Teachers can make a great impact by recognizing and rewarding students who possess different kinds of intelligence.

ISSUES AND PROBLEMS FOR DISCUSSION

ISSUES   Here are some issues for you to debate.

1. How can schools help families to have a positive impact on their children's education?
2. To what extent should schools and teachers assume any of the normal family functions, such as nurturance, caring, and intimacy?
3. How can schools and teachers offset or overcome the effects of poverty, lack of home supervision, child neglect or abuse, low parental and child expectations toward education, gender stereotyping, crass materialism, or other negative factors?
4. How involved should teachers get when students are at risk?
5. How can teachers accommodate developmental, learning style, and ability differences among children?
6. Is it sound to reduce diversity by grouping students for instruction according to one or more of their characteristics—for example, interests, abilities, or learning styles? Or should groups be intentionally diverse?
7. Are exceptional children better off with similar or dissimilar peers?

8. Should more money be invested in educating certain children? Which ones?

9. To what extent should students themselves be responsible for raising their own efforts to achieve?

10. Is it reasonable for society to expect schools to resolve social ills?

11. How well prepared are you to teach others radically different from you?

PROBLEMS   The following are some related, verbatim, day-to-day problems that teachers have shared with us. How might you resolve them?

Problem 1:   When school started today, one of the children came into the room in tears. She was so poorly dressed that she was just about frozen. She wore no gloves or boots and had a very thin scarf on her head. Her hands, ears, and feet were very cold. She came from a home without heat.

Problem 2:   Today got off to a frustrating start. Many children had runny noses, red eyes, and seemed drowsy. Some children had no breakfast, since their parents are still out or are asleep when they leave home.

Problem 3:   When the lesson began, many children were unable to provide a paper and pencil, since it was late in the month and their parents' welfare money had run out.

Problem 4:   A student from a migrant family is having trouble with subtraction facts. The other students make fun of him. I think the student considers this a racial thing, and he has become resentful and defensive.

Problem 5:   There are several non-English-speaking children in class. They are well-behaved but need an inordinate amount of individual attention, which I don't have the time to provide.

Problem 6:   In the midst of a math lesson, an emotionally disturbed boy throws all his math disks on the floor. After I pick them up, he throws them down again. He then decides to walk around the room for the rest of the period.

Problem 7:   Carolyn stays or walks beside me the entire recess and as often as possible in the classroom. She will not move from my side.

Problem 8:   Eight students never seem to understand the science lesson. Just when I think they understand, a quiz reveals otherwise. With forty-three students, there simply is not enough time to give them individual help.

Problem 9:   One boy refuses to leave the room, fearful that boys from another school are waiting to kill him. He says the problem is the result of an incident that occurred over the weekend.

Problem 10:   A boy came into the room in obvious pain with strips of cloth wrapped around his right hand. He says that his mother's boyfriend held his hand on a toaster.

Problem 11:   One of the girls in gym class is very upset that she cannot participate in square dancing. Her parents do not condone any kind of dancing.

Problem 12:   A seventh-grade boy asks to be transferred to another class or school because he thinks the other boys don't like him. He stays by himself and does not seem to seek the friendship of others.

ACTIVITY 2.1: Personal Feelings about Teaching Diverse Students   Write a paragraph or so on the topic "What I think it will be like to teach diverse children in a diverse society." Share your thoughts with your class.

ACTIVITY 2.2: Five Student Types   Scholars (Good & Power, 1976) have identified five types of students. If you are in a field experience, with the help of your mentor teacher try to identify one of each type. How might you serve each?

1. *Successful.* These students are academically successful in school. They work hard and cause few problems. They like school and teachers.
2. *Social.* These students are more interested in the social aspects of school life than in the academic. They are popular and friendly. Their socializing can cause problems.
3. *Alienated.* These students may be openly hostile toward the school and teachers, or they may be passive and withdrawn.
4. *Dependent.* Such students are emotionally and/or academically insecure. They need approval and help.
5. *Phantom.* Such students are quiet, independent, and seldom seen or heard.

   Names of students I have identified and how I would work with each:

1. Successful _____

2. Social _____

3. Alienated _____

4. Dependent _____

5. Phantom _____

ACTIVITY 2.3: Obtain Classroom Teachers' Views about School and Classroom Diversity   Talk with one or more classroom teachers about student diversity. Perhaps they would respond to questions such as:

- Have you noticed any changes in the population of the neighborhood in which the school is situated? Explain.
- Have you noticed any changes in the families of students in your classes? Explain.
- Do you think children are changing in any way? Explain.
- How is this school changing in order to foster such things as student equity, improved learning among all children, improved parent support, the celebration of diversity, use of technology, or other goals related to better education?
- How is this school helping teachers to become more aware of student diversity? How is it reacting to student diversity?

ACTIVITY 2.4: The Implications of Family and Student Diversity for Teaching After reading this chapter, make a list of five to ten *major* things you have learned and their possible implications for classroom practice. For example:

Major Learning	**Possible Implication**
1. Students differ from one another in many ways.	1. To be effective as a teacher, I need to know how my students vary and how I can accommodate their differences. I certainly can't expect to teach them all successfully without using different approaches from student to student and from time to time.
2.	2.
3.	3.
4.	4.
5.	5.
6.	6.
7.	7.
8.	8.
9.	9.
10.	10.

REFERENCES

A profile of American 8th graders. (1990). Washington, DC: U.S. Government Printing Office.

Alderman, M. K. (1990, September). Motivation for at-risk students. *Educational Leadership, 48*(1), 27–30.

Alter, H. (1953). A study of high school students with scores of 130 and above on the California Test of Mental Maturity; unpublished paper.

American Council on Education. (1989, May). *One-third of a nation: A report of the Commission on Minority Participation in Education and American Life.* Denver: Education Commission of the States.

Armstrong, T. (1996, February). ADD: Does it really exist? *Phi Delta Kappan, 77*(7), 424–428.

Armstrong, T. (1996, February). A wholistic approach to attention deficit disorder. *Educational Leadership, 53*(5), 34–36.

Beck, J. (1990, June 12). Getting to children early must be stressed. *Columbus Dispatch,* 11A.

Biddle, B. (1997, September). Foolishness, dangerous nonsense, and real correlates of state differences in achievement. *Phi Delta Kappan 79*(1), 9–13.

Biehler, R., & Snowman, J. (1997). *Psychology applied to teaching.* 8th ed. Boston: Houghton Mifflin.

Bower, E. M. (1978). *Teachers talk about their feelings.* Rockville, MD: Center for Studies of Child and Family Health, National Institute of Mental Health.

Bracey, G. (1995, March). The myth of school failure. Paper presented at the Association for Supervision and Curriculum Development Conference, San Francisco.

Bradley, A. (1990, April 25). Delinquency research affirms benefits of two parents. *Education Week.*

Brandt, R. (1990). On learning styles: A conversation with Pat Guild. *Educational Leadership, 48*(2), 10–13.

Brophy, J. (1985). Interactions of male and female students with male and female teachers. In L. Wilkinson & C. Marrett (Eds.), *Gender differences in classroom interaction* (pp. 115–142). Orlando, FL: Academic Press.

Brown, B. F. (1980, April). A study of the school needs of children from one-parent families. *Phi Delta Kappan, 62*(8), 537–540.

Butler-Por, N. (1987). Underachievers in schools: Issues and intervention. New York: John Wiley & Sons.

Caplan, N., Choy, M. H., & Whitmore, J. K., (1991). *Children of the boat people: A study of educational success.* Ann Arbor: University of Michigan Press.

Carter, D. B. (1987). The role of peers in sex role socialization. In D. B. Carter (Ed.), *Current conceptions of sex roles and sex typing* (pp. 101–121). New York: Praeger.

Center for the Study of Social Policy. (1992). *What the 1990 census tells us about children.* Washington, DC: The Center for the Study of Social Policy.

Checkley, K. (1997, September). The first seven and the eighth. *Educational Leadership, 55*(1), 8–13.

Children's Defense Fund. (1991). *Latino child poverty in the United States.* Washington, DC: The Children's Defense Fund.

Children's Defense Fund. (1992). *Child poverty data from the 1990 Census.* Washington, DC: The Children's Defense Fund.

Clode, D., & Jacobson, J. (1989, April). The future and America's schools: What do these trends mean for education? *School Administrator, 45*(4), 15–16, 18.

Cohen, D. (1993, September 22). Frequent moves said to boost risk of school problems. *Education Week, 13*(3), 15.

Cruickshank, D. (1990). *Research that informs teachers and teacher educators.* Bloomington, IN: Phi Delta Kappa.

Cushner, K., McClelland, A., & Safford, P. (1992). *Human diversity in education.* New York: McGraw-Hill.

Dahmke, B. (nd.) Aaron, a child at risk. (unpublished).

Della-Dora, D., & Blanchard, L. J. (Eds.). (1979). *Moving toward self-directed learning.* Alexandria, VA: Association for Supervision and Curriculum Development.

Dembo, M. H. (1991). *Applying educational psychology in the classroom.* New York: Longman.

Diagnostic and statistical manual of mental disorders. Third Edition (1980). Washington: American Psychiatric Association.

Dimensions. (1993, September 29). Children in poverty. *Education Week, 13*(4), 3.

Dowd, F. S. (1990). *Latchkey children in the library and community: Issues, strategies, and programs.* Phoenix, AZ: Oryx Press.

Dunn, R. (1984, Winter). Learning style: State of the science. *Theory Into Practice, 23*(1), 10–19.

Dunn, R., Dunn, K., & Price, G. (1987). *Learning style inventory.* Lawrence, KS: Price Systems.

Dusek, J. (1987). Sex roles and adjustment. In D. B. Carter (Ed.), *Current conceptions of sex roles and sex typing* (pp. 211–222). New York: Praeger.

Educational Testing Service. (1997). ETS gender study: How females and males perform in educational settings. Princeton, NJ: Educational Testing Service.

Education Week. (1992, August 5). The N.E.A. released a new report, *11*(40), 12.

Elias, M., Zins, J., Weissberg, R., Fry, K., Greenberg, M., Haynes, N., Kessler, R., Schwab-Stone, M., & Shriver, T. (1997). *Promoting social and emotional learning.* Alexandria, VA: Association for Supervision and Curriculum Development.

Elkind, D. (1981). *The hurried child: Growing up too fast too soon.* Reading, MA: Addison-Wesley.

Elkind, D. (1982, January). The hurried child. *Instructor,* 41–43.

Erikson, E. (1963). *Childhood and society.* Second Edition. New York: Norton.

French, L. (1996, Fall). Haircuts and hyperactivity. *Rochester Review, 59* (1), 33.

Fritz, R. L. (1992). *A study of gender differences in cognitive style and volition.* (ERIC Document Reproduction Service No ED354379).

Fuchs, R. F., & Reklis, D. M. (1992, January). America's children: Economic perspectives and policy options. *Science, 255,* 41–46.

Gardner, H. (1983). *Frames of mind: The theory of multiple intelligences.* New York: Basic Books.

Gardner, H. (1988). Beyond the IQ: Education and human development. *Harvard Educational Review, 57,* 187–193.

Gardner, H. (1995). Reflections on multiple intelligences. *Phi Delta Kappan, 77*(3), 200–209.

Gardner, H., & Hatch, T. (1989). Multiple intelligences go to school. *Educational Researcher, 18*(8), 4–10.

Gelardo, M. S., & Sanford, E. E. (1987). Child abuse and neglect: A review of the literature. *School Psychology Review, 16,* 137–155.

Goleman, D. (1995). *Emotional intelligence.* New York: Bantam Books.

Goleman, D. (1995, September 17). successful people demonstrate high "nice guy" quotient. New York Times Wire Service. *Columbus Dispatch,* 6B.

Good, T., & Brophy, J. (1990). *Educational psychology: A realistic approach.* New York: Longman.

Good, T., & Power, C. (1976). Designing successful classroom environments for different types of students. *Journal of Curriculum Studies, 8,* 1–16.

Gowan, J. (1955). The underachieving gifted child: A problem for everyone. *Exceptional Children, 21,* 247–248.

Hacker, A. (1982). Farewell to the family? *New York Review of Books, 29,* 37–45.

Hamburg, D. A. (1992). *The family crucible and healthy child development.* New York: Carnegie Corporation.

Hamburg, D. A. (1995). *A developmental strategy to prevent lifelong damage.* New York: Carnegie Corporation of America.

Headden, S. (1997, October 20). The Hispanic dropout mystery. *U.S. News & World Report, 123*(15), 64–65.

HM Inspectors of Schools. (1978). *Primary education in England.* London: HMSO.

Hofferth, S. (1987, February). Implications of family trends for children: A research perspective. *Educational Leadership, 44*(5), 78–84.

Hyde, J., & Linn, M. (1988, April 5–8). Gender differences in verbal ability: A meta-analysis. Paper presented at the annual meeting of the American Educational Research Association in New Orleans.

Jencks, C., et al. (1972). *Inequality: A reassessment of the effect of family and schooling in America.* New York: Basic Books.

Kagan, J., et al. (1966). Modifiability of an impulsive tempo. *Journal of Educational Psychology, 57,* 359–365.

Kauffman, J. M. (1985). *Characteristics of children's behavior disorders.* Third Edition. Columbus, OH: Merrill.

Keefe, J. W., & Farrell, B. R. (1990). Developing a defensible learning style paradigm. *Educational Leadership, 46*(2), 57–61.

Knapp, M. S., Turnbull, B. J., & Shields, P. M. (1990, September). New directions for educating children of poverty. *Educational Leadership, 48*(1), 4–8.

Kohlberg, L. (1981). *The philosophy of moral development.* New York: Harper and Row.

Kohn, A. (1994). The truth about self-esteem. *Phi Delta Kappan 76*(4), 272–283.

Kolb, D. (1985). *Learning style inventory (LSI).* Boston: McBer.

Kozol, J. (1990, Winter-Spring). The new untouchables. *Newsweek Special Issue,* 48–49, 52–53.

Languis, M., Sanders, T., & Tipps, S. (1980). *Brain and learning: Directions in early childhood education.* Washington, DC: National Association for the Education of Young Children.

Louv, R. (1990). *Childhood's future.* Boston: Houghton Mifflin.

Maccoby, E., & Jacklin, C. (1974). *The psychology of sex differences.* Stanford, CA: Stanford University Press.

Masten, A S., Best, K. M., & Garmezy, N. (1991). Resilience and development: Contributions from the study of children who overcome adversity. *Development and Psychopathology, 2,* 425–444.

Meichenbaum, D. (1977). *Cognitive behavior modification: An integrative approach.* New York: Plenum.

Metropolitan Life. (1992). *Ready or not: Grade level preparedness: Teachers views on current issues in education.* New York: Metropolitan Life Insurance Co.

National Center for Children in Poverty. (1990). *Five million children: A statistical profile of our poorest young citizens.* Washington, DC: The National Center for Children in Poverty.

National Center for Education Statistics. (1997). *Fathers' involvement in their children's schools.* Washington, DC: Government Printing Office. (Document NCES # 98091)

O'Neil, J. (1990). Findings of styles research murky at best. *Educational Leadership, 48*(2), 7.

Pellegrini, A. D., & Horvat, M. (1995). A developmental contextualist critique of attention deficit hyperactivity disorder. *Educational Researcher, 24*(1), 13–20.

Piaget, J. (1964). *The moral judgment of the child.* New York: Free Press.

Pipho, C. (1997, September). Reshaping special education. *Phi Delta Kappan 79*(1), 5–6.

Postman, N. (1983, March). The disappearing child. *Educational Leadership, 40*(6), 10–16.

Plucker, J. & Omdal, S. (1997, June 18). Beyond boredom. *Education Week, 16*(38), 32.

Poverty and Wealth Statistics Branch. (1991). *Poverty in the United States 1990; Money income of households, families, and persons 1990; Measuring the effect of benefits and taxes on income and poverty 1990.* Washington, DC: U.S. Bureau of the Census.

Ramerez, M., & Price-Williams, D. (1974). Cognitive styles of children of three ethnic groups in the United States. *Journal of Cross-Cultural Psychology, 5*(2), 212–219.

Raspberry, W. (1993, January 14). Parents must instill kids with will to learn. *Columbus Dispatch/Forum,* 13A.

Renzulli, J. (1979). *A guidebook for evaluating programs for the gifted and talented.* Los Angeles: National State Leadership Training Institute of the Gifted and Talented.

Resnick, M. (1997, September 10). Protecting adolescents from harm. *Journal of the American Medical Association, 278*(10), 823–832.

Richardson, J. (1993, May 19). Teachers in poll seek greater federal push for parent education. *Education Week,* Vol. 12 p. 10.

Richardson, J. L., et al. (1990, September). Characteristics of eighth grade students who initiate self-care in elementary and junior high school. *Pediatrics, 86*(3), 448–454.

Select Committee on Children, Youth and Families. (1989). *U.S. children and their families: Current conditions and recent trends, 1989.* Washington, DC: U.S. Government Printing Office.

Slavin, R. (1988). *Educational psychology: Theory into practice.* Second Edition. Englewood Cliffs, NJ: Prentice Hall.

Slavin, R. (1991). *Educational psychology: Theory into practice.* Third Edition. Englewood Cliffs, NJ: Prentice Hall.

Steinberg, L., Brown, B., & Dornbusch, S. (1996). *Beyond the classroom: Why social reform has failed and what parents need to do.* New York: Simon and Schuster.

Stevenson, H. W., Chen, C., & Lee, S. (1993, January 1). Mathematics achievement of Chinese, Japanese, and American children: Ten years later. *Science, 259,* 53–58.

Suransky, V. (1982). *The erosion of childhood.* Chicago: University of Chicago Press.

Tannen, D. (1991, July 19). Teachers' classroom strategies should recognize that men and women use language differently. *Chronicle of Higher Education, 37*(40), B1, B3.

Taylor, R. N. (1989, August–September). A promise at risk. *Modern Maturity, 32*(4), 32–41, 84–90.

U.S. Department of Health, Education and Welfare. (1966). *Equality of educational opportunity. Summary report.* (The Coleman Report). Washington, DC: U.S. Government Printing Office.

Walberg, H. (1984, May). Improving the productivity of American schools. *Educational Leadership, 41,* 19–27.

Walberg, H., & Fowler, W. (1987, October). Expenditure and size efficiency of public school districts. *Educational Researcher, 16,* 5–13.

Waldrop, J., & Exter, T. (1990, March). The legacy of the 1980's. *American Demographics, 13*(3), 32–35.

Wallis, C. (1994, July 18). Life in overdrive. *Time, 144*(3), 50.

Wang, M. C. & Gordon, E. W. (Eds.) (1994). *Educational resilience in inner-city America: Challenges and prospects.* Hillsdale, NJ: Lawrence Erlbaum Associates.

Weisman, J. (1990, September 19). Latchkey 8th graders likely to possess emotional risk factors, study discloses. *Education Week, 10*(3), 6.

Werner, E. E., & Smith, R. S. (1992). *Overcoming the odds: High-risk children from birth to adulthood.* Ithaca, NY: Cornell University Press.

Whitmore, J. (1980). *Giftedness, conflict and underachievement.* Boston: Allyn and Bacon.

Whitmore, J., & Maker, C. (1985). *Intellectual giftedness in disabled persons.* Rockville, MD: Aspen Systems Corporation.

Willis, S. (1993, September). Multicultural teaching. *Curriculum Update,* 1–8.

Winfield, L. F. (1991, November). Resilience, schooling and development in African-American youth: A conceptual framework. *Education & Urban Society, 24,* 3–14.

Wingert, P., & Kantrowitz, B. (1990, Winter-Spring). The day care generation. *Newsweek Special Issue,* 86–92.

Witkin, H. A., et al. (1962). *Psychological differentiation.* New York: Wiley.

Witkin, H., Moore, C., Goodenough, D., & Cox, P. (1977). Field-dependent and independent cognitive styles and their educational implications. *Review of Educational Research, 47,* 1–64.

Woolfolk, A. (1990). *Educational psychology.* Englewood Cliffs, NJ: Prentice Hall.

Wynn, R., & Fletcher, C. (1987). Sex role development and early educational experience. In D. B. Carter (Ed.), *Current conceptions of sex roles and sex typing* (pp. 79–88). New York: Praeger.

You and the system. (1990, April). *Teacher Magazine, 7*(1), 10.

Zimiles, H. (1986). The changing American child. In T. Tomlinson & H. Walberg (Eds.), *Academic work & educational excellence, etc.* (pp. 61–84). Berkeley, CA: McCutcheon.

Three Schools of Thought about Learning and Teaching

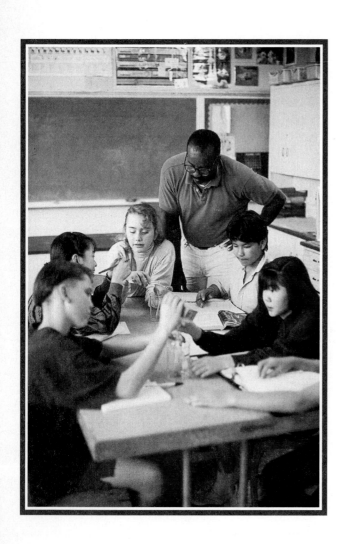

Contents

Have you been in classrooms where a teacher was teaching, but not all students were learning? This could happen to you. If it does, you will ask yourself, "what should I be doing that I'm not doing?" Hopefully, when you ask that question, you will have answers. Many of the answers come from learning theory—what we know about learning. That's why the information about learning contained in this chapter is so important to your success. You simply cannot fail at teaching if you put it to use.

Be warned at the outset that there is much to know about learning that cannot be included here. Since, as Wittrock (1987) notes, "models of instruction derive largely from the behaviorist, cognitive, and humanistic psychological perspectives" (p. 69), we limit ourselves to summarizing those major schools of thought. Figure 3.1 depicts them. Although the schools appear to be independent, you will see they share many beliefs.

After completing the chapter, you should be able to (1) describe the beliefs and findings associated with each school of thought and their implications for teaching, (2) denote some significant educational practices with roots in cognitive,

3.1 What do you recall about how we learn from previous course work and experience?

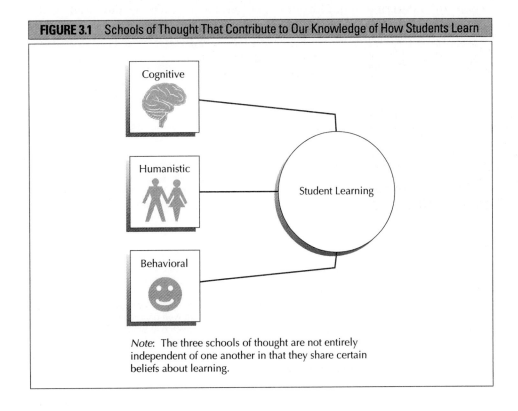

FIGURE 3.1 Schools of Thought That Contribute to Our Knowledge of How Students Learn

Cognitive

Humanistic

Student Learning

Behavioral

Note: The three schools of thought are not entirely independent of one another in that they share certain beliefs about learning.

humanistic, and behavioral learning theory, (3) compare and contrast the three schools of thought, and (4) describe ideas you will use from each of them.

The Cognitive School of Thought

The first school of thought we will examine has its roots in cognitive science, a field that emerged in the 1960s to study how people think. Cognitive scientists try to fathom what goes on inside our heads when we are learning. They have contributed two important, wide-ranging ideas that help us understand how people learn and remember: information processing and meaningful learning.

Information processing refers to the study of how we mentally take in and store information and then retrieve it when needed. Thus, if we understand and use what we know about information processing, we should be able to help our students become better at taking in and remembering information. **Meaningful learning** involves the study of how new information can be most effectively organized, structured, and taught so that it might be used, for example, in problem-solving situations. Let's look at these two somewhat different and sometimes overlapping ideas.

INFORMATION PROCESSING

If you have taken a psychology or educational psychology course, you already know that cognitive scientists—persons interested in information processing—study how we *attend to, recognize, transform, store, and retrieve information.* They develop models, such as the one shown in Figure 3.2, to illustrate how they believe information is processed. Essentially models such as this one suggest that although we encounter many stimuli, we pay attention to only some of them. Of the stimuli we notice, some will be discarded almost immediately, while the rest go into our short-term, or working, memory. **Short-term memory,** as the term suggests, is a storage system that holds only a limited amount and certain kinds of information for a few seconds. When these stimuli reach our short-term memory, the items we use to any degree are transferred to our long-term, or permanent, memory and saved. As the

---

FIGURE 3.2   How Learners Gain or Lose Information

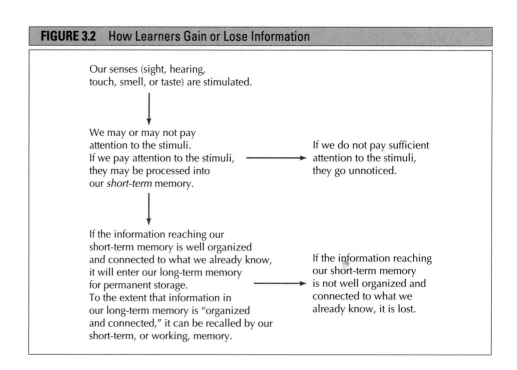

Our senses (sight, hearing, touch, smell, or taste) are stimulated.

↓

We may or may not pay attention to the stimuli. If we pay attention to the stimuli, they may be processed into our *short-term* memory.

→ If we do not pay sufficient attention to the stimuli, they go unnoticed.

↓

If the information reaching our short-term memory is well organized and connected to what we already know, it will enter our long-term memory for permanent storage.
To the extent that information in our long-term memory is "organized and connected," it can be recalled by our short-term, or working, memory.

→ If the information reaching our short-term memory is not well organized and connected to what we already know, it is lost.

name implies, long-term memory is where we keep information for a long time. Information that we do not use to any degree, and that therefore does not reach **long-term memory,** is forgotten as if we had never been exposed to it in the first place. We're sure there are many things that, for lack of proper storage and use, haven't stuck in your memory.

As you might expect, cognitive scientists often try to answer questions that are very important to teachers, such as: What attracts and holds a student's attention? How can more information be placed into short- and long-term memory? How should we organize and present information to make it more memorable? How can students best study or learn new information? Following are some major beliefs and findings of cognitivists that are related to such questions. These beliefs and findings should have direct bearing on the way you teach.

Beliefs about Attention   Getting students to "pay attention" to information is a very real, everyday concern. Cognitivists suggest teachers use the following guiding principles to gain and hold learners' attention:

- Learning experiences should be as pleasant and satisfying as possible. Students are more likely to attend to something (mathematics, music, sport) when they have had previous positive experiences with it. If a learner's previous experience with that stimulus has been unpleasant, the experiences you give him must be especially good.

- Whenever possible, lessons should take into account the interests and needs of students. Students are more likely to pay attention to lessons that focus on what they want to know or what they want to be able to do. A major task for you will be to encourage or motivate them to attend to things they have little interest in.

- The attention of learners can be gained and held longer by making use of different sensory channels and through movement. A student is more likely to attend to lessons that employ a variety of stimuli, that is, when shifts occur from listening to talking to doing, and so forth. Novelty also helps. Avoid monotony!

- Learners can attend for only so long, and they differ in their ability to attend. Younger children and those with dyslexia (a reading impairment) and attention deficiency disorders (described in Chapter 2) have shorter attention spans (Sylwester 1995: Sylwester & Cho, 1993).

- Since it is easier to maintain attention when learners are alert, schedule work that requires intense concentration during the morning and work that may be more intrinsically interesting and/or may require less concentration in the afternoon. For this reason, elementary teachers try to teach art, music, and physical education later in the day.

- Distractions interfere with attention. Therefore, find ways to eliminate the many interruptions to learning that students, other teachers, and administrators can cause.

- Learners can attend to only so much information at any one time. Students should not be overwhelmed, otherwise they may become so confused that they attend to nothing.

To the extent that you can get learners to pay attention by applying these guidelines, the information and experiences they have will enter their short-term memories.

Beliefs about Short-Term Memory   The stimuli we attend to find their way into short-term memory. But, how do we get some of this information beyond short-term and into permanent memory? Cognitivists believe the following principles to be true.

- Short-term memory capacity is severely limited. Estimates are that adult learners can hold only about 5 to 9 bits of new information at one time. Therefore, it is difficult to remember a meaningless series of numerals, such as a long-distance

3.2   Can you describe instances when your teachers either followed or violated one of the principles for gaining attention?

"First, you have to get their attention."

3.3   What should teachers most keep in mind about attention?

"I knew the answers. I just couldn't retrieve them from my memory bank."

3.4 Which beliefs about short-term memory have been most useful to you?

telephone number or a social security number. Young children's short-term memory is much more limited, usually 3 to 5 bits.

- To overcome the limited capacity of our short-term memory, new information can be both *organized* and *connected* to what we already know; for example, learners can be helped to combine, or "chunk," new information. Thus a 10-bit, long-distance telephone number is placed into three chunks, such as (614) 292–1280. Chunking a 9-bit-long social security number also aids short-term memory. Consequently, if it were important to remember the names of the first nine U.S. presidents, we might group them in threes: (Washington, Adams, Jefferson), (Madison, Monroe, Adams), (Jackson, Van Buren, Harrison). Short-term memory also is enhanced by using mnemonics, or systems to aid memory; for example, we more easily recall the names of the Great Lakes if we use the familiar word *HOMES* (*H*uron, *O*ntario, *M*ichigan, *E*rie, *S*uperior) to spur our recall.

- To illustrate how information can be remembered better by connecting it with what students already know, consider the following task. You are helping students learn multiplication facts. They know that six 6's are 36. You help them see that seven 6's is one 6 more.

- To forestall forgetting new information, we must manipulate it or, as cognitive scientists say, engage in active "rehearsals" with it. Such rehearsals can involve either practicing repeatedly or simply thinking about the information. When we engage in recurrent practice, we can move information to our long-term memory through sheer repetition or memorization. Many of us learned multiplication facts in this way, repeating $9 \times 7 = 63$ ad infinitum. Spaced rehearsal, however, seems preferable. Thus, repeating $9 \times 7 = 63$ every hour for five hours is better than repeating it five times in one minute. We might also think about the information, for example, questioning "How can we prove nine 7's are 63?".

Beliefs about Long-Term Memory   As noted, information that learners process extensively, or use in a meaningful way, finds its way into long-term memory. Cognitivists believe the following to be true with regard to long-term memory:

- The capacity of our long-term memory seems to be limitless. We never run out of room to learn.

- We are best able to retrieve information from our long-term memory if that information relates to something we knew previously.

- We can call up, or recollect, related information from long-term memory when processing new information in short-term memory. For example, as you receive new information about how people learn, you can compare it with information you have already learned. In this instance, as you go along, you are able to compare what you already know about short-term memory with what you are learning about long-term memory.

General Beliefs about the Memory Process   The general beliefs of cognitivists with regard to memory include the following:

- Information in short-term memory is lost either when that memory is overloaded or with the passage of time.

- When information in short-term memory is lost, it cannot be recovered. If we forget a telephone number, we must relearn it. In contrast, information in long-term memory can be retrieved and used when conditions are right.

- Retrieval, or remembrance, of information in our long-term memory is enhanced if we connected the information to something we already knew at the

3.5 Why do we forget?

FIGURE 3.3 Information Processing: Key Concepts

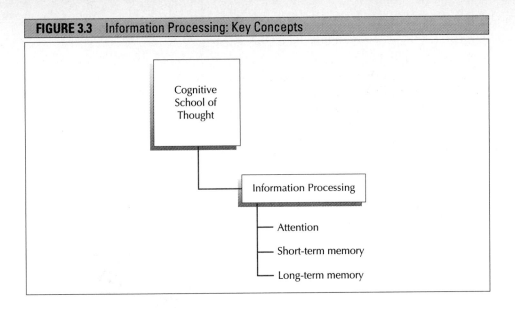

time we originally learned the new information. Additionally, retrieval is easier when the information is originally presented in an organized way.

Figure 3.3 depicts key concepts and key words associated with information processing.

MEANINGFUL LEARNING

While some cognitive scientists are interested in information processing (attention, short- and long-term memory), others are concerned with how information can be made more meaningful so that it can be better understood and subsequently used. These scientists address **meaningful learning.** Among other things, they see the benefits of certain cognitive approaches to teaching which maximize learner understanding, such as reception learning, reciprocal teaching, discovery learning, and problem solving. Let's look briefly at each of these approaches to meaningful cognitive learning.

FOUR COGNITIVE APPROACHES TO LEARNING

Reception Learning **Reception learning** refers to learning that takes place when we present students with new information that is carefully organized and structured (see chapter 6 on "presentations"). The better organized and structured a lesson is, the greater the likelihood that learning will occur (Ausubel, 1977). Since (rightly or wrongly) many, if not most, lessons in K–12 classrooms are teacher-presented, it is important that we know what cognitivists believe about reception learning. Some principal beliefs follow.

"I know my seven-digit phone number, my nine-digit zip code, my four-digit address, and my three-digit area code. There's just one thing I don't know. What's a digit?"

- At the outset of an **expository lesson,** that is, one in which you intend to present facts, ideas, and explanations, present learners with the learning objectives. These objectives alert learners to what they are supposed to know and to be able to do as a result of the presentation.

- An expository lesson should begin with some form of **advance organizer.** An advance organizer is a teaching ploy that prepares learners for the new information that follows. A variety of organizers exist. According to Ausubel (1977), the best kind of advance organizer is one that relates new information to information already contained in the learner's long-term memory. This makes the new information more comprehensible. Leinhardt (1992) agrees that what *can* be learned is determined by what *is already known*. To illustrate, if you are going to teach young children something about the world's oceans, you should determine what they already know about various sizes and bodies of water and connect the new information to their knowledge. A second kind of advance organizer prepares learners for new information by giving them necessary or useful background information. For example, before we can understand word processing, we need to know something about how the computer works. A third kind of advance organizer prepares learners to attend to certain parts of the new information. To illustrate, you might say, "In this film, we will see outstanding defensive basketball players. Notice what they do in common." Yet another kind of advance organizer provides learners with a schema to assist them in organizing new information. For example, with middle school or high school students, you might say, "Here is an incomplete outline. As we learn about the world's oceans, record new information about their sizes, locations, and characteristics in appropriate places on the outline."

- Present new information in an organized, clear, sequential (step-by-step) manner.

- Even though they are primarily teacher-directed, reception learning and expository teaching should be characterized by numerous teacher-student interactions. Ask learners many questions and prompt learners to ask questions, too.

- Make use of both examples and nonexamples of what students are to learn: "Good defense in basketball is characterized by . . ." and "Poor defense is characterized by . . ."

- Reception learning usually proceeds best when structured deductively, that is, from the general to the specific: "First we will learn about the world's oceans in general, then we will find out about main ocean currents and how they affect shorelines."

3.6 Describe instances when your teachers have either violated or applied one of the principles of reception learning?

3.7 What is your opinion of reception learning?

- A review or closure should come at the end of the lesson so learners can reflect on the new information, its application, and personal meaning. "What have we learned? How is the material we have learned useful to us?"

In summary, reception learning, done well, is characterized by (1) telling students what they are expected to know or do, (2) presenting information in an organized, sequential way, (3) moving from general to specific knowledge, (4) utilizing advance organizers, (5) encouraging student involvement and interaction, (6) using both examples and nonexamples when presenting new concepts, and (7) asking learners to reflect on the personal meaning and use of the new information. Figure 3.4 illustrates key concepts and words associated with reception learning.

Reciprocal Teaching   **Reciprocal teaching** is a form of teaching wherein the teacher gradually shifts teaching responsibility to learners (Nuthall, 1995; Palincsar, 1986). Perhaps some of your teachers have done this. At first, the teacher models and/or explains to the learners how to do something, for example how to summarize. As the learners catch on, the teacher selects one or more to demonstrate or explain to others how to summarize and how *they* summarize. During this process, the appointed teacher may ask learners questions to assure their understanding and, conversely, learners may comment and raise questions. Meanwhile, the teacher stands aside, ready to provide any encouragement or assistance needed. This teaching act is called "scaffolding" since it helps and supports learners. You probably remember when former teachers, after teaching a concept or process, asked class members to go to the chalkboard and demonstrate or describe how to do something such as multiplying fractions or diagramming a sentence. If,

FIGURE 3.4 Reception Learning: Key Concepts

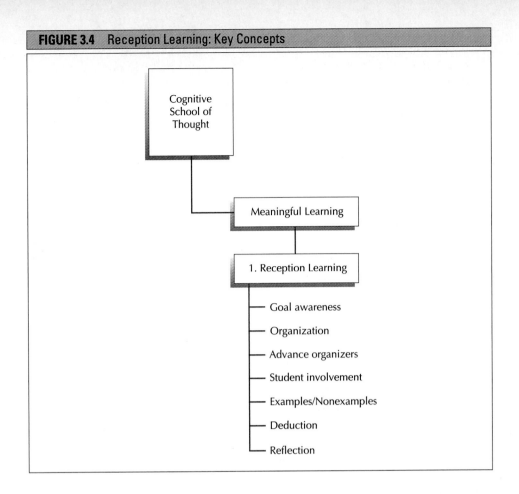

when those demonstrations and explanations occurred, student interchanges followed that increased understanding, then you have already experienced a variation on the theme of reciprocal teaching. Figure 3.5 depicts related key concepts.

Discovery Learning   According to Piaget (1964) and Bruner (1966), students should be encouraged to learn on their own rather than be given or fed information, as they are with reception learning and expository teaching. Piaget notes, "We need pupils who are active, who learn early how to find out for themselves, partly by their own spontaneous activity and partly by [experiences] set up for them; who learn early to tell what is verifiable and what is simply the first idea to come to them" (p. 5). Piaget and Bruner's point of view encouraged the development of discovery learning as another way to make information meaningful. **Discovery learning** refers to learning that takes place when students engage in experiences and experiments from which they derive their own knowledge and meaning. For example, rather than describe what *force* is and why it occurs, a science teacher might ask students what the idea means to them and what forces they think are at work in their everyday world ("What does *force* mean to you? What are some forces you commonly experience?"). After the students had reflected on these two questions, the teacher would ask them, "Suppose you toss a ball. What kinds of forces act on the ball?"

In K–12 schools, much less instruction occurs through discovery learning. This is partly because discovering knowledge takes longer than simply receiving it. Also, we teach as we are taught, and most of the teaching we have been exposed to has been direct and expository in nature. However, authorities in certain subject

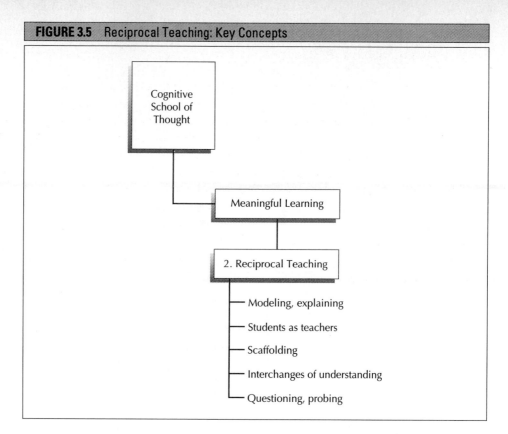

FIGURE 3.5 Reciprocal Teaching: Key Concepts

Cognitive School of Thought

Meaningful Learning

2. Reciprocal Teaching

- Modeling, explaining
- Students as teachers
- Scaffolding
- Interchanges of understanding
- Questioning, probing

fields—namely science, social studies, and more recently, mathematics—are encouraging the use of discovery learning and teaching to make those subjects more meaningful.

Following are some situations in which discovery learning might appropriately be selected as the instructional strategy of choice:

- Why does the water level in the class aquarium recede? Do the fish drink it?
- What happens when you mix different watercolors together—for example, blue and yellow?
- Where is the population center of the United States? Where was it 100 years ago? What factors may have led to the change?
- Why do you suppose some things float and others do not?
- How could the human body be improved?

3.8 What are some things in your teaching field that students could discover?

Wilcox (1989) presents many useful discovery methods. All require that students do more than merely sit quietly and pay attention. Rather, the methods shift responsibility to the students to discover and learn through their own physical and mental activity.

A term closely related to discovery learning is **constructivism,** which has grown out of the work of the aforementioned Swiss theorist Jean Piaget and Russian psychologist Lev Vygotsky. According to O'Neil (1992) and Brooks and Brooks (1993), constructivists believe that for learners to gain deep understanding, they must actively come to know or find out something for themselves. They must act on new information with their present knowledge, and if the new doesn't square with the old, they must resolve the discrepancies. In order to allow learners to know something by themselves, O'Neil suggests we provide time and numerous opportunities for them "to explore phenomena or ideas, to conjecture, to share their hypotheses with others and, where necessary, to revise

CASE 3.1
Constructivism in Action

Deb O'Brien introduced the new science unit on heat by asking her 9-year-olds, "What is heat?" She intended, through the question, to have them draw from their experiences, and this they did. They recalled that heat came from the sun and from fires, radiators, and assorted other sources. However, one boy posited that heat came from clothing such as coats and sweaters. His peers readily agreed. Deb recognized that to a 9-year-old, the observation seemed reasonable. After all, when they put "warm" clothing on, they were warmer. But how to correct this misconception? Should she tell them the truth? No. She felt it more appropriate that they learn it for themselves. So the class constructed an experiment. They wrapped thermometers in coats and sweaters and assumed the temperature thereon should rise. When it didn't, they sealed the clothing and thermometers in plastic bags. Still the thermometers recorded no heat change.

After numerous failed efforts to prove that clothes gave off heat, the learners were willing to entertain an alternative hypothesis—that clothing merely holds or contains the heat given off by those wearing them. These fourth graders constructed for themselves knowledge about what causes and what contains or traps heat (Watson & Konicek, 1990).

their original thinking" (p. 4). The classroom scenario presented in Case 3.1 illustrates how one teacher handled a situation wherein her learners held the misconception that heat comes from clothing.

Those who advocate that learners should find out or discover something for themselves admit this places greater demands on class time and teacher preparation. However, they are confident that when teachers use discovery-constructivist approaches, they enhance the quality of learning and make it more memorable than when a reception learning procedure is followed. For example, it is much more straightforward and less time-intensive for math teachers to tell students that *pi* is a constant equal to about 3.14 than to have learners discover this by manipulating various spheres, measuring, graphing, and so forth. However, the discovery-constructivist procedure probably results in greater meaning and recall (Danielson, 1996).

To summarize, the major beliefs about discovery learning include the following:

- Discovery learning is particularly useful when the learning objectives involve or could involve higher-order thinking, such as analysis, evaluation, and problem solving.
- You should regularly arouse students' curiosity about things and events, as Deb O'Brien did in Case 3.1.
- Discovery learning activities should include both independent and collaborative, or peer group, activities.
- When learners come to understand something on their own, it is more meaningful to them than when someone else presents it to them.
- When learners have regular opportunities to discover knowledge for themselves, they learn *how* to learn.
- When learners share how they think about things and how they see things and solve problems, they grow intellectually.

Overall, discovery learning is more likely to occur when (1) learners have ideas or objects to manipulate, (2) teachers encourage learners to be curious by using comparison ("How does this compare with that or those?"), (3) teachers stimulate informed guessing ("What do you think would happen if we did this?"), (4) teachers encourage learners to react to their own and other learners' thinking, and (5) learners are asked to analyze their own thought processes ("How did you come to that conclusion or position?").

3.9 How might learners discover such things as (1) why nations differ in power, (2) how a wood screw works, or (3) how to solve
$$274 + 274 + 274 + 274 + 274 = ?$$
5

FIGURE 3.6 Discovery Learning: Key Concepts

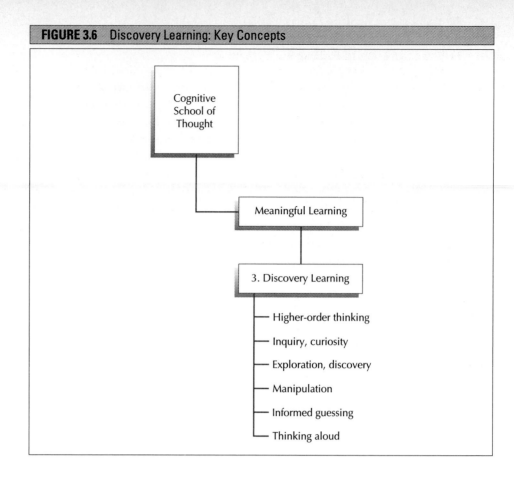

3.10 How do you react to discovery learning?

3.11 Can you think of any "well-structured" problems in the subject matter you will be responsible for teaching?

3.12 What are some other "ill-structured" problems students face?

Figure 3.6 depicts key concepts associated with discovery learning and its place in the cognitive school of thought. In Chapter 7, you will learn more about discovery learning as an instructional alternative.

Problem Solving A fourth method of learning cognitive scientists advocate is problem solving. **Problem solving** requires that (1) a situation exist wherein a goal is to be achieved and (2) learners be asked to consider how they would attain the goal (Cruickshank & Associates, 1980). Frederickson (1984) maintains there are different types of problems, and Biehler and Snowman (1997) describe two of them. One type, which is often encountered when studying mathematics or science, is a "well-structured" problem that "can be solved by recalling and applying a [mathematical or scientific] procedure" (Biehler & Snowman, p. 374). Undoubtedly you can recall working on well-structured mathematical problems that required the application of an algorithm such as multiplication or division to obtain an answer: for example, if you have 18 apples and wish to fill gift boxes with 6 apples each, how many boxes can you fill? Preparing a lesson plan can be thought of as a well-structured problem, since there is a goal we hope to achieve (writing the plan) and there are specific procedures to be followed (described in Chapter 5).

A second type of problem is "ill-structured." It occurs more often in daily living, and comes up when studying people-oriented subjects like psychology or education. With these problems, no specific, simple procedure exists that can be applied to obtain a finite solution. Examples of ill-structured problems include: How can I manage my time better? or How can I make this lesson meaningful to my students? Teachers face ill-structured problems when they expect students to achieve or to behave in a certain way and they don't. Students also

Dom Christoff was regularly assigned students who, for one reason or another, seemed to find school unpleasant. One morning, the school principal appeared at the classroom door with Gary Ross. Mr. Waters introduced Gary to Christoff and noted that Gary would reenter school the next day. Looking over his shoulder as he left with Gary, Mr. Waters suggested, "Let's get together before you leave this afternoon." Christoff acknowledged with a nod of the head.

Later, in the principal's office, Mr. Waters described Gary as a 13-year-old with school phobias. On several occasions he had run away from school, even jumping from classroom windows.

Christoff recognized this as an ill-structured kind of problem. He knew he was expected to keep Gary in school and, particularly, from leaping out the window. He recognized Gary's fear of school and flight syndrome. The next day Christoff talked with Gary, telling the boy that he wanted to help Gary enjoy school. Christoff sug-

gested that Gary give a signal, inconspicuously, by placing his arm across the top of his head whenever he felt he was about to panic. Further, he told Gary to sit next to the door and to leave the class at any time after he gave the signal. Gary agreed to this plan and promised that if he felt compelled to leave the building, he would inform the school office, which would notify Gary's parent.

To everyone's astonishment, Gary—perhaps secure that he could leave whenever he wished—never again did.

face ill-structured problems such as: How can I get the other kids to like me? or How can I pass math when I hate it?

To summarize, major beliefs about problem solving include the following:

- A major goal of education is to help students learn to solve all types of problems, both subject-matter-related (well-structured) and people- or life-related (ill-structured).

- Some problem-solving strategies tend to be subject-area-specific, such as procedures for solving mathematical or scientific problems. For example, we apply the quadratic formula in order to solve a quadratic equation, or a procedure for solving "train problems" involving distance-rate-time calculations (Schoenfeld, 1989, p. 88).

- Other problem-solving strategies are more useful when dealing with ill-structured problems. A general problem-solving strategy might include the following steps: (1) State the goal to be achieved, (2) identify the obstacles standing in the way, (3) project alternative ways to achieve the goal, (4) consider the consequences of each possible solution, (5) decide how to implement the best proposed solution and do so, and (6) evaluate your degree of satisfaction with the problem resolution (Cruickshank & Associates, 1980).

A classroom scenario illustrates how a teacher and student resolved an ill-structured problem (see Case 3.2). Figure 3.7 illustrates key concepts associated with problem solving and the place problem solving has in the cognitive school of thought.

3.13 How prepared are you to teach problem solving?

3.14 What is your opinion of cognitive approaches to learning?

Try Activity 3.1

The Humanistic School of Thought

A second school of thought about learning and instruction is based upon humanistic education, which borrows heavily from social psychology. Persons who champion humanistic or affective education focus on the personal and social learning and development of students. While the humanistic approach recognizes the importance of cognitive learning, it feels that schools focus too much on accumulating knowledge and too little on helping students learn to become psychologically healthy persons.

3.15 What do you think about the criticism that schools are too academically oriented and too little interested in students' personal development?

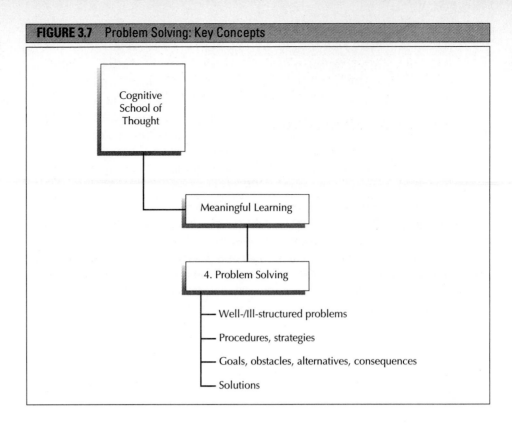

FIGURE 3.7   *Problem Solving: Key Concepts*

Disciples of this school of thought mostly want to make children feel better about themselves and become more accepting of others. To accomplish these goals, followers say that first we need to accept each child as unique and as possessed of individual feelings and ideas, and that, second, we need to help him perceive himself and others as worthwhile and able. Teachers with such an orientation truly believe that "each child counts" and that "each child can do it in his own way."

BELIEFS OF THE HUMANISTIC SCHOOL

The humanistic school holds several core beliefs:

- Having good feelings about oneself is essential to positive personal development. Therefore, engender in students a sense of self-respect, self-worth, and **efficacy,** or having a feeling of control over one's life and destiny.
- Having good feelings about others is also essential to healthy development. Thus, aspire to help learners build respect for and accept others, even when their opinions and behavior may be different.
- The humanistic school believes that "the school should be made to fit the child rather than that the child made to fit the school (Neill, 1969). Therefore, personalize education by giving learners considerable latitude in deciding what to do (learn) and how to do it. Relatedly, create an environment that provides choices and then help students make choices that seem wise to them.
- The school and classroom environment must help youth satisfy such essential human needs as personal safety and security, love, belonging, and achievement (Maslow, 1968); and autonomy, competence, and social relationships (Deci and Ryan, 1990). Failure to meet these needs will be counterproductive to personal development and will have a negative impact on learning.
- Accept learners as they are, that is, with their unique behaviors, feelings, and opinions (Rogers, 1983).

3.16 How will you help learners have confidence in and feel good about themselves and others?

- Place yourself "in the shoes" of learners in order to see and understand a learning situation from the students' perspective (Combs, 1965).
- Use techniques that help learners better understand their feelings and values. Such techniques include active listening, invitational learning, and values clarification—all of which are discussed in the following section.

3.17 How will you show you accept your learners as they are?

HUMANISTIC APPROACHES TO TEACHING

Advocates of the humanistic approach to learning often advocate specific programs and ideas that promote personal development; they include: Teacher Effectiveness Training (TET) (Gordon, 1974), Inviting School Success (Purkey, 1978), values clarification, moral and character education, and multiethnic education.

Teacher Effectiveness Training   TET was developed to encourage teachers to establish open, honest communication in the classroom using such techniques as active listening and conflict resolution. **Active listening** occurs when a teacher permits or encourages a learner to express some feeling and then paraphrases and repeats what the learner said. For example, a student says, "I hate math!" And the teacher might respond, "Bob, you really get upset when math is being taught, and now, just the thought of math makes you feel angry." The teacher gives no advice during active listening. However, **conflict resolution** can also be brought to bear. The teacher and student or the class can talk about how a student might form a negative attitude toward math or another subject and how he or she might change it. In this case, the teacher employing a humanistic approach can draw from knowledge about problem solving and meaningful learning.

Inviting School Success   Inviting School Success was developed to get teachers to communicate to learners that they are "responsible, able, and valuable" people (Purkey, 1978, p.3). To convey this, **invitational learning** calls upon teachers to (1) know learners' names, (2) have individual contact with each learner, (3) show learners they respect them, (4) be honest with learners and themselves, (5) not take a student's rejection personally, and (6) respect themselves as teachers.

Values Clarification   Values clarification refers to techniques by which learners (1) identify how they feel or what they believe about something, (2) value that feeling or belief and, (3) if valued, act on it (Simon, Howe, & Kerschenbaum, 1972). The intention is for learners to become conscious of the values they hold, since those values influence their behavior. Then, they consider the legitimacy or goodness of that which they value. For example, learners could be asked to what extent they believe in gun control. After stating their preference, they are encouraged to share and explain their position and why they hold it. Once they have examined their value in relationship to the values others hold, learners are now better able to prize their value or to modify or reject it. Once the value is prized, learners are expected to go the next step and act on the value. For example, learners might be asked, "All right, if you believe that strongly about gun control, what can *you* do?"

Moral Education   Moral education is akin to character education, values education (not value clarification), and citizenship education. All these techniques are designed to help learners develop more responsible behavior both in and out of school. According to Lickona (1988), teachers can do a number of things to enhance higher levels of students' morality and character, such as (1) serving as role models who are always respectful and caring of others and who intervene as necessary to get students to be respectful and caring, too, (2) creating a family or community atmosphere in the class so that all students feel worthwhile and care about one another, and (3) encouraging students to hold high academic and behavioral

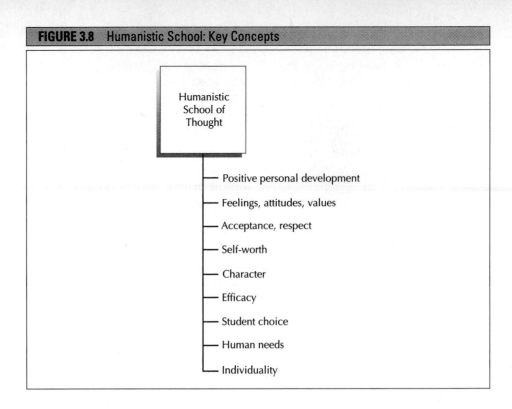

FIGURE 3.8 Humanistic School: Key Concepts

Humanistic
School of
Thought

— Positive personal development

— Feelings, attitudes, values

— Acceptance, respect

— Self-worth

— Character

— Efficacy

— Student choice

— Human needs

— Individuality

3.18 Have you had experience with any of the humanistic approaches to education? Which ones?

3.19 What is your reaction to humanistic approaches to learning?

Try Activity 3.2

standards in order to teach the value of work as a way to develop oneself and contribute to a community (p. 9).

Multiethnic Education Multiethnic education refers to educational practices that encourage learners to revere their roots and culture—ideas, customs, skills, arts, and so forth—*and* to revere the culture and diversity of others. Proponents want learners to see the advantages of a pluralistic society. Related educational practices include helping learners become aware of the various contributions of ethnic and national groups to a nation's development and well-being, and encouraging learners to find out more about their own ethnic and cultural backgrounds.

Figure 3.8 illustrates key concepts associated with the humanistic approach to learning and teaching.

The Behavioral School of Thought

The third school of thought about learning, teaching, and education is behaviorism. **Behaviorists,** as the name implies, help us understand why we behave as we do. They are interested in finding out how external, environmental stimuli cause overt or observable learner behavior and how modifying a learner's environment can change behavior.

If you have studied psychology or educational psychology, you probably learned something about contiguity, classical conditioning, operant conditioning, and social learning—concepts of prime interest to behaviorists.

CONTIGUITY

Contiguity refers to simple stimulus-response (S-R) pairings, associations, or connections, such as lightning and thunder, which occur closely together. When one thing, a stimulus, is regularly associated with another, a response, an S-R connection is established. Like the combination of lightning and thunder, the S-R connection usually occurs within a very brief time span. Thus, the *contiguity* label. We can learn by simple S-R pairing such facts as Columbus landed in America in 1492 and $9 \times 7 = 63$. A great many concepts and facts are learned through simple stimulus-response learning, for example:

STIMULUS	RESPONSE
Einstein	Theory of Relativity
Sodium chloride	Salt
Van Gogh	Artist
Andersonville	Infamous Civil War prison
Eiffel Tower	Paris
Gershwin	Composer

CLASSICAL CONDITIONING

Classical conditioning refers to learning that occurs when we already have an established connection (contiguity) between a primary or original stimulus and a response, and then we pair a new, secondary stimulus with the original stimulus long enough that it begins to evoke the original response even when the original stimulus is absent. Remember Pavlov's dogs? Pavlov, a Russian psychologist, found that his experimental dogs naturally salivated (responded) when his lab assistants fed them meat powder (a stimulus). Later, he found that the mere presence of his lab assistants (new stimulus) caused the dogs to anticipate being fed and to salivate. Let's consider a school example. Students and teachers alike associate a bell (stimulus) with the ending of a class period. Teachers often assign homework at or near the close of class. Thus, the mere assignment of homework (new stimulus) will elicit many behaviors or responses associated with the ringing of the bell—packing book bags and so forth. For this reason, some teachers assign homework at the beginning of class.

3.20 What kinds of S-R responses might you want from your learners? How can the responses be associated with something desirable so that they occur?

OPERANT CONDITIONING

Operant conditioning refers to learning facilitated through reinforcement. A learner does something correctly or appropriately and, consequently, receives a reward. Operant conditioning presumes that if we do something we are rewarded for or which is rewarding in itself, we will do it again. Conversely, if we do something that is not rewarded or rewarding, we will be less likely to repeat the behavior. Operant conditioning is based upon a pleasure-pain view of human behavior. To illustrate, consider Jason, a learner who has turned in a homework essay on gun control. The teacher has dutifully analyzed the essay and responded to it as follows: "This assignment is complete and well written. You have found and used many references. You have presented the major points on both sides, and you have drawn your own thoughtful conclusions. Obviously, you enjoy studying issues and responding to them. May I place your paper on our bulletin board?" Assuming Jason finds the teacher's comments and the display of his paper rewarding, he likely will want to write another essay. Chapters 11 and 12 will discuss more about reinforcement.

3.21 How is reinforcement used by your instructors?

SOCIAL LEARNING

Social learning is also called **observational learning.** Its main tenet is that you can learn a lot by watching others. According to its chief theorist, Bandura (1986), for observational learning to be effective, learners must attend to someone's behavior, retain what they observed the "model" doing, imitate or reproduce the behavior they saw, and experience reinforcement or satisfaction as a consequence. We know learners are most likely to model after persons who are somewhat like themselves and whom they perceive as competent, warm, or powerful. Thus, primary children frequently identify with parents, television, or movie characters, especially super-heroes, and mimic what they do. A kindergarten teacher describes an example of social learning:

> The resurgence of Batman: Raymond brought in a "cape" and all the children were anxious to wear it and run around the room in it. During free play, children were busy making Batman equipment. Story time and singing time were always interrupted by children who were busy describing Batman antics. The entire morning was Batman-oriented and the children could not be interested in much else.

If an elementary school has a Halloween parade, characters such as Scooby-Doo, Snow White, Superman, or the Cookie Monster readily appear. On the other hand, if middle and secondary students have the occasion to wear costumes, they would more likely dress and act like rock or rap personalities or athletes.

Social learning also occurs when we see something good or bad happen to another person. For example, if we were to see a friend praised for her schoolwork, we might try to imitate what she does so we can be praised, too. Conversely, we might avoid doing what another student does if her behavior is not well received.

Behaviorists hold several core beliefs; they would advise the following:

- Try to associate academic learning with things most students of a given age like—for example, you could associate poetry with popular contemporary music such as rap.

- Encourage fearful or shy students to perform. For example, have a child who has "math anxiety" teach younger pupils a mathematical process he has learned. Or, if students are fearful of being in front of the class, let them give reports from their desks.

- Be open and clear about the academic objectives and standards you expect learners to meet, and write those objectives and standards in "behavioral terms." (See Chapter 5, Planning Instruction.)

- Reinforce the learning behavior you expect from students. For example, praise work that is complete and up to the learner's ability level (assuming praise is reinforcing to that child).

- Recognize and praise improvement. Don't expect all students to learn at the same rate.

- Be certain that students have the basic knowledge or skills that new learning is built upon. As suggested earlier in the sections on memory and reception learning, the new should relate to the old.

- When presenting a new task, organize the material to be learned in small, sequential steps.

- When a task is new or difficult, provide more regular reinforcement than when behavior is based on prior learning. Once learners have mastered the new task, they need only occasional reinforcement.

- Demonstrate, or model, the behavior you want students to imitate. For example, demonstrate enthusiasm for learning and for the subject(s) you teach.

- Draw students' attention to others who demonstrate, or model, desirable behaviors. For example, point out ways other students or adults were able to solve a problem or write an effective essay.

- Ask parents to reinforce desired behaviors at home—for example, to recognize perseverance or praise a student's enthusiasm in carrying out an assignment.

BEHAVIORAL APPROACHES TO TEACHING

Behaviorists advocate certain educational practices they believe can be used to increase learning. These include programmed instruction, computer-assisted instruction, mastery learning, precision teaching and applied behavioral analysis.

"Of course I believe that a teacher should offer a positive role model; however . . ."

3.22 To what extent do you believe you will model a former teacher(s)? In what ways?

3.23 What behavioristic beliefs do your teachers seem to use most and least?

FIGURE 3.9 An Illustration of Programmed Instruction That Follows an Operant Conditioning Pattern

Fill in the blank in each frame (1 to 5) and then check the answer against the correct answer "hidden" at the right, proceeding downward on the page.

1. The third prominent school of thought about learning is _____.

   | Behaviorism |

2. This school of thought is interested in our _____ behavior.

   | Overt or observable |

3. When one stimulus is regularly associated with a response, a bond or _____ is formed.

   | Contiguity |

4. When a second stimulus has been associated with the original stimulus, that second stimulus may evoke the same response. This is called _____ conditioning.

   | Classical |

5. When we watch others and mimic their behavior, we call this _____ learning.

   | Social or observational |

Programmed instruction (PI) involves organizing material to be learned or practiced into small parts called *frames* (see Figure 3.9).

Learners respond to a question or problem (stimulus) in each frame; if their response is correct, they receive positive reinforcement and the next frame is presented. When learners respond incorrectly, they may be asked to repeat or be given more information to help them produce a correct response. Learners utilizing programmed instruction typically work at their own pace.

Computer-assisted instruction (CAI) refers to the use of computers to present programmed instruction or to otherwise assist learners with specific learning tasks. Many different kinds of CAI programs are available, and most require learners to engage in lots of drill and practice. Although most CAI programs follow an operant conditioning, stimuli-response-reinforcement pattern, CAI also can be used as a cognitivist approach; some CAI programs, like programmed instruction, teach new concepts, and others engage learners in creative tasks and problem solving. For example, some computer software programs encourage children to make up stories and to illustrate them.

Programmed instruction and CAI seem to be a little more effective than normal educational practices, probably because they make extensive use of practice and reinforcement. Classroom *use of reinforcement is highly related to student learning* (Ellson, 1986; Walberg, 1984).

Mastery learning is a third educational practice based upon behavioral theory. It, too, allows students to learn academic material at their own pace. In practice, all students in a class might be expected to reach a certain level of proficiency, for example, at least 80 percent correct responses on a geography test. Those who fail to reach that criterion level may receive additional time and corrective instruction until they obtain that score. The general intent is to give immediate, additional help to low or slow achievers so they stay even with higher or faster achievers. While low or slow achievers receive corrective instruction, high or fast achievers engage in enrichment work on the same or on a similar topic.

Block and Anderson (1975) propose that mastery learning requires you to (1) prepare a lesson with clear, specific objectives, (2) use learning material that allows students to accomplish those objectives, and (3) prepare not one, but two, tests. Following instruction, students take test 1. Those that meet some preestablished passing criterion, such as 80 percent, move on to supplementary enrichment activities, while those falling short receive corrective instruction based on a different instructional approach or using different instructional materials. After additional instruction, a second, similar test (test 2) is given to the lower achievers. When a large majority of all students (perhaps 80 percent) have passed either test 1 or test 2, the class moves on to new work. The cycle can be repeated until you, the teacher, feel that a large enough majority has reached mastery to permit going on.

According to Walberg (1984), use of mastery learning in science is highly related to student learning. Slavin (1986), concludes that its primary weakness is the amount of time needed to bring almost all students to mastery. That additional time must come from somewhere. He therefore concludes that mastery learning is most important when the material to be learned is critical or "high stakes" material, for example, the basic information or skills in any content field.

Precision teaching occurs when learners master a fact or skill (such as correctly spelling a word or applying an arithmetic algorithm such as division), and then continue practicing these skills until they achieve a high level of precision or fluency. "Practice makes perfect." Precision teaching is reported to help children gain two years of academic growth in one (Sulzer-Azaroff, 1995). Its tenets derive from principles of information processing (see the section on short-term memory).

Applied behavioral analysis (ABA) also is based upon behavioral beliefs and findings and is informed by principles of operant conditioning. It is used mostly in clinical settings (hospitals, prisons, schools) to modify the behavior of clients toward more normal or acceptable patterns. ABA follows a prescribed procedure. First the practitioner—for example, you the teacher—identify a student (client) and the student's behavior that is to be changed. You then determine how often the student presently performs the desired behavior—for example, completing homework. This is called the **baseline.** Next, you introduce an **intervention.** An intervention is usually some reinforcement the student receives every time she performs the desirable behavior. Use of reinforcement encourages your student to behave appropriately more often, that is, more than the client did at the outset or baseline.

3.24 What is your reaction to the behavioral approach to learning?

Try Activity 3.3

Here is an illustration of ABA in a classroom. Jane produces very little when given a writing assignment, even one of her choice. In most cases, her text amounts to a few short sentences. Because she is fairly conversational, you decide you might encourage her to be more forthcoming by having her tell you what she would like to say. As she does, you prompt her to write down the ideas she is expressing. Each time Jane writes her ideas in a writing assignment, you praise her for any increase in the number and range of her ideas. When you evaluate her written work, you comment that, increasingly, Jane's compositions are more complete and interesting. You may even share one or more with the class.

Behavioral analysis always uses the principles of operant conditioning. A close cousin is **behavior modification,** which is also an attempt to change behavior but is a more general concept that includes use of hypnosis, drug therapy, and electroconvulsive shock treatment as well. Figure 3.10 presents key concepts associated with the behavioral approach to learning and teaching.

Is There a Single Best Approach to Student Learning?

We have identified three views of learning that influence the approaches teachers take to instruction. Figure 3.11 brings them together for comparison. Each approach has been defined, and its major beliefs and findings noted. Some have fostered the development and use of specific educational practices, which are briefly described. Table 3.1 compares the three approaches.

A great deal of controversy exists as to which of the approaches to learning is superior (Viadero, 1996). If you ask your university instructors, you may be surprised at the strength of their feelings. You may especially find those espousing cognitive or humanistic beliefs to shun behaviorism, although the reverse is also true.

FIGURE 3.10 Behavioral School: Key Concepts

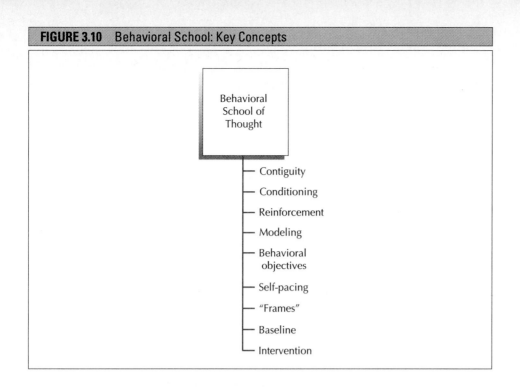

```
Behavioral
School of
Thought
            ── Contiguity
            ── Conditioning
            ── Reinforcement
            ── Modeling
            ── Behavioral
               objectives
            ── Self-pacing
            ── "Frames"
            ── Baseline
            ── Intervention
```

TABLE 3.1 A Comparison of Cognitive, Humanistic, and Behavioral Views

	Cognitive	Humanistic	Behavioral
Focus	Understanding how knowledge is acquired	Understanding how persons come to develop feelings, attitudes, and values	Understanding how observable behavior is modified by changing the environment
Topics/Themes	Information processing Meaningful learning	Basic needs Affect (emotions, feelings, attitudes, values, predispositions, morals) Self-worth Efficacy	Contiguity Classical conditioning Operant conditioning Social, observational learning
Special concepts	Attention Short-, long-term memory Remember/Forgetting Advance organizers	Active listening Conflict resolution	Reinforcement
Instructional approaches that support . . .	Reception learning Reciprocal teaching Discovery learning, constructivism Problem solving	Teacher Effectiveness Training Inviting School Success Values clarification Moral/Character education Multiethnic education	Programmed and computer instruction Mastery learning Precision teaching Applied behavioral analysis

Teachers who work with exceptional individuals, especially those with learning and behavioral deficiencies, often have found that the behaviorist school of thought has been most helpful. There certainly is strong research support for applying its beliefs and findings. For example, Walberg (1986) reports that 98 percent of studies investigating the effects of behavioral learning on students have positive findings. At the same time, Walberg tells us good support also exists for cognitive and humanistic approaches to instruction (p. 222).

Dembo (1991) reminds us there are differences of opinion about learning not only among but also within the various schools of thought. He also points out what

3.25 Which features of which schools of thought about learning attract you? Why?

FIGURE 3.11   Three Schools of Thought about Learning

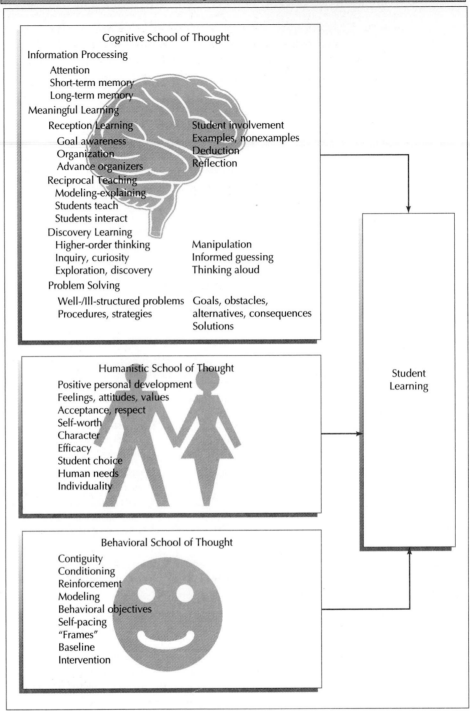

Cognitive School of Thought

Information Processing
  Attention
  Short-term memory
  Long-term memory
Meaningful Learning
  Reception Learning   Student involvement
    Goal awareness   Examples, nonexamples
    Organization   Deduction
    Advance organizers   Reflection
  Reciprocal Teaching
    Modeling-explaining
    Students teach
    Students interact
  Discovery Learning
    Higher-order thinking   Manipulation
    Inquiry, curiosity   Informed guessing
    Exploration, discovery   Thinking aloud
  Problem Solving
    Well-/Ill-structured problems   Goals, obstacles,
    Procedures, strategies   alternatives, consequences
                                     Solutions

Humanistic School of Thought

Positive personal development
Feelings, attitudes, values
Acceptance, respect
Self-worth
Character
Efficacy
Student choice
Human needs
Individuality

Behavioral School of Thought

Contiguity
Conditioning
Reinforcement
Modeling
Behavioral objectives
Self-pacing
"Frames"
Baseline
Intervention

Student
Learning

you have probably already concluded by now, that most educators draw from all three schools of thought. The secret, Dembo informs us, is to have a knack for knowing "when to use ideas from the various perspectives because each has strengths and weaknesses, depending on the purpose you may have in mind" (p. 219). Anderson, Reder, and Simon (1996) agree. Speaking to the same point, Biehler and Snowman (1997) note that advocates of discovery learning, such as Bruner, "do not suggest that students should discover every fact or principle or formula they need to know . . . but rather that "certain types of learning outcomes . . . can best be achieved through personal discovery" (p. 364).

Some Final Thoughts

Helping your students learn is the "bottom line." However, as you can recall from your own school experiences and from the teacher-reported problems that follow, doing so is not always simple. Therefore, you need to learn all you can about learning and teaching and to recognize that the two are inextricably bound together. You can be an excellent teacher *only* when you understand what is known about each and can put that knowledge to work every single time you arrange a learning experience. If your students experience difficulty or failure, you must "go back to the books" and analyze what may be interfering with learning. Never shrug your shoulders or give up on a single child. The knowledge needed to help each child learn is available; it is up to you to find and use it. Reflect on each incidence of failure to learn, and then regroup and try again and again. Remember, teachers are professionals with the opportunity, knowledge, and responsibility to make a difference.

CHAPTER SUMMARY

- Three major perspectives, or schools of thought, on learning and teaching are the cognitive, humanistic, and behavioral perspectives.
- Cognitivists are interested in how knowledge is acquired. Their study centers around information processing and meaningful learning. Information processing looks at the phenomena of attention, short-term memory, long-term memory, remembering, and forgetting. Meaningful learning focuses on reception learning, reciprocal teaching, discovery learning, and problem solving.
- Humanistic proponents are interested in personal development, the self, and the way feelings, attitudes, and values are acquired. They are concerned that school learning focuses too much on academic learning to the detriment of learning about oneself. Therefore, humanists advocate educational and teaching practices that encourage self-knowledge and enhance self-concept. These practices include Teacher Effectiveness Training, Inviting School Success (invitational learning), values clarification, moral and character education, and multiethnic education.
- Behaviorists are interested in how the environment can be changed or manipulated in order to change behavior in a desirable direction. They study contiguity, classical conditioning, operant conditioning, and social or observational learning as means to behavioral change. Educational practices that support the behaviorist school of thought include programmed instruction, computer-assisted instruction, mastery learning, precision teaching and applied behavioral analysis.
- Most teaching draws from all three schools of thought according to the learning task at hand and the characteristics and needs of the students.

ISSUES AND PROBLEMS FOR DISCUSSION

ISSUES   Here are some related issues for you to debate.

1. Which school of thought—cognitive, humanistic, or behavioral—seems best under what circumstances?
2. Should biases we hold toward a particular school of thought be encouraged or reduced?
3. What seem to be the most critical findings about learning that you should know and apply?
4. How should you be held personally accountable for using what is known about learning?

PROBLEMS   Following are some verbatim daily learning-related problems that teachers have shared with us. How might you resolve them? How does each relate to what we know about learning?

Problem 1:   "Today, during a lesson on fractions, the class became rowdy. Since fractions seem especially difficult for them, they become frustrated. One of the girls blurted out, 'You can't make people learn who don't want to.'"

Problem 2:   "The incident that caused me the greatest concern today happened during a reading class while working with a group of eight third-grade children. These children are unable to read or write above a first-grade level at best. The frustrating part is that they don't know words they have gone over and over before."

Problem 3:   "Today I tried to teach the concepts of 'first, middle, and last' to the slow children in my kindergarten. Many approaches were used—three pictures placed on the chalkboard, three objects placed on the floor, three children standing behind each other in a line. Only a few got the concepts."

Problem 4:   "The thing that bothered me today was brought to mind by something another middle school teacher said in the faculty lounge. She stated that nearly all her students can read and spell but do not understand what they are reading or the meaning of words they are spelling. During the next few days, I paid attention to the teacher's comment when working with my students. Yes, they can read and spell words, but half the time they have little or no understanding."

Problem 5:   "A mother came to the door before 9 o'clock dragging her seventh-grade son. She had to hit him just to get him into the room. The boy is a truant and just sits in class without participating in work or activities. This upsets me because I have tried sincerely and affectionately to get him involved."

Problem 6:   "I am concerned with the poor quality of handwriting. Only about a half-dozen students seem to be able to turn in readable work. Even though standards are set up for handwriting quality and handwriting is considered as part of the grade, it makes very little difference."

Problem 7:   "Many of the students I teach have very low self-esteem. They don't think much of themselves and have little confidence in their ability to learn or do anything. Some are just waiting to drop out."

Problem 8:   "Mary is such a shy girl who is very easily embarrassed. Consequently, she avoids performing publicly. That is very difficult in a foreign language class. Yet, she seems to enjoy learning and does all right in other ways."

THEORY INTO ACTION ACTIVITIES

ACTIVITY 3.1: Cognitive Approaches   How do teachers use the cognitive approach? If you are assigned to a classroom, observe your mentor teacher and describe how he or she uses any of the following cognitive approaches and related beliefs or findings.

1. Reception learning

   _____

2. Reciprocal teaching

   _____

3. Discovery learning

   _____

4. Problem solving

_____

5. Related beliefs or findings

_____

ACTIVITY 3.2: Humanistic Approaches   How do teachers use the humanistic approach? If you are assigned to a classroom, observe the mentor teacher and describe how he or she uses any of the following humanistic approaches and related beliefs and findings.

1. Teacher Effectiveness Training (or related ideas)

_____

2. Inviting School Success

_____

3. Values clarification

_____

4. Moral education

_____

5. Multiethnic education

_____

6. Related beliefs and findings

_____

ACTIVITY 3.3: Behavioral Approaches   How do teachers use the behavioral approach? If you are working in a school, observe your mentor teacher and describe how he or she uses any of the following or other behavioral approaches and related beliefs and findings.

1. Programmed instruction

_____

2. Computer-assisted instruction

_____

3. Mastery learning

_____

4. Precision teaching

_____

5. Applied behavioral analysis

_____

6. Related beliefs and findings

_____

ACTIVITY 3.4: Which School of Learning Theory Most Appeals to You? Are you mostly a cognitivist, humanist, or behaviorist, or are you about evenly some of each? Below are twenty-one statements related to learning. Although you may agree with most or even all of them, pick only seven by placing seven check marks on the corresponding blanks. Then go to the key that follows to find out which school of thought each statement you checked is most closely related to.

_____ 1. Students must make connections between new information and the information they already possess.

_____ 2. Anxious students should be given successful academic and social experiences.

_____ 3. Teachers should give greater attention to helping students learn more about themselves.

_____ 4. New information must be logically organized and presented to students.

_____ 5. Information presented to students should be associated with something they like or want.

_____ 6. Students' behavior is mostly the result of their feelings of confidence, self-worth, and personal dignity.

_____ 7. Students forget information unless they rehearse or think about it.

_____ 8. Students should be made aware of *specifically* what they must know and be able to do at the end of instruction.

_____ 9. Students should be encouraged to believe that they are academically and socially capable.

_____ 10. Students should interact with teachers and be encouraged to ask questions.

_____ 11. Reinforcement of appropriate student learning behavior is essential.

_____ 12. Students should be given a secure environment in which they are encouraged to make wise academic and social choices.

_____ 13. When students discover something on their own, they learn better.

_____ 14. Students need to see other students and/or the teacher demonstrating appropriate learning behavior.

_____ 15. Students should be accepted regardless of their school achievement, feelings, or other behavior.

_____ 16. Students need to learn how to learn.

_____ 17. Parents must reinforce their children's learning behavior.

_____ 18. Students should learn to respect themselves and others.

_____ 19. A most important goal of education is to help students become better problem solvers.

_____ 20. Material to be learned should be presented in small, sequential steps.

_____ 21. Students should be encouraged to pursue their own interests.

Key
Cognitively oriented statements are 1, 4, 7, 10, 13, 16, 19
Behaviorally oriented statements are 2, 5, 8, 11, 14, 17, 20
Humanistically oriented statements are 3, 6, 9, 12, 15, 18, 21

REFERENCES

Anderson, R., Reder, L. & Simon, H. (1996). Situated learning and education. *Educational Researcher, 25*(4), 5–11

Ausubel, D. P. (1977). Facilitation of meaningful verbal learning in the classroom. *Educational Psychologist, 12,* 162–178.

Bandura, A. (1986). *Social foundations of thought and action: A social cognitive theory.* Englewood Cliffs, NJ: Prentice Hall.

Biehler, R. F., & Snowman, J. (1990). *Psychology applied to teaching.* Sixth Edition. Boston: Houghton Mifflin.

Block, J. H., & Anderson, L. W. (1975). *Mastery learning in classroom instruction.* New York: Macmillan.

Brooks, J. G., & Brooks, M. G. (1993). *The case for constructivist classrooms.* Alexandria, VA: Association for Supervision and Curriculum Development.

Bruner, J. S. (1966). *Toward a theory of instruction.* New York: Norton.

Combs, A. W. (1965). *The professional education of teachers.* Boston: Allyn and Bacon.

Cruickshank, D. R., & Associates (1980). *Teaching is tough.* Englewood Cliffs, NJ: Prentice Hall.

Danielson, C. (1996). *Enhancing professional practice.* Alexandria, VA: Association for Supervision and Curriculum Development.

Deci, E. & Ryan, R. (1990). In R. Dienstbier (Ed.), A motivational approach to self. *Nebraska symposium on motivation.* (pp. 240–250). Lincoln: University of Nebraska Press.

Dembo, M. H. (1991). *Applying educational psychology in the classroom.* New York: Longman.

Ellson, D. (1986, October). Improving productivity in teaching. *Phi Delta Kappan, 68,* 111–124.

Frederickson, N. (1984). Implications of cognitive theory for instruction in problem solving. *Review of Educational Research, 54*(3), 363–408.

Gordon, T. (1974). *T.E.T.: Teacher effectiveness training.* White Plains, NY: Longman.

Leinhardt, G. (1992, April). What research on learning tells us about teaching. *Educational Leadership, 49*(7), 20–25.

Lickona, T. (1988). Educating the moral child. *Principal, 68,* 6–10.

Maslow, A. H. (1968). *Toward a psychology of being.* Second Edition. Princeton, NJ: Van Nostrand.

Neill, A. S. (1969). *Summerhill: A radical approach to child rearing.* New York: Hart.

Nuthall, G. (1995). Heuristic models of teaching. In L. Anderson (Ed.), *International encyclopedia of teaching and teacher education* (pp. 122–127). Oxford, UK: Elsevier Science Ltd.

O'Neil, J. (1992, March). Wanted: Deep understanding. *ASCD Update, 34*(3), 1, 4–5, 8.

Palincsar, A. (1986). The role of dialogue in providing scaffolding instruction. *Educational Psychologist, 21,* 73–98.

Piaget, J. (1964). Development and learning. In R. E. Ripple & V. N. Rockcastle (Eds.), *Piaget rediscovered.* Ithaca, NY: Cornell University Press.

Purkey, W. W. (1978). *Inviting school success.* Belmont, CA: Wadsworth.

Rogers, C. R. (1983). *Freedom to learn in the 80's.* Columbus, OH: Merrill.

Schoenfeld, A. H. (1989). Teaching mathematical thinking and problem solving. In L. Resnick & L. Klopfer (Eds.), *Toward the thinking curriculum* (pp. 83–103). Alexandria, VA: Association for Supervision and Curriculum Development.

Simon, S. B., Howe, L. W., & Kerschenbaum, H. (1972). *Values clarification. A handbook of practical strategies for teachers and students.* New York: Hart.

Slavin, R. E. (1986). *Educational psychology: Theory into practice.* Englewood Cliffs, NJ: Prentice Hall.

Sulzer-Azaroff, B. (1995). Behaviorist theories of teaching. In L. Anderson (Ed.), *International encyclopedia of teaching and teacher education.* (pp. 96–100). Oxford, UK: Elsevier Science Ltd.

Sylwester, R. (1995). *A celebration of neurons.* Alexandria, VA: Association for Supervision and Curriculum Development.

Sylwester, R., & Cho, J. (1993, January). What brain research says about paying attention. *Educational Leadership, 50*(4), 71–75.

Viadero, D. (1996, May 22). Debate over how children learn is reignited. *Education Week,* 5. Vol. 15, No. 35, p. 5

Walberg, H. J. (1984, May). Improving the productivity of America's schools. *Educational Leadership, 41,* 19–27.

Walberg, H. J. (1986). Synthesis of research on teaching. In M. C. Wittrock (Ed.), *Handbook of research on teaching* (pp. 214–229). New York: Macmillan.

Watson, B., & Konicek, R. (1990, May). Teaching for conceptual change: Confronting children's experience. *Phi Delta Kappan, 71,* 680–685.

Wilcox, R. T. (1989). Rediscovering discovery learning. In K. Cauley, F. Linder, & J. McMillan (Eds.), *Educational psychology: Annual editions 89/90.* Fourth Edition (pp. 87–90). Guilford, CT: Dushkin.

Wittrock, M. C. (1987). Models of heuristic teaching. In M. J. Dunkin (Ed.), *The international encyclopedia of teaching and teacher education* (pp. 69–76). Oxford: Pergamon.

Getting to Know Your Students

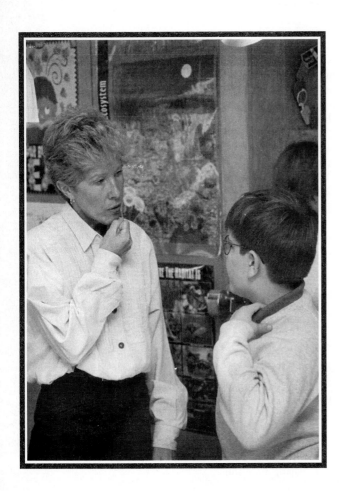

Contents

Chapter 2 addressed the increasingly important circumstance of student diversity and reported some of the many ways in which your learners will differ. This chapter will help you learn how to get to know and size up students, that is, how to recognize individual differences and take them into account when planning and carrying out instruction. You will learn about a variety of approaches to obtain information on your students and how to use that information wisely.

The Importance of Getting to Know Students

In the classic Rodgers and Hammerstein production *The King and I,* Anna, the English-born tutor of the King of Siam's children, sings them the following song:

> It's a very ancient saying but a true and honest thought,
> That if you become a teacher by your pupils you'll be taught.
> As a teacher *I've* been learning (you'll forgive me if I boast),
> And I've now become an expert on the subject I like most—
> *Getting to know you.*
> Getting to know you, getting to know all about you,
> Getting to like you, getting to hope you like me.
> Getting to know you, putting it my way, but nicely,
> You are precisely my cup of tea.
> Getting to know you, getting to feel free and easy,
> When I am with you, getting to know what to say.
> Haven't you noticed, suddenly I'm bright and breezy
> Because of all the beautiful and new things I'm learning about
> you, day by day.

Just as Anna proclaims, a major responsibility and delight for most teachers is getting to know their students. Scholars concur: knowing your students is extremely important if you expect to become an expert teacher (Doyle, 1986; Emmer, 1987; Shulman, 1987). One of the things that normally separates novice from more experienced teachers is that new teachers do not know much about their students (Berliner, 1986; Borko & Livingston, 1989; Carter et al., 1987; Zheng, 1992). Among other things, knowing your students enables you to organize them into a functional class, to interact with them more sensitively, and to teach them more effectively (Airasian, 1991).

Although there are many ways to obtain information about your students, the information itself falls into two general categories: (1) information already contained in existing school records and (2) information you can obtain yourself. You gain personally obtained information by spending time with your students, by observing and interviewing them, and by using questionnaires, sociometric studies, cases, autobiographies, and parent conferences. Let's look more closely at the various methods of getting to know students.

4.1 How important to you is getting to know students? What do you most need to know about them?

Using Existing Records

CUMULATIVE RECORDS

Chris Zajac had received her fifth-grade children's cumulative records, which were stuffed inside salmon-colored folders. . . . For now she only [looked at] her new students' names and addresses, and resisted looking [at other information contained in the records]. It was usually better at first to let her own opinions form. But she couldn't help noticing the thickness of some of the "cumes." "The thicker the cume, the more trouble," she told [another teacher]. (Kidder, 1989, pp. 8–9)

The major source of information about your students will be their cumulative or permanent school records. The **cumulative record** is a depository of information and documents that most school districts require for each child. That record begins when a student enters kindergarten and follows the learner until he or she leaves school or graduates. A student's cumulative record contains a variety of data: *personal information* (address, age, place of birth, special interests, hobbies); *home and family data* (names of parents or guardians, their occupation(s); names and ages of siblings, unusual home conditions); *school attendance records; scores on standardized tests* of aptitude and achievement; *year-end academic grades, teacher anecdotal comments* on students and comments written following parent conferences; and miscellaneous information such as health data, psychological reports, and written communications between school and home.

4.2 What might you want to know about students beyond the information usually contained in a cumulative record?

If you are now assigned to a school, chances are that cumulative records exist for the students you work with. Your mentor teacher may be willing and able to share them with you. If not, you will find five cumulative records in the appendix at the end of this chapter so that you can see what these records are like. The records have been minimally altered to protect the target students (for example, the photographs are not those of the student in the record). Two of the five students, Jack Brogan and Kathleen Glovak, are in fifth grade in a suburban school. The others, Benny Gamble, Julio Rivera, and Debbie Walker, are middle school sixth graders in an inner-city school. Take a moment to find the records and look them over, as we will refer to them later. For now, however, let's briefly consider two of the most important kinds of data contained in a "cume record"—scores on standardized tests and teacher anecdotal comments.

Standardized Test Scores A **standardized test** compares a student's score on that test with the scores of a very large number of similar students who have taken the same test. Thus, a standardized test score enables you to see how your students'

"When my teachers told me that my records would follow me through life, I thought they were exaggerating."

scores compare to the scores of a much larger sample of similar students, such as other eighth graders locally or nationally. Standardized tests that measure potential, or aptitude, for learning are called aptitude tests, while those that measure how much students actually know are called achievement tests.

Aptitude Tests   Aptitude tests that measure general potential to learn are referred to as general ability tests, or intelligence tests. These tests provide you with comparative information about such things as a student's ability to deal with abstractions and to solve problems (Snyderman & Rothman, 1987). Look at Jack Brogan's cumulative record (at the end of this chapter, beginning on page 100). You will see he has taken two mental ability tests. His scores of 103 and 104 become meaningful only when compared against the national average of 100 on the same tests. All students whose records appear in the appendix score about average on their mental ability tests. Scores 20 or more points higher or lower than 100 are usually indicative of higher- or lower-than-average learning potential. Thus, Jack's scores are quite average.

For the past few decades, there has been increasing debate over the use of general ability tests. Some argue the tests are culturally biased favoring white, middle-class Americans—that the tests are written so that nonwhite and/or low SES students would be less likely to do well on them. Most school districts, however, continue to use aptitude tests, although they caution against placing too much confidence in such scores by themselves.

In Chapter 2, we learned about multiple kinds of intelligence (Figure 2.7), including interpersonal insight, physical aptitudes, and the ability to learn in specific fields such as music. In this chapter's appendix, you may notice that the Madison School District students (Jack and Kathy) also took a musical aptitude test. Both scored at the 6th percentile, which means they did as well as or better on this test than only 6 percent of students who have taken it. Based on the test result alone, they would seem to have limited musical aptitude.

Achievement Tests   Standardized tests are also used to measure achievement, that is, how much a student already knows compared to similar students. Again, turn to Jack Brogan's record (page 100). He has taken achievement tests in grades 1 through 4. In grade 1, he received a score of B (high normal) in readiness to read. In grade 2, Jack scored at the 40th percentile, which means his reading score was the same as or better than 40 percent of other students who have taken this test. In grades 3 and 4, we encounter another way to present standardized test scores. This form is called the grade level, or grade equivalent, score. A **grade equivalent score,** according to Airasian (1991), is one that "actually represents the pupil's level of performance relative to pupils in his or her own grade" (p. 438). An example will make this definition clear. In fourth grade, Jack Brogan received a score of 4.2 on the "Middle Grades Achievement Test" (this name was substituted for the real test name). What does 4.2 mean? A grade level or grade equivalent score of 4.2 means that, compared to other fourth graders for whom the test was intended and on whom the test was "normed," Jack is average. Let's look at Benny Gamble's record (page 109). In grade 3, he took the "Metropolitan Achievement Test" in several subjects. In reading, his grade equivalency score was 5.3. This means that, compared to other third graders for which the reading test was intended, Benny did very well; it does *not* mean that Benny necessarily is reading at a fifth-grade level, as the 5.3 might seem to indicate. Standardized tests will be discussed further in Chapter 8.

Teacher Anecdotal Comments   A second kind of information found in cumulative records are teachers' **anecdotal comments,** or the written descriptions teachers write about their students. According to Prescott (1957),

> In general, the description should give a cross-section [showing] how [the learner] acts in a variety of situations. Some children behave so differently in different classes

with different teachers that one can hardly recognize them as the same individuals. It is as important to see what bores a child as to see what excites his interest . . . [The description] would show him in action when things are going well and when they are not going well; interacting with his teacher, other adults, peers, and younger and older children; studying, loafing, creating, sulking, or pursuing an interest alone; interacting with parents, siblings, and neighborhood children; in informal situations such as eating lunch [and while] playing. In short, samplings from the whole range of his life experiences in and around school are needed. (p. 155)

Teachers hardly ever have the time, inclination, or training to pursue Prescott's ideal. In reality, they may make a once-a-year statement about the student in twenty-five words or less. The comments often are interpretive and judgmental and do not reveal in any detail *how* the interpretation or judgment was made.

Touliatos and Compton (1983) suggest the following guidelines for writing anecdotal comments:

4.3 Teacher Chris Zajac (p. 82) resisted looking at her students' cumulative files until she had formed her own opinions. What do you think are the advantages and disadvantages of learning about students from school records?

- Cover only a single incident in the anecdote.
- Record it as soon as possible, with the date and time indicated.
- Begin with a description of the place where the situation occurred, the people who were involved, and the circumstances.
- Describe what transpired (events, reactions, responses—use direct quotes if possible). Try to write in a reportorial style; that is, describe, but do not interpret or editorialize, what you viewed. Be objective—avoid personal judgments.
- Describe how the episode concluded.
- If the episode is related to other episodes, state how and why.

When you look at the "teacher comments" and "personal comments" on the five appended cumulative record cards, it is clear that the teachers who wrote them did not provide all the information Touliatos and Compton suggest. Nevertheless, the comments tell us something about these teachers' perceptions of:

- A student's learning characteristics (Jack Brogan has a "short attention span")
- A student's work habits (Jack is "not finishing his work")
- A student's social and personality characteristics (Jack "is quite immature, constantly talking, fools and daydreams," and so on)
- A student's achievement (Kathy Glovack "is doing strong average work, does very well in school")
- A student's problems ("Kathy doesn't like the student teacher")
- A student's maladies (Benny Gamble "complains of illness")
- A student's interests (Julio Rivera "likes science and music")
- A student's family (Debbie Walker's "stepfather has left home and is trying to get the baby daughter from the mother")

4.4 How might you be affected by reading the student folders in the appendix?

Try Activity 4.1

Unearthing New Information about Students

There may be occasions when you have no cumulative records or when they are inadequate for your needs. At such times, you may want to find out some things about students for yourself. There are several ways you can do so.

OBSERVING STUDENTS

Observation, that is, looking and listening, is an excellent way to learn about students. You can observe them talking, reading, working independently and in groups, listening, and so forth. These observations can be either formal or informal.

Formal observation refers to carefully planned efforts to obtain specific information about a target student or students. The teacher, a teacher aide, another teacher, or a university student involved in a field experience could do formal observation. The use of a carefully designed observation instrument permits you to observe a student or students and then make subsequent observations in order to compare the results. Conversely, **informal observation** refers to casual, unplanned observations done incidentally. Such spontaneous observations, which are made under conditions that were not controlled and thus cannot be closely replicated, are nonetheless valuable to teachers.

Examples may make the distinction between formal and informal observation clearer. Suppose Jack Brogan is your target student. You note from comments in his cumulative record (pages 100–104) that he has difficulty interacting with other students ("minds other people's business, bothers people, has become sullen with other students"). To get a more complete profile of Jack, you decide to observe him. Now the choice of formal or informal observation comes into play.

If you observe Jack formally, you need to specify what you intend to look for. You must also decide how, when, and under what conditions you will make these observations. You might decide to observe his interactions with other students for one complete day: before he enters the building; when he enters and goes to his room; during the time before class begins; during class activities, recess, and lunch; and as he leaves the class and the building. You might even want to make up your own observation instrument or checklist (see Chapter 8). The following are questions you could use to focus your observation:

Try Activity 4.2

- With whom does Jack interact most and least?
- What circumstances surrounded positive interactions?
- What circumstances surrounded neutral interactions?
- What circumstances surrounded negative interactions?
- With whom were the positive, neutral, and negative interactions?
- Were the different kinds of interactions (positive, neutral, negative) related to different times of day, different activities, or other factors or circumstances?

On the other hand, if you observe Jack informally, your observations will not be systematic. You will only be describing spontaneous events and situations that you feel are interesting or important. Thus, informal observation is casual, impromptu, and general. Teacher comments made on cumulative record cards and on report cards (see, for example, page 102) are usually the result of informal observation.

Only from carefully structured, formal observation can you obtain the kind of information you need to address a true concern you may have about a student. Since formal observation is labor- and time-intensive, most teachers reserve it for special circumstances, such as when a student or students need academic or social help.

INTERVIEWING STUDENTS

Humans have an insatiable desire to find out about others. This assertion seems well supported by the number of radio and television talk shows in which persons of all kinds answer questions about what they are like and why. Certainly, one way to find out about persons is to talk with them directly.

Likewise, teachers can find out about their students both by talking casually with them and by formally interviewing them. Interviews may be particularly useful in uncovering personal information that cannot be obtained through observation. For example, you can observe Jack Brogan and try to deduce possible causes of his unsatisfactory interaction with his peers, or you can interview him in an attempt to uncover the cause.

4.5 If you were Kathleen Glovack's student teacher, why might you want to interview her?

Like observations, interviews can be formal or informal. A **formal interview** is a structured, face-to-face meeting to obtain specific information about the interviewee's experiences, views, likes, and so forth. The key characteristics of a formal interview are *purpose* and *structure*. There are particular things you wish to find out, and in order to do so, you must frame your questions accordingly.

An **informal interview** is a face-to-face meeting that is more like casual conversation. The intention is to allow talk to flow naturally and spontaneously in more or less any direction. Perhaps you can categorize prominent interviewers such as Barbara Walters, Larry King, Oprah Winfrey, Sam Donaldson, Ed Bradley, and Jay Leno on a continuum between formal and informal.

What procedures are interviewers expected to follow? TenBrink (1974) offers the following guidelines; think about how you might follow them if you were interviewing Jack Brogan or Kathleen Glovack.

- *Be prepared.* Remember, if you are conducting the interview for a specific purpose, it must be carefully structured. In Kathy's case, you may want to find out how she feels about her student teacher and why. Have explicit, thoughtfully constructed questions ready.
- *Put the student at ease.* Begin by establishing a friendly, relaxed atmosphere. Use a warm-up period to talk for awhile about pleasant, nonthreatening things.
- *Guide the student.* Once you seem to be comfortable with each other, gently lead the child through your thoughtfully planned questions and probe for further, related information if that seems prudent. However, do not push too hard. You may recall times when teachers or parents "interviewed" you and perhaps met with resistance.
- *Know when to quit.* You may have to back off or stop if the interviewee feels threatened.

Try Activity 4.3

4.6 Beyond the information usually found in a cumulative record, what else might you want to know that possibly could come out of an interview?

You can also obtain much useful information about a student through interviewing other teachers and through parent conferences. As with student interviews, the amount of useful information you obtain will be directly related to how well you prepare for the interview and how skillfully you follow good interviewing procedures.

In summary, if you are properly prepared and sensitive to others, the use of interviews can provide you with much needed information that can help you understand and work more effectively with your students.

USING QUESTIONNAIRES

Thus far, we have suggested that you can obtain information beyond that contained in the school's cumulative record folders by watching, listening, and talking to your students. Another way you can acquire student information is to have students complete questionnaires. Questionnaires normally are given to an entire class rather than to an individual. However, individuals can be targeted.

Questionnaires range from asking open-ended questions to asking students to respond to very specific items. Some examples will make this distinction clearer. Open-ended questions, such as the following, allow students greater freedom of response. (Of course, questions would be modified according to the student's developmental characteristics, such as age.)

4.7 What might a teacher want to know that could be discovered through a questionnaire?

- What are you like?
- What is your favorite activity, hobby, sport, TV show, place, food, or subject? What are your least favorite things?
- How do you feel about yourself as a student?
- How would you describe your behavior in class?
- How do you get along with other students?

- What do you want teachers to be like?
- What do you like most and least about school?
- When do you enjoy class most and least?
- What is it like for you at home?

Closed-ended items on a questionnaire are more specific. The respondent often is asked to read each item and then indicate to what extent he or she agrees with it. The respondent is forced to make a choice. The sample of items on the following mock questionnaire are all related to school attitude. They are adopted from Lewis (1986).

	Strongly Agree	Agree	Disagree	Strongly Disagree
1. I like school.				
2. My teachers care about me.				
3. School helps me feel good about myself.				
4. The things I learn in school are important to me.				
5. My teachers praise and reward me.				
6. I need more teacher help.				
7. School is boring.				

Following is another sample of closed-ended items. This time, yes or no answers are required. The items, adopted from Fraser and Fisher (1986), are intended to find out how students feel about the class they are in.

1. Pupils enjoy this class.	Yes	No
2. The difficulty of the classwork is about right.	Yes	No
3. Students get along with each other in this class.	Yes	No
4. This class is very competitive.	Yes	No

Try Activity 4.4

USING SOCIOMETRY

Sociometry is a technique used to obtain information about the social acceptability of individuals within a group. A **sociogram** is a diagrammatic representation of the social relationships that exist within a group at a *particular point in time* (see Figure 4.1).

Suppose you are the teacher of Jack Brogan and Kathleen Glovack, or the teacher of Benny Gamble, Julio Rivera, and Debbie Walker. Furthermore, assume you wish to know more about how their peers feel about each of these students, and how the students feel about their peers. If so, you might ask each class member to name three students they would like to sit near. As Figure 4.1 shows, the responses of the twenty-nine students in Jack and Kathleen's class reveal that:

- No one chooses Jack.
- Four students would like to sit near Kathleen (three girls, one boy).

Ronald, the most nominated student in the class, was selected nine times. Five students other than Jack were not selected by anyone. Can you identify them?

Beyond frequency of nomination (popularity), teachers are also interested in attractions. Who nominated whom? Who chose each of the students? To what extent are the choices mutual? Are there cases of "unrequited love" or instances when students choose others who reject or spurn them?

FIGURE 4.1 Sociogram

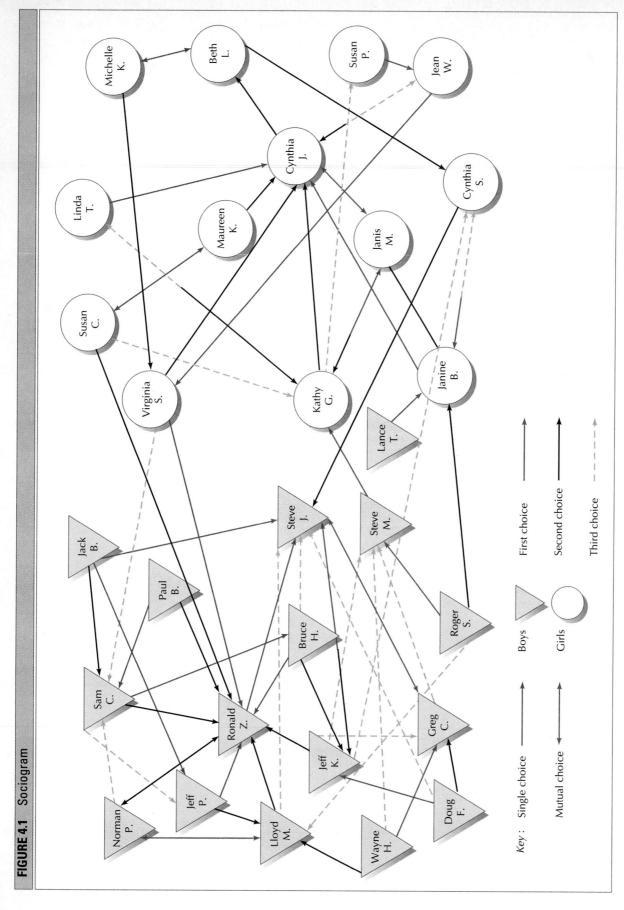

Key: Single choice ——————

Mutual choice ◄————►

First choice ————►

Second choice ————►

Third choice ----►

Boys △

Girls ◯

Question: Name three children in your classroom whom you would most like to sit next to. (Note: Not all children made three choices.)

Although sociometric nominations are one of the most dependable rating techniques (Anastasi, 1988), Touliatos and Compton (1983) urge caution when interpreting sociometric data. The information actually may indicate desired rather than real associations among class members, and "too often high sociometric status is interpreted to mean leadership ability and good personality adjustment, while receiving no sociometric choices is commonly equated with maladjustment. Receiving many choices actually could . . . mean high conformity to the group, and [isolation] could be [a sign] of independence and creativity" (p. 201).

USING AUTOBIOGRAPHY

Autobiography can provide a rich source of knowledge about its author. Thus, another way to obtain information about students is to ask them to write about some aspect of their lives. However, use of this technique is limited since it depends on students' verbal and writing ability. Additionally, it is time-consuming for the writers. Therefore, should you wish to obtain autobiographical information, limit the focus of the story. Ask students to recall and write about such topics as:

- Who am I?
- The best day I ever had
- My favorite year in school
- My favorite teacher
- My life at home
- My life in the neighborhood
- My life at school
- My most memorable experience
- My favorite things

USING PARENTS AND GUARDIANS AS SOURCES

Parents and guardians are important sources of information about students. Normally, parents know more about their children than anyone, and most teachers have opportunities to tap this supply of information. Formally, there are parent-teacher conferences. Some school districts mandate conferences and give teachers time to conduct them. For example, in the Madison School District where Jack Brogan and Kathy Glovack are students, yearly conferences are required. You probably noted the section titled "Parent-Teacher Conference Summaries" in the cumulative record folders. In the Urban School System where Benny, Julio, and Debbie are students, conferences are not required and the folders have no specific place to record them. Of course, Urban teachers do confer with parents. You will note in Debbie Walker's folder that there is a request from her third-grade teacher for a parent conference or a letter from the parent. Mrs. Walker indicated she had received the request, but there is no evidence that a conference took place or that she responded with a letter.

Unfortunately, most parent-teacher conferences are held only to provide information to parents and not also to obtain information from them. Certainly, it was important for Kathy Glovack's fourth-grade teacher to learn that Kathy didn't want to come to school because she didn't like the student teacher. Also, Kathy's third-grade teacher learned from Mrs. Glovack that there was a new baby in the home. This is potentially useful information. In Jack Brogan's case, parent conferences revealed that his father is strict, that his parents want him to behave and learn, and that they are cooperative and helpful.

What might teachers need to know about students that could be learned from parents and guardians? Parents can tell teachers about a student's behavior at home, about his or her likes and dislikes, habits, responsibilities, and so forth.

4.8 How might you put sociometric information to good use?

Try Activity 4.5 or 4.6

4.9 How would your teachers benefit from autobiographical information about you? What kinds of information would you want them to have?

Try Activity 4.7

4.10 What do teachers absolutely *need* to know about a student's family background? What might they *want* to know that isn't absolutely necessary? What kinds of information are helpful? What family information is no one else's business?

"I said, 'Your son doesn't seem to listen very well'."

While parents do not know everything about their children, they can aid you tremendously in getting to know your students needs' and abilities.

What might teachers need to know about parents and guardians that, in turn, would help them understand more about their students? Touliatos and Compton (1983) suggest the following: parental background and current family status, personal characteristics of parents ("the Brogans are strict"), parental perception of their relationship with each other and with the student, the roles of both parents and students in the home, and parental attitudes toward the student and any siblings. To find out about the personal characteristics of parents and other family members, teachers might ask them to tell what they are like as people and as parents, then ask how that may affect their son or daughter. To know how parents perceive their own and their children's roles and relationships in the home, teachers might ask them how family responsibilities and decisions are shared.

Try Activity 4.8

It is particularly useful to know how parents or guardians feel toward parenting and child rearing. You might consider asking them what it is like to be parents or guardians, how being a parent has affected their lives, what it is like to be the target student's parent or guardian, what they believe in as parents or guardians, and so on.

USING CASES

The **case approach** pieces together all existing information to form a comprehensive profile of the target student. Thus, a case pulls together information from cumulative records, observations, interviews, questionnaires, sociometric studies, autobiographies, parent conferences, and any other source and synthesizes it.

Normally, the best existing source of case history information is the cumulative record since it contains several kinds of information and is updated from time to time. When other data are available to fill in the blanks, teachers are able to complete the case. If other data are not available, they must collect the missing information.

Touliatos and Compton (1983) suggest that to have an overall picture of a student, you need the following data:

4.11 Would you like to have a complete study of all the students you teach? What benefits would this offer?

- Identifying information (name, address, telephone, age in years and months, place of birth, gender, grade, race, nationality, religion)
- Family history (relationship of the parent, guardian, or caregiver to the student; parents' age, race, nationality, religion, cultural background, and language spoken in the home; family physical and health concerns; education; present work status; homeowner or renter; adequacy of housing; interests; pastimes)
- Student's medical history (general health, record of prominent illnesses and injuries)

- Student's school history (schools attended, level of performance in general and in specific subjects such as reading and math, aptitude test scores, achievement test scores, special interests, attitudes, relationships with others, friends)

A teacher-written case study of Debbie Walker is contained in Case 4.1. Her cumulative record folder is appended at the end of the chapter.

Try Activity 4.9

Evaluating and Using Information

It is one thing to need or want accurate student information to aid you in your teaching. It is another thing to understand and to use it wisely.

EVALUATING INFORMATION

Several questions should challenge you when you examine student data: Is this information suitable for my purpose? Just what is it that I want to know? Does this information supply the answers? Suppose you want to know about your students' aptitude for learning: to what extent are they likely to be able to deal with abstractions, solve problems, and learn? In this case you would need to have the results of a standardized test that measures learning aptitude. Because it has been constructed for the purpose of measuring learning potential, such a test is considered valid for that purpose. On the other hand, a standardized test that measures student achievement—what a student already knows—would not be suitable for that purpose. Although students' scores on achievement tests are often closely related to their scores on learning aptitude tests, these tests measure different things. A student may perform well on a learning aptitude test, thus revealing the potential to learn, yet may not do well on an achievement test. Conversely, another student may earn a high achievement test score but a low learning aptitude test score. Can you see how this could happen? Since standardized tests have been carefully developed to measure what they are supposed to measure, you need to make certain that you have the right test results for your needs.

A second question related to student data involves correctness. Here you need to ask: Is this information really accurate? Two major factors can contribute to inaccuracy. One relates to whether the information is biased, while the other relates to whether the information is stable. For decades, certain standardized tests have been criticized as biased, usually in terms of culture or gender considerations. As previously mentioned in the section on aptitude tests, some tests appear to be easier for students brought up in white, middle-class communities because they use Standard English and draw from typical middle-class experiences. Others supposedly exhibit gender bias, usually meaning they are easier for males than females. To the extent that such tests are biased, it is impossible to obtain truly accurate student scores. School districts are increasingly aware of the need to find objective tests that provide unbiased, culture- and gender-fair results.

Unfortunately, some degree of bias exists in everyone. Accordingly, be cautious about accepting any interpretation of student data provided by others, including teachers. Although most teachers have no intention of providing slanted information, they naturally become attracted to certain students and are put off by others. They tend to identify with and praise the "attractive students" and to reject and punish the "unattractive" ones. To some extent, the attraction teachers feel toward certain students is a function of their own background and personality. Generally, we tend to like those who are like us. We feel more comfortable around them (the "birds of a feather" syndrome).

Teacher bias is particularly evident when such things as race, nationality, gender, looks, and dress unfairly and incorrectly influence the teacher's perception of students. Can you recall instances of possible teacher bias toward you or a friend based on one of these factors?

 4.12 How will you become aware of your personal biases? How will you deal with them?

CASE 4.1

A Study of Debbie Walker, Written by Her Teacher

Debbie Walker, Grade 5, Edison School. One November morning, Debbie Walker, a transfer student from Baker Middle School, arrived hobbling on crutches and accompanied by her mother. Mrs. Walker explained that Debbie had broken her leg while helping carry furniture into the house from a moving truck. As a result of the accident, Debbie had missed almost two months of school. As soon as she entered our classroom, the children immediately accepted her. This was probably partially a result of her incapacitation. Lynette Overmire and several other children were anxious to help and made plans to escort Debbie to and from classrooms and to her home. This was the first indication that Debbie was able to exert a subtle yet profound effect on the behavior of her peers.

Debbie Walker was born in the city of Urban and has lived in inner-city ghetto areas all her life. During this time, she has attended eight different schools and has been a pupil in eighteen different classrooms. As a result of this continuous shifting, Debbie has never experienced any sense of security or permanency. Her home conditions (the family has fourteen children) are in a constant state of turmoil. In a fatherless home until recently, Debbie and her siblings have moved from one area of the inner-city ghetto to another. Often, the only concern of such families is to eke out a day-by-day existence.

Until recently, Debbie lived only with her mother and six of her twelve siblings. However, within the last two years she also had a "stepfather." More recently, the stepfather left the home and is seeking court action to obtain custody of his baby daughter. Debbie knows nothing of her biological father. She does not even remember one. She has grown up on public assistance. This family has packed up its belongings and criss-crossed the city almost as many times as Debbie has counted birthdays.

Physically, Debbie is relatively tall for her age. She is an African American and a member of the Baptist church. Her personal appearance varies from one day to the next. She does not seem to know how to be neat, clean, and well groomed.

Debbie's general attitude has been pleasant until recently. She has enjoyed helping in the classroom and about the school, and the children elected her to the position of class treasurer. Debbie has been assisting in the arts and crafts program in our after-school program at the Social Center. The arts and crafts teacher has praised Debbie's work.

Very recently, however, Debbie appears to be disturbed. Just last month, she was suspended from school for two days for encouraging two girls to fight each other outside the school building during lunch period. As a result of her suspension, she became sullen and would not complete her academic assignments. Now she has had her school and after-school responsibilities taken away from her.

Debbie had been relatively happy in school until these events occurred. This was reassuring, since she has been retained in the first, third, and fifth grades. She seems to enjoy art, music, and arithmetic the most. However, she claims she likes all her subjects.

Debbie uses fair Standard English. The mark of inner-city linguistic characteristics is evident in her speech pattern.

In a recent conversation with Mrs. Walker, we discussed Debbie's attitudes, general behavior, and failure to follow through with classwork. I indicated that this behavior was jeopardizing Debbie's school success. Her mother thinks that her friendship with Felicia Ault is the reason behind her change for the worse. It is true that Debbie and Felicia are close and have a somewhat negative influence upon each other and the other children. As mentioned earlier, Debbie is able to affect the behavior of her classmates through manipulation and subtle pressure.

Debbie's school achievement has been weak. She has taken three Kuhlman-Anderson IQ tests. The results reveal an IQ range from 86 to 103. Her achievement test scores are recorded on her cumulative record folder and should be interpreted according to her age and grade rather than just grade alone.

One hopes that Debbie's recent failure to complete her work and to behave in more appropriate ways in the school setting may pass. Now that she is encountering more homework, some provisions will have to be made for a quiet place at home for her to study. In a family as large as hers, this circumstance is improbable. Coming to school as she has recently with unfinished assignments may well have led to her frustration and antisocial behavior. Debbie must be continually encouraged to do her best to complete her work and to complete it on time. If she is able to develop this habit, she may soon be eligible to become a hall guard. This status, if attained, may ease her frustrations.

Source: D. R. Cruickshank. (1969). *Inner-city simulation laboratory.* Chicago: Science Research Associates.

Teacher bias also can be positive but inaccurate. Each of us has a friend or relative whom we are attracted to for some particular reason. Sometimes we admire that person so much for one or two positive qualities that we overlook any negative qualities he or she may have. To us, that individual wears a halo. You will find certain students seem to wear halos, too. They can do no wrong. This bias phenomenon is aptly termed "the halo effect." Although it is difficult to detect and control, you must strive to observe and report the truth, the whole truth, and nothing but the truth about learners. This is a tall order.

Inconsistent information about students also presents a problem. Consider Benny Gamble's "general ability tests" (page 111). He took these aptitude tests in grades 1, 2, and 3 and received intelligence scores ranging from 97 (about average) to 116 (above average). Similarly, you might receive conflicting perceptions of a student from different teachers. One might report an eager hand-raiser as an aggressive attention seeker, while another might interpret the same behavior as that of a motivated learner. Which should you believe? Generally speaking, when information about a student is inconsistent, err on the positive side: accept Benny's high score as indicative of what he can do under optimal conditions. And, for the same reason, believe the best about any learner with mixed credentials.

In summary, if teachers are to be effective, they must learn to obtain and use only the information about their students that suits their purpose, is unbiased, and is consistent or stable.

USING INFORMATION PROPERLY

The information we obtain affects the perceptions and expectations we have of students. Moreover, some types of information are more influential than others. Dusek and Joseph (1983) identified and compared the results of seventy-seven studies that were conducted to find out what most influences the academic and personal expectations teachers have for their students. The investigators looked for relationships between teachers' expectations and student gender, gender-role behaviors, physical attractiveness, race and social class, name stereotypes, conduct, and the teacher's previous experiences with a sibling. Five of these factors seem to significantly influence a teacher's judgment: student attractiveness, class conduct, race, social class, and cumulative record information, particularly test scores and teachers' anecdotal comments. To see how, turn to Table 4.1.

In contrast, Dusek and Joseph note that it is unclear whether a student's name (desirable versus undesirable), gender-role behaviors (whether their behavior follows a gender-role stereotype), or a teacher's previous experiences with a student's sibling influence teacher expectations. The researchers conclude that teachers, on average, are not influenced by a student's gender.

TABLE 4.1 Factors That Influence Teachers' Perceptions and Expectations of Students

Variables	Type of Influence
Student attractiveness (physical)	Influences teachers' expectations for both academic achievement and social-personal relationships.
Student classroom conduct	Influences teachers' expectations of future conduct.
Race	Generally, white students are expected to outperform black students.
Social class	Generally, middle-class children are expected to perform better than lower-class students.
Cumulative record information	Teachers' expectations are influenced mainly by test scores and other teachers' comments.

Source: From J. B. Dusek & G. Joseph. (1983). The bases of teacher expectations: A meta-analysis. *Journal of Educational Psychology, 75* (3) 327–346.

Since certain information about students influences the perceptions and expectations of teachers, just how much should they read or hear about their students *before* classes begin? Airasian (1991) says that in the course of interviews with teachers, he found most of them wanted at least three kinds of information early on. They want to know about (1) any physical or emotional problem, (2) learners' special needs, learning problems, or disabilities, and (3) problematic or atypical parent custodial arrangements.

Fortunately, many teachers adjust their perceptions and expectations of students after working with them, after "getting to know them" (Good & Brophy, 1990). Yes, as teachers we tend to believe what we read, but we change those impressions in light of our experience.

4.13 Are you able to change your mind about people?

Some Final Thoughts

As we have seen, sizing up students has its benefits and pitfalls. We have already alluded to the potential danger of relying exclusively or too heavily on certain kinds of information, such as standardized test scores and teacher's comments. Airasian (1991) offers suggestions on how teachers can overcome these and other possible problems. Our modifications of Airasian's suggestions follow:

- Be sensitive to the possibility that you will make poor initial judgments about students from biased, incomplete, or erroneous information or from having a poor first impression. Give each student a second chance to make a good impression.

- Do not rush to judgment about what any student is like. Over time, collect as much information as you can in order to find out who that person really is.

- Rather than relying on recorded information, how the student dresses or looks, and what others say, observe the student and try to get close enough to find out the truth for yourself. Looks can be deceiving!

A large number of formal instruments have been developed for assessing students. Using them can provide knowledge about your students' (1) cognition (intelligence, readiness to learn, maturation, language and number skills, cognitive style, and so on), (2) personality and emotional characteristics, (3) perceptions of the environment, (4) self-concept, (5) attitudes and interests, and (6) social behavior. These instruments are well described in a two-volume set edited by Johnson (1976).

CHAPTER SUMMARY

- Getting to know students is important to teachers. Expert teachers seem to know far more about their students than novice teachers do.

- While there are many ways to get to know students, the information they yield falls into two main categories: information obtained from existing student records and information teachers can obtain for themselves.

- The major source of existing information is the cumulative ("cume") records or folders (five examples are in the chapter appendix). Cumulative records normally contain personal information about a student, home-family information, school attendance data, academic grades, standardized test scores, teacher comments, and so forth. Generally, teachers seem most interested in obtaining standardized test scores and reading former teachers' comments.

- To interpret standardized test scores, it is necessary to know what the test attempts to measure and to understand terms such as *standardized test, percentile,* and *grade equivalent.* To judge teachers' comments, it is necessary to know something about the people who made them and how they reached their conclusions about the student. Teachers' comments are often brief, incomplete, and, at times, inaccurate.

- A second source of information about students is knowledge teachers obtain from observations, interviews, questionnaires, sociometrics, autobiographies, parents, and cases.

- Student observations can be formal (intentionally planned and carried out) or informal (spontaneous and unplanned). Formal observation requires the teacher to specify who will be observed and how the observation will take place. Informal observation requires only occasional and impromptu records of whatever catches the teacher's attention. Most teacher observations are informal.

- Interviews allow teachers to collect information that is difficult to gain through mere observation. Interviews also can be formal or informal. Following certain interviewing procedures increases both the amount and the quality of information obtained.

- Questionnaires are structured using either open- or closed-ended questions. Open-ended questions ask students to broadly describe their perceptions of themselves, their relationships with peers, and their school and home lives. Closed-ended questions force students to answer according to some preconstructed scale or by responding yes or no; they permit no elaboration.

- Sociometry is used to find out how students perceive their social and/or work relationships with peers. A sociogram is a visual representation of those relationships.

- Autobiographical writing provides students with the opportunity to tell about themselves. Use of autobiographical writing is somewhat limited because of the literacy demands it places on some students.

- Parents and guardians can tell teachers much about their charges, and the teacher should tap them for this information. Knowledge of parents and family also helps us understand students.

- The case approach is a technique used to bring together all information about a student in order to create a more complete picture. Thus, a good case contains a mixture of information obtained through all the techniques just mentioned.

- Teachers must be able to evaluate information about students. Of prime importance is how closely the available information relates to the decisions teachers must make. Information that fits the purpose is *valid* information. Also important is the accuracy and stability of information, which is referred to as its *reliability*. Being able to judge the validity and reliability of information is crucial to using it in decision making.

- Certain types of information influence teachers' perceptions and expectations of students more than other kinds. The most influential types of information seem to be class conduct, student attractiveness, social class, race, and cumulative records. All teachers seem to want to gain information about learners' physical, emotional, learning, or home problems early on. Fortunately, teachers adjust their early impressions of students based upon long-term, daily experience with them. Airasian (1991) offers suggestions for overcoming the tendency to think and act on first impressions.

ISSUES AND PROBLEMS FOR DISCUSSION

1. When should teachers receive cumulative record information?
2. What kinds of information about students *must* a teacher have? What kinds *shouldn't* a teacher have?
3. How much confidence should teachers place in standardized tests? How should teachers use test data?

4. What are the advantages and disadvantages of showing students and parents standardized test results?
5. How can a teacher reduce his or her bias toward certain students?
6. How can teachers find time to collect and use student information?

THEORY INTO ACTION ACTIVITIES

ACTIVITY 4.1: Review Some Cumulative Records   If you are in a field experience, ask your mentor teacher if you can see the cumulative records for that class. If so, make a list of the kinds of information they contain. Make a second list of other kinds of information about students that might be helpful to you.

If you are not in a field experience, study the five cumulative records in the appendix and make the same two lists. What else do you need to know in order to understand or interpret specific information contained in the records? Be prepared to share your investigation with other students in this course.

ACTIVITY 4.2: Plan and Conduct a Formal Observation   If you are in a field experience, ask your mentor teacher if you might formally observe a student. Ask your teacher to help you identify the target individual. Then, prepare for the observation by answering the following questions.

- Who is the target student, and why has he or she been targeted? What is the concern or problem?
- What useful information might be gained by watching and listening to the student?
- Specifically when will the student be observed?
- What will be recorded? A list of questions or a checklist is usually required.

ACTIVITY 4.3: Plan and Conduct an Interview   If you are involved in a field experience, you may be able to plan and conduct an interview with a student. It can focus on gaining information on a number of things, including the student's qualities (depicted in Figure 4.2). Beyond those, you can obtain knowledge of the learner's likes and interests, home environment, life outside of school, and personal aspirations.

Use these questions to guide you in preparing the interview:

- Who will the target student be?
- Specifically why was this student chosen? What is the interest or concern?
- What useful information might be gained by conversing with the student?
- When and where will the interview take place?
- What questions will you need to ask to obtain the critical information?

ACTIVITY 4.4: Develop and Use a Questionnaire   You might enjoy constructing your own questionnaire in order to find out more about students. If you are in a school, begin by finding out what student information is already available. You can determine this with the help of your mentor teacher. If you are not in a school, use the five cumulative record cards in the chapter appendix.

Next, determine what else you wish to know. Again, Figure 4.2, Selected Student Qualities, might provide ideas.

Third, construct the questionnaire items. These may be either open- or closed-ended. Keep the items few in number, short, clear, and as nonthreatening as possible. For example, if you wish to gain information about the student's attitude

FIGURE 4.2   Selected Student Qualities

1. Academic

Easy to educate	vs.	Hard to educate.
Interested in studies	vs.	Not interested in studies
Good study habits	vs.	Weak in study habits
Achieves wll	vs.	Limited achievement

2. Citizenship

Prideful of school, class	vs.	Little concern for school, class
Willingly performs class duties and assignments	vs.	Shirks responsibilities
Takes initiative, leads	vs.	Complacent

3. Social Interaction

Popular	vs.	Unpopular
Friendly, likeable	vs.	Withdrawn, difficult to like
No conflicts	vs.	Many conflicts

4. Personal Traits

Self-confident	vs.	Anxious
Understands self	vs.	Lacks self-understanding
Agreeable	vs.	Stubborn
Disciplined, respects authority	vs.	Undisciplined
Persevering	vs.	Distractible
Organized	vs.	Disorganized

5. Home Interaction

Prideful of, identifies with family	vs.	Little concern for, identification with family
Good family relationships	vs.	Weak relationships
No conflicts	vs.	Many conflicts

Source: Suggested in part by D. R. Kadyrbaeva & I. L. Engels (1990).

toward school or home, use open-ended questions like those on the left rather than closed-ended questions like those on the right:

"What are your most enjoyable moments at school?"   versus   "Do you enjoy school?"

"What are your most enjoyable moments at home?"   versus   "Do you enjoy being at home?"

After completing your questionnaire, have a few peers look it over and then share it with your mentor teacher and university instructor. Finally, decide if, or how, you or your mentor teacher should or could collect and use the new information.

ACTIVITY 4.5: Studying a Sociogram   If you are in a field experience, ask your mentor teacher if he or she has made a sociogram of the present class. If so, ask if you could see it and find out how it was done. Ask your mentor teacher to discuss the results. Were they as expected? How were they used? You may wish to make a transparency of the sociogram to share with others in this course.

ACTIVITY 4.6: Develop and Administer a Sociogram   If you are in a field experience, see whether you may develop and administer a sociogram. If so, follow this procedure or one similar to it:

1. Select one student question from the following:
    a. "Which two persons in the class are your closest friends?"
    b. "If you were working on a group project that would receive a grade, with which two persons would you want to work?
    c. If you were in some kind of difficulty, which two persons in the class would most likely help you?
2. Explain to the students that you are trying to find out more about the class in order to be a better teacher.
3. Ask the students to privately answer the question you have selected (a, b, or c).
4. Record the choices each student has made on a chart similar to this one:

RESPONDENT'S NAME	FIRST CHOICE	SECOND CHOICE
a. Julio		
b.		
c.		
d.		

5. Record who chose each student.
    a. Julio was chosen by Robert and Malcolm.
    b.
    c.
    d.
    e.
    f.
6. Select symbols to represent males and females (see Figure 4.1).
7. Place the symbols representing the most oft-chosen students toward the center of the page and those least chosen toward the outer edges. Since males often choose males and females choose females, it may be helpful to place boys on one half of the page and girls on the other (see Figure 4.1).
8. Draw different colored lines with arrows to represent first choices, second choices, and mutual choices (arrows go both ways—see Figure 4.1).

ACTIVITY 4.7: Obtaining Autobiographical Information   If you are in a field experience, you may be able to gain some idea of how autobiographical information is obtained and used. Ask your mentor teacher if he or she obtains student information by way of autobiography. *If so,* find out what the teacher obtains and how. Also, ask how that information is most useful. *If not,* try to obtain permission to collect some. Then, decide what you most need to know and the subsequent topic or topics students should address. For example, assuming you want to know what their lives are like outside school, you might ask them to write about "My Afternoons and Evenings" or "My Weekends."

ACTIVITY 4.8: Using Parent-Supplied Information   If you are in a school assignment, ask your mentor teacher how he or she has used parent contacts to find out about students and their families. What has the teacher found out? Where is it recorded?

If such data are recorded in cumulative records, you may be able to read and reflect on them. What kinds of information have teachers obtained? What additional information could be useful?

ACTIVITY 4.9: Reading Cases You may be able to obtain access to one or more cases. If you are involved in a field experience, ask your mentor teacher whether he or she has written any. Ask what caused the teacher to write the case and how he or she did it. Also, ask about the value of these cases. Perhaps you can share one of the cases with your peers in this course without revealing the student's identity.

REFERENCES

Airasian, P. W. (1991). *Classroom assessment.* New York: McGraw-Hill.

Anastasi, A. (1988). *Psychological testing.* Sixth Edition. New York: Macmillan.

Berliner, D. C. (1986). In pursuit of expert pedagogy. *Educational Researcher, 15*(7), 5–13.

Borko, H., & Livingston, C. (1989). Cognition and improvisation: Differences in mathematics instruction by expert and novice teachers. In T. Russell & H. Munby (Eds.), *Teacher and teaching: From classroom to reflection* (pp. 49–70). London: Falmer Press.

Carter, K., Sabers, D., Cushing, K., Pinnegar, S., & Berliner, D. (1987). Processing and using information about students: A study of expert, novice and postulant teachers. *Teaching and Teacher Education, 3,* 147–157.

Cruickshank, D. R. (1969). *Inner-city simulation laboratory.* Chicago: Science Research Associates.

Doyle, W. (1986). Classroom organization and management. In M. C. Wittrock (Ed.), *Handbook of research on teaching* (pp. 392–431). New York: Macmillan.

Dusek, J. B., & Joseph, G. (1983). The bases of teacher expectations: A meta-analysis. *Journal of Educational Psychology, 75*(3), 327–346.

Emmer, E. (1987). Classroom management and discipline. In V. R. Koehler (Ed.), *Educators handbook: A research perspective.* New York: Longman.

Fraser, B. J., & Fisher, D. L. (1986). Using short forms of classroom climate instruments to assess and improve classroom psychosocial environment. *Journal of Research on Science Teaching, 23*(5), 387–413.

Good, T., & Brophy, J. (1990). *Educational psychology: A realistic approach.* New York: Longman.

Johnson, O. (1976). *Tests and measurements in child development: Handbook II. Volumes 1 and 2.* San Francisco: Jossey-Bass.

Kadyrbaeva, D. R., & Engels, I. L. (1990, December). Psychological-pedagogical characterizations of the school child. *Soviet Education, 32*(12), 32–44.

Kidder, T. (1989). *Among school children.* Boston: Houghton Mifflin.

Lewis, J. L. (1986). Failing students: Can we identify them in advance? Paper presented at the annual meeting of the American Educational Research Association in San Francisco (ERIC Document Reproduction Services ED 278 145).

Prescott, D. A. (1957). *The child in the educative process.* New York: McGraw-Hill.

Shulman, L. (1987). Knowledge and teaching: Foundations of a new reform. *Harvard Educational Review, 19*(2), 4–14.

Snyderman, M., & Rothman, S. (1987). Survey of expert opinion on intelligence and aptitude testing. *American Psychologist, 42,* 137–144.

TenBrink, T. D. (1974). *Evaluation: A practical guide to teachers.* New York: McGraw-Hill.

Touliatos, J., & Compton, N. H. (1983). *Approaches to child study.* Minneapolis: Burgess.

Zheng, J. (1992). An exploration of the pedagogical content knowledge of beginning and experienced ESL teachers. Master's thesis, Queens College of the City of New York (ERIC Document Reproduction Services ED 343 903).

PERSONAL DATA

Student's Name __BROGAN, Jack Robert__

Present Address __280 Falcrest Rd.__

Telephone __354-7520__

Present Age __9__ years __11__ mos.

Proof of Age __Birth certificate__

Place of Birth __Monroe__

Most Recent Picture

Special Activities, Interests, and Hobbies
__Enjoys mythology__

Special Health Conditions

TRANSFER RECORD

Transferred to M.S.D. from

Grade left M.S.D. __Lakeside for grade 2__

Transferred to __Lakeside__

Reason __Reentered from Lakeside__ in grade __4__

The name and data in this student record folder do not apply to the student's
picture except for purposes of the teacher-training program.

All data pertaining to this student study are based on
actual files; however, the names and dates, and locations
have been changed and the person pictured is a child
actor/model.

FAMILY DATA

	Father's Name __Maxwell__	Mother's Name __Helen__
Birthplace	__Elton__	__Bloomington, IN__
Occupation	__laboratory technician__	__retail sales__
Employer	__Harley-Ryan__	__Talbot's__

OTHER CHILDREN

	Name	Present age
1.	__Cheryl__	__8__
2.		
3.		
4.		
5.		
6.		
7.		
8.		

SPECIAL HOME CONDITIONS

__Grandmother (maternal) living in the home__

MADISON SCHOOL DISTRICT

Student's Name __BROGAN, Jack Robert__

__Longacre__ School

ATTENDANCE RECORD

	Kdg.	1st	2nd	3rd	4th	5th	6th	7th	8th
Total days present	170	180	182	179	183				
Possible no. of days attendance	185	185	185	183	183				

ACHIEVEMENT

Primary
V—Very good progress
G—Good progress
N—Needs to improve

Grades 2-8
A—Excellent
B—Above average
C—Average
D—Below average
E—Failing

SUBJECT AREAS	1	2	3	4	5	6	7	8
English	G	B	C	C				
Social Studies		B	C	C				
Science		C	C	B				
Mathematics	G	B	C	C				
Reading	G	C	C	C				
Spelling		B	C	B				
Writing	V	B	C	C				
Teacher's initials	MC	HM	JH	FM				
PROMOTION	A	A	S	A				

PROMOTION
F—Fast
S—Slow
A—Average
U—Unearned

TESTING PROGRAM

Ability Tests

Grade	Test Given	Age	IQ
1	Mental Ability	6	104
3	Mental Ability	7	103
4	Musical Aptitude (raw score 260/137 6 %ile)		

Reading Tests

Grade	Test Given	Score
1	Readiness Test	B (high normal)
2	Primary Reading	40 %ile

Other Achievement Tests

Grade	Test Given	Score
3	Upper Primary	2.8
4	Middle Grades	4.2

TEACHER COMMENTS

Needs to control his loud voice. Still immature. Attention span improving; good progress in reading and writing!

　　　　Maria Carrillo—grade 1

Sometimes fails to finish work because he fools and daydreams. Minds others' business more than his own. Too talkative. Forgets to wait his turn to speak.

　　　　Holly Maybee—grade 2

Jack shows little improvement in finishing his work. He still bothers other people. He does respond well when I ask him to take on a special responsibility or give him some extra attention. I would like to see him take more responsibility for his work and behavior.

　　　　Janice Hsieh—grade 3

Jack has shown slight improvement in completing assignments. He still needs an extra push most of the time. Is occasionally sullen with other students, but shows improvement in solving problems with his classmates.

　　　　Frances Markle—grade 4

PARENT-TEACHER CONFERENCE SUMMARIES

Grade

K   Short attention span. Work is quite immature. Father is very strict. Sharon Wertz

1   Parents are disturbed because Jack is not finishing all his work and is a behavior problem because of constant talking. They want unfinished work sent home to do. They say they will follow through at home. Maria Carrillo

2   Parents very cooperative. Jack needs to be given responsibilities for jobs he can do for himself and needs discipline to follow up. Holly Maybee

3   I had a parent conference with Mr. and Mrs. Brogan. They were told Jack was not finishing enough work to keep up with his classmates or to be as successful as he should be in fourth grade. The difficulty seems to be immaturity, short attention span, and his tendency to daydream. He is too talkative and does not seem mature enough to follow directions and accept third-grade responsibility. I worked on giving Jack some responsibilities at school, and he picked up and improved the last month of school. His parents are encouraged. Janice Hsieh

Grade

4   Jack is still immature. Work not always completed without an extra "push." An assignment book is to be used so parents can check work not completed at night, and I will check it each morning. Both parents are very willing to help. Frances Markle

SPEECH REPORT TO TEACHERS

STUDENT'S NAME _Brogan, Jack_____

GRADE _3_____

SCHOOL _Lakeside_____

CLASSROOM TEACHER _____

DISORDER _Interdental lisp-tongue_
thrust. Distorted sh sounds.
No conference.

WORK DONE IN
SPEECH CLASS _Jack was in a group of five third grade children who worked for correction of the s sound. The s in isolated words is now quite good. Jack can make the_ (below)

DISPOSITION
OF CASE _Continue if fall reevaluation shows the need. There may be continued improvement over the summer._

Speech Therapist

correction nicely. In conversation he is using quite good carryover. However, some s sounds are now a distortion in place of a lisp.

Jack has five s words which he thinks he will use frequently this summer. He is to try to say them right always.

PERSONAL DATA

Student's Name ___ GLOVACK, Kathleen ___

Present Address ___ 142 Sellers Rd. ___

Telephone ___ 359-9874 ___

Present Age ___ 10 ___ years ___ 1 ___ mos.

Proof of Age ___ Birth certificate ___

Place of Birth ___ Elton ___

Most Recent Picture

Special Activities, Interests, and Hobbies

Special Health Conditions

TRANSFER RECORD

Transferred to M.S.D. from ___ Elton in grade 1 ___

Grade left M.S.D. ___

Transferred to ___

Reason ___

Reentered from ___ in grade ___

The name and data in this student record folder do not apply to the student's picture except for purposes of the teacher-training program.

FAMILY DATA

Father's Name ___ Donald ___   Mother's Name ___ Virginia ___

Birthplace ___ Elton ___   Columbus, OH

Occupation ___ machinist ___   parapro

Employer ___ Elton Goods ___   M.S.D.

OTHER CHILDREN

Name	Present age
1. Roberta	14
2. Todd	9
3. Teresa	4
4. Nicky	1
5.	
6.	
7.	
8.	

SPECIAL HOME CONDITIONS

All data pertaining to this student study are based on actual files; however, the names and dates, and locations have been changed and the person pictured is a child actor/model.

MADISON SCHOOL DISTRICT

Longacre School

Student's Name **GLOVACK, Kathleen**

ATTENDANCE RECORD

	Kdg.	1st	2nd	3rd	4th	5th	6th	7th	8th
Total days present		168	175	176	172				
Possible no. of days attendance		185	185	183	183				

ACHIEVEMENT

Primary
V—Very good progress
G—Good progress
N—Needs to improve

Grades 2 - 8
A—Excellent
B—Above average
C—Average
D—Below average
E—Failing

SUBJECT AREAS	1	2	3	4	5	6	7	8
English	G	B	B	B				
Social Studies	G	C	B	B				
Science	G	C	B	B				
Mathematics	G	B	B	A				
Reading	G	C	A	B				
Spelling	G	C	B	A				
Writing	V	A	A	B				
Teacher's initials	RP	MG	DA	FM				

PROMOTION
F—Fast
S—Slow
A—Average
U—Unearned

	1	2	3	4	5	6	7	8
	A	A	A	A				

TESTING PROGRAM

Ability Tests

Grade	Test Given	Age	IQ
1	Mental Ability	6/3	97
3	Mental Ability	8/2	99
4	Musical Aptitude (raw score 260/137 6 %ile)		

Reading Tests

Grade	Test Given	Score	Grade
1	Reading Readiness	B (high normal)	
2	American Reading	2.4	
2	American Reading	4.3	

Other Achievement Tests

Grade	Test Given	Score	Grade
3	Middle Grades	5.5	
4	Middle Grades	5.4	

Kathy is a good average worker. Sometimes she is too thorough and has trouble finishing the work. She is quiet, but pleasant.

Ruth Parks--grade 1

Very quiet, dependable. Good worker. Always smiling!

Margarita Gascona--grade 2

Kathy is a quiet, but very good student. She is very polite and pleasant.

Donna Amity--grade 3

Kathy is an excellent student. Very dependable; lovely child. Beginning to overcome her shyness.

Frances Markle--grade 4

PARENT-TEACHER CONFERENCE SUMMARIES

Grade _____

1 With Mrs. Glovack. Progress report. Kathy doing strong
   average work. Ruth Parks

2 Conference with Mrs. Glovack. Kathy is doing well. Should
   speak up so she can be heard; rather shy. Mother is
   pleased with good work habits. Margarita Gascona

3 No conference—new baby in home—but discussed Kathy's
   good progress with mother at PTA. Donna Amity

4 Conference with mother. Kathy does very well in school.
   For a while, Kathy didn't want to come to school each
   morning. In speaking with her, we found she didn't like
   our student teacher. After our talk, she was fine. She
   has had some problems lately with her best friend, Janis
   Murdock, who has buddied up with Cynthia Jordan.
   Frances Markle

URBAN PUBLIC SCHOOL CUMULATIVE RECORD

(Elementary and Middle School Form)

Name <u>Gamble   Benny</u>   I.D.# <u>1092056</u>

(Last)   (First)   (Middle)

Present age <u>11</u> yrs. <u>1</u> mos.

Place of Birth <u>Urban</u>

Pupil lives with ☐ Both parents ☒ Mother ☐ Father

☒ Other (explain) <u>grandmother</u>

Father's name <u>Morris</u>   Employer <u>Post Office Department</u>

Mother's name <u>Lydia</u>   Employer _____

Address	Phone	Address	Phone
3526 Seneca Parkway	343-6580	5106 Hertel	266-4843
998 35th Street			
3526 Seneca Parkway	343-6580		
5245 College	266-4843		

Siblings (List names of brothers and sisters in order of birth. Indicate sex by G for sister, B for brother. Express age differences as plus (+) or minus (−). Examples: +5 means five years older, −5 means five years younger.)

Sibling's Name	Sex	Age	Sibling's Name	Sex	Age	Sibling's Name	Sex	Age
None								

In case of emergency notify:

Name _____   Phone _____

Address _____   Relationship _____

All data pertaining to this student study are based on actual files; however, the names and dates, and locations have been changed and the person pictured is a child actor/model.

ELEMENTARY AND MIDDLE SCHOOL PROGRESS RECORD

Reporting Code

ACHIEVEMENT: The letter represents the degree to which the child has met the grade standards.

E = excellent	U = unsatisfactory
G = good	GL = grade level
F = fair	BL = below grade level

EFFORT: The numeral indicates the effort the child is making.

1 = doing his best
2 = could work harder
3 = making little effort

Progress Record, Grades K–2

Semester Beginning	Grade	Weeks in Grade	Days Present	Promoted to Grade	Reading	Oral Language	Composition	Spelling	Handwriting	Social Studies	Arithmetic	Science	Art	Music	Physical Education	Conduct	School	Room No.
FALL	Kg	20	85	Kg												F	COLERIDGE	108
SPRING	Kg	20	83	1			FAIR PROGRESS									F	COLERIDGE	107
Fall	1	20	65	1A	F	F			E	G	G	E	F			G	Coleridge	205
Spring	1A	20	80	2	E	E			G	G	E	G	E	F		G	Coleridge	205
Fall	2	20	80	2G	G	G	G	G	G	G	G	G	G	G		G	Coleridge	120
Spring	2	12	53	2G	G	G	G	E	G	G	G	G	G	G		G	Coleridge	120
SPRING	2	8	34	3	E	G	G	E	G	G	E	E	G	G		E	COLERIDGE	209

Progress Record, Grades 3–6

Semester Beginning	Grade	Weeks in Grade	Days Absent	Promoted to Grade	Reading	Reading Level	Math	Math Level	Listening	Speaking	Writing	Spelling	Science	Social Studies	Art	Music	Physical Educ.	Conduct	School	Room No.
FALL	3	20	9	3	G	G	G	G	G	G	E	G	G	G	G	1	G	ALEXANDER	205
SPRING	3	12	7	3	G	G	G	H	G	G	G	E	G	G	G		G	"	"
Spr.	3	7	14	E	G	F	G	G	F	F	E	F	F	F	F	F	F	EDISON	204
Fall	4	20	7	4	E		F	GL	G	G	E	G	G	G		F	Edison	106
Spring	4	20	4	5	E		F	GL	F	F	G	E	G	G	GF		F	Edison	106
	5				attending school in the South (USA)												– – –		
	5	21	12	6	E₁	GL	F₂	GL	E₂	E₂	E₂	E₂	G₂	G₂	E₂	E₂	F₂	F	Edison	209

General Ability Tests

Gr.	Name of Test	Form	C.A.	M.A.	I.Q.
1	KA		6.3	7.3	116
2	KA		7.1	7.8	110
3	KA		8.1	7.9	97

Achievement Test

Gr.	Name of Test	Subtest	Score
1	Metropolitan Readiness		82% LE
3	Metropolitan Achieve.	Reading	5.3
		Spelling	5.1
		English	4.1
		Arithmetic	3.6

Bureau of Child Study Individual Exam Data

Gr.	

Personal Comments

Gr.	Remarks
2	Often complains of illnesses.
5	Claims pains in his back.

Special Activities, Abilities, Honors

Gr.	Remarks
5	Loves to read. Hall Guard Award.

Other Pertinent Information

Gr.	Examination	Evaluation	Gr.	Examination	Evaluation
1	Vision	Should wear glasses and be given front seat placement.			
1	Hearing	Pass			
4	Hearing	Pass			
5	Hearing	Pass			

Notes:

_____

_____

_____

_____

_____

_____

_____

_____

_____

_____

_____

_____

_____

_____

URBAN PUBLIC SCHOOL CUMULATIVE RECORD
(Elementary and Middle School Form)

Name Rivera   Julio   Jesus   I.D.# 2783168
     (Last)   (First)   (Middle)

Present age ___11___ yrs. ___9___ mos.

Place of Birth Puerto Rico

Pupil lives with [X] Both parents   [ ] Mother   [ ] Father

[ ] Other (explain) _____

Father's name José   Employer Lakeside Metals

Mother's name Juanita   Employer Barkley Fish Co.

Address	Phone	Address	Phone
1241 Yale	273-7408		
12 Sword			
5142 Aldine	641-1059		

Siblings   (List names of brothers and sisters in order of birth. Indicate sex by G for sister, B for brother. Express age differences as plus (+) or minus (−). Examples: +5 means five years older, −5 means five years younger.)

Sibling's Name	Sex	Age	Sibling's Name	Sex	Age	Sibling's Name	Sex	Age
Maria	G	-2						
Luchina	G	-5						
Felice	G	-8						

In case of emergency notify:

Name _____ Phone _____

Address _____ Relationship _____

All data pertaining to this student study are based on actual files; however, the names and dates, and locations have been changed and the person pictured is a child actor/model.

Reporting Code

ACHIEVEMENT: The letter represents the degree to which the child has met the grade standards.

E = excellent	U = unsatisfactory
G = good	GL = grade level
F = fair	BL = below grade level

EFFORT: The numeral indicates the effort the child is making.

1 = doing his best
2 = could work harder
3 = making little effort

Progress Record, Grades K-2

Semester Beginning	Grade	Weeks in Grade	Days Present	Promoted to Grade	Reading	Oral Language	Composition	Spelling	Handwriting	Social Studies	Arithmetic	Science	Art	Music	Physical Education	Conduct	School	Room No.
FALL	K	20	92	K	— Good —											F	McNULTY	104
SPRING	K	20	94	Prim 1	— Good —											G	McNULTY	104
Fall	Pri 1	5	23	1B	— Good —											G	McNULTY	106
Fall	1B	20	91	1	G	G			E	G	G		G	F		E	University	4
Spring	1	20	90	2	G	G			G	G	G		G	F		F	University	4
Fall	2	20	88	2	F3	F3		U3	F2	G2	G2	F1	F1	F2		F	University	10
Spring	2	20	95	3	G2	G		G	G	E	E1	E	E	G	G	F	University	10

Progress Record, Grades 3-6

Semester Beginning	Grade	Weeks in Grade	Days Absent	Promoted to Grade	Reading	Reading Level	Math	Math Level	Listening	Speaking	Writing	Spelling	Science	Social Studies	Art	Music	Physical Educ.	Conduct	School	Room No.
Fall	3	20	2	3	G1	G	G1	G	G1	G	G2	G	G	G1	E	G1	G2	F	University	16
Sp.	3	20	1		G	E	G	G2	G	G2	G2	G1	G	G	G1	G1	G1	F	University	16
Fall	4	20	0	1	F2	BL	F3	GL	F2	F2	F2	F3	F3	U	G2	G2		F	Edison	202
Spring	4	20	2	5	G2	GL	F3	GL	F2	F2	F2	G1	F3	F3	E2	E2	G	F	Edison	202
	5	40	4	6	F1	BL	F3	BL	F2	G2	F2	G2	E1	F2	E2	E2	G1	F	Edison	209

Name Rivera, Julio Jesus

All data pertaining to this student study are based on actual files; however, the names, dates, and locations have been changed and the person pictured is a child actor/model.

24

ID# 2783168

General Ability Tests

Gr.	Name of Test	Form	C.A.	M.A.	I.Q.
1	KA		5-11	6-0	104
3	KA		9.4	8.6	91

Bureau of Child Study Individual Exam Data

Gr.	

Achievement Test

Gr.	Name of Test	Subtest	Score
1	Metropolitan Readiness		60%ile
3	METROPOLITAN ACHIEVEMENT	WORD KNOWL.	3.6
		WORD DISCRIM	3.2
		READING	2.6
		SPELLING	4.0
		LANG.	3.2
		COMPUT.	3.0
		PROBLEM SOLVING	2.7

Personal Comments

Gr.	Remarks
5	Interested in science and music. Will need to watch carefully or else he will run around the room or the building or sneak out. Motivation hinges on praise and close supervision. Wants to please

Special Activities, Abilities, Honors

Gr.	Remarks
5	Winner of 5th grade Science Award

Other Pertinent Information

Gr.	Examination	Evaluation	Gr.	Examination	Evaluation
2	Teeth	Oral hygiene fair. Dental care needed.			
2	Hearing	Pass			
4	Hearing	Pass			

Notes:

_____

_____

_____

_____

_____

_____

_____

_____

_____

_____

_____

_____

_____

REFERRAL FOR PUPIL HEALTH SERVICES

Pupil's name Julio Rivera   Date   10/16

Address   5142 Aldine

School   Edison

Room   209

Reason for Referral:

Julio has trouble seeing the chalkboard assignments

in the classroom. He complains of headaches.

Report: Eye referral given to pupil to take home for vision test.

Teacher Nurse   Mary Martin

Vision Record on Child not Wearing Glasses

Urban Public Schools

Child's name   Julio Rivera   Date   10/16

Address   5142 Aldine   Age   11

Parent's name   Juanita   Grade   five

School   Edison

To the Doctor:

    Please fill in the following for the guidance of the class-room teacher.

1. Should the child wear glasses?   Yes X   No ___
   If so, when   __constantly__

2. Should the child wear an occluder? Yes ___   No X
   If so, over which eye _____ when _____ duration _____

3. Should the child have front seat placement?
                              Yes ___   No X

4. Should the amount of close work done by the child be limited?   Yes ___   No X
   If so, to what extent? _____

5. Vision test
   Uncorrected visual acuity   R 20/60   L 20/40
   Best corrected visual acuity   R 20/25   L 20/25

Doctor's Signature

R J Manville

URBAN PUBLIC SCHOOL CUMULATIVE RECORD
(Elementary and Middle School Form)

Name _Walker_ _Debbie_ _____ I.D.# _2585866_____

(Last) (First) (Middle)

Present age __14__ yrs. __1__ mos.

Place of Birth _Urban_____

Pupil lives with ☐ Both parents ☐ Mother ☐ Father

☒ Other (explain) _Mother and stepfather_____

Father's name _Gilliam_____ Employer _____

Mother's name _Janice_____ Employer _public assistance_____

Address	Phone	Address	Phone
5924 Brass	278-8113	3708 Park	
1343 New York	215-7788	1260 52nd Street	542-2275
702 31st Street			
947 33rd Street			

Siblings (List names of brothers and sisters in order of birth. Indicate sex by G for sister, B for brother. Express age differences as plus (+) or minus (−). Examples: +5 means five years older, −5 means five years younger.)

Sibling's Name	Sex	Age	Sibling's Name	Sex	Age	Sibling's Name	Sex	Age
Dewey	B	+10	Scott	B	+5	Melanie	G	−1
Carlton	B	+8	Gary	B	+4	Bishop	B	−4
Donald	B	+7	Louise	G	+3	Keith	B	−5
Douglas	B	+6	Todd	B	+2	Richard	B	−6
						Lori	G	−12

In case of emergency notify:

Name _____ Phone _____

Address _____ Relationship _____

All data pertaining to this student study are based on actual files; however, the names and dates, and locations have been changed and the person pictured is a child actor/model.

ELEMENTARY AND MIDDLE SCHOOL PROGRESS RECORD

Reporting Code

ACHIEVEMENT: The letter represents the degree to which the child has met the grade standards.

EFFORT: The numeral indicates the effort the child is making.

E = excellent   U = unsatisfactory
G = good   GL = grade level
F = fair   BL = below grade level

1 = doing his best
2 = could work harder
3 = making little effort

Progress Record, Grades K–2

Semester Beginning	Grade	Weeks in Grade	Days Present	Promoted to Grade	Reading	Oral Language	Composition	Spelling	Handwriting	Social Studies	Arithmetic	Science	Art	Music	Physical Education	Conduct	School	Room No.
Fall	K	13	48	/			Satisfactory									E	Edison	120
Fall	1B	6	27				Satisfactory									G	Seward	107
Spring	1B	9	90	1B			Satisfactory									G	Seward	107
Fall	1B	17	31		U	F			F		U					G	SEWARD	117
Fall	1B	3	9	retain	U	F			F		U					G	LASALLE	215
Spring	1B	12	56	/	G	G			G		G					G	LaSalle	105
SPRING	1B	8	38	1A	G	G			G		G					F	LaSalle	103
FALL	1A	15	58	2B	E	G			G		E					U	LASALLE	109
Fall	1A	5	33	2B	G	G			G		G					G	Martin	101
Spring	2B	20	91	CDP	Promoted to Primary Continuous Development Program											F	Martin	101
Fall	2A	20	96	3B	G	G	F	F	G		U					F	Martin	203

Progress Record, Grades 3–6

Semester Beginning	Grade	Weeks in Grade	Days Absent	Promoted to Grade	Reading	Reading Level	Math	Math Level	Listening	Speaking	Writing	Spelling	Science	Social Studies	Art	Music	Physical Educ.	Conduct	School	Room No.
SPRING	3B	20	97	3A	F	BL	F	BL	F	G	U	U	F	F	F	F	F	F	MarkJm	212
Fall	3A	8	32	retain	F	BL	U	BL	F	F	F	F	F	F	F	F.		F	Markum	302
Fall	3a	12	54	3a	4	BL	U	BL	7	G	7	U	7	U	7	E	U7	7	Corcoran	309
Spg	3A	10	45	retain	F	BL	U	BL	F	F	F	U	U	F	G	E		F	Corcoran	208
SPRING	3a	9	44	4	U	BL	U	BL	F	F	U	F	F	U	G	G		G	Hess	205
Fall	4	20	3	4A	F	BL	F	BL	G	G	G	G	G	G	G	G	G	6	Hess	310
Spring	4A	20	4	5B	F	BL	F	BL	G	G	G	G	G	G	G	G	G	G	Hess	310
	5B	16	10		F	BL	F	BL	F	F		F	G	F	F	G	G	F	Hess	318
	5	4	3	No grades given due to late entrance.															Baker	316
	5	20	5		U	BL	U	BL	U	U		U	U	U	U			E	Baker	316
	5	29	11	6	C/2	BL	G2	G4	E2	G2		G2 E2	C2	G2 E2	E2	E2	F	EDISON	209

Name __Walker, Debbie__

All data pertaining to this student study are based on actual files; however, the names, dates, and locations have been changed and the person pictured is a child actor/model.

General Ability Tests

Gr.	Name of Test	Form	C.A.	M.A.	I.Q.
1	KA		6.0	5.8	94
1	KA		6.5	6.7	103
3	KA		9.2	7.11	86

Bureau of Child Study Individual Exam Data

Gr.	

Achievement Test

Gr.	Name of Test	Subtest	Score
3	Stanford Pri. "M"	Rdg	2.9
3	Metro Achievement	Reading	2.6
		Spelling	2.4
		Comp.	3.1
		Prob Solv.	2.8
4	METROPOLITAN ACHIEVEMENT	WORD KNOWL.	3.8
		WORD DISCRIM.	4.1
		READ'G	3.6
		SPELLING	4.6
		COMPUTE	4.1
		PROB. SOLVING	4.3

Personal Comments

Gr.	Remarks
5	FAILING TO COMPLETE ASSIGNMENTS. SUSPENSION FOR TWO DAYS. STEPFATHER HAS LEFT HOME AND IS TRYING TO GET BABY DAUGHTER FROM THE MOTHER. CASE IS PENDING IN COURT.

Special Activities, Abilities, Honors

Gr.	Remarks

Other Pertinent Information

31

ID# 2585866

121

CORCORAN SCHOOL

Date __Jan. 14__

Dear Parent:

Your child __Debbie Walker__ is doing failing work __X__
(grade 3) poor work ____

in the following subjects:

Reading __X__   Social Studies _____

Arithmetic __X__   Spelling _____

Science _____   Penmanship _____

I believe this condition is caused by:

Inattention in class __X__

Poor conduct __X__

Poor study habits __X__

Health reasons _____

Absenteeism _____

I am available each school morning at 8:30 o'clock. You
may come to see me if you wish or you may write me a letter
telling me your plan to help your child.

Please sign this letter and return it to me.

Mrs Janice Walker   _Geraldine Phillips_
Parent's Signature   Teacher's Signature

Lois Enright
Principal

September 23

Dear Parents:

Hess School is one of the schools in District 21 which has been selected to provide after-school instruction in reading for pupils who need such help. We are recommending that your child, _Debbie Walker_ take part in this program.

These classes are to be held from 3:30 p.m. to 4:30 p.m. on Mondays, Tuesdays, Wednesdays, and Thursdays, from September 27 to June 23. Will you please remind your child that there will be no patrol boys on duty at 4:30 p.m. and that he/she should be especially careful when returning home.

We sincerely hope that you will take advantage of this opportunity for your child. Please sign the lower section of this letter immediately.

Very truly yours,

Geo. Mancuso

George Mancuso
Principal

.. ..

Date _____

I hereby give my permission for my child, _Debbie Walker_ to be enrolled in the after-school classes at Hess School on Mondays, Tuesdays, Wednesdays, and Thursdays, from 3:30 to 4:30 p.m. beginning September 27, to June 23. I will remind my child that there will be no patrol boys on duty at 4:30 p.m. and that he/she should be especially careful when returning home.

Present Room __318__   Grade ___5___   _____
                                             Signature of Parent

After-school Room

I do not want Debbie to go because I am going to the hospital every day now. Mrs Janice Walker

_____

Dear teacher,
Debbie has my permission to go to reading class.
Thank you
Her mother   Mrs Janice Walker

31

123

Gr.	Examination	Evaluation	Gr.	Examination	Evaluation
1	Hearing	Pass			
1	Teeth	Carious			
2	Hearing	Pass			
3	Hearing	Pass			
4	Hearing	Pass			

Notes:

Needs to work on personal grooming and hygiene

The Act of Teaching

PART TWO

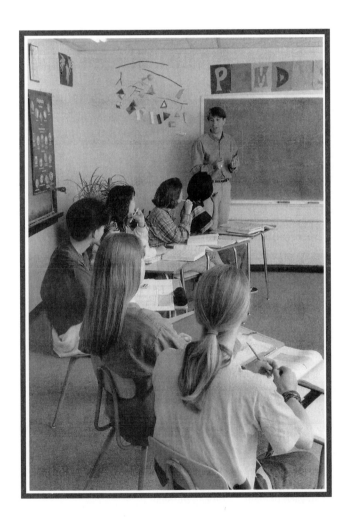

Teaching should be a conscious, deliberate act resulting from thoughtful decision making about what to teach and how students learn best. The five chapters in Part Two are intended to help you become an accomplished teacher. Chapter 5, Planning Instruction, will make you aware of factors that influence what is taught. Mostly, however, it concentrates on showing you how to make good decisions about planning *what* and *how* you will teach. Chapter 6, Three Instructional Alternatives, and Chapter 7, Four More Instructional Alternatives, contain readily usable information about seven prominent teaching strategies, as well as brief references to many others. Chapter 8, Evaluating Students' Learning, will inform you of the importance of assessing student learning and show you how you can do so effectively. Finally, Chapter 9, Reflecting on Teaching, addresses the importance of being a reflective practitioner, that is, a lifelong student of teaching.

Planning Instruction

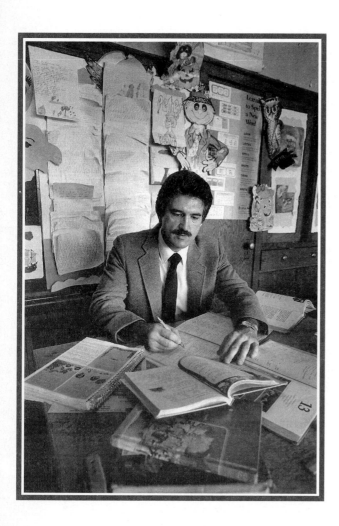

Contents

You have heard the adage "an ounce of prevention is worth a pound of cure." In the realm of teaching, that translates easily to "planning good instruction will prevent countless problems from arising in your classroom." To be a successful teacher, you *must* have the ability and motivation to generate good learning experiences for students.

This chapter looks at instructional planning in detail in order to help you meet this challenge. At the conclusion of the chapter, we hope you will value planning, know that teachers differ in their approach to planning, know which factors determine what is taught, be able to write suitable instructional objectives, be able to construct long-range course plans, intermediate-range unit plans, and short-range lesson plans, and be conversant with the planning issues and problems teachers face.

> "Would you tell me, please, which way I ought to go from here?" asked Alice. "That depends a good deal on where you want to get to," said the Cheshire Cat.
>
> Lewis Carroll. (1963). *Alice's Adventures in Wonderland.*
> New York: Macmillan, Classic Series, p. 59.

Teachers spend a good deal of time deciding "which way to go." Ask them; planning dominates their lives. Among other things, they plan pupil seating, transitions between classroom activities, classroom rules, parent conferences, recess, and the opening and closing of the school year. They also plan what resources they will need; where materials and equipment will be kept; how to make their classrooms attractive; and how best to take attendance, distribute and collect materials, and maintain student records. However, most of the time they devote to planning is given to planning instruction, that is, deciding what and how students will learn.

Some Benefits of Instructional Planning

Instructional planning is the process teachers use to decide how best to select, organize, and deliver a learning experience to maximize both teacher and student achievement and satisfaction. In other words, before they begin teaching, good teachers consider both *what to teach* and *how to teach it* so that teaching and learning are worthwhile for all.

PLANNING BENEFITS TEACHERS

Although beginning teachers sometimes find planning a time-consuming, tedious activity, we cannot overstate the importance of planning. Shavelson (1987) notes that decisions teachers make during instructional planning have a profound influence on their classroom behavior and on the nature and outcomes of the education their students receive.

When teachers take time to think seriously about what their students should know and be able to do and how such learning should take place, the result is likely to be greater creativity and the elimination of "dry as dust" teaching. Such thoughtfulness can free teachers from long-time habits and personal prejudices and enable them to use their full imaginative powers. Once they have developed a good instructional plan, teachers can enjoy greater confidence, security, and enthusiasm for putting the plan into action. Once they have thoughtfully planned, or *thought teaching through*, teachers should feel better and more excited about the teaching that will ensue.

PLANNING BENEFITS STUDENTS

Thoughtful planning promotes learning because it causes us to take into account the diverse backgrounds, interests, and abilities of students, as described in Chapters 2 and 3. Thus a thoughtful plan is more likely to attract and maintain students' attention and to facilitate learning and satisfaction given the instructional goals and available resources. Planning therefore increases the likelihood that students will be *interested*, will *learn*, and will be *satisfied*. Further, a thoughtfully planned lesson is more likely to maximize the use of time and, thereby, to minimize confusion and disruptions. If something goes wrong with your teaching, it probably can be traced to your ability to plan inviting lessons.

Instructional Planning May Be Mandated

As a new teacher, you will find that you are encouraged but sometimes required to develop instructional plans. Albert Shanker, late head of the United Federation of Teachers, underscores the need for and benefits of instructional planning. He wrote in *The New York Times* (September 28, 1980) that "no one quarrels with the idea that teachers must plan lessons in advance." Moreover, he notes that probably only a few teachers are so expert that they can teach effectively without overt planning. Among other things, Shanker urges teachers to: (1) plan the sequence of their lessons, (2) provide for pupil motivation, (3) formulate clear and unambiguous questions, (4) present examples that move from the simple to the complex, (5) review, (6) provide for individual pupil differences, and (7) formulate worthwhile assignments.

Many principals and instructional supervisors require teachers to create and record written instructional plans. Sometimes teachers are required to submit "plan books" spelling out probable lessons one or two weeks in advance. These evidences of advance planning help principals, supervisors, and presumably teachers themselves in several ways. Most importantly, they provide assurance that teachers have thought about what they will do and how they will do it. Additionally, when observing beginning teachers, supervisors often follow the teacher's plan to see how well he or she carries it out. Finally, when teachers are absent, written plans are available for the substitute. This enables the substitute teacher to maintain instructional continuity.

As you saw in Chapter 2, the federal government, as a consequence of the Individuals with Disabilities Education Act (Public Law 101-476), requires detailed, written instructional plans for students with special needs. The resultant Individual Education Program (IEP) is jointly prepared by the teacher, pupil, parent, someone who has recently evaluated the child (perhaps a psychologist), and usually the building principal or a special education teacher.

Since planning is so important to all students, it is essential that you learn to do it efficiently and effectively. Student teachers and beginning teachers, especially, are well advised to plan their teaching in considerable detail, leaving little to chance. Remember, plans are not mere window dressing or hoop jumping, they are a most vital part of the act of teaching.

"Are we that desperate for substitute teachers?"

Planning is so essential that many teacher educators, classroom teachers, school administrators, and state department of education officials have written about the need to plan. Consider some of their statements:

> The importance of planning—both long-range and daily—cannot be overemphasized. In each case, teacher candidates need to see how careful planning supports the learning process. Teacher candidates should observe how [their] clinical supervisors [cooperating or mentor teachers] choose effective teaching strategies to complement content and meet the needs of students.
>
> During any preservice teaching experience, the first several weeks of daily plans should result from the sharing of ideas by the teacher candidate and the clinical supervisor.
>
> This procedure will set a pattern which can be altered as teacher candidates' plans improve and as they achieve greater independence in planning. Most beginners profit greatly from detailed lesson plans but they need help in making steady progress toward a type of planning they can carry on as beginning teachers. This may require planning for a self-contained classroom with eight or more preparations or with as many as six secondary classes and five preparations.
>
> Each plan should be flexible to meet changes that inevitably occur during lessons. Teacher candidates should be encouraged to anticipate potential difficulties in the teaching strategy and be prepared to handle any difficulties which may occur. This rehearsal will reduce the need for a change in the lesson. (Baltimore Area Committee, 1991)

5.4 What is your reaction to this advice about planning?

Different Approaches to Planning

Teachers approach instructional planning in different ways; but this is true of nearly everything people do, including taking vacations.

Picture it: You and a friend, Pat, decide to take a trip to the Eastern United States. As you discuss the trip, it becomes apparent the two of you are approaching this trip in very different ways. You have a carefully thought-out, detailed agenda with specific destinations in mind and a list of things you want to do once you arrive at each stop. You know how far you will need to drive each day, where you will stay each night, and approximately what your expenses will be. Although you will visit a few attractions along the way, you're careful not to let these brief excursions detract from the main purpose of the trip, to see the Eastern United States. You believe that if you pretty much follow the plan you've developed, you'll have a worry-free trip, you'll be able to visit most of the major attractions you want to see, and you'll stay within your budget.

Your friend Pat looks at you in sheer amazement! Pat's idea is to get in the car and *go*, stopping on the spur-of-the-moment to see attractions along the way. Rather than be restricted by advance motel reservations, your friend wants to find a place to stay wherever you find yourselves at the end of each day. When you do get to the East Coast, your friend wants to "play it by ear," enjoying whatever you happen to do each day until your vacation time or money runs out. Pat prefers a less structured trip because "you never know what you'll find, and unplanned discovery is part of the adventure of a vacation."

You may chuckle at these different approaches to planning, but as a teacher, they will become familiar to you. That is because the different personal approaches to vacation planning parallel the different ways in which we teachers make instructional plans for our classrooms.

THE PROCESS APPROACH

There is no magic formula for approaching instructional planning. When we engage in planning, however, we locate ourselves somewhere along a continuum. One end of the continuum we'll call the "process approach." Remember your vacation mate who wanted to see the Eastern United States but who didn't want to do a lot of detailed planning? Pat said, "Lets go! The trip is worthwhile. We'll adjust along the way. Play it by ear."

Many teachers are like Pat. They see the value of certain learning experiences, but they plan these experiences only in a general way—a field trip to the historical society, a discussion of a major current problem or issue, a book to be read, an experiment to do. They believe such activities should be almost spontaneous, with little or no prearranged agenda. If not, the activity will be too teacher-structured, too predictable, and thus downright boring to students. Beyond enjoying spontaneity, teachers who favor this process approach have a strong desire to be flexible and are confident and trusting that all will turn out well.

THE PRODUCT APPROACH

The other end of the continuum can be labeled the "product approach." For the sake of comparison, let's assume that's your approach. You want to go on an East Coast trip and you know precisely what you want to get out of the trip from beginning to end. You feel better and safer when you have a detailed plan. Similarly, as a teacher, you not only plan to generally engage your class in discussion of a topic such as "homelessness," but you also devise a set of questions to ensure depth and breadth of thought. Your questions include: What is homelessness? Who are the homeless? Why are some persons homeless? What are some consequences of homelessness? How do you feel toward homeless people? What are some ways the homeless might be treated? You are willing to sacrifice some flexibility and spontaneity for your feeling of security that your students will likely gain specific knowledge and insight. So, in contrast to the process-oriented teacher, your learning experience is structured to ensure that students will successfully reach what you see as important preconceived goals.

WHICH APPROACH TO USE WHEN

On the surface, these two approaches to instructional planning seem very different—perhaps incompatible. However, you will find both approaches effective, depending upon the situation. Many believe the process-oriented approach to instructional planning enhances student creativity, encourages independence and choice, and is more motivating and satisfying to students. This approach is considered most appropriate by its advocates when the primary goals are to develop students' higher-order thinking and problem-solving skills and to help students learn how to learn. On the other hand, advocates of the product-oriented approach

"And then, of course, there's the possibility of being just the slightest bit too organized."

5.5 Are you more attracted to the process or the product approach? Why might you have such a preference?

FIGURE 5.1   Factors That Influence the Content of the Curriculum

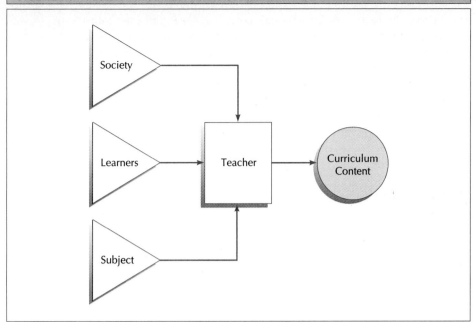

maintain that it provides the structure essential to learning and that predetermined objectives will produce more efficient instruction. It probably is safe to say that the process and product approaches both have advantages and disadvantages and that neither is clearly superior at all times and with all students.

Deciding What to Teach

Regardless of whether you mostly follow the process or product approach to instructional planning, one of the earliest decisions you must make is *what is to be learned*. More precisely, what knowledge, skills, or attitudes are the students to learn? This is a *curriculum* question.

FACTORS THAT INFLUENCE WHAT WE TEACH

Three things strongly influence curriculum content, or what is to be learned: society, the nature of learners, and the nature of the knowledge in a subject or discipline (see Figure 5.1) (Tyler, 1949).

Society   At the societal level, all kinds of international and national events influence what is taught in schools. Some of the curriculum you have studied in school was shaped by scientific and political events. For example, in 1957, the world was stunned when the Soviets launched the first satellite, Sputnik. That event introduced the space age and the space race. It also prompted changes in American school curriculum. Because the Soviets beat the Americans into space, the American school curriculum was judged inferior, especially in science. As a result, since the late 1960s, tremendous efforts and federal monies have been devoted to teaching more science, making the science curriculum more rigorous and developing new ways of teaching that curriculum. For example, emphasis has moved away from the memorization of scientific facts toward the use of laboratory experiences that encourage problem solving, the discovery of cause-and-effect relationships, and the application of scientific principles to practical purposes.

The rapidly developing technology associated with the space industry has also impacted the school curriculum. The availability of inexpensive, handheld calculators has brought about the demise of relatively inaccurate slide rules and led mathematics educators to reexamine the curriculum. Calculators offer a high degree of computational proficiency and can eliminate endless drudgery that many mathematics educators believe serves no practical purpose. Time formerly spent on computation can now be focused on other mathematical learning activities such as problem solving. Further, the widespread use of personal computers in classrooms and the instant accessibility of information via computers and satellites is changing America's curricular priorities.

More recently, dramatic political and economic changes in Eastern Europe, Asia, and Africa have required schools, teachers, and textbook publishers to alter the social science curriculum.

As a preservice teacher, you are experiencing some of this societal influence in your professional preparation. By the early 1980s, declining pupil test scores were blamed on, among other factors, poor teaching in elementary, middle, and secondary schools. The resulting national outcry for changes in the way teachers are educated has affected university education programs. Consequently, your teacher education program probably requires more general education prior to entering your professional course work; more study in the subject areas you plan to teach, such as mathematics, science, or English; more fieldwork in schools; and a thorough grounding in what is known about effective teachers and teaching (see Chapters 10 and 11). Relatedly, an increasing number of states require that teacher education students pass standardized proficiency tests to receive a teaching credential. These tests measure your general knowledge, knowledge of the subjects you will teach, and knowledge of how to teach, including planning.

While society expects schools and teachers to respond to timely events by altering the curriculum, it also wants you to preserve and pass along traditional information referred to as the "basics." Of course, not everyone in our society agrees on what knowledge, skills, or attitudes are basic and should be preserved in the curriculum. As a result, great arguments occur (Hirsch, 1989).

Nature of Learners The second factor influencing what is taught is the nature of today's learners. Each generation of youth differs from the last. Part of this difference is attributable to changes in society. In Chapter 2, you learned that society is becoming more diverse and that today's children are emblematic of this diversity. Increasingly, students are minority children from low-income, single-parent homes where English is not spoken as a first language. In addition, today's youth is increasingly exposed to television violence and sexual intimacy, and they are exploited by advertising. The result is that children often are confused and victimized.

Another factor contributing to differences in youth today is earlier physical and social maturity. This phenomenon is traceable both to human evolution and to societal forces that encourage kids to grow up faster. Early maturity means that children are more likely to be independent, open and assertive, and better informed at an earlier age.

To be effective when planning and teaching, you must take into account your students' experiential and cultural backgrounds, developmental levels (intellectual, social, emotional, and physical), interests, and preferred ways of doing things. *Know thy students!* They need curriculum and learning experiences that are developmentally appropriate if you expect them to learn and to connect that learning to their personal lives and experiences (Willis, 1993).

Subject Field or Discipline The third factor influencing the curriculum is what knowledge experts consider essential in each field or discipline. For example, in 1985, the American Association for the Advancement of Science (AAAS) launched

5.6 What other recent international or national political, economic, social, or scientific events or discoveries are, or will likely be addressed in school curricula?

5.7 How could you modify the content you will teach for different kinds of learners described in Chapter 2?

5.8 Can you think of anyone (perhaps yourself) whose personality and experience needed to be more closely considered to help them learn?

FIGURE 5.2   Source of Subject-Matter Curriculum Standards

Subject Field	Document
Arts	*National Standards for Arts Education*
	MENC Publications, 1806 Robert Fulton Drive, Reston, VA 22091
Civics	*National Standards for Civics and Government*
	Center for Civic Education, 5146 Douglas Fir Rd., Calabasas, CA 91302
Economics	*Voluntary National Content Standards in Economics*
	National Council on Economic Education, 1140 Avenue of the Americas, New York, NY 10036
English	*Standards for the Assessment of Reading and Writing*
	International Reading Association, 800 Barksdale Rd., P.O. Box 8139, Newark, DE 19714–8139
Foreign Languages	In process
Geography	*Geography for Life*
	National Geographic, P.O. Box 1640, Washington, DC 20013–1640
Health	In process
History	*U.S. History Standards*
	World History
	K-4 History
	National Center for History in the Schools, 10880 Wilshire Blvd., Suite 761, Los Angeles, CA 90024–4108
Mathematics	*Curriculum and Evaluation Standards for School Mathematics*
	Professional Standards for Teaching Mathematics
	NCTM, 1906 Association Drive, Reston, VA 22091–1593
Physical Education	*Content Standards and Assessment Guide for School Physical Education*
	NASPE, 1900 Association Drive, Reston, VA 22091
Science	*National Science Education Standards*
	National Research Council, (202)334-3159 or e-mail scistand@nas.edu
Social Studies	*Expectations of Excellence: Curriculum Standards For Social Studies*
	Fulfillment House, Whitehurst & Clark, 100 Newfield Ave., Raritan Center, Edison, NJ 08837

Project 2061. The report this learned society prepared represented the scientific community's effort to answer the question: What knowledge about science, mathematics, and technology should learners acquire by the time they graduate from high school? Similar reports have sprung-up from the National Council of Teachers of Mathematics, the Music Educators National Conference, the National Council of Teachers of English, and other professional organizations (see Figure 5.2). These reports are very influential in shaping the school curriculum. Have you seen them?

The Formal and the Taught Curricula

THE FORMAL CURRICULUM

Eventually, all three factors affecting the curriculum trickle down into documents that teachers use when planning instruction. These documents mainly take the shape of state department publications, school district courses of study, and textbooks. State syllabi are often available for each field of study: reading, science and math, physical education, home economics, music, art, foreign language, health, and so forth. Larger school districts may have localized versions of these documents that are more responsive to the unique wants of individual communities. It is common for teachers of a particular subject and/or grade level to devote many hours of thoughtful committee work toward producing grade level courses of study.

Both state and local curriculum guides may focus on *philosophy* (what a field or subject of study is about and its importance), *goals* to be attained in that subject or field, the *scope and sequence* (what is to be taught and in what order), recommended *instructional activities,* recommended available print and nonprint *materials,* and ideas on how to examine learners and evaluate programs. These curriculum guides vary considerably in detail and specificity and, consequently, in length.

The most used (and sometimes overused) source for determining what students should learn is the textbook. This is so for several reasons. First, textbooks usually are readily available to teachers and learners alike. Second, textbooks are generally written by persons who have expertise both in the subject itself and in methods for teaching it. Third, teachers are often so overwhelmed by the demands of their jobs that they willingly accept the textbook's ready-made teaching materials and step-by-step instructions. Textbook packages are particularly attractive to beginning teachers who may receive little help on the job in learning how to create lessons using a variety of resources.

Some states engage in "statewide adoption" of texts. This means that a central committee selects one or more texts all school districts in the state must use. Other states allow local school districts or individual schools to make textbook adoption decisions. In these states, teachers are heavily involved in the process of textbook selection. Localized adoptions allow schools to compare the content of each textbook with both state and local curriculum guides and to take into consideration the nature of their learners and the demands of the community.

If you have access to a professional education library, it may have a curriculum library that contains copies of curriculum guides and textbooks in your area. It is a very good idea to begin to familiarize yourself with these materials.

5.9 Do you have access to a curriculum library? What materials does it contain, and how could you use them?

THE TAUGHT CURRICULUM

Regardless of state and community efforts to standardize or guarantee a common curriculum, teachers can and do go off on their own. For example, in an alternative school in a large Northeastern city, the teacher and class in a course in American government might branch into a study of Native American government. Teachers have their own preferences and interests that affect what is or is not taught. Glatthorn (1987) refers to what teachers actually teach as the "taught curriculum." Said another way, the teacher, as shown in Figure 5.1, is the final curriculum filter.

In summary, we find that the curriculum, or what is to be learned, depends on societal needs, the subject to be learned, and the personal needs of learners. Although these three factors affect what appears in curriculum guides and textbooks, teachers unofficially decide what is ultimately taught based upon their own assessments of their students and their own teaching abilities and interests. You are the final filter.

5.10 To what extent do you feel you should follow the formal curriculum? Why?

Writing Instructional Objectives

Once you have determined what is to be learned, you are ready to begin planning in earnest. However, as the Cheshire Cat explained to Alice, the plan you develop "depends a good deal on where you want to get to." Thus, the foundation of good planning is the preparation of good goals or objectives. An **instructional objective** or **learning outcome** is a statement of the concepts, attitudes, or skills that students are expected to accomplish by the end of some period of instruction. In other words, if you are to plan effectively, *you must first decide what your students need to know or be able to do as a result of the learning experience.* The question is, *why* are you going to teach or initiate the learning experience?

We cannot overemphasize the importance of writing and then sharing your instructional goals with your learners. You learned in Chapter 3 that telling students what they must know or what they should be able to do at the close of a learning activity increases learning. Research indicates that teachers who are able to identify the specific objectives of their lessons and take time to communicate them to their students are perceived as clearer, and teacher clarity relates both to student achievement and satisfaction (Cruickshank & Kennedy, 1986). Make certain your learners know precisely what is expected of them. As Confucius said, "Ignorance of purpose leads to mediocrity."

Writing good instructional objectives is really not difficult, but it does take understand and practice. Three considerations are essential. First, you must decide the kinds of learning outcomes you want to express in the objective. Second, you must determine whether a general or specific objective is appropriate. Third, you must consider the information that needs to be included in the objective. Let's look at these three tasks more closely.

KINDS AND CLASSIFICATIONS OF LEARNING OUTCOMES

As you begin to write your instructional objectives, your first consideration is to determine what types of learning outcomes you seek. Do you want students to gain knowledge, skills, or attitudes?

Bloom and his colleagues (1956) developed a much used formal classification system, or taxonomy, for learning outcomes. Bloom's *taxonomy of educational objectives* classifies learning outcomes into three types or domains: cognitive (knowledge), psychomotor (skill), and affective (attitude). A description of each follows.

Cognitive Domain   Educational objectives in the cognitive domain cause learners to engage in intellectual tasks. For example, learners given certain information might be called on to recall, understand, apply, break down, combine, or judge that information. Thus, a learner might be expected to recall the sum of the angles of a triangle, to analyze the events surrounding Columbus's voyage to America in 1492, or to identify and discuss the themes found in Jane Austen's novels.

Besides being classified according to type or domain (cognitive, affective, or psychomotor), instructional objectives are also classified *within* type according to the level or complexity of the learning outcome. Bloom's cognitive domain includes six levels, ranging from simple to complex, or, from lower- to higher-order types of thinking. Let's look at an example for each level:

1. *Knowledge.* Learners have knowledge of and the ability to *recall* or recognize information. Example: The learner can recite multiplication facts.
2. *Comprehension.* Learners *understand* and can explain knowledge in their own words. Example: The learner can explain why 6 sevens and 7 sixes are equivalent.
3. *Application.* Learners *apply* knowledge, that is they are able to use it in practical situations. Example: The learner can calculate the cost of purchasing six envelopes costing seven cents each.
4. *Analysis.* Learners are able to *break down* complex concepts or information into simpler, related parts. Example: The learner can break the numeric statement "6 × 7" into subparts or possible combinations (for example, 3 × 2 × 7).
5. *Synthesis.* Learners are able to *combine* elements to form a new, original entity. Example: The learner can hypothesize that if 6 sevens are 42, 7 sevens can be determined by adding another 7 to 42.
6. *Evaluation.* Learners are able to *make judgments.* Example: The learner can devise a strategy for evaluating the accuracy of solutions to multiplication problems with 7 as one integer.

Many educators believe that, unfortunately, teachers require mostly lower-order types of learning (knowledge and comprehension): *When* did Columbus reach America? Teachers much less frequently seem to prod students to develop higher-level, or higher-order, thinking (application, analysis, synthesis, and evaluation): *Why* did Europeans discover America in 1492? Although low-level knowledge is an essential foundation for higher levels of thinking, it is

5.11 What do you think is the value of being able to develop a cognitive *objective* at each of Bloom's six levels?

5.12 Why do you think teachers tend to focus more on lower- rather than higher-order cognitive tasks?

important that you develop objectives and prepare lessons that challenge students to reach all levels of cognitive ability.

Affective Domain Bloom calls a second type or domain of learning outcomes affective. Bloom's **affective domain** deals with attitudinal, emotional, and valuing goals for learners. Although teachers most often associate their instructional outcomes with the cognitive domain, almost all teachers try to promote some change in student affect. For example, most teachers hope that their students come to enjoy and value the subject they teach, as well as learning in general.

Bloom organizes the affective domain into five levels, and again arranges them hierarchically. The five levels of the affective domain and examples of each follow:

1. *Receiving or attending.* Learners are willing *to attend to, concentrate on,* and *receive* information. Example: The learner listens attentively to Marjorie Kinnan Rawlings's story, *The Yearling.* (*The Yearling* is a novel about a young boy, Jody, who lives in the scrub and swamp of the hammock country of Florida. To survive, the family depends on a meager crop. Jody becomes attached to a tame fawn, Flag. However, to protect their crop from Flag, his parents are forced to kill the yearling.)

2. *Responding.* Learners *respond positively* to the information by *actively engaging* with it. Example: The learner participates in a discussion of *The Yearling.*

3. *Valuing.* Learners *express an attitude or belief* about the *value* of something. Example: After reading *The Yearling,* the learner may express the belief that life can be unfair and cruel and that life's worth is sometimes lessened by unkind circumstances.

4. *Organization.* Learners *compare* and *integrate* the attitude or value they have expressed with attitudes and beliefs they hold, thus internalizing the value. Example: The learner considers whether the attitudes or values they expressed after reading *The Yearling* are consistent with other values they or others hold.

5. *Characterization.* Learners *act out* their values. Example: The learner behaves in ways consistent with espoused values. If the learner believes that life is valuable but is often treated as a cheap commodity, he or she may join some group concerned with the preservation of life, such as the Society for the Prevention of Cruelty to Animals.

5.13 What do you think is the value of being able to develop an *affective* objective for each of Bloom's levels?

Psychomotor Domain According to Bloom, objectives in the third, or psychomotor, domain relate to learning physical skills. Courses in child or adolescent psychology taught you that as children grow, they are able to accomplish successively more complex physical tasks. For example, early on, students learn how to hold a large crayon, then to hold a thinner pencil. First, they learn to print, then how to write. Later, they learn to type and to use a word processor. Most subjects require some degree of psychomotor learning. In science, students learn how to organize and manipulate laboratory equipment. In music, they may learn how to use their voice or play an instrument.

Seven levels of the psychomotor domain have been identified (Simpson, 1972). Following are illustrations of possible objectives in this domain.

1. *Perception.* Learners *use sensory cues* (such as vision) to guide their later attempt to perform a skill. Example: The learner notices how to hold and move a brush to create a particular brushstroke.

2. *Set.* Learners are *ready to perform* a skill or an action. Example: The learner is mentally, physically, and emotionally prepared to perform the brushstroke.

3. *Guided response.* Learners *practice* the skill under the supervision of an expert. Example: The learner practices while the instructor coaches.

4. *Mechanism.* Learners *become more proficient* in the skill through practice. Example: The learner becomes more confident as the skill becomes second-nature or habitual.

5. *Complex or overt response.* Learners *perform* the skill with a high degree of proficiency. Example: The learner makes a great number of brushstrokes accurately and quickly.

6. *Adaptation.* Learners *modify* previously learned skills to perform related skills. Example: Building on previous skill, the learner creates different kinds of standard brushstrokes.

7. *Origination.* Learners *create* new, original performances based on previously learned skills. Example: The learner creates brushstrokes the teacher has not demonstrated or suggested.

5.14 What do you think is the value of being able to develop a *psychomotor* objective at each level Simpson suggests?

Try Activity 5.1

ANOTHER WAY OF CLASSIFYING LEARNING OUTCOMES

Gagné and Briggs (1988) provide another arrangement for thinking about and classifying learning outcomes, or objectives. Their system contains five groups of learning outcomes compared to Bloom's three:

1. *Verbal information.* This term is used to describe the vast amount of information obtained and stored in our memory. It is similar to the knowledge level in Bloom's cognitive domain. Example: Pupils learn factual information such as principles of physics or chemistry that they can retrieve as needed. Cognitive scientists refer to this as *declarative knowledge.*

2. *Intellectual skill.* This refers to learning how to do something mentally. It encompasses knowing how to do something rather than merely knowing about something. Example: Learners are able to create a balanced menu or devise a scale model based upon what they know about nutrition or about the object the model is based on. Cognitive scientists refer to this as *procedural knowledge.*

3. *Cognitive strategies.* This refers to learning ways of thinking and solving problems, including learning how to learn. Example: Learners learn to use an inductive approach to solve problems. Thus, knowledge of how to use induction would be a cognitive strategy. Problem solving usually combines the use of declarative and procedural knowledge.

4. *Motor skills.* Although Gagné and Briggs do not refer to the Bloom or Simpson designations of psychomotor skills, they seem to be the same type of learning outcome as Gagné and Briggs's motor skills.

5. *Attitudes.* Gagné and Briggs liken attitudes to Bloom's affective domain.

5.15 Which group of learning outcomes appeals more to you—Bloom's, or Gagné and Briggs's? Why? Could you make use of both?

GENERAL (BROAD) VERSUS SPECIFIC (NARROW) OBJECTIVES

Once your instructional objectives are chosen, a second decision you must make is whether general or specific objectives are more appropriate. This decision brings us back to the two earlier-mentioned approaches to instructional planning—*process* and *product.* Remember, process-oriented persons are more interested in planning only a general learning experience: "Let's go on a trip to Alaska." On the other hand, product-oriented persons like to make detailed plans: "Let's go on a trip to Alaska to accomplish a, b, and c." Therefore, it is quite likely the former will be less interested in preparing specific instructional objectives for their lessons.

For decades, educators have argued over exactly how precise objectives should be (Tyler, 1956). Early in this century, teachers were required to write objectives with great detail and specificity. An example might be "Learners will know 6 sevens are 42." You can imagine the results—literally thousands of detailed objectives! By 1930, an overcorrection occurred and objectives were written so broadly that it became difficult for both teachers and test makers to choose between overly broad and overly narrow objectives. An example of an overly broad and unclear objective might be "Learners will be able to think independently."

Both general and specific objectives are valid and have their place. Since general objectives are more skeletal in nature, they make more sense when people are discussing the broad goals or aims of education or instruction. For example, general objectives are useful at the national and state levels, where the intention is to broadly define what schools should teach.. Consider, for example, one of the six educational goals set by state governors and former President Bush in February 1990 for America to attain by the year 2000:

> By the year 2000, American students will leave grades 4, 8, and 12 having competency in English, math, science, history, and geography; they will learn to use their minds, will be prepared for responsible citizenship, further learning, and productive employment. (National Governors' Association, 1990)

Unfortunately, due to their skeletal nature, general objectives are written using terms that are open to interpretation. In the goal statement above, "having competency" and "being prepared" are examples of general objectives. How will the nation know whether American students are "competent"? Specifically what must they know and be able to do in each subject area? Moreover, how will we determine whether students can "use their minds" and are "prepared for responsible citizenship" and so on?

While such objectives indicate *what the learners will do,* they do not explicitly indicate *what pupils are to learn.* This is unfortunate since it focuses attention on the means of instruction (what the teacher or students will do), not on the ends (what learners will learn). Activities are not ends in themselves, but a means to an end. The real purpose of instruction is to change pupils' behavior and enable them to do things they couldn't do before instruction occurred. To help keep the real purpose of instruction in mind, teachers should write statements that describe the behaviors instructional activities are intended to help pupils learn (Airasian, 1991).

Again, general objectives are useful when making a skeletal outline of what students are to accomplish. Often teachers write them when engaged in long-range planning for the semester or year or when deciding what to accomplish during a month-long unit of instruction. Following are three examples of general objectives:

- Students will know what a verb is
- Students will enjoy music
- Students will be able to swim

WRITING SPECIFIC OBJECTIVES

The third determination you must make as you begin to write instructional objectives is what information to include in your objectives. Remember, a good objective informs students precisely what they are expected to know and to be able to do. Well-written instructional objectives are usually presented in sentence form and *usually* contain four parts or types of information, which we can think of as A, B, C, and D. Here is an instructional objective with these letters marked beneath it:

When given a paragraph, the learner will identify every verb by circling it correctly.

| | C | | A | | B | | D |

A stands for the *audience* the objective is written for. For most objectives, the audience will be "the learner" or "the student." Note that objectives are mostly written as measures of individual performance, not group performance. That is, each member of the class or group is held responsible for reaching the objective. "The class," then, usually is not an appropriate audience for an instructional objective.

B indicates the behavior or kind of *learning outcome expected* from each student. This is perhaps the most important part of the objective statement because it describes exactly what the student must do to demonstrate that she or he has learned. This behavior is exemplified in a verb, but not just any verb. This action must be observable. The verbs in our objective are "identify" and "circle." While verbs such as "know," "understand," "enjoy," "appreciate," and "study" may be acceptable in general objectives, they are inappropriate for specific objectives because they are too open to interpretation and too difficult to measure. Figure 5.3 presents a list of verbs appropriate for learning outcomes at various levels of each of Bloom's three instructional domains.

The designation *C* specifies the *condition* under which the learner is to exhibit the learned knowledge, skill, or attitude. Sometimes the condition is explicitly described. In other cases it is inferred. In our example it is explicit ("given a paragraph").

The *D* states the *degree* of proficiency the student must exhibit. This part of the objective sets a standard which each learner's performance can be compared against in order to determine if sufficient learning has taken place. In our example, 100 percent proficiency is expected.

Here are more examples of objectives stated in specific terms:

1. Given ten sentences containing twenty misspelled words, the learner will
                                C   A
   underline at least sixteen of the misspellings.
     B   D

2. The learner will solve at least eight of ten binary addition problems.
      A   B   D   C

3. Given a100-word speed test in class, the student will type at a rate of no
                  C   A   B
   less than thirty words per minute with fewer than four errors.
                       D

4. When presented flash cards of words containing the letter combination "ph"
                         C
   the student will pronounce the words on eighteen of twenty cards correctly.
     A   B   D

(handwritten note:)
A - the learner
B - outcome expected
C - condition
D - degree of proficiency

Try Activity 5.2

Counterpoint Specific educational objectives derive from general objectives, and give instruction clearer direction in terms of measuring learning outcomes.

However, not all educators advocate the use of specific objectives. Some feel that

- Teachers will focus only on learning outcomes that are easily observed and measured. Thus they will concentrate on teaching simple, factual information at low levels of the cognitive domain. This focus will distract students from learning other things, especially higher-order knowledge and skills that may be more difficult to describe.

- Spontaneity of learning may be lost. There are times when students should be provided with situations or problems without predetermined, specific learning outcomes. For example, taking a walk through the school neighborhood could be a very different experience for each student in the class. Comparing uniquely individual observations and impressions after the walk might lead to discussion opportunities that could not, and perhaps should not, be forecast.

- The mere ability to write specific objectives does not ensure that a teacher will be effective in implementing them.

5.16 Can you think of ways to write specific learning outcomes yet still maintain a focus on higher-order thinking, spontaneity, and implementation of those outcomes?

WHEN ARE OBJECTIVES GOOD?

When developing any instructional plan, you prepare a sequence of related instructional objectives. However, it is essential that you also stop and reflect on those objectives to judge their appropriateness to the curriculum and your learners. You can judge instructional objectives by asking yourself the following questions:

- Are the objectives relevant to the curriculum for which students will be held accountable?

- Can this group of students achieve the objectives? Do the objectives correspond to the readiness and ability levels of students? Do the objectives take individual differences into account?

1. **Cognitive domain**
   a. *Knowledge level*
      1. Objective: to know about
      2. Verbs to use: list, tell, define, identify, label, locate, recognize, describe, match, name, outline, reproduce, state
   b. *Comprehension level*
      1. Objective: to understand
      2. Verbs to use: explain, interpret, illustrate, describe, summarize, expand, convert, measure, defend, paraphrase, rewrite, apprehend, comprehend
   c. *Application level*
      1. Objective: to use knowledge and understanding
      2. Verbs to use: demonstrate, apply, use, solve, choose appropriate procedures, modify, operate, prepare, produce, construct
   d. *Analysis level*
      1. Objective: to break down
      2. Verbs to use: analyze, debate, differentiate, generalize, conclude, organize, break down, dissect, diagram, separate, subdivide, relate
   e. *Synthesis level*
      1. Objective: to combine, to create
      2. Verbs to use: create, combine, plan, design, produce, compile, develop, compose, devise, modify, organize, rearrange, reconstruct
   f. *Evaluation level*
      1. Objective: to judge
      2. Verbs to use: judge, evaluate, conclude, contrast, develop criteria, appraise, criticize, support, decide, compare

2. **Affective domain**
   a. *Receiving level*
      1. Objective: to be willing to attend to and to receive information
      2. Verbs to use: listen, be aware of, observe, be conscious of, recognize, realize, be tolerant
   b. *Responding level*
      1. Objective: to be willing to respond
      2. Verbs to use: respond, cooperate, appreciate, find pleasure in, comply, discuss
   c. *Valuing level*
      1. Objective: to develop attitudes and beliefs
      2. Verbs to use: value, opine, appraise, estimate, approve, appreciate, assess, believe, size up (See also "Evaluation level" under "Cognitive domain.")
   d. *Organizational level*
      1. Objective: to act out values
      2. Verbs to use: demonstrate, perform, act out, engage in, uphold

3. **Psychomotor domain**
   a. *Perception level*
      1. Objective: to notice, recognize, sense
      2. Verbs to use: notice, recognize, sense, perceive, detect
   b. *Set level*
      1. Objective: to be ready to try
      2. Verbs to use: be ready, be prepared, take steps, make preparation, desire
   c. *Guided response level*
      1. Objective: to try
      2. Verbs to use: try, perform, practice
   d. *Mechanism level*
      1. Objective: to improve
      2. Verbs to use: improve, become proficient, change, increase, decrease
   e. *Complex or overt response level*
      1. Objective: to be proficient
      2. Verbs to use: excel, master, perfect
   f. *Adaptation level*
      1. Objective: to adapt
      2. Verbs to use: adapt, adjust, accommodate, modify, modulate
   g. *Organization level*
      1. Objective: to create
      2. Verbs to use: create, originate, produce

- Do the objectives promote learning outcomes across all learning domains (cognitive, affective, psychomotor)?
- Do the objectives promote a range of levels of understanding or performance (low or high) within each domain?
- Are the objectives written in terms of what learners are expected to know or do? Are they specific enough that students will be aware of exactly what they need to know and do?

Preparing Instructional Plans of Varying Duration

Once you have decided what to teach and have prepared good instructional objectives, you need to ask yourself, *How much* and *what kind* of instruction do students need to accomplish these objectives? This question could be asked in reverse order as well. For example, do you first decide how learning should take place and then allocate sufficient time as if the latter were variable? Or, conversely, do you decide how much time you have as if time were a constant and then decide how much or in what manner, you can teach within that time span? Since the allocation of time to instruction or of instruction to time is often a burning issue, you may wish to discuss it in class. Perhaps you recall a course you were enrolled in, or a trip you took that ran out of time and was not completed. Let's turn our attention to the duration or scope of planning.

THE "LONG AND SHORT" OF PLANNING

As a teacher, you will regularly engage in long-, intermediate-, and short-range planning. Our vacation example can be used to illustrate this. You and your friend planned to take a vacation to the Eastern United States. This was your long-range plan. Then you determined the cities you would visit, the route you would take, and approximately how many days you would spend at various sites. This was the intermediate-range plan. Finally, for each day and site, you decided which specific things you wanted to do or see. Thus, you were also concerned with the daily and hourly routine. This was your short-term plan. Similarly, as a teacher, you will engage in long-range, intermediate-range, and short-term instructional planning for your students.

FIGURE 5.4   Plans of Different Duration

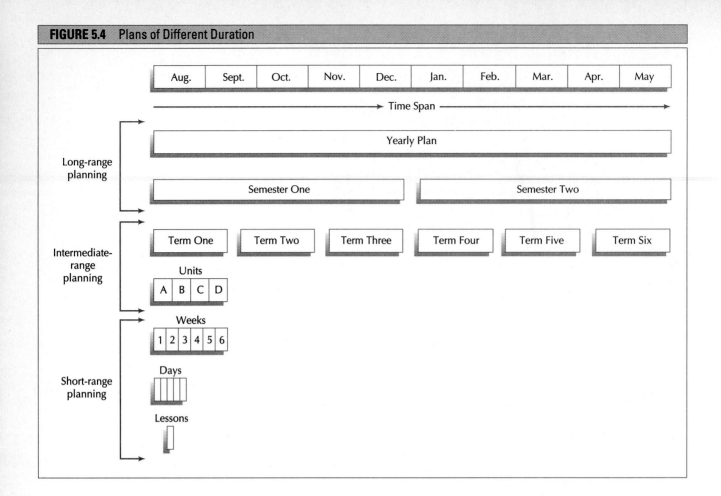

When teachers engage in long-range planning, they are deciding how generally to approach teaching either for an entire year or for a semester-long course. Teachers doing long-range planning first must choose a focus. The focus might be local history, American or Canadian literature, or fourth-grade arithmetic. Second, the teacher needs to determine how many weeks, days, or hours are available for instruction. Interruptions such as holidays, vacations, or exam weeks are taken into account. Third, the teacher must select the content of instruction. For example, long-range planning for an American history course involves deciding about which topics and information, out of all historians know about American history, should be included in this course, given the time available.

Intermediate, middle-range, or unit planning involves decisions about how courses can be broken into chunks, parts, or units, each with a particular theme. In intermediate or unit planning, teachers arrange units or topics in a meaningful order, thus determining the sequence of the course. The history course could be broken into historical periods that students can examine chronologically. Arithmetic for fourth graders might be broken into a series of units on arithmetic processes that are sequenced from simple to complex. A university course outline or syllabus provides an example of long-range and intermediate-range planning.

Once intermediate planning is completed, teachers next plan for the short range; that is, for the week and for daily lessons. During short-range planning, you decide in detail what students must learn and how that can most effectively be accomplished. It is at this level of planning that specific instructional objectives are needed.

5.17   How will you use long-, intermediate-, and short-range plans?

Figure 5.4 depicts plans of different duration (long-range, intermediate-range, and short-range), while Figure 5.5 shows the relationships among subjects, courses, units, and lessons.

FIGURE 5.5 The Relationships among Subject, Course, Unit, and Lesson

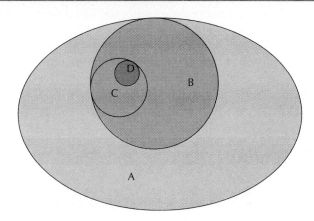

- The large ellipse (A) represents a *subject,* such as arithmetic.
- The large circle (B) represents a particular *course* of study, like fourth-grade arithmetic.
- The medium-sized circle (C) represents a segment or *unit* of study therein, such as multiplication of whole numbers.
- The smallest circle (D) represents an element or *lesson* within the unit on multiplication of whole numbers, such as multiplying by a one-digit number.

RESOURCES USEFUL WHEN PLANNING

As a novice, you may well ask, how do teachers know exactly what topics to address in their courses and in what order to sequence them? Thankfully, many guidelines and sources of help are available. First, as mentioned in a previous section, The Formal Curriculum, each state and school district has usually adopted or prepared a *course of study* which contains broad outlines of the topics and main points to be taught in each subject at each grade level. Additionally, *resource units* are available from state departments of education, federal agencies, professional education associations, and special-interest groups including businesses and industries. Resource units are much more detailed than courses of study; they elaborate on ways to teach a topic in depth.

Instructional resources also include *textbooks* and other print or nonprint materials such as *audio materials* (radio, language laboratories, tape and disk recordings, telephone, telelecture), *visual materials* (illustrations, photographs, flash cards, charts, maps, posters, exhibits, bulletin boards, magnetic boards, dioramas, models, slides and filmstrips, transparencies), and *audiovisual materials* (television, videotape, and CD-ROM interactive video). Many resources are available in public libraries, in your education libraries and media centers, on the Internet, and in the school district where you will be assigned. Finally, don't neglect the possibility of using knowledgeable human resources such as parents and community persons.

COOPERATIVE OR TEAM PLANNING

Normally, you alone will plan what and how your students will learn. However, at some time when planning, you, like all teachers, will solicit the assistance of other teachers or your students. You will use either teacher-team or teacher-pupil planning.

Teacher-team planning often occurs when courses of study or units are being prepared. The principal benefit is that two or more teacher heads often are better than one. Team planning results in sharing purposes, materials, expectations, and instructional ideas. Since teachers tend to be social and gregarious, team planning also can satisfy the need for affiliation and interaction, discussed in Chapter 13.

Teacher-pupil planning is based on the notions that students should learn how to guide or direct their own learning and that they have the motivation and ability to do so. Teacher-pupil planning derives credibility from the fact that pupils are more likely to be responsive to events they helped plan than to events planned for them. Relatedly, teacher-pupil planning provides the opportunity to plan activities that students perceive as more engaging and interesting. Last but not least, advocates note that the process can be an exercise in citizenship and responsibility.

A few cautions about teacher-pupil planning. Such planning should not stray too far from course, unit, or lesson objectives. Consequently, a secure teacher who can hold students to responsible, reasonable boundaries and standards should monitor and guide the planning process. Not all classes and students may be ready for this responsibility, and teacher-pupil planning must be tempered accordingly. While time-consuming on the front end, advocates claim it results in greater student interest and time on task.

Overall, teacher-pupil planning requires skill and considerable forbearance. Teachers who use this technique must be able and willing to provide time, support, guidance, ideas, and resources. Time and effort aside, assisting students in planning what and how they may learn makes a great deal of sense if one of our goals as teachers is to help students become self-directed learners.

5.18 How do you feel about planning with collegues and/or students?

PREPARING LONG-RANGE PLANS

As you have learned, teachers do long-range planning to determine what a year-long or semester-long course should include and how it may be taught. As mentioned, developing a long-range plan for teaching a course is similar to developing a vacation plan. Once you have a general vacation destination in mind, you start to collect ideas. Many will come from books and travel brochures. Other ideas may come from talking with people who have taken similar vacations. You use these ideas and materials as resources. You sit down with them and consider things such as:

1. *Your objective.* Where specifically do you want to go and what do you want to accomplish? Is your aim to spend considerable time at a few sites, to see all the sites you can, or to experience the local culture?

2. *Your timeline.* How much time can you spend in each place you wish to visit? Where do you want to be by certain dates in order to get everything done?

3. *Needed resources.* What will you need to take along or secure along the way to ensure that the vacation is successful?

In other words, you take into account your goals, the order in which you think they can best be achieved, the time required, and the resources needed.

Similarly, when developing a course, you consider what it is your students are expected to know and to be able to do; what activities they might engage in and in what order; how much time is available (weeks, days, hours) to be divided among the various activities; and, finally, what resource materials are at hand. When engaged in long-range planning you should keep in mind that:

- The course primarily should be derived from the established, formal curriculum; that is, it should fit into state and school district curriculum plans.

- The course should be developed to reflect what is known about the subject area. Thus, the content of the course should be up-to-date and reflect what experts in the field think is important.

- The course should be developed to take into account what you know about your learners. To some extent, then, each course you teach will be custom-made. There is no one course that is good for all students because of the differences among learners noted in Chapter 2.

- Decisions regarding what to teach are value-laden. Consequently, you must constantly guard against teaching only personal beliefs or biases about a subject or issue. Likewise, guard against teaching what seems to be "politically correct," that is, presenting a position or information that presents only what special-interest groups regard as true or valid while ignoring or depreciating what others of different persuasions believe or know.

Try Activity 5.3

Glatthorn (1987) presents a model to follow when developing a course. At this point, you might try your hand at constructing a long-term plan. If you'd like to do so, turn to Activity 5.3 at the end of this chapter.

PREPARING UNIT PLANS

Once you have created a long-range plan for the course, the intermediate stage of planning begins. Ultimately you must divide the course into parts, or units; then you must plan the units. A unit or **unit plan** is a more detailed plan for teaching a major section or topic within a course. At the secondary level, units normally are taught over a period of weeks and are limited to one topic. For example, in an American history course, the content might be divided into topics based on chronological periods such as the colonial, federal, and early industrial eras. Several weeks would be allocated to learning about each period. Units developed for elementary grades are often shorter, only a few days or weeks long.

As a teacher, you will likely develop several types of units such as the following:

- *Resource units* are mostly prepared by and are available at minimal or no cost from state education departments, special interest groups, government agencies, and businesses. Consequently, they must be adapted to the particular classroom they are used in to ensure that the level of difficulty and the general appeal are appropriate. An example of a science resource unit is a package that might contain a set of lesson plans, slides, transparencies, student worksheets, and a teacher's guide on natural gas produced by the regional gas company. Of course, resource units are likely to favor the viewpoint of the governmental or commercial group that produced them. They may possess a subtle, "hidden" curriculum bias.

- *Teaching units* are prepared by a teacher or teachers for use with a particular group of learners. Ideas may come from resource units, but they primarily arise from the teachers and from learners who may help develop the unit. (We discussed such collaborative or team efforts earlier.) Although teaching units, like resource units, are prepared before teaching occurs, they are flexible and often modified in use.

- *Subject matter units* are a subtype of either a resource or teaching unit. They are developed and used for teaching academic subject matter that requires a sequential or linear approach. A course may consist of several subject matter units, each prerequisite to the next. Students must master the content of one unit before moving on to the next. Mathematics often involves subject matter units. A unit on square roots and radicals, for example, would be prerequisite to another unit.

- *Experience units* are more of a "happening" than a preplanned unit. No one defines in advance what students are to learn. Teachers and students merely decide what they will generally do from day to day and from lesson to lesson. The learning experiences evolve. An experience unit might revolve around the theme "Sound Surrounds Us." What the students are *experiencing* is of the greatest importance, so students keep journals of what they have learned as their adventure with sound unfolds. Experienced teachers and teachers who are process-oriented probably are more comfortable and adept with experience units. Your friend and travel companion Pat may like to use these units.

- *Integrated units* are especially appropriate at the elementary level. Integrated units combine study from several fields such as social studies, language arts, science, and art around a central theme or topic. For example, an integrated unit on the Crusades might combine a historical and religious study of that period. Students might also read translated literature from that era, study life and customs during the Crusades, and depict them through art.

Parts of a Unit Plan   Although there are many types of units and unit plans, the typical unit plan includes the following parts or sections:

1. The *title* denotes the topic or theme under study, for example, "Sport in America." The topic usually is one the school district's curriculum or course of study requires. However, it may be one introduced for enrichment.

2. The *introduction* provides the rationale or reason why the unit is important to the course and in its own right. It should explain, in terms meaningful to students, why this unit is important, answering the ubiquitous student question: "Why do *we* have to know this?" The introduction also presents the parameters or scope (breadth) and sequence of the unit. By reading the introduction, one should be able to discern what main ideas or subtopics are addressed in roughly what order. The scope and sequence show how the main ideas build on each other and how the unit flows.

3. The *general objectives,* as noted earlier, broadly state the knowledge, skills, or attitudes students will acquire as a result of engaging in this unit. Before establishing the general objectives of a unit, you need to find out what your students know about the topic at hand so that the unit is neither too familiar nor unfamiliar, neither too easy nor difficult. Preassessment also enables you to remediate weaknesses or gaps in students' understanding of the topic and to increase the unit's appeal by building it around students' interests and perceived needs. You can preassess students in a number of ways, including informal observations, discussion, or questioning; formal pretesting of skills, knowledge, and attitudes; or examination of the curriculum previously studied by this group of students.

4. The *body* describes the unit's content, activities, and sequence of instruction. Included in the body are a topical outline, activities, resources, and a time frame.
   - The *topical outline* presents the main points and supporting points of the content. A detailed outline can become the wellspring for daily lessons.
   - The *activities* section denotes in general what the class or individuals can do in order to accomplish the unit objectives. What activities might they undertake to engage in learning the skills, knowledge, and attitudes the unit encompasses?
   - Also included in the body is the list of instructional *materials* and other *resources* that might be useful.
   - A *time frame* describes when the unit will begin and end and when students will undertake particular activities.

5. The *evaluation* section describes how learners will be evaluated in terms of achievement and satisfaction. To what extent do they know what they are expected to know? Can they do what they are expected to do?

6. A *bibliography* presents a list of resources useful to teachers in preparing and teaching this unit. A second list of references useful to students also should be prepared. If the unit will likely be revised and used again, it is a good idea to provide complete bibliographic references. In addition, it is helpful to make a note of where you obtained the resource (that is, your personal library, the school library, a friend's collection, or some other source) so that you can find it again.

Try Activity 5.4

Sometimes teachers break down the general information for a unit plan and present it in the form of **daily** or **block plans.** A block plan shows general objectives, learning activities, evaluation plans, and resources. Each block plan represents one class and serves as the outline or basis for one lesson plan. Figure 5.6 shows a sequence of two block plans for a second-grade unit on dinosaurs.

Benefits of Unit Planning   Developing a unit or several unit plans, especially early in your teaching career, can be time-consuming. However, it also tends to be an engaging and worthwhile exercise because of the flow of ideas and resources generated. Many benefits result from preparing and using units:

- Once completed, unit plans give clear direction for short-term planning—for a week, day, or lesson. An ounce of unit planning now may save a pound of work and classroom anxiety later.
- Good unit planning makes you more aware of your learners' unique qualities.
- Unit planning causes you to think imaginatively about how to get the job done using a variety of instructional materials and activities. It weans you away from mere textbook teaching.
- Unit planning asks you to consider how to help students study some topic or phenomenon in an *interdisciplinary,* or holistic, way. Through use of units, you can incorporate writing, reading, reporting, and so forth into learning activities.

PREPARING LESSON PLANS

A **lesson plan** describes specifically what and how something will be learned within a brief period, usually one or a few class hours. Think back to the earlier analogy of vacation planning. The long-range plan is to tour the Eastern United States. The intermediate plan could be to visit Boston and would cover what you want to accomplish only within that part of the trip. The short-term plan is the day-to-day, hour-to-hour, minute-by-minute formulation of what you would do: for example, a daily plan could be to walk the Freedom Trail during the day Monday, attend a Boston Pops Concert Monday evening, shop Tuesday and see a Red Sox game, and so forth.

Lesson planning further defines a daily plan. It is even more detailed. It is an effort to ensure that that day, every activity will go well.

Parts of a Lesson Plan   A large number of formats for lesson plans are used. A sampling of six is shown in Table 5.1. By comparing the formats, it is obvious that they have a lot in common. The lesson plan format we like appears in Figure 5.7. Keep in mind that eventually you will need to choose your own lesson plan format unless your school district prescribes one.

Let's consider each part in our recommended lesson plan format:

Try Activity 5.5

1. *Objectives.* The challenge here is to write objectives at the lesson level that meet as many of the criteria for good objectives as possible. Remember, the objectives should be relevant to the curriculum; promote learning outcomes across the cognitive, psychomotor, and affective domains; promote a range of levels of understanding (low and high) within each domain; be written specifically enough that it is clear what each student must know and be able to do; and be achievable by your students.
2. *Resources.* Assemble all the available human and material resources that might be used to help your learners gain the objectives. Many were noted in the earlier section entitled Resources Useful When Planning. In practice, many teachers do this first, before they write specific objectives. In any case, the lesson plan should specifically denote which resources you and the learners will use in order to accomplish the specific instructional objectives.

FIGURE 5.6   Sample Daily Block Plans for Dinosaur Unit

Day One
Topic: Dinosaur Days

General Objectives
1. The student will define the term *dinosaur.*
2. The student will describe what the earth was like when dinosaurs lived.

Learning Activity
Discussion: What is a dinosaur? What do you know about them?

Independent study: Distribute resource materials on dinosaurs. Have students find out what life on earth was like when dinosaurs lived.

Evaluation
Independent activity: Make a drawing showing what the earth was like when dinosaurs lived.

Resources:
W. Lindsay. (1991). *The great dinosaur atlas.* London: Darling Kindersley.
T. Dewon. (1993). *Inside dinosaurs.* New York: Doubleday.
Crayons, paper for each student

Day Two
Topic: Dinosaur Diets

General Objectives
1. The student will identify things dinosaurs probably ate.
2. The student will differentiate between meat-eating (carnivorous) and plant-eating (herbivorous) dinosaurs.
3. The student will cooperate and contribute while working on a small group activity.

Learning Activity
Discussion: What do you suppose dinosaurs ate?

Cooperative groups: In groups of three, students classify characteristics of meat-eating vs. plant-eating animals using animal pictures; then they decide if dinosaurs ate meat or plants by examining pictures of dinosaurs.

Evaluation
Sort dinosaur pictures into carnivorous and herbivorous dinosaurs and justify their grouping.

Resources:
H. Marsh. (1987). *Dinosaurs: Those terrible lizards.* Morristown, PA: Science Action Press (public library).
National Geographic. (1993, January). Twelve sets of animal pictures; twelve sets of dinosaur pictures (personal library at home).

3. *Set induction.* **Set induction** and **anticipator set** are terms used to indicate the need to start the lesson by capturing learner attention and interest. During this part of lesson planning, we must think of ways to do so. One idea is to relate what is to be learned to what learners are interested in and/or have previous knowledge of (see *advance organizer* in Chapter 3). It has long been assumed and has now been confirmed that people work harder on tasks related to their knowledge and interests (Renninger, Hidi, & Krapp, 1992). Interest contributes to learning because, among other things, it stimulates a personal, emotional network of associations. By relating new learning to prior knowledge,

TABLE 5.1   Selected Formats for Lesson Plans Listed by Author or Source

Callahan (1971)	Center for Vocational Education (1977)	Department of the Air Force (1984)	Eby (1992)	Gagné & Briggs (1988)	Hunter (1985)
1. Lesson topic	1. Lesson topic	1. Objectives	1. Title	1. Objectives	1. Objectives
2. General objectives	2. Objectives	2. Main lesson points	2. Subject	2. Events, activities	2. Set induction
3. Specific objectives	3. Introduction	3. Instructional method	3. Grade level	3. Resources needed	3. Input and modeling
4. Introduction	4. Instructional method	4. Support material	4. Description	4. Notes and reminders	4. Checking for understanding and guided practice
5. Content	5. Learning activity	5. Lesson beginning and ending	5. Objectives		5. Independent practice
6. Activities	6. Resources	6. Final lesson outline	6. Materials needed		
7. Materials	7. Evaluation		7. Procedures		
8. Conclusions	8. Summary		8. Evaluation		
9. Evaluation					
10. Assignment					

FIGURE 5.7   Parts of a Lesson Plan

1. Objectives—Indicates the lesson's objectives
2. Resources—Denotes resources and materials to be used
3. Set Induction—Describes how the lesson will be introduced
4. Methodology—Describes how teaching and learning will take place
5. Assessment—Makes clear how student learning will be determined
6. Closure—Provides for lesson ending

associations and connections also are more apparent. Chapter 11 details how to provide set induction, while Unit 1 (Microteaching Lesson Two) in part IV provides a practice exercise.

4. *Methodology.* Here you describe how learning will take place. Chapters 2 on student diversity and 3 on learning should be particularly useful in planning your methodology because they describe what is known about students and how they learn. Chapters 6 and 7 on instructional alternatives also are very relevant.

5. *Assessment.* This includes two things: how you plan to monitor students' learning during instruction and how you plan to evaluate learning at the lesson's conclusion. While instruction is ongoing, a teacher should "read" the students. To what extent does each one seem interested and engaged? Is the pace of the lesson appropriate? Are students learning? Your plan should include how you will determine such things. Informal indicators of interest and engagement might include facial expression, body language, and verbal responsiveness. Informal assessments can also be made by asking questions which check understanding and by observing how well and how frequently students apply what they have learned. Formal assessments, frequently used at a lesson's conclusion, include worksheets, homework, and quizzes. No matter which assessment technique you use, remember that it must provide evidence of the students' progress toward the lesson's objectives. See Chapter 8 for more help.

Kagan and Tippins (1992) asked five elementary and seven secondary student teachers at the University of Georgia and the University of Alabama to assist them in answering this question. Because they wanted to see what would happen naturally, the researchers asked the cooperating teachers not to require their student teachers to use any particular lesson plan format. However, Kagan and Tippins gave the student teachers a format with six components: objectives, motivation, major activities, closure, student evaluation, and homework or follow-up. They then asked the student teachers to modify the format so that it worked for them.

As the semester went on, Kagan and Tippins found that (1) elementary teachers' plans became briefer and less detailed, while secondary teachers' plans became more detailed; (2) elementary teachers' plans focused more on learning activities, while secondary teachers focused more on incorporating an outline of a lecture into their plan, and (3) elementary teachers regarded written plans as ways of organizing for the lesson, but preferred to behave spontaneously rather than according to a "script."

The investigators cite the limitations of their study, particularly that only twelve student teachers were involved.

However, they conclude that lesson plan formats probably differ not only between novice elementary and secondary teachers but also as a function of the lesson's academic content. Furthermore, Kagan and Tippins suggest that "it would probably be more productive to define lesson plans as lists of major instructional procedures" (p. 487) and that planners should not be required to list "objectives" and "materials" if they are self-evident in the instructional materials. They also suggest that requiring a section on "evaluation" may promote overuse of formal testing.

6. *Closure.* All lessons need a good finish. But what is a good finish? Normally it takes the form of a review that gets students to summarize what they have learned and connect it to prior and future learning. In Chapter 3, you saw that when information is well-organized and connected to students' prior knowledge, it likely enters their long-term memory. You also learned that a review should require learners to think about the new information, to reflect on its application and its personal meaning. Many teachers conduct their review by asking students what they have learned or discovered.

Try Activity 5.6

Figure 5.8 contains an abbreviated lesson plan designed to help learners discriminate between the terms *theme* and *variation*. How would you improve the lesson if you were teaching toward the same objective?

As mentioned earlier, you eventually need to develop your own style of lesson format unless the school district in which you teach mandates a particular one. Kagan and Tippins (1992) followed elementary and secondary student teachers into their classrooms to find out how they planned. Their study is reported in Spotlight on Research 5.2.

Try Activity 5.7

Additional Points to Keep in Mind When Planning Lessons   Here are four more points to keep in mind when planning:

Plans Should Take into Account What We Know about Learning   Again, information in Chapter 3 is vital. Overall, you should ensure that each lesson provides four elements of learning: drive, cue, response, and reinforcement.

Drive refers to the learner's need to want something from, or see some advantage in the learning experience. This underscores the importance of communicating the objectives of the lesson in terms relating to the student's needs and interests. Further, it suggests that your anticipatory set (Chapter 3) should demonstrate to students how the new information builds on what they already know and how it will help them now as well as later. Convincing students of the usefulness of the

Objectives

1. Given several objects of a common kind or theme—for example, automobiles or sunglasses—the learner will see likenesses and differences among them.

2. The learner will demonstrate understanding of *theme* by drawing six objects with the same shape.

3. The learner will demonstrate understanding of *variation* by varying characteristics of the objects.

Resources

1. Pictures of a variety of automobiles

2. A variety of sunglasses

3. Paper, crayons or markers

Set Induction   (preparing learners to grasp the concepts *theme* and *variation* by causing them to think of themes and variations within their personal experience)

1. Show pictures of automobiles.
"What is the same about each object in our pictures?" (all are automobiles)
"What is different about the automobiles?" (color, shape, size)

2. Show sunglasses
"What is the same about these objects?" (all are sunglasses)
"What is different about them?" (color, shape, size)

3. "Can you think of other objects that have something in common yet are somewhat different?" (people, animal, toys)

4. "Today, we are going to learn two new words we can use to describe things that have something in common yet are somewhat different."

Methodology

1. "The two new words we want to explore are *theme* and *variation*. Print words on chalkboard.

2. "If I said that these pictures [hold up automobile pictures] have a common theme, what do you suppose I mean?" (They are alike in some way.) "What is the common theme?" (They are all automobiles.) Underneath the word *theme* on the chalkboard, write *automobiles*.

3. Repeat steps 1 and 2 with sunglasses.

4. "We know that things with something in common can also be different, or vary, in certain ways. As you said, automobiles and sunglasses have variations." Point to the word *variation* on the chalkboard. "how did you say they vary?" (They vary in size, shape, color.) Write *size, shape, color* underneath the term *variation* on the chalkboard.

5. "Do you think you can show that you understand the words *theme* and *variation*? Draw a group of objects that have a common theme but also show variation. Perhaps you could draw six leaves or six books or anything else that comes to mind."

6. "What ideas do you have for showing *theme* and *variation*, or what we call `variations of a theme'?"

7. Pass out paper. Instruct students to fold paper into six sections and to draw one object in each section.

8. Circulate to guide, monitor, and assess understanding. Ask individuals, "What theme are you using?" and "What variation?"

9. Ask learners to share their themes and variations.

Assessment

1. See Methodology steps 8 and 9.

Closure

1. "What two new words did you learn today?"

2. "What does each word mean?"

3. "Why do you think these words are important? Why is it important to be able to notice likenesses and differences?"

lesson is especially important when working with low-achieving students, who may have less interest in school learning.

Cue refers to the fact that learners must notice something before they can learn it. As previously mentioned, the anticipatory set is intended to initially capture the students' attention. However, their attention must also be maintained throughout the lesson by using cuing words or phrases such as "notice this," "this is important," "you need to know," and "the third step is similar to the second."

Response suggests that the learner must be *actively* involved in the lesson. Each student must be provided with adequate learning experiences. It is also important to check for understanding and, when necessary, to provide guided, supervised practice. It is important to plan for and integrate these assessment activities carefully within the lesson.

Reinforcement means students must feel they have gained something from the learning experience. Throughout the lesson, individual learners should be provided with specific feedback on how they are doing, including both strengths and areas that need improvement. Of course, the reinforcement you provide may vary depending on your students' characteristics such as age, gender, cultural background, and socioeconomic status. The appropriate use of praise and reteaching, essential to student motivation and learning, are discussed more in Chapters 11 and 12.

Regardless of how you will conduct your lesson, ask yourself, "Does my plan provide for drive, cue, response, and reinforcement?"

Plans Should Take into Account What We Know about Learners A good lesson fits students rather than forcing students to fit the lesson. Chapters 2 and 4 provide knowledge about student diversity and how to find out more about your students.

First you must ask yourself, "Do I know my students?" Then, "When I planned my lesson, did I take that knowledge into account?"

Plans Should Be Considered Tentative and Should Be Flexible Shavelson (1987) notes that once teachers launch a lesson plan, they tend not to deviate from it. "Damn the torpedoes. Full-speed ahead!" seems to be the battle cry. If this is true of you, you could have problems. Scottish poet Robert Burns's adage "The best laid plans of mice and men often go astray" is better kept in every teacher's mind. When you are teaching, anything can go wrong. Unplanned school assemblies, fire drills, bomb threats, weather emergencies, and accidents may crop up; sometimes, you'll just hit one of those dog days when, lesson in hand, you look at your students and tell yourself "this just isn't going to work." Consequently, you must exhibit flexibility, adjusting the lesson to the moment or even casting it aside.

Ask yourself, "Am I adaptable enough to make on-the-spot lesson adjustments?"

Plans Should Take the Teaching Environment into Account Lessons frequently fall apart when teachers fail to provide for orderly movement from one activity to another and for the effective distribution of materials. In other words, it is as important to think over the routines and movement patterns during the lesson as it is to plan the content. Specific information on how to plan and develop these important classroom routines is discussed in Chapter 12.

Ask yourself, "Have I planned for routines and movement?"

Plans Should Take into Account What We Know about Good Lessons Spotlight on Research 5.3 describes a study of a group of British teachers and their students, informing us of what they believe constitutes a good learning experience.

FIGURE 5.9 Lesson Planning Resources on the Internet

Since planning lessons is a challenging daily activity, teachers look for sources of ideas for rich, relevant lessons. One fine source is the Internet. Take a look at the following websites.

1. *The Lesson Plan Page*
   http://libits.library.ualberta.ca/library_html/libraries/coutts/lessons.html
   This site, located at the University of Alberta, has links to key sites on lesson planning, including some of our favorites:
   a. *Lesson Plans from CanaDisk*
      For example, check out "Exploring Our Roots," appropriate for middle and secondary students, located at:
      http: //school net.carlton.ca/cdisk/Lesson Plans/ExploringOurRoots
      Also, "Oral Reports Through Personality Bags" at
      http://schoolnet.carlton.ca/disk/lesson Plans/OralReportsPersonality
   b. *Lesson Plans from Teachnet*
   c. *Teacher Talk Forum: Lesson Plans*
   d. A variety of links to sites containing plans specific for use in math, science, English and social studies

2. *Locating lesson plans*
   One of the best ways to find a specific lesson plan is to use search engines such as Hotbed or AltaVista.

3. *K–12 Lesson Plans*
   http://teams.lacoe.edu/documentation/places/lessons. html
   This website is maintained by the Los Angeles County Office of Education and, like the Lesson Plan Page site, has lots of links to explore. Start with: *Ask Eric Lesson Plans*. If you and/or your instructor think you have developed a lesson plan that others might want to know about, you can submit it to *Call for Lesson Plans* at
   gopher://ericir.syr.edu:70/00Lesson/Call4_Lessons

4. *Encarta Lesson Collection*
   http://encarta.msn.com/schoolhouse/lessons/default.asp
   Search this lesson collection by grade level and/or subject.

Internet Resources on Lesson Planning   For those of you with Internet skills who wish to see lesson plans on a variety of topics, see Figure 5.9.

Try Activity 5.8

REVIEW OF PLANS OF VARYING DURATION

Yinger (1980) outlines the levels of instructional planning. Table 5.2 incorporates his ideas with ours.

TABLE 5.2 Plans of Varying Duration

	Purposes	Sources of Helpful Information	Form of the Plan	Criteria for Judging Planning Effectiveness
Yearly planning	1. Establish yearlong general content (fairly general and framed by district curriculum objectives) 2. Establish basic curriculum sequence 3. Order and reserve resource materials	1. Students (general information about numbers and nature of returning students) 2. Curriculum guidelines (district objectives) 3. Resource availability 4. Personal experience with specific curricula and materials	General outline listing basic content and possible ideas in each subject matter area	1. Comprehensiveness of plans 2. Fit with own goals, district objectives, and learners
Term planning	1. Spell out details of content to be covered in next school term 2. Establish weekly schedules that conform to the goals and emphases for the term	1. Direct contact with students 2. Time constraints set by school schedule 3. Availability of resources	1. Elaboration of outline constructed for yearly planning 2. A weekly schedule outline specifying activities and times	1. Outlines: comprehensiveness, completeness, and specificity of elaborations 2. Schedule: comprehensiveness fit with goals for term balance 3. Fit with goals for term 4. Fit with learners
Unit planning	1. Develop a sequence of well-organized learning experiences built around a topic or theme 2. Present comprehensive, integrated and meaningful content at an appropriate level	1. Students' abilities, interests, etc. 2. Materials, length of lessons, setup time 3. Facilities available for activities 4. District objectives	1. Activity and content lists of outlines 2. Sequenced activity lists 3. Notes in plan book	1. Organization, sequence balance, and flow of outlines 2. Fit with yearly and term goals 3. Fit with anticipated student interest and involvement
Weekly planning	1. Lay out the week's activities within the framework of the weekly schedule 2. Adjust schedule for interruptions and special needs 3. Maintain continuity and regularity of activities	1. Student performance in preceding days and weeks 2. Scheduled school interruptions (for example, assemblies, holidays) 3. Continued availability of materials, aides, and other resources	1. Activity names and times entered into a plan book 2. Day divided into four instructional blocks punctuated by morning recess, lunch, and afternoon recess	1. Complxteness of plans 2. Degree to which weekly schedule has been followed 3. Flexibility of plans to provide for special time constraints or interruptions 4. Fit with goals, learners
Daily planning	1. Set up and arrange classroom for next day 2. Specify activity components not yet decided upon 3. Fit daily schedule to last-minute intrusions 4. Prepare students for day's activities	1. Clarity of instructions in materials to be used 2. Setup time for activities 3. Assessment of class "disposition" at start of day 4. Continued interest, involvement and enthusiasm	1. Schedule for day written on the chalkboard and discussed 2. Preparation and arrangement of materials and facilities in the room	1. Completion of last-minute preparations and decisions about content, materials, etc. 2. Involvement, enthusiasm, and interest communicated by students
Lesson planning	1. Relate to previous lesson 2. Progress to new, specifically designed task 3. Evaluate attainment (in individual terms) 4. Project to next lesson and relate to broader plan	1. Evaluation of previous lesson 2. The larger units of planning (daily, weekly, unit, etc.) 3. Feedback from class	See Table 5.1 and Figure 5.6	1. Learner accomplishment of objectives 2. Evaluation during the lesson; at end of lesson; sometime later

Some Final Thoughts

At this point we have thought a good deal about planning. However, reading and talking about instructional planning, and even being skilled at planning does not make one a good teacher! *Planning is necessary but not sufficient for good teaching.* It is a means to an end, not an end in itself. On the positive side, planning helps keep objectives clear and decreases ad lib, off-the-cuff teaching. Although an impromptu approach may work for some teachers some of the time, it does not work for any teacher all of the time. On the negative side, the teacher with a plan must carry it out, and that requires more than planning knowledge. Teachers can plan extraordinary lessons, but they may not have thorough knowledge of what they will teach, or they may lack the instructional abilities to implement the plan. Chapters 6 and 7 will acquaint you with some of the best known and most powerful ways to teach.

CHAPTER SUMMARY

- Teachers devote considerable time and energy to planning or thinking through teaching, in order to maximize both their own and their students' achievement and satisfaction. Planning benefits you because it gives you greater confidence in what and how you are teaching and encourages more instructional variety and creativity. It benefits students by helping teachers take student diversity into account. In short, planning benefits everyone because it results in better use of class time and reduces uncertainty.

- Because of its benefits, school districts often require instructional planning. You may be required to keep plan books to ensure desired content coverage and to provide for instructional continuity when you are absent. Public Laws 94-142 and 101-476 require additional instructional planning for students qualifying for special educational assistance.

- Teachers differ in their approaches to planning. Some prefer a very general plan to guide their actions because a detailed plan might be too restrictive. Others like a detailed plan because it provides a feeling of confidence and security. Although both approaches have advantages, novice teachers are advised to plan in detail, at least until they have more professional experience and knowledge.

- When planning, you must first decide what to teach. Societal factors, the nature and diversity of your students, and subject matter experts and interest groups (such as the American Association for the Advancement of Science and the National Council for Teachers of English) largely determine teaching content.

- Planning requires you to write instructional objectives that indicate what students should know and be able to do at the close of the lesson or unit. There are three categories or domains of objectives: cognitive objectives focus on what learners should know and understand; affective objectives focus on what learners should feel or value; and psychomotor objectives focus on what physical skills learners should possess.

- Instructional objectives may be general or specific. General or broader objectives are most useful in long-range planning, but specific objectives are preferable when writing objectives for a particular lesson. Since specific objectives are clear in regard to what learners should know and be able to do, they are the objectives of choice for newer teachers who are short on professional experience.

- Well-written instructional objectives contain four kinds of information. They designate the audience, the learning outcomes expected of the audience, the conditions under which the audience is to exhibit the learned ability, and the degree or amount of proficiency expected.

- The quality of instructional objectives improves when they are relevant, when they promote diverse learning outcomes, and when they are clear and achievable.
- There are three major kinds of plans: long-range course plans, intermediate-range unit plans, and short-range lesson plans.
- All three major kinds of planning are useful, especially since they cause teachers to think about teaching and consider the best way to facilitate student learning and satisfaction. Therefore, you should be able to craft each type of plan.

ISSUES AND PROBLEMS FOR DISCUSSION

ISSUES   Here are some questions worthy of debate in your class.

1. Which orientation to planning—process or product—is preferable?
2. Should written planning be mandated?
3. How specific should objectives be?
4. What *must* a teacher think about when planning instruction?
5. To what extent should planning be cooperative?
6. What kinds of persons under what circumstances might be able to teach off-the-cuff, that is, without a lesson plan?

PROBLEMS   Following are some planning problems teachers report. What would you do in each circumstance?

Problem 1:   "I planned a lesson in which the class would watch and discuss a televised program. My class was highly motivated to watch. Unfortunately, the TV didn't work."

Problem 2:   "I assigned seatwork to the students so that I could work with each reading group. It soon became apparent I had underestimated how long the independent work would take. Students finishing early became noisy and interruptive."

Problem 3:   "Today students were removed from the room in groups to take hearing tests. I could not continue with my plans because so many children were continually gone. Then, many of the children had to be retested because the tests were invalid. My daily plans were completely altered, and I accomplished very little teaching."

Problem 4:   "Today was a terribly rainy, wet day. Many of our students don't have proper raincoats and do not come to school on such days. Over one-third of my class was absent. I had planned to begin a new unit of work, and my entire day was disrupted."

Problem 5:   "There are times when regular teachers are absent and substitutes are not available. This means we have to break up and distribute the class of the absent teacher. Today I received three boys from another grade. They were unable to work with my children but obviously couldn't be expected to sit all day and do nothing. This meant that I had to devise and correct assignments for them and make out passes for the ones who eat in the school lunchroom."

Problem 6:   "Our lesson required use of the textbook and a state map. Many pupils arrived without one or the other, claiming they had forgotten them."

ACTIVITY 5.1: Recognizing Domains and Levels of Instructional Objectives   Given the following specific objectives, identify the level of each according to Bloom or Simpson by placing an X in the correct boxes.

1. Given a list of spelling words, each learner will use each word in a sentence and spell it correctly.
   Domain: ☐ cognitive   ☐ affective   ☐ psychomotor
   Level: ☐ knowledge   ☐ comprehension   ☐ application
   ☐ analysis   ☐ synthesis   ☐ evaluation

2. Given a reading assignment in Rawlings's novel *The Yearling,* each learner will make a judgment about the correctness of the Baxters' decision to kill Flag the fawn.
   Domain: ☐ cognitive   ☐ affective   ☐ psychomotor
   Level: ☐ receiving/attending   ☐ responding   ☐ valuing
   ☐ organization   ☐ characterization

3. At the conclusion of the typing course, each learner will demonstrate proficiency by typing 60 words a minute with 5 or fewer errors.
   Domain: ☐ cognitive   ☐ affective   ☐ psychomotor
   Level: ☐ perception   ☐ set   ☐ guided response   ☐ mechanism
   ☐ complex or overt response   ☐ adaptation
   ☐ origination

ACTIVITY 5.2: Recognizing Well-Written Instructional Objectives   Read each of the following objectives and determine whether it is well-written. If it is, label the parts A, B, C, D. If it is unclearly written, rewrite it as a good-quality specific instructional objective and label the four parts.

- When dissecting a frog, the student will identify organs of the digestive system.
- Given a worksheet containing twenty addition examples requiring regrouping, the student will correctly complete seventeen.
- The class will know how to use a dictionary for an in-class oral quiz tomorrow.
- Students will be able to list and describe four types of soccer kicks or passes with 100 percent accuracy.

ACTIVITY 5.3: Developing a Long-Range Plan   Do the following to learn more about long-range planning.

- Talk with classroom teachers or your college instructors about how they plan for a yearlong or semester-long course.
- Look through state or local school district courses of study, curriculum guides, and subject matter curriculum standards (Figure 5.2) to see how they can help you in course planning.
- Develop a long-range plan for something you likely will teach during your field experiences or that you hope to teach as a beginning teacher. As part of that long-range plan, it might be helpful to:
  a. Consult the state or school district course of study to learn the requirements for such a course.
  b. Talk with teachers who teach this course to determine what they include in the course and how and why they make those decisions.
  c. Collect and file as many related resources (print and nonprint) as you can.
  d. Determine the main topics the course will include and establish the order in which you will present them.

e. Think about who the learners will be in the course and their interests, aptitudes, and past experiences.

f. Write *general* objectives you want to accomplish in the course.

g. Subdivide the course topics into parts or units and assign a time for each.

h. Decide how you will be able to tell whether learners have accomplished the course goals and are satisfied with the course.

ACTIVITY 5.4: Developing a Unit Plan Do the following activities to learn more about unit planning.

- If you are working in a school, talk with your mentor or cooperating teacher about unit planning. How does he or she organize various activities, experiences, and types of learning around topics, central problems, or areas of interest?

- Look over units your mentor teacher or university professor may have. Also, check to see if any are available through the professional education library or a materials resource center on campus.

- Develop a unit plan that contributes to the long-range plan you developed for Activity 5.3. If you didn't design a long-range plan, design a unit on some topic you probably will teach.

ACTIVITY 5.5: Recognizing Variations on the Theme of Lesson Planning Look at different lesson plans that are available to you from your mentor teacher, education instructor, or other professional education students.

- What format similarities do they share?
- What is different about each lesson plan?
- Which format would be most useful to you when teaching?

ACTIVITY 5.6: Obtaining Classroom Teachers' Views of Lesson Planning If you are doing fieldwork, talk with your mentor teacher about how he or she plans a lesson. You might consider asking some of the following questions.

- When do you develop your lesson plans? How much time does it take each day or each week?
- What information do you write out in the lesson plan?
- Do you have the lesson plan in front of you when you teach?
- How do you know when to change or vary the lesson you have planned?
- What advice would you give a new teacher about planning?

ACTIVITY 5.7: Observing the Implementation of a Lesson Plan Observe a fellow student or teacher implementing a lesson. Did the teacher provide for each of the following? If so, describe briefly what the teacher did with regard to each:

- Set induction
- Communication of objective(s)
- Methodology
- Provision for diverse students
- Closure or summary
- Assessment
- Practice

ACTIVITY 5.8: Developing and Evaluating a Lesson Plan   Develop a lesson plan for something you likely will, or hope to, teach. If you have developed a unit plan, as suggested in Activity 5.4, plan a lesson for use within that unit. Or you might develop a lesson plan for one of the Reflective Teaching Lessons contained in Unit 2 of the Practice Teaching Manual. Follow the format for lesson plans presented in this chapter. Be sure to include all the essential parts.

When you have completed the lesson plan, use the following checklist to evaluate it.

Yes	No	a. Does the lesson plan derive from, and is it obviously related to, the unit of study?
Yes	No	b. Are the objectives clear and measurable?
Yes	No	c. Are the objectives appropriate to the learners?
Yes	No	d. Are the lesson activities interesting and effective?
Yes	No	e. Does the lesson take into account what we know about learners and learning?
Yes	No	f. Are the materials and resources adequate?
Yes	No	g. Does the plan provide a clear lesson beginning (preparing the student for what he or she is to learn), middle (learning activities), and culmination (summary, conclusions, and application)?
Yes	No	h. Does the plan account for where the activities will take place and for transitions (changes and movement)?
Yes	No	i. Does the plan allow you to assess learners on the extent to which they have accomplished the lesson objectives?
Yes	No	j. Is the lesson likely achievable within the time available?

REFERENCES

Airasian, P. W. (1991). *Classroom assessment.* New York: McGraw-Hill.

Baltimore Area Committee on Student Teaching. (1991, Spring). *Student teaching field experience handbook.* Baltimore, MD: The Committee.

Biehler, R., & Snowman, J. (1997). *Psychology applied to education.* Eighth edition. Boston: Houghton Mifflin.

Bloom, B., et al. (1956). *Taxonomy of educational objectives. Handbook I: Cognitive domain.* London: Longman.

Callahan, S. (1971). *Successful teaching in secondary schools.* Glenview, IL: Scott, Foresman.

Center for Vocational Education. (1977). *Developing a lesson plan: Module B–4.* Athens, GA: Engineering Center, American Association for Vocational Instructional Materials.

Cooper, P., & McIntyre, D. (1994). Patterns of interaction between teachers' and students' classroom thinking. *Teaching and Teacher Education, 10*(6), 633–646.

Cruickshank, D., & Kennedy, J. (1986). Teacher clarity. *Teaching and Teacher Education, 2*(1), 43–67.

Department of the Air Force. (1984). *Training handbook for Air Force instructors.* Washington, DC: Headquarters, U.S. Air Force.

Eby, J. W. (1992). *Reflective planning, teaching and evaluation for the elementary school.* New York: Macmillan.

Gagné, R., & Briggs, L. (1988). *Principles of instructional design.* Forth Worth, TX: Holt, Rinehart and Winston.

Glatthorn, A. (1987). *Curriculum renewal.* Alexandria, VA: Association for Supervision and Curriculum Development.

Hirsch, E. D. (1989). *A first dictionary of cultural literacy: What our children need to know.* Boston: Houghton Mifflin.

Hunter, M. (1985). *Mastery teaching.* El Segundo, CA: TIP Publications.

Kagan, D. M., & Tippins, D. J. (1992). The evolution of functional lesson plans among twelve elementary and secondary student teachers. *The Elementary School Journal, 92*(4), 477–490.

National Governors' Association. (1990, February). Report adopted by members of the National Governors' Association.

Renninger, K. A., Hidi, S., & Krapp, A. (1992). *The role of interest in learning and development.* Hillsdale, NJ: Erlbaum.

Shavelson, R. (1987). Planning. In M. Dunkin (Ed.), *The international encyclopedia of teaching and teacher education* (pp. 483–486). New York: Pergamon Press.

Simpson, E. (1972). *The classification of educational objectives: Psychomotor domain.* Urbana: University of Illinois Press.

Slavin, R. (1988). *Educational psychology: Theory into practice.* Englewood Cliffs, NJ: Prentice Hall.

Tyler, R. (1949). *Basic principles of curriculum and instruction.* Chicago: University of Chicago Press.

Tyler, R. (1956). The curriculum—then and now. *Proceedings, Invitational Conference on Testing Problems.* Princeton, NJ: Educational Testing Service.

Willis, S. (1993, November). Teaching young children: Educators seek developmental appropriateness. *ASCD Curriculum Update,* 1–8.

Yinger, R. (1980). A study of teacher planning. *The Elementary School Journal, 80,* 114–115.

Three Instructional Alternatives: Presentation, Discussion, and Independent Study

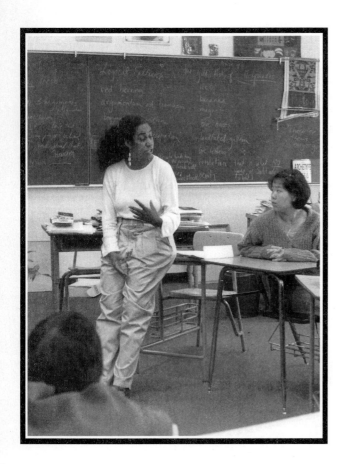

Contents

Instructional Alternatives Defined

Presentations: Teaching as Telling and Showing

Discussion: Learning through Informative Interaction

Independent Study: Teaching as Giving and Guiding Seat-Work and Homework Assignments

The "Best" Instructional Alternatives

Overview of Twenty-Nine Instructional Alternatives

Some Final Thoughts

Chapter Summary

Issues and Problems for Discussion

Theory into Action Activities

References

Can you think of one or more of your teachers who helped you learn and even to enjoy learning? Now can you think of teachers who were not very effective? How did these teachers differ? Probably one thing that characterized the effective teachers was their ability to use a variety of instructional alternatives or strategies. Like acclaimed actors and actresses who can play a large number of roles, *good teachers are multitalented.* On one day, they may have involved your class in a debate. On other days, you may have watched a demonstration, played an academic game, listened to an oral report, or used an individual learning module. The classroom always seemed varied and lively, and while this alone does not ensure effective teaching, it surely helps.

In this chapter and the next, we hope to put you on the road to becoming a multitalented, versatile teacher. In Chapter 6, you will take an in-depth look at the three most commonly known and used instructional alternatives, namely, *presentation, discussion,* and *independent study.* Then, at the end of the chapter you will find a brief overview of twenty-nine instructional alternatives, including these three. In Chapter 7, you will learn about four more of the twenty-nine: *cooperative learning, discovery learning, direct instruction,* and *individualized instruction.* Being aware of all the possible ways to teach and gaining in-depth knowledge of seven will serve you well.

We look in on presentation, discussion, and independent study simply because they are the staples in almost all teachers' instructional repertoires (Goodlad, 1983). They seem to persist over time. Accordingly, you need to be well-versed in each and skillful in its use.

Instructional Alternatives Defined

Just what is an instructional alternative? An **instructional alternative** is any teaching maneuver used to facilitate student learning and satisfaction. Over the centuries, a number have been developed, modified, and even combined (Broudy, 1963; Connell, 1987). We have identified twenty-nine. If you can't wait to find out what they are, turn to the section in the back of this chapter entitled Overview of Twenty-Nine Instructional Alternatives, which contains a brief, alphabetically organized description of each.

Presentations: Teaching as Telling and Showing

In this information age, it is critical that students have more and more knowledge. Teacher presentation is one way knowledge can be obtained. Therefore, presentation of information is one of a teacher's most important instructional functions (Rosenshine, 1987). Presentation is a form of **reception learning**, which falls within the cognitive school of thought described in Chapter 3, pages 59–60.

WHAT IS A PRESENTATION?

By definition, a **presentation** is an informative talk a more knowledgeable person makes to less knowledgeable persons. You will present, or lecture, if you tell less informed students when to use a semicolon, what a peninsula is, why the seasons change, or how to multiply fractions.

Showing can enhance telling, so teachers often accompany their talks with demonstrations. For example, in addition to telling students why the seasons change, you might also use a film, videotape, computer graphic, or mechanical model to provide a visual demonstration.

PURPOSE AND CHARACTERISTICS OF TEACHER PRESENTATIONS

The purpose of a presentation is *to inform an audience of certain facts, ideas, concepts, and explanations*. However, talks can be very different in terms of length, formality, and who does the talking. In other words, teacher talks have a number of characteristics. Think of the many different kinds you have experienced.

In terms of length, some were long and some were short. At times, a teacher presented or talked for a whole class period, without interruptions or questions. Perhaps the teacher said he would answer your questions at the end, but by then you had forgotten what to ask. Other talks were of short duration.

Teacher presentations also vary according to degree of formality. Speeches are, of course, more formal than talks, and talks interspersed with teacher questions or student questions are even less formal. When teachers talk in order to force students to think or reflect, they are practicing a version of what is called the Socratic technique. Socrates taught by questioning his listeners about their views and opinions (What do you think?) and then interrogating them further about what they said (Why do you think that?). He talked in order to probe his listeners' minds and to force them to confront their thoughts and ideas.

A third dimension of teacher presentation has to do with the presenter. Is she the teacher, a guest, perhaps another teacher, or a parent or community figure? Teachers working together to share their expertise engage in what is called **team teaching** or collaborative teaching. Sometimes the collaborator isn't even present. An image and voice may reach us by television, computer, radio, or telephone. When this occurs, the process is referred to as *distance education*. When prerecorded presentations are used as part of individualized, self-paced instructional programs, they are referred to as audio, or audiovisual, tutorials. To illustrate, a student doing independent study in Spanish might watch a videotaped analysis of a classic novel such as Cervantes's *Don Quixote*.

Figure 6.1 depicts the purpose and key attributes of a presentation.

6.1 Think of presentations you have experienced. What made some good and some bad?

FIGURE 6.1   Purpose and Key Characteristics of a Presentation

Purpose —— To orally present information, ideas, explanations

Characteristics {
Teacher or other person may present
Presentation may be live or recorded
Presentation may vary in length
Presentation may be formal or informal
}

GOOD PRESENTERS

How can you become a good presenter? Let's pursue the answer by looking first at the related research literature. It seems that on a personal level, you should be friendly, humorous, enthusiastic, verbally fluent (in other words, talk effortlessly and smoothly), and clear (Kindsvatter et al., 1988; Brown, 1987). Unfortunately, while such characteristics are helpful, they are not sufficient to make you a good presenter. You must also possess knowledge of your students (particularly with regard to their diversity) and, of course, have mastery of the subject you are presenting. In short, being a friendly, funny, dynamic, and talkative person will not do the job if you don't know your audience or what you are talking about. Don't be alarmed! Few people have all or even most of these desirable qualities. So everyone simply has to make the best of what they have and keep trying to improve. You cannot learn to teach overnight or even during your university preparation; it is a lifelong affair. You will find out how to be more humorous, enthusiastic, and clear in Chapters 10 and 11.

GOOD PRESENTATIONS

Persons who have thought about and studied the quality of teacher presentations tend to analyze them according to three primary factors: preparation, delivery, and closure (Brown, 1987; Gage & Berliner, 1976; Gilstrap & Martin, 1975; Rosenshine & Stevens, 1986). The following discussion centers on these three characteristics.

Preparation   As with any form of instruction, you must first establish your topic and general purpose and then set the specific learning objectives you want learners to achieve. Once you have done that, and once you are satisfied that a presentation truly is your best instructional alternative, you should collect, review, and organize the available subject matter resources. Also consider the kinds of examples and illustrations you will need in order to make the information understandable to your diverse students.

Suppose your presentation topic is "Dinosaurs." What is the general purpose of your presentation? It could be to introduce the topic, to provide students with knowledge of dinosaurs, or to promote critical thinking. Let's say your presentation aims to provide knowledge of dinosaurs. If so, what information do you want to present? What should students know? Will they need to understand what a dinosaur was and the various kinds that existed, how they lived, why they became extinct, or perhaps how paleontologists study them? Once this question is answered, your teaching objectives should come into focus. Let's assume that your purpose is twofold: to tell what a dinosaur was and to talk about the kinds that existed. You must now decide what specific knowledge, skills, or attitudes you wish to foster in your learners. Suppose you

 6.2   Given the characteristics of good presenters, which do you feel you have and which must you further develop? How might you do so?

6.3   To what extent do you think you are gaining knowledge about the things you will teach?

 6.4   What to you are the most important characteristics of a good presentation?

TABLE 6.1 Improving Teachers' Presentations with Visual Aids

Visual Aids	Uses
Printed material that serves as advance organizers: handouts, outlines, "questions to think about"	Give these to your students before you begin your presentation to help students focus their attention and to guide their note taking during the presentation.
Overhead transparencies: outlines, drawings, charts, diagrams, maps, cartoons, quotes, key words and ideas	Use these at key times in your presentation to emphasize a point, to review, to organize and categorize information, to stimulate interest, to add a touch of humor, and to summarize.
Pictures and prints: photographs, paintings, posters, slides	Photographs or posters of important people, places, objects, and artwork can greatly aid student comprehension and stimulate interest.
"Clips" on videotape	Showing a segment of a newscast or some televised special can bring events and people to life.
Maps, wall charts, and globes	These can be especially useful if students have desk-size versions or their own small copies.
Concrete objects (manipulatives)	When possible, have examples for students to look at and handle. A lesson on trees could include different types of leaves and bark.

Source: The content of this table is attributed to Dr. Jeffrey Peck, Gardner-Webb University.

decide that learners should be able to (1) define *dinosaur* as the name for two groups of reptiles that lived millions of years ago, (2) name the two groups, (3) describe the physical characteristics and living habits of the two groups and the species therein, and (4) locate where each group lived. Furthermore, you want students to compare how dinosaurs ruled the earth with how people rule the earth today. Once you have your purpose and learning objectives for the presentation in mind, you probably want to identify and collect instructional resources. What kinds? Look for computer software, books, articles, films, videotapes, models, exhibits, pictures. The use of visual aids can particularly increase students' interest and learning since we live in a visually oriented society. Sources of such instructional materials include the classroom, school library, public library, Internet, museums, and knowledgeable students. Students of all ages love dinosaurs. Tell students you are going to teach about dinosaurs, and you will be pleasantly surprised to see what they bring to class to share. Table 6.1 suggests how selected visual aids can improve your presentations.

With purpose and objectives in mind and resources collected, you are now ready to review your subject and create a plan for your talk. Keep in mind the diversity of your students—their interests, abilities, and background knowledge. *Be especially prepared to introduce concepts or ideas that are new to them.* Figure 6.2 provides important information about how to teach a new concept.

In summary, preparing a presentation includes: (1) establishing the general purpose of the presentation and the specific learning objectives, (2) collecting and reviewing information to be presented, and (3) organizing or planning delivery.

Delivery Now we are talking about performance, about the presentation itself. Here you want to do many important things: get your students' attention, tell them what they are going to learn and what they are expected to know and be able to do, make the presentation clear, emphasize important points, monitor their understanding, and promote questions and comments. Do these things supportively, enthusiastically, and perhaps with a touch of humor and fun.

Do you remember the cartoon in Chapter 3, "First you have to get their attention"? Attention is where it all starts and, believe us, nothing good happens without it. In Chapter 3, you found that getting students' attention is easier when

The term *concept* is used to refer to a group of ideas or objects that are alike and thus share a common name or label, such as tables, clouds, dogs, or dinosaurs. We learn many concepts through everyday experience rather than in school. Examples include hot, cold, wet, dry, loud, and quiet. However, a major function of formal education is to teach concepts. Remember when you were taught such concepts as "a meter," "carbon dioxide," "poetry," "the color wheel," "treble," and "long jump"? If your concepts were well taught, you learned and remembered them.

Teachers can present concepts in two ways, either through **expository teaching** or **discovery learning**. Since this section of the chapter is about presentations (expository teaching), the following classical concept-teaching procedure relates to the discussion. The concept *peninsula* is used in this example.

1. Begin with a clear definition that describes the attributes of the concept: "A peninsula is a *land area almost entirely surrounded by water* and *connected to the mainland* by a single strip of land or isthmus." (The attributes are in italics)

2. Next, provide examples of the concept and relate the examples to the definition: "Look at the map. Arabia and Alaska are the largest peninsulas in the world. India is a peninsula with a very large mainland connection. The Baja Peninsula in lower California is a typical peninsula. Florida is a peninsula. Each is an area of land almost circled by water."

3. Now provide nonexamples or negative examples:
   "Mexico is not a peninsula. It is connected to land on two sides. Australia is not a peninsula. It is completely surrounded by water."

4. Check for understanding:
   "Which of the following are peninsulas? Korea, Turkey, Italy, Scandinavia, Newfoundland, Greenland, South America? Why?"

For an in-depth look at concept learning, see Hamilton and Ghatala, 1994, pp. 149–166.

---

learners have had pleasant, rewarding school experiences (especially ones that relate somehow to your presentation) and when they have had some prior interest in your topic. As a learner, if I'm a "happy camper" and if I have a dinosaur model collection, I'm with you. If I'm an underachiever who thinks dinosaurs are like old teachers, watch out! That is why in Chapter 5, Planning Instruction, our lesson plan format contains a section on set induction. Winning coaches are great motivators. So are winning teachers.

As noted earlier, presentation fits the descriptions of expository teaching and reception learning from Chapter 3. Therefore, the rules given in Chapter 3 for good expository teaching apply here. They include: (1) present the learners with the learning objectives—tell them what they are expected to know and to be able to do, (2) use an advance organizer (relate new information to what they already know), (3) present information in an organized, step-by-step manner (don't overwhelm or underwhelm), (4) expect pupil interaction in the form of questions and comments, (5) move from general to specific ideas or information, (6) when teaching a new idea or concept, use both examples and nonexamples of it (Figure 6.2), (7) use good explanations, and (8) encourage learners to reflect on and apply what they have learned ("Are there differences between the way dinosaurs and humans have ruled the earth?").

Figure 6.3 provides three simple rules to follow in order to make an explanation understandable.

Handouts You have undoubtedly attended presentations where the presenter distributed handouts containing some kind of related information and material. You probably found them helpful when they did any or all of the following: (1) made clear the purpose of the talk and what you were expected to know or to be able to do, (2) provided questions that helped you focus on important points, (3) contained an outline of the main points, or (4) included a quiz to check your understanding.

FIGURE 6.3 Making a Good Explanation

Teachers use explanation for at least two purposes. In one case, we explain a concept, idea, procedure, or rule so as to make it understandable. Thus, we explain a concept (global warming), a procedure (how to subtract), or a rule (we raise our hand to be recognized). In a second case, we explain something in order to account for its occurrence: why global warming occurs, how the subtraction algorithm works, or why the class must raise hands. Here explanation is akin to giving reasons.

A good explanation has three characteristics: It must be

- Complete
- Accurate
- Clear

When you give an explanation, remember C-A-C.

Of course, students should be called on to give explanations too. The quality of their explanations can also be judged according to C-A-C guidelines.

Source: D. Cruickshank & K. Metcalf. (1995). Explaining. In T. Husen & T. N. Postlewaite (Eds.), *International encyclopedia of education.* Second Edition. Oxford: Pergamon Press.

Closure   Everything has to end. So how should you conclude the dinosaur presentation? Several recommendations are consistent with what we know about short- and long-term memory and reception learning. Since you told learners what they *would learn* at the outset, now tell them what they *have learned.* Review and summary are appropriate. Reiterate the major concepts, facts, and generalizations that you want learners to recall. Of course, you might consider drawing this information out of your students by way of questioning or **recitation.** Make them rummage around in their own minds.

Next, connect what students have learned about dinosaurs to what they knew prior to the presentation ("This is what you knew then. This is what you know now."). Help students see how their knowledge has grown with regard to what a dinosaur is, how dinosaurs are grouped, and so forth. This effort to tie new information to old enhances long-term memory and information retrieval.

Finally, check for understanding. Be especially sensitive to whether your students can use the information at the higher cognitive levels, demonstrating application, analysis, synthesis, and evaluation, as described in Chapter 5. For example, if it is your purpose, can learners generalize what they have learned about the lives of dinosaurs to other species? To what extent were the habits of dinosaurs similar to those of today's creatures?

A summary of the qualities of good presenters and good presentations is contained in Table 6.2. This is one of several tables contained in this and the next chapter that you will want to keep handy for future reference.

ADVANTAGES AND LIMITATIONS OF PRESENTATIONS

Try Activities 6.1 & 6.2

We may choose a particular instructional alternative such as presentation for a number of reasons. Two especially come to mind. First, we may feel attracted to it because it meets or satisfies our *personality needs.* Second, it may meet our *professional needs.*

All of us have basic personality needs. Murray (1963) has been the most influential person to identify and classify them. (See Figure 6.4.) In part, then, the use of a given instructional alternative is beneficial to the extent that it meets these needs. This would be true for teachers (users) and students (recipients) alike.

TABLE 6.2   Qualities of Good Presenters and Good Presentations

Good Presenters Are . . .	Good Presentations Include . . .
• Knowledgeable about the subject matter • Aware of learner diversity • Friendly • Humorous • Enthusiastic • Verbally fluent and audible	*When preparing:* • Choose the topic • Establish the general purpose • Set specific learner objectives • Collect, review subject matter and useful material • Plan the presentation *When delivering:* • Get students' attention • Tell students what they will learn and what they must be able to do • Relate new information to that in students' long-term memory • Present information step-by-step • Move from the general to the specific • Don't overwhelm or underwhelm • Emphasize important points • Use examples and illustrations to make things clearer • Use variety, such as visual aids, to maintain attention • Monitor understanding by promoting questions, comments • Avoid digressions *When closing:* • Review and summarize important points • Secure new learning to previous knowledge • Check for ability to use new knowledge at a higher cognitive level

FIGURE 6.4   Our Personality Needs According to Murray

Among other things, people have the need for:

Achievement: To do difficult tasks well and quickly
Acquisition: To acquire [in this case, knowledge]
Affiliation: To form friendships, cooperate, join groups
Autonomy: To strive for independence and freedom
Cognizance: To explore, read, seek knowledge
Construction: To organize and build
Deference: To admire, respect, cooperate with, or follow others
Dominance: To influence, control, lead, direct others
Exhibition: To attract attention, make an impression, excite, amuse
Exposition: To give information, relate facts, explain, demonstrate
Failure or harm avoidance: To avoid shame, humiliation, anxiety
Orderliness: To arrange, organize
Play: To relax, enjoy, have fun, seek diversion
Recognition: To seek praise, reward
Similance: To agree with and believe others, to empathize
Succorance: To seek acceptance, help, or protection

Source: H. Murray. (1963). *Explorations in personality.* New York: Oxford University Press.

Beyond having personality needs, teachers also seem to share professional, job-related needs or goals (Cruickshank et al., 1980). They result from the circumstances of being a teacher and conducting a teacher's work, and they include:

- **Affiliation**—The need to establish good relationships with others in the school (students, teachers, administrators, staff)
- **Control**—The need to have students behave appropriately (for example, to be relatively orderly and courteous)
- **Parent relationships**—The need to have good relationships with significant others in the lives of students
- **Student success**—The need to help students succeed academically and socially
- **Time**—The need to have enough and to use it wisely

6.5 Which of these personality and job-related needs might affect you the most? How might they affect your teaching?

Now the questions become: (1) What teacher personality and professional needs is a given instructional alternative likely to meet? (2) What student personality needs might it similarly satisfy? Let's look at the possibilities for the instructional alternative at hand, that is, presentations.

Benefits for Teachers   Looking over Murray's list (Figure 6.4), we hypothesize that planning and giving presentations might satisfy teachers with the following personality needs:

- **Cognizance**—The need to explore, read, and seek knowledge
- **Orderliness/construction**—The need to arrange, organize, and build
- **Dominance**—The need to direct and to be in charge
- **Exposition**—The need to give to others, to share information, to relate facts, to explain and demonstrate
- **Exhibition**—The need to receive attention, praise, and commendation

6.6 Would making presentations satisfy any of *your* needs?

Considering the professional, job-related needs that come with teaching (Cruickshank et al., 1980), we think many teachers may perceive presentations as meeting their need for:

- **Control**—Presentations likely enable teachers to monitor the class better.
- **Student success**—Presentations by definition should be informative and increase student understanding.
- **Time**—Presentations are considered to be an efficient use of time.

Benefits for Students What student personality needs might good presentations meet? We speculate that there are several:

- **Acquisition**—The need students have to acquire information
- **Deference**—The need to admire others, in this case, the presenter
- **Similance**—The need to agree with or believe others
- **Succorance**—The need to seek help

Additionally, good presentations can help students develop important learning skills, including the ability to listen, take notes, and think critically. (See Spotlight on Research 6.1.)

Limitations   On the downside, teacher presentations can fail to involve learners sufficiently, be boring, be overwhelming in terms of content or length, and trigger frustration in learners who do not have good attention, note-taking, or memory skills (Freiberg & Driscoll, 1996).

WHEN TEACHER PRESENTATIONS SHOULD BE USED

Gage and Berliner (1976, 1991) tell us when to lecture. They believe that it is an appropriate instructional alternative when (1) information dissemination is the main goal, (2) the information to be disseminated is not readily available in another form, such as a book, (3) the information must be especially selected, organized, and presented for a specific group of learners, (4) it is important to arouse interest in the information, and (5) the material need not be remembered for a long time.

Although these factors define when presentations should be used, in actuality you will probably make use of them (1) if your former teachers frequently presented, and for the most part you liked and learned from them, (2) if you have prior knowledge about the topic or subject, (3) if you like to talk and have a knack for it, (4) if you believe your students will learn the material best this way, (5) if you have few related instructional resources, (6) if you lack time or competence to facilitate learning in another way, and (7) if presentations meet your personal and professional needs.

SUMMARY ON PRESENTATION

You have learned that informative teacher talks are common occurrences and that they differ in many respects. For example, they differ in degree of formality and length, with informal and shorter talks generally preferable. Presentations also differ according to whether they are live or recorded. To conduct a good presentation, the presenter should demonstrate certain qualities and follow certain procedures, as Table 6.2 noted. Like all instructional alternatives, teacher presentations have advantages and disadvantages for both teachers and learners. In general, when dissemination of information is the goal, they are efficient and economical. Like any instructional alternative, teacher presentations have their place and contribute to learner achievement and to teacher and learner satisfaction.

Try Activity 6.3

6.7 How do you feel about using presentation?

Discussion: Learning through Informative Interaction

Lots of people, perhaps even you, think teachers talk too much. Scholars have provided evidence that teachers talk two-thirds of the time that class is in session (Flanders, 1970). Do you get tired of constantly hearing what someone else has to

TABLE 6.3 Recitation and Discussion Compared

	Recitation	Discussion
Definition	When a teacher asks students a series of relatively short-answer questions	When a student or students and a teacher converse to share information, ideas, and so forth
Purpose	To determine what students remember or understand	To review what students have learned, encourage students to reflect on their ideas or opinions, explore an issue, resolve a problem, or improve face-to-face communication skills
Conceptual level	Questions are usually lower-level, cognitive domain. *Examples:* "When was America discovered?" "What is the sum of the angles of a triangle?" "What are the themes of Fitzgerald's novels?"	Discussion usually is at a higher cognitive level or may be in the affective domain. *Examples:* "What leads to exploration and discovery?" "Are exploration and discovery bad or good?" "If we find life on another planet, should we try to improve it?"
Role of the teacher	"Quizmaster"	Facilitator-moderator, participant, or observer-recorder

say? Do you get squirmy if you have to sit and listen too long? To make matters worse, you may already have acquired from books or other teachers some of the information you are hearing. Listening can become boring, boring, boring! "Why doesn't the teacher let us talk about what we know and how we feel?" For this and other sound reasons, astute teachers include discussion as part of their repertoire.

WHAT IS A DISCUSSION?

6.8 How do like discussions? What has been your experience with them?

A **discussion** is a situation wherein students, or students and a teacher, converse to share information, ideas, or opinions or work to resolve a problem. Conversely, a discussion is not a situation wherein a teacher asks a question, a student or students answer, and then the teacher asks another question. This question-answer-question format is called **recitation.** Its purpose is mainly to quiz students to determine what they know or understand. Some differences between a true discussion and a recitation are illustrated in Table 6.3.

PURPOSES AND CHARACTERISTICS OF DISCUSSION

Purposes of Discussion   A discussion can serve a variety of purposes (Gall, 1987; Gall & Gall, 1990; Roby, 1981). One purpose is to review and extend what students have learned in order *to ensure their mastery of a subject.* Hill (1977) presents us with a discussion model for subject matter mastery that follows certain steps. First, your students see, hear, or read something. Perhaps they view a documentary on using animals in medical research. Then they discuss what they have seen and heard. Among other things, they give attention to terms and concepts that need explanation, to the major ideas presented, and to the major message. Of course, the discussion could go well beyond merely processing (clarifying and rehearsing) the information received. You could, Hill advises, engage students in higher-order thinking by getting them to talk about the authenticity of the message or its effect if carried out. Such discussions primarily help us learn through rehearsal, that is, recalling and talking about things so they become more firmly fixed in our memories.

A discussion can also be held when the purpose is *to have students examine their ideas or opinions.* After studying about the use of animals in medical research, students could be asked to share their views about its appropriateness. The following questions would prompt students to examine what they think and feel about other topics. Is television helpful or harmful? Should persons be assisted in committing suicide? Should the United States make stronger efforts to stop illegal immigration? Should teacher tenure be abolished? Should persons who have not completed a professional education program be allowed to teach?

A third purpose a discussion might have is *to solve a problem*. Students are presented with political, economic, or social problems to discuss and resolve, such as: How can better relationships be established with China? How can we reduce the national debt? How can violence by children be reduced? Closer to home, you and your classmates could address such questions as how to work with students at risk, how to locate instructional resources, or how we can become better classroom problem solvers.

Sometimes a discussion can help students *to improve their face-to-face or interpersonal communication skills.* The purpose is for learners to become better at being good contributors and active listeners, making a point, handling disagreements and conflicts, overcoming fear of speaking in public, and so forth.

Certainly, these are four good reasons for including discussion in your teaching repertoire. Can you think of others?

Characteristics of Discussions   We can consider discussions on the basis of a number of attributes or characteristics: the interaction pattern, the teacher's role, group size and composition, and group arrangement.

Interaction Pattern   We have said that discussion differs from recitation, or the teacher question-student answer technique; interaction during discussions is less formal and more conversational. Moreover, the conversation can occur among students as well as between students and teacher. In the most lively discussions, everyone is an active participant.

Group Size and Composition   The whole class can engage in a common discussion, or it can be divided into groups. All other factors being equal, small groups are preferable since they allow more potential for participation. The composition of a group is also at issue. That is, should members be similar (homogeneous) or dissimilar (heterogeneous)? Arguments can be made for either position.

Group Arrangement   One rule seems to hold: To converse, participants should be face to face. Thus, arranging discussion participants in a circle is a common occurrence. On occasion, a panel discussion makes sense. A panel discussion is carried on when a preselected group of students discusses in front of others who observe. Students on the panel should be arranged face to face. Students who observe

6.9 When, for the purpose of discussion, might it be preferable to form heterogeneous and homogeneous groups?

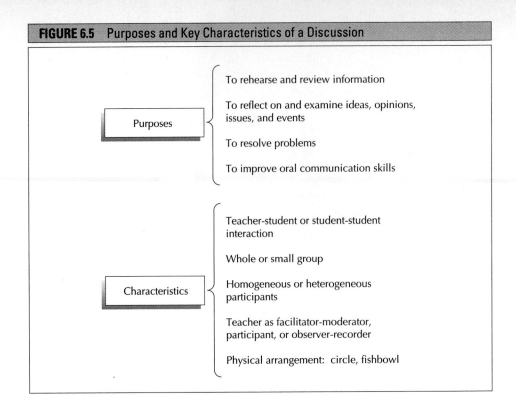

FIGURE 6.5 Purposes and Key Characteristics of a Discussion

Purposes
- To rehearse and review information
- To reflect on and examine ideas, opinions, issues, and events
- To resolve problems
- To improve oral communication skills

Characteristics
- Teacher-student or student-student interaction
- Whole or small group
- Homogeneous or heterogeneous participants
- Teacher as facilitator-moderator, participant, or observer-recorder
- Physical arrangement: circle, fishbowl

might surround the panel. This procedure and arrangement is referred to as a fishbowl—everyone is watching the panel or "fish."

Role of the Teacher   Of course, the interaction pattern suggests a number of different teacher roles and responsibilities. If the interaction is strictly among students, the teacher serves as observer, recorder, and perhaps arbitrator. At other times, you will want to be a member of the discussion group but not its official leader. You merely want to participate. Other occasions may call for you to be the facilitator-moderator. In this case, according to Van Ments (1990), the duty of the teacher is to "enable learners to reflect critically on their experiences . . . to explore different perspectives, to consider how their knowledge is rooted in personal experiences" (p. 12). The role you choose to play—observer, participant, or facilitator—will vary according to circumstances such as the purpose of the discussion and the maturity and experience of the students.

For a visual summarization of the purposes and key characteristics of a discussion, see Figure 6.5.

GOOD DISCUSSION LEADERS

What does it take to be a good discussion leader? We believe you need to possess an assortment of beliefs and skills. First, let's look at four beliefs. Basically, discussion leaders should believe that students, like most persons, desire to communicate with others (Gall & Gall, 1976). We noted previously that teachers like to talk. Well, students like to talk, too, don't they? Persons who utilize discussion as an instructional alternative use it in part to legitimatize classroom conversation, that is, to make it acceptable and purposeful.

Teachers who use discussion also believe in the purposes of discussion: review and extension of what students have learned, examination of ideas and opinions, problem solving, and increased interpersonal communication skills. Democratic forms of government depend on persons so educated.

In addition to believing in the purposes of discussion, discussion users must have confidence in their students' capacities to think effectively. They have faith that, with guidance, students will employ higher-level cognitive skills such as application, analysis, synthesis, and evaluation. Discussion users also believe that by engaging students in discussion, they can accomplish many affective goals, such as encouraging students to respond and value. You may recall that these terms were introduced in the section entitled Writing Instructional Objectives in Chapter 5.

A fourth belief held by persons who favor discussion is that involving students in a well-conceived group experience will enhance their psychological and social growth. In such situations, they can learn to feel good about themselves and to accept others. In addition, shy students can often be encouraged to participate, especially in smaller discussion groups. Good discussion leaders encourage and enhance student pride, dignity, sense of efficacy or personal power, and caring.

Beyond holding to these beliefs, you will be a better discussion leader if you have related skills. For example, can you limit your own talk? Remember, this is the students' conversational opportunity. Persons who have observed discussion remind us that frequently teachers talk too much even during discussions (Dillon, 1985, 1988). Could it be that many of us simply need to rein in our compulsion to talk? We must learn how to get *students* to ask more questions, explore and speculate more, make more references to *their* personal experiences, and so forth.

Additionally, you must be a facilitator, human relations expert, clarifier, and summarizer. As a facilitator, you are responsible for beginning the discussion, moving it briskly, and keeping the group on task and attentive. As a human relations expert, your job is to make everyone feel comfortable and important and to encourage full and equal participation. You must also moderate differences of opinion. As a clarifier, you must ensure that everyone's message is heard and understood. This might require that certain students' comments be limited, rephrased, or probed. Finally, as a summarizer, you need to be skillful in drawing the conversation together and ensuring that everyone sees the progress they have made toward the stated goal.

Bridges (1979) tells us that you also need skill in teaching three kinds of communication skills to your students. You must be able to help them know how to make remarks that are reasonable, to know when and for how long to speak, and to know how critical they should be of the remarks others make.

GOOD DISCUSSIONS

Can you recall thinking to yourself, Wow! That was a good discussion! What makes a discussion good? As is true of any instructional alternative, a discussion is good when it results in learning and satisfaction. Both of these outcomes depend on how the discussion was prepared, presented, and concluded (Bridges, 1979; Dillon, 1988, 1995; Gall, 1987; Gall & Gall, 1976; Jacobson et al., 1985).

Preparation   First, you need to decide whether you should use a discussion and why you want to use one. Do you remember the four purposes—to review and extend knowledge, examine ideas, solve problems, and improve communication skills? For illustration, let's say your purpose is to review what students have learned and to extend that knowledge. More specifically, let's say your goal is for students to review and extend what they have learned about dinosaurs from reading a hypothetical article called "The Age of Dinosaurs" in *National Geographic World,* a magazine written for students. From the article, the students ascertain how scientists have learned about dinosaurs and what they have learned. Consequently, students could discuss a number of things. Some are basic and factual. When did dinosaurs live? Where did they live? What kinds of dinosaurs existed when? How did dinosaurs live? What do scientists do to study dinosaurs?

6.10   Which of the four beliefs of good discussion leaders do you hold?

6.11   How do you feel about your abilities as a facilitator, human relations expert, clarifier, summarizer, and teacher of communication skills?

At a higher level, you can ask participants to analyze, synthesize, and evaluate using the following ploy. "Dinosaurs haven't really become extinct—birds belong on the dinosaur family tree. So, you have a dinosaur bath in your backyard, you dine on roast dinosaur at Thanksgiving, and you munch on dinosaur nuggets at McDonalds. . . . What is a family tree? How do you suppose paleontologists decided birds and dinosaurs are related?" Another premise for discussion might be "Finding out about dinosaurs is both very time-consuming and expensive. Why is it so important? Couldn't the time and money be spent on other things society needs more urgently?" The last questions move the discussion into the realm of reason-seeking and addressing an issue.

Another early consideration when preparing for a discussion relates to student preparation. Are they ready? Perhaps you will need to remind the class or individuals about the need to listen, to take turns, and to be clear, reasonable, considerate, and so forth. Some older children may have watched *Firing Line, Meet the Press,* or *The McLaughlin Group* on television. As a result, they may believe a discussion is a verbal "knock-em-down" that stops just short of mental, if not physical, fisticuffs. Of course, if students have already been involved in discussions with good leaders, they should be more effective participants.

Try Activity 6.4

Next, you must think about your role, which raises questions about grouping, physical arrangements, and time management. If your students are not familiar with discussion, you will have to play the role of facilitator-moderator. Relatedly, you may want to hold a *whole-class* discussion with a less experienced group. That way you can exercise more control over such matters as staying on task, providing for equitable participation, and ensuring that everyone enjoys psychological safety. Students more experienced and mature in discussion enable you to take less dominant, directive roles.

Delivery   Once you have determined your purpose, students' readiness, your role, group arrangements, and time constraints, you are now ready to deliver. This means (1) making certain your students understand the purpose of the discussion ("Let's think further about the material on dinosaurs we have read"); (2) ensuring that you have related the discussion to something students previously learned or to something upcoming; (3) informing them of the discussion questions and potential information sources they can use in preparation ("Some discussion questions can be answered directly from the reading; for others, you will need to come up with your own answers or opinions"); reminding them of discussion rules (perhaps by handing out or posting a set of guidelines such as those in Figure 6.6); and (4) organizing the participants. If several small groups will discuss, you may want to appoint or ask each group to select a facilitator and a recorder, and, of course, the students in these roles must know what is expected of them.

FIGURE 6.6   Discussion Guidelines for Students

- Everyone should have an equal opportunity to contribute.
- Encourage your classmates to join in.
- Ensure that everyone contributes by waiting your turn and taking part about as much as everyone else.
- Listen carefully to what others say and feel.
- Work to understand and, whenever possible, to support what others say and feel.
- Understand that your knowledge and ideas may not always be right.
- Stay on target and help others do the same.
- Be gracious. Avoid attacking and belittling your peers.

Throughout a discussion, effective performance of your role as either facilitator-moderator, participant, or observer-recorder is critical. You will especially need to remember that this is the students' time to talk: Your role is to encourage participation and elevate the cognitive or affective level of the discourse. *Give the discussants a purpose, a plan, and freedom to operate.*

Use of discussion as an instructional technique draws support and direction from various learning theories (described in Chapter 3), depending upon the purpose of the discussion. To illustrate, suppose the purpose of the discussion is to rehearse or practice. Such learning tasks are easier for students when teachers put to work beliefs and findings related to information processing and behaviorism. Or, suppose the purpose of the discussion is to reflect on events, ideas, or opinions. In such cases, we would want to apply the beliefs and findings from the humanistic school, particularly those relating to values clarification. If the purpose is to engage in problem solving, we might want to use what researchers know about meaningful learning.

Closure   At the appropriate moment, the discussion should end. Sometimes it is fitting to close a discussion earlier than planned—for example, when the discussion has accomplished its purpose or when it is failing to do so. In any case, with the possible assistance of the participants, you need to pull the learning together. At this stage, review with students the extent to which they accomplished the purpose of the discussion. Point out where they need to go from here, that is, how the discussion will tie in with future work. A summary of the qualities of good discussion leaders and good discussions appears in Table 6.4.

6.12   What do you think are the most important characteristics of a good discussion?

TABLE 6.4   Qualities of Good Discussion Leaders and Good Discussions

Good Leaders	Good Discussions
• Believe students want and need to engage in purposeful talk • Believe students should be asked to review and use information, explore issues, and resolve problems • Believe students are capable of thinking and doing for themselves • Believe students can be helped to develop via discussion • Control their own talk • Get students thinking • Serve as skillful facilitators, human relations experts, clarifiers, and summarizers • Are skillful in teaching communication skills	*When preparing:* • Establish the general purpose • Set specific learner objectives • Consider the readiness of the class and individuals for discussion • Decide what role you will play, the class grouping, physical arrangements, and time allowance • Plan the discussion *When overseeing:* • Get students' attention • Ensure that participants understand and see the value in the purpose or goal • Relate the goal and task to previous knowledge and future work • Set out the specific questions or statements to be discussed • Remind participants of discussion rules • Monitor to ensure on-task behavior, balanced participation, and understanding • Encourage participants, elevate the level of discourse *When closing:* • Do so at the most appropriate time rather than at a specific time • Summarize progress toward the goal(s) • Tie new learning to previous knowledge • Establish what the participants might next want to know or be able to do

ADVANTAGES AND LIMITATIONS OF DISCUSSION

What are the advantages and limitations of using classroom discussion? Again, we will consider psychological and professional benefits for teachers first.

Try Activity 6.5

Benefits for Teachers   We think discussions offer quite different psychological benefits than presentations do. Unlike presentations, they probably do not seem to meet teachers' needs for cognizance, orderliness, dominance, exposition, exhibition, and recognition. On the other hand, planning and conducting discussions likely do meet the following personal needs Murray posited (Figure 6.4):

- The **construction** need to arrange and organize.
- The need to **play** or seek diversion, change, and relaxation. Teachers sometimes need a break from being in charge and standing "front and center." They occasionally enjoy "giving the ball" to students and letting them carry on. Use of discussion allows teachers to lean back and enjoy a little of what students do.
- The **affiliation** need to get closer to others (students).

6.13   How do you feel about using discussion?

- The need to **avoid failure,** embarrassment, shame, or ridicule. On occasion, teachers admit that they may not be knowledgeable enough in some subject to give an informative presentation. In such instances they may decide to let learners obtain the information from another source and then discuss it with them.

Discussions can also help teachers meet certain professional, job-related needs (Cruickshank et al., 1980):

- The **affiliation** need to establish good relationships with students
- The need for **student success**—the need to help students succeed academically and socially

The need for affiliation seems powerful. It appears to exist as a teacher personality need, a teacher role-derived need, and, as we shall see shortly, a student personality need.

An added job-related benefit of using discussion is that it enables us to (1) prepare students for roles as active citizens who can think analytically and critically about information, ideas, and opinions and form personal perceptions and judgments; (2) encourage effective interpersonal relationships among students; and (3) meet legitimate student needs.

Benefits for Students   The advantages that presentations have for some students—**acquisition, deference, similance, and succorance**—can also accrue through discussion. Students still are able to acquire knowledge, admire and emulate others, and cooperate with and depend on others—only the "others" are their peers rather than their teachers. However, the list of advantages does not end here. Additionally, discussions will probably appeal to learners who have:

6.14   As a student, what advantages do discussions seem to have for you?

- The need to **play,** to seek diversion, change, and relation
- The **exposition** need to give others information
- The **exhibition** need to attract a certain amount of attention to oneself
- The **recognition** need to receive praise and commendation
- The **dominance** need to lead and direct; a need that is particularly well met when the discussion leader or leaders are students
- The **affiliation** need to form associations and friendships

6.15   Why do you think discussions are not nearly as prevalent as teacher presentations?

Since discussion offers so many benefits to students, you might wonder why it isn't used more (Gall, 1987). Perhaps a partial answer is that certain teacher personality and professional needs are better met using another instructional alternative.

Only a small number of studies of discussion have taken place in elementary and secondary classrooms. The rest have been conducted using university students, workers in business and industry, and adult volunteers for psychological studies. Gall (1987) provides us with the most recent summary of those findings. The interpretations and explanations, if any, are ours.

- Discussion generally is more effective than teacher presentation or lecture for promoting retention of knowledge and higher-level thinking (such as analysis, synthesis, and evaluation). This likely is true because the opportunity for rehearsing or using information is greater during discussion.
- Use of discussion generally results in increased motivation to learn. This probably is because engagement in discussion meets the personality needs of many students.
- Discussion is effective in changing attitudes and, to some extent, in advancing moral reasoning. Discussion can create a forum for ideas and idea changes.
- Discussion is less effective than lecture in helping students acquire factual knowledge. Presentations appear to be superior for sheer communication of information.
- After a discussion group reaches consensus, it tends to disregard any further, high-quality ideas that are presented. The group probably has struggled to reach a consensus and fears that new ideas would distract from it.
- Less capable but socially aggressive individuals may dominate discussions.
- Small group size results in more participation, increased satisfaction among members, and greater academic achievement.
- Groups in which members are more alike or homogeneous are more cohesive, communicate more, and experience greater self-esteem.

Heterogeneous groups may be more effective in performance. Birds of a feather may feel more comfortable together, but they may not challenge or assist one another sufficiently.

- Groups without a teacher leader or assertive members interact more often. They also achieve greater satisfaction from the discussion and are effective in handling complex tasks.

Watson's (1983) study is not among those that Gall reviewed. Watson observed ninety "discussion lessons" in English secondary school classrooms and concluded, somewhat negatively, that (1) students were mostly held accountable for knowing facts; (2) teachers did most of the higher-level thinking such as making generalizations, hypothesizing, and synthesizing; and (3) teachers did most of the talking. Watson concludes that most English teachers prefer whole-class discussion, which in this case amounted to a euphemism for teacher question-student answer, or recitation.

Beyond meeting student psychological needs, discussions also meet certain learning and educational requirements. For example, good discussions should capture and maintain attention; help students develop listening, thinking, and speaking skills; promote social and psychological development by encouraging assertiveness, self-confidence, cooperation, and tolerance; and facilitate moving information into long-term memory through rehearsal.

Limitations   On the negative side, poorly conceptualized or poorly conducted discussions are aimless, time-consuming, and therefore inefficient and unpleasant (Van Ments, 1990; Battistich, Solomon, & Delucchi, 1993).

Spotlight on Research 6.2 summarizes recent findings as to what makes an effective discussion. To find out what students say about discussion, see Spotlight on Research 6.3.

WHEN DISCUSSIONS SHOULD BE USED

A few guidelines will help you know when to select the discussion alternative from your teaching repertoire, dust it off, and put it to use. As a general rule, you should use discussion when any of its purposes coincide with your goal. Consequently, engage students in discussion when your goal is to review information, examine ideas and opinions, solve problems, or improve oral communication skills.

When researchers at Stanford University (Phelan, Davidson, & Cao, 1992) asked high school students questions about their school experiences, they received many comments on both teachers and teaching. From these comments, the researchers concluded that "both high- and low-achieving students prefer teachers who draw them into the learning process by holding discussions in which ideas are explored and thoughts, feelings, and opinions are shared" (p. 700). Furthermore, the researchers concluded from students' remarks that during discussions, learners feel important and feel that what they think counts. Students are particularly complimentary of teachers who make the classroom a place where they feel comfortable in expressing themselves. As one student reported,

> [The teacher] makes the class feel comfortable talking about themselves and really expressing their feelings. Like if you read something and everyone interprets it differently, she wants to hear everyone's opinion. (p. 700)

You should also use discussion when you are more interested in long-term memory, higher-order thinking, motivation, attitude change, or moral reasoning. Finally, use discussion when it best meets your students' social and psychological needs. Discussion is effective when students have been mostly inactive listeners, when a more relaxed atmosphere is warranted, and when it would be beneficial to enhance student-to-student friendships and affiliation.

Since there is no research evidence on when or how teachers actually use discussions, our guess is that teachers initiate discussions mostly when pursuing the above goals. However, we are sure you will be guided by other things in your selection of discussion. One is your past experience. Have you been involved in many discussions, and are your remembrances of those experiences positive? Second, how adept are you as an interaction leader, facilitator, or participant? Are you pretty skillful with group interaction? Third, what is your willingness to give up or share the "chalk and talk"? Many teachers, and not just novices, are afraid to let students participate for fear of losing their intellectual or even managerial authority.

SUMMARY ON DISCUSSION

Discussions serve at least four purposes: they can review and extend knowledge, examine ideas and opinions, solve problems, and improve oral communication skills. Most classroom discussions serve the first purpose; that is, students review information they have previously learned from a presentation or from reading. Even then, however, students should review the material at the highest cognitive level. They should be prompted to analyze, synthesize, and evaluate information rather than merely be asked to respond to lower-level, factual questions as in a prototypical recitation.

Try Activity 6.6

In addition to their many purposes, discussions are characterized by multiple interactions, with the teacher assuming the role of either facilitator-monitor, participant, or observer-recorder. Discussions may be whole-class or small-group in nature, and groups may vary in size and composition. For maximum effectiveness, participants must be arranged face to face.

Good discussion leaders need to hold certain beliefs and possess special abilities which are summarized in Table 6.4, column 1. Discussions can be improved by following the guidelines for preparation, delivery, and closure found in Table 6.4, column 2.

A number of advantages accrue from using discussion. Discussion provides personal and professional benefits for teachers and personal and educational benefits for participants. Research shows that discussions promote retention of knowledge and high-level thinking. They also contribute to learner motivation, attitude change, and somewhat enhanced moral reasoning.

Guidelines help teachers determine when to use discussions. Most likely, your actual use of discussion will be affected by past experiences, related abilities, and confidence in sharing teaching and learning with students.

Independent Study: Teaching as Giving and Guiding Seat-Work and Homework Assignments

A third commonly used instructional alternative is independent study or work which, at times, is referred to as "seat work." We all can recall the countless hours we have spent, mostly alone, working on school assignments. Estimates are that students spend 70 percent of their in-class time working independently (Fisher et al., 1978). Add to that the time given to homework, and it's obvious that teachers rely heavily on independent study or practice (Dunkin, 1987).

WHAT IS INDEPENDENT STUDY?

We define independent study as any school-related assignment students do more or less alone. Examples include reading, writing a composition, rehearsing words for a spelling test, and preparing a report. When we think of students "working," we often envision them engaged in some kind of independent study or practice assignment.

PURPOSE AND CHARACTERISTICS OF INDEPENDENT STUDY

We can describe independent study on the basis of its purposes, types, teacher role, and the context in which it takes place.

Purposes of Independent Study   Teachers involve students in independent study for many reasons, some more justifiable than others. It is most justifiable *when students need to rehearse or practice something*. In Chapter 3, you saw how important it is for learners to rehearse what they are learning by thinking about it or repeating it. That is partly why we have interspersed questions and activities in the margins of this book. Rehearsal is part of information processing: it gets new information into our long-term memories.

As a teacher, you will probably use independent practice when you want to be certain that your learners gain specific knowledge or skills. Thus, if you are an elementary or middle school teacher, your students definitely will rehearse or practice reading comprehension skills, language arts skills such as writing paragraphs, and mathematics skills such as solving story problems and computation. Secondary teachers provide students with practice too, as do athletic coaches. If you have

6.16 What good and bad personal school experiences come to mind when you think of independent study?

"It's moments like this—when they're all so very, very quiet—that I get a strange, uneasy feeling."

participated in sports, think of the innumerable times you have practiced shooting foul shots, dribbling a soccer ball, or flutter kicking until these acts became part of your motor memory.

There just is no way to avoid the need to provide students with opportunities to learn through rehearsal or practice. Obviously, students can also rehearse or practice information in a group discussion, but we cannot be sure students know something until they show they can use it independently.

The ultimate goal of formal education is to *help students learn how to learn* so that eventually they are not dependent upon schools or teachers. This is a second purpose served by independent study since it encourages students to acquire study skills that will serve them throughout life. These skills include how to locate, analyze, synthesize, and evaluate information. The more opportunities learners have to dig out, judge, and use information, the better equipped they will be to learn on their own. The curious child who was helped to learn about life in a pond at age 10 is more likely to want and be able to find out about our disappearing wetlands at age 20.

Independent study is also used, and occasionally misused, as a means to other ends. For example, teachers can use it for convenience. This would be the case *when learners are given work to keep them busy ("busy work") because their teachers must do something else*. The something else might be working with other students or simply taking a breather. Working with other students, of course, is necessary and therefore justifiable. Furthermore, all teachers expect their learners to work independently at times so they may work with an individual or a group.

good

The worst misuse of independent study we have observed occurred in a school where one of the authors was principal. Stanley I., a teacher, loved to read. In fact, he often gave his middle school students independent work so that *he* could read. After giving his class the assignment, Stanley went to his desk, sat down, and opened the middle drawer where he always kept a novel. Students were not permitted to interrupt or to come to his desk. When someone came to his door, Stanley rose slowly and, with his upper legs, inconspicuously closed the drawer to conceal his covert activity.

bad

It may take learners a while to catch on to the misuse of independent study or practice, but they can and do, as evidenced from the student's comment in Case 6.1.

Types of Independent Study   By *type* of independent study, we refer to whether the teacher prescribes the work assignment or learners freely choose it. Teachers normally determine the material to be rehearsed. However, when the purpose is to provide

CASE 6.1
"That Wasn't Really Teaching"

I remember a history teacher in high school. I really liked her because her class was so organized and orderly. When we came in there were *x* number of questions on the chalkboard. We read a certain section of the book and wrote out the answers. When time ran out she would ask, "Do you have any questions?" As she said the word *questions,* the bell always rang. Now I've figured out she taught that way just to keep us busy. We didn't have time to do anything but write out answers. That wasn't really teaching! There was no interaction of ideas and people. No real class.

Source: E. M. Bower. (1973). *Teachers talk about their feelings* (p. 17). Rockville, MD: National Institute of Mental Health, Center for Studies of Child and Family Health.

FIGURE 6.7   Purposes and Key Characteristics of Independent Study

Purposes
- To rehearse, practice
- To provide opportunity to learn how to learn
- To occupy students legitimately so the teacher can undertake another task

Characteristics
- Learning assignment is designated by teacher or selected by students
- Teacher serves as facilitator, guide
- Assignment is to be accomplished in school or at home

opportunities to develop and practice independent study skills, students could select the work. For example, suppose you are teaching a unit on biography. Students could read a common biography you assign, or they could select one of personal interest.

Teacher's Role   As with presentation and discussion, the objective of independent study is to facilitate students' learning and satisfaction. Clearly, learning and satisfaction during independent study are in jeopardy if you are not available *to guide and monitor your students' work.* Failure to monitor independent work is a tragic error. Students left entirely on their own may not only fail to learn but learn incorrectly. Of course, when independent study takes the form of homework, monitoring is not possible. Increasingly, however, parents are being asked to supervise and assist students with their homework. Unfortunately, parental availability, interest, and capacity to assist students varies. Some may be better teachers than we are; others might not have a clue about helping a child.

Context   We have already alluded to the fact that students can do independent work either in school or as homework. In-school assignments can be accomplished at a variety of times and in different places. Students reading biographies could work on them during class, during study or library periods, or after other class work has been completed. Some schools even have before- and after-school arrangements that give students an additional time and place to do independent work.

Figure 6.7 reviews the purposes and key characteristics of independent study.

"Omigosh! My science project is gone!"

GOOD INDEPENDENT STUDY LEADERS

If you are going to use independent study well, you must believe in its purposes and values, particularly as a way to provide rehearsal or practice and as a way to help students learn how to learn. Furthermore, you must have confidence in your students' ability to work alone.

Additionally, you must know how to get and keep learners involved in worthwhile independent activities. Kounin (1970) is most helpful here. He and his colleagues observed the behavior of teachers whose students stayed engaged in their seat-work assignments. The teachers had several things in common. They demonstrated valence and challenge arousal, variety and challenge, withitness, and overlapping. Since these terms are Kounin's inventions, they require definition.

Valence and challenge arousal is the ability to engender students with curiosity and enthusiasm and to get them involved in the independent work. Obviously, teachers who are enthusiastic themselves are more likely to beget enthusiasm in their learners. In Chapter 10, you will learn more about teacher enthusiasm.

Variety and challenge is the ability to identify and assign independent study assignments that vary enough to be interesting and are challenging enough to maintain attention. Such assignments need to be demanding but not defeating. What we know from Chapter 3 about gaining and holding attention applies here.

Withitness is the ability to communicate to learners that we know what they are doing even when we are not nearby or looking at them. Perhaps you can recall teachers who seemed to have eyes in the back of their heads. Withitness is this kind of sixth sense.

Overlapping is the teacher's ability to attend to more than one thing at a time. In a sense it is akin to being a juggler. This ability is especially important when working with one or more students, such as when you are directing a group activity while the rest of the class works independently. In such cases, you work with one group while simultaneously monitoring the other students. You will learn more about overlapping and withitness in Chapter 12.

GOOD INDEPENDENT STUDY

Considerable agreement exists about what must be done to ensure good independent study (Anderson et al., 1984; Brophy & Good, 1986; Emmer et al., 1981; English, 1984; Fisher et al., 1978; Gilstrap & Martin, 1975; Rosenshine, 1980; Rupley & Blair, 1987; Slavin, 1994). Let's review that opinion in terms of the preparation, delivery, and closure of independent study assignments.

eyes behind the back of head

6.17 How do you feel about your *ability to use valence and challenge arousal, variety and challenge, withitness,* and *overlapping?*

Preparation   After determining a general purpose and specific instructional objectives, you must determine whether independent study is the instructional alternative of choice. As mentioned earlier, independent study seems preferable when the purpose is to have learners (1) practice or rehearse information, (2) acquire better self-study or learning skills, or (3) remain occupied in some legitimate way so you can undertake another teaching task, perhaps work with a reading group.

Try Activity 6.7

Next, determine the assignment type. Should all students receive a standard assignment, or should they be able to select one of their choice? In either case, we are advised to make sure their assignments are interesting, concise, and at the correct level of difficulty. Of course, older students can work independently for longer periods of time than younger ones, but it is wise to ensure that the assignment does not outlive the learner's interest in it. With regard to the assignment's level of difficulty, scholars suggest that the learner success rate should be somewhere between 80 and 100 percent. In other words, the assignment should be within the students' reach.

Whether the assignment is teacher-mandated or learner-selected, resources must be available so that students can undertake the task comfortably and successfully. If your assignment of choice is to have each student read a biography, a large assorted collection must be available so that the needs of diverse students are met.

Delivery   Delivery involves making the study assignment and guiding it to a satisfactory conclusion. When making the assignment, attention, valence and challenge arousal, and clarity are most important. Clarity is discussed in detail in Chapter 11. Clarity requires that you inform learners of the lesson's rationale, that is, why the assignment is important. To be clear, you must also ensure that students know specifically what they are to do and how to accomplish it. Instructions should also include time limits and indicate what students must or may do if they complete the assignment early. Learners should also be told precisely when and how they may get help. Can you remember times when you couldn't get help and how debilitating that was? This often happens when the independent work is to be done outside class.

What is your role during independent study? Foremost, it is to actively guide and facilitate learning. This cannot be done as novel-loving teacher Stanley I. did. Rather, you must be alert ("withit") and, whenever possible, be on your feet, moving, monitoring, interacting with individual learners, and diagnosing their progress. Even when you assign independent study in order to work on another teaching task, you cannot closet yourself from your students nor shirk the responsibility of making sure they are doing all right. Thus, as Kounin (1970) notes, you need to have or to develop the capacity of overlapping—the ability to deal with more than one thing at a time. Finally, if your students are to be on task in their independent work, you must protect them from each other's needless, distracting interruptions. Properly delivered, independent study may require more of you than giving a presentation or guiding a discussion. Giving students something to do and ensuring their success is not that simple.

Like presentation and discussion, independent study draws support from learning theory. When its purpose is to rehearse or practice, follow the principles outlined in Chapter 3 for information processing and behaviorism. However, when the purpose is to help students learn how to learn, you will find assistance in the cognitive and humanistic or affective schools of thought. To illustrate, if you want students to independently learn something that is mostly cognitive, or knowledge-related, key principles from the cognitive school of thought should guide them. When they are to learn something mostly affective or relating to attitudes or values, the beliefs and findings of the humanistic school apply.

TABLE 6.5 Qualities of Good Independent Study Leaders and Good Independent Study

Good Leaders	Good Independent Study
• Believe independent study enhances learning through rehearsal • Believe independent study enhances learning how to learn • Believe students can work successfully independently • Exhibit clarity, valence and challenge arousal, variety and challenge, withitness, and overlapping	*When preparing:* • Establish the general purpose • Set specific instructional objectives • Consider the ability of individual learners to work independently • Plan the assignment so that it is interesting and at the optimal level of difficulty and length • Collect, prepare instructional resources *When delivering:* • Get students' attention • Inform learners of the rationale for the assignment and of the objectives • Relate assignment to previous and upcoming work • Make sure learners know what to do and how to do it before work begins • Make certain learners know when and how they may get help • Make sure learners know what to do if they finish early • Be alert, move about to monitor and interact with learners • Diagnose students' progress and provide assistance when needed *When closing:* • Collect assignments • Assess assignments • Provide feedback to students • Count assignments toward the grade

6.18 Now that you are aware of what it takes to have good independent study, what would you suggest the teacher in the Case 6.1 scenario needs to do?

Closure A major error many teachers make is to underestimate the importance of correctly closing a lesson. An independent study assignment is no exception. You cannot just create a worthwhile assignment, give it, and then forget it. You have to "close the deal." But what does that mean? Experts say you must collect the assignment, assess it, count it, and give learners feedback on how well it was done. Reteaching may also be in order. Reteaching is not done often enough. Failure to do any of these things sends a message that independent work is not serious business—just busywork intended to occupy the learner's time. Remember the teacher (Case 6.1) who left no time at the end of class for students' questions? Perhaps you can recall teachers who gave you busywork. Without a doubt, students eventually catch on. When they sense that your assignment doesn't count, don't expect them to take it seriously. Would you?

Try Activity 6.8

Expect and collect the assignment on time, holding the learner accountable. Assess the assignment, and go over it with students as soon as possible. Some whole-class, in-class assignments can be reviewed immediately. For example, if students take time for in-class practice in mathematics, go over the answers with them right away. Provide imediate feedback. And, don't forget to count independent study assignments as part of the grade. Walberg (1984) finds that when homework assignments are graded, student achievement improves.

A summary of the qualities of good independent study leaders and good independent study is contained in Table 6.5. Spotlight on Research 6.4 also explores what makes for good independent study.

What Makes Independent Study Effective?

Fortunately, little more research on this instructional alternative is available than is available for either discussion presentation. The studies have taken place in K–12 schools, although mostly in elementary and middle grades. While Scott (1989) provides the most recent general literature review, the individual studies of Emmer et al. (1982), Fisher et al. (1980), Good & Grouws (1975), Gump (1967), Kounin (1970), Gartland (1986), and Rosenshine (1980), are most helpful. Most investigators have looked at independent study when its purpose is to rehearse or practice information just received through presentation or recitation.

Gump (1967) reports on the incidence of independent study, a strategy he finds commonly employed in elementary school classrooms. Rosenshine (1980) notes that independent assignments are usually both appropriate and at the correct level of difficulty. As we have already learned, Kounin (1970) finds that learners are more likely to be on task during independent study when teachers demonstrate valence and challenge arousal, variety and challenge, withitness, and overlapping. Several scholars found that the ingredients of good independent study are clarity of purpose, assignment, and procedures; good monitoring; and the provision of immediate feedback to learners (Emmer et al., 1982; Fisher et al., 1978, 1980). With regard to monitoring, Fisher et al. (1980) found that when teachers interact briefly but meaningfully with students during independent work, the students' on-task time increases by about 10 percent. Relatedly, Good and Grouws (1975) report that teachers whose students achieve more have more contacts with learners at work. Furthermore, these teachers take monitoring opportunities to give students relevant feedback and so help them be successful. Finally, Gartland (1986) finds that teachers should not provide student with more whole-class practice during a teacher presentation but instead should provide them with more monitored independent practice.

ADVANTAGES AND LIMITATIONS OF INDEPENDENT STUDY

What are the pluses and minuses of independent study in terms of teacher's personal and role-derived needs?

Benefits for Teachers   What personality needs of teachers might the use of independent study meet? We believe it would meet the following needs (see Figure 6.4):

- The need to **play,** to seek diversion, change, and relaxation. Use of independent study provides teachers with a change of pace, adding variety and stimulation to their work.

- The **recognition** need to obtain praise and commendation. Recognition is likely to follow independent study when learners have engaged in significant work with good results. Teachers like nothing better than to be able to show off the good-quality independent work students have done.

- The **affiliation** need to get closer to others. Independent study provides teachers with the opportunity for one-on-one dialogue. It allows them to be helpful and supportive.

- The **autonomy** need for independence and freedom. When teachers make worthwhile independent work assignments that intrigue and benefit students, they are free to do other teacher tasks.

Additionally, we believe careful use of independent study meets teachers' job-related needs, including:

- **Affiliation,** or establishing good relationships with students
- **Control,** or having students behave appropriately, in this case being task-oriented and relatively orderly
- **Student success,** or helping learners to succeed academically and socially
- **Time,** or having the opportunity to perform other teaching tasks while students are engaged in legitimate learning activity

Use of independent study as an instructional method can also help us meet selected professional expectations. First, properly presented and monitored, independent study helps students learn. You may recall from Chapter 3 that rehearsal and practice are important elements of learning. Therefore, independent study that requires practice serves students well. Second, independent study has the potential to help students become lifelong learners. The highest goal of education is probably "to shift to the individual the burden of pursuing his own education" (Gardner, 1964, p. 12). Education should help individuals learn how to learn on their own so that they may eventually continue to learn free of institutionalized teaching.

Benefits for Students   Independent study also benefits students. When the purpose of the work is to have learners develop and practice independent study skills, as they might do when preparing a report, then this instructional alternative appeals to students who have the following needs:

- The need for **cognizance**—to explore, read, and seek knowledge
- The need for **orderliness** and **construction**—to arrange, organize, and build something
- The need for **achievement**—to do difficult tasks well and quickly
- The need for **recognition**—to receive praise and commendation
- The need for **autonomy**—to be independent

Our learners can see benefits when the independent study activity helps them rehearse or practice information so it gets into long-term memory or rehearse or practice independent study skills so students will be successful independent learners.

We thought it might be useful to make a chart that compares presentation, discussion, and independent study in terms of their likely ability to meet teacher and student personal needs. It appears as Table 6.6.

Limitations   Perhaps the greatest drawback to independent study is not with the technique itself but with its intentions, conduct, and assessment. If the intentions of such study are not clear and reasonable, students may resist the assignments or exert minimal effort. Said another way, when learners do perceive the task as meeting some need or having value, they will not honor it.

In terms of the conduct of independent study, be forewarned that you must monitor the study, provide feedback, and help students see that the assignment is as valuable as other work (Anderson, 1981; Anderson et al., 1984; Dembo, 1991; Seifert & Beck, 1984).

6.19   How do you feel about use of independent study?

WHEN INDEPENDENT STUDY SHOULD BE USED

To reiterate, independent study should be used (1) when learners need to rehearse or practice information or a skill to get it into long-term memory, or (2) when learners need to learn how to learn independently. In the first case, we are saying that students need to practice: remember the old adage "Practice makes perfect." In the second case, we are saying that a major, if not the ultimate, goal of education is to assist students in learning *how* to learn so that they no longer need schools and teachers. *They* are empowered!

Although we lack evidence to support our assumption, we believe independent study is used mostly in K–12 schools as a means to practice or rehearse. We think it is used much less to prepare students for lifelong learning, although everyone recalls working on self-propelling independent reports. We also believe many teachers use this practice for a third purpose: to keep some students legitimately occupied so that teachers can work with other students in, say, a reading or math

TABLE 6.6 Some Teacher(T) and Student(S) Personal Needs That Presentation, Discussion, or Independent Study May Meet

Key: Column 1 contains sixteen personality needs. Columns 2, 3, and 4 represent the three instructional alternatives presented in this chapter, namely, presentation, discussion, and independent study. The letter T represents teachers, while S represents students. A *T* or an *S* in columns 2 through 4 indicates that we believe that the particular instructional alternative meets the T (teacher) or S (student) need parallel to it in column 1. For example, the top or first *S* in column 4 means that we think Independent Study meets the student personality need for achievement.

Personality Needs (1)	Presentation (2)	Discussion (3)	Independent Study (4)
1. Achievement			S
2. Acquisition	S	S	
3. Affiliation		T/S	T
4. Autonomy			T/S
5. Cognizance	T		S
6. Construction	T	T	S
7. Deference	S	S	
8. Dominance	T	S	
9. Exhibition	T	S	
10. Exposition	T	S	
11. Failure avoidance		T	
12. Orderliness	T		S
13. Play		T/S	T
14. Recognition	T	S	T/S
15. Sibilance	S	S	
16. Succorance	S	S	

Source (for personality needs): H. Murray. (1963). *Explorations in personality.* New York: Oxford University Press.

group. The key word is *legitimately.* Unfortunately, it is too easy to give students work that is nothing more than busywork; in other words, its sole intention is to keep students occupied.

One of the authors recalls visiting in a daughter's first-grade classroom on parents' night. The teacher was entertaining questions. One mother asked, "Why do the children spend day after day coloring dittoes and cutting them out?" The teacher, stymied for a moment and perhaps feeling found out, stammered a possibly suitable but unlikely answer: "To improve eye-hand coordination."

SUMMARY ON INDEPENDENT STUDY

Independent study is an excellent instructional alternative that serves several important purposes. Mostly teachers use it for practice or rehearsal of information. However, it also helps students acquire study and inquiry skills that will serve them throughout life. During independent work, your role is to facilitate and guide learning. To do so, you must not only be available, but must actively monitor. When you are not available or cannot monitor, as with home assignments, you must find someone else to fill this role.

Since considerable consensus exists regarding the benefits of independent study and how to conduct good independent study assignments, you should make use of this instructional alternative. Doing so will make you a better teacher and help your students achieve and be satisfied.

Try Activity 6.9

The "Best" Instructional Alternatives

What do teachers think are the best instructional alternatives for different kinds of students? Are certain alternatives better suited to high- or low-ability learners? Are some better suited to independent vs. (as opposed to) conforming learners? Shuell and his colleagues undertook two studies in order to find answers (Shuell et al., 1988).

In the first study, ninety-one suburban elementary teachers received information about four different kinds of hypothetical students. The information portrayed each of the students as either (1) high ability-independent, (2) high ability-conforming, (3) low ability-independent, or (4) low ability-conforming. For example, the hypothetical high ability-independent learner was characterized as follows:

> Robby is an independent, productive worker. He is doing very well in all his subjects, and is usually ahead of [them] in tasks requiring complex verbal skills. His classmates look up to him for leadership. The teacher has assigned the class to read *Black Beauty* and asked them to be ready for a quiz. (p. 354, paraphrased)

After reading the four hypothetical student characterizations, the ninety-one teachers were asked to decide which of several instructional alternatives would be best suited for each student when engaged in a verbal learning task such as reading. The instructional alternatives teachers were to consider were lecture/explanation, seat work (supervised study), discussion, one-to-one teaching (individualized instruction), peer tutoring (individualized instruction), homogeneous grouping, or praise. We do not consider the last two areas to be instructional alternatives, and the investigators did not claim "praise" was one either. Still, it was included.

In the second Shuell study, twenty fourth- and fifth-grade teachers participated. First, they were asked to think about each of their present students with regard to five attributes: general academic ability, achievement orientation, classroom participation, motivation, and prior knowledge. Next, the teachers were asked to describe which instructional alternative was most appropriate for each student when engaged in a verbal learning task. The instructional alternatives teachers could choose among were the same as in the first study except that "homogeneous grouping" was replaced by "games," and "small-group work" displaced "discussion."

The investigators acknowledge that the two studies differ somewhat but believe the following conclusions are in order:

- Teachers believe different instructional alternatives work best for different learners.
- Teachers consider lecture/explanation and seat work most beneficial for high-ability students.
- Teachers consider one-to-one work, peer tutoring, and praise more appropriate for children of low ability.
- Teachers present mixed perceptions with regard to discussion. In study 1 (the hypothetical students), they felt it was equally inappropriate for either high- or low-ability learners. In study 2 (real students), they reported it appropriate for high-ability students.

Shuell and associates conclude that teachers do have definite ideas regarding how best to teach different learners and that, generally, these ideas are consistent with what we know about learning and teaching.

Overview of Twenty-Nine Instructional Alternatives

At the beginning of the chapter, we indicated that a brief overview of twenty-nine instructional alternatives would follow the in-depth information on presentation, discussion, and independent study. Here they are, presented alphabetically. You will note that some have characteristics in common with others. For example, presentations and recitations are both normally led by the teacher.

- **Academic games or competitions**—Learners compete with each other one-to-one or team-to-team to determine which individual or group is superior at a given academic task such as in "spelldowns," anagrams, or project completion. Some well-known commercially available academic games include *Probe* (vocabulary and spelling) and *Rook* (mathematics). Cooperative learning, presented in the next chapter, may incorporate games and competition.

- **Brainstorming**—To generate creative ideas, learners are asked to withhold judgment or criticism and produce a very large number of ways to do something, such as resolve a particular problem. For example, learners may be asked to think of as many ideas as they can for eliminating world hunger. Once they have generated a large number of ideas, the ideas are subjected to inspection in respect to their feasibility.

- **Cases**—Students make detailed analysis of some specific, usually compelling, event or series of related events so that learners will better understand its nature and what might be done about it. For example, learners in a science class might investigate the occurrence of El Niño, or a disaster of human origin such as the infiltration of the zebra mussel in the Great Lakes.

- **Centers of interest and displays**—Collections and displays of materials are used to interest learners in themes or topics. For example, children may bring to school and display family belongings that reflect their ethnic heritage. The intention may be to interest the class in the notion of culture. Or, the teacher might arrange a display of different measurement devices to prompt interest in and exploration of that topic.

- **Colloquia**—A guest or guests are invited to class to be interviewed. Thus, a guest musician might serve as a stimulus for arousing interest in music and musical performance.

- **Contracts**—Written agreements students and teachers may enter into describe the academic work students plan to accomplish in a particular period of time such as over a week or month.

- **Cooperative learning**—See student-team learning.

- **Debates**—In this form of discussion, a few students present and contest varying points of view on an issue. For example, secondary students could debate the issue "Should public schools be financed by real estate tax, sales tax, or tax on personal income?"

- **Demonstrations**—In this form of presentation, the teacher or learners show how something works or operates, or how something is done. For example, a teacher could demonstrate how to use a thesaurus, how to operate a hand-held calculator, or what happens when oil is spilled on water (as when an oil tanker leaks).

- **Direct instruction**—A teacher gives explicit, step-by-step instruction (Rosenshine, 1987). The advocated format or regimen is demonstration followed by guided practice and independent practice. Thus, the teacher might teach a reading, mathematics, or geography concept or skill; following that, students practice under teacher supervision; and finally, students practice independently to the point of mastery. (See Chapter 7.)

- **Discovery**—As noted in Chapter 3, in discovery learning, students are encouraged to derive their own understandings or meanings. For example, students might be asked to find out what causes golf, tennis, basketball, and bowling balls to bounce differently on different surfaces. Experiments rather than teacher demonstrations are a part of discovery learning.

"It was a very successful field trip. I managed to lose five of them."

- **Discussion**—Described in this chapter, discussions occur when a group assembles to communicate with one another by speaking and listening about a topic or event of mutual interest. To illustrate, a group of learners convenes to discuss what it has learned about global warming. (See Chapter 7.)

- **Drill and practice**—In this form of independent study, the teacher explains a task and then learners practice it. After students learn how to use a thesaurus, for example, they could be asked to locate and use synonyms.

- **Field observation, fieldwork, field trips**—Students make observations or carry out work in an outside-the-school setting. Students might visit the local museum of natural history to see displays about dinosaurs, or they might begin and operate a small business to learn about production and marketing.

- **Independent study or supervised study**—Described in this chapter, independent study requires learners to complete a common task at their desks or as a home study assignment.

- **Individualized instruction**—Any of a number of teaching methods that tailor teaching and learning to meet a learner's unique characteristics. (See Chapter 7.)

- **Learning modules**—These are a form of individualized instruction that allow students to use a self-contained package of learning activities. The activities guide learners to know or to be able to do something. Students might be given a learning module that contains activities intended to help them understand good nutrition.

- **Mastery learning**—As a class, students are presented with information to be learned at a predetermined level of mastery. The class is tested, and individuals who do not obtain adequate scores are retaught and retested. Those who pass undertake enrichment study while classmates catch up. (See Chapter 3.)

- **Oral reports**—Individuals or groups of learners are assigned or choose topics. For example, each may be asked to find out about one planet in our solar system. They share what they learn with other class members through oral presentations.

- **Presentations and lectures**—Students listen to a person who talks about a topic. The teacher, or a guest speaker, might tell the class all about the artist Dali. Presentations are described in this chapter.

- **Problem solving**—Individuals or groups of learners are presented with a perplexing, difficult question or situation and are asked to think about and try to resolve it. (See Chapter 3.)

"Please feel free to call on me if any of you need individual attention."

- **Programmed and computer-assisted instruction**—In this form of individualized instruction, students learn information in small, separate units either by reading programmed texts or by using computer-presented teaching programs. A correct answer to a question or problem enables the learner to advance, while an incorrect response requires repetition or relearning. (See Chapter 3.)

- **Project or activity method**—In this form of individualization, learners choose and work on projects and activities on related topics. Students might write on or present in graphic presentation "Life in the South" or "Life in the North during the Civil War." Learners not only choose topics but also the project that will show what they've learned. (See Chapter 7, Independent Study.)

- **Protocols**—Learners study an original record or records of some important event and then try to understand the event or its consequences. They might watch a film depicting actual instances of discrimination and then consider its causes and effects.

- **Recitation**—Students are given information to study. They then recite what they have learned when the teacher questions them. For example, students might read about what causes different weather patterns, and the teacher might then question them to determine the extent and nature of their knowledge and understanding. (See Table 6.3.)

- **Role playing**—Learners take on the role of another person to see what it would be like to be that person. Thus, a student could play the role of an imaginary student no one likes or the role of an individual with handicaps.

- **Simulation games**—Students play a specially designed, competitive game that mirrors some aspect of life. For example, they might play the *Ghetto* (Toll, 1969) to find out about the problems and pressures ghetto dwellers face and, relatedly, to sense how difficult it is to improve one's lot in life. Another commercially available simulation game is *Gold Rush* (life and adventure in a frontier mining camp). Some simulation games are computerized, for example, *Oregon Trail* and *Amazon Trail*.

- **Simulations**—Learners engage with something intended to simulate—to give the appearance or have the effect of—something else. Thus, students may engage in a simulation of the United Nations General Assembly in order to have "firsthand" experience with how the Assembly works and what its delegates do.

- **Student-team, pupil-team, cooperative learning**—Learners are placed in groups or teams of four to six. Sometimes the groups are as diverse or heterogeneous as possible. In such cases, team members are often rewarded for the team's overall success. Under one type of cooperative learning, student teams might

6.20 Which instructional alternatives do you seem to prefer? Why?

FIGURE 6.8   Wheel of Instructional Choice

- Topics shaded in purple are discussed in detail in Chapter 6.
- Topics shaded in gray are discussed in detail in Chapter 7.

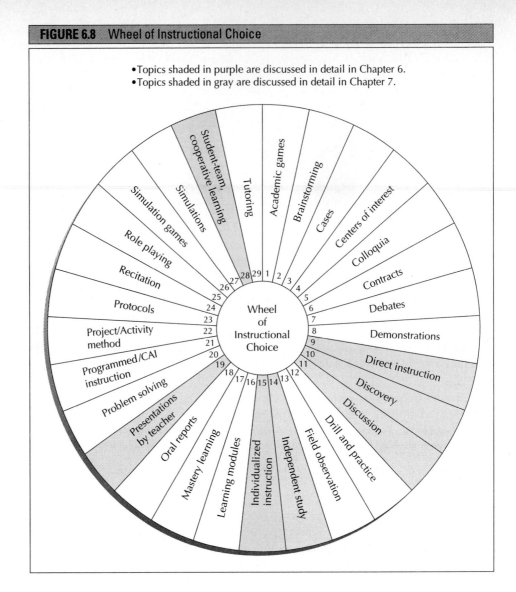

see a teacher presentation on division of fractions. They would then receive worksheets to complete. Team members would work together to find the answers. Finally, team members would take a quiz on division of fractions, and the team members' scores would be added to make up a team score. (See "Cooperative Learning" in Chapter 7.)

- **Tutoring**—In this form of individualization, either a teacher or a fellow student provides a learner or small group of learners with special help, usually because the student is not learning well enough with only conventional instruction (Medway, 1987).

The instructional alternatives we have briefly described are depicted on the Wheel of Instructional Choice in Figure 6.8.

Some Final Thoughts

This chapter is intended to put you on the road to becoming a more multitalented, versatile teacher. Now you are generally aware of twenty-nine ways to teach, and you have special knowledge about three that are considered teaching staples.

For these three, you have learned their purposes and characteristics, what you must do to excel at each, and what benefits research tells us will accrue. We hope you have had the opportunity to try out each one and/or to observe a master teacher demonstrating each one. Furthermore, we hope you have reflected on how you feel about each. Consider yourself part way out on the diving platform leading to successful teaching. After Chapter 7, we think you will be ready to take the plunge.

CHAPTER SUMMARY

- An instructional alternative is a way of teaching intended to facilitate student learning and satisfaction. The most familiar alternatives are presentations, discussion, and independent study. Other notable alternatives (presented in the next chapter) are direct instruction, individualized instruction, inquiry teaching, and cooperating learning. As many as twenty-nine instructional alternatives exist and are depicted on the Wheel of Instructional Choice (Figure 6.8)

- Presentations are informative talks a more knowledgeable person makes to less knowledgeable persons. These talks draw their strength from the cognitive school of thought, especially information processing and reception learning. They can be long or short, interrupted or uninterrupted, formal or informal, given by a teacher or by another person, and either live or recorded.

- Good presentations have three parts: preparation, delivery, and closure. Preparation requires the presenter to establish the general purpose and specific learning objectives, collect and review the information to be presented, and organize and plan delivery. Delivery requires the presenter to obtain students' attention, present the learning objectives and expectations, use an advance organizer, present the information in an organized, step-by-step manner, expect and promote pupil interaction, move from general to specific ideas, use examples and nonexamples when teaching new concepts, ask learners to reflect on what they have learned, and then ask them to use the information. Closure requires the presenter to review, summarize, relate the new learning to what students already knew, and check learner for understanding.

- Presentations may be particularly attractive to teachers who have strong personal needs for cognizance, construction and orderliness, dominance, exhibition, exposition, and recognition. Use of presentations probably also meets teacher job-related needs such as control, student success, and time management. Finally, presentations are advantageous when teachers can present the information better or more efficiently than other sources could or when the information is not available elsewhere.

- Students who have strong personal needs for acquisition, deference, sibilance, and succorance may like presentations. They are also advantageous when students need or wish to develop listening, note taking, and critical thinking skills. Presentations lose their value if students are not involved or if the presentation fails to take into account student diversity.

- Research indicates that the presenter's style is important, that good presenters are often friendly, humorous, enthusiastic, and verbally fluent, that attention falls off rapidly after fifteen minutes, that note taking aids long-term memory, that presentations are good for transmitting information and not as good for promoting students' thinking, and that underachievers need special consideration when using presentations.

- A discussion is a conversation wherein students, or students and teacher, interact to share information, ideas, or opinions, or work to resolve a problem. Discussions also are guided by learning theory. However, the theory the discussion leader draws from will vary according to the discussion's purpose, that is, whether it is mainly cognitive, affective, or some combination of the two. Discussions may take place between teacher and students or solely among students, and the teacher may be actively involved as leader or participant or merely serve as the observer. Finally, a discussion may involve the whole class, small group, or a panel.

- Good discussion leaders usually believe that students' participation in purposeful conversation is normal and healthy, that students must think aloud about information, ideas, issues, and problems, that students are able to think effectively, and that by thinking and interacting effectively, students experience psychological and social growth. Additionally, good discussion leaders control their own talk and are skillful facilitators, human relations experts, clarifiers, and summarizers.

- Good discussions include preparation, delivery, and closure. Preparation requires the leader to determine the purpose and specific objectives; determine students' readiness for discussion, particularly this discussion; decide what kind of interaction is best (teacher-student, or student-student) and, relatedly, what the teacher's role should be (leader, participant, or observer); and decide whether the discussion should involve the whole class or a small group and what the time parameters should be. Delivery requires that the leader ensure that students understand the purpose and objectives of the discussion, set the task, remind students of guidelines for behavior during discussion, organize the participants, and let them "have at it" as the leader fulfills his or her role. Closure requires the discussion leader to summarize and organize findings, conclusions, solutions, or whatever the objectives called for as well as assess students' learning and satisfaction.

- Discussions probably are attractive to teachers who have personal needs for construction, play, and affiliation or to those who may want to avoid giving a presentation because they do not know the subject well enough. Discussions also may help meet teacher job-related needs such as affiliation and student success. Furthermore, discussions could be advantageous when teachers want to encourage students to think analytically and critically or when they want to encourage optimal interpersonal interaction. Discussions probably are advantageous for students who have strong needs for acquisition, affiliation, deference, dominance, exhibition, exposition, play, recognition, sibilance, and succorance. They also are advantageous because they capture and maintain learners' interest, help them develop communication and social-psychological strengths, and help them learn through rehearsal. When they are not well-conducted, discussions can be purposeless, rambling, confrontational, and wasteful of time.

- Research on discussions shows, among other things, that they generally are motivating, promote retention, foster higher-order thinking, and are effective in altering attitudes and advancing moral reasoning.

- Independent study includes any school-related assignment students do more or less alone. It is guided mostly by information-processing and behavioristic theories. The purposes of independent study are to provide rehearsal and practice, opportunities to learn how to learn, and to occupy students legitimately so the teacher can perform other important tasks. Characteristics of independent study include the type (teacher-prescribed or student-chosen), the teacher role (the availability of the teacher to guide), and the context (in school or home).

- Good independent study leaders believe that the purposes of independent study are valuable. They have confidence in students' ability to work alone and are able to demonstrate valence and challenge arousal, variety and challenge, withitness, and overlapping.

- Good independent study includes preparation, delivery, and closure. Preparation requires the teacher to establish the general purpose and specific objectives, settle on the assignment's nature and type, and ensure that it is within learners' interest and ability. Delivery requires that the teacher be absolutely clear regarding the assignment's purpose, objectives, relationship to what has or will be learned, procedures, and time limit. Closure requires the teacher to collect, assess, and evaluate the work, giving learners specific feedback and reteaching when necessary.

- Independent study may seem particularly beneficial to teachers who have strong needs for affiliation, recognition, play, and autonomy. It also helps teachers meet job-related needs for affiliation, control, student success, and time management. Furthermore, it is beneficial when the intention is that students either rehearse information or practice skills or when they need to learn how to learn.

- Independent study may be advantageous for students who have strong needs for achievement, autonomy, cognizance, construction, orderliness, and recognition. It also may be beneficial when students feel independent study would help them achieve mastery or independence.

- Research on independent study finds that it is commonly used, that it is more effective when teachers demonstrate certain leadership behaviors, and that its most important ingredients are (1) clarity of purpose, assignment, and procedures, and (2) monitoring, grading, and provision of immediate feedback.

ISSUES AND PROBLEMS FOR DISCUSSION

ISSUES   Several issues and problems are related to instructional alternatives. Here are a few you might like to discuss in class.

1. Which instructional alternatives do you expect to handle most skillfully?

2. Which instructional alternatives work best for which purposes?

3. When deciding which alternative to use, are teacher or student needs more important?

4. How can you become more competent in using a given instructional alternative?

5. Why do you suppose there is a dearth of useful research-based knowledge about instructional alternatives?

PROBLEMS   Teachers regularly report that they have difficulty "learning to use alternative methods of instruction" (Cruickshank et al., 1980). What would you have done in each of the following situations?

Problem 1:   "I spent the whole weekend reading about Geronimo and preparing to tell the class about him as part of Cultural Awareness Week. I chose Geronimo because there are no Native Americans in the class and I wanted to broaden the kids' perspectives. Well, I'll tell you, very few of the students had any interest whatsoever! Finally, I just cashed it in. So much for giving an 'interesting' talk."

Problem 2:   "No matter how many times we use group discussion, the same old problems crop up. Rashawn and Lawrence think they know everything and won't let others talk or respect what others say. Melody, Arnold, Diane, and Mary won't participate, and Barney sleeps."

Problem 3: "Students really like to do individual study. They can't wait to get started. After that, some just sit, some carry on conversations with neighbors, some just copy word-for-word from a book. A few hurry through so they can fool around. Out of twenty-six, I'd say I can count on fourteen."

Problem 4: "We have some pretty good software and audiovisual materials available. To add variety, I like to have the students use these resources instead of just listening to me. They waste so much time finding what they want and settling down that I usually wish I had done whole-class teaching."

THEORY INTO ACTION ACTIVITIES

ACTIVITY 6.1: Prepare a Presentation. Utilizing what you now know about learning (Chapter 3), good presenters, and good presentations, prepare a brief presentation for a group of peers on a topic chosen from group A or B below. The presentation should be no longer than ten minutes.

A. *Topics from this text*
  1. Attention
  2. Short-term memory
  3. Long-term memory
  4. Reception learning
  5. Bloom's taxonomy
  6. Writing a unit plan
  7. Writing a lesson plan
  8. (your choice)

B. *School curricula topics*
  1. Homophones
  2. Characteristics of Picasso's paintings
  3. The electoral college
  4. The musical scale
  5. Wilderness survival
  6. Peninsulas
  7. Triangles
  8. (your choice)

Assessment: Did you establish your general purpose, set specific learning objectives, collect and review related materials, and plan the presentation with student diversity in mind?

ACTIVITY 6.2: Deliver a Presentation Deliver your Activity 6.1 presentation to a small group of your peers.

Assessment: To what extent did you

  1. Obtain learners' attention and interest?
  2. Inform learners of what they need to learn?
  3. Relate new information to what they know?
  4. Present information step-by-step?
  5. Move from the general to the specific?
  6. Provide just the right amount of information?
  7. Emphasize important points?
  8. Use examples and illustrations?
  9. Use variety to maintain attention?
  10. Ask questions and call for comments?

Were you

1. Friendly?
2. Humorous?
3. Enthusiastic?
4. Fluent and audible?
5. Able to take learners' differences into account?
6. Knowledgeable?

How well do your learners feel you did these things?

ACTIVITY 6.3: Observe a Teacher Presentation   Now that you have learned about presentations, it would be very helpful to observe one or more in a K–12 classroom. If you are enrolled in a field experience, find out when your mentor teacher will be giving a presentation. Talk with him or her about how it would help if you could see a presentation in action. If not so enrolled, perhaps you can obtain a videotape of a presentation made by a teacher or student teacher.

As you observe, record answers to these questions:

- What characteristics of a good presenter did the teacher demonstrate? (See Table 6.2, column 1)

- What qualities of good presentations were evident in this one? (See Table 6.2, column 2)

- In your opinion, what teacher and student personality or role-derived needs did the presentation meet?

- Were any of the research findings on presentations borne out?

Additionally, talk with a student who was attentive and find out how he or she feels about presentations. Conversely, talk with another who was off-task or not attentive to determine his or her perceptions about this instructional alternative.

Finally, ask the teacher how well he or she felt the presentation facilitated learning and satisfaction.

ACTIVITY 6.4: Plan a Discussion   Plan a discussion for this class focusing on any one of the following topics. Plan it so that it has one of the following purposes: to review information; to examine ideas, opinions, or issues; to solve problems; or to improve communication skills. Reread the section Good Discussions for assistance.

Topics from this text

1. Factors influencing how we teach
2. The changing nature of childhood
3. Student diversity
4. Three schools of thought about learning
5. Presentations or discussions
6. (your choice of topic)

Assessment: Did you have a clear purpose and outcomes in mind, take into account learners' differences, decide what role you would play, work out the physical arrangement, and establish the time frame?

ACTIVITY 6.5: Conduct a Discussion   Conduct the discussion you planned in Activity 6.4.

Assessment: Did you

1. Obtain learners' attention and interest?
2. Inform learners of the goal of the discussion and its value?
3. Relate what learners will discuss to their previous knowledge and experience and/or tie it to something they will learn?

4. Remind participants of the rules of (this) discussion?
5. Obtain a facilitator-moderator and recorder for each small group if small-group discussion was used?
6. Monitor understanding and participation?
7. Elevate the level of thinking and discourse?
8. Summarize?
9. Tie what was discussed to previous knowledge?
10. Connect the discussion to what will happen next?

Were you

1. Able to get learners thinking?
2. Able to keep your own talk under control?
3. A facilitator, human relations expert, clarifier, or summarizer as necessary?
4. Able to improve group communication skills?

ACTIVITY 6.6: Observe a Discussion   Try to observe a discussion involving K–12 students. If you do not have access to a K–12 classroom, perhaps your college instructor has a videotape of one. As you observe, record answers to these questions:

1. Which of the four purposes of a discussion seemed to be in play—to review, to examine ideas and opinions, to solve problems, or to improve oral communication skills?
2. What were the characteristics of the discussion? Was the interaction between teacher and students or among students only? Was the teacher a facilitator-moderator, participant, or observer-recorder? Was it a whole-class or small-group discussion? If small group, what was the composition of the group? What was the physical arrangement?
3. What beliefs and abilities related to good discussion did the teacher demonstrate?
4. What teacher and student personal, role-derived, or educational needs did the discussion seem to satisfy?
5. To what extent did the discussion bear out any of the research findings on discussion?
6. To what extent did student learning and satisfaction occur?

ACTIVITY 6.7: Plan an Independent Study   Using what we know about learning and independent study, prepare an assignment for a group of peers on a topic chosen from purpose 1 or 2:

1. *Purpose:* To have peers independently rehearse or practice what you have learned about
   a. Presentation
   b. Discussion
   c. Independent study
2. *Purpose:* To have peers independently learn more about other instructional alternatives appearing on the Wheel of Instructional Choice (Figure 6.8).

In either case, did you establish your general purpose, set specific learning objectives, consider the diversity of the learners, and make the task interesting?

ACTIVITY 6.8: Conducting Independent Study   Conduct the independent study activity you planned in Activity 6.7.

Assessment: Did you

1. Get student attention?
2. Present the assignment's rationale and objectives?
3. Relate the assignment to previous or upcoming work?
4. Ensure that students knew what to do and how to do it?
5. Tell them how they could get assistance?
6. Ensure that they had something to do when they finished?
7. Monitor and interact with learners?
8. Diagnose individual progress and provide assistance?
9. Collect assignments?
10. Provide students with specific feedback?
11. Give credit for the work?

ACTIVITY 6.9: Observe Independent Study   If you are enrolled in a field experience, arrange to visit a classroom to see a scheduled independent study.

1. Which of the purposes for using independent study seemed to be in play (to provide rehearsal or practice of information, provide opportunities to learn independently, or keep students legitimately occupied so the teacher could do something else)?
2. Which of the behaviors of good independent study leaders did the teacher demonstrate?
3. Which of the qualities of good independent study were present?
4. What teacher and student needs did the assignment seem to meet?
5. Which of the research findings on independent study was the teacher able to apply?

Additionally, talk to two students, one who seemed to be very much on-task and another who was more off-task. Ask them how they feel about studying alone. Finally, get the teacher's reactions to the independent study. You might task, "Do you feel the students accomplished what you wanted them to?"

REFERENCES

Anderson, L., Brubaker, N., Alleman-Brooks, J., & Duffy, G. (1984). *Making seat work work. Research Series 142.* East Lansing, MI: College of Education, Michigan State University.

Anderson, L. M. (1981). *Students respond to seat work: Implications for the study of students' cognitive processing.* East Lansing, MI: Institute for Research on Teaching, Michigan State University.

Battistich, V., Solomon, D., & Delucchi, K. (1993, September). Interaction processes and student outcomes in cooperative learning groups. *The Elementary School Journal, 94*(1), 19–32.

Bower, E. M. (1973). *Teachers talk about their feelings.* Rockville, MD: National Institute of Mental Health, Center for Studies of Child and Family Health.

Bridges, D. (1979). *Education, democracy, and discussion.* Windsor, England: National Foundation for Educational Research.

Brophy, J. E., & Good, T. L. (1986). Teacher behavior and student achievement. In M. C. Wittrock (Ed.), *Handbook of research on teaching.* Third Edition (pp. 328–375). New York: Macmillan.

Broudy, H. S. (1963). Historical exemplars of teaching method. In N. L. Gage (Ed.), *Handbook of research on teaching* (pp. 1–43). Chicago: Rand McNally.

Brown, G. A. (1987). Lectures and lecturing. In M. J. Dunkin (Ed.), *The international encyclopedia of teaching and teacher education* (pp. 284–287). Oxford: Pergamon Press.

Connell, W. F. (1987). History of teaching methods. In M. J. Dunkin (Ed.), *The international encyclopedia of teaching and teacher education* (pp. 201–214). Oxford: Pergamon Press.

Cruickshank, D., Applegate, J., Holton, J., Mager, G., Myers, B., Novak, C., & Tracey, K. (1980). *Teaching is tough.* Englewood Cliffs, NJ: Prentice Hall.

Cruickshank, D., & Metcalf, K. (1995). Explaining. In T. Husen & T. N. Postlewaite (Eds.), *International encyclopedia of education.* Second Edition. Oxford: Pergamon Press.

Dembo, M. H. (1991). *Applying educational psychology in the classroom.* New York: Dembo, Longman.

Dillon, J. T. (1985). Using questions to foil discussion. *Teaching and Teacher Education, 1*(2), 109–121.

Dillon, J. T. (1988). *Questioning and discussion: A multidisciplinary study.* Norwalk, NJ: Ablex.

Dillon, J. T. (1995). Discussion. In L. W. Anderson (Ed.), *International encyclopedia of teaching and teacher education* (pp. 251–254). Oxford: Pergamon Press.

Dunkin, M. (1987). Lesson formats. In L. W. Anderson (Ed.), *International encyclopedia of teaching and teacher education* (pp. 251–254). Oxford: Pergamon Press.

Emmer, E., Everston, C., Sanford, J., & Clements, B. (1982). *Improving classroom management: An experimental study in junior high classrooms.* Austin: The University of Texas. (ERIC Document Reproduction Service 261 053)

Emmer, E., Sanford, J., Evertson, C., Clements, B., & Martin, J. (1981). *The classroom management improvement study: An experiment in elementary school classrooms.* Austin: The University of Texas. (ERIC Document Reproduction Service ED 226 452)

English, C. S. (1984). Measuring teacher effectiveness from the teacher's point of view. *Focus on Exceptional Children, 17,* 1–15.

Fisher, C., Berliner, D., Filby, N., Marliave, R., Cahen, L., & Dishaw, M. (1980). Teaching behaviors, academic learning time, and student achievement: An overview. In C. Denham & A. Lieberman (Eds.), *Time to learn: A review of the beginning teacher evaluation study* (pp. 7–32). Washington, DC: National Institute of Education.

Fisher, C. W., Filby, N., Marliave, R. S., Cahen, L. S., Dishaw, M. M., Moore, J. E., & Berliner, D. C. (1978). Teaching behaviors, academic learning time and student achievement: Final report of Phase III-B, *Beginning teacher evaluation study.* San Francisco: Far West Laboratory for Educational Research and Development.

Flanders, N. A. (1970). *Analyzing teacher behavior.* Reading, MA: Addison-Wesley.

Freiberg, H., & Driscoll, A. (1996). *Universal teaching strategies.* Boston: Allyn and Bacon.

Gage, N. L., & Berliner, D. C. (1976). The psychology of teaching methods. In N. L. Gage (Ed.), *The psychology of teaching methods* (pp. 1–20). Chicago: University of Chicago Press.

Gage, N. L., & Berliner, D. C. (1991). *Educational Psychology.* Fifth Edition. Boston: Houghton Mifflin.

Gall, J., & Gall, M. (1990). Outcomes of the discussion method. In W. W. Wilen (Ed.), *Teaching and learning through discussion: The theory and practice of the discussion method* (pp. 25–44). Springfield, IL: Charles C Thomas.

Gall, M. D. (1987). Discussion methods. In M. J. Dunkin (Ed.), *International encyclopedia of teaching and teacher education* (pp. 232–237). Oxford: Pergamon Press.

Gall, M. D., & Gall, J. P. (1976). The discussion method. In N. L. Gage (Ed.), *The psychology of teaching methods* (pp. 166–216). Chicago: University of Chicago Press.

Gardner, J. (1964). *Self-renewal: The individual and the innovative society.* New York: Harper.

Gartland, D. (1986). The effects of varying amounts of teacher-directed instruction and monitored independent seat work on the acquisition of syllabication rules by severely disabled readers. Unpublished doctoral dissertation. University Park: Pennsylvania State University.

Gilstrap, R. L., & Martin, W. R. (1975). *Current strategies for teachers.* Pacific Palisades, CA: Goodyear.

Gold Rush. Post Office Box 997, Lakeside, CA: Interact.

Good, T., & Grouws, L. (1975). *Process-product relationships in fourth grade mathematics classrooms.* Columbia: University of Missouri.

Goodlad, J. I. (1983). *A place called school.* New York: McGraw-Hill.

Gump, P. (1967). *The classroom behavior setting: Its nature and relation to student behavior.* Lawrence: University of Kansas. (ERIC Document Reproduction Service ED 015 515)

Hamilton, R., & Ghatala, E. (1994). *Learning and instruction.* New York: McGraw-Hill.

Hill, W. F. (1977). *Learning through discussion: Guide for leaders and members of discussion groups.* Beverly Hills, CA: Sage.

Jacobson, D., Eggen, P., Kauchuk, D., & Dulaney, C. (1985). *Methods for teaching.* Columbus, OH: Merrill.

Kindsvatter, R., Wilen, W., & Ishler, M. (1988). *Dynamics of effective teaching.* New York: Longman.

Kounin, J. (1970). *Discipline and group management in classrooms.* Chicago: Holt, Rinehart, and Winston.

McLeish, J. (1975). The lecture method. In N. L. Gage (Ed.), *Psychology of teaching methods* (pp. 252–301). Chicago: University of Chicago Press.

Medway, F. J. (1987). Tutoring. In M. J. Dunkin (Ed.), *International encyclopedia of teaching and teacher education* (pp. 243–245). Oxford: Pergamon Press.

Murray, H. (1963). *Explorations in personality.* New York: Oxford University Press.

Phelan, P., Davidson, A. L., & Cao, H. T. (1992, May). Speaking up: Student's perspectives on school. *Phi Delta Kappan, 73*(9), 695–704.

Roby, T. W. (1981, April). Bull sessions, quiz shows and discussions. Paper presented at the annual meeting of the American Educational Research Association, Los Angeles.

Rosenshine, B. (1980). How time is spent in elementary classrooms. In D. Denham & A. Lieberman (Eds.), *Time to learn: A review of the beginning teacher evaluation study* (pp. 107–126). Washington, DC: National Institute of Education.

Rosenshine, B. (1987). Direct instruction. In M. J. Dunkin (Ed.), *International encyclopedia of teaching and teacher education* (pp. 257–262). Oxford: Pergamon Press.

Rosenshine, B., & Stevens, R. (1986). Teaching functions. In M. C. Wittrock (Ed.), *Handbook of research on teaching* (pp. 376–391). New York: Macmillan.

Rupley, W., & Blair, T. (1987, January). Assignment and supervision of reading seatwork: Looking in on 12 primary teachers. *The Reading Teacher, 40,* 391–393.

Scott, Rose Mary. (1989). The relationship between elementary teachers' use of theoretical knowledge about seat work during reading instruction and students' on-task behavior. Unpublished doctoral dissertation. Columbus: Ohio State University.

Seifert, E. H., & Beck, J. J. (1984, September–October). Relationship between task time and learning gains in secondary schools. *Journal of Educational Research, 78,* 5–10.

Shuell, T. J., Brown, S., Watson, D. G., & Ewing, J. A. (1988, March). Teachers' perceptions of the differential appropriateness of various teaching methods. *The Elementary School Journal, 88*(4), 339–356.

Slavin, R. E. (1994). *Educational psychology.* Fourth Edition. Boston: Allyn & Bacon.

Toll, D. (1969). *Ghetto.* Indianapolis, IN: Bobbs-Merrill.

Van Ments, M. (1990). *Active talk.* London: St. Martin's Press.

Walberg, H. (1984, May). Improving the productivity of America's schools. *Educational Leadership, 41,* 19–27.

Watson, K. (1983). Some aspects of classroom discourse in English. Paper presented at the annual meeting of the Canadian Council of Teachers of English. (ERIC Document ED 233 365)

Four More Instructional Alternatives: Cooperative Learning, Discovery Learning, Direct Instruction, and Individualized Instruction

Contents

Chapter 6 introduced twenty-nine instructional alternatives (illustrated in the Wheel of Instructional Choice) and elaborated on three commonly known and used: presentation, discussion, and independent study. In this chapter, we turn our attention to four additional alternatives: cooperative learning, discovery learning, direct instruction, and individualized instruction.

Although the alternatives in this group are important components in a well-rounded teaching repertoire, they are not as commonly known and used as the preceding three. As you will see, each of the four alternatives introduced here is a bit more difficult to understand and complex to use. That might explain why, although each has staunch supporters, they are less easy to spot on the teaching scene.

Cooperative Learning: Teaching Learners to Like and Care for One Another

In a number of classrooms in which you have been a student, there has probably been a degree, perhaps a high degree, of competition among your peers. After all, nearly everyone in a class wants to get a good grade, and usually there are not enough to go around. Competition for good grades, however, may result in jealousy, even hostility, among learners. In an effort to reduce or eliminate competition and, relatedly, to build a sense of community, educators have searched for less competitive, nonconfrontational instructional alternatives. Mostly, they find some form of group work a suitable alternative. The group work of choice now is called cooperative learning.

7.1 How do you feel about classroom competition and cooperation?

WHAT IS COOPERATIVE LEARNING?

Cooperative learning (a variation on the theme of student-team learning) is the term used to describe instructional procedures whereby learners work together in small groups and are rewarded for their *collective* accomplishments. Does that remind you of a team sport such as volleyball or basketball? The whole team does or doesn't do well depending on the performance of each individual player and the extent to which they help one another. Cooperation is critical!

In cooperative learning, the groups or teams typically number from four to six. Their usual tasks are either to collectively learn or master content the teacher has previously presented, or to complete a teacher-assigned project as a team. In the first case, learners might work together to master spelling words the teacher has introduced. In the second, sometimes referred to as *group investigation* (Sharon & Sharon, 1989/1990), or *work groups* (Good et al., 1989/1990), they might work to learn about Native Americans of the Southwest or to solve a complex mathematical problem.

7.2 Have you ever experienced cooperative learning? What was it like for you?

PURPOSE AND CHARACTERISTICS OF COOPERATIVE LEARNING

7.3 How important is the purpose of cooperative learning?

Instructional procedures bearing the title or resembling cooperative learning have something in common with all instructional alternatives: they encourage students to learn. However, in contrast to the others, cooperative learning encourages learners to work together for both the common and individual good. This purpose may remind you of the famous line d'Artagnon speaks in Alexandre Dumas's novel *The Three Musketeers,* "All for one, one for all, that is our device, is it not?"

What are the key characteristics or attributes of cooperative learning systems? How is this "all for one, one for all" purpose achieved? Such systems are generally characterized by (1) the way the groups or teams are made up; (2) by the kinds of tasks they do; (3) the groups' rules of behavior; and (4) their motivation and reward systems.

According to advocates, including Slavin (1990, 1991a), groups must be heterogeneous in terms of gender, academic ability, race, and other traits. Heterogeneity is promoted for at least two reasons. First, cooperative learning is based partly on the humanistic school of thought about learning. That school of thought, as you recall from Chapter 3, focuses on the importance of personal and social development. One of its major objectives is to make students feel better about themselves and to be more accepting of others. Mixed groups offer a major means of achieving this goal.

Another reason to form heterogeneous teams is so that each member will have an equal opportunity to learn, since "talent" is about equally distributed to each group. Finally, heterogeneity is fostered because students with lower abilities are more likely to improve their achievement in mixed groups than in homogeneous groups (Hoffer, 1992; Slavin, 1990). Thus, heterogeneous teams would seem especially beneficial for students who are at risk of academic failure.

A second way cooperative learning can be characterized is by the kinds of tasks teachers typically assign to the teams. The most common assignment requires each team to master material the teacher presented previously. For example, Mrs. Braggins does a presentation on why the seasons change. She then asks the teams to review and learn the material in preparation for a quiz. Another common task is to ask teams to work on projects. Mr. Cruz asks his teams to read about the settling of California and then to collaboratively compose a letter as if a settler were writing to relatives in Spain describing the conditions of mission life.

Third, cooperative learning is characterized by rules of behavior required of team members: individual responsibility and accountability to oneself and the team, support and encouragement of team members, peer helping and tutoring, and, of course, cooperation. You can see how well the "all for one, one for all" analogy fits.

FIGURE 7.1 Purpose and Key Characteristics of Cooperative Learning

Purpose — To cause students to work together for both the individual and common good

Characteristics —
Heterogeneous (mixed) groups

Group tasks, usually either mastery or project work

Rule of behavior is "all for one, one for all" — members help each other

Group reward is shared equally by individual members

Finally, cooperative learning is characterized by a unique system of rewards. Rather than a mark based on personal effort, the individual receives a mark based on the team's achievement. If the students studied for and took a quiz on why the seasons change, the team's mark may be the average score for all team members. In the letter-writing assignment, all team members receive the score the letter earns. Again, we can liken such a situation to a sport where the team has a collective score and thereby wins or loses. Of course, this arrangement usually arouses peer pressure to do well and to help others do well. Thus, we think cooperative learning also derives some of its ideas from the behavioral school of thought, particularly operant conditioning and social learning.

In some cases, as you will see, cooperative teams can compete against one another. In other cases, teams compete against themselves and get a better mark only when they surpass some earlier achievement. Figure 7.1 illustrates the purpose and key characteristics of cooperative learning.

7.4 How do you feel about cooperative learning's key characteristics?

VARIATIONS ON THE THEME OF COOPERATIVE LEARNING

There are many versions of cooperative learning. (Aronson et al., 1978; Cohen, 1986; Johnson, Johnson, & Holubec, 1990; Sharon & Sharon, 1976; Slavin, 1990; Solomon et al., 1990). We will briefly describe a few. More elaborate descriptions are available elsewhere (Arends, 1999; Johnson, Johnson, & Holubec, 1990; Kauchak & Eggen, 1993; Slavin, 1990).

Student Teams, Achievement Divisions (STAD) Of the variations, the simplest to understand is STAD. In STAD, the student teams must master some content, usually presented by the teacher (perhaps new vocabulary). Students work in teams to ensure that all members can perform well on an upcoming quiz. The STAD process involves teacher presentation, team study, individual quizzes, determination of team scores, and team reward or recognition. To arrive at a team score, an individual's score is often compared to past work she or he has done. If the work is better than comparable past work, the person earns "improvement points." The team score is the sum of the improvement points individual members earn. This kind of scoring is most easily done when students take quizzes in spelling, arithmetic, and other subjects with easily quantified scores.

Teams, Games, Tournaments (TGT) The procedure for TGT follows STAD except that, instead of an individual quiz being given, the teams compete against one another. Thus, the TGT procedure is: teacher presentation, teamwork, team-versus-team competition, scoring, and team reward. In the team-versus-team competition phase, each member of a team is assigned to a table where he or she will compete against members from other teams. Top members from each team compete against one another in *equal competition;* the winner at each table is usually bumped up to the next higher level or table of competition. Think of this as comparable to the "ladders" used in sports competition—if you lose, you move down. Thus, competition always occurs among matched or somewhat like-achieving students. To some extent then, TGT loses the characteristic of heterogeneity, at least during academic competition.

Team-Assisted Individualization and Team-Accelerated Instruction (TAI) TAI combines the notions of cooperative learning and individually paced instruction. The latter means that students do not stay together academically, but instead learn or move through the material they are to master at their own pace. For instance, at the outset all students take a proficiency test in arithmetic. Based on the results, they are placed on mixed-ability teams. However, instead of working together, each team member works on a different aspect or unit of arithmetic according to her or his needs. The unit usually contains some guide pages that provide information essential to completing the work. Thus, a unit on division of fractions would contain pages illustrating how to divide fractions. The unit also would contain practice exercises, a short test or tests, and an answer sheet. In TAI, team members check one another's work, and more advanced students serve as tutors. Rewards may be based upon the number of units each team has completed, the number of final tests they have passed, or other criteria. An important element of TAI is that while teams are at work, the teacher is free to pull together students working on similar units to diagnose their progress and further assist them.

7.5 Which form of cooperative learning appeals to you most? Why?

Cooperative Integrated Reading and Composition (CIRC) CIRC is mainly used to teach reading and composition. In the typical CIRC procedure, the teacher sets a lesson in some specific area of reading or composition, for example, identifying the main characters and ideas in a piece of literature such as *Romeo and Juliet.* Student teams are then asked to read the story and to note the main characters and ideas. Team members, who may work in pairs, interact to check each other and gain consensus. They then may check their understanding with another pair on their team or against an answer sheet. While these paired and team activities are going on, the teacher convenes members from each team who are at a comparable proficiency or skill level in order to teach them a new reading skill, and the cycle continues. As with other forms of cooperative learning, points are given to teams based on individual members' performances on the activities and/or tests. The four forms of cooperative learning described are compared in Table 7.1.

GOOD LEADERS OF COOPERATIVE LEARNING

Cooperative learning procedures demand a lot from teachers. These approaches, depending on the type, require teachers to be responsible for presenting information, creating suitable group and possibly independent work assignments, establishing and maintaining cooperative groups, monitoring individual and group progress, convening and teaching small groups of learners, devising and maintaining progress records, and providing rewards.

Foremost, as the leader of any instructional alternative, you must believe in its purpose. You must have faith! In this case, you must subscribe to the "all for one, one for all" philosophy. Relatedly, you must be able to organize heterogenous teams and ensure that team members also value cooperative, collaborative learning. Also, since STAD, TGT, and CIRC incorporate teacher whole-class or small-group presentation, you must be a good presenter (see Table 6.2). Finally, since

TABLE 7.1 Four Forms of Cooperative Learning and Their Individual Characteristics

STAD	TGT	TAI	CIRC
		Proficiency testing of students, team assignment	
Presentation of information	Presentation of information	Individual but team-assisted study	Pairs work and teams work
Individual student quizzes	Team-vs.-team competition	Individual student quizzes	Individual student quizzes
Team scoring	Team scoring	Team scoring	Team scoring
Recognition	Recognition	Recognition	Recognition

all these variations of cooperative learning utilize some amount of independent study, you will also need to be good at facilitating this (see Table 6.5).

All forms of cooperative learning call for teachers who have the organizational skills to plan, monitor, facilitate, and track the work of disparate groups. Monitoring and facilitation are best accomplished when you have diagnostic and clinical skills, that is, when you are able to identify and help students and teams as they encounter problems. You must be a good juggler.

A subtle, yet very real, challenge teachers face when they use small-group instruction is the need to ensure that high-achieving students do not dominate the heterogeneous groups they are in. In a study of cooperative learning, King (1993) reports that "high-achieving students assumed dominant roles in the undertaking of group tasks, in group decision making, and in the frequency and quality of contributions" (p. 399). To avoid passivity on the part of low achievers, King suggests that teachers must create positive expectations that low achievers "can do." As you can see, utilizing cooperative learning is not for the faint of heart.

7.6 What beliefs and abilities do you have that might help you implement cooperative learning? What might inhibit your use of it?

GOOD COOPERATIVE LEARNING

Since there are several forms of cooperative learning, each requires a somewhat different kind of teacher preparation, delivery, and closure. Therefore, we will restrict our comments to STAD since it is the simplest, best known, and most frequently used form. Furthermore, Slavin (1990) recommends it as "a good model to begin with for teachers who are new to the cooperative approach" (p. 54).

Preparation   STAD, you may recall, is the form of cooperative learning in which the teacher presents information and then places students in heterogeneous groups to learn or master that information. Thus, two kinds of preparation are essential: (1) you must be prepared to provide information in the most effective way, and (2) students must be prepared to engage in group work so they can master the information.

Since a teacher presentation is called for, the information on good presentations in the previous chapter is useful. You may recall from Table 6.2 that as you prepare for a presentation, you must establish both its general purpose and its specific learner objectives (what learners should know and be able to do as a consequence of receiving the information). Johnson and Johnson (1976) offer a few questions useful in guiding teacher planning. They include: What do I want students to learn? What cognitive and affective outcomes should they achieve? What are some learning activities that can best accomplish these ends? What resources and assistance will learners need? Relatedly, you must collect and review materials

what you want them to learn, outcome.

FIGURE 7.2 Skills That Cooperative Learning Team Members Need

Johnson and Johnson (1989/1990) caution us that "people do not know instinctively how to interact effectively with others. Nor do interpersonal and group skills magically appear when needed. Students must be taught these skills and be motivated to use them. If group members lack interpersonal and small group skills . . . cooperative groups will not be productive" (p. 30).

The skills Johnson and Johnson feel are most necessary are to:

- Know and trust one another
- Communicate clearly and accurately
- Support one another through praise and encouragement
- Resolve conflicts constructively

that provide the knowledge you will present and, having taken these steps, plan the presentation. Finally, since a team assignment is to be undertaken following the presentation, you must organize that assignment and be ready to deliver it. You also must create a quiz.

Try Activity 7.1

Students must also be oriented to engage in STAD. Prior to its first use they must be told why it is being used, how it works, and, particularly, what is expected of them. Thereafter, each time STAD is used, learners need to be organized into heterogeneous groups and motivated to help one another learn. In some cases, students will need to be taught or reminded of the social skills they need to use. Figure 7.2 lists some of these skills and discusses their importance.

Delivery Delivery of STAD involves two steps: (1) your presentation and (2) initiation and monitoring of the teamwork. Once more, the information on good presentations from Chapter 6 is applicable. To review, when delivering a good presentation you should get students' attention, tell them what they will learn and, as a result, what they should be able to do after learning; relate the new information to ideas learners already know; present the information in a step-by-step manner; don't overwhelm or underwhelm; emphasize the most important points students need to remember or use; use examples and illustrations to increase clarity; use variety to maintain attention; and make sure learners understand by asking them questions.

Following your presentation, teamwork begins. You must then accomplish the following:

1. *Set the team goals.* The major function of the team in STAD is to prepare its members to learn as much as possible in order to obtain a high team quiz score.

2. *Prepare students for teamwork.* In STAD, this requires forming them into heterogeneous groups, reminding them of the "all for one, one for all" philosophy of cooperative learning, communicating your expectations for individual and group behavior, and jogging their memories concerning the interactive or social skills they will need to use.

3. *Give the teams the assignment.* Depending upon the nature of the assignment, you may have prepared handouts, worksheets, or a practice quiz for the teams to work on collaboratively.

4. *Monitor the teams.* Although the intention is that students teach and help one another, you must be sure that this, in fact, is happening. Therefore, you must be up and about, observing and listening, and intervening when necessary. One of the biggest mistakes you can make is to assume students know what to do and to assume they are doing it correctly. An ounce of prevention *is* worth a pound of cure.

5. *Quiz the students.* At a previously designated time, individual team members take the quiz. Although students have worked together to get ready for the quiz, they must take it independently.

6. *Score the quizzes.* Students may score one another's papers, or you may want to collect and score them yourself. (There are advantages and disadvantages either way. Can you think of some of them?) Once you have scored individual quizzes, you need to calculate team scores. There are at least two ways to derive team scores. In one, you calculate an "improvement score" by comparing each learner's achievement on this quiz with her or his achievement on a similar, earlier quiz. If the score is better, the student receives one or more improvement points. Then you add all individual improvement scores to get the team improvement score. Another way to calculate a team score is simply to add the members' scores together. Most advocates of cooperative learning procedures favor the use of improvement scores.

7. *Recognize team accomplishment.* When improvement scores are used, teams that have improved performance receive some recognition. Thus, teams compete with themselves to improve, rather than against other teams to win. This is more gentle than rewarding teams that outperform other teams. Forms of recognition and reward can include printed certificates of achievement, recognition as "super team" of the week, or special privileges. As mentioned earlier, cooperative learning draws also from the behavioral school of thought and particularly from operant conditioning. If you do something well, you get rewarded.

Closure Little is said in the literature on cooperative learning about what, if anything, to do after you give grades and rewards. Considering what we know about short- and long-term memory (Chapter 3), we presume that students should be reminded of what they have just learned, the new information should be securely related and attached to what they already know or what they will learn next, and they should have the opportunity to apply the information in some way.

A summary of the qualities of good cooperative learning leaders and of the elements of good cooperative learning appears in Table 7.2.

7.7 How do you feel about your ability to use any of the forms of cooperative learning?

Try Activity 7.2

TABLE 7.2 Qualities of Good Cooperative Learning Leaders and of Good Cooperative Learning (STAD)

Good Leaders of Cooperative Learning . . .	Good Cooperative Learning (STAD)
• Believe in the importance of getting learners to work together for the individual and common good	*When preparing:* • Prepare the presentation utilizing elements of a "good presentation" (Table 6.2)
• Are able to get diverse learners to work cooperatively	• Prepare the team assignment (Table 6.5)
• Are competent presenters and use independent study assignments effectively (see Tables 6.2 and 6.5)	• Prepare students for future engagement in cooperative learning by explaining effective interpersonal and interactive skills (see Figure 7.2)
• Are especially effective organizers and coordinators of work	*When delivering:* • Make the presentation utilizing elements of a "good presentation" (Table 6.2)
• Are especially effective diagnosticians and clinicians, i.e., are able to identify and help students and teams having difficulty	• Set team goals
	• Prepare students for work with their team
	• Give the teams the assignment
	• Quiz the students
	• Recognize team accomplishments
	When closing: • Remind students of what they learned
	• Relate new learning to past or future learning
	• Provide opportunity for practical use of information

ADVANTAGES AND LIMITATIONS OF COOPERATIVE LEARNING

What do you think makes cooperative learning appealing to teachers and students? What personal and professional needs does it seem to satisfy for the teacher? What needs does it meet for the student?

Benefits for Teachers   Let's begin once more by considering which of Murray's needs cooperative learning seems to help teachers meet. This is difficult to do because the several forms of cooperative learning have some striking differences. The forms cumulatively encompass presentation, discussion, independent study, and individualized instruction—another alternative presented at the end of this chapter.

Given the variations, we will highlight only the teacher personality needs that *all* cooperative learning forms seem to meet. They include:

- The **achievement** need to do difficult tasks as well as possible. Good teaching of any type is difficult; and teachers who use cooperative learning believe it is worth the additional effort because it produces improved learning and satisfaction.
- The **recognition** need to obtain positive attention. Teachers want to be well-thought-of for using promising professional practices, even when these practices may be somewhat more complicated and demanding.
- The **affiliation** need to be liked. Most students like group or team activities, and they like teachers who provide them.

7.8 Which of the teacher needs met by cooperative learning are important to you?

Throughout his book, Slavin (1990) sprinkles testimonial letters from elementary, middle school, and high school teachers who have succeeded using forms of STAD, TGT, TAI, and CIRC. Overall, the teachers extol cooperative learning because it (1) requires students to develop and use group or social skills, (2) challenges able students to help less able students, (3) requires learners to give one another good explanations, (4) fosters individual accountability, (5) raises the pride and self-esteem of students, particularly less able pupils, (6) satisfies students' needs for recognition, and (7) raises students' achievement.

Of the five professional needs Cruickshank and associates (1980) cited, cooperative learning seems most likely to meet the teacher goal of **student success**.

Benefits for Students   Like other instructional alternatives, cooperative learning benefits some students more than others. Those who write about it mostly mention its benefits for low-achieving and mainstreamed students. Augustine, Gruber, and Hansen (1989/1990) provide case reports of how it specifically aided a variety of children. Synopses of these cases appear in Case 7.1.

Cooperative learning meets quite a few of the personality needs of students:

- The need for **play**—to seek diversion, change, and relaxation.
- The **exposition** need to give others information.
- The **achievement** need to do academic tasks as well as possible.
- The **recognition** need to be praised and recognized.
- The **failure avoidance** need, especially for lower-achieving students.
- The **inviolacy** need to maintain one's self-respect, again, a need felt more acutely by students who perform less well academically.
- The **affiliation** need to form associations and friendships with other students.
- The **deference** need to conform and follow the lead of others. This would apply to students with lower ego needs.
- The **nurturance** need to help others. Students who enjoy giving information would benefit here.
- The **succorance** need to seek help from others. Information recipients gain on this count.

7.9 Which of the student needs met by cooperative learning are most important to you?

As you can see, cooperative learning would seem to be quite appealing to students.

CASE 7.1
Cooperative Learning Success Stories

Three teachers (Augustine, Gruber, & Hansen, 1989/1990) provide sketches of three kinds of students positively affected by cooperative learning.

Andy is a low-achieving elementary school student. He was failing several subjects and needed supervision to stay on task until cooperative learning was introduced. The changes are astonishing. His grades have improved to the point where he is passing all subjects. Additionally, Andy has become a "cheerful, confident child."

Susan, a child with handicaps mainstreamed in a regular classroom, was placed in a cooperative learning group. The group's task was to prepare for a chapter test. When the group's study time was over, Susan still was not ready. Instead of taking recess, her group colleagues stayed to work further with her. They also helped her the next day before the test was given. On the test, Susan and all her teammates received perfect scores.

Angela, a gifted student, excelled at school and also in piano, gymnastics, and dance. Her parents questioned how working in a group where she would be held to a group norm would be beneficial. After all, Angela did outstanding work on her own. After a conference, Angela's parents were convinced she might benefit from learning how to interact with less capable peers. Her group work has helped Angela become more tactful, respectful, and sharing.

Limitations The success of cooperative learning depends upon a number of conditions. First, research shows that for a cooperative learning activity to succeed, team members must not simply share answers but, more importantly, explain how they derived the answers and why they are correct (Slavin, 1990). Without this step, students are not able to apply or use the information later. Therefore, some students in each group must be "good teachers." Relatedly, for a successful learning experience, high achievers must care for and help or nurture low achievers. The implicit assumption is that good students wish to help less able students.

A second important condition is that individual team members be accountable to the team. This "one for all" expectation is not what students have been accustomed to; what they are accustomed to is a high degree of interpersonal competition.

Third, in order for cooperative learning to have a chance, team members must stay on task, since time on task is consistently related to students' learning (see Chapter 11). Students tend to get off task when the teacher is not present. Teachers must regularly monitor individual and small-group work during cooperative learning.

Fourth, in any team, individuals must get along with one another. In every classroom, certain students will find this difficult. There may also be students who will do less work or work less hard, thereby causing the team to suffer or cover-up. Brophy and Good (1986) remind us that any form of small-group instruction is more difficult than teaching the class as a whole because these and other management problems are compounded (see Chapter 12).

Finally, teaching arrangements that encourage some children to provide assistance and others to receive it appear likely to increase dependency (Biemiller, 1993).

WHEN COOPERATIVE LEARNING SHOULD BE USED

Properly conducted, cooperative learning is an instructional alternative with strong support. It seems to reduce competition and increase cooperation and achievement. When should it be used? Our answer is, often—but not always. As indicated in Chapter 6, variety in instruction is extremely important. Teachers' comments interspersed throughout Slavin's book (1990) indicate that although students do not seem to tire of cooperative learning, the possibility of boredom exists. Consequently, teachers who use this instructional alternative make certain adjustments. For example, they vary team membership, tasks, and rewards.

A second reason to avoid putting all our eggs into the cooperative learning basket is that different kinds of educational objectives are best achieved using different instructional alternatives. Supporting this view, Stallings and Stipek (1986) note that TGT does not seem to produce as much achievement when used in social studies. Furthermore, they cite Sharon (1980), who questions whether the use of cooperative learning, specifically STAD and TGT, can be as effective when the goal is to teach or use higher-level thinking skills such as analysis, synthesis, and evaluation.

Keeping these restrictions in mind, cooperative learning is probably best utilized when the class needs to develop a sense of harmony and community building (all for one, one for all), when students are at risk or generally suffer from low self-esteem, and when teachers want to help integrate mainstreamed students.

Teachers who select cooperative learning strategies probably believe in the "all for one, one for all" philosophy, feel they have good leadership and interpersonal skills, know that their organizational and monitoring abilities enable them to do more than one thing at a time (overlapping), and believe that this approach works.

Internet Resource   At present, there is a website maintained by the Cooperative Learning Center at http://www.clcrc.com/. The site has several links, including one to "Cooperative Learning." Here, the following questions are addressed: What is cooperative learning? Why use it? What makes cooperative groups work?

SUMMARY ON COOPERATIVE LEARNING

At the outset, we characterized cooperative learning as teaching learners to like and care for one another. We stated the method is analogous to creating teams of musketeers who come to one another's assistance and who succeed together no matter what the circumstances. Cooperative learning seems to have a hint of romanticism about it when compared to its more common instructional cousins such as presentation, discussion, and independent study. In business jargon, it seems to have more "sizzle."

We also learned there are a number of different cooperative learning approaches but that most have four characteristics in common (see Figure 7.1): (1) they utilize teams that are mostly heterogeneous in composition; (2) the task the teams undertake usually involves either mastering material presented by a teacher, mastering written materials, or working on a project; (3) accountability is twofold—to oneself and to assisting the team and its members; and (4) rewards are generally tied to overall team improvement.

As with any instructional alternative, teachers who use this approach need certain attributes. They need to be good presenters, to be insightful in developing worthwhile team assignments, and to be able to monitor teamwork, diagnose problems, and prescribe remedies. Since the various forms of cooperative learning differ, each has a set of best procedures to follow. The qualities of good procedures for STAD appear in Table 7.2.

Like each instructional alternative on the Wheel of Instructional Choice (Figure 6.8), cooperative learning (student-team learning) has unique advantages and limitations. Its advantages mirror those offered by discussion, another student-centered alternative that meets a large number of students' needs. However, cooperative learning seems to be better than discussion at meeting students' needs to achieve academically and socially.

Try Activity 7.3

Certain cooperative learning processes have been subjected to controlled study, and most prove to contribute to student success, that is achievement and satisfaction (see Spotlight on Research 7.1). Little consensus exists concerning how frequently cooperative learning is used; estimates range from 7 to 20 percent of the time. However, we can assume from its repeated mention in the professional literature that cooperative learning is very much alive and well. One of its better known proponents sums it up, although perhaps a bit too optimistically: "Cooperative learning seems to be an extraordinary success. It has an excellent research base, many viable, successful forms, and hundreds of thousands of enthusiastic adherents" (Slavin, 1989/1990, p. 3).

There are differences of opinion regarding the effectiveness of cooperative learning. Its founders and proponents give it very high marks.

Johnson and others (1981) reviewed 122 studies that compared the effectiveness of four instructional alternatives: cooperation, cooperation with intergroup competition, interpersonal competition, and independently done individual work. When cooperation and competition were compared, researchers found that the average student's achievement in a cooperative program equalled that of students at the 78th percentile who worked in either a competitive or individualistic arrangement. This means that a middle-achieving student in cooperative learning does as well as a higher-achieving student under the other two forms of instruction. Other findings indicate that the average student in the cooperative programs achieved at a level (1) equal to that of students at the 64th percentile in interpersonal competitive programs and (2) equal to that of students at the 69th percentile in individualistic programs. Johnson and associates did not find achievement differences between students in cooperative groups and students involved in intergroup competition. Relatedly, no differences in achievement have been found between interpersonal competition and independent work (Runkel & Schmuck, 1982).

Similarly, Slavin's (1991a) findings strongly support cooperative learning processes as facilitating student achievement, He found sixty-seven "high-quality studies" that compared achievement of elementary and high school students taught by cooperative processes to the achievement of similar students taught by traditional methods. In forty-one studies, or 61 percent of the research, the cooperatively taught students performed significantly better. In fact, in only one of the sixty-seven studies did traditionally taught students excel. Slavin notes, "In studies of methods such as STAD, TGT, TAI, and CIRC, effects on achievement have been consistently positive" (p. 76).

Slavin goes on to say that when students are rewarded according to the group's achievement, which depends on how much each learner learned, students learn even more. Achievement improves regardless of grade level, subject area, or geographic location of the school—urban, suburban, or rural.

In addition to the positive effects cooperative learning has on achievement, Slavin (1991a, 1995) also notes that it produces many beneficial side-effects including higher self-esteem, better intergroup relationships, greater acceptance of others, better attitudes toward school, and improved ability to work cooperatively.

After reviewing research on STAD, TGT, and Jigsaw (a form not presented here but described in Slavin, 1990), Stallings and Stipek (1986) agree that these forms of cooperative learning seem to have positive effects on achievement. However, they warn us that many other variations on the theme of cooperative learning have not yet been investigated. Furthermore, Stallings and Stipek feel that the most important outcomes of cooperative learning may be in the affective domain of learning and include such things as greater mutual concern, more friendships with diverse students, a better feeling about school, and a sense of greater peer support.

Other caveats come from Webb (1982) and Battistich, Solomon, and Delucci (1993). Webb reminds us that, contrary to what Slavin and others have reported more recently, Michaels (1978) found individual competition promotes better achievement than group work does. Battistich and his colleagues, who are advocates of cooperative learning, note "that cooperative learning does not invariably lead to positive outcomes" (p. 20).

Discovery Learning: Figuring Things Out for Yourself

You have probably heard of Sherlock Holmes, the famous detective created by Sir Arthur Conan Doyle. As you may recall, Holmes was regularly faced with baffling cases such as the sudden, mysterious death of Sir Charles Baskerville in the novel *The Hound of the Baskervilles* (Doyle, 1901). According to his great friend Dr. Watson, Holmes—as was his custom—demanded the facts. After gathering them, he would retreat into seclusion in order to "weigh every particle of evidence, construct alternative theories, balance one against the other, and make up his mind as to which points were essential and which immaterial" (p. 35) to solving the mystery. Holmes was the consummate inductive reasoner, always "putting two and two together" in order to reach some logical explanation or conclusion.

Many times we, too, face situations where we have to figure things out for ourselves. What is the meaning of a new word we find in a sentence? How can we get the word processor to double-space? Why did we get a C in the course instead of a B? How can we get a B next time?

Psychologists and educators (Bruner, 1961; Dewey, 1933; Joyce & Weil, 1986; Strike, 1975; Suchman, 1961; Taba, 1966) make the case that reasoning skills—Sherlock Holmes's, ours, or our students'—can be improved through use. They propose that we utilize discovery learning to give learners the opportunity to collect, organize, manipulate, and analyze data. Discovery learning is the instructional alternative many educators tout as the choice for teaching social studies, science, and more recently, mathematics.

WHAT IS DISCOVERY LEARNING?

You may recall that we introduced the term *discovery* in Chapter 3, as an example of meaningful learning. (Reviewing that section now would be useful.) Here it is described more fully as an instructional alternative.

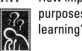

7.10 Do you prefer having someone teach you something or figuring it out for yourself?

We define **discovery learning** as learning that takes place when students are asked to derive their own meaning and understanding from experiences presented to them. This contrasts with **reception learning** and **expository teaching,** in which the teacher tells or gives information. An example might make the distinction clearer. In reception learning, you would describe to your students the life cycle of a frog, perhaps using illustrations. In discovery learning you would *ask* students to find out for themselves, probably through observation, what stages a frog's life moves through. Essentially, you would ask them to conduct an investigation in the manner of Sherlock Holmes.

PURPOSES AND CHARACTERISTICS OF DISCOVERY LEARNING

7.11 How important are the purposes of discovery learning?

Teachers use discovery learning to accomplish three related educational purposes. The major one is to provide students with opportunities to think independently in order to obtain knowledge for themselves. This means we want to wean students away from dependence upon others in order to learn something. The second purpose is to help students discover how knowledge becomes known. This means helping them see for themselves how to formulate knowledge through collecting, organizing, and manipulating data (Joyce & Weil, 1986). Third, discovery learning promotes higher-order or critical thinking skills such as analysis, synthesis, and evaluation. As with other instructional alternatives, these purposes give discovery learning its unique, key characteristics. We think it is different in terms of the teacher's role, the student's role, and the intellectual skills it promotes.

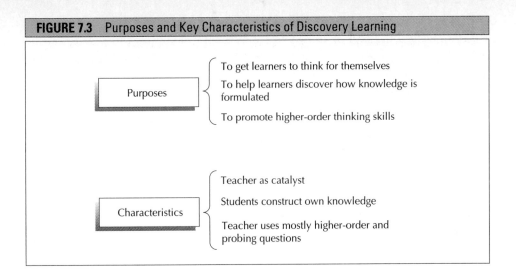

FIGURE 7.3 Purposes and Key Characteristics of Discovery Learning

Purposes
- To get learners to think for themselves
- To help learners discover how knowledge is formulated
- To promote higher-order thinking skills

Characteristics
- Teacher as catalyst
- Students construct own knowledge
- Teacher uses mostly higher-order and probing questions

In any instructional alternative, the role of the teacher is to be a catalyst, or change agent (see Figure 7.3). However, in no other teaching maneuver is this role so critical as it is in discovery learning. Whether students are able to learn by discovery is a direct function of how well the teacher sets the stage by *arranging an environment that encourages and rewards independent thought and exploration.*

The student role is also different in discovery learning. Students are expected to develop or construct their own knowledge. We mentioned constructivism in Chapter 3, when discovery learning was introduced. You may recall Deb O'Brien, the teacher who avoided telling students what heat is and what holds and captures it. Instead, she helped them to find out for themselves, to construct their own meaning (see Case 3.1). Essentially, **constructivism** describes learning that is active, engaging, and arouses curiosity. Students are given the responsibility to search for their own meaning through hands-on activities. They ask questions, explore, and discover, thereby constructing new understandings and incorporating them into what they already hold in long-term memory.

A third key characteristic of discovery learning is that it is concerned with raising the students' level of thinking. Rather than ask them to recall or remember, ask them to analyze, synthesize, and evaluate. This concern is translated into action by the teacher, who poses higher-level questions. Deb O'Brien asked, "What is heat?" "How can we find out if heat comes from clothing?" and, finally, "If heat doesn't come from clothing, why do clothes make us feel warmer?"

7.12 How much do you value the key characteristics of discovery learning?

GOOD FACILITATORS OF DISCOVERY LEARNING

To be effective with this instructional alternative, you must believe in its purposes. Do you think a major goal of education is to get students to think for themselves? Do you believe students have the ability to think for themselves? Even if you answer the first question affirmatively, you may be stymied by the second. After all, you have probably been in classrooms where some of your peers seemed less than able intellectually. However, keep in mind that the cause of their apparent ineptitude may stem from their never having the opportunity to build confidence in their own thinking ability. Belief in one's power to think *must* be planted and cultivated.

A second purpose of discovery learning is to get learners to find out how knowledge is constructed. Do you want them to know how concepts, facts, generalizations, rules, and laws are formulated? If you do, you have intellectual aspirations for your learners. You expect them to understand the very origin and nature of knowledge rather than just memorize facts.

7.13 When your students don't understand, are you more likely to give them the answer or help them discover it?

A third purpose of discovery learning is to get learners to develop their higher-order or critical thinking skills. Do you want them to know how to analyze, synthesize, evaluate, and solve problems? Can you persist in encouraging them to explore, investigate, search, observe, scrutinize, inspect, classify, measure, define, interpret, infer, predict, and hypothesize? If so, you will make an indelible mark on their minds and lives.

Aside from believing in the purpose of discovery learning, to be a good practitioner you need certain qualities. For example, you must enjoy inquiry yourself: you should be naturally curious and have "a strong interest in the discovery of truth by an empirical, critical, rational, 'intellectual' approach" (Anastasi, 1989, p. 488). Relatedly, you should believe that your learners are or can be curious, too. Moreover, you should be nurturing, thoughtful, patient, and accepting of learners' ideas while holding high expectations for them.

GOOD DISCOVERY LEARNING

Suppose you are sold on discovery learning and feel you have the ability to pull it off. What process or regimen would you follow? Persons either reviewing or advocating this instructional alternative suggest several stages and steps (Gilstrap & Martin, 1975; Harmin & Gregory, 1974; Joyce & Weil, 1986; Kauchak & Eggen, 1993; Orlich et al., 1990).

Preparation   When preparing any learning activity, you should have some broad purpose in mind. Perhaps it is to have students learn about pulse rate or rate of respiration. With that in mind, you decide *specifically* what students should know about either or both. Let's say you want them to know the meaning of pulse and respiration (concepts), how pulse and respiration are measured (procedures), the range of pulse and respiration rates (facts), normal rates (facts), and conditions that affect the rates (generalizations). To ensure your own knowledge of these areas and to have related resources available, you need to collect material on these topics.

Now you are ready to generate the discovery lesson. How can you create situations where students can find out these things for themselves? More specifically, how can you create interest? What do you want students to notice or discover? How can they do so? Here we take into account all we have learned about lesson planning from Chapter 5, Planning Instruction.

Finally, in the preparation stage you need to be sure your students are ready to use scientific methods such as observation, recording, and analyzing. If they have not previously had experience with inductive and deductive reasoning, you will have to provide greater guidance and simplification.

Delivery   When you studied information processing in Chapter 3, you learned how essential it is to obtain and maintain students' attention. In Chapter 5, Planning Instruction, this message was reinforced by the concept of **set induction,** that is, doing something at the start of the lesson to grab the learners' attention. Can you think of something that would cause students to focus on learning about pulse and respiration? It could be a question such as, "What are some things our body must do to stay alive?"

Having gained your students' attention, you next might present a situation, real or hypothetical, that is challenging or baffling. Again, you can use questions such as: "What do physicians do to find out if our systems are OK?" "How do they know?" "How do we know when our pulse rate and respiration are normal?" "What is normal? How can we find out?" "What might make our pulse and respiration rates change? How can we find out?" Depending on the specific objectives of your lesson, you would phrase questions that invite learners to discover answers. Getting them to phrase questions is even better. Table 7.3 reminds us of four forms of knowledge and provides examples of questions that promote each form.

Try Activity 7.4

"How do you expect me to learn anything when you're the one who keeps asking all the questions?"

TABLE 7.3 Four Forms of Knowledge and Illustrative Questions That Could Be Used to Promote Discovery of Each

Form of Knowledge	Questions That Promote Discovery
1. *Concepts.* A concept is the name that describes a class of ideas or objects.	1.1 What is a mammal? 1.2 What is luck? 1.3 What is rap music? 1.4 What is a democrat?
2. *Facts.* A fact is a truth.	2.1 What is the average pulse rate? 2.2 What is the life history of the frog? 2.3 What is the sum of the angles of a triangle? 2.4 What happens when blue and red mix?
3. *Generalizations.* A generalization is an inference that may not be universally true but is widely supported.	3.1 How are families changing? 3.2 How should lessons be prepared? 3.3 What are the attributes of good teachers? 3.4 Why do students go south for spring break?
4. *Rules/laws.* A rule or law is an unchanging principle that governs a particular situation or set of conditions.	4.1 How are words divided into syllables? 4.2 How is table tennis played? 4.3 How are fractions divided? 4.4 Why do certain objects float?

7.15 How would you help learners discover *any one* of these concepts, facts, generalizations, or rules/laws?

Once you have presented students with a challenge, you need to ensure that they have a clear idea of how to investigate the question. "What can you do to discover the answers to these questions?" "Which ones might you be able to find out for yourselves without reading books?" "How could you do so?"

When students are ready to proceed with their observation, data collection, analysis, and so forth, your task is to monitor and display the qualities of a good discovery learning teacher. These include holding high expectations that students can learn on their own, nurturing them, being patient and accepting of their ideas, and causing them to be thoughtful and reflective. It is particularly urgent that you develop a secure environment that supports risk-free thinking. Fear of ridicule, failure, or criticism must be removed or your learners may be intellectually paralyzed. This does not mean that the environment is evaluation-free. Rather, it means that judgments result from thoughtful consideration and perhaps from the testing of all ideas.

Closure Following open and substantial consideration of the data they have unearthed, learners need to draw conclusions. "After your investigation, what can you conclude about pulse and respiration rates?" Here your task is to help learners organize and phrase the discoveries. To ensure that the discovery has become embedded in long-term memory, you next need to provide an opportunity to use it. In the case of pulse and respiration, perhaps students could assess family members' pulse rates.

Table 7.4 is a summary of the qualities of good discovery learning teachers and of good discovery learning procedures.

Try Activity 7.5

FACILITATING DISCOVERY LEARNING ONLINE

You can accomplish the outcomes of discovery learning by utilizing certain computer software programs and by using the computer to search for information. The Dalton School in New York City exemplifies how (Wallis 1995).

A software program called *Archaeotype,* developed at Dalton, is a computer simulation of an archeological dig, complete with shovel sounds. Groups of four or five

TABLE 7.4 Qualities of Good Facilitators of Discovery Learning and of Good Discovery Learning

Good Facilitators . . .	Good Discovery Learning
• Believe in the purposes of discovery learning	*When preparing:*
• Tend to be inquirers (curious) themselves	• Determine the general purpose of the lesson
• Are optimistic and confident in students' ability to inquire	• Determine the specific lesson objectives: identify the concepts, facts, generalizations, rules, or laws to be discovered
• Hold high expectations of students	
• Are nurturing	• Collect useful resources and material
• Are thoughtful	• Plan the discovery lesson
• Are patient	• Ensure that learners are ready to use inductive methods
• Accept students' ideas	*When delivering:*
• Are reflective	• Obtain students' attention via set induction
	• Present the challenging or baffling situation
	• Utilize questions that will promote discovery (see examples in Table 7.3)
	• Ensure that learners know what they are supposed to do
	• Monitor and guide student activity and thinking
	• Encourage observation, collection and organization, manipulation, analysis of ideas and data, and so forth
	When closing:
	• Help learners to organize and phrase what they have concluded: the concepts, facts, generalizations, and so forth
	• Provide opportunity to use the new knowledge

students are assigned a "lot" to unearth at an ancient Syrian site. The purpose: to locate what is buried, analyze it, and create and defend a thesis about the site and its inhabitants. To support the theories generated, the group has online access to libraries and art museums containing stores of related information. Thus, rather than receiving information about life in ancient Syria, students discover the knowledge for themselves. Quite literally, they construct it.

Another class at Dalton, after reading Shakespeare's *Macbeth,* is able to delve more deeply into the text and its characters by connecting online to various databases containing related information. For example, a group of students working on a paper on Lady Macbeth is able to access illustrations of the character, scenes in which she is portrayed in motion pictures, and dozens of essays about her. Obviously, the information obtained is far more extensive than would otherwise be available, and having it permits the group to formulate knowledge, to derive their own meaning about who this person was.

ADVANTAGES AND LIMITATIONS OF DISCOVERY LEARNING

The psychological and professional advantages of having teachers and students use discovery learning are presented next.

Benefits for Teachers   Teachers who have the following personal needs would seem more likely to employ discovery learning:

• The **cognizance** need to explore.
• The **construction** need to organize and build.

- The **recognition** need to obtain praise. Discovery learning is viewed as an exemplary instructional alternative because of its focus on promoting higher-order thinking.
- The **exhibition** need to excite others. Encouraging discovery excites others and thereby attracts positive attention to the teacher.
- The **affiliation** need to form associations with students. This is one of several instructional alternatives that promote teacher-student and student-student interaction.
- The **nurturance** need to nourish and aid others. Discovery learning requires and rewards teachers who help students find out for themselves and to learn how to learn.

In addition to meeting these personality needs, discovery learning helps teachers live up to professional, job-related expectations. For example, good teachers are supposed to engage their students in meaningful learning. In Chapter 3, meaningful learning was described as learning that maximizes learner understanding. Certainly, when students discover the meaning of concepts, determine facts, and make generalizations from data, the knowledge they obtain is infinitely more understandable and consequently more easily remembered. Nuthall and Snook (1973) and Tamir (1995) agree, noting that knowledge discovered from personal experience is very special, more meaningful, and stays with us longer than knowledge gained in other ways. Additionally, we transfer this knowledge more easily to other situations; it earns a more important place in our minds.

Today, teachers are urged to engage students in constructing their own knowledge. Discovery learning provides a vehicle. Using it, learners can construct concepts, facts, generalizations, rules, and laws, or they can see how such constructs are formed. Furthermore, they can compare their constructs to the constructs of others, both peers and experts.

Helping students learn how to learn and how to develop higher-level cognitive skills is another expectation good teachers hold. As students construct knowledge, they learn how to learn through analysis, synthesis, and evaluation. Finally, to the extent possible, good teachers employ *interactive teaching*, that is, teaching that causes students to act reciprocally—to give and take with other students and the teacher. Said another way, good teachers involve their learners in active classroom dialogue.

7.16 What are the major advantages of discovery learning for you as a teacher?

Benefits for Students Students who have the following personality needs would seem to benefit from engaging in discovery learning.

- The **cognizance** need to explore.
- The **construction** need to organize and build.
- The **achievement** need to do difficult tasks well and efficiently. The tasks of discovery learning normally are challenging, sometimes almost baffling.
- The **exposition** need to organize and present information, to explain and demonstrate. Discovery learning is intrinsically rewarding to students who possess higher-level thinking ability.
- The **recognition** need for attention. Learners have the opportunity to gain recognition for their ability to use the reasoning processes.
- The **autonomy** need to strive for independence and freedom. The idea is to encourage speculation and independence of thought.
- The **affiliation** need to form friendships and associations. When properly structured and monitored by the teacher, discovery learning encourages and supports positive student interactions.
- The need to **play**—to seek diversion. Discovery learning can be great fun and quite a change of pace from normal teacher-centered instruction.

What student educational needs does discovery learning seem to meet? Most importantly, it causes students to learn how to find things out for themselves. It begins the process of emancipating the student from the teacher. It encourages students to draw their own inferences and conclusions As Szent-Gyorgyi (1965) describes it, "Discovery consists of seeing what everybody has seen and [perhaps] thinking what nobody else has thought" (p. 225).

Limitations   It is too bad that so promising an alternative also has formidable shortcomings. Most notably, not everything students must learn is amenable to classroom discovery. Students in most classrooms cannot be expected to discover chemical elements, the themes of famous writers and artists, or the way a computer works. Such knowledge is probably too complex for the minds of K–12 students. Even when they have the capacity to discover complex knowledge, there may not be sufficient time or appropriate resources to make the investigation. Perhaps that is why teacher presentations are still so common. They provide a fairly efficient way of getting complex knowledge to a large group of diverse learners.

Another shortcoming is that some teachers simply do not have the experience or aptitude for this approach (Tamir 1995). Neither do all of their students—it may just not be your or their "style." In this case, perhaps teachers and students would like it more if they simply tried it more. Maybe it just needs getting used to.

Finally, discovery learning allows students to make errors. Unless these errors are corrected, serious confusion can result. Consequently, the teacher must closely monitor the results of discovery learning.

WHEN DISCOVERY LEARNING SHOULD BE USED

Given what we know, when should discovery learning be used? We believe it should be employed when your instructional goals coincide with its main purposes: (1) to get students to think for themselves, (2) to help them to discover how knowledge is created, and (3) to promote higher-order thinking. Additionally, discovery learning should be used when it best serves the personal and educational needs of you and your learners. Finally, it should be used only when you have developed the qualities of a good facilitator and you know and can follow the regimen for good discovery learning.

Of course, all the above is based on the premise that your learning objectives can be most effectively gained using this alternative. If that is not the case, you must be convinced that the time and energy it demands are worth it. Said another way, the ends of discovery learning should justify it as the means.

All teachers probably use some modified or abbreviated forms of discovery learning because of the influence of educational philosopher John Dewey (1933) and psychologist Jerome Bruner (1960, 1961). Both theorists admonished teachers to get students to think for themselves. Consequently, when you observe a reading class in an elementary school, you will often hear the teacher ask students to figure out the meaning of a new word from the sentence and paragraph the word is embedded in. In another classroom, you might see students investigating the leaves of different trees. Joyce and Weil (1986) note, "Probably nothing has been more consistently pursued yet remains more elusive than the teaching of thinking" (p. 42). However, even though discovery learning is widely recommended for this purpose, most teachers use it incidentally, as a part of recitation or discussion. For the most part, teachers persist in telling students what to think.

SUMMARY ON DISCOVERY LEARNING

As a student, if you have been exposed to discovery learning, you have been asked to take on the role of a detective. You were asked to investigate a situation in order to figure it out. Almost every day, you are faced with perplexing academic and nonacademic situations, and for the most part, you must cope with them on your

What does research on discovery learning tell us? The results are mixed. Hofwolt (1984) reports that compared to more traditional teacher- and textbook-centered techniques, inquiry teaching produces significant learner achievement in science. Negatively, Wittrock (1966) strongly questions its use with slower learners. Slavin, Karweit, and Madden (1989) find more direct forms of instruction better for teaching concepts. (The next section of this chapter will introduce direct instruction.)

Nuthall and Snook (1973) conclude that, "it is still necessary to find the experimental evidence which demonstrates convincingly that the discovery procedure is superior [to expository teaching or teacher presentations]" (p. 63). Merwin (1976) puts it all in perspective when he writes, "The research related to discovery learning is neither conclusive nor convincing enough to warrant its universal adoption. . . . However, one cannot ignore the successful learning outcomes as recorded in several [research studies]. For many students and teachers, discovery learning provides an exciting and rewarding [experience]; for others, it is fraught with frustration and failure" (p. 391).

own. Thus, any previous experience you have had with inductive thinking should be of help. If you have had teachers who mostly told you what to do and think, you are disadvantaged. Such teachers may have given you much knowledge but not taught you how to think.

Discovery learning holds promise in ensuring that your learners will be able to think for themselves. Its major purpose is to help students learn how to find out for themselves. To use this alternative effectively, you need to believe in its purposes, you must have certain qualities such as curiosity, optimism, and confidence in students' abilities to think and inquire, and you must have patience. Finally, you need to know and follow the discovery learning regimen or procedure illustrated in Table 7.4.

Discovery learning appears well-suited to certain teachers and students. It may be well-suited to others who have had little experience or bad prior experiences with the method. As teachers, one of our toughest jobs is to remediate bad past experiences students have had. Spotlight on Research 7.2 describes the negatives and positives of discovery learning.

Try Activity 7.6

Direct Instruction: Teaching in the Most Efficient Way

Direct instruction is not precisely *an* instructional alternative. Rather, it is a description of what teachers do to utilize what is known about successful teaching and about learning. However, we include it here because it provides a very clear scenario about how you can teach so that students learn.

The basic idea of **direct instruction** is to get students to learn as much academic content as efficiently as possible. There are two schools of thought about how to do this. One school suggests that the best means is to observe the most effective teachers to find out what they do and then prepare other teachers to teach likewise. The other school tells us to have teachers put into practice what we know and believe about how students learn. In other words, have them implement the learning theories described in Chapter 3. We will call the first school the *research-based school* and the second the *learning theory-based school*. These schools are not mutually exclusive. As you will see, effective teachers utilize what research tells us about learning. Figure 7.4 illustrates the two schools of thought, or kinds of direct instruction, and prototypes of each.

Since the two schools of thought about direct instruction are based on different approaches, we will present them consecutively.

FIGURE 7.4 Two Kinds of Direct Instruction

WHAT IS RESEARCH-BASED DIRECT INSTRUCTION?

At one time or another, we have all tasted something especially good and asked ourselves: "What's in this, and how was it made? We ask because we appreciate the food a great deal and might like to prepare it ourselves.

Likewise, in schools, we see certain teachers who are especially good at helping students learn. We want to know how they do it—what is their "recipe"? We call these teachers "effective." What they do—their recipe—has been referred to as direct instruction, an overarching generic term (Rosenshine & Meister, 1995), and as Basic Practice (Murphy, Weil, & McGreal, 1986), Explicit Teaching (Rosenshine, 1986), and Active Teaching (Good, Grouws, & Ebmeier, 1983), its subtypes.

Research-based direct instruction is used to describe the practices of teachers who are more effective in bringing about student academic learning. You may ask, how do we know what effective teachers do? To find the answer, we must locate teachers who consistently produce greater learning gains than other teachers who teach comparable students. Next, investigators descend on these teachers' classrooms to observe, record, and analyze what they do. Chapter 11, Effective Teachers: Professional Skills and Abilities, contains a description of many procedures effective teachers follow. Thus, that chapter ties in closely with this section. Here we will merely mention the attributes of effective teachers. You may wish to review Chapter 11 simultaneously.

PURPOSE AND CHARACTERISTICS OF RESEARCH-BASED DIRECT INSTRUCTION

7.19 How important is the purpose of direct instruction?

What is the purpose of direct instruction, and what are its key attributes? Clearly, the purpose of direct instruction is to help students learn basic academic content such as reading, mathematics, and so forth in the most efficient, straightforward way.

The six key characteristics or key elements of research-based direct instruction have been compiled by Weil and Murphy (1982) and Murphy, Weil, and McGreal (1986), among others. Murphy, Weil, and McGreal (1986) call them teacher centrality, task orientation, positive expectations, student cooperation and accountability, nonnegative affect, and established structure.

Teacher centrality means that teachers exert strong instructional direction and control. The teacher decides what is to be learned and how, and is visibly in charge. **Task orientation** requires that the primary emphasis be on academic learning. Effective teachers engage learners in the pursuit of basic knowledge. **Positive expectations** indicate that effective teachers show concern for the academic progress of each student, and they expect each student to be successful. **Student cooperation and accountability** means that students are held accountable for their academic work and, furthermore, that they are expected to assist one another and to share materials. **Nonnegative affect** means these teachers ensure that learners feel psychologically safe and secure—that is, not threatened. Finally, **established structure** refers to the fact that effective teachers establish class rules and ensure that they are followed.

The purpose and key characteristics of research-based direct instruction are illustrated in Figure 7.5.

 7.20 What is your reaction to the key characteristics of direct instruction? Do you believe you can successfully implement each?

VARIATIONS OF RESEARCH-BASED DIRECT INSTRUCTION

Previously, we noted that direct instruction goes by different subtypes and names, including Basic Practice, Explicit Teaching, and Active Teaching (see Figure 7.4). Let's take a look at each variation.

The Basic Practice Model (Murphy, Weil & McGreal, 1986) has four steps to follow: lesson introduction, development, structured or guided practice, and independent practice.

In the introductory, or *orientation phase,* the teacher clearly establishes the content area to be studied, the instructional objectives, and the procedures to be followed. Additionally, the teacher communicates expectations to the students.

During the *development phase,* teachers present the information to be learned (concept, fact, generalization, skill, and so on). Regardless of the kind of research-based direct instruction, *teacher presentations are a constant.* Teachers provide clarity of presentation by demonstrating and by using examples. They also reinforce newly learned procedures and rules, and check students' understanding regularly to ensure progress.

Next, learners begin *structured, controlled practice.* Students try out or rehearse the information or skill the teacher has presented under the teacher's supervision. The teacher reinforces correct practice immediately and addresses incorrect practice, misunderstandings, and misconceptions as soon as they occur.

After teachers are satisfied that learners know or can do what is expected of them, the learners are set free to *practice independently.* However, even then, effective teachers move about the classroom, constantly monitoring and checking the work.

Explicit teaching is a second kind of direct instruction. It is described by Rosenshine (1987), Rosenshine and Meister (1995), and Rosenshine and Stevens (1986) as consisting of six phases of instructional activity: review and

"Ms. Perkins certainly has a way with children."

FIGURE 7.5 Purpose and Key Characteristics of Research-Based Direct Instruction

Purpose — To directly cause students to learn academic content or skills

Characteristics
- Teacher provides strong direction
- Orientation is very academic
- Concern is for achievement; high expectation that students can/will learn
- Student accountability, cooperation demanded
- Students made to feel psychologically safe
- Student behavior is controlled

check homework, present new content/skills, guide student practice, provide feedback and correctives, move to independent practice, and conduct weekly and monthly reviews.

First, effective teachers *review* the previous day's work and homework, if assigned, and *reteach* when needed. This review of prior learning ensures that students are ready for the presentation of new information or skills. Such reviews often take the form of teacher questioning and recitation.

In the *presentation* stage, effective teachers inform their learners of the lesson's objectives, that is, what learners must come to know or be able to do. Good teachers provide an overview of what will happen during the lesson and how. Then the presentation proper begins with the teacher proceeding in small steps but at a rapid pace. A rapid pace is also referred to as gathering and maintaining *lesson momentum.* The teacher provides many detailed examples and illustrations, highlights or reinforces major points to notice and remember, and regularly raises questions to check for understanding. Most importantly, throughout the presentation, the teacher must be clear.

Following the presentation and a quick check for understanding, *teacher-guided whole-class practice* begins. Guided practice often takes the form of a public recitation whereby the teacher asks a question, a student or students answer, and then the teacher asks another question (see Table 6.3). The teacher directs the questions to all students and provides them adequate time to think (see Chapter 11, wait time, on p. 341). When students have difficulty, the teacher prompts or helps them think aloud. Guided practice continues until the class and individuals are responding correctly over 80 percent of the time.

Providing *feedback and correction* are part of the presentation. Investigators who observe effective teachers report that they use specific praise in moderation ("That is a good answer because . . ."). Correction of misconceptions may require review, reteaching, or more practice.

Having determined that their learners seem to know or be able to do whatever is needed, effective teachers provide opportunity for *independent practice.* Their intention is to have students rehearse the information or skill in order to get it into long-term memory. Independent practice should continue until learners' responses are rapid, confident, and highly accurate. Effective teachers hold students accountable for independent work, and they monitor it whenever possible.

Finally, effective teachers periodically engage their learners in *review* so that the information or skill is further embedded in long-term memory.

Active teaching is a third variation of research-based direct instruction (Good, Grouws, & Ebmeier, 1983). Mostly constructed from observations of effective mathematics teachers, it contains five instructional phases: the opening, development, independent work, homework, and continued review.

Opening refers to reviewing the concepts or skills recently taught and collecting homework. During lesson *development,* effective teachers do a number of things. They ensure that students have the knowledge needed to understand the new information to be presented. They develop the new concepts and skills using numerous lively illustrations and explanations. They make skillful use of questioning, examples, and problems. And, importantly, they repeat and elaborate as necessary. Good and Grouws (1977) found that when fourth-grade teachers spend about half of the mathematics class time on lesson development and increase students' participation in the lesson, learning gains are dramatic.

The *independent work* stage is characterized by uninterrupted practice. Students are forewarned that their work will be examined. The difficulty level of assigned work is intended to produce 80 percent or higher accuracy. During independent practice, effective teachers are careful to keep everyone involved and on task.

Effective elementary school teachers give about fifteen minutes of homework each night, Monday through Thursday. The assignment allows students to practice newly acquired information and review the old. Finally, effective math teachers use *continued review.* They have students recall and use earlier learning by holding in-class weekly and monthly reviews.

As you can see, the three types or variations of the direct instruction approach—Basic Practice, Explicit Teaching, and Active Teaching—are nearly indistinguishable (see Table 7.5). This *should* be the case since the persons proposing the variations created them after having read essentially the same research studies on effective teaching.

GOOD DIRECT INSTRUCTORS

Good direct instructors are, by definition, effective teachers. So, what are effective teachers like? What are their personal attributes? As you shall see, we have devoted all of Chapter 10 to answering these questions. Briefly, effective teachers are enthusiastic, warm and accepting, and humorous. They hold high expectations that their students can learn. Furthermore, they are supportive and encouraging, businesslike, adaptable-flexible, and knowledgeable. If you want to find out more at this time, skip directly to Chapter 10.

 7.21 Which of the qualities of good direct instructors do you now have? Which qualities would you like to achieve or improve?

GOOD RESEARCH-BASED DIRECT INSTRUCTION

Following are summaries of procedures that good direct instructors follow as they prepare, deliver, and close lessons.

TABLE 7.5 Three Variations of Research-Based Direct Instruction

Basic Practice	Explicit Teaching	Active Teaching
• Introduce lesson	• Review previous work, check homework	• Review, check homework
• Develop lesson	• Introduce lesson	• Develop lesson
• Supervise practice	• Develop lesson	• Check on understanding
• Provide feedback, correction	• Check on understanding	• Provide independent work in class
• Provide independent practice	• Supervise practice	• Review
	• Provide feedback, correction	
	• Provide independent practice	
	• Review	

Preparation Authors of the various forms of research-based direct instruction give little specific attention to lesson planning or preparation. This probably is because the study of effective teachers focused on observing what they did in their classrooms when delivering instruction. However, it is probably true that effective teachers follow the preparation regimen good presenters use; that is, they establish the general purpose of the lesson, set specific learning objectives, collect and review subject matter and useful, related materials, and plan the presentation.

Delivery There are many maneuvers effective teachers know and use. Direct instruction usually seems to begin with a review of homework or of an independent assignment. The review helps to determine the level of learners' understanding and accuracy. When either are low, reteaching is appropriate.

Following homework review and collection, the effective teacher ensures that learners are ready for the new material. That readiness may result from the homework review. If not, it is necessary to go over earlier related information or skills. When readiness is evident, the specific objectives of the lesson are communicated in terms of what the students are to know and to be able to do. The students are oriented to the lesson and its parts and to the way it will be conducted.

Now that the students are ready and aware of what is to be accomplished and how, the presentation is given. Instructional clarity is critical. The notion of clarity is fully developed in Chapter 11, and the behaviors characterizing clear teachers appear in Table 11.5. These behaviors include a step-by-step presentation, use of examples and illustrations, cuing learners to important elements to notice and remember, and using numerous questions directed to all students in order to encourage participation and check understanding.

After the learners have achieved a good level of understanding, guided whole-class practice of the information or skill begins. The teacher provides exercises, and students respond to them aloud so that everyone is on the same page, so to speak, and the teacher is able to hear what students are thinking. The teacher acknowledges correct responses and reminds students specifically why their responses are right. Should misunderstandings and errors occur, the teacher reteaches, often using a different approach.

As soon as the teacher feels that learners are able to work on their own with a high level of accuracy, independent practice starts. At the outset, learners are informed that their work will be examined and that a high level of accuracy—for example, above 80 percent—is expected. After the work is assigned, the teacher monitors to help students stay on task and reduce errors. Practice continues until responses are both rapid and accurate and learners are confident.

Closure In the closure stage, a research-based direct instruction lesson fulfills two requirements. One is the assignment of related homework. Assignments should be short, but regular. Secondly, the teacher reminds students of the importance of the lesson's objectives and the need to be able to recall and use the newly acquired information or skill. The teacher plans dates and times of weekly and monthly reviews.

7.22 What is your reaction to the approaches good direct instructors use?

Slavin (1991b) notes that the regimen and principles of research-based direct instruction fit closest to expository teaching and reception learning, described in Chapter 3. Rosenshine and Stevens (1986) agree, pointing out the correspondence between the results of research on direct instruction and what we know about information processing, including the limits of short-term memory, the importance of elaboration and practice, and the need for continued practice. That research confirms the need to review previously learned information and skills, the need to limit the amount of new, difficult information presented, the need to

TABLE 7.6 Qualities of Good Leaders of Research-Based Direct Instruction and of Good Direct Instruction

Good Leaders of Research-Based Direct Instruction Are . . .	Good Research-Based Direct Instruction
• Enthusiastic	*When preparing:*
• Warm, accepting	• Research on effective teaching hardly addresses what teachers do to prepare. We might assume they do the same things they would do when preparing a good presentation. (See Table 6.2.)
• Humorous	
• Supportive	*When delivering:*
• Encouraging	• Collect, review homework
• Businesslike	• Review earlier, related information
• Adaptable-flexible	• Communicate to learners what they are to know and be able to do
• Knowledgeable	• Present an overview or orientation of how the lesson will be conducted
• Hold high expectations for student success	• Present information/skill to be learned
• See also Table 6.2, Qualities of Good Presenters and Good Presentations	• Proceed in small steps
	• Maintain a quick pace
	• Use many illustrations, examples
	• Encourage involvement of all students
	• Ask many questions to check for understanding
	• Repeat and elaborate on major points to notice, remember
	• Provide teacher-guided whole-class practice
	• Provide feedback and reteach to eliminate misunderstandings
	• Ensure that students can practice with at least 80 percent accuracy
	• Provide independent practice
	• Let students know the work will be examined
	• Monitor the work to keep students involved and to eliminate errors
	• Continue practice until learners are confident and their responses are both rapid and accurate
	When closing:
	• Assign short, regular, related, homework
	• Establish when this information or skill will next be reviewed

proceed in small steps, the need to rehearse, elaborate, and summarize in student words and language, and the importance of overlearning.

A summary of the qualities of good research-based direct instructors and direct instruction appears in Table 7.6.

ADVANTAGES AND LIMITATIONS OF RESEARCH-BASED DIRECT INSTRUCTION

Benefits for Teachers Probably the overriding advantage of research-based direct instruction for teachers is that it meets the need to achieve. Murray (1963) defines **achievement** as the need to overcome obstacles and to do difficult tasks as well and as quickly as possible. Certainly, helping students to succeed is the primary challenge many teachers face. Obviously, effective teachers feel that what they do—what we call research-based direct instruction—is the most efficient and effective way to get students to learn.

Additionally, due to its characteristics, research-based direct instruction is probably well-suited to teachers with the following compelling personal needs:

- The **exposition** need to give facts, explain, and demonstrate.
- The **construction** need to organize and build. Remember, good research-based direct instruction calls for developing the lesson step-by-step.
- The **nurturance** need to nourish or aid. Users of direct instruction probably feel it is the best way to help students academically.
- The **dominance** need to lead, direct, organize, and control others.

7.23 What advantages does research-based instruction offer you?

What professional demands does research-based direct instruction meet? Most particularly, **student success**—it helps lower-socioeconomic status children learn. Especially since the 1960s, there has been enormous pressure on teachers to get children at risk to learn and to stay in school. Additionally, when teachers use research-based direct instruction, they are seemingly in control, and that is viewed as very important nowadays.

Benefits for Students   What personality and educational needs would direct instruction seem to satisfy for learners? From the students' perspective, this instructional alternative might be particularly well-suited for anyone who has any of the following strong needs:

- The **acquisition** need to acquire knowledge or skill.
- The **deference** need to be a follower, to cooperate.
- The **succorance** need to seek and depend on help.
- The **similance** need to agree, believe, emulate, and imitate.

7.24 What advantages does research-based instruction offer students?

Research-based direct instruction, by definition, meets the students' need to achieve academically. If doing well on tests is the major goal, most teachers will utilize the processes of good direct instruction. Of course, merely doing well on tests is not what education is all about.

Limitations   Of course, research-based direct instruction has its critics. Slavin (1991a, b) points out that it deemphasizes students' autonomy. Gersten and Keating (1987), advocates themselves, acknowledge critics who say the tight structure may stifle children. Peterson (1979b) informs us that this approach does not promote achievement in creativity, abstract thinking, and problem solving or higher-level cognitive skills. Stallings and Kaskowitz (1975) feel it is not as good as other instructional alternatives for improving cooperation, attitude toward school, and, relatedly, school attendance. Spotlight on Research 7.3 reviews the findings on research-based direct instruction.

Perhaps the most damning criticism points to the fact that the promising practices of effective teachers, on which direct instruction is built, mostly derive from observations of effective elementary teachers teaching reading and mathematics. These content areas are more structured; that is, they follow a more sequential, step-by-step learning process than other content areas such as social studies, art, and science.

WHEN RESEARCH-BASED DIRECT INSTRUCTION SHOULD BE USED

Peterson (1979a) and others address the question, when should direct instruction be used? She concludes that it is superior when the goal is to improve achievement in basic skills as measured on tests. Rosenshine (1986) agrees, and specifies that it is most valuable when teaching knowledge and explicit concepts and procedures. He provides examples such as teaching factual historical information (such as the chronology of the colonization of Africa), teaching grammatical concepts (what a sentence is), and teaching mathematical processes or procedures (how to solve an algebraic equation). *In other words, use direct instruction when the content to be learned is well-structured, clear, and unambiguous.* Berliner (1982) feels that direct instruction is more suitable when the material is arranged in a hierarchical or sequential manner. He also feels it is most useful during the first stages of instruction with unfamiliar material.

Peterson (1979a, 1982) also addresses the related question, with whom should direct instruction be used? In response, she notes this approach has been shown to be very effective for teaching younger, less able learners. She also suggests it may be the instructional alternative of choice when teaching children who need direction from others. This supports our contention that students with high needs for deference, similance, and succorance would be attracted to research-based direct instruction.

Peterson (1979a) suggests that direct instruction is similar to "traditional teaching." To some extent, this is true. Generally speaking, traditional teaching is directed toward learning academic content. It is also characterized by a teacher-centered and teacher-dominated classroom. However, if traditional teaching equalled direct instruction, all "traditional" teachers would be effective, and we know that is not the case. Only a few traditional teachers are able to outperform the rest when teaching comparable students. So we can only say that traditional teaching is like direct instruction in kind but falls short of it in implementation. Specifically, direct instruction demands not only teacher direction but *strong* teacher direction, not only an academic orientation but *strong* academic orientation, and so forth. Consequently, it is probably safe to say that traditional teaching would have to be ratcheted up to have characteristics identical to those of research-based direct instruction. This kind of direct instruction probably is used only by teachers determined to help their students achieve academically.

WHAT IS LEARNING THEORY-BASED DIRECT INSTRUCTION?

While the first school of thought about direct instruction is based on research on teaching, the second is based on learning theory. By that, we mean its advocates have constructed instructional procedures that are based upon and mimic what we know about human learning.

Theory-based direct instruction describes the approach teachers use to put into use what is known about learning. Sponsors of this school of thought are less interested in what teachers do than in what they ought to do. What they ought to do, advocates say, is to use the beliefs and findings of one or more schools of thought about learning described in Chapter 3.

PURPOSE AND CHARACTERISTICS OF LEARNING THEORY-BASED DIRECT INSTRUCTION

The purpose of both types of direct instruction is identical: to help students learn academic content in the most straightforward way. The two types also seem to share the same overall characteristics (see Figure 7.5).

VARIATIONS OF LEARNING THEORY-BASED INSTRUCTION

The two best known and most widely used forms of learning theory-based direct instruction, as depicted in Figure 7.4, are the Mastery Teaching Program (Hunter, 1982, 1984) and the Direct Instruction System in Arithmetic and Reading, or DISTAR (Becker, 1986).

The Mastery Teaching Program Hunter seems to have based her teaching model mainly on learning theory, particularly instructional theory as proposed by Gagné (Rosenshine & Stevens, 1986). Her program has the same purpose (to foster academic learning) and shares most of the key characteristics of research-based direct instruction programs (teacher centrality, task orientation, and so forth; Figure 7.5). *A major difference is that Hunter suggests that instructional alternatives other than teacher presentation may be just as effective, depending on the lesson objectives.*

Slavin (1991b) notes the stages or steps in Hunter's (1982) version: getting students set to learn, input and modeling, checking understanding, and guided practice. Do they sound familiar? Obviously, they are quite similar to those advocated by educators who take the research-based road.

The Direct Instruction System for Teaching and Learning (DISTAR) The developers of DISTAR believe your task is to find out what children need to know to succeed in school and then to teach it to them following principles of learning theory that come mostly from the behavioral school of thought (Chapter 3). The program was developed mainly for use with low SES children.

A major difference between DISTAR and all other forms of learning theory-based direct instruction is that it is very heavily scripted. Teachers are told precisely what to say and do from lesson beginning to end. Benjamin (1981) describes DISTAR as leaving nothing to chance. "Every action by the teacher—verbal and nonverbal—is specifically outlined; every student response is similarly choreographed" (p. 72). Consequently, DISTAR is said to be teacher-proof. Any instructor can use it and obtain the same result.

Stallings and Stipek (1986) refer to Bereiter-Englemann DISTAR programs as "carefully structured, highly verbal, patterned drill and practice" (p. 734). These authors provide an extensive description of the background, development, and use of DISTAR.

It seems that regardless of whether we generalize from the observation of what effective teachers do in their classrooms, or whether we speculate what teachers should do from learning theory, when academic learning is the goal, we end up with many of the same principles and ideas.

GOOD LEARNING THEORY-BASED DIRECT INSTRUCTORS

The qualities of teachers who use direct instruction based on learning theory are not documented. However, we can presume they are like the qualities of effective teachers, so Table 7.6 and Chapter 10 may be helpful.

Do students of teachers who use learning theory-based direct instruction learn more? We would presume so, but let's look at the research.

Research on the Mastery Teaching Program has not generally shown "that the students of teachers especially trained in this variation have learned more than other students" (Slavin 1991a, p. 253). Slavin suggests this may be because at some time *all* teachers have been exposed to and use learning theory and associated instructional maneuvers. Therefore, when it comes to learning theory, all teachers teach about the same way, anyway. However, Hunter, the developer of the Mastery Teaching Program, feels that the reason her program has had limited success is that it has not been properly implemented.

What does research on DISTAR reveal? Much to the alarm of its critics, DISTAR has mostly been very effective in its purpose. Stallings and Stipek (1986) tell us that when low SES students spend four years (kindergarten through grade 3) in the Direct Instruction Follow-Through Model, they achieve close to national norms on achievement tests, performing much better than similar students who received other kinds of instruction. Meyer (1984) reports that students from an inner-city Brooklyn, New York, school that used DISTAR in grades 1 through 3 were more likely to complete secondary school. Gersten and Keating (1987) also found positive long-term effects such as lowered dropout rates and increased proportions of students applying for college. Stallings and Stipek conclude, "One implication for elementary [teachers] is that a structured, carefully sequenced program for low-achieving children in the lower grades helps them to succeed academically" (p. 741).

GOOD LEARNING THEORY-BASED DIRECT INSTRUCTION

Good direct instruction, according to the Mastery Teaching Program (Hunter 1982, 1984), requires following a specific procedure: getting students ready to learn, providing input, modeling, checking for understanding, and providing and guiding practice. Inasmuch as these steps are very similar to those which effective teachers use, the information in Table 7.6 can again be our guide.

ADVANTAGES AND LIMITATIONS OF LEARNING THEORY-BASED DIRECT INSTRUCTION

The DISTAR form of direct instruction has essentially the same benefits and drawbacks as the Basic Practice, Explicit Teaching, and Active Teaching variations since all utilize mostly teacher presentation. Since the Mastery Teaching Program does not specify a single best way to teach, we are not able to address its advantages and limitations. Therefore, the advantages and limitations of all the instructional alternatives selected for inclusion in Chapters 6 and 7 apply.

Spotlight on Research 7.4 discusses the findings on learning theory-based direct instruction.

WHEN LEARNING THEORY-BASED DIRECT INSTRUCTION SHOULD BE USED

Studies of DISTAR (Gersten & Keating, 1987) seem to support its use in much the same ways we would use direct instruction based on effective teaching. It seems mostly to benefit students at risk of school failure.

Studies of the Mastery Teaching Program offer less clear direction. The Mastery Teaching Program is more likely to be utilized with children of different SES, while DISTAR is used almost exclusively with low SES students. Perhaps for this reason, DISTAR seems very popular in large metropolitan districts.

SUMMARY ON DIRECT INSTRUCTION

Rather than being one precise instructional alternative, direct instruction is a label given to related efforts to improve the *academic learning* of K–12 students.

There are two major kinds of direct instruction. The first kind, research-based, derives from observing effective teachers to see what they do to bring about consistently higher levels of student learning. There are three variations on this kind of direct instruction: Basic Practice, Explicit Teaching, and Active Teaching. Advocates who developed these variations believe that you should be educated and trained in direct instruction according to their particular model. Doing so, they say, should increase your ability to bring about student learning.

The second kind of direct instruction derives from learning theory—what we know and believe about how people learn. There are two popular variations of this kind: the Mastery Teaching Program and the Direct Instruction System for Teaching and Learning (DISTAR). Scholars who developed these forms believe that you should be educated and trained according to their model. Furthermore, they believe that after education and training, you will know how to use what is known about learning and, consequently, your students will benefit academically.

Both kinds of direct instruction have the same purpose, which is to help students learn academic content. They also share common characteristics, including strong teacher direction, an academic orientation, high expectations for student achievement, student accountability and cooperation, a psychologically safe classroom atmosphere, and strict classroom rules and regulations.

Within the first kind of direct instruction, good instructors must have the qualities of effective teachers, which are elaborated in Chapter 10. These include enthusiasm, warmth, and humor. They must also be supportive and encouraging, businesslike, adaptable, and knowledgeable in their teaching area. Within the second kind of direct instruction, the requisite teacher qualities are not as clear.

Both kinds of direct instruction require teachers to follow regimens mostly characterized by three words—practice, practice, practice. Effective teachers use many and varied kinds of practice, which is one of the four major elements of learning: drive, cue, response or practice, and reinforcement (terms introduced in Chapter 5) Direct instruction is advantageous to teachers and students who have certain personality dispositions. It also meets certain teacher professional and student educational needs.

Try Activity 7.7

For the most part, research findings support direct instruction, especially for low SES students in highly structured subjects such as reading and mathematics. DISTAR has been extended for use in many subjects. Over forty DISTAR programs are available commercially from Science Research Associates, a subsidiary of McGraw-Hill.

Individualized Instruction: Tailoring Teaching

7.25 How do you feel about individualism as opposed to conformity? To what extent should teachers tailor instruction to fit individuals?

If you want to get teachers upset, remark that classrooms in Japanese schools have many more students, as many as fifty. Why is the thought of large classes so distressing? Because American teachers, among others, believe that individual students cannot be well served when classes are large. After all, individuals and individualism is what America is all about. So we have striven to provide for individuals and individualism. How? Through individualized instruction.

WHAT IS INDIVIDUALIZED INSTRUCTION?

Individualized instruction is the term used to refer to any instructional maneuver that attempts to tailor teaching and learning to a learner's, or a group of like learners', unique strengths and needs. Said another way, individualized instruction means responding educationally to individuals. In Chapter 2, we found out that teachers must, according to the Individuals with Disabilities Education Act, develop an individualized educational program (IEP) for each student with educational challenges or handicaps. Of course, to a lesser extent, teachers try to meet the special needs of all children. You can probably recall some teachers who, more than others, took into account your strengths and needs.

As you will soon see, various types of individualized instruction exist. Each type more or less individualizes instruction. By "more or less," we mean some types do more, or go farther than others, in addressing learners' strengths or meeting learners' needs.

PURPOSE AND CHARACTERISTICS OF INDIVIDUALIZED INSTRUCTION

Individualized, personalized instruction has unique attributes. As the name implies, its most unique purpose is to tailor teaching to an individual's peculiar strengths and needs. No other instructional maneuver does just that.

The characteristics of individualized instruction also set it apart. Consider the role of the teacher. When individualizing instruction is the goal, the teacher's role is to know and care about individuals, about the diversity of students. The teacher can't teach the class as though everyone in it is alike any more than parents can treat their children as if they are all the same. It just won't do.

Another characteristic that sets individualized instruction apart is the unique way in which it deals with these five variables: the *goals of instruction, learning activities, resources, mastery level,* and *time.* When learners have a great deal of autonomy in regard to these five factors, we can say that instruction really has been *tailored, customized,* or *personalized.* Let's consider each variable.

Goals of Instruction   As we learned in Chapter 5, the "formal curriculum" is set by the state and local school district. For the most part, teachers teach that curriculum. Perhaps all fourth grade classrooms study the history of Native Americans, while in the tenth grade everyone studies American government. However, what if one or more fourth graders is interested in learning about the discovery of gold in California and Alaska or some tenth graders want to study African-American history? To the extent that teachers allow students to choose the topic or subtopic of study, they are individualizing instruction, that is, meeting individual needs.

Learning Activities   In most classrooms, all students are asked to follow a similar learning procedure. For example, if the teacher's goal is to study the history of Native Americans, the teacher usually spells out how the class will do this. However, the teacher, after setting the goal, could permit a good deal of autonomy with regard to how individual students might attain the goal. In this case, the instructor could say, "We are going to study Native Americans. How would you like to do this? Would some of you prefer to read? to look at recorded documentaries? to interview Native Americans?" The greater the instructional autonomy teachers grant, the more they are individualizing and personalizing.

Resources Even though students have individual preferences about how they want to learn, they need further individualization. For example, if several students want to learn about Native Americans through reading, a number of different kinds and levels of reading material must be made available. Providing autonomy to choose how to learn carries individualization only so far. Providing a variety of resource materials for different ability levels takes it further.

Mastery Level Another way you can individualize is to accept different levels of performance from different students. This is complicated because you also need to have high expectations for all. Perhaps the best way to put it is to have high expectations for all learners but even higher expectations for some. Thus, you might want all children to achieve at some agreed-upon level but want others to surpass that level—to excel. In studying the history of Native Americans, children with little previous related knowledge could be expected to reach level X, while children who have had a keen interest in and prior knowledge of Native Americans could be expected to reach level Y. As Brophy and Evertson (1976) note, "The very idea of individualized instruction implies that there is a certain level of difficulty or content specificity that is optimal for each student" (p. 61).

7.26 In which ways are you most likely to individualize instruction?

7.27 Which of the various forms of individualized instruction have you experienced? What were they like for you?

Time The final variable that can be manipulated for individuals is time. You can, as is usually the case, expect all students to accomplish the goal in the same amount of time. Or time can be flexible, with some students taking more than others.

To repeat, individualized instruction has a unique purpose and characteristics. Its purpose is to serve the individual rather than the entire class. Consequently, the teacher is called upon to know and care about student diversity. The nature or character of individualized instruction is a function of several factors. It can differ according to the amount of autonomy given students to select what they will do and how they will do it. It can also differ according to the resources they have available, the level of mastery they are expected to achieve, and the time they are given to complete the task. Figure 7.6 depicts the key characteristics of individualized instruction.

TYPES OF INDIVIDUALIZED INSTRUCTION PROGRAMS

We have identified a number of procedures and programs that have been generated to individualize instruction. As you read about each, ask yourself, "To what extent does this idea really get at individual strengths and needs?"

FIGURE 7.6 Purpose and Key Characteristics of Individualized Instruction

FIGURE 7.7   A Contract Format

Sixth-grade teacher John Swang (1993) has students use contracts in his middle school science classes. A modified form is shown here. Note that the student, parent, and teacher must all sign.

The National Student Research Center Scientific Research Contract

Date: _____

Student's signature: _____

Parent's signature: _____

Teacher's signature: _____

1. I would like to do a scientific research project on _____

    _____

2. I am interested in this topic because _____

    _____

3. Some of the questions I want to answer are _____

    _____

    _____

    _____

4. I will collect information from these sources:

    ____Encyclopedia   ____Journals

    ____Trade books   ____Atlas

    ____Textbooks   ____Almanac

    ____Newspapers   ____Other. Name: _____

    ____Databases

5. My project will be ready by _____

The Dalton and Winnetka Plans   Two of the earliest efforts toward individualization were called the Dalton and Winnetka plans. The Dalton plan divided the school day into two instructional parts. In the morning, students had free time to work, often independently, without interruption, and at their own pace on contracted monthly assignments (Lawry, 1987a). In the afternoon, groups of learners engaged in social, vocational, and physical activity. The **contracts** were agreements students signed attesting that they would do certain prescribed academic work in mathematics, social studies, English, foreign language, or science. More recently, individual student contracts also prescribe, rather than leave open-ended, the time frame in which the work must be completed. Learners may also contract work at different levels of achievement and difficulty. Work contracted at a high level of achievement, when properly completed, would earn the learner a grade of A. Less demanding and difficult work would earn a lower grade. A format for a contract is shown in Figure 7.7.

The Winnetka plan also set aside the morning for the study of academic subjects such as arithmetic, reading, and language arts, which included handwriting, spelling, writing, and grammar. Students learned these subjects mostly through

Ameritech is one of several companies trying to support computer instruction in America's classrooms. It has a traveling display that demonstrates newer ways computers can help students learn. Stratton (1993) describes three of them.

Jason, a high school freshman, opened a computer window and looked inside a storm cloud. The cloud was a model projected on the screen. Jason could rotate the image so he could see the column of heat in the cloud's center. Furthermore, he would vary the temperature or wind speed to see how the cloud would react.

Ten-year-olds Teruko and Sam talked to each other over speakerphones while viewing a world map on their separate computer screens. In this way, they could collaborate on a homework assignment on mapping.

Pupils in two Ohio cities were connected by a large-screen computer and telephone that enabled them to jointly study tissue and genetics. They could not only see and hear each other but also see and hear the teacher and see slides and other materials the teacher used.

self-instruction. Consequently, many self-instructional textbooks and other materials were specially written, and students were only periodically tested on their knowledge and skills (Lawry, 1987c). The Winnetka scheme of self-instruction using specially prepared materials was the forerunner of programmed and computer-assisted instruction and Individually Prescribed Instruction, described next.

Programmed and Computer-Assisted Instruction Programmed and computer-assisted instruction are outgrowths of the Winnetka plan (Lawry, 1987b). They were described in Chapter 3 as examples of instruction following the behavioral school of thought.

Both programmed instruction (PI) and computer-assisted instruction (CAI) use self-instructional formats. The material to be learned is broken down into small, easily learned segments. When students finish one segment correctly, they go to the next. If a student does not understand, he is redirected to try again or is provided additional information that facilitates understanding. Newer programs actually diagnose students' mistakes and provide them with highly individualized feedback. Some computer-assisted instruction has become very creative (see Case 7.2).

Individually Prescribed Instruction (IPI) IPI is described by Jeter (1980). At the beginning of a school year, IPI students are pretested in several subject areas to find out what they already know. According to the results, students are assigned work at appropriate academic levels. Students do not necessarily work alone; they may be given tasks to complete with other learners who are at the same level. At set intervals in the curriculum, learners take tests. If they are successful, they move on. If not, instruction is repeated.

Individually Guided Education (IGE) IGE is another form of individualized instruction. A major difference between IGE and other systems is that IGE is done in a "nongraded" school. A **nongraded school** is one in which grade levels are blurred or nonexistent. In IGE schools, several teachers may be assigned to a unit of 100 to 150 students who would typically span several grade levels in achievement. The team of teachers develops and evaluates an instructional program for each child. "Ideally, each child's program is based on how and at what pace he learns best, and where he stands on mastering specific skills and concepts" (Rossmiller, 1976, p. 403).

Tutoring **Tutoring,** or coaching, is perhaps the oldest and best known means of individualizing instruction. It is used either to give remedial instruction to a student or to provide supplementary information. In the first case, a child could be

CASE 7.3
Project-Based Learning

According to a report in *Education Week* (Olson, 1993), the project method is enjoying a renaissance. Olson notes that virtually all persons connected with the reform movement under the sponsorship of the New American Schools Development Corporation "have embraced some form of project-based learning" (p. 6). Project-based learning occurs when students plan and carry out the study of some topic or theme which causes them to investigate it using an interdisciplinary, cross-subject approach. The following examples are cited.

- Members of a class map the downtown area, interview store owners, and then write guidebooks for children's use
- Students who are working on a three-month unit of work entitled "Designing Spaces for People" design and build model structures for people living under peculiar climatic conditions

Olson informs readers that the project method was advocated and used by progressive educators in the 1930s and 1940s. She cites the Eight-Year Study done in 1942, which found that college students who had gone to progressive high schools outperformed their peers from more traditional schools in which they studied everything in separate subjects.

---

tutored if she or he couldn't count to 100 by an appropriate age or developmental level. In the second case, a child might be instructed as to how to create a crossword puzzle.

Many different persons serve as tutors, including teachers, teacher aides, students, and parents. Cross-grade tutoring occurs when older children work with younger ones. This is a fairly popular approach, although some question its academic value to the student tutor. Nixon-John (1994) describes how she effectively used peer tutoring to increase student enthusiasm about writing and improve their writing performance.

Distance Education   Another variation of individualized instruction is distance education (Feasley, 1982). As the name implies, the intention is to make education more accessible to persons not located near an instructional facility such as a public school. Distance education programs are used widely in Alaska and Australia where they serve rural or outback children. The means for providing instruction include telephone, radio, television, computer programs (CAI), and printed materials such as texts and guidebooks. Most of us are familiar with the concept of correspondence courses and correspondence study. This was, and is, the most popular form of distance education. When a student is ill or homebound, teachers often engage in distance education.

The Project Method   All six examples of individualized instruction described thus far have something in common: They intend to bridge the gap between what society expects students to know and what they actually know. In contrast, the Project Method allows students autonomy to pursue their own interests by engaging in an activity within the larger curriculum framework. A student or cluster of students decides what task they want to undertake. The task could be cognitive or knowledge seeking, affective or values-related, or psychomotor skill building. Often it contains all three elements. The student or cluster then decides how they will undertake the task and even how it will be evaluated (Lawry, 1987b). Interest in the Project Method is on the rise, especially in science education where constructivist approaches to learning are popular. Olson (1993) reports on state-of-the-art project methods in Case 7.3.

Individualization, then, is not any one kind of program. It eschews whole-class or mass teaching and embraces instead *group practices, adaptation of subject matter to the individual,* and, at its extreme, the *emancipation of students from the*

7.28   What values, knowledge, and abilities do you have that would help you implement individualized instruction?

constraints of the curriculum planned by others. Its tenets include self-direction, initiative, freedom, and responsibility and a preference for constructivist learning theory (Gibbons, 1971).

GOOD USERS OF INDIVIDUALIZED INSTRUCTION

To be really good at individualizing instruction, we think you must have particular values, knowledge, and abilities. Foremost, you must prize diversity. Heck and Williams (1984) note, "you must comprehend, accept, value, and affirm respect for all people regardless of sexual, racial, cultural, ethnic, religious, and physical differences" (p. 53). Relatedly, you must value individualism by encouraging your students to think and do for themselves.

Gaining knowledge of your students is essential. The more you know about them, the better your potential to address their strengths and needs. Therefore, you must be inclined toward being a diagnostician and clinician. Chapter 4 provides suggestions for getting to know learners better.

You also need knowledge of and ability to use the various types of individualized instruction such as the Dalton and Winnetka plans, Individually Guided Education, the Project Method, and so forth. Finally, you will need interpersonal skills, including the ability to listen, to accept, and to encourage.

GOOD INDIVIDUALIZED EDUCATION PROGRAMS

Given the definition of individualized instruction and its purpose and characteristics, the following criteria should help you decide how good an individualized program really is.

- Is the program tailored to meet a learners' unique strengths and needs?
- How much autonomy do learners have with regard to the goals of instruction, the learning activities, resources, and time?
- Does it result in equity (academic, social, emotional) without hurting participants by stigmatizing, causing loss of self-esteem, or restricting friendships? (Corno & Snow, 1986)

A summary of what good users of individualized instruction and good programs are like appears in Table 7.7.

ADVANTAGES AND LIMITATIONS OF INDIVIDUALIZED INSTRUCTION

Let's look at the benefits for teachers and for students when individualized instruction is utilized.

Teacher Benefits   As you can imagine, following individualizing instruction is demanding. As a consequence, the rewards must match or exceed the effort. We

7.29 Which of the advantages of individualized instruction are most important in your eyes as a future teacher?

TABLE 7.7   Qualities of Good Users of Individualized Instruction and of Good Individualized Programs

Good Users . . .	Good Programs . . .
• Prize diversity	• Are tailored to meet individual learners' strengths and needs
• Value individualism	
• Know learners' strengths and needs	• Permit considerable learner autonomy with regard to goals, means, resources, time
• Have knowledge of and ability to implement such programs	• Result in greater equity
• Have strong interpersonal skills	• Have no damaging side effects

think they do. If you have the following needs to any great extent, using individualized instruction may be very satisfying to you:

- The **achievement** need to overcome obstacles, to do difficult tasks well and quickly.
- The **recognition** need to obtain praise and commendations (in this case, for doing the right thing, that is, meeting students' needs).
- The **affiliation** need to be liked and accepted (by students). We all like persons who try to meet our needs.
- The **nurturance** need to nurture or aid another (in this case, students).

Using individualized instruction also satisfies certain professional demands on teachers. First and foremost, it helps teachers respond to the challenge to recognize and encourage diversity among learners. What better way to do so? Additionally, it seems professionally correct when teachers:

- Encourage students to pursue their interests within the mandated curricular framework.
- Allow students to decide how they will best learn their targeted objectives.
- Hold students accountable for choices and progress.

7.30 How do you feel about individualization as a teacher?

Student Benefits   Depending upon the form used, individualized instruction programs can meet a number of student needs:

- The **construction** need to organize and build. This need would be met when individuals or group of students interested in learning about the discovery of gold in Alaska learn how prospectors decided where to pan for gold and then build a model of a cradle used to separate gold from worthless stone.
- The **cognizance** need to explore, to read, and to seek knowledge. This need would be filled when students want to find out what causes strife in places like Israel, Northern Ireland, or South Central Los Angeles.
- The need to **play**—to seek diversion, change, and relaxation.
- The **exposition** need to give information, to relate facts, to explain and demonstrate. This need would be met when individuals or groups report to others on what they have discovered.
- The **achievement** need to do well.
- The **failure avoidance** need to avoid failure and shame.
- The **recognition** need to obtain praise and notice.
- The **exhibition** need to attract attention to oneself.
- The **autonomy** need to strive for independence and freedom.
- The **contrariness** need to act differently from others, to be novel or unconventional.
- And, if a group is involved, the **affiliation** need to form friendships.

In addition to meeting students' personality needs, good individualized instruction has educational benefits.

- It can capture and maintain attention and interest.
- It may deliver instruction in a way compatible with the student's learning style.
- It promotes independence and self-discipline.
- It can help students learn how to learn.
- It can give students confidence in their ability to learn.

7.31 How do you feel about individualization as a learner?

Limitations   The overwhelming disadvantage of individualization is, of course, that it is very time-consuming when done properly. You cannot just give students any old thing to do, even on an attractive computer. Neither can you simply allow students to do whatever they please. Individualizing means responding responsibly to each individual as a person with unique educational needs.

WHEN INDIVIDUALIZED INSTRUCTION SHOULD BE USED

Obviously, individualized instruction should be used whenever teachers hope to serve a student's unique strengths and needs. "OK," you say, "But isn't that all the time?" Of course, but human and material resources are not available to meet this ideal. Thus, you will need to compromise, using individualized, personalized instruction whenever a child is at risk of school failure and beyond that as often as possible.

From your experience, you know that, in almost all classrooms, teacher presentations and recitations prevail. In some instances, discussion is an occasional alternative of choice. Most likely, individualized instruction is underutilized, even with children at risk. The only pervasive effort to compel its use is contained in the Individuals with Disabilities Act, which, as you know, requires that Individual Educational Programs (IEPs) be drawn up and followed for students with disabilities. That is not to say that teachers are unaware of the needs and strengths of individual students, nor that they totally ignore such information. Rather, for the most part, teachers do not in a regular and conscious fashion individualize. What they tend to do is ability-group children with similar needs or similar strengths. However, and sometimes unfortunately, the practice of homogeneous grouping is drawing fire from those who claim it has negative side effects such as stereotyping students in the less advanced groups.

Spotlight on Research 7.5 summarizes the research findings on individualized instruction.

SUMMARY ON INDIVIDUALIZED INSTRUCTION

We have learned what individualized instruction is, and we have seen it takes many different forms. Most of the forms are fairly prescriptive and controlled. By this, we mean that students have little or nothing to say about what or how they will learn. The only part of individualized instruction that may be truly individualized is the *time* needed to learn. The forms are often tight programs that students move through as quickly as they can. However, in terms of student learning, these programs seem to work.

Few forms of individualized instruction allow students any real autonomy in deciding what they will learn and/or how. We mentioned one exception: the Project Method, a standby for generations, that seems to work for teachers and learners alike. You will see many classrooms, particularly in elementary and middle schools, where individuals or groups of children address themselves to topics they have an interest in and decide how they will learn about some aspect of the topic.

We have said that when teachers instruct students one-on-one, they must know the students and accept and prize their diversity. Furthermore, they have to value individualism and have good interpersonal skills, especially the ability to listen and encourage. If the individualized program you use is a good one, it will be tailored to each learner's strengths and needs, give students as much autonomy as possible, and help children achieve without causing personal embarrassment.

Good individualized instruction seems to be a standout approach. It can meet a great many personal, professional, and educational needs for teachers and students. This instructional alternative also has good support from research.

Try Activity 7.8

Some Final Thoughts

At the outset of Chapter 6, you were asked to think of a teacher who helped you learn and enjoy learning. We assumed that those teachers that you targeted would have a number of admirable personal and professional qualities and, further, that one of those qualities would be the ability to use a wide repertoire of instructional alternatives.

So that you may someday be thought of as an exceptional teacher, too, you have learned about seven teaching strategies in Chapters 6 and 7, namely: presentation, discussion, independent study, cooperative learning, discovery learning, direct instruction, and individualized instruction. If you have had the opportunity to reflect on these practices and especially to try the end-of-chapter activities related to each method, then you have reached some degree of competence with them. Of course, practice makes perfect, and knowledge does not always equate with skill. To truly be skillful with any instructional alternative, you must work with it over time. In the months and years ahead, we hope you will find these two chapters particularly useful desk references as you strive to be the best teacher you can be.

7.32 How would you rank the seven instructional alternatives presented in Chapters 6 and 7? What accounts for your attraction to your top two choices? How does your ranking compare with your classmates'?

CHAPTER SUMMARY

- Cooperative learning describes instructional procedures that place learners in small work teams that are rewarded for what they collectively accomplish. The purpose of cooperative learning is to engender in students a collective caring, an "all for one, one for all" philosophy. Principal characteristics include small, heterogeneous teams and tasks that revolve around either mastering some knowledge or skill or participating in a group academic project. Cooperative learning draws on the cognitive, behavioral, and humanistic schools of thought, and its variations include STAD, TGT, TAI, and CIRC.

- Good leaders of cooperative learning believe in its purpose; they are able to get students to work together, are competent presenters, effective organizers, and good work coordinators; and they are able to identify and help students and teams having difficulty.

- Good cooperative learning includes preparation, delivery, and closure. In STAD, preparation requires planning a good presentation, preparing the teams' assignments, and getting students ready to engage in teamwork. Delivery requires making a good presentation, setting team goals, preparing for teamwork, giving teams their assignment, quizzing students, and recognizing team accomplishments. Closure requires that students be reminded of what they have learned, that they relate new learning to earlier learning and that students have the opportunity to use new learning.

- Cooperative learning is beneficial for teachers with strong personality needs for achievement, recognition, and affiliation. It also meets demands placed on teachers to develop students' interpersonal skills, to make students more accountable to themselves and their peers, to raise student pride and self-esteem, and to improve achievement.

- Students with strong personal needs for play, exposition, achievement, recognition, failure avoidance, inviolacy, affiliation, deference, nurturance, and succorance seem to benefit from cooperative learning. This instructional alternative appears most advantageous for students, and research has been mostly positive in terms of students' achievement.

- Cooperative learning has certain limitations. It requires higher-achieving students to assist low achievers and presumes high achievers are willing to do so. Additionally, since cooperative learning is a group activity, substantial teacher monitoring is necessary to keep teams on task.

- Discovery learning takes place when students are presented with experiences and are asked to derive their own meaning and understanding from them. Its purposes are (1) to provide students with the opportunity to think for themselves in order to figure something out, (2) to help students discover how knowledge is gained, and (3) to promote higher-order thinking skills such as analysis, synthesis, and evaluation.

- In discovery learning, the teacher is a catalyst who causes students to construct their own knowledge rather than spoon-feed it to them. Teachers ask many, mostly higher-order questions: "Why?" "How come?" "What would happen?" and so forth. Good discovery learning teachers believe in its purposes, tend to enjoy inquiry, are optimistic that students are inquiry-oriented and capable of learning in this fashion, and hold high expectations of students; they are nurturing, thoughtful, patient, reflective, and accepting of students' ideas.

- Good discovery learning includes attention to preparation, delivery, and closure. Preparation includes determining the general purpose and specific objectives students are to accomplish, collecting useful materials, and planning lessons around inductive procedures. Delivery includes obtaining students' attention; presenting the baffling situation that requires investigation; promoting inquiry through use of observation, manipulation, analysis, and so forth; ensuring that learners know what to do; setting them free to inquire; monitoring; and, when necessary, guiding their inquiry and encouraging positive student interaction. Closure includes helping learners organize and define what they have found out and draw conclusions from it.

- Discovery learning is advantageous for teachers who have strong personal needs for cognizance, construction, recognition, exhibition, affiliation, and nurturance. Use of discovery learning is most advantageous when trying to teach students how to construct their own knowledge.

- Discovery is beneficial to students who have strong personal needs for cognizance, construction, achievement, exposition, recognition, autonomy, affiliation, and play. It is educationally beneficial since it tends to emancipate students from dependence on teachers and to make them independent life-long learners.

- Among the limitations of discovery learning are that not all things are amenable to classroom discovery, some discovery is too complex for K–12 student minds, and time constraints often limit the ability to explore.

- Research results on discovery learning are mixed and inconclusive. It seems a viable alternative that will enhance learning for some children while frustrating others.

- *Direct instruction* is one of several terms used to describe the sequence of instructional events (1) that "effective" teachers have been observed to follow or (2) that teachers should follow if they want to utilize what is known about learning. Two major kinds of direct instruction are consistent with this definition. The first derives from observing effective teachers and includes three major subtypes: Basic Practice, Explicit Teaching, and Active Teaching. The second kind derives from analyzing and applying learning theory and has two major subtypes: the Mastery Teaching Program and DISTAR. The primary purpose of all these variations is to maximize learning of academic content or skills.

- Direct instruction teachers provide strong academic direction, have high expectations that students can and will learn, make students feel psychologically safe, urge them to cooperate, hold them accountable for their work, and closely monitor and control students' behavior. Good leaders of direct instruction are enthusiastic, warm and accepting, humorous, supportive, encouraging, businesslike, adaptable or flexible, and knowledgeable.

- Good direct instruction has three phases: preparation, delivery, and closure. The preparation that direct instruction teachers engage in is not clear. We can only assume it equates to preparing a good presentation. In DISTAR, preparation requires being well acquainted with the teacher's instructional manuals. Delivery requires some very major tasks including (for most variations) collection and review of previous work, reteaching when necessary, presentation of new material, teacher-guided practice and, finally, independent practice until 80 percent or higher proficiency is achieved.

- Direct instruction probably benefits teachers with strong personal needs for construction, exposition, nurturance, and dominance. It also seems to satisfy the professional demand to help low SES children learn and to maintain manageable classrooms.

- Direct instruction is probably advantageous for students with strong personal needs for deference, similance, acquisition, and succurance. It seems to be one of the best instructional alternatives for helping low SES children acquire academic knowledge. Its most notorious limitations are that it deemphasizes students' autonomy, it may stifle more able learners, and it doesn't do much to improve creativity, abstract thinking, and problem solving.

- Generally, research on direct instruction is encouraging. All of its variations have been investigated; with the possible exception of the Mastery Teaching Program, they have proven to be more or less successful in increasing academic achievement in the basic skill areas such as reading and mathematics.

- Individualized instruction refers to a number of instructional maneuvers that attempt to tailor teaching and learning to a learner's unique strengths and needs. There are many types of individualized instruction, including the Dalton and Winnetka plans, programmed and computer-assisted instruction, Individually Prescribed Instruction, Individually Guided Education, tutoring, and the Project Method. In some, individuals with like abilities are grouped.

- The teacher's role in individualized instruction is to know and care about the diversity of students and to see that the learning tasks are varied or modified for each individual. Good users of individualized instruction prize diversity, value individualism, know learners' strengths and needs, know about and have the ability to implement individualized instruction programs, and have good interpersonal skills.

- Good individualized instruction programs are tailored to meet individual learners' strengths and needs, permit considerable autonomy, result in greater equity, and have no damaging or harmful side effects on students.
- Individualized instruction is probably advantageous to teachers who have strong needs for achievement, recognition, affiliation, and nurturance. It also satisfies some professional demands, such as encouraging students to define areas of interest, allowing them to decide how they learn best, and holding them accountable for their choices and progress.
- Individualized instruction is beneficial to students who have strong needs for construction, cognizance, play, exposition, achievement, recognition, exhibition, failure avoidance, autonomy, contrariness, and affiliation. Individualized instruction can capture and maintain students' attention and interest, deliver instruction compatible with student learning styles, promote independence and self-discipline, help students learn how to learn, and increase confidence in their ability to learn.
- Research on individualized instruction makes it clear that its use is worth the extra time and effort. Its major limitation is that when it is properly conducted, it is very time-consuming.

ISSUES AND PROBLEMS FOR DISCUSSION

1. Some instructional alternatives foster competition, others cooperation. Which is preferable?
2. Some instructional alternatives depend upon whole-class instruction. Others depend upon the use of groups or independent work. Which is preferable?
3. Some instructional alternatives require teachers to teach directly (see Chapter 1). Others, more indirect, require teachers to draw things out of their students. Which is preferable?
4. Some instructional alternatives are more suitable to our personality and professional, job-related needs. Which alternatives are most attractive to you?
5. Some instructional alternatives meet different learners' needs. Which learner needs are the most important to you? to your classmates?
6. Given your responses to these questions, which instructional alternatives appeal most to you?

THEORY INTO ACTION ACTIVITIES

ACTIVITY 7.1: Prepare a Cooperative Learning Lesson   Although a cooperative learning activity generally spans several class periods, one can be developed to fit a short period of time. Following the STAD procedure, plan a cooperative learning activity for use in this class. Explain how you plan to briefly present information, establish teams and charge them to master the material, give team members a quiz, determine scores, and provide recognition and reward.

Assessment: Did you follow the planning procedures for good presentations and good cooperative learning? (See Tables 6.2 and 7.2.)

ACTIVITY 7.2: Conduct a Cooperative Learning Activity   Deliver the lesson you prepared in Activity 7.1.

Assessment: To what extent did you actually follow the procedures for good presentations and good cooperative learning? (See Tables 6.2 and 7.2.) To what extent did you model the personal qualities of good facilitators of cooperative learning? (See Table 7.2.) How well do your peers feel you succeeded?

ACTIVITY 7.3: Observe Cooperative Learning   It would be advantageous for you to see cooperative learning used in K–12 classrooms. Such observations would serve to confirm or deny what you have read and also help fix the concept in your long-term memory.

If you are assigned to a K–12 classroom, find out if and when your mentor teacher plans to use cooperative learning. If your mentor does not plan to do so, try to arrange a visit to a class where some sort of cooperative learning activities are in effect. If you cannot arrange to see this instructional alternative, perhaps your university instructor has a videotape on it. Videotapes are available from the Johns Hopkins Team Learning Project, Johns Hopkins University, 3505 N. Charles Street, Baltimore, MD 21218–7570, and from Teaching Inc., P.O. Box 788, Edmunds, WA 98020.

As you observe, record answers to these questions:

- Did the cooperative learning session have these identifying characteristics: heterogeneous groups, group cooperation, and group reward? How effective were these characteristics?—did they work?
- What qualities of good cooperative learning were most obvious? (See Table 7.2 for ideas if STAD was the process used.)
- Did certain students seem to benefit more and others less? Why?
- What teacher and student needs seem to have been most fully met?

Additionally, talk with students about how they feel about cooperative learning and ask the teacher his or her perceptions of it.

ACTIVITY 7.4: Prepare a Discovery Lesson   Using what you have learned about meaningful learning in general and about discovery learning in particular, prepare a discovery lesson that might be used with a group of your classmates. The lesson should be as brief as possible and should require your learners to discover some form of knowledge, either a concept, a fact, a generalization, a rule, or a law. (See Table 7.3 for ideas.)

Assessment: Did you follow the procedures for good discovery learning?

ACTIVITY 7.5: Deliver a Discovery Lesson   Deliver your discovery lesson to a small group of your peers.

Assessment: Following the lesson, have your learners respond to these questions. To what extent did you:

- Challenge learners by presenting them with the need to find something out for themselves?
- Ensure that learners knew what they were to do?
- Provide them with useful resources if needed?
- Monitor and guide their activity and thinking?
- Encourage inductive processes: observation, organization, manipulation, and analysis?
- Encourage supportive peer interaction?
- Assist learners in phrasing their conclusions?
- Provide opportunities for learners to use their new knowledge?

ACTIVITY 7.6: Observe Discovery Learning   Hopefully, you will be able to observe a discovery lesson. If you are assigned to a field experience, ask your mentor teacher if one is scheduled. Perhaps the teacher would conduct one just for you. Don't be afraid to ask. If a live discovery lesson is not available, perhaps your university instructor has captured one on videotape. In making your observation, whether real or recorded, answer the following questions:

- To what extent did the lesson possess the characteristics of discovery learning: the teacher acting as catalyst, students constructing their own knowledge, and the discovery revolving around mostly higher-order thought provoking questions?
- What did the teacher do to prepare the lesson?
- What qualities of good discovery teaching were displayed by the teacher?
- What qualities of good discovery learning were most evident?
- In your opinion, what teacher and student needs did discovery learning seem to meet?
- Why do you believe that some students seemed to benefit more than others?

Interview students who seemed to benefit most and least. Ask them how they feel about discovery learning. Finally, ask the teachers how they like this instructional alternative and what they think are its advantages and disadvantages.

ACTIVITY 7.7: Observe Direct Instruction   A number of schools are attempting to put into practice what is known about effective schools, educational practices, and teaching (Cruickshank, 1990). Many of those schools are the ones most likely to be implementing one or more of the direct instruction approaches you read about in this chapter.

If you are involved in a field experience, you may have the opportunity to observe one or more teachers using Basic Practice, Explicit Teaching, Active Teaching, the Mastery Teaching Program, or DISTAR. If not, perhaps your instructor has a videotape.

As you observe, record answers to these questions:

- To what extent were the characteristics of direct instruction evident: the teacher providing strong academic direction, the teacher holding high expectations for student achievement, the students being held accountable for their work, the students expected to be cooperative, the students feeling psychologically safe, and the teacher controlling behavior?
- What qualities of a good leader of direct instruction were evident? (See Table 7.6.)
- To what extent was the teacher able to follow the regimen for good direct instruction? (See Table 7.6.)
- What teacher personality and professional needs did the instruction seem to meet?
- What student personality and educational needs did the instruction seem to meet?

Talk with the teacher about his or her feelings about direct instruction. Finally, ask a few diverse students whether they like to be taught this way.

ACTIVITY 7.8: Observe Individualized Instruction   If you are presently involved in a field experience, find out if your mentor teacher or another teacher is using some form of individualized instruction. Should you be able to observe, answer the following questions.

- How would you describe the setting, the class, and the lesson?
- Which of the following were altered to meet students' strengths and needs?

  1. The goals and content of instruction
  2. Learning activities, or how students could choose to learn
  3. Materials and resources

4. Mastery level, or how much students were expected to learn

5. Pacing or time

6. Other

- To what extent did the lesson seem to accomplish the purpose of individualization, that is, to meet students' individual strengths and needs? Explain. Also, talk to the teacher and students. How do they feel about individualization of instruction?

REFERENCES

Anastasi, A. (1989). *Psychological testing.* Sixth Edition. New York: Macmillan.

Arends, R. I. (1999). *Learning to teach.* Fourth edition. New York: McGraw-Hill.

Aronson, E., Blaney, N., Stephan, C., Sikes, J., & Snapp, M. (1978). *The jigsaw classroom.* Beverly Hills, CA: Sage.

Augustine, D. K., Gruber, K. D., & Hansen, L. R. (1989/1990, December–January). Cooperation works. *Educational Leadership, 47*(4), 4–7.

Battistich, V., Solomon, D., & Delucci, K. (1993, September). Interaction processes and student outcomes in cooperative learning groups. *The Elementary School Journal, 94*(1), 19–32.

Becker, W. C. (1986). *Applied psychology for teachers.* Chicago: Science Research Associates.

Benjamin, R. (1981). *Making schools work.* New York: Continuum.

Berliner, D. (1982). Issue: Should teachers be expected to learn and use direct instruction? *ASCD Update, 24,* 5.

Biemiller, A. (1993) Lake Wobegon revisited: On diversity and education. *Educational Researcher, 22*(9), 7–12.

Brophy, J., & Evertson, C. M. (1976). *Learning from teaching.* Boston: Allyn and Bacon.

Brophy, J. & Good, T. L. (1986). Teacher behavior and student achievement. In M. C. Wittrock (Ed.), *Handbook of research on teaching* (pp. 328–375). New York: Macmillan.

Bruner, J. S. (1960). *The process of education.* Cambridge, MA: Harvard University Press.

Bruner, J. S. (1961). The act of discovery. *Harvard Educational Review, 32,* 21–32.

Cohen, E. G. (1986). *Designing group work: Strategies for the heterogeneous classroom.* New York: Teachers College Press.

Corno, L., & Snow, R. E. (1986). Adapting teaching to individual differences among learners. In M. C. Wittrock (Ed.), *Handbook of research on teaching* (pp. 605–629). New York: Macmillan.

Cruickshank, D., Tracey, K., Novak, C., Mager, G., Holton, J., Applegate, J., & Myers, B. (1980). *Teaching is tough.* Englewood Cliffs, NJ: Prentice-Hall.

Cruickshank, D. R. (1990). *Research that informs teachers and teacher educators.* Bloomington, IN: Phi Delta Kappa.

Dewey, J. (1933). *How we think.* Boston: Heath.

Doyle, A. C. (1901). *The hound of the Baskervilles.* New York: Grosset & Dunlap.

Ellson, D. (1986, October). Improving productivity in teaching. *Phi Delta Kappan, 68,* 111–124.

Feasley, C. E. (1982). Distance education. In H. E. Mitzel (Ed.), *Encyclopedia of educational research.* Fifth Edition (pp. 450–458). New York: Free Press.

Gersten, R., & Keating, T. (1987, March). Long-term benefits from direct instruction. *Educational Leadership, 44*(6), 28–31.

Gibbons, M. (1971). *Individualized instruction: A descriptive analysis.* New York: Teachers College Press, Columbia University.

Gilstrap, R. L., & Martin, W. R. (1975). *Current strategies for teachers.* Pacific Palisades, CA: Goodyear.

Good, T., & Grouws, D. (1977). Teaching effects: A process-product study in fourth grade classrooms. *Journal of Teacher Education, 28,* 49–54.

Good, T. L., Grouws, D., & Ebmeier, H. (1983). *Active mathematics teaching.* White Plains, NY: Longman.

Good, T. L., Reys, B. J., Grouws, D. A., & Mulryan, C. M. (1989, December; 1990, January). Using work groups in mathematics instruction. *Educational Leadership, 47*(4), 56–62.

Harmin, M., & Gregory, T. (1974). *Teaching is.* . . . Chicago: Science Research Associates.

Heck, S., & Williams, C. R. (1984). *The complex roles of the teacher.* New York: Teachers College, Columbia University.

Hoffer, T. B. (1992, Fall). Middle school ability grouping and student achievement in science and mathematics. *Educational Evaluation and Policy Analysis, 14*(3), 205–227.

Hofwolt, C. A. (1984). Instructional strategies in the science classroom. In D. Holdzkom & P. Lutz (Eds.), *Research within reach: Science education* (pp. 41–58). Washington: National Science Teachers Association.

Hunter, M. (1982). *Mastery teaching.* El Segundo, CA: TIP Publications.

Hunter, M. (1984). Knowing, teaching, and supervising. In P. Hosford (Ed.), *Using what we know about teaching.* Alexandria, VA: Association for Supervision and Curriculum Development.

Jeter, J. (1980). Individualized instruction programs. In J. Jeter (Ed.), *Approaches to individualized education* (pp. 402–407). New York: Bowker.

Johnson, D. W., & Johnson, R. T. (1976). *Learning together and alone: Cooperation, competition, and individualization.* Englewood Cliffs, NJ: Prentice-Hall.

Johnson, D. W., & Johnson, R. T. (1989/1990, December/January). Social skills for successful group work. *Educational Leadership, 47*(4), 29–33.

Johnson, D. W., Johnson, R. T., & Holubec, E. J. (1990). *Cooperation in the classroom.* Revised Edition. Edina, MN: Interaction.

Johnson, D. W., Maruyama, G., Johnson, R., & Nelson, D. (1981). Effects of cooperative, competitive, and individualistic goal structures on achievement: A meta-analysis. *Psychological Bulletin, 89*(1), 47–62.

Joyce, B., & Weil, M. (1986). *Models of teaching.* Englewood Cliffs, NJ: Prentice-Hall.

Kauchak, D. P., & Eggen, P. D. (1993). *Learning and teaching: Research-based methods.* Boston: Allyn and Bacon.

King, L. H. (1993). High and low achievers' perceptions of cooperative learning in two small groups. *Elementary School Journal, 93*(4), 399–416.

Lawry, J. R. (1987a). The Dalton plan. In M. J. Dunkin (Ed.), *The international encyclopedia of teaching and teacher education* (pp. 214–215). Oxford: Pergamon.

Lawry, J. R. (1987b). The project method. In M. J. Dunkin (Ed.), *The international encyclopedia of teaching and teacher education* (pp. 217–219). Oxford: Pergamon.

Lawry, J. R. (1987c). The Winnetka scheme. In M. J. Dunkin (Ed.), *The international encyclopedia of teaching and teacher education* (pp. 216–217). Oxford: Pergamon.

Merriam-Webster Dictionary of Quotations. Springfield, MA: Merriam-Webster.

Merwin, W. C. (1976). The inquiry method. In S. E. Goodman (Ed.), *Handbook on contemporary education.* New York: Bowker.

Meyer, L. A. (1984). Long-term academic effects of the Direct Instruction Project Follow-Through. *Elementary School Journal, 84,* 380–394.

Michaels, J. W. (1978). Classroom reward structures and academic performance. *Review of Educational Research, 47,* 87–98.

Murphy, J., Weil, M., & McGreal, T. (1986). The basic practice model of instruction. *The Elementary School Journal, 87,* 83–95.

Murray, H. A. (1963). *Explorations in personality.* New York: Oxford.

Nixon-John, G. D. (1994, Summer). The high school writing center: A room for one-on-one student tutoring. *Teaching and Change, 1*(4), 369–379.

Nuthall, G., & Snook, I. (1973). Contemporary models of teaching. In R. M. Travers (Ed.), *Second handbook of research on teaching* (pp. 47–76). Chicago: Rand McNally.

Olson, L. (1993, February 17). Progressive-era conception breaks mold: NASDC schools explore "project learning." *Education Week, 12*(21), 6.

Orlich, D. C., Harder, R. J., Callahan, R. C., Kauchak, D. P., Pendergrass, R. A., Keogh, A. J., & Gibson, H. (1990). *Teaching strategies: A guide to better instruction.* Lexington, MA: Heath.

Peterson, P. (1979a, October). Direct instruction: Effective for what and for whom? *Educational Leadership, 37,* 46–48.

Peterson, P. (1979b). Direct instruction reconsidered. In P. Peterson & H. Walberg (Eds.), *Research on teaching: Concepts, findings, and implications.* Berkeley, CA: McCutchan.

Peterson, P. (1982). Issue: Should teachers be expected to learn and use direct instruction? *ASCD Update, 24,* 5.

Rosenshine, B. (1986). Synthesis of research on explicit teaching. *Educational Leadership, 43*(7), 60–69.

Rosenshine, B. (1987). Direct instruction. In M. J. Dunkin (Ed.), *The international encyclopedia of teaching and teacher education* (pp. 257–263). Oxford: Pergamon.

Rosenshine, B. & Meister, C. (1995). Direct instruction. In L. Anderson (Ed.), *International encyclopedia of teaching and teacher education.* Second Edition (pp. 143–148). Oxford: Elsevier Science Ltd.

Rosenshine, B., & Stevens, R. (1986). Teaching functions. In M. Wittrock (Ed.), *Handbook of research on teaching*. Third Edition (pp. 376–391). New York: Macmillan.

Rossmiller, R. A. (1976). Individually guided education. In S. E. Goodman (Ed.), *Handbook on contemporary education* (pp. 402–407). New York: Bowker.

Runkel, P. J., & Schmuck, R. A. (1982). Group processes. In H. E. Mitzel (Ed.), *Encyclopedia of educational research*. Fifth Edition (pp. 743–755). New York: Free Press.

Sharon, S. (1980). Cooperative learning in small groups: Recent methods and effects on achievement, attitudes, and ethnic relations. *Review of Educational Research, 50,* 241–271.

Sharon, S., & Sharon, Y. (1976). *Small group teaching.* Englewood Cliffs, NJ: Educational Technology Publications.

Sharon, Y., & Sharon, S. (1989, December; 1990, January). Group investigation expands cooperative learning. *Educational Leadership, 47*(4), 17–21.

Slavin, R. E. (December 1989/January 1990). Here to stay or gone tomorrow: Guest editorial. *Educational Leadership, 47*(4), 3.

Slavin, R. E. (1990). *Cooperative learning: Theory, research, and practice.* Englewood Cliffs, NJ: Prentice-Hall. A division of Simon & Schuster.

Slavin, R. E. (1991a, February). Synthesis of research on cooperative learning. *Educational Leadership, 48*(5), 71–82.

Slavin, R. E. (1991b). *Educational psychology.* Third Edition. Englewood Cliffs, NJ: Prentice-Hall.

Slavin, R. E. (1995). Cooperative learning. In L. Anderson (Ed.), *International encyclopedia of teaching and teacher education.* Second Edition (pp. 139–143). Oxford: Elsevier Science Ltd.

Slavin, R., & Madden, N. (1989, February). What works for students at risk: A research synthesis. *Educational Leadership, 46,* 4–13.

Slavin, R. E., Karweit, N. L., & Madden, N. A. (1989). *Effective programs for students at risk.* Boston: Allyn and Bacon.

Solomon, D., Watson, M., Schaps, E., Battistich, V., & Solomon, J. (1990). Cooperative learning as part of a comprehensive classroom program designed to promote prosocial development. In S. Sharon (Ed.), *Cooperative learning: Theory and research* (pp. 231–260). New York: Praeger.

Stallings, J., & Kaskowitz, D. H. (1975, April). A study of follow-through implementation. Paper presented at the annual meeting of the American Education Research Association, Washington.

Stallings, J. A., & Stipek, D. (1986). Research on early childhood and elementary school teaching programs. In M. D. Wittrock (Ed.), *Handbook of research on teaching.* Third Edition (pp. 727–753). New York: Macmillan.

Stratton, L. (1993, February 19). Pupils see computer's classroom potential in action. *The Columbus Dispatch,* p. D1.

Strike, K. A. (1975). The logic of learning by discovery. *Review of Educational Research, 45,* 461–483.

Struthers, D. B. (1990, October). Cooperative learning: Fad or foundation for learning? *Phi Delta Kappan, 72*(2), 158–162.

Suchman, R. J. (1961). Inquiry training: Builds skills for autonomous discovery. *Merrill Palmer Quarterly, 7,* 147–171.

Swang, J. (1993, April/May). Ensuring success in science. *Learning, 93,* 24–27.

Szent-Gyorgyi, A. (1965). *An anthology of partly baked ideas.* New York: Capricorn.

Taba, H. (1966). *Teaching strategies and cognitive functioning in elementary school children.* Cooperative Research Project 2404. San Francisco: San Francisco State University.

Tamir, P. (1995). Discovery learning and teaching. In L. Anderson (Ed.), *International encyclopedia of teaching and teacher education.* Second Edition (pp. 149–155). Oxford: Elsevier Science Ltd.

U.S. Department of Education. (1986, 1987). *What works: Research about teaching and learning.* Washington, DC: U.S. Department of Education.

Walberg, H. (1984, May). Improving the productivity of America's schools. *Educational Leadership, 41,* 19–27.

Wallis, C. (1995, Spring). The learning revolution. *Time, 145* (12), 49–51.

Webb, N. M. (1982). Student interaction and learning in small groups. *Review of Educational Research, 52*(3), 421–445.

Weil, M. L., & Murphy, J. (1982). Instruction processes. In H. Mitzel (Ed.), *Encyclopedia of educational research* (pp. 890–917). New York: Free Press.

Wittrock, M. C. (1966). The learning by discovery hypothesis. In L. S. Shulman and E. R. Keislar (Eds.), *Learning by discovery: A critical appraisal.* Chicago: Rand McNally.

Evaluating Students' Learning

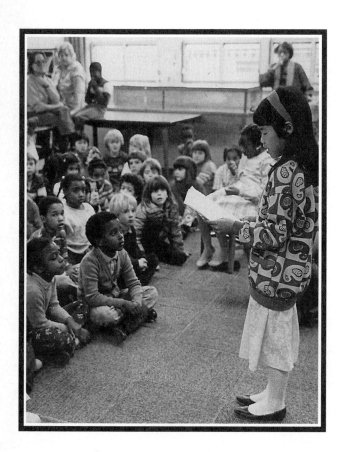

Contents

At many points during the instructional process, teachers make decisions about how well their students are learning and how effective their instruction has been. These assessment decisions, while often difficult, are important in helping teachers improve their performance and their students' learning (Goodwin & Klausmeier, 1975; MacDonald, 1992). They require teachers to measure student learning in one or more of several ways and to use that information to make judgments about the effectiveness of their instruction.

In this chapter, we examine ways teachers can more accurately assess student learning and thereby make judgments about the effectiveness of their own instruction. We begin by defining instructional assessment and underscoring its importance in effective teaching. Next, we examine several factors which influence the quality of assessments, and then we look at the principal types of assessment. The next sections then deal respectively with standardized tests and testing and with teacher-made tests and test construction. In the final section, we discuss systems for grading student performance and ways to effectively and fairly assign grades.

Defining Classroom Assessment, Measurement, and Evaluation

When teachers think of instructional assessment, they most often think of paper-and-pencil tests administered to students at the end of instruction. However, good classroom assessment requires more than that. It requires teachers to continually gather information about their students' progress from a variety of sources, to synthesize that information, and then to make a judgment or evaluation about how well or how much each student has learned.

Classroom assessment serves at least two important purposes for effective teachers. First, it provides information about the effectiveness of instruction. By gathering information before, during, and after instruction, teachers are able to plan and adapt instruction to better meet students' needs. Second, the information gained through assessment helps them make more accurate determinations about what an individual student has or has not learned and why. Thus, they can reteach when necessary, avoid unnecessary repetition, and help the student correct or modify misconceptions, errors, and inaccurate strategies.

The process of gathering objective information or data about students' performance is referred to as **measurement.** Measurement merely describes, usually in the form of a number or score, how much students have learned or how well they have performed. For example, students' scores on a twenty-item quiz represent a measurement of how well the students understand the material. In themselves, these numbers do not represent good, bad, acceptable, or unacceptable performance. The "goodness" of a student's score is determined by making a judgment about the measured score, that is, by comparing the score obtained through measurement to some standard or to other students' scores. This judgment is referred to as an **evaluation.**

The process of collecting, synthesizing, and interpreting information to aid in decision making is called **assessment.** While measurement is generally considered objective and nonjudgmental, assessment is always subjective to some degree. As the teacher, you must decide what your students' scores indicate. For example, does a numerical test score of 85 represent good, average, or poor performance? In making this decision, you must consider each student's score either in relation to how well other students did or in relation to some minimum score you have established. You may also consider other factors, not directly measured, which affect a student's score. For example, was the child feeling ill at the time of measurement? Did the child's performance improve from the last measurement, even if it did not meet the minimum acceptable score? Did you feel that the measurement was somehow unfair to the student?

While assessment of student performance often involves more than measurement, you must remember that the more you allow personal opinions or biases to influence how you interpret the results of measurement and make judgments, the less accurate your assessments will be. Further, even if you attempt to be objective in interpreting information, both the methods you use to gather your information and the sources you use influence the accuracy of your assessment. Let us now examine the factors more closely and then turn our attention to the various types of assessment.

Factors Influencing Assessment Quality

To use assessment effectively, teachers must consider several factors which influence the accuracy and usefulness of their assessments. First they must select appropriate sources of information, then they must ensure that their measurements and judgments are accurate, and finally they must determine how and why they will use the assessment.

SOURCES OF INFORMATION

In Chapter 4, we discussed several sources of information, such as cumulative records, observations, and interviews, that allow teachers to get to know their students better. These and other information sources help teachers find out about students' strengths and weaknesses, likes and dislikes, and problems and successes. Teachers use this information to organize their classrooms and plan their curricula. In this chapter, we are most interested in sources of information that help determine what a student has learned and in what areas or ways the student may need more instruction. Although some of the more informal sources discussed in Chapter 4 can be used to assess academic achievement, teachers mostly gain this kind of information by analyzing students' work or through testing.

Analysis of Students' Work Obviously, a great deal of useful information about academic achievement is gained through analyzing students' work. In contrast to merely examining the score a student obtains on a given piece of work, such as a homework assignment, teachers often want to know how a student arrived at an answer. For example, what process or method did the child employ, and how accurately did he or she employ it? By looking closely at the process the student employed, the teacher can identify errors that prevent the student from completing the work accurately. Homework assignments, projects, worksheets, and even tests or quizzes can be designed so that teachers can observe and analyze students' work. When teachers do this, it is important that they give students feedback about their performance (see Chapter 11).

"I see many of you anticipated a sneak quiz today."

Testing Testing is the most recognized source of assessment information. Tests require students to demonstrate how well they have learned the targeted content and allow teachers to describe their students' performance. Tests, like other instructional activities, can also be structured so that students are forced to demonstrate how they solve problems or arrive at conclusions. Thus, tests are a rich source of information. As with information from any source, however, the information tests provide is useful only when it is accurate and unbiased. Further, tests provide only one measure of students' progress.

Effective assessment requires that teachers collect and synthesize as much accurate information from as many sources as possible. They must integrate the data they gain from informal observations and interactions with students with the more formal measurements they obtain through testing, student projects or performances, and other available sources. However, the value of these teacher judgments depends largely on the accuracy of the information they obtain.

ACCURACY OF INFORMATION

The data that teachers obtain about students and their progress is never completely accurate. For a variety of reasons, no measure is ever totally free of bias or error. In fact, some of the information sources just noted are easily identified as subject to inaccuracy. For example, opinions from teachers or parents are likely to be somewhat inaccurate because they are highly subjective. Likewise, teachers' observations of their students are inevitably selective and incomplete; they are influenced by personal values and, consequently, are open to error and bias. Thus, teachers must take care to identify potential biases or errors when gathering and using information from these and other sources.

Even tests are subject to error. No test precisely measures a given student's knowledge or achievement in a subject area. First of all, tests are selective. They normally measure only part of what a teacher attempts to teach. Also, they do not test for knowledge that a student may have acquired from other sources such as books, friends, or other teachers. They may also omit some incidental things that a student has learned from the test-giving teacher. Furthermore, the student's internal condition at the time of testing can influence results. Perhaps the student was tired or ill when taking the test. Or perhaps the test emphasizes material that the student happened to review just before taking the test. In each case, the score obtained is not a full or accurate measure of the student's total knowledge on the subject.

A teacher's primary considerations when determining the accuracy of information gained from tests are (1) does the test measure what it was intended to measure *(validity)*, and (2) does the test provide consistent measurements *(reliability)*?

We shall discuss these two factors as they relate to tests, although they are equally important in judging information collected from any source.

Validity Validity is the term used to describe the *degree* to which a test measures what it was intended to measure. Validity is based upon the extent to which a test meets three criteria. First, a valid test measures understanding or mastery of what was actually taught and nothing more. In other words, the knowledge or tasks the test addresses should include as much of the content covered during instruction as possible, but it should not include content the students were not exposed to. Specifically, a valid test measures students' mastery of *each* of the teacher's major instructional objectives.

Second, a valid test measures performance in whatever *domains* (cognitive, affective, psychomotor) and at whatever *levels* (see Bloom's taxonomy in Chapter 5) the teacher's instructional objectives targeted. For example, if a history teacher reviews lessons that focused on knowledge (facts) about the American Revolution and then spends considerable time getting her or his students to analyze, synthesize, and make evaluations based on these facts, then the tests, to be valid, should emphasize these three higher cognitive levels.

Third, just as a valid test reflects the balance between the various domains and levels of instruction, it should also reflect the emphasis the teacher places on various content areas. For example, if social and economic conditions in the American colonies receive roughly equal instructional time as prevailing ideologies of the period, then a valid test should cover both bodies of content in roughly equal proportions.

Perhaps an extended example would be useful. Let's suppose that you teach a three-week unit on slavery and that you base your instruction on four cognitive objectives—one at the knowledge level, two at the synthesis level, and one at the evaluation level. During instruction, you spend one day on the reasons for slavery in the United States, three days on the practice of slavery, three days on causes of the demise of slavery, and two days on the impact of the Emancipation Proclamation on slaves and the Southern economy. A valid test would require your students to demonstrate understanding of each of these topics: reasons, practices, causes of demise, and impact. Further, the test would ask students to use their knowledge to (1) recall some information (the knowledge-level objective), (2) synthesize some information, and (3) evaluate one or more situations. The test should place the greatest emphasis on the topics of the practice and demise of slavery (three days on each of these), somewhat less emphasis on the impact of the Emancipation Proclamation (two days), and the least emphasis on reasons for slavery (one day). Students would not be asked questions related to other topics, for example, the impact of slavery on African cultures, even though there might have been incidental learning in this area.

To summarize, validity is the accuracy with which a test measures what you want it to measure. It thus gives you information about your students' learning and the success of your instruction. You have probably noticed from our discussion that a test cannot perfectly meet every criterion for validity. Validity is not either-or, but rather a matter of degree, so you must decide whether a given test is *sufficiently* valid for your purposes. In later sections, we discuss the ways you can make your tests more valid.

Reliability In addition to measuring what you want it to measure, you probably hope that your test provides you with *consistent* measures of your students' learning. This consistency is referred to as *reliability*. Specifically, reliability means that a test will yield nearly the same scores if the individuals were to take the test repeatedly. As with validity, no test can be expected to provide exactly the same scores for someone taking the test at different times, and so reliability, like validity, must be thought of as a matter of degree.

A test that lacks reliability produces scores that do not accurately reflect students' understanding or ability due to some error in the test itself. An analogy might help clarify. Let's assume you want to measure the dimensions of the bookshelves in your classroom. You locate a thin metal yardstick that was left lying in the bright sun on the windowsill and begin to measure the shelves. You record the dimensions of four shelves, but then you are interrupted by a call from the office. You lay the yardstick on the air-conditioning duct and go to the office. When you return, you realize that you left the paper you were recording the measurements on in the office. Rather than return to get it, you pick up the yardstick from the air-conditioning duct and remeasure the first four shelves. Sometime later in the day, you find the original paper and notice that the two sets of measurements for the shelves are not the same: The shelves are slightly smaller in the earlier measurements than in the later ones. You might conclude that the shelves changed length during that time. However, the real explanation is that the metal yardstick did not give you reliable measures because it expanded from lying in the sun (thus making the shelves appear smaller) and contracted from lying on the air-conditioning duct (thus making the shelves appear larger).

This same problem can occur when a test is not reliable. Unreliable tests lead us to draw inaccurate conclusions about student learning. If they have taken a flawed test which produces unreliable results, students may appear to have made little academic progress when, in fact, they may have learned quite a lot. Reliability is difficult to assess. Manufacturers of commercially available tests usually provide statistical indications of the reliability of their tests called **reliability coefficients.** These coefficients range from .00 to 1.00, with zero representing no reliability and 1.00 indicating perfect reliability. Generally, reliability coefficients above .85 are considered acceptable. Although you may be unable to compute the reliability coefficient of your own tests, you can improve their reliability by increasing the number of questions they contain and by being certain to score objectively and consistently. Guidelines for constructing reliable tests appear in a later section.

8.2 Did you ever feel that a teacher had made an inaccurate assessment of your performance? Why do you feel the assessment was inaccurate?

TYPES OF ASSESSMENT: FORMATIVE VERSUS SUMMATIVE

We have seen that instructional assessments use information from a variety of sources and that this information can have various degrees of accuracy. Instructional assessments also vary in terms of their use. Typically, we think of assessment as occurring after instruction with the results used to determine students' grades. However, Scriven (1967) pointed out that assessment conducted *after* instruction is completed is not very useful in improving learning. Although necessary to assign grades, postinstructional assessment does not help the teacher or the student correct deficiencies. More important, according to Scriven, is assessment conducted *during* instruction. This type of assessment can be used to adapt instruction to meet the needs of the student while learning is taking place.

Scriven introduced two terms to describe these different types of assessment. **Formative assessment** refers to assessment conducted during the course of instruction. Such assessment provides feedback while it is still possible to influence the instructional and learning process. Although student performance may be graded during formative assessment, the primary purpose is to provide feedback that can be used to plan or alter instruction. Formative assessment enables the teacher to *form* effective instruction and thereby improve students' performance. Formative assessment consists of both informal teacher observations and examples of student work, including responses to teachers' questions or any work students might complete within a larger unit of instruction. The feedback provided through formative assessment allows the teacher to adjust instruction and improve students' performance before a final assessment of learning is conducted.

Summative assessment is the term used to describe assessment conducted *after* instruction is completed. This type of assessment is used to make final judgments

TABLE 8.1 Characteristics of Formative and Summative Assessments

	Formative	Summative
Purpose	To monitor and guide a learning process while it is still in progress	To judge the success of a learning process at its completion
Time of assessment	During the process	At the end of the process
Type of assessment technique	Informal observation, quizzes, homework, pupils' questions, worksheets	Formal tests, projects, term papers
Use of assessment information	Improve and change a process while it is still going on	Judge the overall success of a process; grade, place, and promote

Source: From P. Arasian. (1991). *Classroom assessment.* New York: McGraw-Hill.

about a student's learning. Its primary purpose is not to adapt instruction or to remedy learning deficiencies; rather, it attempts to *summarize* a student's achievement or progress, generally in the form of a grade or score. Summative assessment generally involves information gathered from unit examinations, final examinations, or other projects due at the end of the term. In many cases, formative assessment of similar but less encompassing student work has taken place prior to this final assessment.

Effective teachers use both formative and summative assessments. However, formative assessments conducted and then communicated to students through a variety of formal and informal methods is most closely related to improved learning (Brophy, 1981). Table 8.1 provides a brief comparison of formative and summative evaluation.

Standardized Testing and Standard Scores

You may remember from Chapter 4 that a common type of assessment in schools is **standardized testing.** We all remember the days we spent in classrooms, our No. 2 pencils sharpened and ready on our desktops, waiting with trepidation for the teacher to finish reading the directions and to tell us to "open your test booklets and begin." Perhaps more recently, you remember taking the Scholastic Aptitude Test (SAT) or the American College Test (ACT) before entering college. In each case, you were taking a standardized test. The results were to be used to help others make judgments about how much or how well you had learned. They made these judgments by comparing your scores with those of similar students who also had taken the test.

Standardized testing has become increasingly common in U.S. public schools in recent years. Calls for greater accountability for students' learning and more rigorous standards have prompted many states to require students to pass standardized tests at several grade levels. It is estimated that 127 million standardized tests are administered to students in the United States each year. Nearly $900 million per year is spent on developing, administering, and scoring these tests (Willis, 1990). Because teachers are routinely expected to administer and interpret the results of standardized tests, we now turn our attention to this form of assessment. We will examine the standardized testing process and discuss how the scores from such tests are reported and used.

8.3 What standardized tests have you taken?

THE STANDARDIZED TESTING PROCESS

Standardized tests get their name because they are administered and scored in consistent, uniform ways. Any student taking a nationally standardized test will take the test under roughly the same conditions as any other student, no matter where or when the test is administered. This uniformity includes all controllable factors that might influence a student's performance on the test: the materials used, the time limits, oral instructions, preliminary demonstrations, policies for handling questions from students, and any other detail believed to affect test performance (Anastasi, 1988).

For example, when you took the SAT or ACT, you completed the test under the same conditions as all other students who took the exam. You were given the same instructions, the test booklet and scoring sheets were the same, the questions you answered were of equivalent difficulty and type, the equipment you were allowed to use was the same (pencils, calculators, and so on), you had the same amount of time to complete each section, and your scores were reported in the same ways. As a result, you are able to compare your performance with that of all other students who took the exam, even if they took it at another time or in another place. This ability to make comparisons across large groups of pupils is the greatest benefit of standardized tests.

Standardized tests offer several benefits in addition to allowing comparisons of students. They are efficient in measuring a wide range of student learning relatively quickly and inexpensively. They are fairly and objectively scored. They tend to be more reliable than teacher-made tests, and they can be developed to assess higher-order thinking. In spite of these benefits, standardized tests are often criticized for emphasizing low-level basic skills and for cultural, racial, and gender bias (e.g., Linn, 1991; Wiggins, 1989). Often, the harshest criticisms of standardized tests arise when the tests are misused or their results misinterpreted.

Each standardized test has been developed for use with targeted groups of students and is appropriately used only with similar students. For example, some standardized tests, like the Iowa Test of Basic Skills (ITBS) or the California Aptitude Test (CAT), are meant to assess broad learning outcomes for students of particular grade levels across the United States. Because every student taking the ITBS takes it under the same conditions, and because scores are always reported in standard ways, it is possible to compare the achievement of students from all across the country.

As a classroom teacher, you will probably be expected to administer standardized tests and to interpret their scores to students and their parents. When administering a standardized test, it is important that you exactly follow the directions provided. Failure to do so makes the results of the test less accurate and may put your students at a disadvantage. A major responsibility when administering the test is to allow all students an equal opportunity to do well. Thus, you must ensure that each student has the necessary materials, desk space, and time. Further, you should carefully read the instructions using a calm, clear, relatively slow speaking voice that all students in the room can hear. Voice inflection, tone, and facial expression should reinforce the instructions. You must also monitor students as they complete the examination, making sure that students begin and end at the appropriate times and do not cheat. Each standardized test will provide instructions for administering the exam, and you are well advised to follow them.

You can help your students improve their performance on standardized tests even if you do not know the exact content to be tested. By helping them develop good test-taking skills, you enable them to better convey what they do know. Students who are knowledgeable about how to efficiently complete standardized tests can be expected to achieve higher scores than students who are not (Anastasi, 1988). While this level of **test sophistication** does not change how much your students know about the content, it gives them a better opportunity to demonstrate their knowledge. That's why you should prepare your students for upcoming standardized testing by providing them with opportunities to respond to questions of similar types and under similar conditions. You may also wish to give students suggestions about when or if to guess at the correct answer and how to manage their

8.4 Do you get anxious or nervous about taking standardized tests? Why or why not?

"It's exam week, and they're not in a good mood. Let's be careful out there."

time. Such guidance helps students feel more comfortable and confident when taking the test and—especially for disadvantaged students—can substantially improve their test performance (Anastasi, 1981; Wahlstrom & Boersman, 1968).

INTERPRETING STANDARDIZED TEST RESULTS

The use of standardized tests has increased greatly in recent years and so has the responsibility of the teacher to convey the meaning of the results to students and parents. While most of you are familiar with the standardized testing process, few of you have ever had to interpret the results of a standardized test to anyone. In this section, we examine the various ways of reporting standard scores. Knowing this, you can then use this information to evaluate your students' progress and improve your own teaching.

Criterion- Versus Norm-Referenced Scores   To interpret test scores, you must compare a particular score to some standard. The two most widely used standards are: (1) the scores of other students or (2) an established, fixed criterion. When you compare students' scores to one another, you are using a **norm-referenced** approach. In this approach, the number of items a student answered correctly or incorrectly (called *raw score*) is less important than how the child's performance compares to other students who took the test. Norm-referenced test scores provide little information about what specific learning a student has gained or in what areas the student may need remediation. What they do show is how well the student's achievement compares with other students in the class, school, district, state, or nation who have taken the test. Because comparisons of all students who took the test are possible, even if the students were in different schools or different parts of the country, schools or state agencies often use the results of norm-referenced testing to make policy decisions.

When you compare students' raw scores to an established standard or criterion, you are using a **criterion-referenced** approach. In this approach, the number of items answered correctly or incorrectly is used to determine whether a student has mastered specific learning objectives. When a student's score is lower than the established criterion, the testers believe that the student has not sufficiently mastered the objectives. The results of criterion-referenced testing provide very detailed information about the specific learning the student has gained and the particular areas in which the student needs more work. Thus, criterion-referenced test results can be of tremendous benefit in evaluating, planning, or adapting classroom instruction. However, they give little information about how well your

TABLE 8.2 Comparison of Norm-Referenced and Criterion-Referenced Tests

Norm-Referenced Test	Criterion-Referenced Test
Reports the student's performance in relation to other students who took the test	Reports the student's performance in relation to a fixed, usually predetermined standard
Provides information about general learning and achievement	Provides information about specific learning and mastery of particular objectives
Is useful in making policy decisions at the national, state, and local levels	Is useful in designing the most appropriate instruction for individual students

students' performance compares with that of other students. A comparison of norm-referenced and criterion-referenced tests appears in Table 8.2.

TYPES OF STANDARD SCORES

The results of standardized tests are most often reported as norm-referenced scores. Remember that such scores indicate how the student did in comparison to others who took the test. This comparison, or **norming group,** can be limited to the class, school, or district, or it can be statewide or even national in scope. To interpret standard scores accurately, you must be aware of the comparison, or norming, group. Then you should discuss your student's performance only in relation to this other group. You must also know what standard test scores mean.

Standard scores are reported in one or more of five ways: as z scores, T scores, percentile rank (PR) scores, stanine scores, or score bands. Detailed descriptions of each type of score and its computation are available in other sources (see Arasian, 1991; Anastasi, 1988). However, we will briefly discuss each type.

All standard scores are norm-referenced: They indicate how well a student did in comparison to other students. Specifically, standard scores compare a raw score to the arithmetic mean or average score for the norming group. For example, the score would indicate whether a student did as well as, better than, or more poorly than the average student taking the test. The standard score indicates whether a particular score is above or below the mean score and how far above or below. Importantly, because each type of standard score is compared to the mean, it is possible to compare all types of standard scores with one another. For instance, a z score of +1 is the same as a T score of 60, a percentile rank score of 84 percent, and a stanine score of 7.

Standard scores are based upon several known characteristics of the **normal curve** (see Figure 8.1). This bell-shaped graph depicts the expected frequency of particular scores. The peak of the curve, in the middle, indicates that a large number of scores can be expected at or near the mean. As you move further in either direction from the middle or mean, you see that fewer and fewer people can be expected to obtain these very high or very low scores.

The **standard deviation** for a group of scores is an indication of how widely the scores vary from the mean. A small standard deviation indicates that the scores do not differ greatly, with most falling very near the mean. A large standard deviation indicates much variation in the scores, or a number of very high and very low scores.

Standard scores use both the mean and the standard deviation when making comparisons between student scores. As previously noted, all standard scores indicate how a particular score compares with the mean of the norming group. They indicate: (1) whether the score is above or below the mean and (2) how far above or below the score is in terms of standard deviations. To make the reporting more uniform, each type of standard score assigns a particular set of numbers or scale to the normal curve and reports individual scores along the scale. This is not unlike measuring distance. You can measure a shelf in inches, centimeters, arm lengths,

FIGURE 8.1 The Normal Curve and Standard Scores

Standard deviations	−3	−2	−1	Mean	+1	+2	+3
z scores	−3	−2	−1	0	+1	+2	+3
T scores	20	30	40	50	60	70	80
Stanine scores		1	3	5	7	9	
Percentile rank scores	1st	3d	16th	50th	84th	97th	99th

or by using other scales, but the shelf remains the same length. Although it sounds very complex, it will become clearer as we examine some common standard scores.

A **z score** is the most basic type of standard score. On this scale, the mean is zero and each standard deviation one unit (see Figure 8.1). Positive numbers indicate scores above the mean; negative numbers indicate scores below the mean. The larger the number, the more the raw score differs from the mean. Thus, if a student achieved a raw score equal to the mean, his z score would be 0.00. If he achieved a score that was one standard deviation above the mean, the z score would be +1.00. On this scale, a z score of −2.00 would indicate a raw score two standard deviations *below* the mean. Notice that we don't know the student's raw score, only how his score compares with the norming group. It should also be pointed out that z scores are reported to two decimal places. A z score of −1.50 indicates a score falling one and one-half standard deviations below the mean.

T **scores** assign a scale which uses 50 as the midpoint (mean) of the normal curve, with each standard deviation representing 10 points (see Figure 8.1). A student whose raw score was equal to the mean would be assigned a *T* score of 50. A score which was one standard deviation above the mean would be 60, two standard deviations above would be 70, and so forth. An advantage to this scale is the elimination of negative numbers and decimal places. Even scores below the mean are reported as positive numbers. For example, a score falling one and one-half standard deviations below the mean (a z score of −1.50) would be reported as a *T* score of 35 (50 minus 15).

Another common form of standard score is **percentile rank (PR).** When you received the results of your ACT or SAT, they were likely reported as percentile rank scores. Percentile rank also makes use of some known and stable characteristics of the normal curve. A percentile rank score indicates what percentage of people taking the test scored at or below a given score. In the normal curve, exactly half the scores fall above the mean and half below. Thus, a percentile rank of 50 indicates that the student's raw score was the same as the mean, that her score was equal to or better than 50 percent of the people in the norming sample. A PR of 70 suggests that the student scored as well as or better than 70 percent of the people in the norming sample. Percentile rank scores above 50 indicate raw scores above the mean, PR scores lower than 50 indicate raw scores below the mean. Although some percentile rank scores may look similar to T scores because both scales have a midpoint of 50, they are not the same and should not be confused. Just as with other standard scores, percentile rank scores do not indicate how many items a student answered correctly. They merely indicate how the student did in relation to others who took the test.

Stanine scores are commonly used to report the results of standardized tests in education. Stanine gets its name from the scale it applies to the normal curve. In this scale, 5 is the midpoint, or mean, and each standard deviation is 2. The entire scale contains nine values, hence, it is a "standard nine," or "stanine," scale. Stanine scores, like T scores, eliminate negative numbers and decimals. They are typically considered easier to interpret because they are somewhat less precise than z scores or T scores. Using this scale, a stanine of 5 indicates that the raw score was equal to the mean. A stanine of 9 indicates a raw score two standard deviations above the mean. A raw score one standard deviation below the mean would be a stanine of 3.

Grade equivalent (GE) scores are easily interpretable and particularly common in education. Grade equivalent scores compare a student's performance with the scores of other students of varying grade levels who took the same test. For example, if a student's raw score is similar to that obtained by seventh graders who took the test, the grade equivalent score would be 7. Decimal places are used to indicate months of the academic year, with 1 referring to the first month of the academic year and 10 typically referring to summer. Thus, a GE of 7.6 would mean that the student scored as well as a seventh grader in the sixth month of the school year (roughly February). The scale for grade equivalent scores is created by administering the test to large numbers of students at various grade levels and computing average scores for students at each month of each grade.

It is important to note that the students at various grade levels all take the *same* test. If the test is intended for students in the fifth grade, all students in the norming sample take this fifth-grade test, *not* a more or less advanced version. In this example, if a fifth-grade student achieved a GE of 9.1, her score on this fifth-grade test was roughly equal to that of students in the first month of ninth grade. This score means only that the fifth grader has mastered the fifth-grade material as well as the typical ninth grader. It does *not* mean that the fifth-grade student is capable of doing ninth-grade work.

Remember that no test is completely accurate in measuring a student's knowledge or ability. Some error is always present. Because of this, many test manufacturers now report student performance not as a single score, but as a range of scores which the student would likely obtain if he or she took the test several times. This **score band** includes the student's actual score (usually at the middle of the band) and indicates how much above and below that score the student might have performed. Although less precise than other types of scores, score bands are a useful way to use the results of standardized tests. They prevent us from attempting to make very fine judgments between students whose scores did not differ much.

Try Activity 8.1

SUMMARY OF STANDARDIZED TESTING

Teachers are commonly required to administer standardized tests, interpret the results to students and parents, and utilize the results to improve instruction. It is important that you be aware of the appropriate uses of such tests in order to avoid misusing them. Elementary teachers, especially, are expected to present and interpret the results of standardized tests to parents on a regular basis. You must know what standard scores mean and do not mean, and you must be able to convey this information to parents.

Fill in

Teacher-Made Tests

Standardized tests are increasingly important in determining educational policy at the national, state, and district levels. However, the most common form of classroom assessment remains the teacher-made test (Borich, 1992). It has been estimated that students spend well over 10 percent of classroom time in teacher-developed evaluation activities (Crooks, 1988). Well-made teacher-constructed tests have several advantages over standardized tests. First, since the classroom teacher develops them, they can be keyed to the specific content and objectives that teacher has taught rather than to general content "most" teachers teach at that grade level. Second, teacher-made tests are far less expensive than commercially produced tests. Third, when they are well-constructed around the instructional objectives, teacher-made tests provide more detailed and specific information on how well students have mastered the course content. However, in spite of these advantages, teacher-made tests are often poorly constructed and thus often provide inaccurate information (Haertel, 1986).

Because teacher-made tests are so common and potentially valuable, we now engage in an extended discussion of how best to develop and use the two primary types of teacher-made tests: pencil-and-paper tests and observational or performance assessment. After defining and describing each type of assessment, we will discuss the specific strengths and weaknesses, note considerations in selecting or developing appropriate instruments, and suggest methods of scoring.

PENCIL-AND-PAPER TESTS

The most recognizable type of teacher-made assessment is the pencil-and-paper test. Each of us has spent countless hours frantically writing our responses to essay questions or using our pencils to fill in the dots on a scoring sheet. And, perhaps just as often, we have spent time after the exam thinking about how unclear some of the questions were or wondering why the instructor asked so many questions about one aspect of the content while totally neglecting other aspects. In each case, we were prevented from giving a true account of how much we had learned because of a poorly developed test. It is your ethical responsibility as a teacher to make sure that your students have the opportunity to make a valid showing of how much they have learned.

Pencil-and-paper tests most often use items of two types. One type requires students to select a correct response from a list of possible answers called **selected response items.** Multiple-choice, true-false, matching, and completion items are all selected response types. The other type of item requires students to develop or create a response in their own words. These are called **created response items.** Essay or short-answer questions are examples of created response items.

Each item type possesses advantages and disadvantages depending on the ease or difficulty of construction and scoring. In other words, one type of item is easier to write but more difficult to score, while the other is just the opposite. Many people believe that one item type is inherently better than another, for example, that essay items are more valuable than multiple choice. However, Moore (1992) writes,

> A common misconception is that selected response items test only for facts or knowledge-level behaviors. In truth any type of test item can be used to measure any instructional outcomes at any level. Although it is often difficult to write selected response items at the higher levels, it is also difficult to write high-level items of any kind. (p. 123)

Thus, we should know about and be able to use items of each type when appropriate.

Created Response Items   Created response items require students to compose an answer, generally in their own words, rather than select the appropriate answer from a list. Created response items can require students to generate anything from a short sentence to a multiple-page essay. Well-written created response items can allow students to demonstrate learning at all cognitive levels—from recall through evaluation. They can push students to organize or reorganize ideas and concepts, apply content in unique ways, and solve problems. Poorly written created response items may discourage creativity, confuse and frustrate students, and result in unfair and inaccurate judgments about students' progress.

Created response items possess several advantages. First, they are easy to write—much easier, in fact, than selected response items. This is especially true when the teacher is attempting to assess higher-level cognitive processes. Thus, created response items require less time to construct. Second, because students must organize and express their answers in their own words, created response items allow teachers to assess students' ability to communicate ideas. Third, they reduce the likelihood that students will simply guess the correct answer.

Created response items also have disadvantages. Although they can be constructed rather easily and quickly, they are extremely time-consuming to score. Imagine, for instance, the high school teacher who administers a five-item essay exam to four classes, each with thirty students. If the response to each item was only one-half page, this teacher would have to read 300 pages of students' responses! Providing prompt and detailed feedback to students about their performance on this exam would be a daunting prospect.

Another disadvantage of created response items is that they limit the amount of content the test can cover. Because students must be allowed sufficient time to think about the item, compose an answer, and put it on paper, the test can include only a few items. Thus, a test consisting entirely of created response items cannot possibly assess all that has been taught. In essence, the validity of the test is reduced because it does not cover all important aspects of the content.

The final and most troubling disadvantage of created response tests is that they are difficult to score reliably. Created response items require teachers to make judgments about the quality of students' responses. Several factors can bias these judgments and result in unfair scoring. For example, the quality or legibility of the students handwriting, grammar, writing style, or length of response are known to influence the score that teachers assign to created responses (Stanley, 1958). This may be a particular problem for young students or for students with limited English proficiency. In addition, teachers' opinions and expectations of students can lead them to score responses unfairly. For instance, a student who has contributed to class discussions and seems motivated and interested is likely to receive a higher score than another student who is perceived as uninterested and unmotivated but makes the same response.

Created response items can be written as **restricted response** or **extended response items.** Restricted response items set explicit parameters within which students are to respond. Such items may restrict the topic or topics to be included or the length or space devoted to the response, and they often make specific suggestions about aspects of the content the response should address. Restricted response items do not allow students as much flexibility or creativity in responding. However, because they reduce variability in the style, length, and topics of students' responses, they are generally more reliable and fair than extended response items.

Extended response items often do not place any restrictions on students' responses. As a result, they allow much greater creativity and flexibility in creating the response. Students can write as much or as little as they wish and can include all aspects of the content they deem necessary. Extended response items give us a better picture of how well students can communicate and approach problems

FIGURE 8.2 Created Response Items: Restricted versus Extended Response

Restricted Response
List, describe, and present an example of each of three literary devices Poe uses to set the mood in the introductory paragraph of "The Fall of the House of Usher." Use no more than five complete sentences.

Extended Response
Discuss and provide examples of the literary devices Poe uses to set the mood in the introductory paragraph of "The Fall of the House of Usher."

creatively, but they are more open to biased and unfair scoring. As a result, you should use restricted response items in most situations. Examples of restricted and extended items are shown in Figure 8.2.

Once you have decided that your instructional objectives can best be assessed through created response items, you can do several things to improve the validity, reliability, and thus the accuracy of your test. First, key the test to your instructional objectives. Your goal should be to create assessment instruments that provide accurate measures of how well each student has mastered all the objectives. The test should be representative of the breadth, depth, and emphases of the objectives and should require students to perform or respond at cognitive levels matching your objectives. If you have written clear and complete instructional objectives, constructing a created response test is a relatively easy procedure. Just follow these guidelines.

"I didn't understand half of what you wrote—I like that in a thesis."

- First, consider which objectives are most important to your assessment. As noted earlier, created response items take students longer to complete, so you may be unable to assess all objectives. In that event, you should select those most critical to students' mastery of the material, those that were most emphasized in instruction, or those that are broad enough to encompass other objectives. However, you must be realistic in determining how many created response items students can handle. All students should be able to answer all questions in the time allowed.

- Second, write restricted response items for each objective. Always begin these items with the verb from your objective (compare, contrast, list, and so on), and provide specific information about the length, components, and style to be used. It is also a good idea to indicate whether spelling or grammar will be considered, whether an outline is acceptable, and how much weight you will apply to each element of the response.

- Third, after writing the item, it is a good idea to immediately compose a complete model response that can serve as your guide in scoring students' responses. Make a note about the time it took you to construct your answer, and use this to determine how much time students will need to answer the item. (Remember, it will take students much longer to think about, create, and write their answers.) Then, after making sure that your response provides a satisfactory answer, identify and list the characteristics or components that make it exemplary.

- Fourth, try to use several items requiring relatively short answers rather than a few questions requiring extensive answers. This allows you to assess more of your objectives (improving the validity of the test) and gives students a better opportunity to accurately demonstrate what they know (better reliability). It is also wise to construct the test in such a way that all students are expected to answer all items.

Before duplicating the test, write instructions for completing the test that include guidelines for composing and writing each response, information about how you will score the items, and the weight you will give each item. When appropriate, suggest the amount of time students should spend on each item as well. Then carefully proofread the test, perhaps asking a colleague to read through it for clarity and to ensure that your time frame is reasonable.

As noted earlier, a major weakness of created response tests is that they are difficult to score reliably and objectively. Using restricted rather than extended response items helps by more clearly defining the range of information and detail that students should include in their responses. In addition, judging each student's response against the components and characteristics you identified in your model response makes scoring more consistent and objective. Guidelines for improving your scoring of created response items follow.

- First, attempt to score the tests without knowing which student made the response you are reading. You might have students put their names only on the last page of the test, assign each student a code to use in place of the name, or cover the students' names until you have scored all items.

- Second, score only one item at a time for all papers. This allows you to more consistently apply the same criteria to all students' responses. It also reduces the likelihood that you will allow your opinion of an early answer to influence your scoring of one you read later.

- Third, don't score all papers at once. Scoring essay examinations takes a great deal of time and energy. If you become fatigued, you are less likely to be objective and accurate in your scoring. It is best to score all students' responses to one particular item, then move to another item, and so on until you begin to feel tired. Do not attempt a marathon session in which you sit for hours in order to "get through" a stack of papers.

- Fourth, after scoring all responses, reread all or a random sample of the papers to ensure that you have scored them accurately. It is often a good idea to organize the papers into high, moderate, and low scores and then to reread some papers in each category to check your scoring.

- Fifth, when necessary, adjust your scoring to reflect poor teaching. When no student is able to respond to an item with reasonable accuracy, you may wish to eliminate the item or reconsider the criteria you used to score it.

Created response items serve a useful purpose in classroom assessment. Because they are easy to construct, they are less time-intensive up front. They are also easier to adapt to higher-order cognitive processes. However, they are extremely time-intensive to score, and highly susceptible to scoring bias. These characteristics have led some to suggest that created response items, in spite of their intuitive appeal, are appropriate only when selected response items *cannot* be used (Borich, 1992). Table 8.3 briefly summarizes the guidelines for writing and scoring created response items.

Try Activity 8.2

Selected Response Items   Selected response items require students to select the most appropriate answer from a list of alternatives or to complete the item with a single, short answer (usually a word or short phrase). Students are not asked to compose a new or unique response, as in created response items. As noted earlier, many people believe that selected response items are not effective in assessing students' higher-order cognitive skills. However, such items, when written carefully, can be as effective as any other item in encouraging students to use high-level thinking skills. One way to do this is to write items that require students to identify metaphors or to answer questions about an extended, detailed scenario or problem.

Selected response items possess many advantages. Probably the most important is that they are less subject to scoring bias—the student either does or does not select the appropriate alternative. Reliability and fairness are increased because

TABLE 8.3 Guidelines for Writing and Scoring Created Response Items

Writing Items	Scoring Items
1. Key all test items to your instructional objectives.	1. Compose a model response immediately after writing each item.
2. Select the most important objectives, and write at least one item for each.	2. Identify components that make your response exemplary.
3. Begin each item with the verb from your objective.	3. Score all student responses against the model.
4. Write restricted rather than extended response items.	4. Score items without knowing which student constructed it.
5. Include as many items as students can reasonably complete.	5. Score only one item at a time for all papers.
6. Indicate whether spelling and grammar will be considered in scoring.	6. Avoid becoming fatigued.
7. Proofread carefully before duplicating.	7. Review a sample of the tests to check the accuracy of your scoring.

scores are not based upon the judgment of the scorer. Also, since selected response items take less time for students to complete, they allow the teacher to assess more content and objectives. As a result, tests that use these items tend to be more valid. Scoring is easy, quick, and less subject to bias. Because they do not require students to compose an answer, selected response items measure students' mastery of the content rather than their ability to write or communicate effectively.

On the other hand, selected response items are difficult and time-consuming to write. They are much more time-intensive up front than created response items are. A major weakness of selected response items is the difficulty of constructing items that encourage students to apply higher-order cognitive skills. While such items can be written, they usually take considerable thought. As a result, selected response items often emphasize lower-order thinking.

There are four types of selected response items: multiple-choice, matching, true-false, and completion. In the following sections we will examine the construction, uses, and scoring of selected response items.

Most of us have taken innumerable **multiple-choice** tests during our schooling. Nearly all standardized tests use them, as do many teacher-made tests. Multiple-choice items consist of two parts: a **stem** which presents a problem or asks a question, and several **alternative responses.** Students are expected to select the alternative which offers the best solution to the problem or which best answers the question the stem presents.

Multiple-choice items possess several strengths. They are probably the most versatile selected response item in that they can be used to evaluate learning in any content area and at all cognitive levels. Because each item takes relatively little time for students to complete, multiple-choice questions allow teachers to evaluate more instructional objectives than created response items. Similarly, multiple-choice items allow teachers to make fine discriminations in the depth and breadth of students' understanding. In contrast to created response items, multiple-choice items can be easily and reliably scored.

There are two primary disadvantages in using multiple-choice items. The greatest disadvantage is that they are difficult and time-consuming to construct, particularly when writing items to assess learning at the higher levels of thinking. High-level items require teachers to process the information at the more advanced levels, then create a problem or question that is likely to elicit similar processing in students, and finally to generate several *realistic* alternative responses, each requiring high-level thinking. A second disadvantage is that, unlike created response tests, multiple-choice tests do not allow us to evaluate how well students are able to communicate their understanding. Students merely select a response.

There are several things you can do to improve the validity and reliability of your multiple-choice tests. As with any test, you should write your multiple-choice items during the planning process to match your instructional objectives. Using your objectives or instructional plan as your guide, you then determine roughly the number of items to devote to each part of the content. You now have a rough test plan and are ready to begin writing or selecting individual test items.

The process of writing multiple-choice items begins with the stem. It must be clearly written in simple language, and it should ask a question or present a problem—not just make an incomplete statement. The stem should be clear enough that the respondent could generate the most appropriate answer even if the alternative responses were not presented. Be certain that each stem presents a new problem and that neither the stem nor alternative responses provide clues to other items. It is also wise to avoid using negative questions or statements in the stem or alternative responses.

For example, the stem, "The American Revolution could *not* have been won if the British military had not . . ." is confusing. It includes too many negatives and does not ask a question. A better way to write this stem would be, "Which of the following errors the British military made was critical to the outcome of the American Revolution?" This stem avoids negatives, presents a complete question, and uses clearer wording.

After writing the stem, you construct three to five reasonable alternative responses, writing the correct response first and then the others. It is not necessary to include an equal number of alternatives for every item. To reduce the likelihood that students can guess the correct answer, each alternative should present a reasonable answer to the problem presented in the stem, but only one should be most defensible. Avoid responses that are unreasonable and avoid using "none of the above" or "all of the above" since they encourage guessing. Be certain that neither the stem nor the responses provide grammatical clues to the correct response or to other items. This is most often a problem when the stem is an incomplete statement. For example, the stem might be, "George Washington was a . . .". In this example, the correct response must begin with a consonant to be grammatically correct. The response, "affluent land owner" would probably not be the correct answer because it doesn't complete the statement grammatically.

Finally, each alternative should be roughly the same length (in poorly constructed items the longest response is often the most appropriate). Figure 8.3 summarizes the guidelines for writing effective multiple-choice items.

Matching items can be thought of as a series of multiple-choice items with all stems using the same list of alternative responses. Matching items present a list of stems, often called *descriptors,* in the left column, and a slightly longer list of alternatives in the right column. Students are to select for each stem the most closely related or appropriate alternative. Matching items are effective in assessing students' ability to identify relationships between words, terms, or factors. Thus, they are most useful in measuring learning at the knowledge and comprehension levels. Matching items can require students to match terms or words with definitions, short questions with answers, symbols with proper names, descriptive phrases with other phrases, causes with effects, principles with situations in which they apply, and parts or pictorial units with names.

Matching items are less versatile than multiple-choice, but more effective than true-false or short-answer items. They are easy to construct and score. Because students can complete them quickly, a large number of items can be used and, thus, more of the objectives assessed. The most significant disadvantages of matching items are related to the low level of thinking they require. Matching

FIGURE 8.3   Guidelines for Writing Multiple-Choice Items

1. Write the stem so that it presents a complete question or problem. Avoid stems that are incomplete statements.

2. The stem should be sufficiently clear that the learner could generate the correct answer even if it were not provided.

3. Avoid using negative questions or statements in the stem or responses.

4. Avoid placing grammatical cues that suggest the correct alternative in the stem.

5. Write the correct response first, then generate between 2 and 4 reasonable alternatives.

6. Write alternative responses of roughly equal length.

7. Avoid using "none of the above" or "all of the above."

8. To assess higher-order thinking, write items that require students to identify metaphors or to answer questions about an extended, detailed scenario or problem.

9. Avoid establishing a pattern of responses.

10. Proofread all items carefully.

11. Place the entire item (stem and all alternatives) on the same page.

items encourage memorization and recall rather than understanding, and they tend to focus on trivial material.

As with other types of items, it is best to write matching items during the planning stage. As a general rule, a series of matching items should include between ten and twelve stems dealing with a clearly related set of ideas or concepts. When items deal with obviously different topics, students can more easily guess the correct answer to any one stem because some alternatives could not apply. The stem should be the longer of the two-item parts, it should be numbered, and it should appear in the left column. Alternative responses should be shorter in length, lettered, and appear in the right column. The list of alternatives should contain about 25 percent (2 or 3) more items than the list of stems, and the instructions should specify whether alternatives can be used more than once. As with multiple-choice items, each alternative in the list should present a plausible answer to the stem. The entire series of matching items, including the stems and alternatives, should appear on a single page so that students need not go back and forth between pages. Lastly, clear instructions should be given about how to record answers. Generally, space should be provided so that students can record their answers in blanks to the left of each numbered stem. Figure 8.4 depicts an abbreviated series of both good and poor matching items.

True-false items ask students to indicate whether a statement is true or false. Because the response options are limited to one of two choices, these items are sometimes called *alternative choice*.

Alternative-choice items appear often in teacher-made tests. They are easy to construct and score, but they are not very reliable or versatile. They allow the teacher to assess whether students have learned large amounts of material, but they encourage guessing and memorization rather than understanding. Most items of this type are written at the knowledge level, in part because few high-level statements are definitively true or false.

When alternative-choice items are deemed the most effective way to evaluate students' knowledge- (recall-) level learning, the guidelines in Figure 8.5 can improve their quality.

Alternative-choice items are efficient only when assessing student recall of large amounts of content. However, to make true-false items more versatile, some have suggested requiring students to correct false statements or to explain their answers. When these tasks are required, the item more closely resembles a completion or created response item and may push students beyond mere recall.

FIGURE 8.4   Examples of Poor and Good Matching Items

Poor Matching Series

For each numbered item on the left, write the letter of the most appropriate description from the column on the right.

_____ 1. Abraham Lincoln

_____ 2. Jefferson Davis

_____ 3. Gettysburg

_____ 4. John Wilkes Booth

_____ 5. Slave auction

a. A cemetery in Pennsylvania

b. Where slaves were traded

c. President of the Confederacy

d. President of the U.S.

e. Assassinated Lincoln

Good Matching Series

For each numbered description in the left column, write the letter that corresponds to the most appropriately described individual from the right column. Each individual may be described more than once.

_____ 1. President of the Confederacy

_____ 2. Assassinated Lincoln

_____ 3. Confederate General

_____ 4. Killed at Bull Run

_____ 5. Union General

a. Abraham Lincoln

b. John Wilkes Booth

c. Ulysses S. Grant

d. Robert E. Lee

e. Jefferson Davis

f. James Madison

FIGURE 8.5   Guidelines for Writing Alternative-Choice Test Items

1. Write each item as a true statement, and then change some to make them false.

2. False statements should be false because of substantive information rather than trivialities.

3. Keep all items the same length (false items are often shorter than true).

4. Avoid direct quotes from the textbook or lecture notes. Quotation items are nearly always recall level.

5. Avoid using negative statements. Negative statements are more difficult to write clearly.

6. Be careful of specific determiners ("always," "never," and so on). Since few things are "always" or "never" true, a testwise student will guess "false." Likewise, avoid indefinites ("sometimes," "often," and so forth). Since most things happen only some or most of the time, testwise students will guess "true."

7. Limit each statement to one main idea or point. Including too much information in one item will only confuse students.

8. When possible, include the crucial information near the end of the statement to help make the stem clearer.

9. Be certain that each statement is genuinely true or false.

10. Include approximately an equal number of true and false items.

11. Avoid a pattern of responses (for example, alternating true and false).

Completion items require students to supply missing words from a statement or write a short phrase that answers a question posed in a stem. These items may present statements with critical words or phrases deleted and symbolized by blanks, or they may ask simple questions. Although they do not present a list of alternative responses as other selected response items do, neither do they require students to create unique responses.

Completion items are particularly useful with young children who may be able to write but cannot easily create extended responses. Completion items are easier to construct than other forms of selected response items because they do not

Try Activity 8.3

FIGURE 8.6 Guidelines for Writing Completion Items

1. Provide clear instructions regarding the use of synonyms, spelling, and so on.
2. Be certain that only one correct answer is possible.
3. Avoid using direct quotes from the textbook or class notes.
4. When including blanks, try to use no more than one. Multiple blanks in a statement make it less clear.
5. Require only a single word or brief, definitive phrase rather than an extended response.
6. Direct questions generally are clearer than incomplete statements.
7. Be certain each statement is factually correct.
8. Omit only key words or phrases, not trivial information.
9. When using blanks, place the blank at or near the end of the statement to make the statement clearer.
10. When the response is to be numeric, include in the statement the units in which the student is to express the response.

require you to develop plausible alternative responses. Like other selected responses items, they require little response time and thus can be used to assess a large amount of content. Further, because responses are not provided, students don't guess as much. On the other hand, these items typically focus only on recall of specific names or facts. They are also difficult to score objectively. For example, a student may not have provided the expected response because she could not remember the specific term or name, but she did provide a description of the person whose name she could not remember. Is this a correct or an incorrect response?

Completion items are most appropriate for assessing young learners or knowledge-level instructional objectives. Figure 8.6 provides guidelines for writing effective completion items.

Packaging the Test   As noted earlier, the most effective assessments are planned early in the instructional process. Regardless of the type of test items used, it is wise to develop your test items either while planning (shortly after developing instructional objectives) or as you conduct instruction (to match the instructional methods and emphases). In developing a pencil-and-paper test, validity and reliability are primary considerations. You want to ensure that the test accurately measures the breadth, depth, and levels of students' learning. Thus, you should attempt to ensure validity—the closest possible match between your objectives or topical coverage and the assessment.

One way to improve validity is through the use of a **test blueprint.** A test blueprint is a matrix that depicts the relationship between instructional objectives or topics covered, cognitive levels, and items on a test. An example of a test blueprint appears in Table 8.4. As you can see, the topics of instruction are listed in the left column. Across the top are each of the six levels of Bloom's taxonomy of cognitive objectives. The far-right column indicates the total number of test items for each objective, and the bottom row indicates the total number of test items at each cognitive level.

When building a test, you first determine the total number of items you wish to include and put this number in the box at the lower-right corner. Then you determine how many items will address each topic and indicate this in the right column. This judgment should be based on the importance of the topic and on the emphasis you placed on it during instruction. For each topic, you then decide how many questions to ask at each cognitive level and indicate this in the appropriate columns. You can include some test items at cognitive levels *lower* than the instructional objective (because the higher levels require students to use lower-order skills), but it is not appropriate to include items that require higher levels

TABLE 8.4 Test Blueprint for Unit on Dinosaurs

Topic	Recall	Comprehension	Application	Analysis	Synthesis	Evaluation	Totals
Names of dinosaurs	10 (40%)						10 (40%)
Physical characteristics		3 (12%)					3 (12%)
Carnivores	1 (4%)		2 (8%)				3 (12%)
Herbivores	1 (4%)		2 (8%)				3 (12%)
Extinction	2 (8%)	3 (12%)	1 (4%)				6 (24%)
Totals	14 (56%)	6 (24%)	5 (20%)				25 (100%)

FIGURE 8.7 General Suggestions for Test Construction

1. Use a test blueprint to improve the validity of the test.

2. Write several more items than you will use. Then select the items that best fit your test blueprint.

3. Include some questions that all students can answer correctly.

4. Use only two or three item types in each test. Use only one type for young learners. Using several types of questions in a single test can be confusing to students.

5. Be certain to include clear and thorough instructions on the test. These should inform students about recording their answers, scoring, weighting of items, and so forth.

6. Organize all test items of similar type together. For example, keep multiple-choice items separate from completion items.

7. Properly space items to improve clarity. More space should be provided between items than between stems and responses. Created response items must allow sufficient space for students' answers.

8. Include as many items as possible to enhance reliability, but be realistic about the number of items students can complete. Remember that created response items take much longer to complete than selected response items.

9. Keep all parts of each item on the same page. In other words, ensure that each stem and its alternative responses appear on the same page.

10. Check to ensure that there is no predictable pattern of correct responses.

11. Provide space for pertinent information (name, date, course or course number, and so on).

12. *Proofread the test!* Check for clarity of directions, grammatical accuracy (especially among distractor alternatives), typographical errors, spelling, and format.

of thinking than your instruction directly promoted. After completing the test blueprint, you "build" the test to include the number and types of items identified in the blueprint. If you have developed a number of potential test items as you planned or conducted instruction, you construct the test simply by selecting the best of these items.

In the example provided (Table 8.4), the teacher wishes to construct a twenty-five-item test which assesses students' learning in five topical areas of a unit on dinosaurs. The blueprint indicates that the greatest instructional emphasis was placed on helping students learn the names of dinosaurs, because ten items, or 40 percent, of the test, relate to this topic. Slightly less emphasis is placed on the causes of extinction (six items), while roughly equal emphasis is placed on physical characteristics, herbivores and carnivores (three items each). The blueprint also suggests that students will be expected only to recall the names of dinosaurs, perhaps through true-false or completion items. But some higher-level thinking will be required of students on the other topics, probably through multiple-choice or matching items.

In addition to using the test blueprint, you can do several other things to improve the quality of your tests. Figure 8.7 lists all the suggestions.

Administering the Test After constructing the test, you can improve the accuracy of your assessment by providing students with as much information as possible

8.5 Do you prefer to take created response or selected response tests? Why? How might this influence the way you test your own students?

FIGURE 8.8　Guidelines for Administering Classroom Tests

1. Establish test-taking procedures, teach them to students, and then follow them consistently. For example, students should know whether questions will be answered after they begin the test, what to do when they are finished with the test, and so on.

2. Allow sufficient time for all students to complete all parts of the test. Don't let time keep some students from doing as well as they could.

3. Organize the physical setting before students enter the room to begin the test.

4. Before handing out the test, be certain that all students have the necessary equipment or materials to complete the test.

5. Explain or review test procedures or rules (for example, what to do when finished with the test) before handing out the test.

6. Control distribution of the test so that no student receives the test much sooner than others. It is wise to have students wait to begin reading or working on the test until your signal.

7. Note corrections before students begin.

8. Avoid discussion of the test or items after students have begun. If you must provide additional information or guidance about the test or an item to any student, announce this information to all students.

9. Monitor test behavior throughout the testing period.

about the nature of the test and by following preset testing procedures. Students should know well in advance when a test will be administered, what material will be covered, what types of items will be included, and how the test will be scored. This allows them to better prepare. In addition, it is a good idea to establish a set of procedures for test taking and then to follow them consistently. These procedures would include information about what materials are required for tests, whether the teacher will answer questions during the test, what students are to do when they have completed the test, and so on. Establishing these procedures provides continuity for students and allows them to concentrate on the test rather than to have to remember a new set of expectations each time. Figure 8.8 lists several suggestions for administering classroom tests.

OBSERVATIONAL AND PERFORMANCE ASSESSMENT

Sometimes students' learning is not easily measured by pencil-and-paper tests. When the instructional objectives require students to produce a product, follow a set of procedures, or perform a physical task, the most effective form of assessment involves *observing* and *evaluating* the quality of their product, procedure, or performance. For example, an art teacher might evaluate the quality of students' projects, a speech teacher might assess students' ability to make speeches of various kinds, a physical education teacher might assess how well students demonstrate proper technique in throwing a ball, a science teacher might evaluate how well students follow a set of procedures for conducting an experiment, or a music teacher might evaluate students' performance of a piece of music.

Pencil-and-paper tests require learners to perform a *cognitive* task and then to record an answer that indicates the result. Observational assessments require students to apply learning by *performing physical tasks* or *producing concrete products* that the teacher can observe and evaluate. As a result, observational assessments are often believed to be more authentic than traditional forms of testing. Thus, many educators believe that such *authentic assessment* should replace most if not all pencil-and-paper assessment (Choate, Enright, Miller, Poteet, & Rakes, 1995; Fuchs, 1994).

As with other forms of assessment, a primary concern in observational assessment is the accuracy of the information gathered. Although teachers observe students' performance or products in informal ways throughout the learning process, such

FIGURE 8.9   Checklist for Scale Performance

Criterion	B♭	F	G
1. Correct notes	＿＿	＿＿	＿＿
2. Good tone quality	＿＿	＿＿	＿＿
3. Consistent rhythm and tempo	＿＿	＿＿	＿＿
4. Proper instrument position	＿＿	＿＿	＿＿
5. Proper posture	＿＿	＿＿	＿＿
6. Good breath control	＿＿	＿＿	＿＿

"Dad, I got an A+ on my science project!"

informal observations occur spontaneously. By contrast, teachers carefully plan formal observation and evaluation based upon well-defined criteria, permitting the teacher to compare performances or products. This provides greater validity and reliability. Conducting formal observations using written checklists, rating scales, or rubrics is a common way to increase the validity and reliability of observational assessment.

Checklists   A checklist is a written instrument that lists the specific elements deemed necessary for desirable performance. The teacher observes students' performance or products and then marks whether or not each element was present. The overall performance is judged according to the extent to which it included all necessary elements. For example, a music teacher might assess students on their ability to play three scales. An example of the checklist for this performance appears in Figure 8.9

An advantage of checklists is that they can help the teacher and student focus on the most important aspects of a performance. Although the total task may be complex, the checklist can help the student see what things must be done to perform the task. Similarly, the checklist provides specific feedback about elements of the student's performance that are or are not present. Thus, the student and teacher know precisely what the student needs to improve.

The primary disadvantage of checklists is that the quality of each specific element is not evaluated. The checklist allows the teacher to record only whether the element was present not how well the element was performed. For instance, in Figure 8.9, the teacher records whether the student used proper instrument position while playing each scale. However, although some students may have better instrument position than others, the checklist does not provide for differentiation or

FIGURE 8.10 Rating Scales for Scale Performance

Numeric Rating Scale

Circle the number representing the quality of the student's performance (1 = unsatisfactory, 2 = poor, 3 = average, 4 = good, 5 = excellent).

Criterion	Rating				
1. Student plays correct notes.	1	2	3	4	5
2. Student uses good tone quality.	1	2	3	4	5
3. Rhythm and tempo are consistent.	1	2	3	4	5
4. Proper instrument position is used.	1	2	3	4	5
5. Proper posture is evident.	1	2	3	4	5
6. Student uses good breath control.	1	2	3	4	5

Graphic Rating Scale

Place a check on each scale to represent the quality of the student's performance.

Criterion	Rating			
1. Student plays correct notes.	Poor	Fair	Good	Superior
2. Student uses good tone quality.	Poor	Fair	Good	Superior
3. Rhythm and tempo are consistent.	Poor	Fair	Good	Superior
4. Proper instrument position is used.	Poor	Fair	Good	Superior
5. Proper posture is evident.	Poor	Fair	Good	Superior
6. Student uses good breath control.	Poor	Fair	Good	Superior

Descriptive Rating Scale

Criterion	Rating		
1. Student plays correct notes.	Some notes; some in tune	All notes; most in tune	All notes; all in tune
2. Good tone quality is used.	Unclear, fuzzy, soft	Clear, but soft and weak	Clear, strong, and loud

assessment of quality. Another difficulty in using checklists lies in making a judgment about the overall performance. Is each element on the checklist absolutely necessary for effective performance? If so, students must be expected to demonstrate every checklist element in the performance. In some cases, however, there are likely to be some elements that are desirable but not absolutely necessary. In these cases, how many of the elements must be demonstrated for a student's performance to be acceptable? These questions are difficult to address.

Rating Scales   A rating scale is much like a checklist in that it lists the specific elements of desirable performance. However, rating scales allow the teacher to make a judgment about the quality of each element. Rating scales assess not just whether an element was present, but also how well or accurately it was performed. As a result, rating scales possess the strengths of checklists with fewer of the disadvantages.

Three types of rating scales are commonly used in the classroom (see Figure 8.10). In *numeric* rating scales, a number indicates the quality of performance.

A higher number generally reflects greater quality. *Graphic* scales require the observer to place a mark along a continuum indicating performance quality. *Descriptive* scales rate performance on a continuum that includes terms that describe various levels of quality.

Arriving at a grade or overall judgment about a student's performance is somewhat easier using rating scales than using checklists. The teacher makes such judgments by summarizing across the ratings of the specific elements. Typically, summarization produces a single number representing a measure of the overall quality of the performance. Numeric scales are particularly easy to summarize either by adding the item ratings or by computing the mean rating. Graphic and descriptive scales can be summarized numerically by assigning a number to each graphic or descriptive item rating and then proceeding as you would with numeric scale data. It is sometimes useful to summarize the student's performance more descriptively, particularly when graphic or descriptive scales are used. In such cases, the descriptors for each performance element can be combined into a single global scale and an overall rating assigned based upon total performance.

Rubrics   A rubric is a matrix or table which expands on the detail included in descriptive rating scales, the specificity of checklists, and the ease of synthesis of numeric rating scales. In most rubrics, each column represents a particular aspect of performance to be evaluated (for example, grammar, writing style, spelling, and punctuation) and each row conveys descriptions of the characteristics of each element at varying levels of mastery. Usually, the rubric presents a numeric scale or score associated with performance at each level for each element.

Figure 8.11 depicts a rubric for evaluating students' writing. The four columns indicate the five aspects of students' writing we wish to evaluate (grammar, spelling, punctuation, style, and capitalization). For each of these aspects of writing there are four rows, each describing a level of performance. Also, notice the numbers which appear at the top of the columns and to the left of the rows, indicating the total possible score for each aspect and the range of scores associated with varying performance levels within each row. On the basis of these numbers, we can see that the writing assignment is worth a total of 40 points and that each of the four elements are of equal value (that is, they each contribute one-fourth of a student's total score on this assignment). While this rubric allows for some teacher flexibility within each row by applying a range (for example, 8–10 for exemplary) at each level, these ranges are not necessary in a rubric.

Using this rubric, the teacher can more easily and more consistently assign scores to students' work. Importantly, students can also use the rubric to evaluate their own or others' work and to provide more meaningful feedback. The rubric helps both the teacher and the student focus attention on the aspects of the writing considered most important. For these reasons, rubrics are often used in combination with portfolios.

Rating scales, checklists, and rubrics are effective ways to improve the accuracy of your assessment when judging students' performances, products, or projects. They are most accurate when they meet four conditions. First, the specific elements that constitute effective performance or an acceptable product must be identified, delineated, and made known to the learners. Second, each specific element must be observable and described thoroughly in clear terms. Third, the setting or context the performance or product will be judged in must be specified. And fourth, performance is evaluated using predetermined scoring or rating procedures.

Portfolio Assessment   Portfolio assessment is a unique and increasingly popular approach to student evaluation, especially among advocates of authentic assessment. Though the validity and usefulness of portfolio assessment have not yet been established (Elliot, 1994), portfolios are believed to be a promising alternative to traditional standardized tests (Zessoules & Gardner, 1991; Rothman, 1992).

FIGURE 8.11 Rubric for Evaluating Students' Writing

	Grammar 10 points	Spelling 10 points	Punctuation 10 points	Capitalization 10 points
Exemplary 8–10 points	• All sentences are complete thoughts. • All verbs match their subjects. • All pronouns are used appropriately. • No conjunctions are used at the beginnings of sentences.	• Every word is spelled correctly. • Every word is written legibly.	• Each sentence ends with appropriate punctuation. • Commas are used appropriately throughout. • Apostrophes are used correctly to represent plural and singular possessives.	• Each sentence begins with a capital letter. • All proper nouns are capitalized.
Good 5–7 points	• All sentences are complete thoughts • Most verbs match their subjects. • All pronouns are used appropriately. • Few conjunctions are used at the beginning of sentences.	• Most words are spelled correctly. • Every word is written legibly.	• Most sentences end with appropriate punctuation. • Commas are used appropriately throughout. • Apostrophes are used to represent most possessives.	• Most sentences begin with a capital letter. • Most proper nouns are capitalized.
Fair 2–4 points	• Some sentences are complete thoughts. • Some verbs match their subjects. • Some pronouns are used appropriately. • Some conjunctions are used at the beginnings of sentences.	• Most words are spelled correctly. • Most words are written legibly.	• Some sentences end with appropriate punctuation. • Some commas are used appropriately. • Few apostrophes are used to represent possessives.	• Some sentences begin with a capital letter. • Some proper nouns are capitalized.
Poor 0–1 points	• Few or no sentences are complete thoughts. • Few or no verbs match their subjects. OR • No attempt was made.	• Few words are spelled correctly. • Few words are written legibly. OR • No attempt was made.	• Few sentences end with appropriate punctuation. • Few commas are used appropriately. OR • No attempt was made.	• Few sentences begin with a capital letter. • No proper nouns are capitalized. OR • No attempt was made.

A *portfolio* is a "collection of student products designed to show a progression of accomplishments from early undertakings to more recent and advanced efforts" (Eby, 1992, p. 247). In portfolio assessment, the student collects numerous samples of his or her work. These samples can include a variety of products, including papers, projects, quizzes, homework, journals, and even tests. You might also choose to include video- or audiotapes of student performances. In addition to these samples of students' work, the portfolio would include evaluations of the work by the student, by other students, and by the teacher. Thus, the portfolio is a collection of several assessments that collectively provide detailed and descriptive information about how well the individual student is doing or how much she or he has improved.

A critical feature of portfolio assessment is the involvement of the learner in "collecting and documenting, developing and reflecting on the learning" (Crawford, 1993, p. 317). Students are actively involved both in selecting the work to be included in their portfolios and in evaluating their work and progress. A primary goal of portfolio assessment is to help learners become more engaged in and responsible for their own learning (Crawford, 1993; Summer, 1991; Valencia, 1990).

Students' portfolios can be more effective if you make deliberate efforts to keep students and parents informed about the process (Crawford, 1993). It is a good idea to discuss with students at the beginning of the year the process of developing and using their portfolios. You should explain what the portfolio is, why it will be important, and how it will be used. You should also attempt to help students feel a sense of ownership and responsibility for their portfolios by allowing them input on work that might be included. During this early-in-the-year discussion, you should make clear what work or products *must* be included and what supplemental materials students might elect to include.

Portfolios should be kept in a place where students have easy access to them, and time should be provided regularly to allow students to update their portfolios. You should check students' portfolios frequently to ensure that necessary materials have been included and to make assessments about the development of students' work or progress. When you check portfolios, it is helpful to make written notes about students' progress and to include these in the portfolios. Encourage your students to take their portfolios home occasionally so that parents are continually aware of their child's progress and of the development of the portfolio. When used in these ways, portfolios can be a valuable assessment, instructional, and communication tool.

Grading and Assigning Grades true & False

In most cases, the final step in our classroom assessment is assigning each student a grade. Grades represent a simple way to summarize students' performance or learning over time and across a variety of experiences. Thus, while assessment involves both summative and formative techniques, grading is typically a summative process. Ultimately, you must synthesize the information you have about a student's learning or progress, make a judgment about the quality of the progress, and assign a grade that you believe accurately and fairly represents this judgment.

Grading is an important, though often intimidating, part of teaching. Many teachers report anxiety and dread about determining and reporting students' grades (Arasian, 1991; Bradley, 1993). Some of this anxiety is due to the importance parents, students, and school officials place on grades as the primary source of information about the student's progress. Assigning grades is also difficult because it forces teachers to move from the role of facilitator of learning to that of objective observer and judge (Lortie, 1975). Finally, grading is often intimidating to teachers because many teachers do not feel sufficiently prepared to meet this challenge (Hills, 1981).

In spite of the difficulty and anxiety associated with grading, grades are used for several reasons (Arasian, 1991). *Administratively,* grades are used to make decisions about which classes students should take, how well they are progressing, and whether they should be advanced to the next grade or graduated. *Informationally,* grades tell parents, students, and school officials how well students are learning and progressing. For some students, grades serve a *motivational* purpose, pushing them to work harder. For all these reasons, it is a teacher's responsibility to select and implement a grading system that is accurate, fair, consistent, and supportable.

In selecting and implementing a grading system, three factors must be considered. First, what assignments, performances, or projects should you consider in the grade? Second, what standard will you use to make judgments about the quality of the students' performance? And, third, how will you synthesize information from several assignments or sources into a single grade? Let's look at each of these factors.

WHAT SHOULD YOU CONSIDER WHEN ASSIGNING A GRADE?

The grade that you assign represents a summary of how well the student performed in several tasks or situations. The goal is to assign a grade that accurately reflects both the depth and breadth of the student's learning, which, in turn, should match the teacher's instructional emphases.

8.6 Why do you suppose some teachers dislike assigning grades? How do you feel about this aspect of your professional responsibilities?

Generally your grades should include information from as many sources as possible. The more sources of information, the more accurate your "picture" of the student's progress will be. Common information sources include tests, quizzes, homework, performances, portfolios, and projects. By including information from several of these sources, you are better able to judge the quality or extent of a student's progress.

Some teachers also consider attendance records, or informal observations of a student's behavior, attitude, participation, motivation, or effort. However, it is generally best to include in the grade only factors that directly reflect a student's achievement (Arasian, 1991; Borich, 1992). When the grading system combines achievement with other less clearly defined factors, such as motivation or attitude, grades become inconsistent and less informative. To address this problem, some elementary school grading systems assign each student two grades: One reflects achievement, while the second is a judgment about motivational or behavioral factors. When only one grade can be assigned, it should indicate only the student's achievement. Information about other factors can be conveyed through written notes or conferences with the student or the student's parents.

While it is desirable to include information from as many sources as possible, teachers must be realistic about the number of assignments they can evaluate and record. Certainly it is realistic to include all tests scores in the grade as well as scores from all major products, projects, or performances the students completed during the grading term. However, you may need to be selective about how many other assignments to include. For example, if you have daily quizzes or daily homework assignments, it may be unreasonable to include every quiz or homework score in the final grade. Each teacher must decide how many of these factors to consider in the students' final grades.

WHAT STANDARD SHOULD YOU USE?

As noted earlier, grading requires that you make judgments about the quality of students' progress or learning. The information obtained from the sources we have discussed does not tell you whether a student has performed well. You make that determination by comparing students' performance to some standard or criterion. The three most commonly used standards are: (1) the performance of other students, (2) a predetermined fixed standard of performance, or (3) each student's earlier performances.

"I don't know why you're so surprised by his poor grades. Every day you asked him what he did at school, and every day he answered, 'Nothing.' "

Comparison with Other Students You may recall from our explanation of test scores that when a given score is reported as a comparison with other students' scores, it is a _norm-referenced_ assessment. We use the same term to describe grades that compare a student's performance with that of other students. When we talk of teachers who "grade on the curve," we mean that the teacher is using a norm-referenced grading system. In this system, the grade a particular student receives depends upon how well the other students in the class performed. If the student did better than most other students, the grade will be high; if the student did more poorly than most other students, the grade will be low.

Norm-referenced grading systems typically take one of two forms. In a _fixed percentage system_, the grading scale defines what percentages of the class will get particular grades. Generally, the scale is constructed so that most students get C's, somewhat fewer get B's and D's, and the fewest number of students get A's and F's. For example, in the fixed percentage scale that follows, 10 percent of the students would receive an A, 10 percent an F, 20 percent a B, 20 percent a D, and 40 percent a C. Thus, using the sample test scores depicted in Figure 8.12, Bill would get an A; Mary and Joan a B; Karen, Kevin, Pam, and Paul would get C's; Elizabeth and Kaya D's; and Kip an F. This is true even though the difference between Bill and Kip is only 10 points and in spite of the fact that the highest score was only 85 out of 100.

GRADE	PERCENTAGE
A	10%
B	20%
C	40%
D	20%
F	10%

As you can see, in this type of grading system, grades are only an indication of how well the student performed _compared with other students,_ not of how high or low they scored. If all students performed well, those who performed even slightly less well would receive lower grades. Thus, an A on one assignment does not equal an A on another.

More common is a _flexible distribution system._ In this system, students' grades are still based upon comparison with other students, but the percentages of students who will receive each grade are not predetermined. Instead, the percentages are adjusted to reflect situations where all students do well or all students do poorly. Unlike the fixed percentage scale, the flexible scale can be adjusted so that no students receive any particular grade. In the set of scores depicted in Figure 8.12, all

---

FIGURE 8.12 Sample Raw Scores on a 100-Point Test

Student	Score
Bill	85
Mary	83
Joan	83
Karen	82
Kevin	82
Pam	81
Paul	78
Elizabeth	76
Kaya	76
Kip	75

the students performed at roughly the same level. None of them appears to have done particularly well, and none particularly poorly. You might elect to adjust the scale so that no students receive an A, D, or F. Thus, you might award B's to students with scores from 81 to 85, and C's to students with scores from 76 to 78.

Norm-referenced grading systems are commonly used. However, the effects of this form of grading are predominately negative, particularly for less able students. Norm-referenced grading reduces students' motivation, increases anxiety, promotes negative interactions among students, diminishes students' study habits, and reduces learning (Crooks, 1988). Additionally, grades based upon this system are difficult to interpret because they do not provide an accurate indication of subject mastery (Arasian, 1991). For these reasons, it is wise to avoid using this system.

Comparison with a Predetermined Standard   Students' grades can also be determined by comparing performance with a predetermined standard. These grading systems are *criterion-referenced* assessments. In this type of system, a student's grade in no way depends upon the performance of other students. Instead, the grade is based upon the extent to which the performance demonstrates mastery. Usually, this means the proportion of points earned (for example, on a test) out of the total number possible. If a student gets most of the possible points, the grade is high; if the student gets fewer of the possible points, the grade is lower. The teacher determines the proportions associated with particular grades in advance and compares each student's performance with this scale. A common criterion-referenced grading scale follows:

PERCENTAGE	GRADE
92–100	A
84–91	B
76–83	C
65–75	D
00–64	F

Let's use the test scores in Figure 8.12 to see what grades we would assign using this criterion-referenced system. In this example, no students would receive an A, Bill would receive a B, most students would receive a C, and Kip would receive a D. As you can see, using a criterion-referenced scale, any student could receive *any* grade.

The criterion-referenced system is intended to measure students' learning against an objective standard rather than against the performances of other students. Thus, grades assigned using this system are more likely to be accurate indicators of students' achievement (Arasian, 1991). A primary advantage of this system is that the meaning of particular grades is clearer. An A represents a given level of performance regardless of the situation or the ability of other students in the class. Although determinations about the scale are subjective, grades assigned using a criterion-referenced system are considered less subject to bias. For these reasons, the criterion-referenced system is generally the most appropriate system for assigning grades.

Comparison with the Student's Earlier Performances   Norm-referenced and criterion-referenced grading systems assign grades by comparing a student's performance with an external standard. However, these systems do not account for differences in students' abilities or background knowledge. A student who has little aptitude in a subject is graded using the same standard as a student who finds the subject very easy. Thus, some teachers believe that a **self-referenced grading system** is more student-centered and more desirable. In a self-referenced system, grades are determined by comparing a student's current performance with past performance. In other words, the grade is based upon individual improvement. A student who improves a great deal will receive a high grade, a student who improves only slightly will receive a lower grade. This approach is commonly used with cooperative learning (see Chapter 7).

Self-referenced systems predetermine how much improvement is necessary for a student to receive a particular grade. As with criterion-referenced scales, differing amounts of improvement are associated with different grades. The scale below depicts a self-referenced scale for assigning grades based on improvement.

POINTS IMPROVED	GRADES
Perfect score	A
12 or more	A
9–11	B
4–8	C
1–3	D
No improvement or decline	F

Self-referenced scales typically include allowances for students who are already performing at high rates. This is done to avoid penalizing students for doing well. For example, a student who received 98 out of 100 on the previous performance could improve no more than 2 points, earning a D on the scale. However, in the scale, a student could still earn an A if he or she receives a perfect score on the current performance. In spite of this allowance, self-referenced scales are biased against students who do very well in early performances. It is more difficult to improve or maintain performance that is already nearly perfect than to improve very weak performance. Although self-referenced grading systems avoid the competition or rigidity of norm- and criterion-referenced systems, the grades assigned in self-referenced systems do not reflect the level of a student's mastery or ability in the subject. An A may mean near-perfect mastery or only limited mastery from a student who performed very poorly at first. In spite of its intuitive appeal, self-referenced grading systems probably should be avoided. Table 8.5 compares the three types of grading systems.

8.7 Which grading system do you prefer as a student? Why? Which do you as a teacher believe is most desirable?

Try Activity 8.4

HOW WILL ASSESSMENT INFORMATION BE SYNTHESIZED?

In assigning grades that represent an overall judgment about a student's performance, several types of performance (tests, quizzes, homework, projects, and so on) must eventually be combined into a single letter, number, or symbol. After

TABLE 8.5 Comparison of Norm-Referenced, Criterion-Referenced, and Self-Referenced Grading Systems

	Norm-Referenced System	Criterion-Referenced System	Self-Referenced System
What comparison is made?	Pupil to other pupils	Pupil to predefined criteria	Pupil to pupil's earlier performance
Method of comparison	Grading curve; percent of pupils who can get each grade	Standard of performance; scores pupils must achieve to get a given grade	Standard of improvement; amount of improvement pupils must exhibit to get a given grade
What the grade describes	Pupil's performance compared to others in the class	Pupil's percentage of mastery of course objectives	Pupil's improvement from earlier performance(s)
Availability of a particular grade	Limited by grading curve	No limit on grade availability	No limit on grade availability

FIGURE 8.13 Sample Term Grades (Numeric Conversion)

Student's Name	HMK 1	HMK 2	Quiz	Test 1	Test 2	Project
Adams, Bill	✓ (3)	+ (5)	B (4)	A (5)	A (5)	A (5)
Darby, Joan	✓ (3)	✓ (3)	B (4)	C (3)	B (4)	A (5)
Evans, Karen	+ (5)	✓ (3)	A (5)	B (4)	B (4)	B (4)
Stone, Elizabeth	+ (5)	✓ (3)	A (5)	B (4)	B (4)	A (5)
Thompson, Kaya	− (1)	✓ (3)	D (2)	C (3)	B (4)	C (3)

determining which performances to grade, you must then determine how to grade each one. Finally, you must combine the grades from the selected performances and arrive at a single grade that reflects overall learning.

As you prepare to synthesize selected performance scores, remember that the scores reflect different content, objectives, and levels of importance. Not all scores or grades are of equal value. For example, Figure 8.13 presents performance grades for five students. As you can see, the teacher recorded information about students' performance on two tests, two homework assignments, a quiz, and a project. If we were to look only at the grades, each would be considered of equal importance or weight. Bill's grade of A on the first test receives no more weight than Karen's A on the quiz. However, you probably want the test scores and project to carry more weight than the homework or quiz scores.

Synthesizing grades is easier if you establish a grading system that reports all grades in the same fashion, for example, as letters, scores, checks, or pluses. However, some teachers elect to use different symbols for different types of assignments. In Figure 8.13 homework grades are reported as checks, pluses, or minuses; while tests, quizzes, and projects are reported as letter grades. In this case, you must convert each of these different symbols to a single scale. You could do this by converting all symbols to numbers. Using the information in Figure 8.13, you could convert the homework grades to numbers by awarding 5 points for a plus, 3 for a check, and 1 for a minus. Similarly, you could convert letter grades by assigning 5 points for an A, 4 for a B, 3 for a C, 2 for a D, and 1 for an F. Now, all the information is in numeric form and can be synthesized mathematically, typically by computing the average of the scores. However, before doing so, you must decide how important each number or grade is in the overall summary. For example, the project is probably most important, the tests next, and the homework and quizzes less so.

Most teachers weight individual performance grades just prior to synthesizing them. To do this, they multiply each individual performance score by a weight that reflects its importance. Using the converted (numeric) information in Figure 8.13, each individual test score could be multiplied by 2 and the project score by 3. The resulting weighted numeric scores appear in Figure 8.14. You could now use these weighted or adjusted scores in your synthesis.

When all scores have been converted to the same, usually numeric, scale and weighted to reflect differing levels of importance, you are ready to synthesize them into a single grade.

To do this, add the weighted individual performance scores. Then divide this total by the *weighted* number of performances. In our example, the original number of performances was 5, but we multiplied some of these in order to weight

FIGURE 8.14 Sample Term Grades as Weighted Numeric Scores

Student's Name	HMK 1	HMK 2	Quiz	Test 1	Test 2	Project	Average Grade
Adams, Bill	3	5	4	10	10	15	4.7 (A)
Darby, Joan	3	3	4	6	8	15	3.9 (B)
Evans, Karen	5	3	5	8	8	12	4.1 (B)
Stone, Elizabeth	5	3	5	8	8	15	4.4 (B)
Thompson, Kaya	1	3	2	6	8	9	2.9 (C)

them. The *weighted* number of performances is 10 because the tests each count as 2 performances and the project counts as 3.

Try Activity 8.5

Homework 1	=	1
Homework 2	=	1
Quiz	=	1
Test 1 (× 2)	=	2
Test 2 (× 2)	=	2
Project (× 3)	=	3
Weighted total	=	10

Student's grades are determined by comparing their weighted averages to the 5-point scale we originally used to convert symbols and letters to numbers. Figure 8.14 depicts the weighted averages and grade for each of the five students.

Grading is an anxiety-producing but important part of teaching. It is often the final result of your overall assessment program. When well planned and accurately implemented, grading is a fair, accurate, and supportable process that can provide valid information about students' learning and performance.

Some Final Thoughts

An important part of effective teaching is assessing students' learning. Doing so helps teachers determine not only how well or how much students have learned, but also how effective their own instruction has been. Accurate evaluation requires that teachers gather valid, reliable information from diverse sources and then make judgments based on that information. Tests, both standardized and teacher-made, are the most recognized source of assessment information, but most teachers use a variety of other sources, both formal and informal. Their ultimate goal is to make fair, consistent, and valid judgments which give valuable feedback to students, parents, themselves, and other education professionals.

CHAPTER SUMMARY

- The process of collecting, synthesizing, and interpreting information to aid in decision making is called *assessment*. The process of gathering objective information that describes students' performance, usually in numeric terms, is referred to as *measurement*. *Tests* are the most commonly used measurement instruments. The process of making a qualitative judgment (good or bad performance) based on assessment information is referred to as *evaluation*.

- The effectiveness of an assessment depends upon the sources used to gain information and the accuracy of the information. Formal sources of information such as tests, quizzes, homework, projects, or skill performances are more teacher-controlled and can be repeated as needed. Informal sources such as teacher observations of spontaneous student behavior; conversations with students, parents, or other teachers; or access to students' logs and diaries can also be valuable but are more prone to subjective bias and error.

- The accuracy of assessment information depends upon its validity and reliability. *Validity* is the term used to describe the degree to which a test or other data source measures what it is supposed to measure. A valid assessment of student learning (1) measures understanding or mastery of all the important content or skills that were taught and nothing more; (2) assesses them in the same ways and at the same levels as they were taught; and (3) maintains the same content emphasis as the instruction.

- *Reliability* refers to the consistency with which an assessment source, such as a test, yields nearly the same scores for anyone who might take the test repeatedly. The primary way to improve reliability is to obtain information from as many valid sources as possible. Although reliability is often difficult to assess, test manufacturers typically provide information about the reliability of their tests.

- Assessment can be conducted either during instruction or at the conclusion of instruction. Formative assessment is conducted during the instructional process and is used primarily to help improve student and teacher performance. Summative assessment is conducted at the conclusion of instruction and is used primarily to make final judgments about a student's learning. Effective teachers make use of both types of assessment to improve their teaching and make good instructional decisions.

- Standardized testing has become increasingly common in U.S. public schools in recent years, and the results of these tests are often used to make policy decisions at the national, state, and local levels. Standardized tests get their name because they are administered and scored in consistent, uniform ways. They typically control the materials students may use, limit the time they can take, provide the instructions, and control any other details believed to affect test performance. Although standardized tests are effective in measuring a wide range of learning, are scored objectively and fairly, and can be designed to assess higher-level thinking, their results are often misinterpreted and misused. Teachers can help their students perform better on standardized tests by giving them experience in taking similar kinds of tests and by offering suggestions about when to guess and how to manage time.

- The results of standardized tests are commonly reported in one or more of the following ways.

  1. Students' test scores can be reported as a raw score, in relation to the scores of other students, or in relation to some predetermined criterion or standard.

  2. Raw score is the number of items answered correctly. It tells us little about what or how much the student has learned.

  3. A criterion-referenced score compares the student's raw score with an established standard of mastery and provides detailed information about the specific objectives a student has mastered.

  4. A norm-referenced score compares the student's raw score with the performances of other students who took the test (usually reported as standard scores).

- Standard scores compare a raw score to the arithmetic mean or average score obtained by other students who took the same test. These scores indicate how far above or below the mean a particular raw score is. Standard scores are built upon numeric scales to points on the normal curve. The most common types are z scores, *T* scores, percentile ranks, and stanine scores. Grade equivalent scores and score bands are often used in reporting the results of educational achievement tests.

- The most common form of classroom assessment is the teacher-made test. When properly constructed, such a test can be more cost-effective and valid than standardized or commercially produced tests because it reflects the instruction a teacher actually provided to a specific group of students rather than some national norm. Teacher-made pencil-and-paper tests use two types of test items: created response items and selected response items. Created response test items, which require students to compose an answer in their own words, are relatively easy to write. These items not only assess students' understanding but their ability to communicate. However, they are also time-consuming to score and are difficult to score reliably and objectively. Restricted response items make the parameters (expected length and coverage) of students' answers explicit. Extended response items do not impose parameters and thus allow students to be more creative.

- Selected response items, which require students to select the most appropriate answer from a list of alternatives, are easier to score objectively and typically allow the tester to assess a greater range of content. However, these items require more time to write and often elicit only lower-level thinking. Selected response items include multiple-choice, matching, true-false, and completion items.

- Observational and performance assessments require students to apply learning by performing physical tasks or producing concrete products for observation and evaluation. Because students are actually applying their learning to solving real problems, the term *authentic assessment* is often used to refer to this type of assessment.

- Formal observation and product evaluation are most accurate when they are based upon well-defined criteria. Checklists and rating scales are the most common instruments teachers use to guide observational assessment. They each list the specific elements deemed necessary to desirable performance. While checklists allow the observer only to indicate whether or not an element was present, rating scales allow the observer to make a judgment about the quality of each element presented.

- In portfolio assessment, samples of each student's work are collected to see progress or development over time. Portfolios might include tests, quizzes, and papers, as well as evaluations of the products and portfolio by the teacher, the student, or the students' peers. A critical feature of portfolio assessment is the learner's involvement in collecting and evaluating the work samples.

- Grading is an attempt to summarize students' performance or learning across a variety of experiences and over an extended time period. In spite of the anxiety many teachers experience in assigning grades, the grades serve several important administrative, informational, and motivational purposes. Although grades should be based on as many different sources of information as possible, teachers should not become unrealistic about how many student performances they can include in their grading system.

- Although factors such as behavior or attitude can be considered when assigning grades, it is best to limit grades to students' academic achievement. When grades are based upon factors other than achievement, they are less informative. To overcome this limitation, some elementary school grading systems allow the teacher to assign each student a grade for achievement and a grade for behavior or attitude.

- Teachers can also assign grades by comparing students' performances to one another, to a fixed standard, or to themselves. Norm-referenced grading systems compare each student's performance to the scores of other students.

  1. In a fixed percentage system, the percentage of students who will receive each grade is predetermined. Most students in this system get C's.

  2. In a flexible distribution scale, the percentage of students who will receive each grade is adjusted to reflect situations where all students do well or all students do poorly.

  3. Research has shown that norm-referenced grading systems promote several negative consequences, including competition, anxiety, and reduced learning.

- Criterion-referenced grading systems assign grades by comparing students' performance with a predetermined standard that shows how well each student has mastered the targeted objectives or content.

- Self-referenced grading systems compare each student's current performance with his or her previous performance. Many believe this system is more equitable for students of lower ability who fare poorly when compared to other students. However, a problem with self-referenced grading is that the grades assigned do not provide information about how much a given student knows, only how much she or he has improved.

- Ultimately, teachers must synthesize several sources of information in order to assign a single grade that reflects students' overall performance. The process of synthesizing is easier if all grades are recorded in a similar fashion, for example, as letters or numbers. However, when different types of grades have been used, all must be converted to the same, usually numeric, scale.

- To develop an overall course grade, each assignment grade must be weighted to reflect its relative importance within the course.

- The most common way to synthesize assignment grades is to (1) convert them all to numbers, (2) compute the arithmetic mean or average, and (3) convert this numeric average into a letter grade.

ISSUES AND PROBLEMS FOR DISCUSSION

PROBLEMS Teachers made the following comments or described the following incidents. What do you think about each, or how would you deal with it?

Problem 1: "About three weeks into the second grading period I received a telephone call from a parent who was angry about the grade I had given her daughter. She had spoken with another parent whose child had been receiving similar marks throughout the grading period, but who ended up with a higher grade. When I checked my grade book, I remembered that I had given the other student a slightly higher grade than she had earned through points because I felt she had worked very hard. Tomorrow I am to meet with the principal and this parent to explain the discrepancy. I'm a little nervous about what may happen."

Problem 2: "I told my students at the beginning of the year that each grading period they could drop their two lowest scores before I assigned period grades. Now, with two more units remaining in the grading period, several students realize that they can earn a good grade without doing anything for these last three weeks. I'm not sure what to do. These units are important, and I want them to be responsible for the material."

Problem 3: "Our state administers a required standardized test at the end of each school year. The test results are published by school and district in local newspapers. I *hate* giving standardized tests, and *this* one is *awful!* There are so many things that I want students to know and think about that this test just doesn't cover. My principal had been applying a lot of pressure to improve our school's scores, but I don't want to focus on the test."

THEORY INTO ACTION ACTIVITIES

ACTIVITY 8.1: Interpreting Standard Test Scores   Explain what each of the following scores would tell us about the student's performance.

1. A z score of +1.75
2. A percentile rank of 32
3. A score band ranging from the 55th to 63rd percentiles
4. A *T* score of 80
5. A stanine score of 8
6. A grade equivalent score of 6.3

Convert each of the following scores as indicated:

1. If z score is –1.75, $T = ?$
2. If stanine is 3, $z = ?$
3. If PR is 50, $T = ?$
4. If $T = 75$, $z = ?$
5. If stanine is 5, what are z, *T,* and PR?

ACTIVITY 8.2: Writing Created Response Items   Write a broad instructional objective from your subject area. Develop an extended response item that assesses students' mastery of the objective, and write a model response. Next, rewrite the item as a restricted response item using your model response as a guide.

ACTIVITY 8.3: Writing Selected Response Items   Using the instructional objective you developed in Activity 8.2, write at least three selected response items that you could use to assess students' mastery of all or part of the objective. Now, write a single multiple-choice item that requires students to at least synthesize information related to the objective in order to answer.

ACTIVITY 8.4: Developing a Grading System   Develop a reasonable grading system for a course you are likely to teach. Include and justify a variety of sources of information, the way each source will be graded or scored, the weight you will apply to each, and the standard you will use to assign grades.

ACTIVITY 8.5: Synthesizing Assessment Information   Using the grading system you developed in Activity 8.4, randomly assign grades or scores for each assignment to ten imaginary students. Based upon the system you have chosen, synthesize this information and assign a letter grade to each student. You should be able to clearly explain how and why each student is receiving the assigned grade.

REFERENCES

Anastasi, A. (1981). Coaching, test sophistication, and developed abilities. *American Psychologist, 36,* 1086–1093.

Anastasi, A. (1988). *Psychological testing.* New York: Macmillan.

Arasian, P. (1991). *Classroom assessment.* New York: McGraw-Hill.

Borich, G. (1992). *Effective teaching methods.* Second Edition. New York: Merrill.

Bradley, A. (1993). Not making the grade. *Education Week, 13*(2), 1, 19–21.

Brophy, J. (1981). Teacher praise: A functional analysis. *Review of Educational Research, 51*(1), 5–32.

Choate, J., Enright, B., Miller, L., Poteet, J., & Rakes, T. (1995). *Curriculum-based assessment and programming.* Boston: Allyn and Bacon.

Crawford, L. (1993). *Language and literacy learning in multicultural classrooms.* Needham Heights, MA: Allyn and Bacon.

Crooks, T. (1988). The impact of classroom evaluation practices on students. *Review of Educational Research, 58*(4), 438–481.

Eby, J. (1992). *Reflective planning, teaching, and evaluation for the elementary school.* New York: Merrill.

Elliot, S. (1994). *Creating meaningful performance assessments: Fundamental concepts.* Reston, VA: Council for Exceptional Children.

Fuchs, L. (1994). *Connecting performance assessment to instruction.* Reston, VA: Council for Exceptional Children.

Goodwin, W., & Klausmeier, H. (1975). *Facilitating student learning: An introduction to educational psychology.* New York: Harper and Row.

Haertel, E. (1986, April). Choosing and using classroom tests: Teachers' perspectives on assessment. Paper presented at the annual meeting of the American Educational Research Association, San Francisco.

Hills, J. (1981). *Measurement and evaluation in the classroom.* Columbus, OH: Merrill.

Linn, R. (1991). Dimensions of thinking: implications for testing. In B. Jones & L. Idol (Eds.), *Educational values and cognitive instruction: Implications for reform* (pp. 179–208). Hillsdale, NJ: Erlbaum.

Lortie, D. (1975). *Schoolteacher.* Chicago: University of Chicago Press.

MacDonald, R. (1992). *A handbook of basic skills and strategies for beginning teachers.* New York: Longman.

Moore, K. (1992). *Classroom teaching skills.* Second Edition. New York: McGraw-Hill.

Rothman, R. (1992). Performance-based assessment gains prominent place on research docket. *Education Week, 12*(9), 1, 22, 24.

Scriven, M. (1967). The methodology of evaluation. In R. W. Stake (Ed.), *Perspectives on curriculum evaluation. AERA Monograph Series on Curriculum Evaluation, no. 1* (pp. 39–83). Chicago: Rand McNally.

Stanley, J. (1958, April). ABCs of test construction. *NEA Journal,* pp. 224–229.

Summer, H. (1991). Whole language assessment and evaluation. In B. Harp (Ed.), *Assessment and evaluation in whole language programs* (pp. 137–157). Norwood, MA: Christopher-Gordon.

Valencia, S. (1990). A portfolio approach to classroom reading assessment: The why, whats and hows. *Reading Teacher, 43*(4), 338–340.

Wahlstrom, M., & Boersman, F. (1968). The influence of test-wiseness upon achievement. *Educational and Psychological Measurement, 28,* 413–420.

Wiggins, G. (1989). Toward more authentic and equitable assessment. *Phi Delta Kappan, 70,* 703–713.

Willis, S. (September, 1990). Transforming the test: Experts press for new forms of student assessment. *ASCD Update,* 3–6.

Zessoules, R., & Gardner, H. (1991). Authentic assessment: Beyond the buzzword and into the classroom. In V. Perrone (Ed.), *Expanding student assessment* (pp. 47–71). Association for Supervision and Curriculum Development.

Reflecting on Teaching

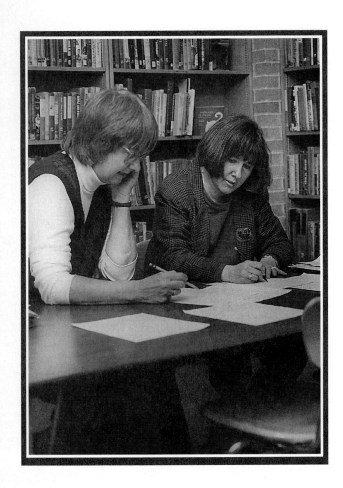

Contents

The previous four chapters in this section presented important information about the most obvious aspects of teaching: planning, implementing plans, and assessing learning. You probably are less familiar with the important, deliberative part of teaching, which is reflecting on the act of teaching after it is done. **Reflection** enables us to learn from experience (Wilson, Shulman, & Richert, 1987). It is the ongoing process of critically examining and refining teaching practice by considering the personal, educational, social, and ethical aspects of teaching and schooling (Han, 1995). Reflection enables teachers to describe and think about what they do, to anticipate and solve classroom problems, and to experience continued professional and personal growth. This chapter focuses on the process of reflection. It will help you realize the importance of reflecting on teaching. Further, it will recommend ways to enhance your own reflective abilities.

9.1 Define reflection, based on your own experience and background.

Try Activity 9.1

A Tale of Two Student Teachers

Let's look into two classrooms to see how two different student teachers deliberate on identical mathematics lessons. In each lesson, the student teacher divides students into groups of three. Using plastic blocks in a variety of shapes and colors, each group of students is to sort the cubes into piles or sets that are alike in some way, describe the characteristics of each set, and determine the number of possible combinations of sets they can make from their assortment of blocks. Throughout the lesson, the students are active and excited. Too quickly, time runs out, and both student teachers dismiss their respective students for lunch.

After the math lesson, Student Teacher A feels proud of the lesson. "That was a great lesson because the students enjoyed it. I wish my supervisor had observed it! I used manipulatives and small groups, just like we were told to do in our education courses."

But the classroom is a mess! Plastic blocks are piled on desks and scattered on the floor. "Now I have to clean this up. There are cubes everywhere!"

As she picks up, she thinks of the students. "I sure hope they got the idea of sets. They have to be ready for a test next Tuesday, and they didn't do very well on the last test." She is concerned about how prepared they are for more difficult math concepts later in the year.

She sighs as she walks to the teachers' lunchroom fifteen minutes late. "Another lesson done. This semester is sure going fast! It's almost the end of the grading period and of my student teaching experience. And I'm surviving!"

After an identical kind of lesson, Student Teacher B responds quite differently. She, too, is pleased with how the lesson progressed and with the enthusiasm the students displayed. This raises questions in her mind. "Why did the lesson go so well? What worked? I guess it was the use of manipulatives. That made math more fun for students. And working in groups—they always seem to enjoy that. Or at least most of them enjoy working in groups. I noticed today that some students seemed quiet or confused, as though they were withdrawing from the group. They weren't involved in dividing the blocks into sets, either. I wonder if they were learning by just watching, or if they were learning at all."

This leads her to question whether she chose the right instructional approach for the lesson. "I wonder if it would have been better to have students work individually with manipulatives instead of in groups. That way I could have circulated around and prevented some students from withdrawing from the lesson. I could have held them all accountable for learning. Why did I decide to put them into small groups? Was it because that's what I was told to do in my college courses, or is it really a better approach for this class of students? No, I think that the students came up with more combinations and sets because they were working in groups. I think I made the right decision."

Her classroom, too, is in disarray. "Look at this mess!" As she collects the blocks, she thinks, "Where could I have saved time so that the students would have had time to clean up? Next time, I think I'll assign one person in each group to gather the supplies. I'll give them a five-minute warning before the end of class, too."

Student Teacher B also thinks about her students' learning. "I wonder what they really learned about sets from this lesson. Tyler seemed to understand; his eyes just lit up! Andre seemed to have problems. He'll need more practice; I can work with him tomorrow. From what I observed, most of them got the idea of sets and the relationships among sets."

Teacher B sighs as she walks to the teachers' lunchroom fifteen minutes late. "I feel good about the lesson, though," her thoughts continue. "Their enthusiasm makes my job a lot easier! Next time, though, I have to make time for cleanup. And I will monitor students in the groups more closely to be sure that everyone is involved. With more difficult math concepts ahead, the students can't slack off now!"

How are the reactions of the two student teachers similar? How do their reactions differ? Both teachers gave good lessons, motivated students, and experienced relatively few problems. Student Teacher A was upbeat about the lesson, and justifiably so. She thought she was doing what good teachers do and that her teaching was effective. As a result, she will probably use precisely the same approach in future lessons.

In contrast, Student Teacher B had deeper afterthoughts about the teaching and learning during the lesson. She pondered: "Am I doing the right things in the right ways? Why am I doing things this way?" By asking herself many self-challenging questions, she was reflecting on teaching. She analyzed her decisions related to the lesson and assessed her personal satisfaction with the lesson. Further, she used her responses to those questions to plan changes in her teaching behavior. As a result of this reflection, it is likely that her future lessons will be even better than this one.

While both of these student teachers are good teachers, Student Teacher B is better. She is a reflective practitioner; she is already developing habits of thought that will make her a wiser teacher and ensure her consistent professional growth in increasingly complex classroom settings.

Characteristics of Reflective Practitioners

9.2 Think of a situation when you questioned a classroom event or theory. How did you respond?

Reflective practitioners, like Student Teacher B, share certain characteristics. They are deliberative, open-minded, responsible, and sincere; they have a spirit of inquiry. Let us examine these qualities more closely.

First, reflective practitioners routinely and purposefully *deliberate* or reflect on teaching. You recall that Teacher B reflected about many aspects of her lesson. Reflection helps you make rational decisions about teaching and learning and helps you assume responsibility for the results of those choices in the classroom (Ross, 1987).

Reflective practitioners are *open-minded* (Dewey, 1933). They are willing to question their own views of and reactions to their teaching practices and the school culture. Student Teacher B showed open-mindedness when she questioned the wisdom of dividing her students into groups for the math lesson. She openly explored, rather than defended, her decision. Open-minded teachers view situations from multiple perspectives, search for alternative explanations for classroom events, and use evidence to support or evaluate a decision or position.

Reflective practitioners take *responsibility* (Dewey, 1933). Student Teacher B assumed responsibility for her teaching decisions. She decided to use group work to teach her students about sets. The result was that some students withdrew from the group and were not engaged in the learning activity. Rather than ignore the struggling students, Student Teacher B accepted responsibility for her decision and resolved to help Andre in class the next day. Further, she took responsibility for running out of time and resolved to work more effectively within the time allotted for math lessons. Thus, reflective practitioners consider and accept the consequences of their decisions and the changes they make in teaching style, in the learning environment, or in the school culture.

Furthermore, reflective teachers are *sincere* as they closely investigate their teaching (Dewey, 1933). They take reflection seriously. Their reflection is purposeful and exciting because it helps them better understand who they are as teachers. Their reflection is not "idle meandering or daydreaming"; rather, it focuses on the goal of improving their effectiveness as teachers (Boud, Keogh, & Walker, 1985). This difference in thinking was evident between the two student teachers. While Student Teacher A's thoughts after the lesson were random and unfocused, Student Teacher B's reflection eagerly probed various aspects of the learning experience her lesson provided. She did not merely accept the fact that students enjoyed the instructional method she selected. She wanted to know why it was successful. Further, she thought sincerely about the individual learning that resulted from the lesson. Goodman (1984) points out that this sincerity enables you to work through any fears or insecurities you may have about questioning your teaching, your beliefs, and the educational values you see in the school environment and in society.

Generally, then, we could say that a *spirit of inquiry* characterizes reflective teachers. Reflective teachers are interested in the subtleties of the art and science of teaching. They want to learn all they can about teaching from both theory and practice. They think deeply about their course work and about how it should impact their teaching. For example, Student Teacher B drew on a theory she learned in her college courses when she decided students would learn more about sets by working in small groups. Inquiring teachers also learn by studying teaching and by observing other teachers, and they continue to learn when they practice and subsequently analyze their own teaching skills (Cruickshank, 1987).

Because of the individual nature of reflective thinking and the uniqueness of each teacher's reflection, reflective practice has been referred to as **inquiry-oriented teaching** (Wellington, 1991). This process of inquiry leads teachers to become "students of teaching" (Dewey, 1904). Dewey contends that it is more important for you as a future teacher to learn to think about your work than it is to master specific techniques of teaching and classroom management.

What distinguishes teachers who are students of teaching from those who are not? To summarize, they inquire into and analyze their own teaching behavior. They are sincerely interested in the fine points of the art and science of teaching, and they want to learn all they can about teaching. They are open-minded and willing to consider why they teach as they do. They take responsibility for the consequences of their teaching. They deliberate on their teaching, and as a result of this reflection they change or modify their patterns of teaching behavior.

9.3 Are you a student of teaching? Why or why not?

Try Activity 9.2

Benefits of Reflecting on Teaching

Reflection may sound like a lot of work. It is important to realize, though, that reflection holds both immediate and long-term benefits for you as a teacher. Even now, reflection can enhance your learning about teaching and increase your ability to analyze classroom events. Later, when you are teaching, reflective thinking can improve your classroom life, enable you to monitor yourself, and stimulate your personal and professional growth.

Perhaps the most important benefit of reflection as you prepare to teach is that it *enhances your learning about teaching.* According to learning psychologists, reflectivity plays a central role in learning from your course work and from your field or school experiences (Han, 1995; Jadallah, 1996; Kolb & Fry, 1975). To learn the most from these experiences, you need four things. First, you must have a concrete learning experience, such as grading homework papers for your cooperating teacher. Second, you must have an opportunity to reflect on the experience by recapturing and evaluating it. Thus, after grading the assignments, you might think back on the distribution of grades, consider the nature of the homework assignment and how students benefited from it, and even challenge why teachers assign homework to students. You might conclude that while good students did well on their homework, less able students did poorly. As a result, you might decide that homework assignments must be individualized to provide a meaningful learning experience for all students.

The next step in the learning process is to integrate your reflections with what you already know and believe about teaching and learning. This leads you to recognize new ways of doing things, resolving problems, or clarifying issues. Finally, you must engage in active experimentation, applying the insights you have gained to make decisions and solve problems (Boud et al., 1985; Kolb, 1981). The experience of grading and reflecting on homework assignments may have led you to clarify your beliefs about homework. As a result, you may begin to consider evaluating students' learning using an authentic strategy discussed in Chapter 8, such as portfolios.

This scenario suggests that one of the best ways to increase your learning about teaching is to strengthen the link between the learning experience and the reflection that follows; that is, by taking time to reflect on the experiences and ideas you have been exposed to in your teacher preparation program (Boud et al., 1985; Emery, 1996).

A second benefit of reflecting on teaching that you can begin to take advantage of now is that reflection *increases your ability to analyze and understand classroom events.* That is, reflection makes you more thoughtful and wise (Cruickshank, 1987; Fien, 1996). Liston and Zeichner (1987) observed that preservice teachers tend to look at classrooms with a wide rather than narrow lens. Perhaps you have experienced this yourself, sitting in the corner of a classroom, observing everything superficially but focusing on nothing closely or critically. The students may appear to be naturally well behaved because you are not concentrating on analyzing and understanding the cues and nonverbal desists the teacher uses to prevent students from drifting off task (see Chapter 12).

Because preservice teachers do not always understand the teaching they observe, Ross (1987) found that most still use whim or emotion as much as logic or evidence in making decisions about how they will teach. Further, most preservice teachers see no logical way to differentiate among conflicting positions or different teaching approaches, such as between direct instruction and discovery learning. They tend to hold tightly to one teaching approach they have observed to be effective, such as discovery learning, rather than to analyze when and how this approach would work best with different groups of students and different instructional tasks.

Reflection enables you to examine and analyze classroom events rather than simply observe them. Reflective teachers such as Student Teacher B are better able to ask themselves basic questions about teaching. They are more analytical and less judgmental when they consider their teaching and that of others. Reflection leads teachers to consider the underlying assumptions about, beliefs about, and implications of the practices they are using and how these practices affect students as they learn (Cruickshank, 1987; Han, 1995)). In short, reflective teachers understand what teaching and learning are all about. Preservice teachers who practice analyzing classroom events by reflecting on them are less anxious about student teaching than are their peers who observe classrooms through a wide, unfocused lens (Cruickshank et al., 1981).

A third benefit of reflection is that reflecting on teaching will *enhance your classroom life* as a teacher by helping you establish an inviting, predictable, and thoughtful environment. This is because reflective teachers are better able to apply what they have learned from course work to their classroom practice (Cruickshank, 1987). This will benefit both you and your students. Hundreds of teachers and administrators who were asked to consider the personal and professional benefits of higher-level thinking, including reflection, support this. They suggest that teachers with good thinking abilities and habits are usually more sensitive, accepting and empathic, tolerant and open-minded, flexible, wise, reasoning, resourceful, creative, informed, objective, observant, aware, and self-understanding (Cruickshank, 1986). In Chapter 12, we will discuss why the attitudes and approaches of such teachers are essential to establishing an inviting, predictable classroom environment in which students feel secure, respected, and free to explore and learn.

Unfortunately, many teachers rely on trial and error rather than reflective thinking when establishing their classroom environments. Dewey (1916) distinguished between trial-and-error activity and reflective activity as two approaches teachers use. With trial and error, he commented,

> We simply do something, and when it fails, we do something else, and keep on trying till we hit upon something which works, and then we adopt that method as a rule-of-thumb measure in subsequent procedure (p. 169).

Using trial and error sets up a random, unpredictable classroom environment which students find upsetting and threatening. In contrast, when teachers consistently use reflective activity to make decisions, their students experience a predictable, inviting classroom environment that makes them eager to learn. Further, when a reflective teacher models thinking and problem-solving skills, students begin to think and to use those skills to resolve their own problems (Martin, 1984). As a teacher, you will indeed enhance your classroom life as students respond to the predictable, thoughtful environment!

A fourth benefit of engaging in reflection is that teachers who use reflective skills become *self-monitoring*. It is impossible for you to be prepared for every situation you may encounter during your teaching career. And, unfortunately, during most of your teaching career you will not receive feedback on your teaching performance, strengths, and weaknesses. By reflecting on your teaching, however, you can assess your needs and monitor your teaching performance and satisfaction (Valverde, 1982). During reflection, teachers learn by studying themselves, and this helps them grow in self-understanding (Boyd & Fales, 1983; Cruickshank, 1987). Reflective thinking helps teachers create and clarify meaning in terms of who they are *per se* and who they are in relation to the world of teaching and education (Boyd & Fales, 1983; Schön, 1983). By extracting personal meaning from their teaching and learning experiences, they direct themselves toward their teaching and professional goals (Cruickshank, 1987).

Teachers who are not introspective and self-monitoring tend to be governed by routine, tradition, and authority (Dewey, 1916). They miss out on *personal and*

 9.4 Have you seen examples of teachers using trial and error? In what ways, and how did it work?

FIGURE 9.1   Immediate and Future Benefits of Reflection

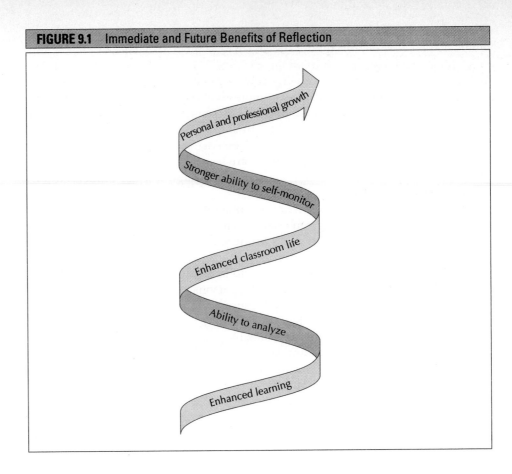

Personal and professional growth

Stronger ability to self-monitor

Enhanced classroom life

Ability to analyze

Enhanced learning

9.5   What values and beliefs about teaching and learning will influence your reflective thinking?

9.6   Which benefit of reflection is most important to you?

Try Activity 9.3

professional transformation, a fifth benefit of reflective thinking (Figure 9.1). Smyth (1989) considers the "spiral of empowerment" resulting from reflective practice as its greatest benefit and as a necessity for teachers. Because a person's preconceptions of teaching, learning, and the purposes of the school will greatly influence how he or she interprets teaching experiences, these beliefs and values must be examined rather than merely accepted. Questioning personal and societal beliefs and values is intended "to raise consciousness, to challenge complacency, and to engender a higher order of professional practice" (Wellington, 1991). As teachers reflect on the factors that affect their teaching behavior, such as those discussed in Chapter 1, they can rid themselves of unfounded beliefs about teaching and learning. They are then able to develop new or revised beliefs more likely to lead to effective teaching and student learning (Cruickshank, 1987).

This sort of reflective practice provides teachers with a better way of understanding the role teachers and schools play in addressing or perpetuating social problems. By examining even deeper issues of ethics, morals, and justice in education, reflective thinking engages teachers in the redesign and reconstruction of their world.

Developing Reflective Abilities

To meet the demands of today's classrooms, you must be willing and able to reflect on classroom events. Your professional growth and satisfaction as a teacher will, in part, be linked to this ability.

How can you develop your reflective abilities? People have suggested and tried many methods. Four of the most promising are presented here.

FIGURE 9.2 Sample Dialogue Journal Entries for Student Teacher B

Student Teacher B Entry

"Today's math lesson on sets went well, but a few things bothered me about it. I broke the students down into groups of three and had them sort the blocks with similar characteristics into groups, then count and describe those sets. I'm glad I had them working in groups because they identified a lot of sets . . . more than we would have as a whole class, I think. The thing that bothered me, though, was that some students weren't involved in the group work. About five students seemed to withdraw . . . and how are they supposed to learn if they don't participate? I thought students were supposed to participate more in small groups, not less!"

Cooperating Teacher Entry

"Your lesson went really well! You had a clear objective and communicated it well to the students so that they knew exactly what they were supposed to do in their small groups.

   I think you are being a little bit hard on yourself about the level of student involvement in the small groups. Because I was observing, I could see perhaps more closely what students in each group were actually doing. Some of the students who seemed to not participate looked to me like they were just participating more sporadically than the more outgoing students in the group. Simon, for example, may have looked uninvolved, but remember that he is a very reflective learner. He just thinks before he acts! If you are concerned about small groups, try to think through how you assigned the students to groups. Are the personalities compatible? Are the ability levels mixed? Are there gender or ethnic considerations? Also, think about what you can do to hold all students accountable for participating in the group in some way. Don't give up . . . small groups are challenging, but also effective!"

Student Teacher B Entry

"I never thought about how complicated it is to assign students to groups, and how that could impact the lesson! I just assigned them randomly for this lesson. They all seem to get along so well together that it never occurred to me that some of them might not work well together in a small-group situation. Can you provide me with any `inside information' you have about potential mismatches so that I can assign the groups more carefully next time?"

Cooperating Teacher Entry

"I have a committee meeting tomorrow at 3:30, but we could meet for about fifteen minutes right after school to discuss my `insights.' Also, I have some notes from a cooperative learning workshop that you might be interested in reading. Keep up the good work!"

DIALOGUE JOURNALS

Writing about a classroom experience can help you develop reflective abilities because it enables you to play back and recreate classroom events and to gain a new perspective on those experiences (Wallace, 1996). A **dialogue journal** goes a step further by providing you with feedback on the experience and on your thinking. In a dialogue journal, you carry on a running conversation that expresses thoughts, questions, and problems related to your roles, responsibilities, and practices as a teacher. A friend, cooperating teacher, or university instructor should respond to your entries on a regular basis by sharing any thoughts, reactions, and questions that come to mind.

A dialogue journal can help you internalize various ideas about teaching and become more flexible and mature in your thinking (Bolin, 1988). It can also help you see alternative ways of dealing with classroom events and recognize the connection between teachers' actions and students' outcomes. Figure 9.2 shows what entries in a dialogue journal might have looked like for Student Teacher B following her mathematics lesson on sets.

Try Activity 9.4

DISCUSSIONS

One way you can construct meaning from your teacher preparation experiences is by talking about them. If your discussion is focused and purposeful rather than random, it can help you engage in higher-level thinking and even in attitude change (Cruickshank, 1986, 1991; Jadallah, 1996).

Some researchers have found that talking about experiences is a better reflective tool than writing about them, partly because of the feedback you receive from your peers (Emery, 1996; Jadallah, 1996; Pultorak, 1996). Schön (1983) and Emery (1996) say that it is most effective to discuss your classroom experiences, especially the methods and strategies you have tried while teaching. To be truly reflective, however, the discussion should be geared toward critical self-reflection and should involve four steps, which we have modified from Smyth (1989):

1. *Describe* what you did by elaborating on one specific lesson or classroom event.
2. *Inform* yourself and others of what is behind this classroom event. What did the event mean? What principles or theories did the event or teaching behavior illustrate?
3. *Confront* the knowledge of teaching, learning, and social theories you identified in the previous step. Ask yourself: Why did I choose this teaching strategy? What causes me to draw from this theory? What interests and objectives does my classroom practice serve?
4. *Reconstruct* the classroom event or lesson by asking how you might have done things differently. It is important that in this step you reconceptualize or refine your understanding of teaching and learning theories as they apply to this specific classroom or school context, and that you bring your teaching practices more in line with those theories.

ACTION RESEARCH

Action research is the process of conducting classroom research to answer questions or solve problems about teaching and learning. Unlike traditional research, which requires you to pore over books and journals in search of information and solutions, action research occurs in schools. Classroom teachers engage in action research to help them better understand their teaching and to solve problems related to learning. In action research, a teacher identifies a classroom-related question, plans classroom-based methods of gathering information related to the question, and then collects information about the phenomenon under study (Eisner, 1985). By reflecting on the information gained, the teacher increases his or her understanding of the event and is able to suggest a course of action.

You can conduct action research during your field experiences by focusing your observations on one particular aspect of the classroom and reflecting on your observations. For example, you could focus on one student, whom we'll call Jennifer, who seems to be underachieving. Your question is, why doesn't Jennifer work up to her potential? To find out, you could observe her during lessons and, every few minutes, record whether she is paying attention and engaged in the learning task. You might also interview Jennifer, querying her about her attitudes toward school, the teacher, and other subjects. Through conversation and by investigating her permanent record, you can gain insights into her home life: how supportive her parents are toward education, whether she has a quiet place in which to study, and what cultural factors may explain her motivation. Taken together, these resources should enable you to reflect on Jennifer's learning and behavior. After careful reflection, you can make inferences about why Jennifer performs as she does in school.

Used in this way, action research can contribute to your professional growth by making your field experiences more meaningful and sharpening your reflective abilities. Later, when you have your own classroom, action research can help you solve some of the "mysteries" of teaching and learning unique to your school situation.

ON-CAMPUS LABORATORY EXPERIENCES

Laboratory experiences are contrived teaching experiences carried out on campus, often with a small group of peers, rather than in an actual classroom setting. Some on-campus laboratory experiences such as microteaching, discussed in Part

Four, Unit 1 of the Practice Teaching Manual, are intended to help you practice and build basic teaching skills. Simulations, discussed in Unit 3, provide you with practice in solving vexing classroom problems.

Reflective Teaching, a program provided in part in Unit 2, was specifically developed to help preservice and in-service teachers become more thoughtful teachers (Cruickshank, 1991). Reflective Teaching provides you with a teaching experience in a supportive environment which serves as the basis for subsequent reflection. In Reflective Teaching, you engage in all aspects of the teaching cycle (planning, implementing, assessing, and reflecting) by presenting a short, content-neutral lesson based on specific objectives to a group of peers. The Reflective Teaching experience is structured to promote analysis and reflection about the teaching and learning processes through small-group and whole-class discussions.

Research on the effectiveness of Reflective Teaching shows that preservice teachers find it enjoyable and that they benefit greatly from the immediate, non-threatening feedback (Bainer & Cantrell, 1992; Peters, 1980). More importantly, research suggests that the Reflective Teaching program can make you a more reflective teacher. Preservice teachers who engaged in Reflective Teaching were better able to think and talk critically about teaching (Cruickshank et al., 1981). Troyer (1988) found that if preservice teachers are informed about the nature and importance of reflective thinking, as you have been by reading this chapter, they are even more reflective in analyzing classroom teaching situations.

Some Final Thoughts

Yes, teaching is a complex activity. But in spite of this, you can increase the likelihood that you will be an effective teacher if you develop the ability to reflect on your teaching and the teaching practices of others. Hopefully, your teacher preparation program and cooperating teachers are helping you to reflect on your own teaching and the teaching you observe. You will surely benefit if, in addition, you take specific steps to develop attitudes essential to reflective thinking. You will enhance your learning and teaching as you make reflection a careful, consistent part of your life.

CHAPTER SUMMARY

- Teaching is a complex activity that requires teachers to think about or reflect on what they do.
- Good teachers can become even more effective by reflecting on teaching.
- Reflective practitioners share certain characteristics.
  1. They routinely and purposefully deliberate or reflect on teaching.
  2. They are open-minded, freely questioning their own views and reactions to their teaching practices.
  3. They consider and accept responsibility for the consequences of the decisions they make in the learning environment.
  4. They are enthusiastic and eagerly focus on ways to improve their teaching.
  5. They become "students of teaching" by inquiring into theory and practices related to teaching and learning.
- Reflective thinking offers immediate and future benefits for preservice teachers.
  1. Reflecting on learning experiences enhances learning.
  2. Reflective thinking increases the ability to analyze and understand classroom events.

3. Reflection enhances the teacher's classroom life by helping him or her establish an inviting, predictable, and thoughtful learning environment.

4. Reflective teachers are self-monitoring, which means they can direct their own personal growth.

5. Reflection leads to personal and professional growth and empowers teachers to redesign teaching and the school culture.

- Teachers can develop reflective thinking skills in many ways.

1. The interaction provided through a dialogue journal can help you internalize ideas and build flexible, mature thinking about teaching.

2. Focused and purposeful discussions can build higher-order thinking skills and attitude changes.

3. Action research, a field-based approach to reflecting on teaching and solving problems related to learning, can contribute to the development of reflective thinking skills.

4. Clinical experiences, such as Reflective Teaching, conducted on campus in a supportive environment can enhance reflective thinking skills.

ISSUES AND PROBLEMS FOR DISCUSSION

1. Do teachers need to be reflective to be effective at bringing about students' learning and satisfaction?

2. Why are many teachers fearful about reflecting?

3. What should teachers reflect about? Should they be compelled to think about some aspects of education more than others?

4. Do you agree with Dewey that it is more important to learn to reflect than to master teaching skills?

5. What could a building principal do to encourage teachers to become more reflective?

THEORY INTO ACTION ACTIVITIES

ACTIVITY 9.1:   Ask your cooperating teachers what it means to reflect on teaching. Ask if they reflect on their teaching. If so, when do they reflect? What do they reflect about? What is the result of that reflection?

ACTIVITY 9.2:   Identify and interview a teacher whom you consider a "student of teaching." Compare the interview results with those your classmates obtain. What commonalities do you find among teachers who are students of teaching?

ACTIVITY 9.3:   Design a weekly schedule for a teacher that would be conducive to reflective thinking. Share it with a teacher or principal for their reaction.

ACTIVITY 9.4:   For two weeks, keep a dialogue journal by carrying on a written conversation with a friend about your preservice teacher education. Reflect back on the experience. What did you learn? How did the exchange help you? What problems existed?

Bainer, D. L., & Cantrell, D. (1992). Nine dominant reflection themes identified for preservice teachers by a content analysis of essays. *Education, 112*(4), 571–578.

Bolin, F. S. (1988). Helping student teachers think about teaching. *Journal of Teacher Education, 39*(2), 48–54.

Boud, D., Keogh, R., & Walker, D. (Eds.). (1985). *Reflection: Turning experiences into learning.* New York: Nichols.

Boyd, E. M., & Fales, A. W. (1983). Reflective learning: Key to learning from experience. *Journal of Humanistic Psychology, 23*(2), 99–117.

Cruickshank, D. R. (1986). Critical thinking skills for teachers. *Teacher Education Quarterly, 13*(1), 82–89.

Cruickshank, D. R. (1987). *Reflective teaching: The preparation of students of teaching.* Reston, VA: Association of Teacher Educators.

Cruickshank, D. R. (1991). *Reflective teaching.* Revised Edition. Bloomington, IN: Phi Delta Kappa.

Cruickshank, D. R., Kennedy, J. J., Williams, E. J., Holton, J., & Fay, D. E. (1981). Evaluation of reflective teaching outcomes. *Journal of Educational Research, 75*(1), 26–32.

Dewey, J. (1904). The relation of theory to practice in education. In C. A. McMurry (Ed.), *The relation of theory to practice in the education of teachers.* Third yearbook of the National Society for the Scientific Study of Education, Part I (pp. 9–30). Chicago: University of Chicago Press.

Dewey, J. (1916). *Democracy and education: An introduction to the philosophy of education.* New York: Macmillan.

Dewey, J. (1933). *How we think.* Boston: Heath.

Eisner, J. (1985). Facilitating action research in school: Some dilemmas. In R. Burgess (Ed.), *Field methods in the study of education.* Lewes: Falmer Press.

Emery, W. G. (1996). Teachers' critical reflection through expert talk. *Journal of Teacher Education, 47,* 110–119.

Fien, J. (1996). Reflective practice: A case study of professional development for environmental education. *Journal of Environmental Education, 27,* 11–20.

Goodman, J. (1984). Reflection and teacher education: A case study and theoretical analysis. *Interchange, 15*(3), 9–26.

Han, E. P. (1995). Reflection is essential in teacher education. *Childhood Education, 71,* 228–230.

Jadallah, E. (1996). Reflective theory and practice: A constructivist process for curriculum and instructional decisions. *Action in Teacher Education, 18,* 73–85.

Kolb, D. A. (1981). Learning styles and disciplinary differences. In A. W. Chickering & Associates (Eds.), *The modern American college.* San Francisco: Jossey-Bass.

Kolb, D. A., & Fry, R. (1975). Towards an applied theory to experiential learning. In C. L. Cooper (Ed.), *Theories of group processes.* London: Wiley.

Liston, D. P., & Zeichner, K. M. (1987). Reflective teacher education and moral deliberation. *Journal of Teacher Education, 38*(6), 2–8.

Martin, D. (1984). Infusing cognitive strategies into teacher preparation programs. *Educational Leadership, 42*(3), 68–72.

Peters, J. L. (1980). The effects of laboratory teaching experience (Microteaching and Reflective Teaching) in an introductory teacher education course on students' views of themselves as teachers and their perceptions of teaching. Doctoral dissertation, The Ohio State University, Columbus.

Pultorak, E. G. (1996). Following the development process of reflection in novice teachers: Three years of investigation. *Journal of Teacher Education, 47,* 283–291.

Ross, D. D. (1987). Reflective teaching: Meaning and implications for preservice teacher educators. Paper presented at the Reflective Inquiry Conference, Houston.

Schön, D. A. (1983). *The reflective practitioner: How professionals think in action.* San Francisco: Jossey-Bass.

Smyth, J. (1989). Developing and sustaining critical reflection in teacher education. *Journal of Teacher Education, 40,*(2), 2–9.

Troyer, M. B. (1988). The effects of reflective teaching and a supplemental theoretical component on preservice teachers' reflectivity in analyzing classroom teaching situations. Doctoral dissertation, The Ohio State University, Columbus.

Valverde, L. (1982). The self-evolving supervisor. In R. Sergiovanni (Ed.), *Supervision of teaching* (pp. 81–89). Alexandria, VA: Association for Supervision and Curriculum Development.

Wallace, J. (1996). Words, words, words . . . *Science and Children, 33*(5), 16–19.

Wellington, B. (1991). The promise of reflective practice. *Educational Leadership, 48*(6), 4–5.

Wilson, S. M., Shulman, L. S., & Richert, A. E. (1987). 150 different ways of knowing: Representations of knowledge in teaching. In J. Calderhead, (Ed.), *Exploring teachers' thinking* (pp. 104–124). London: Cassell.

The Effective Teacher

PART THREE

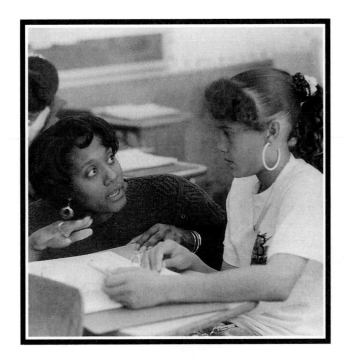

The role of the classroom teacher is critical. The teacher is, after all, the point of contact between the educational system and the pupil: the impact of any educational program or innovation on the pupil operates through the pupil's teachers. Thus, maximizing teacher effectiveness is a major goal of education (Medley, 1986, p. 4).

Most people enter teaching because they want to make a difference in the lives of young people. While concerned about their students' emotional and social welfare, a teacher's most direct obligation is to ensure that students leave their class with greater knowledge, understanding, and appreciation of specific subjects and other people than when they entered.

While all teachers make some difference in their students' lives, some teachers consistently have a greater and more positive influence than others. They seem to relate to students better and to be more successful in producing genuine learning among their students. We would almost certainly call these teachers *effective*.

All teachers want to be effective, to make the greatest possible difference in their students' lives. But what is an "effective" teacher? What makes one teacher more effective than another, and what can be done to improve effectiveness? The next four chapters are devoted to answering these questions. In Chapter 10, Effective Teachers: Personal Attributes and Characteristics, we describe research on teaching and then examine the personal attributes or characteristics associated with effective teachers. In Chapter 11, Effective Teachers: Professional Skills and Abilities, we focus on the professional skills effective teachers use to maximize their students' learning. In Chapter 12, How the Effective Teacher Manages the Classroom, we discuss the organizational and managerial strategies effective teachers use to maintain a positive learning environment. Finally, Chapter 13, The Teacher as a Problem Solver, explains how effective teachers solve classroom problems.

Effective Teachers: Personal Attributes and Characteristics

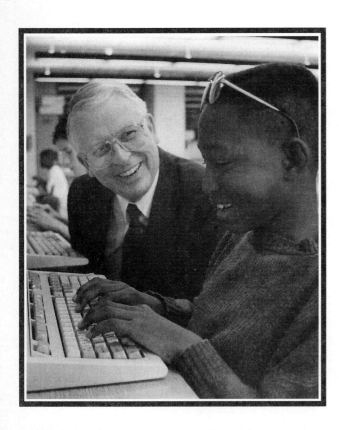

Contents

10

In this chapter we examine the personal attributes or characteristics of teachers whose instruction seems most successful. Our emphasis is on an examination of those personal attributes of a teacher that seem most closely connected to students' learning. Before discussing specific personal attributes, we will examine how researchers have studied effective teachers and defined effective teaching. Then, we will look at eight attributes characteristic of effective teachers:

1. Enthusiastic
2. Warm and humorous
3. Credible
4. Holding high expectations for success
5. Encouraging and supportive
6. Businesslike
7. Adaptable/flexible
8. Knowledgeable

Research on Teaching

To understand the importance of teachers' characteristics and the behaviors associated with effective teaching, it will be helpful if we first determine what the term *effective teaching* means and how effective teachers can be identified.

DEFINING EFFECTIVE TEACHING

There are many ways to define effective teaching. Most people would agree that good teachers are caring, supportive, concerned about the welfare of students, knowledgeable about their subject matter, able to get along with parents, administrators, and colleagues, and genuinely excited about the work that they do (Raspberry, 1993). Certainly, these characteristics are valuable. But they overlook an important aspect of effective teaching—the fact that effective teachers are able to help students learn.

For nearly a century, educational researchers have attempted to identify effective teachers. Early research defined effective teachers as those who received high ratings from their superiors. This research examined the relationship between high ratings and teachers' personality characteristics or traits. Barr (1961) indicates that researchers attempted to link administrative ratings with such traits as teachers' buoyancy, cooperativeness, dependability, emotional stability, expressiveness, forcefulness, judgment, mental alertness, personal magnetism, physical drive, and ethical behavior.

10.1 Why do you think each of us has unique ideas about what good teaching is? What clues does Chapter 6, on instructional alternatives, offer?

Although this type of research continued until the mid-1960s, the results were discouraging. None of these personality traits were consistently tied to the rating levels teachers received. Many scholars concluded at that point that little could be determined about what made teachers effective. In frustration, Biddle and Ellena (1964) expressed a common belief that "it is not an exaggeration to say that we do not know how to select, train for, encourage, or evaluate teacher effectiveness" (p. vi).

Fortunately, several events occurred during the 1960s which prompted valuable and productive research into the definition and nature of effective teaching. Among the most powerful catalysts for more productive research was the "*Equality of Educational Opportunity*" study (Coleman et al., 1966). This study was commissioned by the United States Department of Health, Education, and Welfare to examine the differences between schooling opportunities and resultant learning outcomes for white and black children.

Coleman, the major investigator, and his colleagues found that students attending some schools did indeed achieve more than students attending others. However, when he investigated why this was true, he found that differences in pupils' achievement among schools was associated largely with one factor—the socioeconomic status (SES) of the pupils and community the school was located in. What was even more surprising and disappointing to many educators was Coleman's finding that the usual factors thought to contribute to school achievement, such as class size, textbook quality, the school facility, and teachers' experience, had little impact on student learning.

Reanalysis of Coleman's findings (Jencks et al.,1972) and a more recent finding by Walberg and Fowler (1987) reemphasized that SES overshadows all other variables in its relationship to students' achievement. Perhaps as much as 75 percent of a student's success in school seems to be a result of that student's socioeconomic, family, and cultural background—factors teachers have little or no control over. This finding is increasingly important in light of the current demographic trends noted in Chapter 3, such as reduced parental involvement and more children living in poverty. However, Coleman and others did find a few school, teacher, and pupil characteristics that also contributed to differences in students' learning. These factors included the qualities of the teacher and the educational aspirations or motivation of the students.

Needless to say, educators were extremely disturbed by the news that most of students' school achievement was determined by their SES rather than the school they attended or the teachers they experienced. These reports prompted renewed interest in defining and describing effective teaching. Many educators reasoned that since schools and teachers seemed to have limited influence, it was important to learn how to make the most of that influence. Thus, educational researchers sought to identify the characteristics of teachers and schools that seemed to be making the most difference for their students. Thus was born a second and highly productive era of research on effective teaching. In this second era of research, researchers identified effective teachers not according to supervisor ratings but according to their ability to help students gain the most from instruction.

THE SEARCH FOR EFFECTIVE TEACHERS

Shortly after publication of the Coleman report, educators began to investigate teachers' behaviors and attributes that seemed linked to greater learning. Guided by the notion that students' learning was, in part, the result of these attributes and behaviors, educational investigators began identifying teachers who were consistently able to produce high levels of learning. Often, though not always, the researchers measured learning by performance on standardized achievement tests.

10.2 How would you feel if you were told that you would be hired, fired, promoted, or receive salary increases based on your students' performance on a standardized test? Would it change your approach to teaching? If so, how?

Then the investigators observed these teachers to determine whether they possessed common characteristics or teaching behaviors that might explain their students' success. Thus, in this new era, research considered a teacher who produced more learning than others teaching similar students to be an effective teacher.

Over the past twenty-five years, educational research has identified a number of teacher behaviors and attributes associated with greater learning. These behaviors also seem linked to other desirable outcomes for students, such as increased satisfaction and better attitudes toward school, better self-concept, and higher graduation rates (Needels & Gage, 1991). One of the most exciting things about these findings is that they describe real teachers in real classrooms with real pupils. They are not just theory; they are what living, breathing effective teachers do. By being aware of what these effective teachers are like and aware of what they do, you can learn to incorporate these characteristics and behaviors into your own teaching.

Effective Teachers: Personal Attributes and Characteristics

Although *teachers' personal attributes* are expressed through behavior, they are primarily inherent personality traits which all teachers possess and exhibit to varying degrees. For example, some teachers naturally display greater enthusiasm than others through their speech and actions. This may be the result of greater enthusiasm for their work or simply differences in personality which limit or enhance their ability to express enthusiasm. Some personal attributes, like enthusiasm or warmth, are difficult to acquire or to enhance because they are so firmly rooted in our personalities. Others, such as professional, businesslike demeanor, are somewhat easier to acquire and modify. By becoming more aware of personal attributes that research shows are common among successful teachers and by matching them against your own natural tendencies, you will be able to begin building your own unique teaching persona—one which will maximize your ability to make positive connections with your students.

The remainder of this chapter will deal with eight personal attributes identified by research as common among effective teachers. To guide our discussion, we have organized these attributes under three broad headings: motivating personality, orientation toward success, and professional demeanor. *Motivating personality* includes the attributes enthusiasm, variety, and warmth and humor. These attributes help get and keep students involved and interested in learning. *Orientation toward success* means teachers believe in their own and their students' abilities to be successful. Attributes like expecting success and being encouraging and supportive of students convey this orientation. *Professional demeanor* means that the teacher is focused on helping students learn. Effective teachers are professionally knowledgeable and businesslike; students see them as credible and worthy of trust. As you will see, these three groups of attributes are highly interrelated. For example, being prepared for class conveys confidence, builds credibility, makes the atmosphere of the classroom more businesslike, and enables teachers to more easily adapt their instruction to students' needs.

The following pages will examine these attributes in some depth. First, we will present a definition or description of each, followed by an examination of the research which supports its importance. Finally, we will discuss the specific behaviors which characterize each attribute. As you read these sections, remember that these attributes have been linked to increased student learning. Consider the extent to which you naturally possess and demonstrate each one, and ways in which you might employ them more effectively with your students.

Motivating Personality

Effective teachers possess a motivating, stimulating personality. They seem to enjoy what they are doing, they are supportive of students, and they are believable and easy to trust. In this section, we discuss three particular attributes that are characteristic of teachers with motivating personalities: enthusiasm, warmth and humor, and credibility.

ENTHUSIASM

One of the teacher attributes most closely linked to desirable student outcomes is enthusiasm (Rosenshine & Furst, 1971). Enthusiastic teachers convey to students that they are confident and enjoy what they are doing, that they trust and respect students, and that the subject they teach is valuable and enjoyable (Carusso, 1982). Enthusiastic teaching helps students persist at tasks, motivates them, and leads to increased learning and satisfaction (Bettencourt, Gillett, & Gall, 1983; Denight & Gall, 1989; Wang, Haertel, & Walberg, 1993).

Although enthusiasm is difficult to define, Good and Brophy (1987) indicate that a teacher's enthusiasm has two important dimensions: interest and involvement with the subject matter, and vigor and physical dynamism. Enthusiastic teachers often are described as dynamic, stimulating, energetic, and expressive. Their behavior suggests they are committed to students and to their subject.

People convey enthusiasm through variety in speech, gestures, and facial expressions. As they teach, enthusiastic teachers move around the room, front to back as well as side to side. They are animated and gesture with their hands, arms, head, and shoulders to reinforce or emphasize their points. They maintain eye contact with all students, encourage all students to participate, and solicit and use input from all students. Enthusiastic teachers maintain a brisk lesson pace while allowing and adjusting for students' understanding. They promote interest by varying the speed, pitch, and inflection of their voices, and they use pauses to reinforce points and add variety. Their changes in facial expression (for example, eyes widening or narrowing, smiling or frowning) are frequent and positive and further reinforce what they say.

Maintaining such a dramatic, animated presence from 8:15 A.M. until 3:00 P.M. is a difficult, perhaps impossible task. Fortunately, constant enthusiasm is not necessary. In fact, like other factors, levels of animation are most effective when they vary. A teacher who never ceased moving, always using broad gestures and smiling, would soon become routine or even annoying. Nonetheless, remember Denight and Gall's (1989) advice: While teachers often expect students to be interested in *what* they say, students more often react to *how enthusiastically* it is said.

Remember, you are only enthusiastic if your students perceive you to be. In other words, just feeling enthusiastic about your students and your subject does not ensure that your students will see you as enthusiastic. What behaviors do students perceive as teachers' enthusiasm? Table 10.1 presents teacher behaviors which students use to differentiate between enthusiastic and unenthusiastic teachers. Note that none of these behaviors alone conveys enthusiasm. Rather, they collectively lead students to perceive the teacher as enthusiastic.

WARMTH AND HUMOR

Whether you realize it or not, as the adult authority in the classroom, you will set the tone, define roles, establish parameters, and promote patterns of interpersonal relationship among your students. Teacher warmth and humor are important factors in promoting a supportive, relaxed, satisfying, and educationally productive environment for your students (Murray, 1983; Ryans, 1960; Soar & Soar, 1979). By contributing to a safe and productive environment, warmth and humor

10.3 Do you think it would be better to feel enthusiastic but be unable to convey it to students, or to lack enthusiasm but be able to act enthusiastic? Why?

10.4 Are you an enthusiastic person? Do you easily convey enthusiasm? How is your enthusiasm conveyed?

10.5 Is there something you may have to teach that you feel unenthusiastic about? How will you deal with it?

Try Activity 10.1

TABLE 10.1 Teachers' Enthusiasm

Enthusiastic Teachers . . .	Unenthusiastic Teachers . . .
• Appear confident and friendly	• Appear anxious or defensive
• Establish and convey the relevance of the subject to their students	• Are mechanistic, go through the motions without relating the lesson to the students' interests or needs
• Use broad, animated gestures to emphasize or reinforce points	• Often stand or sit in one spot throughout the lesson
• Are creative and varied in their instructional approach	• Use only one or two instructional alternatives
• Are engaged and dramatic when they teach	• Are disinterested and disengaged
• Maintain eye contact with all students	• Avoid eye contact with students
• Use varied pitch, volume, inflection, and pauses to make vocal delivery more interesting	• Speak in a monotone
• Are patient	• Are impatient
• Are insistent that students successfully complete tasks	• Give up quickly when students do not easily arrive at the correct response
• Are aware of and quickly deal with off-task behavior	• Ignore students' off-task behavior
• Maintain a quick lesson pace	• Use time inefficiently; stall
• Have a sense of humor; can laugh at themselves	• Are frequently critical
• Use movement to maintain interest and attention	• Seldom move from the front of the room

Source: Adapted from V. Carusso. (1982).Teacher enthusiasm: Behaviors reported by teachers and students. Paper presented at the annual meeting of the American Educational Research Association, New York.

indirectly promote learning. In Chapter 12 we will also see that a supportive classroom climate reduces students' misbehavior.

While most people watching various teachers could probably agree on whether they conveyed warmth and humor, it is difficult to explain precisely what constitutes warm behavior or a good sense of humor. However, the two attributes are related.

Warmth A teacher manifests warmth through positive, supportive interpersonal relationships with students. It is important that you allow students to get a sense of your personality. Students often say that good teachers "are real people." Positive classroom relationships are fostered when you are friendly, maintain a positive attitude in your students as individuals, appear to be open and willing to "work things out" with students, and work hard to help them succeed academically. On the other hand, you reduce warmth and injure classroom relationships when students perceive you as unfair, when you are overly judgmental or inflexible, or when you discourage student-teacher interactions.

Specifically, then, what can you do to convey warmth to your students? Many of the teacher behaviors that convey enthusiasm also convey warmth. Figure 10.1 lists suggestions to help you promote a sense of warmth with your students.

Humor An appropriate sense of humor is one of the characteristics students frequently note in the teachers they enjoy (Csikszentmihalyi & McCormack, 1986). These teachers make learning fun. Humor can defuse tension, communicate the teacher's security and confidence, promote trust, and reduce discipline problems.

FIGURE 10.1 Conveying Warmth

1. Greet students by name at the door. Comment on their personal achievements outside your classroom or other aspects of their personal lives.

2. Smile frequently.

3. Be yourself. Convey your personality, likes, dislikes, even opinions.

4. Use nonthreatening physical proximity to students. Moving closer to students can be used to convey a sense of trust and openness.

5. Encourage students to approach you and to be open with you. Keep most in-class interactions on academic topics, but express interest and willingness to talk with students about nonacademic concerns outside of class.

6. Draw out students' opinions, feelings, and ideas, and actively incorporate these into your instruction.

7. Provide remediation and time for all students to master the material and to be successful.

8. While conveying genuine interest, concern, and acceptance of all students, avoid becoming "one of the students" by lowering expectations or joining them socially. This is especially true for new teachers who may be close in age to their students.

Further, effective use of humor in the classroom appears to reinforce learning and improve long-term retention (Desberg, Henschal, & Marshall, 1981; Gruner & Freshley, 1979; Kaplan & Pascoe, 1977).

Effective use of humor has both a spontaneous and a deliberate, or planned, dimension. We convey a sense of humor through our ability to laugh when something funny occurs. During the course of a typical school day, any number of humorous events or accidents occur. Don't be afraid to laugh at these things. You must especially learn to laugh at yourself. All teachers make mistakes. They trip over the cord to the overhead projector and drop stacks of papers as they rush to hand them back. Laugh at these events! Keep them in perspective, and don't take yourself too seriously. On the other hand, avoid sarcasm or cynicism, and be extremely careful about teasing students. Sarcasm and cynicism often send a message of indifference, disinterest, or dislike. And, although some students may respond positively to teasing by the teacher, many may respond negatively by assuming the role of "class clown" or, perhaps more serious, by feeling hurt or embarrassed. Be yourself, be a real person, but remain aware that you set an example for acceptable classroom behavior that students will tend to follow.

While much classroom humor is spontaneous, effective use of humor in the classroom also has a deliberate dimension. Plan lessons which incorporate or point out amusing aspects of the topic. This should go beyond using cartoons and jokes to more substantive aspects of the lesson. For example, a middle school English teacher might use humor to initiate a unit on Edgar Allen Poe's work by humorously drawing attention to his eccentric life and work. The teacher could appear in dark, drab clothes like those Poe might have worn, perhaps with a black plastic bird (a raven) on his shoulder. He could play the role of Poe, exaggerating demented or paranoid speech and mannerisms, to introduce Poe's work in the context of his life. The teacher might talk as Poe would have about the difficulties of his life and writing, introducing the works to be studied in class. The intentional, structured combination of humor and content would make the lesson more memorable and the teaching more effective.

Warmth and humor are means to desirable ends, not ends in themselves. Used in moderation, they help create a relaxed, comfortable environment in which students can learn. However, teachers who place too much emphasis on warmth and humor actually reduce learning (Soar & Soar, 1979). Thus, warmth and humor are best used naturally and sparingly.

10.6 Do you feel comfortable laughing at yourself in front of people? Why or why not?

"If I smile for the yearbook picture, no one will recognize me."

CREDIBILITY

Effective teachers appear to students to be credible and worthy of trust (Rosnow & Robinson, 1967). Once again, it is important to point out that your credibility exists in the eyes of the beholders, your students. Regardless of a teacher's knowledge, experience, education level, or position—all elements that might be expected to ensure your credibility—you are credible only when your students believe you are. In the early grades, teachers, as adult authority figures, have some degree of built-in believability with students. However, as students become more mature, they are less likely to assume that teachers are automatically credible. As university students, you continually make judgments about the credibility and trustworthiness of your instructors. These judgments determine, at least in part, the perceived effectiveness of each instructor.

What can you do to establish yourself as credible and trustworthy? Three elements seem important: your credentials, the messages you send to students, and your behavior (Fisher, 1980). Your credentials are most likely to influence the perceptions of young students who are relatively knowledgeable about the subject or who are highly motivated to succeed. However, even under these conditions, your credentials are only helpful if students are aware of them. The content of the messages you deliver also impacts your credibility. When you are able to demonstrate to students how the topics you present are related to their interests and needs, they view you as more credible. Most important, however, is your behavior. Credibility and trust are the result of being open, honest, and equitable in your dealings with students, and of openly soliciting and accepting students' comments or criticisms, of defining your expectations and the relevance of the subject, of communicating clearly, and of demonstrating interest and concern for your students' success. As you can see, credibility and trust must be earned.

Orientation Toward Success

Effective teachers are positive people. They generally believe in their students' abilities to learn and in their own ability to help students be successful. Importantly, they seem able to communicate a positive attitude and to develop this in their students. Specifically, effective teachers have high expectations of success and are encouraging and supportive of students.

10.7 What factors do you use to determine the credibility of your teachers?

10.8 Have you ever had a teacher who betrayed your trust? What happened? How did it make you feel toward the teacher?

HIGH EXPECTATIONS FOR SUCCESS

Effective teachers hold high expectations of success for themselves and their students. They genuinely believe all students can master the content and that they themselves have the ability to help all students learn. It would appear that teachers' expectations *cause* differences in learning. Research indicates that when teachers' expectations of students rise, students learn more (Brophy, 1981).

It is unclear exactly how teachers' expectations contribute to learning. However, Good (1981) suggests that the expectations teachers have for both themselves and their students affect teachers' behavior, which in turn affects students' learning. For example, if you believe that Joanna is incapable of learning certain material, you are likely to spend less time working with her, focusing instead on other students you believe are more likely to benefit from your help. Thus, Joanna receives less academic guidance and is more likely to fail.

Students are quite adept at sensing cues that subtly communicate your expectations for them. If you hold low expectations for a particular student, not only that student but other students are likely to sense this and to adapt their perceptions and expectations accordingly. In short, students are constantly monitoring teachers' behavior and are likely to sense the attitudes and expectations behind that behavior. As a result, a student is likely to pick up and internalize any teacher behavior that signals low expectations for that particular student and to lower his or her self-expectations (Walberg, 1991). This, of course, increases the likelihood that the student *will not* learn the material.

Most students enter school confident and expecting to be successful, but they quickly learn to adapt their self-perceptions to the expectations of the teacher (Raspberry, 1993; Weinstein & Middlestadt, 1979). Brophy (1982) and others have found that the students most susceptible to the positive and negative effects of teachers' expectations are young, low achievers, students in transition (from elementary to middle school, for example), or students particularly fond of the teacher. Thus, unfortunately, some of the very students who most need their teacher's help and support are those for whom many teachers normally hold low expectations (Brophy, 1982).

Discussions of teachers' expectations and students' success often focus on the idea of **self-fulfilling prophecy**—that you get what you expect. Much of this notion is based upon the work of Rosenthal and Jacobsen (1968) in *Pygmalion in the Classroom* (see Spotlight on Research 10.1). More recently, however, Cooper and Tom (1984) indicate that self-fulfilling prophecy is only one of two ways in which teachers' expectations affect learning and that it is, at most, a minor contributor.

More important are what Cooper and Tom call **sustained expectations.** Initial teachers' expectations may be more or less accurate and thus affect teachers' initial behavior and students' learning. However, expectations can and should be continually modified to more accurately reflect students' ability. The tendency some teachers have to stubbornly refuse to adjust their initially inaccurate (normally low) expectations of certain students can seriously impede learning. Whereas the effects of initial expectations are limited, sustained expectations have a cumulative effect. That is, they continually and repeatedly influence unsuccessful student performance over extended periods of time. The result is a vicious downward spiral—teachers expect certain students to fail, those students fail, the teachers lower their expectations still further, the students again fail, and so on.

You should try to convey to your students that you expect them to be successful and that you will help them be so. You should set realistic goals, convey them clearly, and work to provide each student the opportunity to succeed. A good rule of thumb is to ensure that every student is successful most of the time. This is particularly true for students who are not academically oriented or whose academic self-concept is low (Crawford, 1978). For students who find school difficult and who may not believe they can be successful, you should attempt to

10.9 In what ways did your teachers convey their expectations for you? How did it make you feel? How did it affect your learning?

Robert Rosenthal and Lenore Jacobsen (1968) studied the effects of teachers' expectations on student intelligence test scores. Originally, they were concerned that government programs for disadvantaged youth seemed to promote stereotypes about the academic potential of students in the programs. Specifically, they investigated whether students whose teachers believed they would make great intellectual gains during the school year would make greater gains than other students.

Rosenthal and Jacobsen conducted their experiment in a school serving mostly lower- and middle-class students in a midsized city. Near the end of one school year, all students took a standardized intelligence test. Just before the beginning of the following school year, approximately 20 percent of the students in the school were randomly identified as "potential academic spurters." These students were not really different from the other students in the school, and there was no reason to believe that they would demonstrate any greater intellectual gains than their peers. However, the researchers told teachers that the "academic spurters" were likely to show great intellectual gains during the coming year.

All students took a standardized intelligence test in midyear, at the conclusion of one academic year, and again at the conclusion of a second school year. The results indicated that when teachers were duped into believing certain children were potential "spurters," those children did, in fact, show much greater gains than other students. Further, when teachers were asked to describe these students, they believed they were more curious, more interesting, more appealing, better adjusted, more affectionate, less in need of social approval, and more likely to succeed in later life than other children. Again, remember that these children were initially no different from their peers.

In discussing the results of their study, Rosenthal and Jacobsen concluded that teachers' expectations of increased intellectual gain caused these students to achieve such growth. Interestingly, the gains these children made seem to have resulted from differences in the ways teachers interacted with the children. Rosenthal and Jacobsen noted that the teacher's tone of voice, facial expression, touch, and posture communicated higher expectations for these students. These nonverbal messages "might help the children by changing their conceptions of themselves, their anticipation of their own behavior, their motivation or their cognitive skills" (p. 6).

structure assignments and activities they can complete successfully 80 to 95 percent of the time. This helps build students' confidence in their own abilities, and motivates them to try other, more difficult academic tasks. Even academically oriented students who may be confident of their abilities need to be successful most of the time. A success rate of 70 to 85 percent seems to lead to improved motivation and learning for these students.

Thus far we have discussed students' success in terms of only two types of students—successful and unsuccessful—each needing a specific level of success. You may have noted that academic confidence and optimal levels of success are inversely related. That is, as students' confidence and ability increase, the need for very high levels of success diminishes. To put it another way, less academically able or less confident students need to experience success more often. However, as the unsuccessful student becomes more academically competent and confident, you should structure tasks that take this into consideration. To keep the student challenged and motivated you should gradually make assignments more difficult so that the student is still successful most of the time, but not as often.

You must also be careful to avoid prejudging students or failing to adapt your expectations when necessary. All students have more ability in some areas than in others, even within the same subject. In classes where they feel confident of their ability, students are likely to participate actively and freely. An effective teacher will tune in to a student's strengths and weaknesses and provide opportunities for more success in problem areas and somewhat less success in areas the student is already proficient in. Effective teaching requires the teacher to constantly match students' ability levels with task difficulty.

"Ms. Krenshaw, please send in someone who laughed at me in high school."

Try Activity 10.2

Teachers also convey high expectations for success when they provide **remediation** for students who fail to master material the first time. Your instructional plans should include time for remediation using a variety of alternative instructional sources and materials (old textbooks, magazines, videotapes, computer programs, and so on). You should also be sure to give these students the attention they need in order to succeed. This attention should include both your own time and opportunities for group work and peer tutoring. When you devote time to helping students understand the material, you convey a positive message both about your expectations and about the importance of the material.

When most teachers think about expectations for success, they generally think of teachers' expectations for students. However, the most effective teachers also maintain high expectations for themselves as well. Their own high personal standards motivate them to be well-prepared for class, use class time efficiently, and provide substantive feedback to students. They exhibit thorough knowledge of their subject, convey confidence and calm, dress, act, and speak professionally, and work to correct deficiencies in their own professional ability.

As we have discussed, you will most often convey your expectations indirectly, through your actions rather than your words. How, then, can you convey high expectations to students? Table 10.2 contrasts the behaviors of teachers who hold high expectations of students with those of teachers who hold low expectations.

ENCOURAGING AND SUPPORTIVE

10.10 Do you believe you can help *all* students learn? Explain.

Effective teachers are encouraging and supportive of students, addressing students' needs to belong, to be liked, and to be successful (Wang, Haertel, & Walberg, 1993). Ornstein (1990) defines teachers who are encouraging as those who respect and genuinely believe in students' abilities. They help students feel accepted as individuals, and they recognize effort and potential, not merely correct answers. Thus, encouragement relates to other important attributes like warmth, enthusiasm, and expectations for success. Through encouragement and support, you can help students meet your expectations for success even when they experience some difficulty along the way.

Encouragement is particularly important when students are most likely to experience reluctance and difficulty. This occurs in the early stages of learning a new task or concept, in low-achieving students, and in shy or socially immature students (Brophy, 1981). Encouragement can motivate students to attempt tasks they may be reluctant to start and to continue working when they are struggling or becoming frustrated.

TABLE 10.2 Teachers' Behaviors That Convey High or Low Expectations of Students and Themselves

Teachers with High Expectations . . .	Teachers with Low Expectations . . .
• Clearly inform students of the lesson objectives	• Do not convey the objectives or convey unclear objectives
• Provide extended, organized, well-paced explanations	• Provide explanations which are incomplete and often unclear
• Clearly relate lesson content to student interests	• Make few attempts to relate lesson content to student interests
• Set reasonable standards and modify them frequently	• Set standards which are too high or low and are too rigid
• Plan for and provide remediation when necessary	• Do not provide remediation
• Maintain consistent discipline and task direction	• Do not maintain consistent discipline or task direction
• Solicit and incorporate input from students they instruct	• Discourage or ignore student input
• Frequently smile, nod, and maintain eye contact	• Convey less attention in academic situations
• Call upon all students frequently and equitably to respond	• Seldom and inequitably call on students to respond
• Use wait time to allow students to consider before responding	• Allow students little or no wait time as they attempt to respond
• Help students modify incorrect or inadequate responses	• Frequently provide praise for incorrect or inadequate responses
• Use criticism infrequently	• Frequently criticize students' performance
• Provide extensive, frequent, and specific feedback	• Provide infrequent and vague feedback
• Seldom interrupt students while they are working	• Often interrupt students while they are working

FIGURE 10.2 How to Demonstrate Encouragement and Support for Your Students

1. Use positive comments about students' abilities rather than negative comments about their performance.
2. Be aware of and note improvement, not just perfection.
3. Help students learn to work through their own problems and evaluate their own work.
4. Be optimistic, positive, and cheerful.
5. Demonstrate good, active listening when students are speaking (focus your attention on the student, nod, and so on).
6. Provide several alternative routes to task completion and allow students some degree of choice.

How can you encourage students without being condescending? First, a classroom environment which is supportive, safe, and open will promote students' willingness to begin new or unfamiliar tasks. Students must feel that the tasks you assign are realistic and important, that you will help them succeed, and that they can approach you for assistance if needed. Figure 10.2 lists some ways to demonstrate your encouragement and support.

When students have begun a task but are becoming frustrated and are ready to give up, it is important to help them continue. Words of encouragement such as, "You can do it," "What you've done so far is good. What *could* we do next?" "I understand how frustrating this is, but I know that you can do it," "Let's try the next

10.11 Do you believe *all* students can be academically successful in your classroom? Why or why not?

step together," "Don't give up, you're getting there," or "I *know* you can do it" indicate to students that you are aware of and sympathetic to their struggles but that you are confident they can work through the task successfully. It is important in this situation that you help the students accurately complete the next step in the process with as little direction as possible. Ask questions or point out factors that help the students discover what they need to do next rather than simply give the students the right answer. By helping students work through problems mostly on their own, you build their confidence.

PROFESSIONAL DEMEANOR

Attributes under this heading may be the easiest for you to modify. Effective teachers, while being motivating and positive, also establish and maintain a professional demeanor. They are businesslike and task-oriented, yet flexible and adaptable when necessary to help students be successful. They are knowledgeable not just of the subjects they teach, but also of **pedagogy** and students.

BUSINESSLIKE

A common characteristic of effective teachers is a task-oriented, businesslike classroom demeanor (Cruickshank, 1990; Gabbros, 1979; Rosenshine & Furst, 1971). When you first hear effective teachers described in this way, you may imagine a cold-hearted, unsmiling taskmaster who uses an "iron hand" to force students to do nothing but work seriously on boring, quiet tasks. However, this is not the case at all. In fact, research has found that students often perceive businesslike teachers to exhibit greater warmth and concern than other teachers (Medley, 1977; Ryans, 1960).

The business of the classroom is learning. A businesslike teacher is one who emphasizes and focuses classroom activities on tasks most likely to help students learn. He directs his own behavior and his students' behavior toward the successful and efficient attainment of meaningful, clearly defined learning outcomes. If the teacher does this, learning is likely to improve and the teacher can be considered successful—that is, effective. If the teacher spends too much energy and time on tasks or activities not likely to improve students' learning, the teacher will be unsuccessful.

An analogy may help demonstrate this idea. Imagine for a moment a young boy who has suffered life-threatening injuries in a serious automobile accident. His family accompanies him to the hospital. The physician meets the patient and his distraught family at the emergency room door. She acknowledges the family and immediately begins to determine the nature of the boy's condition. The family is directed to wait in the emergency room lobby, feeling anxious and alone. When the little boy's condition is stabilized, the physician briefly speaks to the child's family. She then instructs a nurse to stay with the family for a few minutes, excuses herself, and immediately begins treating another emergency admission. The physician's behavior toward the family seems somewhat cold, but she has saved the little boy's life.

Now let us assume for a moment that rather than beginning immediately to treat the young boy, the doctor, feeling tremendous sympathy for his family, spends several minutes consoling them. The physician instructs an aide to prepare the little boy for treatment while she remains to talk with the boy's family, build rapport with them, and console them. After several minutes they feel somewhat better, and the physician leaves them to attend to the child. Unfortunately, during this time the little boy's condition has worsened. Although we might consider the physician a caring person, we would probably not consider her an effective physician.

Exaggerated though the analogy may be, it makes the point that the effective physician is the one who most effectively conducts the "business" of medicine. The best doctor would save lives *and* exhibit warmth and caring. However, we would expect a physician to focus on the primary business of the profession. Thus, sympathy and caring are important but not sufficient for effective doctoring . . . *or* for effective teaching.

Ryans (1960) generally describes the businesslike teacher as responsible and systematic. More specifically, Gabbros (1979) notes that a businesslike teacher is goal-oriented, serious, deliberate, and organized.

Goal-Oriented   Businesslike teachers focus their efforts on helping students achieve learning goals. In the chapter on planning instruction, we discussed the importance of establishing the desired outcomes of instruction and of basing our instruction on these objectives. Businesslike teachers establish clear, realistic, specific objectives and communicate these to students. They plan and conduct instruction in ways that efficiently and systematically move students toward the objectives. They actively seek input from students about the reasonableness of the objectives and about problems the students may be having, and they use this information to modify their instruction when necessary. They optimize activities and time devoted directly to helping students reach the established goals and minimize approaches, comments, questions, or behaviors that are not directed toward the goals.

Serious   Businesslike teachers value learning and model this to students through their words and actions. This does not mean that they do not use humor, but their humor is natural and without cynicism or sarcasm. These teachers convey seriousness of purpose through earnest and genuine expressions indicating the value of the tasks at hand, reasonable expectations, guidance in task execution, and efficient use of time. The teacher treats the subject seriously, maintains a professional and confident image, and uses appropriate verbal and nonverbal behaviors.

Deliberate   Also important is a businesslike teachers' ability to establish and maintain a sense of purpose throughout each lesson. Careful planning of instruction allows such teachers to be concise, thorough, and exact in conducting instruction. Businesslike teachers organize instructional activities or tasks in a logical sequence including a clear introduction, presentation, and closure. This type of teacher deliberately conducts instruction in ways that devote equal attention to all students.

Although deliberateness requires systematic planning and implementation of instruction directed toward specific goals, it does not mean that the teacher is inflexible. When the teacher becomes aware that students do not understand or that the planned instructional activities are not working effectively, they adapt the activities. Teachers must adapt as quickly as possible, but not without careful consideration of the learning objectives. In other words, they might ask why the planned activity is not helping students reach the goals, what alternative activities might help, and which alternative can immediately be implemented? Even when teachers deviate from planned instruction, they should remain focused on the original learning goals.

Organized   Businesslike teachers organize the classroom and instruction based upon the established goals. Furniture, resources, materials, equipment, and activities are organized to minimize disruptions. Teachers use available personnel, such as aides or parent volunteers, to promote desirable learning outcomes rather than to reduce their workload. Even classroom management and discipline procedures are intended to promote the established goals.

Generally, then, a businesslike teacher is openly focused upon the business of promoting students' learning. Guided by clearly established goals and objectives, the teacher plans for, implements, and adapts whatever instruction will most efficiently help students reach learning objectives. Although many distractions may arise, the teacher minimizes activities or time not directed toward reaching the

TABLE 10.3 Teachers' Businesslike and Nonbusinesslike Behavior

Businesslike Teachers . . .	Nonbusinesslike Teachers . . .
• Establish clear academic goals and objectives	• Fail to establish academic learning goals
• Communicate the goals and objectives to students	• Do not communicate the goals and objectives to students
• Plan lessons directed at helping students reach the objectives	• Do not plan sufficiently or direct instruction toward objectives
• Seek input from students about the reasonableness of goals	• Disregard or fail to solicit students' input about the reasonableness of goals
• Emphasize activities and time devoted to academics	• Emphasize nonacademic activities and use time inefficiently
• Treat the subject seriously and respectfully	• Are sarcastic or make light of the subject
• Maintain a professional image	• Seem to be "one of the kids"
• Involve all students in the instructional activities	• Neglect some students while focusing mainly on good students
• Organize the room and equipment to minimize disruptions	• Fail to carefully organize the physical setting
• Use aides or volunteers to provide additional academic attention for students	• Use aides or volunteers primarily to deal with administrative tasks

objectives. Remember that this businesslike focus can be maintained without sacrificing genuine warmth and caring for students. Table 10.3 contrasts the behaviors of teachers who are businesslike with those of teachers who are not.

ADAPTABLE/FLEXIBLE

A supervising teacher once told her student teacher, "No matter what you plan for, something else will happen." Teaching may not be quite that unpredictable, but certainly the most effective teachers are prepared for and able to adapt to a variety of circumstances (Walberg, 1990). As you have probably noticed from your years of experience as a student, an effective teacher must be flexible and adaptable.

In the next chapter, we will discuss the importance of systematically building variety into your instruction and instructional activities. However, for now, let us focus on the ability to react appropriately and relatively quickly to changing classroom circumstances.

Flexibility and adaptability in this sense requires that you be *aware* of the need for change and be *able* to adapt to those changes. Hunt (1976, 1979) refers to these capabilities as "reading" and "flexing." As you work with students, you must consciously monitor the effectiveness of the activities you and your students are engaged in. Through a variety of verbal and nonverbal cues, you can ascertain, or "read," the need for adapting or flexing. Nonverbally, students may appear puzzled, confused, frustrated, or bored. Verbally, they may appear unable or unwilling to respond accurately to your questions, to complete assigned tasks, or to ask meaningful questions. In each case, you must first be aware that a problem exists and then be willing to adapt your goals and instruction as needed. In short, you should avoid a tendency to stick with your lesson plan if it is not working. Next, you must determine potential alternatives that will help you reach the established objectives, select an alternative, and implement it, often in a matter of a few seconds. Chapter 11 will present specific skills that will help you read and adapt your instruction.

10.12 Do you feel you can be flexible and adaptable when you teach? How could thorough planning help make you *more* flexible during the lesson?

FIGURE 10.3   Enhancing Flexibility and Adaptability

1. Clearly define goals, objectives, or intentions and make them known to students.

2. When planning instruction, consider students' characteristics, attributes, preferences, and interests.

3. Plan instruction that is interesting to the students and is directed toward the intended learning outcomes.

4. While implementing the planned instruction, systematically and continually monitor students' verbal and nonverbal behavior to determine the appropriateness of your instruction (for example, puzzled or frustrated looks, inability to answer questions or to complete tasks, and student questions or comments that indicate a lack of understanding).

5. When the planned instruction appears to be inappropriate, attempt to determine why and to identify alternatives.

6. When necessary, implement an alternative and again monitor its effectiveness.

Figure 10.3, based upon the work of Hunt (1976, 1979) and others, notes characteristics of the flexible, adaptable teacher. Notice that some of Hunt's suggestions are directed at planning developmentally appropriate instruction to reduce the need for subsequent changes. Still, as noted in Chapter 5 on planning, even the best plans often need some adjustments to fit individual students and classes.

The ability to recognize the need for change and to adapt instruction accordingly is probably the most difficult task for beginning teachers. However, with time and a conscious attempt to develop a varied teaching repertoire, you can improve your ability to adapt your instructional approach, even during the lesson!

KNOWLEDGEABLE

Brief mention should be made of the role of subject matter knowledge in effective teaching. Knowledge of the subjects they teach seems intuitively to be an important attribute of effective teachers. Certainly it is reasonable to believe that good teachers know their subjects well. However, there is little agreement regarding *how much* knowledge a teacher must have to teach well (Cruickshank, 1990; Porter & Brophy, 1988; Rosenshine & Furst, 1971). We have all experienced teachers who were obviously quite knowledgeable about the subject they taught but unable to help students learn it, as well as teachers who effectively facilitate learning with substantial but not overly extensive knowledge of the subject.

Although research findings are mixed, there is some evidence that teachers' knowledge of subject matter can be helpful to their teaching. In a review of research, Druva and Anderson (1983) found that the number of courses teachers had taken in the subject they taught was only marginally related to students' learning. Additional reviews by the General Accounting Office of the United States government (1984) and Evertson, Hawley, and Zlotnick (1984) revealed similar findings. Berliner (1985) concludes from the research on this topic that "we are assured, only, that the relationships between academic knowledge and student achievement are not negative!" (p. 2).

In a more recent review, Porter and Brophy (1988) conclude that knowledge of the subject is important but not sufficient for effective teaching. What seems more important is the teacher's ability to combine knowledge of the subject, knowledge of teaching (that is, pedagogy), and knowledge of students in order to implement effective instruction. Knowledge of the subject and of learners helps make the teacher more aware of the misconceptions students are likely to have or to develop about the subject. Knowledge of pedagogy and of learners allows the teacher to select and implement instructional alternatives that can best address students' misconceptions. Thus, knowledge of subject is most useful when the teacher draws upon it to select and implement instruction.

10.13 Which of the three types of knowledge Porter and Brophy (1988) defined do you feel you most possess? Which do you feel you least possess?

"For that you went to college?"

Some Final Thoughts

In this chapter we have discussed eight teacher attributes or characteristics that help students learn more effectively. We learned that effective teachers are positive and confident about their own and their students' success, are supportive and encouraging of students, and are professional in their demeanor. We also saw that these teachers primarily convey these attributes through behavior and that speech is sometimes at odds with how a teacher really feels. It is important to remember that these attributes and the specific behaviors which seem to communicate them to students are interrelated. When one is modified, the other also changes. Though teachers' attributes are difficult to change, teachers should be aware of how various attributes impact on students and should work to enhance those that have positive effects.

CHAPTER SUMMARY

- Research on effective teaching has been conducted for nearly a century. Early research defined effective teachers as those whom supervisors or administrators rated highly. However, researchers could find no relationship between these ratings and the teachers' personal traits. Many concluded that effective teaching could not be described or taught.

- Civil rights developments during the 1960s prompted a new era of research on effective teaching. The *Equality of Educational Opportunity* study, by Coleman and his associates, spurred increased interest in identifying and describing effective teaching. Coleman found that teaching and schools made little difference in students' achievement. The greatest single contributor to academic success was the student's SES and family background.

- Researchers in this new era began to define effective teachers as those who helped their students learn more than other teachers with similar students. These researchers observed the classrooms and classroom behaviors of effective teachers and found that they shared several common attributes and abilities which tended to increase students' learning and satisfaction with teaching and to enhance students' self-concept.

- Personal attributes are primarily inherent personality traits which everyone possesses and exhibits to varying degrees. Attributes are expressed through verbal and nonverbal behavior, and some, like warmth, are difficult to change because they are so much a part of our personalities. Other attributes, such as businesslike demeanor or flexibility, can be modified through awareness.

- Effective teachers' personal attributes can be organized around three broad characteristics: motivating personality, orientation toward success, and professional demeanor.

- At least three specific attributes are associated with teachers who possess a motivating personality: enthusiasm for their students and their subject matter, warmth and humor, and credibility and trustworthiness.

- Teachers' enthusiasm promotes learning by helping to motivate students, by keeping them persistent at tasks, and by helping them feel more satisfied with the teaching. Enthusiastic teachers vary their voices, gestures, and expressions; they move around the room from front to back and side to side; and they maintain a quick lesson pace involving high levels of interaction with students.

- Warmth and humor seem mostly to influence students' learning indirectly by promoting an environment that makes students feel free and motivated to participate. Teachers convey warmth by being "real" people, by demonstrating concern for students' success, and by being open. Humor can be spontaneous or planned. Teachers should be able to laugh at themselves and their mistakes; they should avoid using sarcasm or teasing students. However, warmth and humor, if overemphasized, actually reduce classroom learning, so they are best used naturally and sparingly.

- Credibility and trustworthiness create a relaxed, supportive environment where students trust the teacher to help them succeed. Teachers develop credibility and trust through open, honest teacher-student interaction, not through a teacher's position or credentials; and these qualities exist only if students perceive them.

- Effective teachers are positive people, oriented toward and optimistic about their own and their students' success. Specifically, effective teachers have high expectations for success and are encouraging and supportive of students. They believe in their own ability to help every student learn successfully. Expectations appear to influence teachers' behavior toward students which, in turn, affects learning. When teachers expect certain students to fail, they tend to reduce the amount of time and attention devoted to those students, thus increasing the likelihood the students will be unsuccessful. Even more critical than inaccurate initial expectations is the failure to modify those expectations when necessary.

- A good rule of thumb for teachers is to ensure that every student is successful most of the time. Students with low academic self-concepts should be successful almost every time, until their confidence improves. Students with strong academic self-concepts should also be successful most of the time, but not quite so often. Remediation, that is, providing reteaching when a student doesn't master the content, is a good way to convey high expectations and to promote success.

- Effective teachers are encouraging and supportive of students and convey a sense of genuine respect for them and for their individual abilities. Encouragement and support are most important when students are reluctant to begin new tasks or when they experience difficulty and frustration. Teachers demonstrate encouragement and support by avoiding negative comments, by noting improvement—not just perfection, and by helping students reach realistic goals.

- Effective teachers exhibit a professional but flexible demeanor in the classroom. Businesslike behavior, the ability to be flexible and adaptable when necessary, and thorough understanding of subject, pedagogy, and learners all enhance professional demeanor.

- Businesslike teachers focus on promoting learning in a variety of ways. They direct classroom activities toward helping students reach the established goals and objectives. They establish the importance and seriousness of the subject and of the goals and convey this importance to students. Instruction and instructional activities are deliberate and carefully planned to allow the teacher to be concise, thorough, and efficient. The classroom and classroom activities are organized to help students reach the desired goals.

- A professional demeanor also includes the ability to calmly and effectively adapt to changing classroom circumstances. This includes the ability to "read" what is happening in the classroom: the level of students' understanding and motivation, changes in the classroom environment, and problems with instruction. When problems arise, teachers must "flex" or adapt their instruction to more effectively reach the established goals.

- Teachers who exhibit a professional demeanor are also knowledgeable of their subject, pedagogy, and students. Knowledge of the subject is most useful when it is integrated with knowledge of pedagogy and knowledge of learners. Only then can teachers select, plan, and implement the most effective instruction.

ISSUES AND PROBLEMS FOR DISCUSSION

PROBLEMS   Teachers commented on the following incidents or problems. Would you have anticipated these situations? What would you do in each situation?

Problem 1:   "Funny incident! I was on playground duty last week with kindergarten, first, second, and third graders. A little kindergarten child got stuck on top of the jungle gym crying his heart out! *Naturally* I climbed in and rescued him. Then the bell rang for kids to come in, and guess what 49-year-old teacher was stuck inside the jungle gym? Yours truly!!! One of the third graders had to tell the teacher how to put her head out first and then the rest of me! Hazardous duty? Nope. Just a funny happening."

Problem 2:   "A student returned with a cast on his lower left arm. Giving him the usual sympathy and understanding was not enough. During class he did many things to draw attention to himself. I was quite irritated at the end of class and had to struggle with myself to keep my temper and irritation under control. He is a very immature student and this demonstrated his immaturity again."

Problem 3:   "I have one little boy who copies even when he knows the correct answer. I'm trying to build his self-confidence; however, he continues to look on others' papers. When I move him away from the rest of the class, his work is very good. He seems to need reassurance by looking at others' work."

Problem 4:   "My greatest concern today was having a change in the regular schedule and having to decide which classes my class would have to omit. The school nurse wanted to show a filmstrip and talk with the class. To reinforce this, I had the children do a work paper and make a paper puzzle. So, we had a long health class. But, because of this, the decision had to be made to have only one of the regular classes of writing, language, or social studies."

ACTIVITY 10.1: Observing Enthusiasm in the Classroom   During your next visit to a classroom, take the time to observe the teacher's level of enthusiasm. Use the behaviors in Table 10.1 as a guide. Did the teacher demonstrate these behaviors? How enthusiastic did the teacher appear to you? If you have an opportunity, ask students how enthusiastic they believe their teacher to be. Do their perceptions match your own? Why or why not?

ACTIVITY 10.2: Maintaining Positive Expectations   If you have friends who are currently student teaching or are in their first year of teaching, arrange to speak with them about maintaining positive expectations. What do they find most difficult? Do they feel they have high expectations for all students? Do they seem to hold high expectations for themselves? What do they do to avoid becoming pessimistic or lowering their expectations too far? What advice might they offer to help you maintain positive expectations?

REFERENCES

Barr, A. (1961). Wisconsin studies of the measurement and prediction of teacher effectiveness. *Journal of Experimental Education, 30,* 16–25.

Berliner, D. (1985). Laboratory settings and the study of teacher education. *Journal of Teacher Education, 36*(6), 2–8.

Bettencourt, E., Gillett, M., & Gall, M. (1983). Effects of teacher enthusiasm training on student on-task behavior and achievement. *American Educational Research Journal, 20*(3), 435–450.

Biddle, B., & Ellena, W. (1964). *Contemporary research on teacher effectiveness.* New York: Holt, Rinehart, and Winston.

Brophy, J. (1981). Teacher praise: A functional analysis. *Review of Educational Research, 51*(1), 5–32.

Brophy, J. (1982). Successful teaching strategies for the inner-city child. *Phi Delta Kappan, 63*(8), 527–530.

Carusso, V. (1982). Teacher enthusiasm: Behaviors reported by teachers and students. Paper presented at the annual meeting of the American Educational Research Association, New York.

Coleman, J., Campbell, J., Wood, A., Weinfeld, F., & York, R. (1966). *Equality of educational opportunity.* Washington, DC: U.S. Department of Health, Education, and Welfare, Office of Education.

Cooper, H., & Tom, D. (1984). Teacher expectation research: A review with implications for classroom instruction. *Elementary School Journal, 85*(1), 77–89.

Crawford, J. (1978). Interactions of learning characteristics with the difficulty level of instruction. *Journal of Educational Psychology, 70*(4), 523–531.

Cruickshank, D. (1990). *Research that informs teachers and teacher educators.* Bloomington, IN: Phi Delta Kappa.

Csikszentmihalyi, M., & McCormack, J. (1986). The influence of teachers. *Phi Delta Kappan, 67*(6), 415–419.

Denight, J., & Gall, M. (1989). Effects of enthusiasm training on teachers and students at the high school level. Paper presented at the annual meeting of the American Educational Research Association, San Francisco.

Desberg, P., Henschal, D., & Marshall, C. (1981). *The effect of humor on retention of lecture material.* Lubbock: Texas Technical University. (ERIC Document Reproduction Service ED 223 118).

Druva, C., & Anderson, R. (1983). Science teacher characteristics by teacher behavior and by student outcome: A meta-analysis of research. *Journal of Research in Science Teaching, 20,* 467–479.

Evertson, C., Hawley, W., & Zlotnick, M. (1984). *The characteristics of effective teacher preparation programs: A review of research.* Nashville, TN: Peabody College, Vanderbilt University.

Fisher, R. (1980). Teacher credibility: A challenge. Unpublished manuscript. Columbus: The Ohio State University.

Gabbros, R. (1979). An analysis of the influence of a training intervention for businesslike behavior on the businesslike behavior and level of warmth of preservice teachers. Paper presented at the annual meeting of the American Educational Research Association, San Francisco.

General Accounting Office. (1984). *New directions for federal programs to aid mathematics and science teaching* (GAO/PEMO-84-5). Washington, DC: General Accounting Office.

Good, T. (1981, February). Teacher expectations and student perceptions: A decade of research. *Educational Leadership,* 415–422.

Good, T., & Brophy, J. (1987). *Looking in classrooms.* Fourth Edition. New York: Harper and Row.

Gruner, C., & Freshley, D. (1979). Retention of lecture items reinforced with humorous and nonhumorous exemplary material. Paper presented at the annual meeting of the Speech Communication Association, New York. (ERIC Document Reproduction Service ED 193 725)

Hunt, D. (1976). Teachers' adaptation: "Reading" and "flexing" to students. *Journal of Teacher Education, 27*(3), 268–275.

Hunt, D. (1979). *Teachers' adaptation to students: Implicit and explicit matching.* Research and Development Memorandum 139. Stanford, CA: Center for Research and Development in Teaching.

Jencks, C., Smith, M., Acland, H., Bane, M., Cohen, D., Gintis, H., Heyns, B., & Michelson, S. (1972). *Inequality: A reassessment of the effect of family and schooling in America.* New York: Basic Books.

Kaplan, R., & Pascoe, G. (1977). Humorous lecture and humorous examples: Some effects upon comprehension and retention. *Journal of Educational Psychology, 69*(1), 62–65.

Medley, D. (1977). *Teacher competence and teacher effectiveness: A review of process-product research.* Washington, DC: American Association of Colleges for Teacher Education.

Medley, D. (1986). Teacher effectiveness. In H. Mitzel (Ed.), *The encyclopedia of educational research* (pp. 1894–1903). New York: Macmillan.

Murray, H. (1983). Low inference classroom teaching behavior and student ratings of college teaching effectiveness. *Journal of Educational Psychology, 75,* 138–149.

Needels, M. & Gage, J. (1991). Essence and accident in process-product research. In H. Waxman & H. Walberg (Eds.), *Effective teaching: Current research.* Berkeley, CA: McCutchan.

Ornstein, A. (1990). *Strategies for effective teaching.* New York: HarperCollins.

Porter, A., & Brophy, J. (1988). Synthesis of research on good teaching. *Educational Leadership, 45*(8), 74–85.

Raspberry, W. (1993, September 27). Children will learn if they're properly taught. *The Columbus Dispatch,* p. 9.

Rosenshine, B., & Furst, N. (1971). Research on teacher performance criteria. In B. Smith (Ed.), *Research in teacher education.* Englewood Cliffs, NJ: Prentice-Hall.

Rosenthal, R., & Jacobsen, L. (1968). *Pygmalian in the classroom: Teacher expectations and pupils' intellectual development.* New York: Holt, Rinehart, and Winston.

Rosnow, R., & Robinson, E. (1967). *Experiments in persuasion.* New York: Academic Press.

Ryans, D. (1960). *Characteristics of teachers.* Washington, DC: American Council of Education.

Soar, R., & Soar, R. (1979). Emotional climate and management. In P. Peterson & H. Walberg (Eds.), *Research on teaching: Concepts, findings, and implications.* Berkeley, CA: McCutchan.

Walberg, H. (1990). Productive teaching and instruction: Assessing the knowledge base. *Phi Delta Kappan, 71*(6), 470–478.

Walberg, H. (1991). Productive teaching and instruction: Assessing the knowledge base. In H. Waxman & H. Walberg (Eds.), *Effective teaching: Current research*. Berkeley, CA: McCutchan.

Walberg, H., & Fowler, W. (1987). Expenditure and size efficiency for public school districts. *Educational Researcher, 16,* 5–13.

Wang, M., Haertel, G. & Walberg, H. (1993). What helps students learn? *Educational Leadership, 51*(4), 74–79.

Weinstein, R., & Middlestadt, S. (1979). Learning about the achievement hierarchy of the classroom: Through children's eyes. Paper presented at the annual meeting of the American Educational Research Association, San Francisco.

Effective Teachers: Professional Skills and Abilities

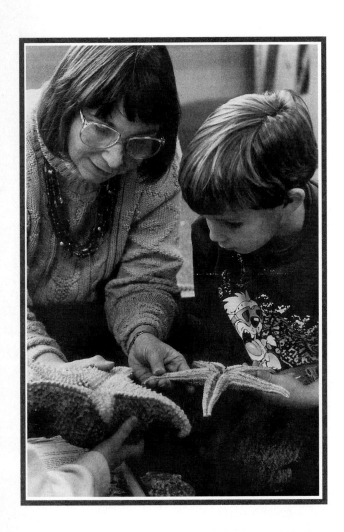

Contents

11

The *personal* attributes of teachers discussed in Chapter 10 are vital in establishing an environment that supports students and encourages them to learn. Although teachers can modify these attributes through awareness and determination, they are often difficult to change substantially. In contrast, teachers can acquire and use a variety of *professional* skills that research shows can have a profound impact on students' learning. In fact, these skills may be among the most critical factors in determining a teacher's effectiveness (Metcalf, 1992; Wang, Haertel, & Walberg, 1993–94). This chapter focuses on the following seven teaching skills, all important in helping students learn (from Cruickshank, 1990):

1. Establishing set
2. Using variety
3. Optimizing instructional time
4. Using questions
5. Providing clear instruction
6. Monitoring students' progress
7. Providing feedback and reinforcement

To guide our discussion of these teaching skills, we will organize them into four broad areas of classroom instruction. First, we will discuss how teachers engage and maintain students' attention; second, how teachers optimize instructional time; third, how teachers go about interactive instruction; and fourth, how teachers use feedback and reinforcement.

As you read this chapter, remember that these are skills that effective teachers use consistently and proficiently. The better you are at incorporating them into your teaching style, the more your students will gain from instruction since research has linked them to students' learning. Further, it has been shown that any teacher can learn to use these skills more effectively to increase learning in his or her classrooms (Brophy, 1982; Cruickshank, 1990; Gage, 1989; Walberg, 1990). Consequently, we have incorporated practice exercises that will help you acquire these behaviors into Units 1, 2, and 3 of the Practice Teaching Manual.

Focusing and Engaging Students' Attention

Effective teachers are able to get students' attention at the beginning of a lesson and to hold their attention throughout the lesson. (Feden, 1994; Wang, Haertel, & Walberg, 1993–94). To accomplish this, teachers must be skilled in establishing set (providing a context for the lesson and instruction) and in using variety.

ESTABLISHING SET

Students learn more when teachers begin their lessons by **establishing set,** that is, by providing a context for the lesson and the instruction. This is variously referred to as **set induction,** providing advance organizers, or lesson entry. Whatever the label, you may recall from Chapter 5 that a teacher uses this skill at the beginning of an instructional segment and generally intends it to do one or more of the following:

1. Capture students' attention or provide them with a framework for the lesson
2. Help students relate new material or information to what they have previously learned
3. Determine students' entry-level knowledge prior to introducing new content

When our purpose is to engage students' attention in a new instructional activity, we are establishing **orientation set.** This type of set may vary from a few minutes at the beginning of a single lesson to a full class period at the beginning of a new unit of study. When the primary goal of a set is to help students understand how the new material relates to what they learned previously, we are using **transition set.** This might include a brief review of previous lessons, a discussion to focus students on what they already know about a topic, or a single sentence that shows the relationship to previous material (that is, "Yesterday we learned two causes of the Civil War. Would someone name them for me?" . . . "Today we'll learn two more reasons . . ."). We use **evaluative set** to establish what students already know about a topic. The teacher might ask students questions about the topic or give a short quiz or pretest to make judgments about how best to teach the lesson.

The notion of establishing set before introducing students to new material relates closely to cognitivist approaches to learning (Perkins, 1993), particularly reception learning (see Chapter 3). Brophy and Good (1986) note that learning increases and becomes more efficient when new material is related to previously learned material. Schuck (1985) and Waxman (1987–88) both report students' achievement and long-term retention is greater when teachers deliberately establish set. Generally, establishing set seems to help students learn more by focusing their attention, improving their ability to self-monitor their understanding, and increasing the likelihood that new information is linked to existing knowledge or schema (Eby, 1992; Feden, 1994).

Luiten, Ames, and Aerson (1980) found that to be effective, information or activities used to establish set must be (1) at a higher level of abstraction or broader in scope than the content to be learned in order to encompass the specific concepts of the lesson and (2) related directly to students' prior knowledge. Thus, the early minutes of a lesson may be used to promote several goals and are critical to establishing a tone and instructional pattern that allows students to learn.

11.1 What is the most memorable lesson entry you've ever experienced? Did it help you learn more?

The beginning of the lesson should accomplish four goals. First, it should be more than a simple, dry introduction, an overview of the material, or a statement like "Open your math books to page 79." Establishing an effective set requires a configuration of several general characteristics (Arends, 1991). First, the topic should be introduced in a way which makes it novel, interesting, or relevant to students. Often teachers begin a lesson by performing a demonstration with a surprising or unexpected outcome in order to stimulate curiosity about the topic of the lesson. For example, at the beginning of a lesson on chemical reactions and their by-products, a teacher might drop a small piece of potassium into a beaker of water and allow students to see the reaction (the potassium will spark, sputter, and eventually burn up).

A second goal of the beginning of the lesson is to establish an interactive climate and tone. It is important that teachers immediately involve students in responding to questions or in thinking and talking about the topic. In the previous

FIGURE 11.1 Establishing Set

1. Review previous material.
2. Ask a curiosity-provoking question or pique students' interest by using a unique problem or scenario.
3. Provide an overview of the major points or topics of the lesson.
4. Demonstrate the concept or ideas of the lesson.
5. Provide a visual schema which depicts the relationship of various aspects or concepts of the lesson.
6. Provide a problem (orally, visually, or by some other means) to engage students in processing the concepts to be learned.
7. Convey interest, enthusiasm, and curiosity about the topic.
8. Inform students of the objectives or goals of the lesson, and point out its relevance to their lives.

example, the science teacher might ask students what they think will happen before the potassium is dropped into the water. After students have observed the reaction, the teacher could ask them what they observed, what might explain it, and gradually guide them toward the major topic of the lesson.

A third objective of the lesson introduction is to direct students' attention to important aspects of the content or communicate the lesson objectives. Sometimes teachers will put a topical outline on the board to highlight important aspects of the lesson. Sometimes they use a demonstration, note the major reasons behind the events in the demonstration, and explain how the lesson will focus on these reasons. For example, after asking students to explain what they observed, the science teacher in our example might use students' responses to note that the chemical reaction produced new compounds, that it is possible to write an equation that depicts this reaction, and that by the end of the day's class they will be able to write equations for reactions like this.

Fourth, the entry should link today's lesson with what students already know. "Remember yesterday we talked about . . . ? How might that explain what we saw in the demonstration? . . . Well, today we're going to talk about . . ." Figure 11.1 presents some specific ways of establishing an effective set for your lessons.

Try Activities 11.1 and 11.2

USING VARIETY

Educators have long believed that variety increases students' motivation and learning. Rosenshine and Furst (1971) and subsequent researchers have supported this belief. Effective teachers use variety in virtually every aspect of their classroom behavior including nonverbal behavior, instructional approaches, classroom organization, questioning, types of assessment, and gestures. We have all experienced teachers who taught every lesson for the entire year in the same way, with the same activities arranged in the same order, using the same, monotonous voice patterns and few gestures. This lack of variety in instructional patterns can negatively affect learning. Imagine a teacher (perhaps you can even remember one) who responded to every student's answer or contribution with, "Exactly!" The first few times you witness a student receiving this response, it seems enthusiastic and encouraging. However, eventually, even if every student's answer is correct, "Exactly!" is no longer effective and may, in fact, become annoying. The same holds true for many other teacher behaviors (Henson, 1980).

Rosenshine and Furst (1971) identified variety as the second strongest predictor of teachers' effectiveness. Many researchers have since agreed that deliberate use of variety is a critical factor in effective classrooms (Couch, 1973; Kintsch & Bates, 1977; Napell, 1978; Williams & Ware, 1977). However, variety probably does not directly improve learning. Instead, it has a positive effect on students' attention and involvement, thus making students more receptive to learning. Teachers

"Go to kindergarten, finger-paint, have quiet time, play with building blocks, eat lunch, listen to a story, take a nap, color, go home from kindergarten—day after day, week after week. I'm 5, and I'm in a rut."

who use variety not only prevent students from becoming bored, they keep them interested and actively involved in the lesson. A teacher's knack for variety fosters interest and engagement on the part of students; this in turn leads to increased learning (Doyle, 1986).

Several researchers have identified specific ways teachers can introduce variety into their classrooms (Brophy & Evertson, 1976; Brophy & Good, 1986; Rohrkemper & Corno, 1988). Their suggestions can be organized into two major categories: variation in instructional activities and materials, and variation in teacher-student interaction.

Instructional Activities and Materials   As we discussed earlier, one way of establishing effective set in your lessons is to pique students' interest by presenting novel situations or problems. In addition, teachers can vary their instruction by using a variety of instructional alternatives: cooperative learning, discussion, seat work, direct instruction, inquiry learning, and so on (see Chapters 6 and 7). Ideally, every lesson should allow students to experience the content through several senses. You might tell students about certain ideas or have them read about them; ask them to conduct an experiment or activity in which they manipulate materials and can see, feel, hear, taste, or even smell the results of their manipulations; then organize them into small groups to write a summary of their observations.

Interacting with Students   In addition to introducing students to content in a variety of ways, Brophy and Good (1986) emphasize the importance of varying the ways teachers interact with students. For example, college teachers shouldn't spend an entire class period standing in one spot in the front of the room lecturing to students. A much more effective lesson would include some teacher talk, some questioning, and some discussion.

Teachers should also vary the ways in which they reinforce or praise students for desirable performance or inform them about their progress. Smiling at students, maintaining eye contact, moving closer, laughing, and gesturing toward students often can be reinforcing and convey support and interest. More explicitly, you can give students rewards for desirable performance. Verbal praise, recognition of outstanding work, free time, or tokens are examples. Brophy and Good note that, just as a single instructional alternative eventually becomes monotonous and ineffective, so too does a single form of reward. Likewise, teachers can and should provide students with information about their performance in a variety of forms—not

11.2   Why do you think it is so easy for teachers to "get in a rut" rather than use variety? What will you do to make sure that you continually incorporate variety?

just in written comments or grades on students' papers. Verbal information from the teacher, peers, and group are important ways of accomplishing this. We will discuss reinforcement and feedback in detail later in this chapter.

Try Activity 11.3

Using Instructional Time Efficiently

The most effective teachers learn to optimize the time available for instruction. It's only reasonable that students learn more when they spend more time engaged in learning activities. Three factors contribute to more efficient use of instructional time: (1) time on task, (2) maintaining momentum, and (3) smooth transitions.

OPTIMIZING TIME

Research has shown that **time on task** is consistently related to increased learning. When teachers and students spend more time actively engaged in academic tasks, students learn more (Brophy & Good, 1986; Doyle, 1986; Harnischfeger & Wiley, 1978; Karweit, 1984; Rosenshine, 1980; Walberg, 1988). Interestingly, however, only a small percentage of available instructional time is actually used for meaningful instruction (Rosenshine, 1980). An examination of the reasons for this can show where time is lost and how to maximize the use of available time.

It is useful to think of instructional time in terms of four levels, somewhat like the target in Figure 11.2. At each level, less time is used for instruction than is available. For example, at the broadest level is **mandated time;** that is, the formal time scheduled for school or academic activities. The length of the school year, day, and periods determine the maximum time available for instructional activities. Teachers are compelled to work within the constraints and schedules established by their state, school district, and school. Schools in most states schedule approximately 185 school days; the typical school day is about 7½ hours in length; and the typical high school period is about 50 minutes. It should be noted, however, that there is much disparity even in amounts of mandated time (Doyle, 1986; Harnischfeger & Wiley, 1978; Karweit, 1984; Rosenshine, 1980). In fact, Harnischfeger and Wiley found a difference of 45 minutes in the length of the school

FIGURE 11.2   The Relationships among the Four Levels of Instructional Time

"They never quit, do they?"

day for second graders *within the same school district!* In this school district, as in many others, the maximum available time for school-related activities is much greater for some students than for others.

Obviously, not every minute of mandated time is used for instruction. Some time is scheduled for lunch, moving from class to class, recess, homeroom, and other noninstructional activities. Thus, only a portion of mandated time is actually allocated to instruction.

Allocated time is the amount of mandated time intended or scheduled for academic activities. Rosenshine (1980) found that less than 75 percent of mandated time is allocated to academic tasks. Nonacademic activities (that is, convocations, field trips, pep rallies, special programs or speakers, and so on) and formal transitions (that is, passing periods, restroom breaks) take over 25 percent of mandated time. Based upon Rosenshine's data, it would appear that only about seven of every ten mandated days is actually available for academic or instructional purposes. The remaining three days are consumed by the nonacademic activities cited above.

The next circle in Figure 11.2 represents the amount of allocated time during which the teacher is actually conducting instructional activities. This is called **academic instruction time.** Just as allocated time is always less than mandated time, the amount of time spent in academic instruction is always less than is allocated. Doyle (1986) reports that less than 60 percent of allocated time in elementary schools and less than 45 percent of allocated time in high schools is spent in academic instruction. While allocated and mandated time are often beyond the control of teachers, maximizing the amount of allocated time spent in academic instruction *is* their responsibility.

Most teachers do not realize how much class time they spend in noninstructional tasks and activities. For example, although a seventh-grade social studies teacher may have 50 minutes of allocated time five days a week, not all of the 250 minutes allocated to instruction will be devoted to it. Some time will be spent socializing, organizing or preparing instructional materials, giving directions, or intervening in discipline problems. Additional time will be lost to absenteeism, administrative requests, and other disruptions. Using Doyle's data, of the 250 minutes allocated over five days, fewer than 145 minutes will be spent in academic activities.

Returning again to Figure 11.2, let's now examine the smallest but most critical circle. This inner circle represents the amount of academic instruction time during which students are *actively* and *successfully* engaged in learning and is referred to as **academic learning time (ALT),** or engaged time. Two factors are considered in determining academic learning time. First is the amount of time a given student is actively engaged in the instruction/learning process. Rather than daydreaming, doodling, or misbehaving, the student is attentive to the learning activity. This attention may be overt, such as answering a question, participating in a discussion, solving pencil-and-paper problems, manipulating concrete materials in an experiment, or talking to another student about the instructional task. It may also be less obvious, as when students are actively thinking about the academic task even if they do not exhibit any outward signs of engagement.

The second factor considered in ALT is a student's success at the activity. If a student is actively engaged in completing an academic activity incorrectly, she may actually be practicing and learning an incorrect process. For academic instruction time to be considered "engaged," or academic learning time, *given learners must be actively engaged in meaningful academic tasks at which they are mostly successful.*

This suggests that, even though teachers may be conducting instruction, it is unlikely that every student will be engaged in the activity at any given time. In fact, no individual student is likely to be engaged 100 percent of the time. Thus, more time is lost. Borich (1992) suggests that an effective teacher probably maintains an academic engagement rate of 80 to 95 percent. However, Rosenshine (1960) indicates that in most classrooms, students spend about 30 percent of instructional time engaged in academic activity under the supervision of a teacher or aide. If we consider Rosenshine's data in terms of our middle school social studies example, of the 145 minutes per week when the teacher was providing instruction, the typical student would be *engaged* for only about 50 minutes.

An examination of the tremendous loss of time between mandated and engaged time shows how critical it is for teachers to take full advantage of the time they have. As previously noted, while state and school officials generally set mandated or allocated time, teachers can increase their students' academic learning time through the skillful application of professional teaching skills.

One way to guard against loss of academic learning time is to be aware of potential detractors (Hargreaves, 1994). At the district level, time is frequently lost to snow days, weather delays, and teachers' strikes. At the school level, fire drills, convocations, trips, passing periods, lunch, recess, and homeroom periods reduce time. At the classroom level, time is lost by starting class late or ending early, by providing unmonitored study time, by spending too much time on administrative tasks, by using films, computers, or games excessively, by spending too much time on discipline problems, by failing to monitor or making too many transitions, or by straying from the lesson at hand.

How, then, can teachers improve their use of time? First, they should deliberately attempt to use most of the available time for instruction rather than other tasks. Begin and end each lesson on time. Have materials, equipment, and activities planned and ready so that you can begin as soon as the period begins. Establish and enforce rules requiring students to be on time and to be prepared for class. To avoid wasting time at the end of the lesson, plan more instruction than you think you will need. If you finish early, spend the remaining time reviewing with students rather than having them do individual seat work or giving them "free time." If individual seat work is assigned, monitor students to be sure they are engaged in the learning task. It is also helpful to use and enforce a signal which indicates to students that they may begin putting away their materials at the end of the lesson or period. This allows you to keep students involved for the maximum amount of time and prevents the problem created when students close their books or stand to leave while you are attempting to finish the lesson. Make sure, however, that you allow students sufficient time to put away materials before leaving the room or moving to another activity.

Try Activity 11.4

11.3 Are you good at managing your time? Do you think you will be better or worse at managing classroom time? How will you know?

Establishing and maintaining rules and procedures for routine activities can also provide more time for instruction by reducing the amount of time needed for giving directions. Chapter 12 provides detailed information about rules and procedures. Briefly, though, you should teach and enforce procedures for obtaining or returning materials and equipment, checking homework, making up missed work, and completing group or individual seat work. Similarly, when you must give directions, explain the tasks and procedures clearly and completely. Check for understanding of these procedures, answer students' questions, and give them feedback *before* telling them to begin.

Another important factor in increasing students' engagement is to create and maintain a highly interactive instructional pattern. Use a variety of instructional behaviors and alternatives. Make assignments interesting, relevant, and at a level that allows most students to complete them successfully without your guidance. Spend the majority of your classroom time in teacher-directed activities where you can more carefully monitor students' engagement. Randomly circulate around the room, especially when students are working in small groups or at individual seat work. Reinforce students verbally and nonverbally for remaining on task, and quickly redirect off-task behavior.

Maintaining Momentum   The concept of momentum is related to the effective use of time. Momentum refers to the flow of activities and to the pace of teaching and learning maintained in the classroom (Kounin, 1970). The most effective teachers maintain a smooth, relatively rapid instructional pace. Their classroom activities are orderly, and changes occur easily without disrupting the instructional flow since these teachers have established effective routines and follow them. The speed at which they conduct instructional activities, while brisk, matches the difficulty of the content and the students' abilities (Brophy, 1979).

Your skill in maintaining momentum is important when considered in light of the research on time. Your goal should be to maximize your students' engagement, to help them work through relevant materials and activities as quickly and as successfully as they can. By adapting the pace of your instruction to students' abilities and success and by working to maintain a smooth flow of classroom activities with few disruptions and little "down time," you help students learn more.

It is easier to maintain momentum in teacher-directed instructional activities than during seat work or small-group work (Gump, 1967, 1969; Walberg, 1991). Teacher-directed instruction allows the teacher greater control of the pace and flow of the lesson, whereas small-group or individual seat work relies heavily on students' motivation to maintain momentum.

You must consider how best to maintain momentum when planning and implementing instruction. The pace of instruction must be adapted to the difficulty or complexity of required tasks. For example, you must plan for and use a slower pace early in the learning process or when the task requires higher-order thinking skills. For lower-order tasks such as drill and practice or recitation, a quicker pace is more appropriate. Further, the pace should vary in your long-term plans, including your weekly and monthly reviews.

Effective teachers must learn to monitor and deal with concurrent classroom activities. While working with a small reading group in the back of the room, they must also be aware of and keep students working at their desks in the front of the room, at learning centers, or on projects. Momentum is enhanced when teachers organize their classrooms to minimize disruptions and time lost to giving directions or reexplaining. Rules and procedures which enable students to complete tasks on their own help reduce disruptions. Teachers must also be careful to avoid getting "bogged down" in unimportant or minor aspects of the topic, digressing from the topic at hand, or spending too much time with a single student or group of students.

Making Smooth Transitions   Instructional transitions are "points in instructional interactions when contexts change" (Doyle, 1986, p. 406). Instructional transitions require that teachers refocus students' attention on changes in the direction of a discussion or lesson. Transitions occur when you change the topic, its focus, or the activity at hand. Major transitions take place between class meetings or lessons (the time from the end of one class to the beginning of the next class), between lessons in the same room (particularly in elementary classrooms), and between different instructional activities within the same lesson (changing from lecture to lab work). Because major transitions often involve changes in equipment or location, they take more time, and when poorly planned, they are a major contributor to classroom disruption. We will discuss major transitions and how to deal with them more fully in Chapter 12.

Minor transitions occur within a lesson when the speaker moves from one aspect of the topic to another, when the speaker pauses, or when the speaker changes (a new speaker begins). These minor transitions are necessary and desirable because they help learners organize their thinking by signaling the move from one topic or aspect of the topic to another. They also allow more people to contribute to the discussion or lesson.

Transitions, particularly minor transitions, are frequent occurrences in classrooms and largely determine the smoothness and momentum of the lesson (Arlin, 1979). Poor transitions can greatly detract from effective use of instructional time. As a result, teachers should work to ensure that their transitions are few in number and that they are as well-organized and as brief as possible. Problems result when transitions are not well-structured, when students do not want to stop what they are doing or have not had sufficient time to complete the assigned task, or when the next instructional segment is delayed for some reason.

To make your instructional transitions smoother, you should practice the following routine. First, plan for the transitions. When preparing your lessons, you can predict points where changes in focus or activity will occur or when waiting is inevitable. You should determine what materials and procedures you will need to begin the next segment as quickly as possible and what both you and your students should do during the transition. An important part of planning for transitions is having all materials and equipment prepared, readily available, and in working order. Also, you can routinize daily or frequent transitions through patterns or procedures. For example, students can be taught what they are to do when they finish a test early, while you take roll, or when they move from one area of the room to another. Establishing these patterns saves time that might otherwise be spent giving directions and allows students to engage in constructive activities rather than just sit and wait. Figure 11.3 lists specific steps you can take to optimize your use of time.

FIGURE 11.3 Optimizing Instructional Time

1. Have materials and equipment ready prior to class.
2. Begin on time.
3. Establish and enforce rules for entering the classroom and beginning class.
4. Establish and enforce procedures for routine tasks and transitions, like turning in work and obtaining or putting away equipment, so that students can do these chores without your direction.
5. Plan more instructional material than you think you will need.
6. Maintain a relatively brisk instructional pace, varying the pace as needed to accommodate learners and match the difficulty of the content.
7. If you finish your planned lesson early, use the remaining time to review with students. Avoid giving students "free time" or individual seat work.
8. Establish a signal that informs students when they are to begin putting away their materials or when they are dismissed.
9. Maintain a highly interactive instructional pattern. Question all students, move frequently, use variety, and convey enthusiasm to help keep students actively engaged.

Conducting Interactive Instruction

Effective teachers are able to conduct instruction that keeps students actively involved in the lesson. In addition to establishing set and using variety to keep students motivated, the best teachers are skilled in questioning, in helping students come to a clear understanding of the content, and in monitoring understanding.

USING QUESTIONS

The most effective teachers establish and maintain highly interactive classrooms—classrooms characterized by student-student and teacher-student dialogue rather than simply teacher talk (Feden, 1994). Integral to this type of classroom is the teacher's ability to use questions effectively. Bellon, Bellon, and Blank (1992) state, "Questioning is the instructional process that is central to verbal interaction in the classroom. The questions teachers ask serve as the interface between teacher expectations and student responses" (p. 308). This interface in interactive teaching is critical because it shifts the focus from the teacher to the students (Moore, 1992).

Effective questions require students *to actively process information and compose an answer.* Good questions increase students' engagement, raise the level of thought, help students organize their thoughts, guide students more successfully through academic tasks, and allow the teacher to monitor understanding and provide feedback. In spite of the obvious value of good questions, it appears that teachers seldom use questions as effectively as they could (Cazden, 1986; Orstein, 1990). Most teachers' questioning patterns include giving information that is unnecessary or confusing, posing more than one question at a time, or failing to specify the nature of the expected answer (Sigel, 1990). What, then, do we know about good questions and questioning patterns?

Although questions comprise about one-third of the classroom interactions between teachers and students (Fisher, et al., 1984), only recently has educational research shown that effective questioning directly and indirectly influences the amount, level, and type of learning. Good and Brophy (1987) reviewed research on questioning and concluded that students learn more when teachers ask frequent questions and include a variety of questions in their lessons. Wilen and Clegg (1986) also reported that teacher questioning is related to increased achievement among students. Particularly important to our knowledge of questioning is Redfield and Rousseau's (1981) review of research on questioning, which revealed that teachers' use of higher-order questions promoted students' higher-order thinking. Morine-Dershimer and Beyerbach (1987) and Good and Brophy (1987) conclude that questions are important because the more frequently students interact with the teacher and their peers about the subject, the more they learn. The following discussion organizes what researchers know about questioning into three areas: asking questions, obtaining answers, and following up questions or reacting to student responses.

How to Ask Questions   If teachers want their questioning to be effective, they must be sure to phrase questions clearly and concisely. Too often, teachers ask questions that are almost impossible for students to answer accurately. They fail to make clear what it is they want to know of students or how they want them to answer. Clear questions use natural, unambiguous language appropriate to the level of the students. They are also concise, including only the words, terms, and information students need in order to answer the questions. They describe the specific points students should attend to, but they do not include unnecessary words or parenthetical expressions. Finally, they are directed toward academic content or the objectives of the lesson.

11.5   When you teach, do you ask lots of questions? Do you ever get nervous about asking questions when you're in front of a group? Why?

To be effective, questions should require students to *process* or think about what they are learning and to *compose* an answer. This means teachers should avoid asking questions which have only one answer or which are rhetorical. Closed-response questions, which can be answered with a simple yes-no or true-false response, allow students to guess at the answer without processing the content. Even when students do process what they have learned in order to answer a closed-response question, they can still *select* a response rather than *compose* one. It is easy to reword closed-response questions to require students to create more thoughtful, detailed responses.

Rhetorical questions, that is, questions asked for effect rather than to generate students' responses, are problematic because they can, over time, inhibit students' responses. Students become unsure whether a question is merely rhetorical or whether they are supposed to respond. For similar reasons, teachers should avoid including the answer within the question or answering a question themselves.

In addition, teachers should take care to ask only one question at a time. Many times teachers ask multiple questions without realizing it. While asking a question, they think of another aspect of the content they also want to address. As a result, it may not be clear whether one answer is expected for all the questions or whether a different answer is expected to each question. Similarly, students probably are confused when their teacher asks a question and then immediately rephrases it. This creates two problems. First, students' thinking about the original question is interrupted and, second, the rephrasing is often sufficiently different from the original to make the students wonder if it is a separate question.

An additional consideration in formulating and asking questions is the *type of question* or level of thought required of the students. Questions can be of several types or levels and are intended for a variety of purposes (Barden, 1995). Questions may be lower- or higher-order, convergent or divergent, narrow or broad, and content or process.

The lower- and higher-order delineations refer to the level of thought required in order to answer the question. Bloom's taxonomy, discussed in Chapter 5, is the most frequently used system for organizing questions along this hierarchy. Lower-order questions require students to respond at the knowledge, comprehension, and sometimes application levels of the taxonomy. Students can generally answer these questions using existing knowledge, either by recalling and then restating them, by rephrasing them, or by performing a task. Higher-order questions require the cognitive skills of analysis, synthesis, or evaluation and thus require more complex and original thinking.

Questions can also be categorized as convergent or divergent—labels which refer to the direction of thought required to reach an answer. In answering convergent questions, students' thought processes proceed from broad or general to narrow or specific. These questions require one or a small number of correct responses. Factual questions asking who, what, when, or where as well as closed-response (yes-no) questions are examples of convergent questions. These questions are most appropriate for helping to reinforce specific, important aspects of the content.

Divergent questions require thinking that moves from the narrow or specific to the broad or general. They require students to identify or generate several potential answers—any of which might be accurate. The difference between convergent and divergent questions is easy to see in mathematics instruction. Suppose students are presented with the numeric statement 7×9. A convergent question might be "What is seven times nine?" Students are expected to arrive at the one correct answer. This example is also a lower-order question. However, the same numeric statement (7×9) might also serve as the basis for a divergent question like "How many different ways could you determine what seven times nine is?" To answer this question, students might use simple addition, commutative property,

Try Activity 11.5

combinations of mathematical principles, manipulative solutions, or other creative methods to generate answers to the question. Rather than focus on the single correct answer, as in the convergent question, students must expand on or diverge from the initial facts to generate the answer.

Questions may also emphasize *content* or *process*. Content questions deal directly with the information being learned and make up about 80 percent of the questions teachers ask (Borich, 1992). The question and the expected answer are drawn directly from the content of instruction, and the teacher generally has a "correct" answer in mind. Content questions are often associated with lower-order cognitive processes. However, because they focus students' attention on important aspects of the content, they have been found to improve students' achievement (Borich, 1992). On the other hand, teachers use process questions to stimulate students' thinking. Although these questions deal with content, they place less emphasis on the "correctness" of answers and more on pushing students to think about the content in different, creative, or complex ways (Mencke & Pressley, 1994). Thus, process questions are generally higher-order and divergent. These questions are used much less often than content questions and are less closely related to achievement. However, they do appear to promote students' abilities to think at higher levels and to solve problems (Redfield & Rousseau, 1981).

Several common recommendations for improvement apply to each of these types of questions. First, just as in other aspects of instruction, you should use a variety of question types. Although most teachers rely heavily on lower-order, convergent questions, the importance of developing students' thinking and problem-solving abilities requires that you deliberately incorporate process, higher-order, and divergent questions into your lessons. Second, you should match the type and level of questions you ask to your objectives and your students. When teaching toward lower-order objectives, lower-order questions make sense. When your objectives include higher-order processes or when you want to promote students' critical thinking, you must integrate higher-order, divergent, and process questions into your lessons.

To ensure good phrasing and appropriate types of questions, you should consider your questions and questioning patterns when planning your lessons. After all, good class discussion and interaction don't just happen. Some questions emerge spontaneously from the lesson as a result of students' comments or questions. These you cannot plan in advance. However, you can write many of the critical questions into your lesson plan. There are at least four important reasons for doing this.

First, integrating planned questions into your lessons increases the likelihood that you will conduct an interactive lesson. Second, when you prepare questions in advance, you are more likely to focus them on the major objectives of the lesson. If you rely totally on spontaneous questions, you can easily get side-tracked and ask too many questions on one aspect of the lesson while neglecting others. Third, including some pivotal questions in the lesson plan makes it more likely that you will ask a variety of questions at a variety of levels. Divergent, higher-order, and process questions are more difficult to develop than are convergent, lower-order, and content questions. That may partly explain why teachers use them less often (Dillon, 1988; Gall, 1984; Pate & Bremer, 1967; Sigel, 1990). Preparing some of these questions in advance, even if you don't use them all, directs your attention toward more advanced levels of thinking. Fourth, writing pivotal questions in advance makes it more likely that you will phrase the questions clearly and concisely.

Obtaining Good Answers After teachers have developed and phrased their questions, they must get students to respond to them. As mentioned, asking clear and varied types of questions at a variety of levels promotes students' participation. Research also suggests that soliciting answers in certain ways can enhance the effectiveness of

FIGURE 11.4 Sequence of Teachers' Questioning

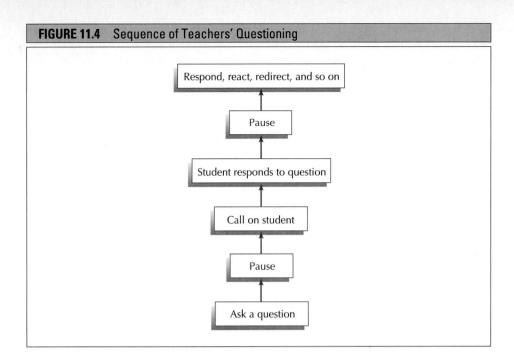

questions and the quality and quantity of students' responses. It is particularly important that teachers use wait time and that all students participate.

Wait time refers to the pauses that effective teachers use when they solicit and react to students' responses. Rowe's (1974) work has served as the basis for most subsequent research on wait time. The early research of Rowe and others focused on the importance of asking a question, pausing, and then calling on a student to respond. More recently, investigators have determined that in addition to pausing after the question is asked, it is also important to pause before reacting to the student's answer or calling on a second student to respond (Tobin, 1987). Thus, wait time includes (1) the pause between the teacher's question and the student's response and (2) the pause between a student's response and the teacher's reaction. Figure 11.4 depicts this sequence.

Rowe (1974) found that after asking a question, most teachers paused for less than 1 second before calling on a student to respond. In contrast, the most effective teachers included pauses of from 3 to 5 seconds after asking a question and before reacting to a student's response. Research on wait time has found that those 3- to 5-second pauses produce the following desirable and important outcomes: students' responses are longer and more thorough, the cognitive level of students' responses is higher (for example, they display more analysis, synthesis, and evaluation), students volunteer more information to support their responses, and students' confidence in their responses is greater. In addition, more students respond to questions, particularly those labeled as "slow." Finally, positive interactions among students and between students and the teacher increase, as do the number of relevant questions students ask (Berliner, 1987; Rowe, 1974; Sadker & Sadker, 1986; Tobin, 1987; Wang, Haertel, & Walberg, 1993–94).

Increasing wait time seems a simple thing to do, but, especially for beginning teachers, it often proves difficult. A pause of 5 seconds can seem like an eternity when you are insecure about the effectiveness of your instruction or unsure whether anyone will answer your questions! Still, as you learn to incorporate these pauses, they become easier, and they give all students increased time to think and participate.

You can do several things to make your use of wait time more effective. First, you should adopt a policy restraining students from shouting out their answers.

11.6 Why might you feel that the pause you use after a question is longer than it really is?

Allowing callouts prevents you from controlling the length of the pause after your question and reduces wait time. After asking a question, count to five in your head while scanning the room, then call on a student to answer. Do not repeat, rephrase, or add to the question until at least several seconds have passed. Doing so interrupts students' thinking and may interfere with their ability to respond. When students respond, it is important you do not interrupt before they have completed their answers, even if they are absolutely correct. When they are finished answering, pause, use a few seconds to think about their answers, allow other students to think about the answer, and consider how best to react or follow up.

The use of wait time must be balanced against the brisk pace needed to maintain the momentum of a lesson. Specifically, teachers should match wait time with the level or difficulty of the question asked. Lower-order, convergent questions generally require shorter pauses than higher-order, divergent, and process questions. Vary wait time to accommodate the students' need to process the question, generate an answer, or consider the response of another student.

The second factor to consider during the response phase of questioning is how to maximize student participation. Morine-Dershimer and Beyerbach (1987) found that students' learning and affect were related to the number of opportunities students had to participate in the lesson and to respond to questions. Thus, a goal of your questioning should be to ensure that all students have an equal opportunity to respond successfully. Questioning can help you monitor understanding, keep students engaged, and serve as a measure of the success of your instruction, but it is imperative that you ask *all* students to respond to your questions. This is especially difficult but important in a class with diverse abilities or cultural backgrounds.

Mastering the effective use of wait time will increase participation in your questioning. However, most teachers still call primarily on volunteers to respond to questions. This practice results in an unfair distribution of questions and unequal opportunities to respond (Coladarci & Gage, 1984). Effective questioning requires that you call on all students, especially nonvolunteers. A good practice is to ask a question, pause to allow all students to think about the question and develop a response, and then to select a student to respond. To ensure an equitable distribution of questions, some have suggested using a pattern in selecting students to answer (Anderson, Evertson, & Brophy, 1979). For example, you might write each student's name on a note card and then randomly select from the students' cards for participation. Using a pattern enables you to know which students have already been asked to respond. To keep all students alert, even when they have already answered a question, it is a good idea to vary your pattern and to call randomly on students to make follow-up responses.

Incorporating wait time and equitably distributing the opportunity to respond work together to improve the effectiveness of your questioning. Wait time allows more students the opportunity to process an answer. While some students can do this relatively quickly (usually those who volunteer most frequently), others require more time to arrive at an answer. Thus, wait time increases the number of students who can respond accurately to the question. Calling on all students, even when they do not volunteer, maintains students' engagement. It allows all students some opportunity to interact with you and to be successful, and provides you with a more complete assessment of how well students understand the material.

Following Up Students' Responses　After a student has responded to your question, you must respond or react to the reply. This phase of the questioning process is called follow-up. Your follow-up behavior will either encourage or discourage thoughtful, successful participation in your lessons and, thus, the long-term success of your instruction (Latham, 1997).

11.7　Does it make you feel uncomfortable when a teacher calls on you to respond when you haven't volunteered? Why or why not? Could the teacher help you feel better about it?

"Say your car gets 23 miles per gallon at 55 miles per hour and your fuel tank holds 16 gallons. If gas costs 86¢ per gallon and you know the capitals of all 50 states, how much will it cost to drive to the capital of Nebraska?"

The most frequent though ineffective teacher's reaction is "okay" or "uh-huh" (Sadker & Sadker, 1986). Instead of such routinized and meaningless responses, you should attempt to clarify, synthesize, expand, modify, raise the level of, or evaluate students' responses. The effective use of follow-up is based upon the accuracy and confidence of the students' responses (Good, 1988; Rosenshine & Stevens, 1986). They can range from correct and confident to wrong and careless. Rosenshine and Stevens (1986) suggest the following responses and reactions:

1. When a student responds correctly and confidently, accept and acknowledge the response and move on. Do not overpraise.

2. When a student responds correctly but hesitantly, provide feedback to the student or use additional questions that encourage the student to determine why the response is correct. Before moving on, be certain the student understands why the answer was correct.

3. When a student responds confidently but incorrectly, reinforce the initial effort, then use additional questions to help the student arrive at the correct answer. Avoid giving the student the answer or calling on another student to respond. You may give reinforcement for participation and effort, but there should be no confusion regarding the fact that you are reinforcing participation, not accuracy.

4. When a student responds incorrectly and carelessly, provide the correct response and move on. You should never avoid following up or correcting an incorrect answer.

Generally then, follow-up is used any time the student fails to respond accurately and/or confidently. These follow-ups can be divided into four types: providing the correct answer, probing, redirecting, or rephrasing. Providing the correct answer is advisable only when a student has responded carelessly and incorrectly. The remaining three follow-up methods deserve discussion.

Probing means asking additional questions of the responding student to help expand or raise the level of the response (Danielson, 1996). Probing questions are often intended to focus attention on important aspects of the question that enable the student to improve the response (see Figure 11.5). In this case, probing should include convergent questions phrased in simple but not condescending terms. Frequently, more than one question is needed to address particular aspects of the original question or response and to guide the student toward a more correct or complete answer.

FIGURE 11.5   Examples of Follow-up Questioning Techniques

Probing (to raise the level of a student's response)

Teacher: "Why might President Ford have pardoned former President Nixon?" (Pause) "David?"

David: "To prevent embarrassment of the Republican party."

Teacher: "Can you explain how the pardon might prevent embarrassment?"

David: "Well, if the investigation had continued, they might have found that there were a lot of other people, mostly Republicans, who were involved."

Teacher: "Why do you think that might be true?"

David: "Hmmm. Well, because since then some others have admitted being involved or named people who were."

Teacher: "Okay, so let's say President Ford doesn't pardon Nixon and all of this is revealed, what do you think would be the result?"

Probing (to help a student answer correctly)

Teacher: "Ball, bed, bug, baby. These are all words that begin with the *b* sound. What are some other words that begin with the *b* sound?" (Pause) "Danielle?"

Danielle: (Silence)

Teacher: "Okay, does Danielle start with a *b* sound?"

Danielle: "No, it's a *d*."

Teacher: "Right. What about Brittany? Does Brittany start with a *b* sound?"

Danielle: "Yeah!"

Teacher: "Okay, Danielle. Think of the sound. What words do you know that start with that sound?"

Danielle: (Pause) "Bunny!"

Teacher: "Right! Bunny!"

Redirecting (after an incorrect response)

Teacher: "What was the name of the Watergate special prosecutor?" (Pause) "Trevor?"

Trevor: "Strom Thurmond?"

Teacher: "No. Thurmond is a senator. What was the name of the special prosecutor?" (Pause) "Steve?"

Steve: "Archibald Cox."

Teacher: "Yes."

Rephrasing (to clarify a question)

Teacher: "Why did Gerald Ford pardon Richard Nixon?"
(Pause)
(No student responses)
"What was the reason Ford gave for the pardon in the speech we just watched?" (Pause) "Kassandra?"

Kassandra: "He said he thought the country needed to put the issue behind us and move on."

Probing can also be used to raise the level of a student's response. As noted earlier, teachers generally ask convergent, content questions at the lower cognitive levels. Further, most students respond with lower-order, convergent answers, even when the teacher has asked a higher-order or divergent question (Cazden, 1986). Probing can be used after such a response to prompt the student to use higher-order processes. Simple ways of doing this include asking students to explain why they responded as they did, to provide an example which supports their answer, or to describe how their response would change if a particular aspect of the original question had been different.

Redirecting is another way of following up an incorrect response. When redirecting, the teacher asks another student to answer the same question (see Figure 11.5). This method of follow-up is highly effective with students whose academic self-concepts are strong. It appears that students who are academically confident are challenged by this technique and motivated to work harder. However, redirecting is not effective with students whose academic self-concepts are weak. In fact, redirecting following an insecure student's incorrect response is likely to result in reduced self-concept, motivation, participation, and learning (Coladarci & Gage, 1984).

TABLE 11.1 The Do's and Don'ts of Effective Questioning

Do	Don't
1. Match questions to the objectives and use a variety of question levels and types.	1. Emphasize only lower-order or convergent questions.
2. Ask lots of questions throughout the lesson.	2. Use questions mainly to review at the end of the lesson.
3. Ask a question, pause, and then call on a student by name to respond.	3. Allow callouts or fail to include pauses after your questions.
4. Ensure that all students get equal opportunities to successfully answer questions.	4. Rely on volunteers.
5. Follow up lower-order, inaccurate, and incomplete answers.	5. Overlook or allow to go uncorrected inappropriate or incomplete answers.
6. Write questions, especially critical questions, into your lesson plan.	6. Rely solely on your ability to generate spontaneous questions during interaction.
7. Keep questions clear, brief, and to the point.	7. Use long questions or ask multiple questions simultaneously.
8. Ask questions to keep students engaged.	8. Ask questions as a punitive, disciplinary tool.
9. Write the objectives and summary of the lesson as questions.	9. Devise questions only on major points.
10. Match nonverbal behavior with the questions you ask.	10. Convey disinterest in asking questions or in students' responses.

Rephrasing simply means restating the same question in different terms. When students fail to respond to a teacher's question, it is often due to poor phrasing of the initial question. Thus, rewording the question can make it clearer, simpler, or focus students' attention on critical aspects (see Figure 11.5). Rephrasing generally is not an effective follow-up technique and should be avoided. A better technique is to elicit some type of response, then use probing questions to help the student arrive at a correct response. While all teachers occasionally ask poorly stated questions, careful consideration of questions during planning, monitoring their effectiveness during instruction, and questioning with confidence will eventually reduce the need for rephrasing.

To summarize, questioning is a vital aspect of effective, interactive teaching. It promotes a number of desirable outcomes and can be used for several purposes. Table 11.1 provides an overview of correct and incorrect questioning techniques.

Try Activity 11.6

PROVIDING CLEAR INSTRUCTION

Throughout this chapter we have focused on teachers' attributes and behaviors that appear to directly or indirectly promote greater learning, achievement, and motivation. Each characteristic or behavior is grounded in research. We now turn our attention to a complex teaching skill that may contribute more to teacher effectiveness than any other.

Instructional clarity has been the focus of much research ever since Rosenshine and Furst (1971) identified it as the "most promising teacher variable related to student achievement" (p. 107). **Instructional clarity** refers to the teacher's ability to provide instruction which helps *students come to a clear understanding of the material*. Thus, clarity is something students achieve, not something the teacher does. However, research has identified specific teacher behaviors that students say help them achieve this clarity of understanding (Bush, 1976; Bush, Kennedy, & Cruickshank, 1977; Kennedy, Cruickshank, Bush, & Myers, 1978; Hines, 1981; Hines, Kennedy, & Cruickshank, 1985).

According to students, clear teachers emphasize important points by repeating them, writing them on the board, pausing after stating them, and reviewing them. They monitor students' clarity of understanding by asking questions and providing students with activities and experiences that allow them to apply their knowledge. When students do not understand, clear teachers repeat, review, or rephrase important points. Not surprisingly, teachers who most often and most proficiently use these behaviors to help students understand are associated with significantly greater student learning and satisfaction than teachers who do not (Gliessman, Pugh, Brown, & Archer, 1989; Good & Grouws, 1977; Hines, 1981; Metcalf, 1992; Metcalf & Cruickshank, 1991; Williams, 1983).

The teachers' behaviors that make instruction clear apply not only to the ability to explain content clearly, but also to the ability to structure presentations. And, importantly, this lesson-structuring problem applies to both teacher-directed and student-directed instruction (Feden, 1994; Metcalf, 1991). These specific behaviors involve: (1) preparing and entering the lesson, (2) introducing and emphasizing content, (3) elaborating on important ideas or concepts, and (4) monitoring students' understanding and remediating when students fail to understand. The following discussion of teacher clarity will be organized around these four topics.

Preparing and Entering the Lesson   Clear instruction is logically organized and is conducted in a way that helps students see the relationships between major concepts or ideas. Accordingly, clear teachers organize their lesson content and activities logically, inform students of the objectives of the lesson, and introduce the content or activities step-by-step. During planning, these teachers determine the most logical way to introduce content based upon their students' abilities, previous learning, and the natural structure of the content. Chapter 5 explained some of the ways this can be done (for example, chronologically). For logical organization to make instruction clearer, the organization must be obvious and logical *to students*.

At the beginning of the lesson, teachers should inform students of the lesson objectives. As noted in our discussion of establishing set, teachers should provide an overview of the lesson to help students establish a mental framework for the concepts or activities and to enable them to monitor their own understanding. Students find instruction clearer when the teacher gives it step by step. In other words, teachers should provide instruction and instructional activities in a way that makes the relationship between the concepts obvious to students. Doing so helps students incorporate the new learning with previous learning more accurately.

11.8 Have you ever had a teacher who was obviously knowledgeable, but not clear in helping you understand? How did you feel? Did the teacher realize the problem?

Introducing and Emphasizing Important Points   Beyond planning and organizing, clear instruction focuses students' attention on important aspects of the instruction. A common way to do this is to write the major points on the board and/or have students record them. It is important, however, that you monitor your use of the board to ensure that you do not overuse it for minor or unimportant points. Students will perceive things you write on the board as important. Consequently, if you fill the board with minor points or fail to put some or all of the major points on the board, the effectiveness of this technique is reduced.

Another way to reinforce important aspects of the lesson is to point them out through verbal structuring or cuing. Enumerating important points helps structure them. For example, "The first point we will discuss is . . ." "Second, . . ." and "Finally, . . ." enables students to organize their thoughts and the content. Likewise, comments such as, "It is important for you to remember this" or "Listen carefully because this is an important point" alert students to pay close attention to what you are about to say. Repeating important points also cues students. You might combine these reinforcers into a pattern in which you state a point, pause or write it on the board, and then repeat it. To provide even more reinforcement, you could note that this is an important point, state it, write it on the board, and then repeat it.

Finally, you reinforce major points when you review or summarize them. In Chapter 5 we applied the term *closure* to this element of the lesson. Upon completing the lesson or important segments of the lesson (immediately preceding a transition), you should summarize or have students summarize the major ideas of the lesson segment. This serves to repeat major points, further identify them as important, help achieve closure, and prepare students for a smooth transition to the next segment.

Elaborating on Important ideas or Concepts In addition to identifying and reinforcing major points for students, you can deepen their understanding of the content by providing examples, explanations, and elaborations. Examples and nonexamples (items that do *not* fit the concept) that illustrate the major points can be vital to students' understanding. Examples can be verbal, written, pictorial, or concrete depending upon the content and the level of the learners. For instance, if learners are familiar with ants, merely noting that ants are an example of an insect may be sufficient. They do not need to see an ant for the example to be useful. However, if you were to use a potentially unfamiliar example of an insect, such as a walking stick, a concrete or pictorial example might be necessary. Further, you would need to make clear how or why the example relates to the concept—in this case, what characteristics classify a creature as an insect. Adding nonexamples, such as a scorpion, would further clarify the concept.

Relatedly, clear instruction helps students see how things are similar or different. You can describe, demonstrate, explain, or show students how two ideas, concepts, examples, or ways of doing things are alike and how they differ. Again, this type of instructional behavior helps students assimilate new information more accurately. When the lesson involves learning a task or skill, it is important that you demonstrate the task and, while doing so, explain what you are doing and why. For example, if you were helping students learn to draw circles with a compass, you might place the pointer and explain why you put it there; explain that the pointer must be kept securely in place with one hand, and show them how to do so; place the marker end of the compass solidly on the paper; and then demonstrate and explain how to turn the compass, ensuring that the mark is complete.

Students also note that clear teachers explain unfamiliar words, whereas unclear teachers often fail to do so. A good rule of thumb is to assume that all new terms are unfamiliar to students and explain or define them *before* using them in the lesson. Finally, students' understanding is enhanced when you briefly pause after introducing something important. Just as wait time allows students to think about a question, pausing after introducing an important point allows students to think about it. It also signals the importance of the ideas.

Ensuring Students' Understanding The final aspect of instructional clarity involves monitoring and correcting students' understanding by providing opportunities for students to apply the concepts or ideas. Critical to this is your ability to use frequent questions at a variety of levels. In addition to asking questions that assess students' understanding, you should build time for student-generated questions into the lesson. Often, if you have established an open and interactive climate, simply including a long pause after a lesson segment will prompt students who do not understand to ask for clarification. You may also call for students' questions by asking "Are there any questions?" However, in such a general call for questions, extended wait time is critical. Many students will have to think through the content to determine whether they need to ask questions, some will need time to formulate the question they want to ask, and some will need time to work up the courage to ask. Thus, after inviting questions, it would not be inappropriate to pause for as long as 5 to 10 seconds while scanning the room. A better alternative would be to ask for specific questions, such as "What questions do you have about the three points we just discussed?" and then follow up to see how well students understand.

FIGURE 11.6 Behaviors That Characterize Clear Teachers

1. The lesson is planned and implemented in an organized manner.

2. Students are informed of the lesson objectives in advance.

3. The lesson is conducted step by step.

4. The teacher draws students' attention to new or important points by writing them on the board, by repeating them, by reviewing them at appropriate points in the lesson, and by incorporating deliberate pauses which allow time for processing and reflection.

5. The teacher presents and works examples that explain and support the concept or ideas being taught.

6. The teacher explains unfamiliar words before using them in the lesson and points out similarities and differences between ideas.

7. The teacher asks students lots of questions and gives application exercises to find out if students understand the content.

8. The teacher carefully monitors students' work for understanding.

9. The teacher encourages and allows time for students to ask questions.

10. When students do not understand, the teacher repeats main points, presents additional examples or explanation, or elaborates until the students achieve clear understanding.

Try Activity 11.7

In addition to allowing time for questions, you should include activities that ask your students to demonstrate examples, then closely monitor their performance and provide corrective feedback as needed. In Chapter 5 this was described as providing guided practice. You can have students work individually at their seats, in small groups, or at the board with the entire class contributing. When a student cannot answer a question, cannot accurately apply the content to the examples, or asks a question indicating misunderstanding, it is important that you correct the misunderstanding. Several of the earlier mentioned behaviors, like repeating things, rephrasing, probing, or providing additional examples and further explanation may help clear up confusion.

To summarize, instructional clarity refers to a broad and important set of teachers' behaviors. The major focus of clarity is on helping students understand what you have taught. Remember, clarity is something the student, not the teacher, achieves. However, by learning to use behaviors which make instruction clearer to students, you can greatly improve the effectiveness of your teaching. Figure 11.6 summarizes ten specific behaviors related to clear instruction.

MONITORING STUDENTS' PROGRESS

Effective teachers are adept at monitoring students' understanding, not just their behavior. They carefully and continually assess students' performance and progress and check for understanding in a variety of ways. If students seem to lack understanding, it cues effective teachers to review and possibly adapt their instruction. Monitoring also conveys teachers' interest in their students' progress and task orientation. If the teacher has established an interactive environment in which students participate freely by asking and answering questions, many opportunities will be available for monitoring understanding.

Research has not directly related monitoring student understanding to improved learning. As noted, however, monitoring is an important element of instructional clarity. It is also closely tied to the effective use of instructional time and to effective feedback, each of which has been found to influence students' learning.

Monitoring is especially critical in the early stages of learning when misunderstandings or lack of background knowledge are most likely to affect students. Monitoring during this time allows teachers to correct students before they learn and habituate improper patterns of thinking or behavior. As we will discuss in detail later, it also allows teachers to provide feedback to help students understand why their performance is correct.

You can monitor student understanding in numerous formal and informal ways. Tests, quizzes, homework, and projects are examples of formal monitoring. Although formal monitoring is important, particularly in determining grades, informal monitoring is more frequent, immediate, and can impact more directly on instructional behavior and learning. Good teachers are constantly aware, or "withit" (Kounin, 1970). They ask many questions of all students, provide a supportive, open environment in which students feel free to ask questions or clarify misunderstandings, and they watch for verbal and nonverbal indications that students do not understand.

Specifically, you can improve your ability to monitor students' understanding in several ways. Establish set and use advance organizers at the beginnings of lessons to help students understand the task and monitor their own progress. Get to know students and call on them by name. Move around the room to monitor attention and stay in closer proximity to all students. Maximize interactive, whole-group instruction and minimize small-group or individual work, especially when no additional adult help is available. Use good questioning techniques: call on all students—not just those who raise their hands; ask questions at a variety of cognitive levels; and allow wait time. Maintain eye contact with all students by scanning the room for both understanding and misbehavior. Convey openness and availability for help. Spend very little time sitting at your desk, even when students are engaged in individual seat work. Instead, move around, scan, avoid turning your back to the class, and be careful not to spend too much time with any one student or group of students. As you will see in Chapter 12, these behaviors are also characteristics of teachers who are effective classroom managers.

PROVIDING FEEDBACK AND REINFORCEMENT

During the instructional process, effective teachers frequently provide students with information about their academic performance. They most commonly do this through feedback and reinforcement. Although similar, feedback and reinforcement are not the same. Reinforcement is meant to improve students' motivation, while feedback is intended to inform students about the accuracy of their performance. In order to use these skills effectively, teachers must understand each of them and how to apply them.

Both reinforcement and feedback are ways of responding to students' performance. They are skills that teachers employ after a student has done something—for example, answered a question, contributed to a discussion, turned in homework, or completed a project. Gagné (1985) notes that in a classroom where the teacher has established an interactive tone, opportunities for teachers to provide feedback and reinforcement arise naturally and almost constantly. Zahorik (1987) indicates that about one-third of classroom interactions are teachers' responding behaviors. Thus, a teacher's ability to respond appropriately can greatly influence students' performance and motivation.

Feedback Feedback (sometimes called *knowledge of results,* or *KR*) is primarily intended to (1) inform students about the quality and accuracy of their performance and (2) help them learn how to monitor and improve their own learning. For example, teachers use feedback on students' papers to inform them of how well they did in comparison to some standard, what could be improved, and how to improve. The information teachers provide through feedback relates directly to the quality or accuracy of the student's academic performance (Walberg, 1991).

For some students, feedback can also provide reinforcement by helping them feel more secure in their ability to complete the task successfully. However, feedback is not always reinforcing, nor is it intended to be.

11.9 Did you ever feel as if a teacher were "clueless" about your lack of understanding? How did it make you feel? Why did the teacher seem to remain unaware?

Teachers must be able to use both feedback and reinforcement effectively. However, skill in providing feedback is more important in helping students learn than ability to provide reinforcement, particularly praise (Wittrock, 1986). According to Bloom and Bourbon (1980), "It is more important to tell students when they are wrong than when they are right, but the most productive approach is to tell them why they are wrong" (p. 543). While feedback helps the learner to accurately understand and successfully complete necessary tasks, it does not necessarily reinforce or reward the student's performance.

Effective feedback includes information about: (1) the *criteria* used to evaluate performance, (2) how the *student's performance relates* to the standard, and (3) specifically how the performance can or should be *improved* (Butler & Nisan, 1986; Elawar & Corno, 1985; Wittrock, 1986). Most people think of feedback as verbal or written comments from the teacher. However, students often learn about the adequacy of their performance simply by observing or comparing their own performance with some standard. Thus, while students can learn from feedback provided by the teacher or peers, they can also learn by watching or listening to their performance through video- or audiotaping. The immediate goal of feedback is to improve students' understanding and performance. A long-range goal is to enable learners to judge for themselves the adequacy of their own work or performance (Wittrock, 1986).

Several principles can make teachers' feedback more effective:

1. Provide feedback as frequently as possible—every day for every student, if possible. It is important that you plan and maintain a highly interactive environment providing a variety of opportunities for students to practice or perform, and that you monitor and provide feedback on these performances.

2. Provide feedback as soon after performance as possible. For example, return papers quickly, try to grade immediately following performance, and provide verbal feedback while monitoring students' practice.

3. Make your feedback specific rather than general. For example, use students' names and comment specifically on their performance instead of simply saying "good job" or writing "weak here."

4. Focus feedback on the *quality* of the student's performance, not on his or her intentions or motivations. Good feedback can convey confidence in a student's ability without giving the impression that incomplete or inaccurate work is acceptable and without appearing cold and impersonal. One way to do this is to include feedback on the process (how to do it better) along with the adequacy of the performance.

5. Design and use feedback that teaches students how to gauge their own progress and performance. Gradually allow students to assume more and more responsibility for assessing their progress. Allow them to score their own or each other's papers and provide mutual feedback, to engage in peer editing as a part of the writing process, to watch or listen to recordings of their performances, and so on.

Reinforcement Reinforcement is intended to strengthen and increase the frequency of a desirable behavior or response, usually by providing some type of reward. Reinforcement lets students know when they have done something well in the hope that they will do it again or with greater frequency. When a normally quiet student voluntarily responds to a question, you might attempt to reinforce him, perhaps through a smile or gesture, in the hope that he will contribute more often in the future. Your focus should be on rewarding the student for his participation (that is, his behavior), not necessarily on the accuracy of his response. Chapter 12 will discuss this type of reinforcement further.

In contrast to feedback, which is directed toward improving the quality of students' performance, reinforcement is directed toward increasing motivation.

Often reinforcement is provided through verbal praise, but it can take many forms. Repeating or paraphrasing a student's comment or answer or including it in your discussion can be reinforcing. Nonverbal expressions like nods or smiles, eye contact, gestures, or proximity may also reinforce students. More tangibly, reinforcement can take the form of free time, candy, tokens, or other rewards.

Reinforcement, particularly in the form of praise or rewards, is only marginally effective in increasing learning (Brophy, 1981; Walberg, 1991). In fact, the relationship between learning and the use of praise seems to be curvilinear. That is, increasing the use of praise will help students learn more only up to a point. After that, increased praise will probably diminish learning. One reason for this may be that praise and other rewards are reinforcing only if the student perceives them to be. If the reward is embarrassing or of no interest to the student, the reward is likely to diminish rather than increase learning (Lepper, 1983; Wittrock, 1986). A second problem with praise and reinforcement is that teachers often unknowingly reinforce the wrong behavior (Callahan, Clark, & Kellough, 1992; O'Leary & O'Leary, 1977). For example, to get an unsuccessful student to contribute more often to class discussions, teachers may praise an incorrect or inappropriate contribution rather than the behavior of participating. The result may be that the student does contribute more often, but also learns inaccurate content.

Because reinforcement focuses on students' motivation and self-concept, it is most important early in the learning process and with low-achieving students. However, teachers seldom use it in these situations (Brophy, 1981). Reinforcement is most likely to be successful (1) when it specifically identifies the behavior or performance being rewarded, (2) when it is contingent upon desired behavior or performance (it is not offered when students respond or behave incorrectly), and (3) when it is believable (O'Leary & O'Leary, 1977). Criticism (the opposite of praise) can be effective with high-achieving students when used in moderation. Generally, however, it is not effective in promoting learning, and it often is counterproductive, diminishing students' self-concept and motivation (Beamer, 1979; Rosenshine & Furst, 1971).

Although a powerful tool, reinforcement should be used sparingly and with caution. Brophy (1981) notes that teachers should try "structuring the classroom in order to elicit good student performances in the first place rather than on reinforcing good performance after it has been elicited" (p. 16). Teachers should provide heavy reinforcement and feedback to all students early in the learning process and to low-achieving students throughout. Especially with older students, reinforcement and praise should be low-key, private, and specific to the student's performance.

Reinforcement can and should focus on both motivation and outcome. However, it should be keyed to desirable performance, and the teacher should make clear the specific behavior being reinforced. Although some students should be rewarded for participation even if the response is incorrect, make clear that the reward is for *participation*, not incorrect *performance*. When offering reinforcement or praise, be certain to match verbal and nonverbal behavior. That is, don't tell a student she did a nice job with a scowl on your face! Closely monitor the effectiveness of your reinforcement of each student. Remember, although you may intend your actions to be reinforcing, the student may not perceive them that way. Finally, allow yourself to be somewhat spontaneous with your use of praise; it is more sincere.

 11.10 Do you agree that feedback is more important in promoting student learning than reinforcement? Why or why not?

 11.11 Why do you think teachers emphasize reinforcement and neglect adequate feedback?

Some Final Thoughts

Running through all the specific behaviors discussed in Chapters 10 and 11 is the notion of providing students with instruction that will maximize their learning and their motivation to learn. Establishing set helps students focus. Momentum, variety, and enthusiasm maintain students' interest and engagement. Questions, when used well, help students process the lesson content in order to better understand it. Thus, although we have emphasized teachers' personal attributes and professional behavior, we must always remember that these are merely efficient means to desirable ends. They are not ends in themselves. For example, questions are not used for their own sake, but to help students learn more and better. However, much evidence indicates that these attributes and behaviors are critical in maximizing learning and motivation. They are the foundation upon which instructional alternatives and classroom management strategies are built. The better you are able to use them, the more effective your use of any instructional method, alternative, or strategy will be.

CHAPTER SUMMARY

11.12 What can you do now to help ensure that you will make use of what is known about effective teaching in your own classroom?

- Effective teachers possess a repertoire of professional skills that enable them to help students learn more. These professional skills are more open to improvement than personal attributes are. They can be organized around four aspects of instruction: engaging and maintaining students' attention, optimizing the use of instructional time, promoting meaningful teacher-student interaction, and providing effective feedback and reinforcement.

- Skilled teachers engage students' attention and maintain their interest and motivation by establishing set at the beginning of the lesson and incorporating variety in their lessons.

- There are three major types of set. Orientation set engages students in a new instructional activity. Transition set helps students see the relationship between past and present learning. Evaluative set establishes what students may already know about a topic.

- The beginning of a lesson is critical because it establishes a climate or tone for the lesson. The beginning of the lesson should engage students' interest through an interesting or provocative problem; should establish an interactive climate that encourages students to participate; should make students aware early in the lesson of the major topics, objectives, or tasks for the lesson; and should make clear the relationship between the current lesson and previous lessons.

- An effective teacher uses variety in nonverbal behavior, instructional approaches, types of assessment, and a host of other areas. Variability, which Rosenshine and Furst (1971) found to be closely related to students' learning, probably increases learning by helping students remain more interested and engaged.

- The most effective teachers maximize the time available for instruction. The three factors most closely related to the efficient use of instructional time are time on task, momentum, and smooth transitions.

- *Time on task* is a broad term that refers to the amount of time students are actively engaged in academic tasks. Generally, the more time students spend actively engaged in academic tasks, the more they learn. However, only a small percentage of available time is actually used for academic tasks.

- Instructional time can be organized around four levels. Mandated time is the formal time scheduled for school or academic activities: for example, the length of the school year, day, or period. Allocated time is the amount of mandated time intended solely for academic activities. It excludes such things as passing or lunch periods. Academic instruction time is the amount of allocated time during which the teacher is conducting instructional activities. This is time left after taking attendance, giving directions, and so on. Academic learning time is the amount of time a given student spends actively engaged in academic tasks she is mostly successful at doing. This eliminates the part of academic learning time when the student may not be paying attention or may be inaccurately learning the content.

- From mandated to academic learning time, much opportunity for learning is lost. Effective teachers maximize students' engagement by beginning and ending on time, minimizing time spent giving directions, establishing rules and procedures that minimize disruptions, and actively monitoring students' engagement. They also create a highly interactive and varied environment that gets students' attention and holds it throughout the lesson.

- Momentum refers to the flow and pace of classroom activities. Maintaining momentum helps maximize academic learning time by maintaining a brisk instructional pace that still allows students to be successful. Momentum must be adapted to students' needs and to the difficulty or complexity of the required tasks. Generally, teacher-directed instruction allows greater control of momentum and instructional time.

- Instructional time is enhanced when teachers plan for and implement smooth transitions. Transitions are points where students' attention is refocused to new topics or activities.

- Teachers should work to minimize the number and length of transitions and to make them as organized as possible. They should develop routines and procedures for frequently occurring transitions, should inform students about what they are to do ahead of time, and should monitor the transition.

- Effective teachers keep students involved in their lessons through questioning, instructional clarity, and monitoring of understanding.

- Questioning involves not only asking good questions but knowing how to obtain answers and how to react to students' responses. The most effective questions require students to process information and formulate a correct answer. Closed-response questions should be avoided or minimized. Questions should be phrased clearly and concisely in direct, natural, unambiguous language and should vary in form and in cognitive level depending upon the objectives of the lesson. Teachers ask more and better questions when they include them in their lesson planning. Teachers can enhance the effectiveness of their questioning by using wait time and maximizing student participation. Wait time refers to the pauses teachers place between the question and a student's response and between a student's response and the teacher's reaction. Ideal wait time appears to be between 3 and 5 seconds, and allows students to think about the question or response.

- We should address questions to all students, not just volunteers. This keeps the class alert, allows everyone to participate, and permits the teacher to better monitor the success of instruction.

- After a student responds to a question, the teacher's reaction is critical. Possible responses include probing, redirecting, rephrasing, or giving the student the answer. Probing means asking the student additional questions to expand or raise the level or accuracy of the response. Redirecting involves asking another student to answer the same question. This should generally be avoided. Rephrasing means rewording the original question to make it clearer. Generally, this should be done only after the student has unsuccessfully attempted to respond.

- Teachers whom students find most enjoyable and helpful provide instruction that leads them to a clear understanding of the material. Instructional clarity is achieved through logical organization, identifying and reinforcing main points, using good examples to elaborate, and monitoring and correcting.

- Clear teachers use logical organization by informing students of the lesson objectives early in the lesson and presenting the content so that students can see the relationships between concepts or ideas.

- Clear teachers help students identify and reinforce important aspects of the lesson by noting and repeating major points and writing them on the board. Reviews and summaries are included throughout the lesson to help reinforce major points and draw broader conclusions.

- Clear teachers elaborate on important ideas and concepts using concrete, verbal, or written examples and by explicitly showing how ideas, concepts, and tasks are similar to and different from one another.

- Clear teachers monitor and quickly correct students' misunderstandings by asking questions and assigning application exercises throughout the lesson to monitor understanding and to allow students to clarify their own misconceptions.

- Effective teachers carefully and continually assess students' understanding through good questioning and by establishing an open, interactive classroom climate in which students are more likely to ask for help.

- Effective teachers provide students with frequent feedback and reinforcement for their academic performance. Although reinforcement and feedback are both means of responding to student performance, they are designed to achieve different ends.

- Feedback is primarily informational and is intended to help students improve their performance. It is probably more important than reinforcement in promoting learning.

- The most useful feedback includes the standard performance was judged against, how the student's performance compares with that standard, and specifically how the performance can be improved. Feedback should be provided frequently, as soon after performance as possible, and should focus on the quality of performance rather than the student's intentions or effort.

- Reinforcement is intended to strengthen or promote desirable behavior by providing some type of reward. Reinforcement is directed toward motivating students. Thus, it is most useful at points where students are most likely to become frustrated and give up (for example, early in the process of learning a task or at any time with less able students).

- Reinforcement in the form of verbal praise is only marginally effective. The most effective reinforcement is specific to the behavior being rewarded, contingent upon the desired behavior or performance, and believable or genuine.

ISSUES AND PROBLEMS FOR DISCUSSION

PROBLEMS   The following are problems and concerns teachers have expressed. How do you feel about them? What would you do in each teacher's place?

Problem 1:   "Today I spent all afternoon on one lesson. I spent from 12:30 to 1:15 and again from 1:30 to 2:15 on math. They were all 'higher than kites' and it was probably due to Halloween. I caught about five kids writing notes instead of paying attention. When I checked to see if they knew what they were doing, they didn't!"

Problem 2:   "We have a good program called 'Book It' to encourage reading. My main concern today is providing my first-grade 'Book It' students with adequate time for oral book reports without neglecting the rest of the class."

Problem 3:   "What concerns me is the way so many of my students won't listen to directions. I gave a math assignment and had about ten kids that didn't know what to do. The lack of inner discipline I see in many students worries me."

Problem 4: "Today's class was disrupted by constant talking. Every time the group was given a new direction or activity, they began talking. I had to remind them more than once to remain quiet."

Problem 5: "I find it difficult to meet with three reading groups all working at different levels in the 60 minutes allotted to reading. I find myself neglecting the top group. Also, I don't like giving the groups busywork since it is wasted time for everyone, including the grader. How do others deal with this?"

THEORY INTO ACTION ACTIVITIES

You have learned about the importance of developing several professional skills to improve your instruction. The following exercises will help you apply your understanding.

ACTIVITY 11.1: Planning to Establish Set   Develop a lesson plan for a 10-minute lesson segment in which you will establish at least one of the three types of set. Then, ask a classmate to evaluate the plan using the guidelines in Figure 11.1.

ACTIVITY 11.2: Establishing Set in the Classroom   Conduct an observation of a teacher, focusing on the teacher's use of set induction. Did the teacher establish set? How long did the set take? Which type or types were used? To what extent did the teacher include the four general aspects of effective set? What, if anything, could be done to establish set more effectively?

ACTIVITY 11.3: Variety in College Instruction   Think about one of your current courses. Keep a running list or journal of the forms of variety the instructor uses over a two-week period. Then, label each type of variation as "variety of instructional materials" or "techniques" or "interaction." Which type of variety is used most often? How effective is the instructor's use of variety? List some specific ways in which the teacher could enhance variety.

ACTIVITY 11.4: Observing and Recording Instructional Time   Make two detailed observations of the use of time during teacher-directed lessons. You will need a stopwatch or watch with a second hand. In the first observation, record the amount of time the teacher devotes to academic tasks (for example, providing instruction, answering content questions, and so forth) and the amount of time devoted to noninstructional tasks (taking attendance, correcting behavior, giving directions). What proportion of the time was devoted to instructional tasks? to noninstructional tasks? What might the teacher do to increase the amount of instructional time?

In a second lesson, use this same procedure to assess the academic learning time of one student. At the beginning of the lesson, select a student to observe. Record the amount of time the student appears to be engaged in academic tasks and compare this with the total length of the lesson. What percentage of the time was the student engaged? Were there particular activities that seemed more or less engaging to the student? What did the student do when not engaged? Do you believe this student is typical of the other students in the classroom?

ACTIVITY 11.5: Asking Clear Questions   Rewrite each of the following questions to make them more effective.

1. "What did we say was the capital of Russia?"
2. "True or false? 6×8 is the same as 8×6."

3. "What is the importance of the Eighteenth Amendment to the Constitution? Today we're going to talk about that."

4. "David, you weren't paying attention. What did Aaron just say?"

5. "What could possibly justify the enormous loss of human life during the Vietnam War?"

6. "Can anyone tell me who wrote *A Christmas Carol*?"

ACTIVITY 11.6: Planning for Effective Questioning Generate a list of questions you might use if you were teaching a lesson on American holidays. Attempt to include questions of each type and level. For example, generate lower- and higher-order questions, convergent and divergent questions, process and content questions, and so on.

ACTIVITY 11.7: Planning for Giving Clear Instructions Develop a plan for a short lesson following the suggestions for instructional planning in Chapter 5. Then make notations to help you improve the clarity of the lesson. For example, underline or highlight specific information you will write on the board, indicate points where you will review and summarize, and include questions you will ask to monitor students' understanding.

REFERENCES

Anderson, L., Evertson, C., & Brophy, J. (1979). An experimental study of effective teaching in first-grade reading groups. *The Elementary School Journal, 79,* 193–223.

Arends, R. (1991). *Learning to teach.* New York: McGraw-Hill.

Arlin, M. (1979). Teacher transitions can disrupt time flow in classrooms. *American Educational Research Journal, 16,* 42–56.

Barden, L. (1995). Effective questioning and the ever-elusive higher-order question. *American Biology Teacher, 57*(7), 423–426.

Beamer, D. (1979). Praise and criticism. Unpublished manuscript. Columbus: The Ohio State University.

Bellon, J., Bellon, E., & Blank, M. (1992). *Teaching from a research knowledge base: A development and renewal process.* New York: Macmillan.

Berliner, D. (1987). But do they understand? In V. Richardson-Koehler (Ed.), *Educators' handbook: A research perspective* (pp. 259–293). New York: Longman.

Bloom, R., & Bourbon, L. (1980). Types and frequencies of teachers' written instructional feedback. *Journal of Educational Research, 74,* 13–15.

Borich, G. (1992). *Effective teaching methods.* New York: Macmillan.

Brophy, J. (1979). Teacher behavior and its effects. *Journal of Educational Psychology, 71,* 733–750.

Brophy, J. (1981). Teacher praise: A functional analysis. *Review of Educational Research, 51*(1), 5–32.

Brophy, J. (1982). Successful teaching strategies for the inner-city child. *Phi Delta Kappan, 63*(8), 527–530.

Brophy, J., & Evertson, C. (1976). *Process-product correlations in the Texas Teacher Effectiveness Study* (Final report) (Research Report 74–4). Austin: University of Texas Research and Development Center for Teacher Education. (ERIC Document Reproduction Service ED 091 094)

Brophy, J., & Good, T. (1986). Teacher behavior and student achievement. In M. Wittrock (Ed.), *The handbook of research on teaching* (pp. 328–375). New York: Macmillan.

Bush, A. (1976). An empirical exploration of teacher clarity. Doctoral dissertation, The Ohio State University. *Dissertation Abstracts International, 37,* 2805A.

Bush, A., Kennedy, J., & Cruickshank, D. (1977). An empirical investigation of teacher clarity. *Journal of Teacher Education, 28,* 53–58.

Butler, R., & Nisan, M. (1986). Effects of no feedback, task-related comments, and grades on intrinsic motivation and performance. *Journal of Educational Psychology, 78,* 474–481.

Callahan, J., Clark, L., & Kellough, R. (1992). *Teaching in the middle and secondary schools.* New York: Macmillan.

Cazden, C. (1986). Classroom discourse. In M. Wittrock (Ed.), *The handbook of research on teaching* (pp. 432–469). New York: Macmillan.

Coladarci, T., & Gage, N. (1984). Effects of a minimal intervention on teacher behavior and student achievement. *American Educational Research Journal, 21,* 539–555.

Couch, R. (1973). Is lecturing really necessary? *The American Biology Teacher, 10,* 391–395.

Cruickshank, D. (1990). *Research that informs teachers and teacher educators.* Bloomington, IN: Phi Delta Kappa.

Danielson, C. (1996). *Enhancing professional practice: A framework for teaching.* Alexandria, VA: ASCD.

Dillon, J. (1988). *Questioning and teaching.* New York: Teachers College Press.

Doyle, W. (1986). Classroom organization and management. In M. C. Wittrock (Ed.), *The handbook of research on teaching* (pp. 392–431). New York: Macmillan.

Eby, J. (1992). *Reflective planning, teaching, and evaluation for the elementary school.* New York: Macmillan.

Elawar, M., & Corno, L. (1985). A factorial experiment in teachers' written feedback on student homework: Changing teacher behavior a little rather than a lot. *Journal of Educational Psychology, 77,* 162–173.

Feden, P. (1994). About instruction: Powerful new strategies worth knowing. *Educational Horizons, 74,* 18–24.

Fisher, C., Berliner, D., Filby, N., Marliave, R., Cohen, L., & Dishaw, M. (1984). Teaching behaviors, academic learning time, and student achievement: An overview. In D. Strother (Ed.), *Time and learning* (pp. 97–122). Bloomington, IN: Phi Delta Kappa.

Gage, N. (1989). Process-product research on teaching: A review of criticisms. *The Elementary School Journal, 89*(3), 253–300.

Gagné, E. (1985). Strategies for effective teaching and learning. In *The cognitive psychology of school learning.* Boston: Little, Brown.

Gall, M. (1984). Synthesis of research on teachers' questioning. *Educational Leadership, 42,* 40–47.

Gliessman, D., Pugh, R., Brown, L., & Archer, A. (1989). Research-based teacher training: Applying a concept teaching model to the development and transfer of a learning-related teaching skill. Paper presented at the annual meeting of the American Educational Research Association, San Francisco.

Good, T. (1988). Research on teacher effects: Uses and abuses. *Elementary School Journal, 89*(1), 3–21.

Good, T., & Brophy, J. (1987). *Looking in classrooms.* Fourth Edition. New York: Harper and Row.

Good, T., & Grouws, D. (1977). Teaching effects: A process-product study in fourth-grade mathematics classrooms. *Journal of Teacher Education, 28,* 49–54.

Gump, P. (1967). *The classroom behavior setting: Its nature and relation to student behavior* (Final report). Washington, DC: U.S. Office of Education, Bureau of Research. (ERIC Document Reproduction Service ED 015 515)

Gump, P. (1969). Intra-setting analysis: The third grade classroom as a special but instructive case. In E. Williams & H. Rausch (Eds.), *Naturalistic viewpoints in psychological research.* New York: Holt, Rinehart, and Winston.

Hargreaves, A. (1994). Time and teachers' work: An analysis of the intensification thesis. *Teachers College Record, 94*(1), 87–107.

Harnischfeger, A., & Wiley, D. (1978). Conceptual and policy issues in elementary school teacher-learning. Paper presented at the annual meeting of the American Educational Research Association, Toronto.

Henson, K. (1980). What's the use of lecturing? *The High School Journal, 64,* 115–119.

Hines, C. (1981). A further investigation of teacher clarity: The relationship between observed and perceived teacher clarity and student achievement and satisfaction. Doctoral dissertation, The Ohio State University. *Dissertation Abstracts International, 42,* 3122A.

Hines, C., Kennedy, J., & Cruickshank, D. (1985). Teacher clarity and its relationship to student achievement and satisfaction. *American Educational Research Journal, 22,* 87–99.

Karweit, N. (1984). Time-on-task reconsidered: Synthesis of research on time-on-task. *Educational Leadership,* 32–35.

Kennedy, J., Cruickshank, D., Bush, A., & Myers, B. (1978). Additional investigation into the nature of teacher clarity. *Journal of Educational Research, 72,* 3–10.

Kintsch, W., & Bates, E. (1977). Recognition memory for statements from a classroom lecture. *Journal of Experimental Psychology: Human Learning and Memory, 3,* 150–159.

Kounin, J. (1970). *Discipline and group management in classrooms.* New York: Holt, Rinehart, and Winston.

Latham, A. (1997). Asking students the right questions. *Educational Leadership, 54,* 84–85.

Lepper, M. (1983). Extrinsic reward and intrinsic motivation. In J. Levine & M. Wang (Eds.), *Teacher and student perceptions: Implications for learning.* Hillsdale, NJ: Erlbaum.

Luiten, J., Ames, W., & Aerson, G. (1980). A meta-analysis of advance organizers on learning and retention. *American Educational Research Journal, 17,* 211–218.

Mencke, D. and Pressley, M. (1994). Elaborative interrogation: Using 'why' questions to enhance the learning from text. *Journal of Reading. 37*(8), 642–645.

Metcalf, K. (1991). Improving problem-solving instruction using research of instructional clarity. *Issues and Trends in Education, 1,* 6–12.

Metcalf, K. (1992). The effects of a guided laboratory experience on the instructional clarity of preservice teachers. *Teaching and Teacher Education, 8*(3), 275–286.

Metcalf, K., & Cruickshank, D. (1991). Can teachers be trained to be more clear? *Journal of Educational Research, 85,* 107–116.

Moore, K. (1992), *Classroom teaching skills.* New York: McGraw-Hill.

Morine-Dershimer, G., & Beyerbach, B. (1987). Moving right along. . . . In V. Richardson-Koehler (Ed.), *Educators' handbook: A research perspective* (pp. 207–232). New York: Longman.

Napell, S. (1978). Updating the lecture. *Journal of Teacher Education, 29*(5), 53–56.

O'Leary, K., & O'Leary, S. (Eds.). (1977). *Classroom management: The successful use of behavior modification.* New York: Pergamon.

Ornstein, A. (1990). *Strategies for effective teaching.* New York: HarperCollins.

Pate, R., & Bremer, N. (1967). Guiding learning through skillful questioning. *Elementary School Journal, 67,* 417–422.

Perkins, D. (1993). Teaching for understanding. *American Educator, 17,* 28–35.

Redfield, D., & Rousseau, E. (1981). A meta-analysis of experimental research on teacher questioning behavior. *Review of Educational Research, 51,* 237–245.

Rohrkemper, M., & Corno, L. (1988). Success and failure on classroom tasks: Adaptive learning and classroom teaching. *The Elementary School Journal, 88*(3), 298–312.

Rosenshine, B. (1960). How time is spent in elementary classrooms. In C. Denham & A. Lieberman (Eds.), *Time to learn* (pp. 107–126). Washington, DC: National Institute of Education.

Rosenshine, B. (1980). How time is spent in elementary classrooms. In P. Peterson & H. Walberg (Eds.), *Research on teaching: Concepts, findings, and implications* (pp. 28–56). Berkeley, CA: McCutchan.

Rosenshine, B., & Furst, N. (1971). Research on teacher performance criteria. In B. Smith (Ed.), *Research in teacher education* (pp. 37–72). Englewood Cliffs, NJ: Prentice-Hall.

Rosenshine, B., & Stevens, R. (1986). Teaching functions. In M. Wittrock (Ed.), *The handbook of research on teaching* (pp. 376–391). New York: Macmillan.

Rowe, M. (1974). Wait time and rewards as instructional variables, their influences in language, logic, and fate control: Part one—Wait time. *Journal of Research in Science Teaching, 11*(2), 81–94.

Sadker, M., & Sadker, D. (1986). Questioning skills. In J. Cooper (Ed.), *Classroom teaching skills* (pp. 143–180). Lexington, MA: Heath.

Schuck, R. (1985). An empirical analysis of the power of set induction and systematic questioning as instructional strategies. *Journal of Teacher Education, 36,* 38–43.

Sigel, I. (1990). What teachers need to know about human development. In D. Dill and associates (Eds.), *What teachers need to know: The knowledge, skills, and values essential to good teaching.* San Francisco: Jossey-Bass.

Tobin, K. (1987). The role of wait time in higher cognitive learning. *Review of Educational Research, 56,* 69–95.

Walberg, H. (1988). Synthesis of research on time and learning. *Educational Leadership, 45*(2), 143–178.

Walberg, H. (1990). Productive teaching and instruction: Assessing the knowledge base. *Phi Delta Kappan, 71*(6), 470–478.

Walberg, H. (1991). Productive teaching and instruction: Assessing the knowledge base. In H. Waxman and H. Walberg (Eds.), *Effective teaching: Current research* (pp. 33–62). Berkeley, CA: McCutchan.

Wang, M., Haertel, G., & Walberg, H. (1993–94). What helps students learn? *Educational Leadership 51*(4), 74–79.

Waxman, H. (1987–88). Effective lesson introductions and pre-instructional activities: A review of recent research. *Journal of Classroom Interaction, 23*(1), 5–7.

Wilen, W., & Clegg, A. (1986). Effective questions and questioning: A research review. *Theory and Research in Social Education, 14,* 153–161.

Williams, E. (1983). The short term stability of teacher clarity. Doctoral dissertation, The Ohio State University. *Dissertation Abstracts International, 44,* 3362A.

Williams, R., & Ware, J. (1977). An extended visit with Dr. Fox: Validity of student satisfaction with instruction ratings after repeated exposures to a lecturer. *American Educational Research Journal, 14,* 449–457.

Wittrock, M. (1986). Students' thought processes. In M. Wittrock (Ed.), *The handbook of research on teaching* (pp. 297–314). New York: MacMillan.

Zahorik, J. (1987). The effects of planning on teaching. *The Elementary School Journal, 71,* 143–151.

How the Effective Teacher Manages the Classroom

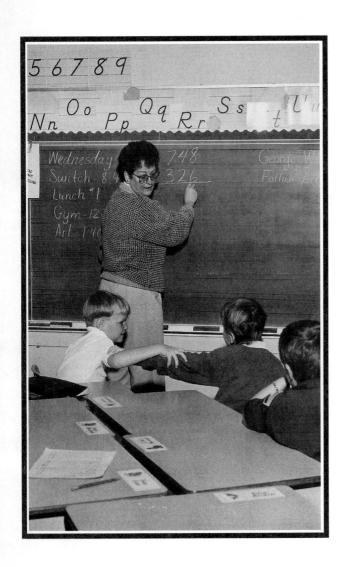

Contents

"I feel ready to teach, but what do I do if some student tells me to shut up?"

The fear and confusion this student teacher expresses reminds us that a common, persistent problem among teachers, and perhaps the greatest fear of new teachers, is student misbehavior.

Feelings of inadequacy are compounded by the realization that teachers are *expected* to be good classroom managers. Administrators expect teachers to effectively manage their classrooms and students, and often equate control of students with good teaching. Likewise, parents and the community expect teachers to control students both at school and at extracurricular events and to teach students self-control. Even students expect teachers to exert classroom control in order to establish a good learning environment. Finally, teachers themselves expect their students to be controlled. In poorly managed classrooms, teachers feel that their goals are thwarted because classroom management takes so much time, energy, and patience that there is little opportunity for instruction. These teachers report feeling frustrated and dissatisfied with teaching (Cruickshank & Associates, 1980).

Because well-managed classrooms are so important to everyone, you should begin developing a classroom management plan at once. Your plan should include four parts. First, you must anticipate and decide *how to prevent management problems* from occurring. Second, you should decide *how to monitor your students behavior* in order to maintain a good learning environment. Third, you should plan *how you will react when students misbehave* in your classroom. Finally, you need to decide *how you will reestablish a positive classroom environment* after correcting misbehavior. This chapter is organized to help you develop specific management strategies in each of these four areas.

12.1 What expectations do you hold for yourself and your students regarding classroom management?

What Is Classroom Management?

Traditionally, classroom management has been viewed as reactive in nature with a focus on how teachers react *after* students misbehave. The emphasis was on **discipline,** or the specific actions teachers or others take in response to a student who disobeys a reasonable classroom or school rule (Wolfang & Kelsay, 1995). Some teachers spend as much as 80 percent of their time and effort trying to control student behavior (Englander, 1986).

Surprisingly, this approach does not seem to work. Teachers who are obsessed with disciplining students or who neglect instructional preparation in favor of total control tend to end up with *more* control problems than teachers who are well prepared and who focus their efforts on helping students achieve academically (Brophy & Evertson, 1976). This may be because teachers, especially novices, frequently believe learning cannot take place until the classroom is organized and the sutdents are under control. They focus their time and energy on controlling students rather than on teaching-learning processes (Anderson 1991; Dollard, 1996).

Research suggests that these control-oriented teachers may be trying too hard and teaching too little. That is, they are not presenting the clear, uninterrupted, brisk-paced lessons essential to students' involvement and learning. Every research study attempting to link learning with some classroom influence shows that effective management skills are positively related to students' achievement. That is, when students spend more time engaged in learning tasks and correspondingly less time engaged in nonacademic behaviors, they learn more. In short, academic engagement is inversely related to students' misbehavior (Hawley & Rosenholtz, 1984).

In the 1970s, research by Kounin shifted attention from reactive disciplinary strategies to **proactive,** or preventive, views of classroom management. Effective proactive management includes establishing clear rules and predictable routines, monitoring behavior, consistently enforcing rules, and anticipating behavior problems and responding immediately (McGinnis, Frederick, & Edwards, 1995). It is clear that the most effective classroom managers are those who prevent problems from arising in the first place (Brophy, 1983; Kounin, 1970). Kounin's work reminds teachers that although they must be able to discipline students when necessary, effective instruction must be the first priority. Indeed, Jones and Jones (1995) estimated that proactive techniques reduce disruptive behavior by at least 75 percent. Doyle (1983) found that the curriculum and daily academic work are an integral part of classroom management because they can motivate students, engage them in challenging activities and thinking, and prevent them from drifting into misbehavior. Effective classroom managers, then, strive to elicit students cooperation and involve them in high-interest activities, thus preventing potential discipline problems.

For today's classrooms, a comprehensive management plan should include both proactive (preventive) and reactive (disciplinary) management strategies. **Classroom management,** then, can be defined as the provisions and procedures necessary to create and maintain an environment in which teaching and learning can occur (Duke, 1987, p. 548). This means that when you plan your classroom management strategies you need to consider the sort of classroom environment you want and the rules and routines you need to establish this environment. Further, you must learn how to hold students accountable for following classroom procedures and how to reinforce and reward students for doing so. Finally, you need to plan how you will intervene when misbehavior does occur.

Preventing Management Problems

Evertson (1989) describes the transition from the world of preservice education to the real world of teaching as problematic and traumatic. Why? Because preservice teachers like yourselves rarely see practicing teachers take an empty classroom, multitudes of raw materials, a designated group of students, and school goals and organize them into a dynamic, safe, cooperative learning environment. Think about the classroom observation experiences you have had thus far. Most education students observe and practice in classrooms that are already well-established. As a result, the issue of how to set up a classroom where students will engage in learning and behave appropriately is generally overlooked in teacher preparation programs.

Fortunately, even if you have not observed a teacher establishing a learning oriented environment, you do not have to depend on your intuition or on trial and error when you attempt to set up your own classroom. Research over the past two decades has produced considerable knowledge about exactly what effective classroom managers do to establish classrooms where teaching and learning occur and to prevent control problems. Effective teachers begin early in the school year to systematically implement a carefully developed plan. They thoughtfully establish

12.2 What are your greatest fears about classroom management?

12.3 How, if at all, have you changed your mind about classroom control?

the physical and psychological environments in their classrooms. Further, they plan and implement classroom routines to make the classroom a more predictable place. Let's focus in more detail on these aspects of preventive management.

ESTABLISHING THE PHYSICAL AND PSYCHOLOGICAL ENVIRONMENT

The classroom environment has a powerful impact on students' behavior, learning, and motivation. Lewin and his associates showed that the interaction between one's needs and the surrounding environmental conditions is a key factor in explaining an individual's behavior (Lewin, Lippitt, & White, 1939).

Teachers can manipulate two elements of the classroom environment to increase learning and improve behavior (Anderson, 1991). The **physical environment** consists of those aspects of the classroom that are independent of the people who inhabit it. The shape and size of the room, the seating arrangement, and the location and availability of equipment and materials are major aspects of the physical environment. Because these are concrete and observable, most of the students in a classroom would describe the physical environment in the same way.

In contrast, the **psychological environment** exists only in the minds of those who occupy the classroom. As a result, the students and teacher may experience and describe the psychological environment in different ways. The psychological environment is sometimes referred to as the classroom **climate**. It includes the emotional tone of the classroom and the comfort level students feel with the teacher, learning tasks, and one another as a social group (Eggen & Kauchak, 1992; Walberg, 1987). Specific, observable teachers behaviors and management skills affect the quality of both the physical and psychological environments in the classroom.

Planning the Physical Environment   Effective classroom management starts with decisions about the physical environment in the classroom. While there is little evidence that classroom materials and equipment strongly influence students' achievement (Wang, Haertel, & Walberg, 1993–94), there is substantial evidence that other factors such as room arrangement and seating patterns can affect the behavior of students and their attitudes toward school and learning (Ainley, 1987; Gunter, Shores, Jack, Rasmussen, & Flowers, 1995). How you arrange your classroom and your students' places within it, then, are important management considerations.

The fact that the classroom environment influences students' behavior and learning makes sense when we recall the ideas of Maslow (1968). As mentioned in Chapter 3, Maslow developed a hierarchy of the needs that motivate and influence human behavior. Maslow's work suggests that everyone, students and teachers alike, has a basic need to feel safe and secure in their surroundings. Further, they need to feel valued as members of the social group and to be challenged by new and varied experiences. Savage (1991) suggests that many incidents of students' misbehavior arise as students seek to have these basic needs met. For example, a student seated near the pencil sharpener may feel threatened when other students cluster there, leaning on her desk and talking while they await their turn. She may verbally or physically lash out at the students to keep them out of "her" space. Thoughtful management of the physical environment can minimize or eliminate this and many other classroom problems.

Seating Patterns   One of the most obvious aspects of the physical environment that teachers can manipulate is the seating arrangement. Students need to know that the classroom is a safe, comfortable place in which they can engage in positive social and academic experiences. They need to have enough space that they can move freely around their desk areas and work at their desks without distractions. What is the best way to seat students to achieve a well-managed, comfortable learning environment?

12.4   Where do you prefer to sit in a classroom? Why?

Although research on seating patterns is incomplete, inconsistent, and often contradictory, there is enough evidence that seating impacts students' behavior and attitudes to warrant your careful consideration of various arrangements as part of your classroom management plan (Weinstein, 1987). Three notable aspects of the classroom environment that seating arrangements impact are peer interactions, teacher-student interactions, and student affect.

It is not surprising that seating arrangement affects peer interaction. Consider how students interact when they are seated in rows. In that case, they tend to be focused on instruction and to persist at independent learning tasks since it is difficult for them to communicate with one another (Wheldall et al., 1981). In contrast, students seated face to face around tables interact more frequently with their peers (Gill, 1977). Further, sitting around a table seems to influence the development of student leadership abilities. Weinstein (1987) found that when students are assigned to sit at tables with two on one side and three on the other, twice as many leaders emerge from the side where only two students sit, perhaps because these students can influence more people.

Peer interactions and leadership show similar effects when students are seated in a circle. In a circular seating arrangement, students are most likely to speak to persons seated directly across from them. They rarely speak to persons seated beside them (Weinstein, 1987). This suggests that teachers can influence communication patterns during discussion by purposefully seating students. For example, when a quiet student sits opposite the leader, chances are that the quiet student will participate more than usual. Conversely, placing an overly vocal student next to the designated leader should prevent that student from dominating the discussion.

Student seating also influences the interactions between students and the teacher. Johnson (1973) found no real differences in the frequency of teacher-student interaction when seats were arranged in rows, crescents, or a circle. However, other researchers examining classrooms with row seating have identified an **action zone** of student-teacher interaction (Adams & Biddle, 1970). That is, students seated in the front and down the middle of the classroom define a triangular area in which most interaction occurs (Figure 12.1). Teachers are physically closer to these students and interact more frequently and more positively with them. While students seated inside the action zone tend to participate more, work more persistently, and hold more positive attitudes toward the class, students seated outside of this zone and farther from the teacher attain lower levels of achievement and hold less positive attitudes toward learning.

In studying this phenomenon, Dykman and Reis (1979) and Walberg (1969) found that students who choose seats outside the action zone tend to have lower self-esteem, to doubt their academic ability, and to feel threatened by the classroom environment or the teacher. Seated along the periphery of the classroom, these students are less engaged with the teacher and the instructional tasks at hand and are more easily distracted. This leads to increased failure, which reinforces their self-doubt and low self-esteem.

In Chapter 11, we discussed the importance of an interactive classroom to learning. When students are involved and interacting in the classroom, they feel a sense of belonging and, because they are occupied, they are less likely to misbehave. This suggests that teachers should consider the student-teacher action zone when arranging students. While allowing students to select their own seats, especially at the secondary level, has some psychological benefits, it may be advisable to gradually move students with academic or behavioral problems into the action zone to increase their academic engagement. Relatedly, teachers should be sure to call on students, especially nonvolunteers, seated in the periphery of the classroom.

Teachers can actually change the location of the action zone by the way they instruct and monitor students. Because the action zone is defined in terms of the teacher's position in the classroom, it can be redefined by simply moving around

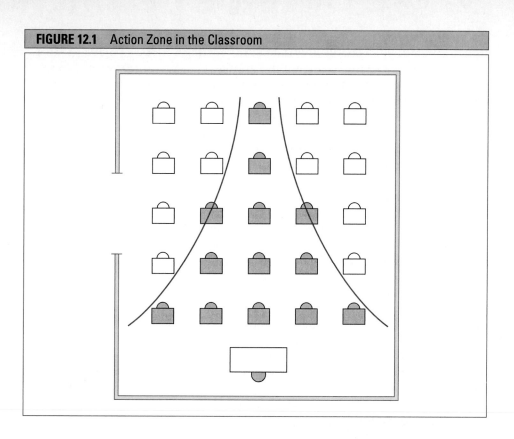

FIGURE 12.1 Action Zone in the Classroom

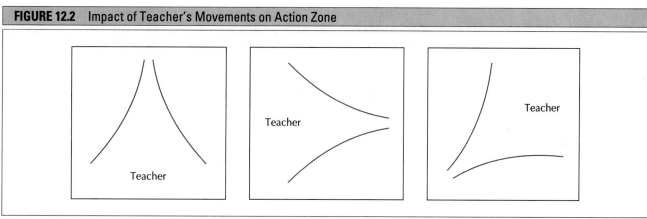

FIGURE 12.2 Impact of Teacher's Movements on Action Zone

Teacher

Teacher

Teacher

Teacher

while teaching, by relocating the teacher's desk or teaching station, or by circulating to all parts of the room while monitoring students (Figure 12.2). Moving around the classroom during instruction makes it possible to monitor all students more closely and to interact with them more equitably (Gunter et al., 1995).

Affective outcomes are the third aspect of the classroom that the seating arrangement influences. Research consistently shows that students sitting toward the front of the class experience greater enjoyment of and interest in the class, are more involved with the class, and like the teacher more. Interestingly, at least at the college level, these results are the same whether the seats are assigned or are selected by the students (Weinstein, 1987). This provides some justification for changing the seat assignments when classes are arranged in traditional rows.

No single seating arrangement is ideal for all classes, learning situations, or individuals. Depending on individual students' characteristics, seating patterns have been shown to affect motivation, communication patterns, and leadership in the

Try Activity 12.1

classroom (Weinstein, 1987). Consequently, it is important that you give serious consideration to how you will seat students in your classroom.

Rather than constantly changing the arrangement of student seats, Musgrave (1975) suggests choosing a "home base formation" that serves as a semipermanent arrangement. This formation should be suitable for many teaching situations and easily moved into alternative formations as needed. Borich (1992) suggests traditional rows as the home base formation because this arrangement conveys a businesslike appearance, is easily monitored, and can be reorganized quickly into small groups, circles, or other formations for increased interaction among students. Weinstein and Mignano (1997) agree that novice teachers should seat students in rows until they feel confident in their management abilities. However, the teacher may later modify the arrangement, they add, based on students' characteristics as well as the level of interaction the teacher expects. If you want to seat students in groups, you will need goals that fit that arrangement and you will need to provide collaboration guidelines to the students.

Number of Students   While teachers have little, if any, control over the number of students in their classes, they can influence the effects of class size. To begin, they can be sure they have an adequate number of desks and lockers. Equally important, the desks should be the right size for their students and should provide ample work space for them. The seating arrangement, then, should consider not only where a student would fit in best academically and socially, but also which desk he or she will fit into most comfortably and safely. Left-handed students and students with physical challenges will need work spaces specifically designated for their safety and comfort.

Equipment and Materials   Where and how you store supplies and equipment will affect their accessibility. Providing students ready access to reference books and supplies will reduce the number of times you need to handle supplies or give instructions about their location and distribution. Students should have access to resources and supplies without reaching across other students' desks or crowding their chairs. Organize your classroom to prevent lines and bottlenecks around storage areas, reference shelves, and supply tables. When several students are waiting or pushing to get supplies, inappropriate behavior is bound to erupt. Putting the wastebasket and the pencil sharpener near the door, for example, creates congestion in that area and increases the likelihood of behavior problems.

Room Arrangement   Research attests to the impact of room arrangement on students' behavior and learning. It suggests that an attractive, well-organized environment leads to more positive attitudes, better grades, and more receptive students. Further, students persist longer at tasks, participate more in discussions, and feel closer to the group in pleasantly arranged classrooms. Conversely, unattractive classrooms have been linked to frequent absenteeism, discomfort, fatigue, and complaints from both parents and students (Brodie, 1964; Horowitz & Otto, 1973; Maslow & Mintz, 1956; Santrock, 1976; Sommer & Olsen, 1980; Wang et al., 1993–94). A pleasant and comfortable physical environment is especially important to students with low self-esteem or with a history of school failure; that is, students who are at risk of failing or leaving school (Raviv, Raviv, & Reisel, 1990). To avoid these problems, the physical environment should be arranged so that students know that they are safe and secure and that their involvement in educational activities can take place without crowding or distractions (Weinstein & Mignano, 1997).

Today, teachers have more physical space to arrange and manage. In 1970, an average elementary school provided 62 square feet for each student. By 1995, each pupil had 111 square feet—a 79 percent increase (White, 1996)! This is due to new teaching methods, increased use of technology, and greater community de-

FIGURE 12.3 Floor Plan of Good Classroom Arrangement

Bulletin board
Chalkboard
Bulletin board
Rug
Student mailboxes
Low bookcases
Teacher's desk
Pencil sharpener
Low bookcase
File cabinets
Study desk
Low bookcase
Study table
Low bookcase
Trash can
Student lockers

mands on school space. Middle and high schools have grown similarly. Regardless of whether your actual classroom space is larger, it will be more complex. Regular classrooms are being outfitted to accommodate disabled students and rewired to incorporate new technology into everyday instruction. Distractions and congestion can be minimized in these complex classrooms by arranging furniture in a way that orients students toward the primary sources of information yet also gives them access to resources and activities without disturbing others (Anderson, 1991). For example, if you do choose to seat students in groups or around tables, be sure all students can see the teaching center of the room without looking around other students, turning their chairs, or uncomfortably twisting their bodies. The teacher should also have an unrestricted view of all students.

When arranging the physical environment, it is also important to consider the types of instructional activities that will occur in the classroom. Use open space or furniture to establish activity boundaries or to separate incompatible activities. For example, you might use low bookcases to separate group work or activity centers from seat work areas. Dividers like these should be high enough to provide an undisturbed work space for students in that area, but low enough for you to see students in all parts of the room. Also, be sure to provide open lanes for movement between frequently used activity areas, such as between students' desks and learning centers or the pencil sharpener. You will also need to determine where to direct student traffic to avoid distractions and congestion where students are working. Figures 12.3 and 12.4 contrast good and poor classroom arrangements.

12.5 Recall a classroom that you think had a good physcial environment. What was it like?

FIGURE 12.4 Floor Plan of Poor Classroom Arrangement

Built-in bookcases, reference and library books

Student lockers

Pencil sharpener

Filing cabinets

Tall bookcase

Couch

Bulletin board

Windows

Teacher's desk

Trash can

Bulletin board

Chalkboard

Student mailboxes

Planning the Psychological Environment   We can think of the psychological environment as the climate or atmosphere of the class that potentially influences what students learn (Walberg, 1987). A positive climate promotes cooperative working relationships and helps prevent control problems (Bellon, Bellon, & Blank, 1992). Three aspects of the psychological environment have been consistently linked with students' learning: emotional affect, or tone; task orientation; and organization (Walberg, 1987; Wang et al., 1993–94).

12.6 What classroom characteristics make you feel energized and ready to learn?

Tone   An **inviting classroom** is an appealing, positive place that provides a sense of physical and emotional safety for students and the teacher. That is, it has a positive tone. Maslow's (1968) hierarchy of needs outlines what motivates and influences human behavior and helps us understand why an inviting classroom is so important (Figure 12.5). Maslow described the most basic human need as that for safety and security, followed by a need for acceptance or esteem and recognition. Only when these needs have been met is it possible to fulfill the human need for aesthetic pleasure and mental challenges. This suggests that students are most able to learn and to behave appropriately when they feel safe, secure, and accepted.

How can you create a classroom where students feel psychologically and emotionally safe? Such a classroom is characterized by three qualities: it is attractive, it encourages prosocial development, and it exhibits ownership.

Effective teachers use color, light, temperature, and displays to create an attractive classroom tone where students feel safe and comfortable (Anderson, 1991).

FIGURE 12.5   Hierarchy of Human Needs

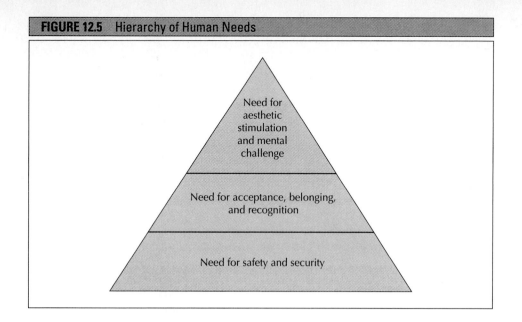

For example, to offset the cold impression that hardwood or linoleum floors, Formica desks, fluorescent lights, and plaster or concrete walls convey, you could use soft, textured bulletin board coverings, plants, family photographs, a rocking chair with a seat cushion, and posters of animals, nature scenes, or poetry. Conveying a sense of softness and safety is especially important for young children. The key is to use elements of light, texture, and color in a coherent, orderly way and in moderation. Overuse may overstimulate students, tiring them emotionally and distracting them from learning.

Even if you share a classroom with other teachers you can create a sense of softness and psychological safety. For example, one teacher carried a small vase of flowers from room to room to soften the mood in any classroom in which she taught her English classes. Carrying a colorful, textured book bag or a personalized coffee mug, wearing colorful neckties or accessories, or wrapping your textbook in a unique cover also conveys a sense of softness to students. Your worksheets and handouts can contribute to the psychological environment if they are duplicated on colored paper, display pictures or cartoons, and contain plenty of space so they don't appear cluttered.

Traditional classrooms are often described as lonely, isolated, silent, competitive, and lacking in spontaneity and interaction (Lyman & Foyle, 1990). In contrast, inviting classrooms are communities of learners that demonstrate trust and mutual respect between teacher and students, cooperative relationships among students, and a sense of student satisfaction (Anderson, 1991; Canter, 1996). This psychological environment encourages prosocial development in students.

You can create such an environment by modeling the trust and respect you want from students. Canter (1996) stresses that you should listen to your students, look them in the eye, and give them your complete attention during interactions. You should speak respectfully with students and be aware of words and actions which students, especially those from different cultural and ethnic groups, consider disrespectful. Further, Canter suggests getting to know your students as individuals by greeting them at the door by name and with a hello and a smile. Acknowledging their birthdays and other events in their lives and attending their sports events, recitals, and concerts shows students that you care about and support them both in and out of the classroom.

Teachers in inviting classrooms use strong human relations skills to build cohesive relationships among their students and to help them work toward consensus

12.7 How do the needs of today's students differ from those of students when you were in school? How could you take these differences into account when planning the classroom environment?

12.8 How can a teacher show students that they are respected?

on issues that impact the classroom community. Negotiating a compromise between two students who are fighting over a basketball and allowing the class to determine at least some of the classroom rules and procedures are the types of teacher behaviors that establish an inviting classroom which encourages prosocial behaviors.

Freiberg (1996) observed that too often classroom environments based on trust and support in the elementary grades are replaced by classroom environments that emphasize compliance and obedience in later grades, especially in urban schools. Without a cooperative, supportive psychological environment, students tend to pass through school without active involvement, commitment, or a sense of belonging (Rogers & Freiberg, 1994) and tend to achieve little. In contrast, inviting classrooms exhibit ownership. Recall that Maslow (1968) suggested that a feeling of belonging and recognition of achievement are basic human needs. Students sense ownership when they help in the classroom, library, and other school functions. Ownership is also apparent when the classroom walls are covered with students' work; when the students rather than the teacher create signs, exhibits, or lists; and when the classroom displays information about and mementos of its members.

12.9 What makes a teacher genuine or real to you?

Your sense of ownership as a teacher should also be exhibited in an inviting classroom. Research suggests that when students perceive their teacher as a "real" human being, they are more receptive to teaching and learning. This is especially true when the teacher and students come from different cultural, ethnic, or socioeconomic backgrounds (Scollon, 1981). By giving students insights into your hobbies, family, pets, and priorities, you contribute to an inviting psychological environment in which it is safe to share and express oneself. The objects on your desk, your personal reaction to the books you read in class, and casual discussion about weekend events, school sports activities, or current events all contribute to your humanness in the students' eyes. Sharing your personality, however, should not interpret or impinge on instructional time.

12.10 What qualities do you have that will enable you to establish an inviting classroom? What skills do you need to acquire?

Task Orientation   A classroom with a positive psychological environment is a busy, task-oriented place. In task-oriented classrooms, students perceive there are definite learning goals to pursue and believe they will be held accountable for reaching those goals. Relatedly, they spend most of the classroom time working toward those goals (Anderson, 1991). Even during free time, the classroom environment should encourage intellectual exploration. For example, learning centers displaying enrichment books and motivational posters add to a task-oriented environment. Simply by placing an unusual object on your desk or on a table, perhaps something from your travels or a trophy you won, you can stimulate such inquiries as "Where did you get this?" and foster interaction and cognitive growth.

Try Activity 12.2

Organization   A classroom with a positive psychological environment is also organized in a predictable way. Clear rules communicate the teacher's expectations for behavior and learning. Routines provide structure to guide students' learning experiences (Anderson, 1991) so that students know where to find supplies, how to turn in papers for grading, when to sharpen pencils, and how to gain the teacher's attention. Teachers who are effective managers organize their classrooms with appropriate rules and routines. This is the focus of our next section.

ESTABLISHING CLASSROOM RULES AND ROUTINES

Effective classroom management is fundamentally proactive. First, by thoughtfully establishing the physical and psychological environments in your classroom, you can prevent much misbehavior. A second way to exercise proactive or preventive management is by organizing the procedures and movement in the classroom. In a well-organized classroom, students clearly understand what behaviors the teacher expects and are guided toward those behaviors by the predictable structure of the classroom. You can prevent misbehavior in your classroom, then, by developing rules and implementing routines that create order and structure. Classroom **rules** are authoritative directions for conduct which create an environment conducive to learning. Classroom **routines** are established procedures which control and coordinate how students move and how events occur.

Jackson (1986) characterizes classrooms as unpredictable and complex. This is especially true of today's classrooms because of increased student diversity (see Chapter 2), more pressure on teachers to ensure that learning takes place, and shifting societal norms. This complex, unpredictable environment complicates learning for many students because they feel insecure or unsafe. Specifically, Jackson contends that many students fail at school, both behaviorally and academically, not because they lack intelligence or needed personality traits, but because they are unsuccessful in deciphering or understanding the classroom routines. According to Evertson and Harris (1992), new activities are especially troublesome because they require students to "read" the required behaviors correctly or else risk negative reactions from the teacher and other students. This suggests the need for explicit classroom rules and routines that are thoroughly communicated to students and that make the classroom less complex.

Teachers also benefit from the rules and routines that create a less complex, more predictable room. A predictable classroom is less stressful for the teacher. Certain routine teacher behaviors, such as taking attendance and collecting papers, become automatic, predictable classroom events and enable teachers to use class time more effectively. Routines help ensure that needed materials are available and that students know how to go about their learning activities. Routines make lessons smoother and more effective by reducing interruptions for questions such as, "Where is the glue?" or "Where should I put my homework paper?"

Given the benefits of classroom rules and routines for students and teachers, it seems wise to consider how to establish them. Indeed, in well-organized and managed classrooms, teachers spend at least as much time early in the year planning and establishing classroom rules and routines as they do on content instruction (Emmer, Evertson, & Anderson, 1980).

Developing Classroom Rules   Too often, teachers develop rules and hope that appropriate student behavior will follow. But rules alone, without a management plan that includes classroom routines and a discipline strategy, have a marginal effect on behavior (McGinnis et al., 1995). Other teachers believe that to have an orderly, well-managed classroom you just get tougher and tougher with students; you impose more rules and harsher consequences to gain the students' attention and respect. This doesn't work, either. According to Canter (1996), more rules won't affect students who see your rules as meaningless, who aren't afraid of your punishments, and who aren't motivated by your praise. As we have seen, in an effective, inviting classroom, the management plan is built on a foundation of trust and respect.

Researchers have provided guidelines for established effective classroom rules (McGinnis et al., 1995). The general consensus is that five rules is the maximum number that students can easily recall, although this number may need to be expanded or reduced based on grade level. Rules should convey exactly what type of student behavior is expected in observable, measurable terms. The wording of the rules should be simple and specific enough to avoid alternative interpretations. It is also best to state rules positively and to explain the desired behavior. For example, "keep your eyes on the teacher" is better than "no looking around." Finally, rules should be posted in a prominent place for all to see. Using pictures to illustrate rules helps young children, those with visual learning styles, and students with reading or language difficulties.

12.11 Think about a typical day. What routines do you follow to organize your life and make it less complex?

12.12 What problems have you had because teachers haven't developed or communicated routines?

Try Activity 12.3

Should students have a voice in developing classroom rules? McGinnis et al. (1995) note that student input is generally beneficial, and Wolfgang and Kelsay (1995) claim it is key in establishing a democratic classroom. You need to be aware, however, that students tend to be more strict, to set behavioral standards too high, to suggest too many rules, and to impose harsher punishments. It is best if the teacher has a basic framework of rules in mind, then incorporates students' input into the list of rules that emerges from the discussion and that all parties agree to.

Developing Classroom Routines Several researchers have observed effectively managed classrooms to better understand the types of routines they have in place (Leinhardt, Weldman, & Hammond, 1987; Yinger, 1979). Their findings suggest that effective managers establish four types of routines in their classrooms: management, activity, instructional, and executive planning routines. For each one, the teacher must predetermine whom the routine applies to, when it applies, and what procedures or steps are involved.

Management Routines **Management routines** involve nonacademic matters such as distributing and collecting materials and papers, leaving and entering the room, making transitions between activities and classes, starting and ending the school day, cleaning the room, and taking attendance. They are the nuts and bolts of a smoothly functioning classroom.

You may notice that many management routines are related to classroom transitions. Transitions are frequent classroom events. Doyle (1986) observed about 31 major transitions each day in most elementary classrooms, and Steele (1988) found that transitions in secondary classrooms occur three or four times per hour. While effective classroom managers conduct transitions in approximately 30 seconds, less effective teachers require up to nine minutes (Steele, 1988). As we learned in Chapter 11, poorly conducted transitions are disruptive, waste instructional time, and encourage misbehavior.

Which procedures lead to quick and easy transitions in your classroom? *First, you must signal the students that a transition is about to begin.* The signal may be verbal or nonverbal. Some teachers, for example, use phrases such as "Attention, please" or "The signal is on" to attract students' attention before beginning the transition. Elementary teachers often use nonverbal cues such as dimming the lights or raising their hand. Songs or clapping sequences are especially effective with primary students. A clapping sequence requires students to stop what they are doing, put all supplies down, and clap their hands while they focus their attention on the teacher. The nature of the signal is less important than what it does. That is, students must be taught to respond with full attention to the teacher as soon as the signal is given. Further, you should never proceed with the transition until all students have responded to the cue and are attending to you.

Second, give clear directions about what students are to do. When students are first learning the transition routine, it is a good idea to reinforce understanding by writing directions on the chalkboard or by asking students to repeat them. With younger students or students with limited English proficiency, it is especially important to demonstrate each step of the directions and to check for understanding. You might, for example, ask everyone to point to where they are to put the glue when they clean up and then to point to where they are to put their finished projects. If you are breaking the class into small groups, ask the students to point to where their group will meet. Never allow students to begin moving during a transition until all students have convinced you that they know exactly what they are to do next.

Third, signal students to make the transition. Perhaps the most difficult aspect of classroom transitions is monitoring students who are in different stages of carrying out the directions. Monitoring is much easier if all students make the transition at once. That is, part of the class should not be finishing the last step of a laboratory experiment while others are cleaning up and still others are assembled in the front of the room awaiting the class discussion. This requires that you manage *three* different groups of students at one time. Some students will inevitably make the transition more quickly than others; therefore, it is important that you monitor all stages of the transition. Circulate around the room prodding the slower students and letting everyone know that you are aware of what is going on throughout the room. Use statements like, "Thanks for doing such a thorough job of cleaning up, Sam. Now you're ready to move to the front of the room,"or "I see that four people are already cleaned up and waiting quietly in their seats for the discussion to begin."

Once students learn the directions and your expectations during transitions, these become management routines that save instructional time and reduce the stress on both you and your students. Further, because students know what they are to do, they are less likely to misbehave.

Activity Routines   Generally, when teachers think about a school day or a class period, they think of it as made up of many different kinds of activities. For example, an elementary teacher may conceptualize the morning as including attendance and announcements, sharing time, silent reading, whole-class reading time, and then recess. These activities are the basic structural units of the classroom (Yinger, 1979). Effective teachers establish **activity routines** that spell out how each kind of activity will be conducted. This includes its location, duration, and participants. Further, activity routines specify the content, structure, and sequence of the activity and let students know what materials are needed. Activity routines also provide important guidelines for appropriate student behavior and interactions. They establish acceptable ways for the students and teacher to gain each others' attention and apprise students of when it is acceptable to interact with one another.

One primary grade teacher, for example, sits in a rocking chair with her students seated around her on a rug while she reads to them. This "rug time" is an established activity with routines. When the teacher announces it is rug time, students know to get up from their desks, push in their chairs, and quietly walk to the rug area, taking nothing with them. At the rug area, students know they are free to choose where they will sit but must avoid crowding other students or sitting near someone who might distract them. Although they do not need to raise their hands to talk, students may not interrupt the teacher or their classmates while they are talking. At the end of the story, students know that rug time is over and they return to their desks in an orderly fashion. The students in this class follow the rug time routines automatically without being reminded of how to behave, where to sit, and so forth. This teacher has a well-established activity routine!

Instructional Routines   **Instructional routines** establish what the teacher will do while teaching. For example, when one mathematics teacher is about to begin teaching a new concept, he sets up the teaching station by pulling down the projection screen and focusing the overhead projector. His overhead transparencies are in a three-ring binder, so he turns to the appropriate lesson and pulls out the sequenced transparencies for that lesson. Immediately following the lesson, he washes and returns the transparencies to the notebook. Routine use of the overhead projector and transparencies is the backbone of this teacher's instruction and signals students that he is about to introduce new information.

Instructional routines such as this correlate with the teacher's strategies or style, making the teaching more predictable and efficient. As a teacher, you should establish routine ways of giving directions, demonstrating, instructing, monitoring, reviewing, and questioning students. Such routines are especially helpful for young students and for those with limited English proficiency or limited attention spans. In these situations, directions must be clearly presented, reinforced, and checked.

Let's examine the instructional routine one kindergarten teacher uses for giving directions in a bilingual classroom. When giving directions for completing one activity, the teacher clearly outlines the three things the students need to do: color the picture of the astronaut, cut it out, and paste it somewhere on the class moonscape mural. As she describes what to color, she prints the key word "color" on the chalkboard and draws a crayon after the word. She then quickly models how to color the astronaut. The teacher repeats this procedure for the next two directions in the sequence, cutting and pasting. After she has told and shown the students what they are expected to do, she checks their understanding of the directions by asking individual students to remind the class of the first, second, and third things they are to do. By the time the children begin the activity, the teacher is certain that they all heard, saw, and understood the tasks. Her predictable approach to giving directions is especially important for her students with limited English skills.

12.13 What personal responsibilities will affect your professional life as a teacher? What executive planning routines will you need to implement to balance these demands on your time?

Try Activity 12.4

Executive Planning Routines   **Executive planning routines** include establishing how, when, and where you will complete your teaching tasks—for example, how and when you will plan for instruction, evaluate students and correct papers, use your preparation time at school, and fulfill clerical responsibilities such as filling out attendance reports and grade cards. Establishing these routines helps you manage time more effectively so that you can balance your professional and personal life.

Because these are such personal routines, they vary tremendously from teacher to teacher. Some teachers stay after school one hour each day to correct papers and to handle clerical chores; others arrive an hour early in the morning or relegate these tasks to preparation periods. Some teachers work in teams one evening each week to plan for instruction, others develop their weekly plans on Saturday morning, while still others plan each evening for the next day's activities. In establishing your own executive planning routines, you may want to talk with expert teachers about how they manage their time and balance their many roles. In this way, you can benefit from their years of experience.

STARTING THE SCHOOL YEAR

Establishing a good classroom environment and developing rules and routines are important ways to prevent management problems and create a positive learning environment. A team of researchers from the University of Texas at Austin suggests that teachers must implement these proactive measures early in the school year and then maintain them if they are to be effective. Following are guidelines for preventing classroom problems based on the researcher's observations of well-managed elementary and secondary classrooms (Evertson et al., 1989; Emmer et al., 1989).

Begin to Establish Routines on the First Day of Class   The first time they meet with students, effective classroom managers clearly demonstrate that they have thought about routines and procedures, and they begin to implement them immediately. As previously discussed, you should plan the way you will arrange your classroom space, furniture, and equipment. You must also plan rules and procedures for their use. To prevent overburdening the students with too many rules at one time, your first meetings with the class should focus on routines that address students' concerns: your attitudes, expectations, and policies as their teacher; guidelines for interacting with others; procedures for meeting basic needs such as using the pencil sharpener, restroom, and drinking fountain.

Clearly Communicate and Model Classroom Routines   Simply announcing or posting classroom routines and rules will not suffice to establish a well-managed classroom. Researchers found that effective managers devote a large amount of time during the first days of school to *teaching* the routines. In fact, effective elementary teachers spend more time during the first days of school teaching about management issues than academics (Leinhardt et al., 1987). They follow up this initial instruction with about three weeks of reviewing and remediating the routines (Emmer, Evertson, & Anderson, 1980). Of course, secondary students more familiar with school routines would not need such a prolonged emphasis on routines.

How do you teach routines and rules? First, you must clearly communicate and model them. Further, you should help students understand *why* the routines are necessary. Especially with secondary students, this rationale should point out how following the rules and routines benefits the students themselves, rather than focus on benefits for the teacher or the class as a whole. Finally, you should provide situations in which the students can practice the routines and give immediate, specific feedback on their performance.

Be Sure Students Feel Good About the Classroom Arrangement and Routines   If students feel comfortable with the classroom arrangement and the availability of supplies, they are more likely to use them carefully and quietly. Similarly, if they feel that the rules and routines are realistic and attainable, they are more likely to follow them. After all, we all like to engage in activities in which we are successful.

You can help ensure that students feel comfortable and successful in their new classroom by providing situations in which they can practice using classroom resources and following routines. Then observe. If an arrangement or routine seems awkward or unnatural for students or if it just doesn't work, invite students to suggest a more appropriate way of doing things. Once you and the students have agreed upon a set of rules and routines it is a good idea to limit instruction to whole-class teaching rather than breaking down into small groups. This will give you time to observe how well your routines fit the class. It will also ensure that all students have mastered the routines before they are placed in small-group or individualized situations that are more difficult for you to manage.

Communicate That You are Prepared and Competent   Your teaching behaviors should always communicate to students that you are well-prepared and capable of instructing and managing. This doesn't mean that you will be a perfect teacher and classroom manager, but it does mean that you will be good and predictable. That is, students will know what you expect of them and how you will react if they do not meet your expectations. This predictability establishes an environment in which you are able to teach, students are able to learn, and misbehavior is less likely to occur.

Hold Students Responsible for Following Routines and Rules   Early in the year, effective classroom managers remind students of appropriate procedures prior to an activity and correct them if they follow routines improperly. Such frequent feedback is essential to learning both the classroom routines and your expectations for students' behavior.

Monitoring Students Behavior

Even when students have settled into your classroom and have learned the routines and procedures, your management work is still not done! Observations of effective classroom managers show us that such teachers monitor students' compliance with the routines throughout the year. Evertson (1987) points out that

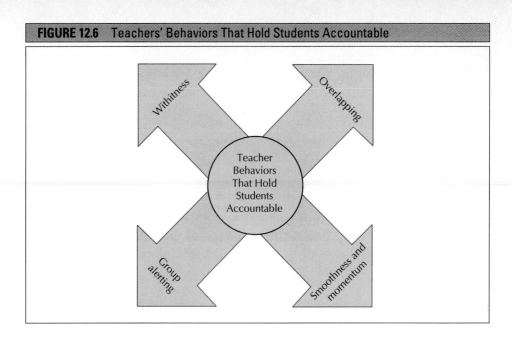

FIGURE 12.6 Teachers' Behaviors That Hold Students Accountable

even the best planned management system can fail if it is not maintained. Monitoring enables you to signal students when they are drifting into inappropriate behavior and to redirect their attention to instruction, thus preventing more serious misbehavior.

HOLDING STUDENTS ACCOUNTABLE

Unfortunately, students tend to take seriously only those things they are held accountable for (Doyle, 1983). As a result, teachers must be alert to follow through and reinforce the norms and expectations they present to students early in the year. Teachers need to develop creative and constructive procedures not only to hold students accountable for their learning and behavior, but also to help them *become* accountable (Evertson, 1987; Good, 1983).

Based on years of classroom observations, Kounin (1970) describes strategies effective classroom managers use to monitor students and to hold them accountable for their behavior throughout the school year (Figure 12.6).

Withitness Effective managers monitor classrooms using **withitness;** that is, they are aware of students' behavior in all corners of the classroom at all times. Such teachers seem to have eyes in the backs of their heads! How can you communicate to your class that you are "withit"? For one thing, try not to turn your back to the class when you are writing on the chalkboard. Instead, stand at an angle to the chalkboard so that you can easily glance over your shoulder to observe students' behavior. Similarly, when working with individual students, remain standing and periodically scan the entire classroom. Establish eye contact with students who seem to have questions or who you sense may begin to act inappropriately. Withit teachers detect inappropriate behavior early and deal with it quickly. They know who started the problem and do not depend on students to tell them what happened. Nor do they scold the wrong student. Withit teachers not only prevent classroom problems (Kounin, 1970), they also produce greater student achievement (Anderson, Evertson, & Brophy, 1979; Brophy & Evertson, 1976).

Overlapping Effective classroom managers are also able to monitor more than one classroom activity at a time, an ability called **overlapping.** Teachers who overlap can, for example, instruct a small group of students while keeping the remaining students busy and quiet. Suppose that you are working with a group of five students on math problems while the rest of the class is working on a review exercise. As you scan the classroom, you notice that two students in the back corner have stopped working and started talking. Using overlapping, you could ask the small group to try the next problem on their own. You then would establish eye contact with the misbehaving students to signal them to get back to work. Or you could walk back to them to determine whether they have a question and to redirect their attention to the review exercise. By the time the students in the small group finish working the next problem, you would be back to continue your instruction.

Smoothness and Momentum   Overlapping is closely related to two other strategies, **smoothness** and **momentum.** These suggest that you should move the class through the lesson at a brisk pace without interruptions. In well-paced lessons, students are less likely to misbehave. In Chapter 11, we discussed how effective teachers use cues—for example, verbally identifying the first, second, and third points in the lesson—to help students focus and proceed smoothly and quickly through the lesson. In addition, effective teachers who demonstrate smoothness focus on the subject at hand rather than attend to irrelevant or intrusive details; they do not interrupt children engaged in learning activities; and they follow through rather than leave activities "hanging in mid-air" (Dunkin & Biddle, 1974). Have you ever been interrupted when taking a test by a teacher announcing a correction of a typographical error? That teacher was not demonstrating smoothness.

Momentum concerns a teacher's ability to avoid behaviors that slow down the pace of the lesson (Dunkin & Biddle, 1974). Such behaviors include overdwelling on students' behavior or on a minor point in the lesson and dealing with students individually rather than as a group. A teacher exhibiting good momentum, for example, gives clear directions regarding an assignment to the entire class, then checks for understanding of those directions. A teacher lacking momentum fails to give clear directions and so must respond to students individually when they question the details or directions of the assignment. While students are waiting for the teacher to answer their questions, they can easily drift into misbehavior.

Group Alerting   You can also monitor students' behavior by using group alerting. **Group alerting** is the process of gaining and maintaining students' attention and holding them accountable for their behavior and learning. As discussed in Chapter 11, you can keep everyone's attention by calling on nonvolunteers as well as volunteers and by using various questioning strategies to keep students in suspense about who will be called on to recite.

You can also keep students alert by asking or reminding them what they should be doing, by having them repeat rules and routines they should be following, and by calling attention to appropriate behavior. Further, general comments such as "I'm still waiting for everyone to put their pencils down and look up here" or "I see that two people need to stop whispering and turn to page 572 and follow along" will alert students regarding their behavior.

Controlling the time available for a task also keeps students engaged in learning activities. When allocating time to group activities and independent work, be sure to give students just enough time to complete the task. Too little time will cause concern, stress, frustration, and perhaps inappropriate behavior. Too much time may allow students to drift into casual conversation or other interfering behaviors. Cuing or reminding students about the time helps them to be accountable for their behavior. Statements such as "We'll begin cleaning up in five minutes, so you should be finishing the last step of your experiment" should prod students who are off task toward more appropriate behavior.

Likewise, using **proximity** or adjusting the amount of space between you and your students can influence their behavior and keep them alert. Moving toward off-task students raises their awareness of your presence and helps them refocus attention on the learning activity. If the inappropriate behavior persists, it may be necessary to pause next to the students until they adjust their behavior and reenter the lesson (Gunter et al., 1995). Think about how you feel when a teacher stands near your desk. Your level of concern can become so elevated that your palms sweat, you are distracted, and learning is actually inhibited. So use proximity for monitoring behavior rather than for intimidation.

Try Activity 12.5

Finally, the visibility of the teacher and availability of materials in the classroom also hold students accountable and alert them to behave appropriately. Circulate randomly around the classroom during independent seat work or small-group projects. Students need to see you are available to answer questions and to redirect their attention. Similarly, supplies and materials that students need should be visible and accessible. This removes one excuse for not engaging in the appropriate activity.

REWARDING AND REINFORCING STUDENTS

A second way to monitor and influence students' behavior in your classroom is by using reinforcement and rewards. According to **reinforcement theory,** which is based on operant conditioning (discussed in Chapter 3), behavior that is rewarded is strengthened and therefore likely to be repeated. Conversely, behavior that is not somehow reinforced will eventually diminish. Early psychologists like Thorndike and Skinner recognized the importance of **positive reinforcement,** that is, providing something that an individual needs, values, or desires, as perhaps the most effective means of influencing that individual's behavior (Goetz, Alexander, & Ash, 1992). The use of reinforcement theory has evolved over the past two decades. Whereas reward systems once emphasized external control of students, they now focus on helping students control themselves. Reward systems have also shifted their focus from inhibiting misbehavior to rewarding positive academic and social performance (Brophy, 1983; Evertson & Harris, 1992). Correctly implemented, reinforcements and rewards provide a systematic and humanistic approach to guiding students away from misbehavior and toward independent self-control.

Unfortunately, because teachers are consumed with other classroom events, many appropriate things students do go unnoticed or at least unrewarded in today's busy classrooms. By monitoring behavior and acknowledging students who behave appropriately, teachers reinforce the importance of such behavior (Cruickshank & associates, 1980). Relatedly, many teachers unintentionally reinforce and thus encourage undesirable behaviors. For example, researchers who studied student out-of-seat behavior observed that the more frequently teachers corrected students by using the command "sit down," the more students got out of their seats (Madsen et al., 1968)! Inadvertently, the teachers were giving students the attention they were seeking only when they got out of their seats, thus reinforcing the unwanted behavior.

Applying Reinforcement Theory Although using reinforcement to influence students' behavior sounds easy, it can be difficult. First, the teacher's delivery is vital in determining a reinforcement's effectiveness. As we learned in Chapter 11, reinforcers must be given immediately after the desirable behavior, not hours, days, or weeks later. Otherwise, the effect of the reinforcer is dramatically reduced. Further, in order to effectively influence students' behavior, the reinforcement must be specific rather than general. At the elementary level, the most powerful reinforcers identify both the individual who is behaving appropriately and the appropriate behavior. For example, it is relatively ineffective to tell Cindy, an impulsive student, that you appreciated how good she was in class today. She does not know specifically what she did right, so she cannot repeat that behavior tomorrow. Further, the reinforcement was too far removed from her appropriate behavior. Instead, tell her five times during the day that you notice she is raising her hand before speaking in class, a real improvement. This specific, immediate feedback encourages her to control herself and to raise her hand in the future.

Second, it is essential to remember that students respond differently to different kinds of reinforcers. In other words, what is rewarding to one student may not be rewarding to others. For example, some students thrive on praise, while others cringe upon receiving public recognition. At least in part, this varied response is linked to cultural and socioeconomic differences among students. Shade's research (1982) found that many minority students value group identity over individual recognition. Individual public recognition is considered disrespectful and inappropriate (Garner, 1989). In these situations, it is appropriate to reinforce group efforts rather than to single out one individual for praise.

Sometimes what is reinforcing to students surprises teachers. For example, in one kindergarten class the teachers used stickers to reward students for following the class routines. To the students, however, the stickers themselves were not sufficient reinforcement. The real reward was in being allowed to wear the stickers on their faces throughout the day! In another situation, a middle school awarded points to students for appropriate behavior. Students could redeem 1,000 points for lunch with the principal at a fast-food restaurant nearby. Teachers soon found that this was not an appropriate reinforcer; while the students wanted the principal to take them to lunch, they wanted to keep it short. They wanted to get back to school early enough to play basketball with their friends during the lunch break!

A wise teacher is aware of the types of reinforcers learners need and want. Four types of reinforcers are commonly used in classrooms: social, activity, tangible, and negative reinforcers (Goetz et al., 1992; Hunter, 1990; Kazdin, 1975). **Social reinforcers** send a positive message to the student from the teacher. Verbal praise, smiles, time spent with students, and appropriate physical contact are social reinforcers that are easy to give, cost nothing, and are seldom overused. These are often the most powerful reinforcers (Hunter, 1990). However, while these are effective in monitoring students' behavior, they may not be strong enough to control misbehavior in some situations.

When dealing with older students, verbal reinforcers should focus on benefits for the student rather than on the teacher's approval (Hunter, 1990). Whereas primary grade students are usually delighted that their behavior pleases the teacher, some older students may not care about the teacher's approval. Some may even prefer to annoy the teacher! While a statement such as "I like the way Max is getting right to work on his math problems" may effectively reward a primary student, it is important to show the benefit of that appropriate behavior to Max if he is an older student. Try saying, "Max you've gotten right to work on your math problems! That means you'll have them finished before the end of the period so you won't have any homework." At the secondary level, it is often preferable to reinforce students quietly or privately rather than aloud in front of the entire class.

Activity reinforcers are privileges not routinely accorded to everyone. Access to the gym or computer, extra free or recess time, and class responsibilities such as taking messages to the office or monitoring the class when the teacher is out of the room are examples of activity reinforcers that many students prefer. The weakness with using such activity reinforcers is that they may not be immediately available. This makes immediate reinforcement impossible and weakens their effectiveness.

Tangible reinforcers are concrete objects that a student needs or wants. Often referred to as external or extrinsic rewards, they include stickers, pencils, records of productive behavior, and points or tokens redeemable for larger rewards or special events. Hunter (1990) suggests that tangible reinforcers be used sparingly and with caution, usually as a last resort when students do not respond to social or activity reinforcers. Because these extrinsic reinforcers have no natural association with the desired behavior, they can divert the student's attention away from being a responsible, productive, self-directed learner. Lepper (1983) found, for example, that to motivate students toward more appropriate behavior it is sometimes necessary to initially use external rewards but to gradually phase them out as the behavior changes. In contrast, if students are already motivated to behave appropriately, Lepper found that using tangible rewards was harmful because it undermined students' motivation to learn and to behave appropriately.

A less positive but often effective reward for shaping appropriate behavior is by using **negative reinforcement.** Negative reinforcement is important in helping students to develop self-control in the classroom because the student is in charge of what happens (Hunter, 1990). With negative reinforcement, something unpleasant is removed from the student's life when they behave appropriately. This reinforces the desirable behavior. For example, if a student who has been giggling with a neighbor reforms her behavior because of the teacher's glare, the student has removed the negative reinforcer (teacher's glare).

As a teacher, how will you know what kinds of reinforcers will work with your students? One way is to observe the students, especially during free time when they display their interests. Also, especially with older students, you can simply ask them. Many teachers use this information to develop a **reinforcement menu** that lists the various reinforcers available to them as they monitor students' behavior in their classrooms.

Scheduling Reinforcement   Most teachers are aware of the need to reinforce appropriate behavior, especially when students are learning a new behavior such as at the beginning of the school year. When it becomes apparent that the students are beginning to behave appropriately and to demonstrate self-control, teachers begin omitting the reinforcement. They expect the students to behave automatically thereafter (Hunter, 1990). Remember, though, that most students have had a lot of practice and reinforcement for behaving inappropriately. As a result, change doesn't happen overnight. Shaping behavior through reinforcement takes time, persistence, and planning. Students need to be reinforced more than once or twice to produce real changes in their behavior. The more frequently behaviors are reinforced, even for small amounts of progress, the faster students' behavior will change.

Teachers who are effective managers are aware of the importance of scheduling reinforcement. **Scheduling** means changing the frequency of reinforcement in response to students' behavior. As students become more comfortable with the classroom rules and routines and their behavior improves, teachers should reinforce behavior intermittently rather than regularly. In most situations, teachers can gradually eliminate external rewards as students increasingly experience academic and social success and become intrinsically motivated (Woolfolk, 1993). McCaslin and Good (1992) suggest that unless the reinforcement schedule and rewards are adjusted as students progressively assume more responsibility and self-control, conflict and tension will erupt in the classroom.

When teachers persist with frequent, regular reinforcement long after students have mastered the desired behaviors, two things generally result. First, the students begin to ignore the teacher and the rewards; then they become bored with what they perceive as manipulation, and their behavior deteriorates. Morgan (1984) pointed out that rewards should not appear to be ends in themselves but rather to be symbols of how much the student is learning and progressing. In other words, although you need to reinforce students for raising their hands in September, you certainly shouldn't still reward that behavior in May!

Many times during the school year, life becomes hectic for teachers and students alike. Holidays, report cards, inclement weather, and sports events are a few examples of events that raise stress levels in the classroom. Teachers often resign themselves to the fact that students are going to forget the rules and routines at such times and behave much as they did at the beginning of the year. While many teachers unconsciously return to a "catch 'em and punish 'em" mode, scheduling suggests a return to a schedule of regular, frequent reinforcement like that used at

12.14   What reinforcers worked for you in elementary school? in secondary school?

Try Activity 12.6

the beginning of the year. Returning to a frequent reinforcement schedule enables a teacher to maintain the strength of the appropriate behaviors during periods of classroom stress.

Criticisms of Reinforcement Theory   Teachers who apply reinforcement theory in the classroom have a powerful tool to influence students' behavior and establish a positive learning climate. Nevertheless, classroom use of reinforcement and rewards has drawn criticism. Critics and advocates of reinforcement theory alike are quick to point out that there is a danger of teachers misapplying these strategies. Brophy (1983), Slavin (1988), and Woolfolk (1993) have described and summarized these criticisms and dangers:

1. Some people object to the application of reinforcement theory because they think it is "bribing" students to do what they should do anyway: follow the classroom rules.
2. Some critics state that teachers frequently use reinforcement theory to overcontrol students. Others emphasize that teachers should focus on academic behavior rather than social control when they attempt to influence students' behavior. After all, a quiet class is not necessarily a learning class.
3. Some charge that reinforcement theory is impractical for classroom use. The financial and time costs associated with implementing a system of rewards and tokens makes this approach unacceptable to many teachers. Further, it is unlikely that teachers can monitor or systematically reinforce more than a fraction of the desirable behaviors occurring in their classrooms.
4. Others suggest it is questionable whether praise and social reinforcement have powerful effects on most students after first or second grade.
5. Critics warn that emphasizing extrinsic rewards may cause students who are already intrinsically motivated to lose interest in learning for its own sake.

Reacting to Misbehavior

The findings of Kounin and others help us understand how to manage the classroom as a whole. They tell us how to establish a management system that involves students in learning and reduces deviancy (Dunkin & Biddle, 1974). While this is an essential aspect of classroom management, it can only reduce instances of misbehavior, not eliminate them entirely. Effective managers couple skills in preventing and monitoring inappropriate behavior with skills in quickly stopping misbehavior (Emmer, 1987). Let us now turn our attention to the skills and techniques that effective teachers use in responding to misbehavior.

Student misbehavior is any action that the teacher perceives as disruptive to the order of the classroom (Bellon et al., 1992). Misbehavior ranges from very subtle actions to physically aggressive behavior. Cangelosi (1993) classifies the most commonly exhibited misbehaviors in elementary and secondary schools as inappropriate talking (that is, excessive talking, talking out of turn, unnecessary talking) and inappropriate movement, such as clowning and out-of-seat behavior. Other common misbehaviors include tardiness, cutting class, not bringing supplies and books, inattentiveness, daydreaming, and mild verbal and aggressive acts (Doyle, 1986). Less frequently, teachers encounter misbehavior such as crying, arguing, fighting, stealing, and cheating (Steele, 1988). With increased frequency, teachers must also react to students' use of narcotics, alcohol, and weapons (Bellon et al., 1992). Responding to misbehavior, then, is the process of helping students control themselves so that they can function productively in group settings such as the classroom (Bellon et al., 1992).

12.15   What type of misbehavior troubles you the most?

It is important to keep in mind that there is no foolproof method for correcting misbehavior. No single discipline technique will solve the variety of behavior problems exhibited in today's classrooms. To respond to misbehavior in an effective, professional way, teachers must carefully consider the context of the misbehavior and the student's motivation before choosing how to react. That is, they must be good classroom problem solvers (see Chapter 13).

WHY STUDENTS MISBEHAVE

Teachers can respond more appropriately to misbehavior if they understand why students misbehave. Dreikers, Grunwald, and Pepper (1982) propose that, whether they are aware of it or not, students misbehave in order to meet four basic needs. Most misbehavior, at least at the elementary level, is due to students *seeking attention* (Albert, 1995; Glasser, 1990; Savage, 1991). These students need extra attention and want to be center stage. They distract teachers and classmates by making noises, using foul language, and causing interruptions during class. Second, some students misbehave because they are *seeking power*. These students want to be the boss and want things done their way. To show the teacher and classmates that "you can't push me around," they refuse to comply with rules or requests and are likely to challenge and argue with others. Third, misbehavior may be caused by a student's *seeking revenge*. The misbehavior often occurs in response to an earlier power struggle in which the student felt embarrassed, humiliated, or treated with disrespect in front of peers. Students seeking revenge may threaten physical harm or get indirect physical revenge by breaking, damaging, or stealing. A fourth reason students misbehave is that they are *seeking isolation*. These students are trying to avoid failure. They feel inadequate and believe they can't live up to their own, their family's, or the teacher's expectations. They procrastinate, pretend to have disabilities, and turn in incomplete work hoping everyone will leave them alone so they won't have to face the fact they aren't working up to their potential. Unfortunately, being left alone further erodes their sense of adequacy.

While much misbehavior is due to students' attempts to meet their needs, Sylwester (1971) points out that some misbehavior is actually caused by teachers. Sylwester identified four teacher behaviors that cause misbehavior in the classroom. *Inadequate preparation* is perhaps the most common. Failure to plan the structure and pace of learning activities causes students to become restless and misbehave. Second, *differential treatment* of students often causes misbehavior because students think the teacher has certain favorites or enemies. *Verbal abuse,* especially "friendly" sarcasm, also causes student reactions and misbehavior. Finally, if students feel that a teacher *responds unfairly* to misbehavior, further misbehavior often results.

In order to manage misbehavior, teachers need to be aware of what motivates students to misbehave and how their own behavior influences the behavior of the students. This suggests that they need to develop sensitivity and a broad range of skills and techniques to draw upon when reacting to misbehavior in their classroom.

DECIDING HOW TO REACT TO MISBEHAVIOR

Teachers who are good classroom managers are also good decision makers (Bellon et al., 1992). When misbehavior erupts, teachers must decide *when* and *how* to intervene. Effective teachers deal with misbehavior as quickly as possible (Albert, 1995; Evertson, 1989). But how do they decide how to intervene? At least four concerns should shape the decision: whether intervention will interrupt the lesson, the nature and severity of the misbehavior, the student involved, and the time the misbehavior occurred.

First and foremost, teachers must decide to what extent the intervention will interrupt or interfere with the instructional activity (Bellon et al., 1992). Doyle (1986) warns that, while most teachers intervene about sixteen times per hour,

12.16 What caused you to misbehave in school?

12.17 How will you determine the cause of a students' misbehavior?

"How come when you say we have a problem, I'm always the one who has the problem?"

interrupting the lesson to deal with misbehavior is "inherently risky" since it distracts from ongoing instruction. For example, the most successful teachers that Kounin (1983) observed kept students on task 98.7 percent of the time. The least successful teachers intervened 986 times a day, which meant the students were engaged in learning only 25 percent of the time.

Further, decisions on how to intervene should be based on the nature and severity of the misbehavior, the student involved, and the time the misbehavior occurred (Doyle, 1986; Wolfgang & Kelsay, 1995). Beginning teachers are often told they must be consistent in how they deal with misbehavior, or students will become confused and the misbehavior will increase. Many teachers find this expectation confining and frustrating, especially at the secondary level where students may challenge the teachers fairness. Dreikers and colleagues (1982) suggest that, since the same teacher-imposed consequences are not equally effective on all students, it is better to develop a range of intervention strategies. A normally responsible student who neglects to turn in one assignment, for example, should not require the same punishment as a student who repeatedly misses assignments. It is essential, though, that the intervention seems logical and fair to the students and their parents. Ideally, the intervention will educate students about how their actions affect their lives and the lives of those who must share classroom space and experiences with them (Wolfgang & Kelsay, 1995). Further, Curwin and Mendler (1988) encourage teachers to discuss with their students the fact that "fair is not always equal." They should point out that just as students require individualized academic plans to meet their different learning needs, they also have varying social needs which require a range of alternative consequences. This enables teachers to be both consistent and flexible when intervening in students' behavior.

TYPES OF INTERVENTION

Unfortunately, little research is available to suggest how effective teachers respond to repeated student misconduct (Reynolds, 1992). Effective classroom managers, however, have a repertoire of intervention strategies that range from subtle, unobtrusive actions to radical strategies such as expulsion. To be effective, intervention strategies must be delivered calmly, firmly, and with intensity immediately after the misbehavior, and must be confined to the offending students (Erickson & Mohatt, 1992). Negative responses to misbehavior, such as criticism, shouting, scolding, ridicule, and sarcasm, are not effective (Canter, 1996; Kounin & Gump, 1961; Swick, 1985). Further, while public reprimands, corporal punishment, and other punitive actions may stop misbehavior temporarily, they are ineffective in the long run

12.18 Describe a classroom incident you observed in which the teachers' intervention distracted from the lesson.

because they fail to teach constructive substitute behaviors (Goldstein, 1989; Wolfgang & Kelsey, 1995). Teachers using these negative and punitive approaches generally find their students become more aggressive and unsettled and less concerned with learning than do effective classroom managers (Kounin & Gump, 1961).

How, then, should we react when students misbehave? The following list of strategies is appropriate for classroom intervention. They are arranged from the most subtle, nonintrusive measures to stronger corrective interventions.

Extinction   Effective teachers generally ignore minor distractions and instances of inattention (Reynolds, 1992). For example, if a student misbehaves to gain the teacher's attention and that attention is withheld, it is likely the behavior will disappear. This intervention strategy is called **extinction.** It suggests that a teacher should ignore minor attention-seeking misbehavior the first time it happens as long as it is not dangerous or distracting to other students (Hunter, 1990).

It is important to understand that extinction is a nondirective response. That is, while students may cease the distracting behavior, they still don't know how they should behave. The key, then, is not how you react to the misbehaving student, but how you respond to the other students in the class who are behaving appropriately. While you ignore the misbehavior, you praise or give attention to the appropriate behavior of another student near the offender. This communicates to offenders what they should be doing (Hunter, 1990; Martin, 1981).

Let's look at an example. As you begin a lesson, Keyla begins to tap her pencil on the desk in an effort to distract you and gain your attention. In applying extinction, you would ignore Keyla's pencil tapping but turn to Ricardo, who sits nearby, and praise him for listening closely to the directions. This suggests to Keyla that in order to gain the teacher's attention, she too must listen closely to the directions.

Although extinction has been used effectively to eliminate disruptive behavior, off-task behavior, tantrums, and aggression (Goetz et al., 1992), it is quite difficult to practice. One reason is that it basically requires you to do something unnatural. You have been trained to be aware of everything going on in your classroom and, upon recognizing misbehavior, to "nip it in the bud." Recall that Kounin's research (1970) shows that effective classroom managers are "withit," or aware of everything that is happening in the classroom, and that they communicate their awareness to students. The principle of extinction suggests that you *not* communicate directly with students if your response provides them with the attention they are inappropriately seeking. Instead you provide attention or positive reinforcement only when a student chooses to act appropriately.

Another problem with the use of extinction is that it takes time to change behavior. Worse yet, ignoring attention-seeking behavior may, at first, actually increase incidents of misbehavior (Cruickshank & associates, 1980; Kounin, 1970). In some cases, ignoring students' behavior leads to aggression, presumably in reaction to increasing frustration (Azrin, Hutchinson, & Hake, 1966). If Sam, for example, gained the teacher's attention in fourth grade by getting out of his seat, it is likely he will try the same method in your fifth-grade class. If you do not respond the way the fourth-grade teacher did, he may assume that you simply don't see him and get out of his seat even more frequently. After all, if he gained attention from teachers in the past by behaving in this way, why should he expect a different reaction now? However, if you consistently ignore the misbehavior and redirect attention toward the appropriate behavior, the misbehavior should eventually disappear. More importantly, you will have prevented interruptions to your lessons.

12.19   How do you feel when a teacher uses mild desists to correct your behavior?

Mild Desists   Effective managers deal with potentially serious disruptions early by using nonverbal intervention and mild desists (Reynolds, 1992). Nonverbal strategies such as establishing eye contact, shaking the head, using facial expressions, moving closer, touching or gesturing, and redirecting attention are highly effective, yet they do not interrupt the flow of the lesson or distract other students in the class. Indeed, a study of middle school teachers found that nonverbal strategies stopped misbehavior 79 percent of the time. Teachers in the study identified as the "more effective managers" had an even higher success rate, stopping misbehavior with nonverbal strategies 95 percent of the time (Lasley, Lasley, & Ward, 1989)!

Subtle verbal desists are also effective. Slowing your speaking rate, pronouncing things more distinctly, speaking more softly, or (even more powerful) pausing briefly and looking around are all nonobtrusive, more private ways of conveying to students that they need to adjust their behavior. Likewise, using the misbehaving student's name, directing short questions or comments to the disruptive student, calling the name and pausing briefly, or redirecting the student back to the lesson ("Open to page 271 and follow along") are effective yet largely nonintrusive verbal interventions. Brophy (1982, 1983) points out that such subtle but direct public interventions are often more effective than ignoring misbehavior or praising appropriate behavior. This is particularly true for older students who bisbehave because they are seeking attention.

Reprimands Verbal reprimands are widely used in classrooms. White (1975) found that teachers in all grades reprimand students once every two minutes. Sadly, the number of reprimands exceeds the amount of praise given in every grade after second grade.

Teachers often reprimand students for not listening, breaking school rules, or creating noise others can hear outside the classroom. The use of reprimands also tends to be highly situational. Teachers seem to be more tolerant, or at least to deliver fewer reprimands, immediately following a lesson and during the last few minutes of the period. Teachers also appear more tolerant when the misbehavior is minor, brief, and not likely to escalate or when it is caused by a usually well-behaved student (Bellon et al., 1992).

Reynolds (1992) outlines the way effective managers deliver reprimands. They talk with misbehaving students in private rather than in front of the class, thus minimizing power struggles and face-saving gestures. They question the students to determine whether they understood their inappropriate behavior, and they ask for explanations. Also, effective managers make sure that students understand why the behavior is unacceptable; they try to get the students to accept responsibility for the behavior and to make a commitment to change. They instruct or model more acceptable ways for the students to behave. Finally, effective managers warn students about the consequences of continuing the misbehavior, help them understand how the consequences of disruptive behavior are detrimental to them and to other students, and follow through with those consequences when the misbehavior does not change.

In summary, effective managers view misbehavior as instances when the student did not learn appropriate behavior. From this view, misbehavior is a situation that calls for corrections that explain and reorient. Misbehavior need not be endured or punished (Emmer & Evertson, 1981; Kounin & Gump, 1961).

Overcorrection Overcorrection, sometimes called positive practice, is the compulsory practice of acceptable behavior as a result of misbehavior (Kazdin, 1982). When a student misbehaves, the teacher can apply overcorrection by having the student repeatedly perform the correct behavior. The teacher may also require the student to make restitution by correcting any damage related to the inappropriate behavior. For example, consider a student who is heading toward the door at the end of the period, pushing desks out of the way and talking loudly the whole way. Overcorrection would require the student to practice leaving the room appropriately and to straighten the desks pushed out of line.

FIGURE 12.7 Types of Intervention

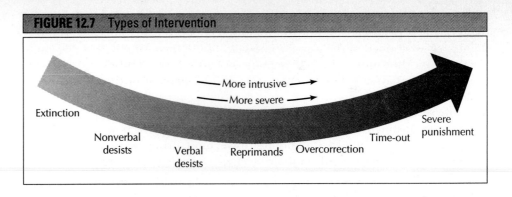

While overcorrection is primarily used to help children with severe problems learn self-help skills, teachers have also used it to deal with disruptive behavior, poor attendance, and failure to share (Azrin & Powers, 1975; Barton & Osborne, 1978).

Time-Out For more serious misbehavior, using a time-out strategy may be effective (Figure 12.7). **Time-out** reduces unwanted behavior by removing the offending student from the situation and, therefore, from the attention and rewards the situation provides. During time-out, the student may be excluded from an activity, asked to put her hands or head on her desk, removed to a desk in the back of the room, removed from the classroom, or sent to a time-out room.

Time-out is especially effective for students who misbehave to draw attention from their peers or who are overly active. If, for example, a student kicks the volleyball across the gymnasium during a physical education class to show off to his classmates, the teacher would ask the student to sit on the bleachers for ten minutes to think about what he has done. If the student enjoys playing volleyball with his teammates, being removed from the situation is punishment. He is likely to consider what he did wrong and resolve to behave appropriately if he wants to reenter the game.

It is important to remember certain guidelines when using time-out. First, the time-out period must be brief, usually from five to twelve minutes, depending on the age of the student. A rule of thumb is that the time-out should be one minute long for each year of the child's age. Longer periods of time do not make the treatment more effective (Kazdin, 1982). An extended time-out period could increase the student's resentment if he or she considers the time-out unfair, or it may cause the student to fall behind in class work.

Second, during time-out, the student must be isolated. It is best to isolate the student in the classroom to retain opportunities for learning (Kazdin, 1982). Asking a disruptive student to leave a math lesson for time-out in the hallway where he gets attention from every passerby may be more of a reward than a punishment, especially if he doesn't like math! However, if the misbehavior is so severe that the student's continued presence is likely to disrupt instruction, the isolation may need to occur outside the classroom. It is important that classmates or other school personnel not talk with the student during isolation. If a student is sent to another classroom or to the office for time-out, school personnel should be asked not to interact with the offending student.

Third, the offending student should be allowed to return to the regular classroom activity after the designated time has elapsed or when she demonstrates appropriate behavior, such as sitting quietly and attending to the lesson. Some teachers ask students to identify what they did wrong and how they should have acted as a condition for returning to the activity.

Finally, students should be held accountable for the work they miss during a time-out. The work should be completed on the students' own time or at home rather than during recess or a special activity, which would serve as a second punishment.

Time-out can be an effective way to influence student behavior if you correctly apply and monitor it. Above all, don't forget about the student! Too many teachers remove distracting students from the situation, return to the lesson, and promptly forget about the student in time-out. The extended, unfocused time in isolation negates the impact of the time-out procedure for the misbehaving student.

USING PUNISHMENT IN THE CLASSROOM

The most common reaction to misbehavior in schools, no matter what the offense, is some form of punishment. Punishments may include verbal reprimands, time-out, detentions, or more severe verbal or physical reactions (Englander, 1986). Yet Reynolds (1992) found that effective classroom managers invoked punishment only as a last resort, and Hamilton and Ghatala (1994) note "there is not much to recommend it as a procedure for eliminating undesirable behavior" (p. 57). **Punishment** is something undesirable, painful, or discomforting that is applied to the student as a result of misbehavior. It is intended to weaken the probability that the inappropriate behavior will recur (Savage, 1991). The most effective punishments are brief and mild; they involve restitution and allow students to quickly regain normal status (Bellon et al., 1992). Punishment should also provide students with information about how to change their behavior (Brophy & Evertson, 1976; Wolfgang & Kelsay, 1995).

Criticisms of Punishment Teachers can easily misuse punishment, and consequently it is a controversial topic in today's schools. Some of the more common criticisms are summarized here:

1. Critics contend that while punishment may restore a student's appropriate behavior temporarily, in the long run it has undesirable side effects on both the offending students and the entire class (Steele, 1988). This is because punishment often stirs negative emotions in students. Some students become resentful of the teacher and vow to avenge the punishment, especially if they consider the punishment unfair or too harsh. Also, by experiencing punishment or seeing others being punished, some students become so anxious and fearful that their academic performance suffers.
2. Another criticism of punishment is that it often strengthens bad behavior, especially if the punishment is administered publicly. This is especially true for students who receive little or no attention at home or who are behaviorally disadvantaged. Punishment may be the only type of attention they know how to gain. To such children, anything, even punishment, is better than being ignored.
3. Others point out that punishment fails to model appropriate behavior and actually models aggressive behavior (Brophy & Putnam, 1979). Punishment also breeds avoidance behavior, which may be counterproductive to learning and socialization (Stipek, 1988). Becker (1986) contends that most of the undesirable behaviors observed in school and society (cheating, truancy, sneaking, hiding, lying) are really escape and avoidance behaviors that children learn in order to avoid punishment at school or at home.
4. Punishment does not remove the underlying causes of the misbehavior (Englander, 1986). Students still do not know how to resolve conflicts, deal with frustrations, or follow classroom rules and routines after punishment. It is important, then, that discipline focus on educating students about appropriate behaviors and social responsibility (Wolfgang & Kelsay, 1995).

Guidelines for Using Punishment Advocates of the appropriate use of punishment point out that, when carefully used, punishment can be effective. For example, softly delivered, firm reprimands for misbehaviors have proven to be much more

12.20 As a student, were you ever punished? How did you feel?

12.21 Are you surprised that teachers use punishment so widely in today's classrooms?

effective than shouting (O'Leary et al., 1970). The following guidelines apply to using punishment in the classroom.

1. *Use punishment sparingly.* O'Leary and O'Leary (1972) suggest that punishment should be reserved for serious misbehavior and generally used as a last resort. Further, a teacher should never punish out of anger or frustration. Effective classroom managers take responsibility for dealing with problem students rather than referring them to others such as the guidance counselor or principal (Brophy & Rohrkemper, 1981). In short, effective classroom managers take responsibility for managing their students' behavior and do so in a professional manner.

2. *Use punishment quickly.* Effective classroom managers react to students' misbehavior quickly—usually when the behavior starts (Walters, Parke, & Cane, 1965). Effective managers don't threaten students or issue warnings unless they follow up on those reminders. Further, Emmer, Evertson, and Anderson (1980) found that effective managers plan their penalties ahead of time and usually discuss those penalties with students.

12.22 What logical consequences would you use for the common misbehaviors discussed in this chapter?

3. *Use punishments related to the misbehavior.* In selecting punishments for possible use in your classroom, it is important to make sure they logically relate to the misbehavior. For example, if a student turns in a poorly prepared paper, the logical consequence is to have him rewrite it, rather than to keep him after school or assign him additional math problems for homework. Punishments that are not related to the offense may be seen as arbitrary to students, and the teacher may appear dictatorial. Illogical punishment may also hinder learning. For example, assigning regular schoolwork as punishment is inversely related to gains in students' learning (Brophy & Evertson, 1976).

12.23 What qualities do you have that will help you deal with misbehavior?

4. *Use punishment after careful consideration.* Since punishment is complex and situational (Bellon et al., 1992), teachers should be aware of the context; they should know how the students will interpret the punishment and what the punishment will require of them. It is possible, for example, for teachers to administer a "punishment" that the student does not perceive as punishment. For some students, being forced to sit out of a physical education class or to stay inside during recess may be a blessing in disguise. Can you see why? Further, as Brophy and Evertson (1976) note, the effectiveness of some forms of punishment differs according to the socioeconomic status of the student.

Try Activity 12.7

5. *Avoid complex, time-consuming punishment systems.* Some teachers try to implement complex intervention systems that require extensive record keeping or time-consuming conferencing. Even if these systems are effective, they may be too complicated to be practical (Bellon et al., 1992). Further, they generally do not provide the immediate reinforcement vital to changing students' behavior (Evertson & Harris, 1992).

Reestablishing the Learning Environment

No matter what intervention you choose to employ in a given classroom situation, you will need to reestablish a positive classroom climate and a positive relationship with the offending student as soon as possible. After all, the message you want to convey is that while the behavior is unacceptable, the student is an acceptable person and an important part of the class. You can use the strategies listed earlier in the chapter to reestablish a positive, cooperative relationship among students and between you and the offending student.

Sometimes the management systems initiated at the start of the year just don't seem to work, and sometimes the reinforcement and intervention strategies you employ are not effective. Don't panic or resign yourself to putting up with a disorganized or unruly class for the remainder of the year. Evertson (1989) recommends reexamining your management system periodically and repairing and restoring the system as needed. These "second beginnings" are best introduced after natural breaks in the school year, such as after a weekend or holiday. They should be implemented using clear communication, careful monitoring, and consistent accountability, just as you would introduce a management plan at the beginning of the school year. There is nothing wrong with making a mistake and starting over, as long as the repaired management system contributes to a more effective learning environment.

Some Final Thoughts

Good classroom management is essential to classroom learning. Effective managers plan how to prevent behavior problems, how to monitor student behavior, how to react when students misbehave, and how to reestablish a positive classroom environment after correcting misbehavior. They know how to review and adjust their management plans. By developing and following proactive behavior management plans, you will help establish an effective learning environment for your students and minimize stress in the classroom.

CHAPTER SUMMARY

- Nearly everyone expects teachers to be good classroom managers. Administrators often consider teachers who exert strong control to be their best teachers, while parents and the community expect teachers to teach students self-control. Likewise, students expect teachers to exert control and to establish a positive learning environment. Finally, teachers who are poor classroom managers feel frustrated and dissatisfied with teaching.

- Classroom management consists of all the provisions and procedures a teacher uses to create and maintain a classroom environment in which teaching and learning can occur. Traditionally classroom management focused on reactive management, that is, how teachers reacted to (or disciplined) students who misbehaved. This approach neglected the close relationship between instruction and classroom management. Today's classrooms stress proactive management, or preventing control problems from erupting in the first place.

- Effective classroom managers prevent control problems by organizing and establishing a classroom environment that is safe and predictable, both physically and psychologically.

- The physical environment consists of those concrete elements that are independent of the people who inhabit the classroom. The psychological environment is intangible and exists only in the minds of teachers and students.

- Seating patterns influence peer interactions, teacher-student interactions, and student attitudes or affect. Students seated at tables interact more than students seated in rows and, consequently, tend to develop better leadership skills. Students seated in a circle speak more to those across from them and less to those seated next to them. An action zone of teacher-student interaction is composed of students seated toward the front and middle of the class. These students enjoy the teacher more and feel more involved in the class. Because no single seating arrangement is ideal, experts recommend a flexible arrangement that the teacher can modify for various activities.

- Although teachers cannot control the number of students in their classes, they should ensure that all students have comfortable desks and lockers and that materials and equipment are readily available without crowding students or making them wait. Likewise, they should arrange their rooms to produce a safe, stimulating environment for students. This includes arranging furniture to (1) minimize distractions and congestion; (2) establish activity boundaries between incompatible activities; (3) allow the teacher to monitor in all parts of the room; and (4) provide open lanes for movement, especially between desks and around supply areas.

- In a classroom with a positive tone, students feel safe, comfortable, respected, and responsible. In such classrooms, (1) students' basic needs are met; (2) color, light, temperature, and displays are used to create softness, stimulation, and emotional safety; (3) mutual respect, cooperation, and student responsibility are present; (4) student and teacher ownership are evident; (5) the environment is busy and task-oriented; and (6) teachers' expectations are clear, and structure is provided.

- Classroom routines, which control and coordinate movement and events, help prevent classroom management problems. These routines fall into four categories: management routines, activity routines, instructional routines, and executive planning routines.

- Management problems can be minimized by arranging the classroom environment and establishing routines early in the school year. The task of establishing classroom rules and routines begins on the first day of class and routines, like instructional lessons, should be clearly communicated, modeled, and taught to students. Teachers should also provide opportunities to practice. Finally, teachers should communicate that they are prepared and competent to manage the classroom and should hold students responsible for following the classroom routines.

- Monitoring students' behavior throughout the year by signaling students who are beginning to misbehave and redirecting their attention to the lesson prevents serious misbehavior. Effective monitoring involves the use of withitness, overlapping, smoothness and momentum, and group alerting techniques.

- Teachers can monitor and maintain students' behavior by using rewards and reinforcement. Reinforcement theory posits that behavior that is rewarded is strengthened and likely to be repeated; behavior that is not rewarded is likely to diminish. To be effective, targeted behaviors must be clearly communicated and must be reinforced immediately after the behavior.

- Since different students respond to different types of reinforcement, teachers should develop a reinforcement menu that meets the needs and wants of individual students. Such a menu should include (1) social reinforcers such as praise, smiles, and physical contact; (2) activity reinforcers such as free time or class responsibilities; (3) tangible reinforcers such as redeemable tokens; and (4) negative reinforcers such as removal from detention.

- As students' behavior improves, teachers must change the reinforcement schedule. Desirable behaviors should be reinforced less frequently following mastery, and more complex behaviors should be reinforced after students have learned simple behaviors.

- Many critics disparage the use of reinforcement in classrooms. Some view reinforcement as bribing students, others as overcontrolling them. Some feel that praise and social rewards are ineffective after the primary grades and that extrinsic rewards may actually reduce internal motivation. Finally, some critics say reinforcement theory is impractical for classroom use because of the time, expense, and complexity involved.

- Even with a well-planned and monitored management system, misbehavior will occur. Such misbehavior can result from a need for attention, power, revenge, or isolation. Also, teachers sometimes cause the misbehavior by failing to prepare, by treating students differently, by verbally abusing them, or reacting in ways that students perceive as unfair.

- Teachers must decide when and how to intervene when students misbehave and must respond quickly. When deciding how to intervene, they should consider the extent to which intervention will interrupt instruction, the nature and severity of the misbehavior, the student involved, and when the misbehavior occurred.

- Effective classroom managers have a repertoire of intervention strategies they can use to respond to students' misbehavior. These include extinction, mild desists, reprimands, overcorrection, time-out, and other forms of punishment.

- Critics charge that punishment has undesirable long-term side effects, that it sometimes strengthens bad behavior, that it teaches aggressive and avoidance behavior, and that it does not remove the underlying cause of the behavior problem. However, punishment may be effective in reducing repeated, serious misbehavior. When using punishment, the teacher should administer it quickly and thoughtfully, should make sure it is logically related to the misbehavior, and should choose the intervention after careful consideration of the context, the way students will respond to the punishment, and the complexity of the intervention system.

- Periodically, it may be necessary to evaluate and reestablish the learning environment in the classroom. For example, after intervening in misbehavior, the teacher needs to reestablish a positive climate of mutual respect and cooperation. It is a good idea to periodically review the effectiveness of the management plan and to adopt new routines when needed.

ISSUES AND PROBLEMS FOR DISCUSSION

1. What should the goal of classroom management be?
2. Should teachers share their personal lives and interests in the classroom?
3. Do students have rights in the classroom? Do teachers?
4. Is it ethical for teachers to influence or control student behavior?
5. Should teachers be responsible for the behavior of students outside the classroom?
6. Should students' behavior be factored into their grades?
7. Should punishment be used in classrooms? Can it be "humane?"
8. Should teachers send misbehaving students to the principal's office?
9. Should principals be expected to support teachers' classroom management practices and decisions?
10. Should states outlaw some forms of punishment, such as paddling?
11. How should teachers respond to the increased violence in today's schools?

THEORY INTO ACTION ACTIVITIES

ACTIVITY 12.1: Observing Seating Arrangements
1. Ask your cooperating teacher what he or she thinks are the most important things to take into account when deciding how to seat students in a classroom.
2. Observe in several classrooms that have different seating arrangements for students. Draw a diagram of the way the desks are arranged. Then make a sociogram by drawing arrows to indicate the conversational flow among students. Keep track of these student interactions for ten minutes. When you compare the student interactions across different seating arrangements, what do you notice?

FIGURE 12.8 Floor Plan of Music Classroom

Two rows of twenty-five folding chairs on risers

Door

Drum set

Piano

Chalkboard

3. Figure 12.8 is a diagram of a music classroom. The fifty students were seated in two rows of folding chairs. The teacher was very frustrated because the students talked and misbehaved so much she could hardly teach. Analyze the seating arrangement and make suggestions about changes that might prevent students from misbehaving. Also suggest instructional behaviors the teacher should adopt to monitor students and hold their attention.

4. Visit a classroom. Observe students and the seats they are assigned to. Do the students seem to "fit" comfortably in their seats? Are left-handed and special-needs students accommodated? Try sitting in a student seat yourself. How does it feel? Could you sit there comfortably for a morning or a day?

ACTIVITY 12.2: Organizing the Physical and Psychological Environments of the Classroom

1. As you enter the classroom, what are your feelings and first impressions? What messages about learning and the teacher does the classroom send? How would you feel about spending many hours each day in this classroom as a student? As a teacher?

2. Draw a floor plan for the classroom. Be sure to include all furniture and workstations in the classroom on your drawing. Now observe the flow of students around the classroom for thirty minutes. Draw those patterns on your floor plan. Identify areas of heavy traffic flow and bottlenecks that may threaten the students' sense of psychological safety in the classroom.

3. Softness in the room helps students to feel safe and meets aesthetic needs. Look around the room for examples of softness and list them.

4. What do you see that communicates something about the people who occupy this room? How is student ownership of the classroom expressed?

5. Now observe the teacher-student interactions in the room, especially during instruction or discussion. Construct a sociogram showing the patterns of interaction. Try to identify the action zone in the classroom. Does the teacher make any efforts to accommodate students sitting outside the action zone?

6. Does the classroom provide an enriched environment? Identify and describe ways the teacher uses the physical environment to stimulate students' growth and learning.
7. Evaluate the physical and psychological environments you have observed. What are the strengths? From your point of view, how could the environment be changed to make it a more accessible and inviting environment?

ACTIVITY 12.3: Developing Classroom Rules

1. Ask your cooperating teacher about classroom rules.
   a. What are they? Are they posted? Why or why not?
   b. How does the teacher develop the rules?
   c. How does the teacher introduce the rules at the beginning of the year?
   d. Analyze the rules for clarity, simplicity, positive tone, and practicality.
2. Ask a student about classroom rules.
   a. What are they?
   b. How were the rules developed?
   c. How did the students learn the rules?
   d. Are the rules enforced? If so, how and when?
3. Compare responses from the teacher and student with your own observations.

ACTIVITY 12.4: Developing Classroom Routines

1. Ask your cooperating teacher what he or she thinks about routines and which are the most critical.
2. Observe and describe the following management routines in an elementary or secondary classroom.
   a. How does the teacher pass out and distribute student papers and work?
   b. What routines are established for student transitions: entering the room, leaving the room, and moving from one instructional activity to another?
   c. How does the teacher begin and end the school day or class period?
   d. What routines are in place for students to sharpen pencils, use the restroom, dispose of trash, or meet other individual needs?
   e. Are students given responsibilities in the classroom? What evidence do you see of this? How are student responsibilities assigned?
3. Observe and describe the following activity routines in an elementary or secondary classroom.
   a. When and how do students gain the teacher's attention? Does this routine change throughout the day based on the type of activity or other factors?
   b. Identify and describe one activity routine in the classroom.
4. Observe and describe the following instructional routines in an elementary or secondary classroom.
   a. What routine or procedure does the teacher use to give directions or assignments?
   b. Listen closely to how the teacher asks questions or leads a discussion. What routines does the teacher follow?
5. Observe or discuss the following executive planning routines your cooperating teacher utilizes.
   a. When does the teacher plan for instruction?
   b. What executive routines does the teacher have in place for grading papers, running dittos, typing tests, and performing clerical tasks?
   c. What advice would the teacher give you about balancing your personal and professional lives as a new teacher?
6. From what you have observed and heard, how important do you think routines will be in your classroom? Cite three specific routines you are now aware of that you plan to adopt in your own classroom someday.

ACTIVITY 12.5: Holding Students Accountable

1. Ask your cooperating teacher what he or she does during the first day and week of school.
2. Observe your cooperating teacher. Describe behaviors the teacher uses to communicate to students that he or she is "withit."
3. Describe how your cooperating teacher exhibited the ability to overlap.
4. When observing in your cooperating teacher's classroom, look for things that threaten the smoothness and momentum of the lesson. How does the teacher deal with each of these?
5. Observe as your cooperating teacher monitors students by using nonverbal behaviors. Describe the nonverbal behaviors you observe.

ACTIVITY 12.6: Reinforcement in the Classroom

1. Observe your cooperating teacher for thirty minutes, focusing on teacher-student interactions. List specific examples of social reinforcers the teacher used. How did students respond?
2. What is the teacher reinforcing? Is it behavior or academic performance? (You may need to keep a tally to answer the question accurately.)
3. List specific examples of activity reinforcers you observed. How did students respond to them?
4. List examples of tangible reinforcers or rewards the teacher used. How did students respond?
5. From your observations, which types of reinforcement seemed to be most effective in bringing about desired behavior? How can you explain this?

ACTIVITY 12.7: Types of Intervention

1. Interview three teachers to determine what they think about using extinction in the classroom. Have they tried to extinguish inappropriate behavior? Do they think the approach works?
2. Observe a classroom for examples of extinction. How does the misbehaving student respond?
3. Observe a teacher interacting with students for thirty minutes. Keep a tally of the nonverbal and verbal mild desists the teacher uses to intervene in misbehavior. Which approach does the teacher use most frequently? Which approach seems most effective with the students in that classroom?
4. Talk with a variety of teachers and ask them what types of intervention they use. Make a list. Does the type of intervention used vary according to grade level? years of teacher experience? other classroom variables?
5. Survey several students, parents, and teachers to see if they agree or disagree with the use of punishment in the classroom. What kinds of punishment do they deem appropriate? What do they think is inappropriate?

REFERENCES

Adams, R. S., & Biddle, B. J. (1970). *Realities of teaching: Exploration with videotape.* New York: Holt, Rinehart, and Winston.

Ainley, J. G. (1987). Equipment and materials. In M. J. Dunkin (Ed.), *The international encyclopedia of teaching and teacher education.* New York: Pergamon.

Albert, L. (1995). Discipline: Is it a dirty word? *Learning. 24*(2), 43–46.

Anderson, L. M., Evertson, C. M., & Brophy, J. (1979). An experimental study of effective teaching in first-grade reading groups. *Elementary School Journal, 79,* 193–223.

Anderson, L. W. (1991). Classroom environment and climate. *Increasing teacher effectiveness* (pp. 36–53). Paris: UNESCO.

Azrin, N. H., Hutchinson, R. R., & Hake, D. J. (1966). Extinction-induced aggression. *Journal of the Experimental Analysis of Behavior, 9,* 191–204.

Azrin, N. H., & Powers, M. A. (1975). Eliminating classroom disturbances of emotionally disturbed children by positive proactive procedures. *Behavior Therapy, 6,* 525–534.

Barton, E. J., & Osborne, J. G. (1978). Development of classroom sharing by a teacher using positive practice. *Behavior Modification, 2,* 231–250.

Becker, W. C. (1986). *Applied psychology for teachers: A behavioral cognitive approach.* Chicago: Science Research Associates.

Bellon, J. J., Bellon, E. C., & Blank, M. A. (1992). *Teaching from a research knowledge base.* New York: Macmillan.

Borich, G. D. (1992). *Effective teaching methods.* Second Edition. New York: Merrill.

Brodie, T. A., Jr. (1964, December). Attitude toward school and academic achievement. *Personnel and Guidance Journal, 153,* 375–378.

Brophy, J. E. (1982). Supplemental group management techniques. In D. Duke (Ed.), *Helping teachers manage classrooms* (pp. 32–51). Alexandria, VA: Association for Supervision and Curriculum Development.

Brophy, J. E. (1983). Classroom organization and management. In D. C. Smith (Ed.), *Essential knowledge for beginning educators* (pp. 23–37). Washington DC: American Association of Colleges for Teacher Education.

Brophy, J. E., & Evertson, C. M. (1976). *Learning from teaching: A developmental perspective.* Boston: Allyn & Bacon.

Brophy, J. E., & Putnam, J. (1979). Classroom management in the elementary grades. In D. Duke (Ed.), *Classroom management.* (The Seventy-eighth Yearbook of the National Society for the Study of Education, pt. 2, pp. 182–216). Chicago: University of Chicago Press.

Brophy, J. E., & Rohrkemper, M. M. (1981). The influence of problem ownership on teachers' perceptions of and strategies for coping with student problems. *Journal of Educational Psychology, 73,* 295–311.

Cangelosi, J. S. (1993). *Classroom management strategies: Gaining and maintaining students' cooperation.* New York: Longman.

Canter, L. (1996). First, the rapport—then, the rules. *Learning, 24*(5), 12–14.

Cruickshank, D. R., & associates. (1980). *Teaching is tough.* Englewood Cliffs, NJ: Prentice-Hall.

Curwin, R. L., & Mendler, A. N. (1988). *Discipline with dignity.* Alexandria, VA: Association for Supervision and Curriculum Development.

Dollard, N. (1996). Constructive classroom management. *Focus on Exceptional Children, 29*(2), 1–12.

Doyle, W. (1983). Academic work. *Review of Educational Research, 53,* 159–199.

Doyle, W. (1986). Classroom organization and management. In M. C. Wittrock (Ed.), *Handbook of research on teaching,* Third Edition (pp. 392–431). New York: Macmillan.

Dreikers, R., Grunwald, B., & Pepper, F. (1982). *Maintaining sanity in the classroom: Classroom management techniques.* Third Edition. New York: Harper & Row.

Duke, D. L. (1987). Environmental influences. In M. J. Dunkin (Ed.), *The international encyclopedia of teaching and teacher education* (pp. 548–553). New York: Pergamon.

Dunkin, M. J., & Biddle, B. J. (1974). *The study of teaching.* New York: University Press.

Dykman, B., & Reis, H. (1979). Personality correlates of classroom seating position. *Journal of Educational Psychology, 71,* 346–354.

Eggen, P. D., & Kauchak, D. (1992). *Educational psychology: Classroom connections.* New York: Macmillan.

Emmer, E. T. (1987). Classroom management. In M. J. Dunkin (Ed.), *The international encyclopedia of teaching and teacher education* (pp. 437–445). New York: Pergamon.

Emmer, E. T., & Evertson, C. M. (1981). Synthesis of research on classroom management. *Educational Leadership, 38,* 342–347.

Emmer, E. T., Evertson, C. M., & Anderson, L. M. (1980). Effective classroom management at the beginning of the school year. *The Elementary School Journal, 80,* 219–231.

Emmer, E. T., Evertson, C. M., Sanford, J. P., Clements, B. S., & Worsham, M. E. (1989). *Classroom management for secondary teachers.* Englewood Cliffs, NJ: Prentice-Hall.

Englander, M. E. (1986). *Strategies for classroom discipline.* New York: Praeger.

Erickson, F., & Mohatt, G. (1992). Cultural organization of participant structures in two classrooms of Indian students. In G. Spindler (Ed.), *Doing the ethnography of schooling: Educational anthropology in action* (pp. 132–174). New York: Holt, Rinehart, and Winston.

Evertson, C. M. (1987). Creating conditions for learning: From research to practice. *Theory Into Practice, 26,* 44–50.

Evertson, C. M. (1989). Classroom organization and management. In M. C. Reynolds, (Ed.), *Knowledge base for the beginning teacher* (pp. 59–70). New York: Pergamon.

Evertson, C. M., Emmer, E. T., Clements, B. S., Sanford, J. P., & Worsham, M. E. (1989). *Classroom management for elementary teachers.* Englewood Cliffs, NJ: Prentice-Hall.

Evertson, C. M., & Harris, A. H. (1992). What we know about managing classrooms. *Educational Leadership 49*(7), pp. 74–78.

Freiberg, H. J. (1996) From tourists to citizens in the classroom. *Educational Leadership, 54*(1), 32–36.

Garner, B. (1989). Southeast Asian cultural and classroom culture. *College Teaching, 37,* 127–130.

Gill, W. M. (1977). A look at the change in open-plan schools in New Zealand. *New Zealand Journal of Educational Studies, 12,* 3–16.

Glasser, W. (1990). *The quality school.* New York: Harper & Row.

Goetz, E., Alexander, P. A., & Ash, M. J. (1992). *Education psychology.* New York: Macmillan.

Goldstein, A. P. (1989). Teaching alternatives to aggression. In D. Biklen, D. Ferguson, & A. Ford (Eds.), *Schooling and disability.* (The Eighty-eighth Yearbook of the National Society for the Study of Education, pt. 1, pp. 168–194). Chicago: University of Chicago Press.

Good, T. L. (1983). Recent classroom research: Implications for teacher education. In D. C. Smith (Ed.), *Essential knowledge for beginning educators* (pp. 55–64). Washington, DC: American Association of Colleges for Teacher Education.

Gunter, P. L., Shores, R. E., Jack, S. L., Rasmussen, S. K., & Flowers, J. (1995). On the Move: Using teacher/student proximity to improve students' behavior. *Teaching Exceptional Children, 28*(1), 12–14.

Hamilton, R. & Ghadala, E. (1994). *Learning and instruction.* New York: McGraw-Hill.

Hawley, W. D., & Rosenholtz, S. J. (1984). Good schools: What research says about improving student achievement. *Peabody Journal of Education, 61*(4), 15–52.

Horowitz, P., & Otto, D. (1973). *The teaching effectiveness of an alternate teaching facility.* Alberta, Canada: University of Alberta. (ERIC Document Reproduction Service Ed 083 242)

Hunter, M. (1990). *Discipline that develops self-discipline.* El Segundo, CA: Theory Into Practice.

Jackson, P. (1986). *Life in classrooms.* New York: Holt, Rinehart, and Winston.

Johnson, R. H. (1973). The effects of four modified elements of a classroom's physical environment on the social-psychological environment of a class. Doctoral dissertation, Oregon State University. *Dissertation Abstracts International, 34* (1002A). (University Microfilms 73–21, 311)

Jones, V. F. & Jones, L. S. (1995). Comprehensive classroom management: Creating positive learning environments. Fourth Edition. Boston: Allyn & Bacon.

Kazdin, A. E. (1975). *Behavior modification in applied settings.* Homewood, IL: Dorsey.

Kazdin, A. E. (1982). The token economy: A decade later. *Journal of Applied Behavior Analysis, 15,* 431–455.

Kounin, J. S. (1970). *Discipline and group management in classrooms.* New York: Holt, Rinehart, and Winston.

Kounin, J. S. (1983). *Classrooms: Individuals or behavior settings?* (Monographs in Teaching & Learning, no. 1). Bloomington, IN: Indiana University, School of Education. (ERIC Document Reproduction Service ED 240 070)

Kounin, J. S., & Gump, P. V. (1961). The comparative influence of punitive and nonpunitive teachers upon children's concepts of school misconduct. *Journal of Educational Psychology, 52,* 44–49.

Lasley, T. J., Lasley, J. O., & Ward, S. H. (1989, April). Activities and desists used by more and less effective classroom managers. Paper presented at the annual meeting of the American Educational Research Association, San Francisco.

Leinhardt, G., Weldman, C., & Hammond, K. M. (1987). Introduction and integration of classroom routines by expert teachers. *Curriculum Inquiry, 17,* 135–175.

Lepper, M. (1983). Extrinsic reward and intrinsic motivation: Implications for the classroom. In J. Levine & M. Wang (Eds.), *Teacher and student perceptions: Implications for learning.* Hillsdale, NJ: Erlbaum.

Lewin, K., Lippitt, R., & White, R. (1939). Patterns of aggressive behavior in experimentally created social climates. *Journal of Social Psychology, 10,* 271–299.

Lyman, L., & Foyle, H. C. (1990). *Cooperative grouping for interactive learning: Students, teachers and administrators.* Washington, DC: National Education Association.

Madsen, C. H., Jr., Becker, W. C., Thomas, D. R., Koser, L., & Plager, E. (1968). An analysis of the reinforcing function of "sit down" commands. In R. K. Parker (Ed.), *Readings in educational psychology* (pp. 79–95). Boston: Allyn & Bacon.

Martin, J. R. (1981). A new paradigm for liberal education. In J. F. Soltis (Ed.), *Philosophy and education.* Chicago: University of Chicago Press.

Maslow, A. (1968). *Toward a psychology of being.* Princeton, NJ: Van Nostrand Reinhold.

Maslow, A. H., & Mintz, N. L. (1956). The effects of esthetic surroundings: I. *Journal of Psychology, 41,* 247–254.

McCaslin, M., & Good, T. L. (1992). Compliant cognition: The misalliance of management and instructional goals in current school reform. *Educational Researcher, 21*(3), 4–17.

McGinnis, J. C., Frederick, B. P., & Edwards, R. (1995). Enhancing classroom management through proactive rules and procedures. *Psychology in the Schools, 32,* 220–224.

Morgan, M. (1984). Reward-induced decrements and increments in intrinsic motivation. *Review of Educational Research, 54*(1), 5–30.

Musgrave, G. R. (1975). *Individualized instruction: Teaching strategies focusing on the learner.* Boston: Allyn & Bacon.

O'Leary, K. D., Kaufman, K. F., Kass, R. E., & Drabman, R. S. (1970). The effects of loud and soft reprimands on the behavior of disruptive students. *Exceptional Children, 37,* 145–155.

O'Leary, K. D., & O'Leary, S. G. (1972). *Classroom management: The successful use of behavior modification.* Second Edition. New York: Pergamon.

Raviv, A., Raviv, A., & Reisel, E. (1990). Teachers and students: Two different perspectives?! Measuring social climate in the classroom. *American Educational Research Journal, 27,* 141–157.

Reynolds, A. (1992). What is competent beginning teaching? A review of the literature. *Review of Educational Research, 62*(1), 1–35.

Rogers, C. R., & Freiberg, H. J. (1994). *Freedom to learn,* Third Edition. Columbus, OH: Merrill.

Santrock, J. W. (1976). Affect and facilitative self-control: Influence of ecological setting, cognition, and social agent. *Journal of Educational Psychology, 68*(5), 529–535.

Savage, T. V. (1991). *Discipline for self-control.* Englewood Cliffs, NJ: Prentice-Hall.

Scollon, R. (1981). *Teachers' questions about Alaska Native education.* Fairbanks, AK: University of Alaska Center for Cross Cultural Studies. (ERIC Document Reproduction Service ED 238 661)

Shade, B. J. (1982). Afro-American cognitive style: A variable in school success? *Review of Educational Research, 52,* 219–244.

Slavin, R. E. (1988). *Educational psychology: Theory into practice.* Englewood Cliffs, NJ: Prentice-Hall.

Sommer, R., & Olsen, J. (1980). The soft classroom. *Environment & Behavior, 12*(1), 3–16.

Steele, B. F. (1988). *Becoming an effective classroom manager: A resource for teachers.* Albany: State University of New York.

Stipek, D. J. (1988). *Motivation to learn: From theory to practice.* Englewood Cliffs, NJ: Prentice-Hall.

Swick, K. J. (1985). *Disruptive student behavior in the classroom.* Washington, DC: National Education Association.

Sylwester, R. (1971). *The elementary teacher and pupil behavior.* West Nyack, NY: Parker.

Walberg, H. J. (1969). Physical and psychological distance in the classroom. *School Review, 77,* 64–70.

Walberg, H. J. (1987). Psychological environment. In M. J. Dunkin (Ed.), *The international encyclopedia of teaching and teacher education.* (pp. 553–558). New York: Pergamon.

Walters, R. H., Parke, R. D., & Cane, V. A. (1965). Timing of punishment and the observation of consequences to others as determinants of response inhibition. *Journal of Experimental Child Psychology, 2,* 10–30.

Wang, M. C., Haertel, G. D., & Walberg, H. J. (1993–94). What helps students learn? *Educational Leadership, 51*(4), 74–79.

Weinstein, C. S. (1987). Seating patterns. In M. J. Dunkin (Ed.), *The international encyclopedia of teaching and teacher education* (pp. 544–548). New York: Pergamon.

Weinstein, C. S., & Mignano, A. J., Jr. (1997). *Elementary classroom management: Lessons from research and practice.* Second Edition. New York: McGraw-Hill.

Wheldall, K., Morris, M., Vaughan, P., & Ng, Y. Y. (1981). Rows vs. tables: An example of the use of behavioral ecology in two classes of eleven-year-old children. *Journal of Educational Psychology, 1,* 171–184.

White, K. A. (1996, October 2). New teaching methods, technology add to space crunch. *Educational Week, 16,* p. 12.

White, M. A. (1975). Natural rates of teacher approach and disapproval in the classroom. *Journal of Applied Behavior Analysis, 8,* 367–372.

Wolfgang, C. H. & Kelsay, K. L. (1995). Discipline and the social studies classroom, grades K–12. *Social Studies, 86,* 175–182.

Woolfolk, A. E. (1993). *Educational psychology.* Needham Heights, MA: Allyn & Bacon.

Yinger, R. J. (1979). Routines in teacher planning. *Theory Into Practice, 18*(3), 163–169.

Problems Teachers Face

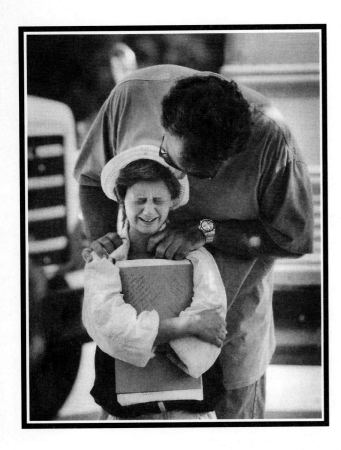

Contents

What Is a Problem?

Sources of Problems

What Are the Professional or Job-Related Problems Teachers Face?

Affiliation

Control

Parent Relationships and Home Conditions

Student Success

Time

How Are the Problems of Teachers Related to Their Personalities?

Preventing and Resolving Classroom Problems

Preventing Classroom Problems

Resolving Classroom Problems

Developing a Problem-Solving Attitude

Some Final Thoughts

Chapter Summary

Issues and Problems for Discussion

Theory into Action Activities

References

At this point, you are well on your way to becoming a knowledgeable and skillful teacher. Among other things, you (1) know what factors will influence your teaching, (2) understand the complexities of teaching diverse learners in a diverse society, (3) can utilize what is known about human learning, (4) have greatly expanded your teaching repertoire, (5) know how to evaluate student learning and how to reflect on your own teaching, (6) are aware of key personal and professional characteristics and abilities requisite of teachers, and (7) have the know-how to manage a classroom. However, there is one more side of teaching—a darker side—that we feel you must have knowledge of and skill in. The dark side consists of the numerous and diverse problems that challenge teachers. In Chapter 13 (we apologize for the number's connotation), you will be made aware of the most commonly reported teacher problems and, more importantly, of a problem-solving process you can use should the dark side of teaching cross your classroom threshold.

What Is a Problem?

Nearly everyone has problems. If someone you know does not, they are either very lucky or very skillful. Fortunately, you can avoid most problems, and resolve many others. However, before we get into that, let's consider what a problem is.

The simplest definition of a **problem** is goal-response interference. We need or want to achieve or have something, and we cannot do it (see Figure 13.1). Can you think of something you need or want that is elusive or unattainable? It could be a good part-time or summer job, a particular friend or friends, better living conditions, or the opportunity to participate in a certain activity. You

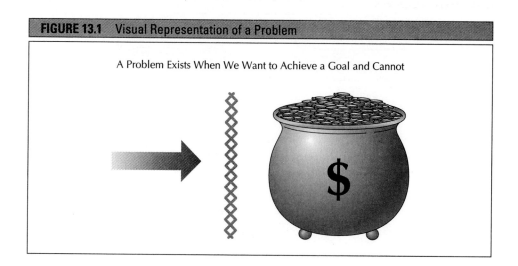

FIGURE 13.1   Visual Representation of a Problem

A Problem Exists When We Want to Achieve a Goal and Cannot

probably need or want to do well in this class to maintain or increase your grade-point average which, in turn, might affect your student teaching assignment and, ultimately, your ability to obtain a teaching position. Of course, most of you care more about learning to teach than you do about grades. You are intrinsically, or inner, motivated.

You may have noticed we are using the terms *need* and *want*. *Need* designates something that is an absolute necessity to you. You need to breathe. On the other hand, *want* designates something that would be nice to have but is not essential to your well-being. Ice cream is a want. Whether the goal you seek is a need or a want is vitally important, for we must attain a need, whereas we can live without a want. Pursuit of either a need or a want that is elusive or unattainable still designates a problem. The difference is one of kind and degree.

Sources of Problems

Our needs can come from virtually any source. However, they all relate to the pursuit of either primary *biological needs* or secondary *learned needs* (Figure 13.2). Thus, some problems result from the inability to satisfy our inborn biological needs for food, water, and rest. We are driven, or motivated, to meet these primary needs on a regular basis. If you have been deprived of any of these needs for any length of time, you know how devastating it can be. The "machine" breaks down.

Unfortunately, you will see students deprived of these basic needs. Teachers working with students of low socioeconomic status (SES) report that such children frequently come to school without adequate clothing and are often hungry and sleepy (Cruickshank, 1969, Cruickshank & Associates, 1980). Teachers report children arriving cold and wet, stealing lunches, and sleeping in class. Be forewarned: such problems are not peculiar to low SES children. The primary needs of high SES children also may go unmet.

On the other hand, some of our problems and those of our students are fueled by the inability to meet secondary or learned needs. In the process of growing up,

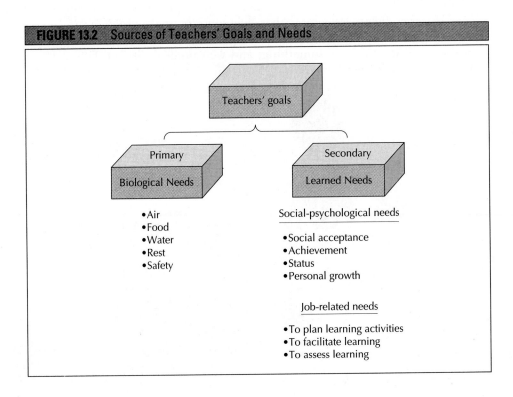

FIGURE 13.2 Sources of Teachers' Goals and Needs

we learn that we "need" to be friendly, to look good, to be successful, and so on. For the most part, we hope to please others and ourselves. Inability to satisfy our learned needs is likely to make us feel personally unfulfilled and unhappy. All of us have felt disappointed or discouraged when our efforts to achieve secondary needs are thwarted. Teachers report that students have many problems as a result of their unmet social and psychological needs. They act out, give up, and sometimes break down.

What we do for a living has a direct impact on our ability to meet our primary and secondary needs. Different kinds of work make life easier or more difficult. When our work enables us to satisfy our needs, it hardly seems like work at all. In such cases, we like our job. Conversely, work that is not fulfilling can be killing. Teaching normally is very pleasant work. It enables us to meet our biological needs fairly well, although some teachers in some situations might argue to the contrary. It also has the potential for helping us meet our learned needs. However, that occurs only when we teach well. This brings us to another subcategory of secondary needs we will call "job-related." To teach well, we must be good at planning learning activities, facilitating or helping students learn, and assessing learning—activities you have learned about in this book. The end results of teaching well are acceptance, achievement, and personal satisfaction.

What Are the Professional or Job-Related Problems Teachers Face?

We have been able to determine what the problems or unmet needs of teachers are as they engage in the act of teaching by asking hundreds of K–12 teachers to record their most difficult problem each day for up to two weeks. When these thousands of teacher-perceived problems were collected and analyzed, we found that there are sixty *common* problems that fall into five larger categories we call "areas of concern": affiliation, control, parent relationships and home conditions, student success, and time (Figure 13.3). Let's look at each area.

AFFILIATION

Affiliation is defined as the teacher's need to establish and maintain good relationships with others in the school. This includes students, faculty colleagues, staff, and administrators.

When we have asked teachers to describe their day-to-day concerns, they report these problems: liking some or all of their students, getting students to like them, getting cooperation and support from their colleagues and the administration,

13.1 Have you had teachers who seemed to have problems in one or more of the five areas of teacher concern? What were these teachers like?

13.2 How important to you is getting along with others?

FIGURE 13.3 Five Areas of Concern for Teachers

- Affiliation
- Control
- Parent relationships
- Student success
- Time

being professional in their relationships with others in the school, having confidence in other teachers, and feeling anxious when being supervised (Bainer, 1986; Cruickshank & Associates, 1980).

Having the comforting acceptance, companionship, and support of others is a very real social-psychological need, as Figure 13.2 indicates. Teachers deprived of human support during their workday feel lonely, unappreciated, ineffective, alienated, and perhaps even rejected. Teachers who report frequent affiliation concerns also report they are dissatisfied with teaching and with the school they are in (Myers, 1980).

The need for affiliation seems to be especially strong in persons like you who elect to teach. According to Super (1970), when teachers are compared to certified public accountants, engineers, lawyers, and clergy, the teachers value four things more highly: (1) having fellow workers whom they like, (2) working under pleasant conditions, (3) having the respect of others, and (4) enjoying job certainty. Thus, three of the things teachers prize seem directly related to the need for affiliation. Similarly, when Holland (1973) compared teachers with persons in other occupations using an instrument that measures personality types, he found that they rank highest on the "social" scale.

Affiliation also probably is of particular importance to us and more difficult to achieve because of the nature of our work. We are constantly in contact with others. Moreover, at certain times we are required to be leaders, while at others we may be equals or followers. Very few occupations regularly require all three interpersonal roles.

Tracey (1980) provides us with some affiliation-related problems that teachers report:

- I have a problem with a student who swore at me in class. Having had this student in classes for two years, I was disappointed with his lack of respect (p. 78).

- The teachers at my grade level had their weekly meeting. Once again, it was them against me. Everything was decided by them. They didn't even know I was there (p. 78).

- I have heard that my principal said to a colleague of mine that he thinks I do not work hard enough—that I should have more students and teach more classes. I am already working so hard. I can't believe he thinks so little of me when I work so hard (p. 79).

As you can see, affiliation concerns seem directly related to our expectations and to those of our students, colleagues, administrators, and staff. Our inability to meet their expectations, and their inability to meet ours, seem to be the root of the problem. Affiliation concerns also come from our inability to interact effectively. Consequently, we need to be aware of what students, colleagues, administrators, and staff expect of us, and we must know and practice good interpersonal skills such as being sensitive to others and generally trying to assist them in meeting their social-psychological and job-related needs.

Tracey (1980) provides a summary on affiliation:

Affiliation problems, those which involve relationships with students, fellow teachers, and administrators, are troublesome to many teachers. It is important to seek solutions to these problems because the quality of interactions and the degree of affiliation with others greatly affect personal and professional satisfaction.

When dealing with an affiliation problem, examine the expectations held by all the people involved. Not meeting expectations of self or others leads to conflict and frustration. . . . Research about [human] interaction provides helpful information. . . .

Affiliation is a critical and complex [area] for teachers. Valuable [related] information can be learned from work in communication, social psychology, psychology, and sociology. There are no simple explanations for human behavior or simple solutions for establishing better affiliation. (pp. 108–109)

CONTROL

Control is the teacher need to have students behave well or appropriately. When teachers define "appropriately" they mean students should be reasonably quiet, orderly, courteous, honest, and show respect for others and for property.

Teachers who have participated in our studies report they have several problems: maintaining order, quiet, and control; not knowing how to respond to improper behavior such as swearing and use of obscenities; controlling aggressive behavior; enforcing considerate treatment of property; getting students to use leisure time well; maintaining students' attention; enforcing values such as honesty and respect; removing students who are sources of frustration; and teaching self-discipline (Bainer, 1986; Cruickshank & Associates, 1980).

When students do not behave appropriately, two things can happen. First, animosity can develop between teacher and student, resulting also in an affiliation problem. Second, teachers can feel like and be perceived by students, teachers, administrators, and parents as ineffective classroom managers.

To complicate matters, we suspect that many persons who decide to teach are not strongly control-oriented. Remember, mostly we are *socially oriented*. We want to like and be liked. In fact, many teachers believe that the classroom should be "democratic" and that students should be empowered or given authority to decide things and, essentially, to control themselves. Complicating matters even further, many teachers simply don't have a clue about how to establish and maintain any kind of order. After all, they enjoyed learning and presume that their students will, too. When students respond to learning negatively by acting up, many teachers are shocked and stymied.

Novak (1980) provides us with examples of teacher-reported, control-related incidents:

> The same boy, DeWayne, who has been causing all the trouble in one of my classes was off and running again today. He had the girl sitting behind him combing his hair. Later in the period, he threw a paper wad across two rows to a boy. And, he was talking to the boys and girls around him. I think that the time has come for the school authorities to be called in. (p. 115)

Chapter 12 contains basic information about organizing, managing, and controlling the classroom that applies to this second area of teacher concern. Novak (1980) provides further help. He proposes five principles that can make control less of a problem (see Figure 13.4):

* *Pursue only classroom goals that are truly important and appropriate.* Then make sure the goals are achievable. Thus, when you teach, modify or scale down overly ambitious intentions. In the case of the above control incident Novak provides, it is very important for DeWayne to behave appropriately. However, he and the teacher may have to work at it over time. Therefore, the teacher might modify or scale down classroom goals and ask DeWayne to make an effort to behave appropriately in meeting these easier goals. Rather than expect immediate perfection, the teacher should look for progress.

13.6 How important is control to you?

13.7 What types of control-related problems do you worry about most?

FIGURE 13.4 Five Principles of Classroom Control

* Pursue only important, appropriate classroom goals
* Analyze what may be affecting the problem situation
* Use positive techniques for managing behavior
* Use punishment sparingly and appropriately
* Teach self-control

- *Analyze the factors that may be affecting the problem situation.* Novak reminds us that the more you know about the circumstances of a problem, the more likely you will be able to select and employ effective techniques to resolve it. Therefore, he asks that you analyze the learning task and the students' ability to do it, consider the events that occurred before and during the problem's onset (what led up to the incident?), and consider what happened following the control incident (was there peer laughter, ineffective punishment?). By analyzing the situations DeWayne misbehaves in, you may deduce some clues that can explain his actions.

- *Use positive techniques for managing behavior.* Novak believes that when students do not act appropriately, they must learn new behavior patterns. This requires teaching students what is expected of them and recognizing and rewarding subsequent desirable behavior.

  Students must have a clear understanding of behavioral expectations and of their importance. Some students will simply misunderstand your expectations unless these expectations are absolutely clear and you are doggedly insistent in their pursuit. Other students will need to learn how to behave somewhat differently to what they are accustomed to in other classrooms or at home, where other behavioral expectations often exist. Yet others may have difficulty with you, and you with them, because of some social or emotional shortcoming.

  Novak has specific advice as you work with students who have a difficult time behaving appropriately. *First,* he urges that you single them out when they are doing the right thing and applaud their efforts. *Second,* recognize and reward them only when they engage in desirable behaviors. Do not give in to or reward undesirable behaviors. *Third,* ignore inappropriate behavior as often as possible. Do not allow your attention or the other students' attention to be drawn to it. *Fourth,* make sure that recognition and reward for desirable behavior is indeed rewarding. Not all learners will see better grades, teacher praise, or the assignment of more difficult work as positive. *Finally,* engage students themselves in problem solving. They, too, need to know how to go about resolving problems. Chapters 3 and 12 contain information you can readily apply in pursuit of Novak's third principle.

- *Use punishment sparingly and appropriately.* Use only punishment that works, use only as much as necessary, and make certain students know what behavior is inappropriate and, conversely, what is acceptable.

13.8 How important will control be in your classroom?

- *Teach students to manage their own behavior.* Teach them self-control. Notes Novak, "Self-control means having students behave appropriately in the absence of external control" (p. 149). When students know that inappropriate and appropriate behavior have predictable consequences and when they can recognize and respond to important classroom rules, they can exhibit self-control. Rules can include "When directions are being given, it is especially important to listen" and "When you borrow something, return it." Finally, Novak implores, "Don't be too controlling. Seek reasonable control. It is a lot easier to achieve and less stressful to you and your students" (p. 150).

PARENT RELATIONSHIPS AND HOME CONDITIONS

We learned in Chapter 2 that most families and caregivers have great influence on children. Therefore, if you are able to involve parents constructively in their child's education, it is more likely that improved attendance, achievement, and behavior will follow (Haynes, Comer, & Hamilton-Lee, 1989; Henderson, 1987; Rich, 1988). Teachers recognize the important role parents and significant others play in the lives of students. Therefore, they want to maintain constructive relationships with them.

Teachers are also aware that the conditions in students' homes impact on their school success. As a result, teachers benefit from knowing what home conditions are like and most teachers would like to influence those conditions positively.

Many teachers who have participated in our surveys tell us that they find it difficult to have good relationships with parents and to find out about and have a positive effect on home conditions. Specifically, they report problems with the following endeavors: improving life for students by correcting conditions both inside and outside school, keeping students away from people and things that may have a bad influence, improving conditions so that students can study better at home, encouraging parental interest in school matters, holding worthwhile parent conferences, understanding the conditions of home and community, and assisting parents who are having difficulty with their children (Bainer, 1986; Cruickshank & Associates, 1980).

Mager (1980) suggests that to achieve constructive parent relationships, teachers and parents or guardians must be mutually supportive. For the most part, this means that teachers must accept and support parental values and behaviors and that parents must do likewise for teachers. Certainly, this is easier said than done, particularly when home and school values and behaviors differ. Mager shares a teacher-written illustration: "I was talking to the class about all the fights they had been getting into. The students told me that their parents tell them to hit anyone who does something they don't like. I suddenly realized that it's the school's no fighting policy versus the parents don't be a sissy policy" (p. 157).

Perceptions of lack of competence also come into play and thus interfere with good relationships. For example, parents may doubt a teacher's decisions. One teacher writes, "I received a phone call from a parent who questioned the worth of an upcoming field trip. I tried to explain why the trip was worthwhile, but I am plagued by the thought that I was not convincing enough" (Mager, p. 156). Conversely, teachers may question the competence of parents. "I understand why Ellen behaves the way she does. These parents just don't care" (Mager, p. 157).

Failure to achieve mutual support may also result simply because barriers prevent teachers and parents from getting together to talk. Teachers may not have the time and energy. They may perceive that parents are too busy, or they may not want parents to "intrude" into their domain. For their part, parents may not wish to visit with teachers because they lack time or energy, they may not want to intrude, or they may perceive teachers as too busy. Additionally, parents may shy away from interactions with teachers because of unhappy childhood memories they may have of school, feelings of insecurity, or guilt that their child is having problems. Parents and caregivers may also be reluctant to talk with teachers because they have personal or family difficulties, because they may not be the child's birth parent, or because they cannot converse fluently in English (Weinstein & Mignano, 1997). Remember, as we learned in Chapter 2, the number of parents with limited English proficiency is increasing.

In discussing the teacher's need to know what students' home and community conditions are like and, relatedly, the teacher's desire to influence them in a positive direction, Mager again points out hindrances. First of all, parents and guardians, not teachers, control home conditions. The following anecdote reveals a teacher's frustration on this count. "Today a student came late to my first hour class for the ninth time in four weeks. The main problem is that most of his excuses are legitimate. His lateness can be directly attributed to his parents. Car won't start, alarm doesn't work, mother got breakfast late, he had to babysit until 2 A.M. and so forth (Mager, p. 161).

Second, home conditions may even be beyond the control of parents. Some parents are forced to live in substandard housing in deteriorating, violent communities. Some parents must raise children without adequate financial and human support. Some children must be left to their own devices. Other parents have limited

13.9 How important is getting along with parents and other caregivers?

13.10 Which problems in parent-teacher relationships seem most noteworthy to you? Why?

intellect and/or education. Mager shares another teacher anecdote. "I visited the home of a new seventh grader coming from a rural school. He is having difficulty academically and socially. The purpose of the visit was to obtain permission to have him tested. I have come in contact with many deprived families but this one is very sad. Both parents are extremely retarded as is another child, a sixteen-year-old who has never even been to school. Neither parent can read or write" (p. 162). Unfortunately, these are realities that neither parents nor teachers alone can overcome.

Mager provides suggestions for helping you build mutual support with parents and improve home and community conditions (see Figure 13.5). To achieve mutual support, he argues that you need to increase the frequency and improve the quality of teacher-parent interactions. Such "interactions" can include sending out a classroom newsletter regularly, perhaps monthly; bringing in parent volunteers; forming a mom and/or dad's club, and so forth. To improve the quality of interactions, you need to learn what parents expect of you and you need to share what you expect of parents. Usually, unpleasant interactions are the result of unrealistic or failed expectations.

To achieve the goal of optimal home and community conditions, Mager advises that you take at least two steps. First, recognize that the relationship between home and community conditions and a student's school experience is complex. Avoid simplistic causal explanations such as "Robert would do better if he could move out of that home and neighborhood." That may or may not be true. Second, remember that the nature of the parents or guardians and the quality of the interactions they have with their children are far more important than the material possessions found in the home. Home and neighborhood trappings do not substitute for quality-of-life relationships. Therefore you should not, as the saying goes, "judge the book [home and community] by its cover."

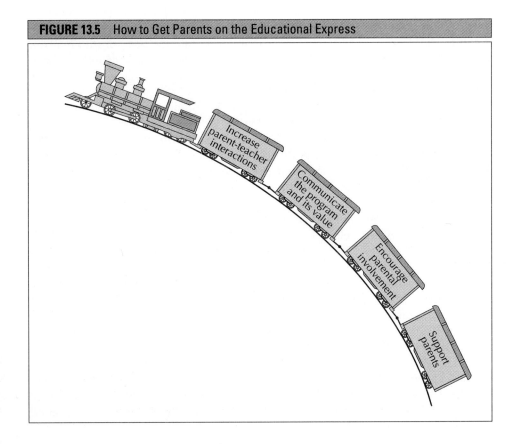

FIGURE 13.5 How to Get Parents on the Educational Express

STUDENT SUCCESS

Student success is defined as the need teachers have to help learners achieve both academically and socially. It is a very important goal because when you are successful in attaining it, you meet your secondary or learned needs for achievement, status, and acceptance in the teaching profession.

Unfortunately, many teachers struggle with student success. In our studies (Bainer, 1986; Cruickshank & Associates, 1980), when teachers have described everyday problems, a great many fit into this category of concerns.

Kinds of Success Problems   Teacher-reported student success problems are of three kinds: those related to insufficient student interest, those related to working with students who have special needs, and those related to a teacher's own instructional shortcomings.

Problems related to teachers' perceptions of insufficient student interest include statements such as "I have a problem having students present and on time; getting students to participate; getting them to work up to their ability; prevailing on them to value grades; and overcoming apathy or even dislike of school and learning."

Problems associated with students who face special challenges include helping children with personal problems; helping those with special physical, social, emotional or intellectual needs; overcoming a student's frustration with self; and getting students to feel they are succeeding.

The third kind of student success problem is related to our personal instructional limitations when planning, teaching, and assessing the learning that has taken place. Specifically, teachers tell us they have trouble planning instruction that adds variety to classroom life, creating student interest, providing for individual differences, using different instructional alternatives, assessing learning, promoting students' self-assessment, and extending learning beyond the classroom.

Obstacles to Student Success   Holton (1980) describes four obstacles to achieving student success. First, "Knowledge about teaching is at best sketchy" (p. 205). Although, as we learned in Chapters 10 and 11, that knowledge about how to teach is accumulating, we still know less than is needed. If we had what we truly need to know, this text probably would consist of at least five volumes!

A second hindrance to student success is students' individual differences. Recall that Chapter 2 was devoted to student diversity. Holton notes that diversity or individual difference is no cliché. He notes that according to G. W. Beadle, a Nobel laureate in genetics, if we calculated all possible human characteristics and the resulting permutations, the number of possible different human individuals would be about 2 raised to the 4-billionth power (that is, $2 \times 2 \times 2 \ldots 4$ billion times) (p. 205). So much diversity exists among our students that it is difficult at best to facilitate the learning of every one (p. 205).

Third, "schools have many, often vague goals and not all of them are consistent with student learning" (p. 205). Some people, Holton notes, want schools to teach "the basics," while others are intent on "developing the whole child." The latter would educate them intellectually, morally, socially, emotionally, and physically. Still others want schools to educate children to change or improve society. Each school of thought about educational goals would have teachers doing different things. Teachers have difficulty working toward student learning if the goals are not well-defined and agreed upon and its character is unclear.

Fourth, says Holton, "Teaching is greater than the sum of its parts" (p. 206). There is some "magic" to it. One can carefully construct lessons and still have them fail; there is no guarantee. Holton attributes this to what he calls the unknown and possibly unknowable *X* factor in teaching. "While we sense the *X*, it has defied our attempts to weigh it, measure it, or catch it. . . . This *X* factor is what

13.11   How important to you is getting students to succeed academically and socially?

13.12   Which problems related to student success do you believe may be troublesome for you? Why?

13.13   What do you think the *X* factor is? Do you think you have or can develop it?

makes the successful classroom greater than the sum of its parts" (p. 206). It is the particular genius of knowing how and when to do something that works.

Teacher Behaviors Linked to Student Success   Holton notes there are important teacher behaviors associated with student academic success. These behaviors are consistent with what appears in Chapters 10 and 11 of this book. He notes that effective teachers are clear, enthusiastic, and businesslike or work-oriented, they use a variety of instructional alternatives and materials, they adjust the material to students' abilities, they recognize the need to arouse interest, they provide adequate opportunity and time to learn, and they help students get the most out of their school experiences.

TIME

Lack of time represents a serious problem for teachers. According to the thousands we have surveyed, teachers do not have sufficient time to prepare for classes, complete the planned work, and diagnose and evaluate learning. Furthermore, constraints on time have increased because of (1) large classes, (2) the number of classes teachers are required to teach, and (3) the assignment of noninstructional tasks such as bus, lunchroom, and playground monitoring. Finally, they tell us they do not have enough time to do personal tasks because of the amount of work they must take home (Bainer, 1986; Cruickshank & Associates, 1980).

Unfortunately, there is little likelihood that demands on schools will lessen, and time is not a commodity we can manufacture more of. Rather, for decades, demands have been on the increase—teachers have more rather than less to do. Thus, teacher personal and professional needs seem to be growing inversely in relation to the time available to meet them.

Applegate (1980) suggests that since time is finite, we must learn to use it better, and she offers a number of suggestions. First, *know yourself.* Know your personal and professional needs. Are you spending enough time on the things that are important to you professionally and personally? Know your optimal work times. Are you a morning, afternoon, or evening person? Do you use your "best time" appropriately to get things done? Know your sleep and exercise needs. Are you skimping on or overdoing sleeping or exercising? Have your habits robbed you of vitality?

Second, *know your goals.* Are some in conflict with others, causing you to be counterproductive? For example, do you want both to be a teacher and wealthy? Additionally, are your goals realistic and attainable? Are you willing to invest heavily in order to accomplish something fairly remote? Do you want to be "teacher of the year" so badly that you will sacrifice nearly everything?

Third, *know your work environment.* What aspects of teaching can you control in order to use time better? Can you share instructional and other responsibilities with a colleague? Is it possible to eliminate interruptions that detract from instruction? Can you use uninterrupted time more effectively?

Fourth, *plan.* Do you plan in order to maximize your productivity and leisure? Do your plans support the things you consider most important?

Fifth, *learn to set priorities and to say no.* Having decided what is important, do you say no when other things try to intrude? Applegate notes, "When you say no to such a request, you are saying yes to yourself" (p. 277).

Sixth, *know your support system.* Are you aware of the kind of human and material help that may be available to you? Are you willing to ask for and give assistance?

Seventh, *concentrate.* Do you reserve time and space for uninterrupted concentration? Do you fool yourself by taking work home but then fiddle with it or merely bring it back undone? Is your work space uncluttered and amenable to work?

Eighth, *act. Don't procrastinate.* Do you indulge yourself or socialize to avoid work? Do you put things off because they are not rewarding? Many teachers say

13.14   What personal characteristics and professional abilities do you have that will probably serve you well? What related shortcomings would you like to have help with?

13.15   What kind of time-related problems do you think you may have as a teacher?

13.16   How do you feel about time? Are you in control of your time?

they do not like to evaluate students' work. By that, they mean they don't like to grade papers. That may be one reason some teachers take so long to return tests and homework.

Applegate's last suggestion is, *follow through. Finish.* Do you follow through on things you begin, or do they often end up incomplete and thus represent wasted effort and time?

13.17 Which of Applegate's suggestions for using time has the most meaning for you?

Try Activity 13.1

How Are the Problems of Teachers Related to Their Personalities?

Myers (1977) wondered what teachers' personalities might have anything to do with the kinds of classroom problems they report. So she asked 432 teachers of grades 7–12 to complete the *Edwards Personality Inventory* (EPI) and our Teacher Problem Checklist containing the sixty most frequent and bothersome teacher-reported concerns (Cruickshank & Associates, 1980). Myers also obtained data from the teachers that related to their job (school) location and job satisfaction. First, let's look at what she discovered when comparing the teacher-perceived frequency and severity of problems with their feelings of satisfaction with their workplace and job.

Teachers who report frequent *affiliation* problems are mostly young, have very few years of teaching experience and teach in rural or suburban schools. Additionally, they are often dissatisfied with teaching and with their workplace. Oddly, teachers who do not report frequent affiliation problems but who do report they are bothered by such problems when they arise *are* satisfied with teaching and the workplace. Apparently, infrequent affiliation problems are manageable, but a regular diet of feelings of alienation and isolation is too much for many teachers.

Teachers who report frequent *control* problems are also less experienced, and they prefer "structured" classrooms. Obviously, the desire to have a structured classroom may make control more difficult to attain. However, these teachers like their jobs. Perceived lack of classroom control, then, does not necessarily lead to job dissatisfaction. Teachers who are *bothered* by lack of control tend to be young, inexperienced, satisfied with work, and female. This is the only area of teachers' concern where gender appears to be a factor.

Myers was unable to find any strong relationships among either the frequency or the severity of *parent relationships/home conditions,* the workplace, or teacher satisfaction.

Most teachers who admit that they have frequent problems in the area of *student success* teach low socioeconomic status (SES) students in inner-city schools. Since low SES frequently is associated with low school achievement, this finding is not surprising. However, teachers who are *bothered* by such problems when they do occur are just as likely to teach in suburban and rural schools as in the inner city. It seems teachers everywhere find that achieving student success is a bothersome, if not frequent, area of concern.

Finally, teachers frequently reporting lack of *time* as a concern are more likely to teach high SES students in suburban or rural areas. They also are more likely to teach large classes and to like their school. Perhaps surprisingly, teachers bothered by lack of time are both satisfied with teaching and their workplace.

Now let's see what Myers found when she compared the kinds of problems teachers reported with their personality characteristics as obtained from the EPI. Teachers who believe they have *affiliation* problems believe others view them as either especially competent or as having undesirable traits such as wanting undue recognition, not being considerate or ethical, not being logical or articulate, or having trouble making friends.

Teachers who told Myers they have *control* problems believe others view them as easily influenced, avoiding arguments, wanting sympathy, and liking set routines. In other words, they think they are perceived as ineffectual teachers.

Teachers who mostly report *parent relationship/home condition* problems believe others view them as easily influenced, not very articulate, and perhaps a bit lax. On the positive side, they think others perceive them as cooperative and as understood.

Teachers who mostly report *student success* problems believe others characterize them as having few cultural interests, lacking persistence, and being lax. Also they think others believe that they don't enjoy being center stage, that they avoid arguments, and that they do not need or want sympathy.

Those 7–12 teachers who reported mostly *time* constraints feel others perceive them as hard workers, anxious to please, and absent-minded. Also, they believe others think they are misunderstood and that they avoid facing problems and want sympathy.

Myers is the first to look for associations between the kinds of problems teachers report, their personalities, and their job satisfaction. Her most notable findings, in summary, are that (1) teachers who perceive themselves as frequently having affiliation problems are dissatisfied; (2) teachers reporting frequent control problems are less experienced, like structure, and are female; (3) teachers everywhere report it is difficult to achieve student success; (4) working with high SES students and teaching large classes frequently cause time pressures; and (5) teachers reporting different kinds of concerns have distinguishable personalities.

13.18 In what ways do you think your personality may reduce or increase classroom problems?

Preventing and Resolving Classroom Problems

At this point we have learned that we have a problem when we need or want something (a goal) but cannot attain it because of obstacles or hindrances. Some of the things we desire we truly need because our biological or social-psychological well-being depends upon our having them. Other goals or objectives, although desirable, are not truly necessary. We merely want them. Additionally, some of our needs are professional, or job-related, such as knowing how to teach well. You are taking this course in large measure because you must learn to teach well in order to get and hold a teaching position. Unfortunately, five categories of problems occur as we engage in teaching. These problems prevent us from teaching as well as we would like. Let's look at how we might prevent these job-related problems from occurring.

PREVENTING CLASSROOM PROBLEMS

How can we avoid problems related to affiliation, control, parent relationships, student success, and time? To be relatively immune to these teacher concerns, we must already possess or acquire specific abilities. Some of the abilities we need in order to prevent problems in each of the five categories are shown in Table 13.1.

Perhaps you are blessed with certain of these attributes already. Most likely those attributes you enjoy are related to affiliation and, to some extent, to time management since you have had years of opportunity to acquire both. Gaining as many of the abilities as possible will put you in an enviable position in any classroom. As the saying goes, an ounce of prevention is worth a pound of cure.

RESOLVING CLASSROOM PROBLEMS

It is doubtful that many, if any, of us have or can acquire all the different kinds of abilities noted in Table 13.1. In our studies spanning three decades (Bainer, 1986; Cruickshank & Associates, 1980), we have come across less than a handful of teachers who claim they have no problems. Unless you are very remarkable or possibly oblivious, you can expect to encounter events that interfere with accomplishing the five major goals teachers share. We can say with assurance that teachers do have problems and that *teaching is tough*. What to do? Obviously, the best way to escape from a problem is to solve it. So let's think about problem resolution.

**TABLE 13.1   Abilities That a Teacher Needs to Prevent Problems
in the Five Areas of Teachers' Concerns**

If You Have Concerns Related to . . .	Then You Must . . .
• Affiliation	• Be accepting, caring, and supportive of others
	• Be cooperative
	• Be professional in relationships
	• Know of and use interpersonal skills
	• Know of and be able to meet reasonable expectations others have for you
• Control	• Appear to students to have reasonable expectations for work and behavior
	• Recognize and reward work and behavior that meet your expectations
	• Get students to monitor and control their own work and behavior
• Parent relationships	• Have good affiliation skills (see above)
	• Be able to establish a system of mutual support
	• Get parents and caregivers involved in the student's education
• Student success	• Be able to create and maintain learners' interest
	• Be able to meet a wide range of individual differences
	• Be thoughtful and skillful in planning and facilitating learning and assessment
	• Have the qualities and abilities of effective teachers
• Time	• Concentrate on doing what is most important
	• Know when during the day you and your learners work best
	• Plan
	• Share mutual work and responsibilities with colleagues
	• Avoid procrastinating and finish what you start

A problem is solved or resolved only when you are able to either give up the goal (need or want) or get closer to it—while, at the same time, avoid unpleasant side effects. With the help of extensive literature on problem solving, we have developed a problem-solving approach or regimen that should be advantageous to any teacher in difficulty.

The Problem-Solving Approach (PSA)   The PSA consists of five stages and ten steps:

Stage 1: Problem identification and ownership. At the outset, it is essential that the problem, goal, and the ownership of both be clear. The first three steps are to

1. State the problem. What is it that is bothersome to you?
2. Identify the goal(s). What specifically do you need or want to have happen that is not happening?
3. Identify the problem's owner. Who has the problem? Who needs or wants the goal? Obviously, if it is your goal that is blocked, it is your problem.

Stage 2: Value clarification. Once the problem has been identified and its ownership established, the fourth step is to

4. Value the goal. Do you really care so much about the goal to continue to pursue it?

Stage 3: Analysis of the problem situation. Assuming that you have found the goal worthy of pursuit, you now enter the problem analysis stage. The three steps in this stage require that you

5. Identify the obstacles preventing you from accomplishing your goal. What specifically seems to stand between your goal and its accomplishment?

6. Project strategies for removing, overcoming, or circumventing the obstacle(s).

7. For each of the potential solutions, list possible negative side effects or consequences. Remember that it is one thing to "get your way" and another to get it in a manner that harms you or someone else. You could "win the battle but lose the war."

Stage 4: Rating the potential solutions. In Steps 6 and 7, you projected strategies for reaching your goal and identified possible harmful side effects.

8. Rate each proposed solution to arrive at the best one or ones. Remember, *a good solution is one that gains or puts you closer to your goal without causing unpleasant side effects.*

Stage 5: Implementing and evaluating the best solution. In the last two steps of our PSA, you are asked to:

9. Decide how you would implement the best solution. What precisely would you do?

10. Decide the extent to which the solution has brought you closer to your goal, thus reducing or eliminating your problem.

Try Activity 13.2

Even if you do not have all the abilities necessary to prevent the occurrence of classroom problems, you certainly can learn how to be a better problem solver. Figure 13.6 provides an outline of the PSA.

FIGURE 13.6   The Problem-Solving Approach (PSA)

Stage 1: Identify the problem and its ownership
1. State the problem. What is it that is bothersome?
2. Identify the goal(s). What specifically do you or does someone else need or want?
3. Identify the problem's owner. Who needs or wants the goal?

Stage 2: Determine the value of the goal
4. Value the goal. After thinking about it, decide whether the goal is of
   ____unquestionable value.   ____little value.
   ____great value.   ____no real consequence.
   ____value but negotiable.

Stage 3. Analyze the problem situation
5. Identify the obstacles to goal achievement.
6. Project ways you might achieve the goal by either getting rid of, overcoming, or circumventing obstacles, or thinking of ingenious creative solutions.
7. List some possible consequences each solution might have.

Stage 4: Rate the proposed solutions
8. Rate each potential solution according to the likelihood it would help reach the goal and cause few, if any, unfavorable side effects.

Stage 5: Implement and evaluate the best solution
9. Decide specifically how to put the best solution to work.
10. Decide to what extent the best solution is working.

DEVELOPING A PROBLEM-SOLVING ATTITUDE

No one wants problems, but when faced with one, how do you react and what do you think? Do you consider it a source of irritation and mostly gripe about it? Teachers' lounges are notorious for hosting this activity. Teachers reportedly often stand around and complain to one another. Although this may be a good way to let off steam, it seldom accomplishes much else. Or, do you consider a problem to be a challenge? Do you have a good problem-solving attitude? If so, you may even avoid this use of the teachers' lounge in order to use the time to work toward solving the problem and attaining your goal.

The way you react to problems reveals your problem-solving attitude. As we have talked with teachers, we find those with a positive problem-solving attitude or outlook have certain characteristics. They

- Have a "let's solve this" approach
- Refuse to blame others for their inability to gain a goal
- Accept their problems and respond, "I have a problem. How do I solve it?"
- Focus on the present or future rather than bemoan the past
- Replace natural emotional, visceral reactions to a problem with goal-oriented, thoughtful ones; they "get the problem out of their stomach and into their head"
- Refrain from jumping to conclusions or solutions
- Search for new approaches, deviate from old habits, and avoid the obvious
- Expect disagreements and accept and respect the views of others
- Ask what they themselves can do to reach their goals rather than depending upon others to act on their behalf
- Accept approximations to a goal: "Half a loaf is better than none"
- Work toward bettering already satisfactory situations to ensure they remain so
- Consciously make use of available time for problem solving

Attitude isn't everything, but it counts a lot in terms of whether we face problems feeling action-oriented or immobilized. Be positive. You *can* do it. Just do it!

 13.19 How do you react when you need or want something and cannot readily attain it?

 13.20 What characteristics of a good problem-solving attitude do you already possess? Which do you need to work on?

Some Final Thoughts

The book *Teaching Is Tough* (Cruickshank and Associates, 1980) leads off with the following statement:

> Teaching is tough. It is difficult to think of many occupations as demanding intellectually, physically, and psychologically. Who else but teachers must keep well-informed in one or more disciplines, must organize and manage one or more groups of workers, and provide for both their success and satisfaction? Who else must be concerned not only with the client but with maintaining good relationships with the client's family? Who else gets blamed when test scores drop and crime increases? What other occupational group is subjected to so much national criticism? Who else is constantly second-guessed by nearly everyone about what to do and how to do it?
> Yes, teaching is tough, and that is why teachers have so many legitimate concerns or problems. (p. vii)

You are well-advised to take problem solving very seriously. Because we do, we have included teacher reported problems at the end of chapters 2, 3, 5, 6, 8, 10, and 11. There also is a simulation in Unit 3 of the Practice Teaching Manual where you can try your hand at resolving representative teaching problems.

CHAPTER SUMMARY

- A problem exists when we need or want something and cannot readily attain it.

- Problems result from our inability to achieve primary *(biological)* or secondary *(learned)* needs. Biological needs include air, food, water, rest, safety, and security. Learned needs are social-psychological, and some are job-related. Social-psychological needs include social acceptance, achievement, status, and personal growth. Job-related needs include the ability to plan, teach, and assess learning.

- Teacher problems occur mostly in pursuit of social-psychological and job-related needs. Teachers commonly report about sixty problems that fall into five categories: *affiliation, control, parent relationships/home conditions, student success,* and *time.* Studies provide us with theoretical knowledge that helps us understand the problems in each category.

- Teachers who report different categories of problems also differ in certain ways. Teachers with frequent affiliation problems are often dissatisfied with their jobs. Teachers bothered by affiliation problems are often younger and less experienced, and they tend to teach in rural areas and suburbs. Teachers with frequent control problems are often younger and less experienced; they prefer structured classrooms and like their jobs. Teachers bothered by control problems are younger, inexperienced, and female; they like their work. Teachers with frequent student success problems generally teach low SES students in city schools. Teachers bothered by lack of control are found in all kinds of school districts. Teachers with frequent time problems more likely teach high SES rural and suburban students. Teachers bothered by time problems are satisfied with their jobs. There also are clear relationships between teachers' problems and teachers' personality characteristics.

- It is important both to be able to prevent problems and to be able to resolve them. Teachers with certain dispositions and abilities are likely to have fewer problems. Teachers who employ a problem-solving approach are more likely to resolve classroom problems, and teachers with a positive problem-solving attitude also are more likely to meet their needs.

ISSUES AND PROBLEMS FOR DISCUSSION

1. How legitimate are the five goals teachers share?
2. Which of the five goals are most important?
3. Should teachers be expected to resolve most classroom problems on their own?
4. How can teachers become better problem solvers?
5. Where can teachers find specific pedagogical help related to the classroom problems they face?

THEORY INTO ACTION ACTIVITIES

ACTIVITY 13.1: Talk With a Teacher About Classroom Problems   If you are involved in a field experience, talk with a teacher about classroom problems. You might ask:

1. What kinds of problems do most teachers in the school seem to have?
2. What might make teaching easier for one teacher and harder for another?
3. What can I do to minimize and resolve the problems I might have?

ACTIVITY 13.2: Record a Teacher's Problem and Analyze It   If you are in a field experience, ask your mentor teacher if you can record a problem and, with the teacher's help, analyze it.

1. With the mentor teacher's assistance, identify a situation where you or the teacher has a goal in mind and there is difficulty achieving it.
2. Write a detailed account of what happened. In other words, what specifically was the problem?
3. With the teacher's assistance, analyze the problem.
   a. What is desirable that isn't happening?
   b. How important is the goal?
   c. What obstacles seem to be in the way of goal achievement?
   d. How might the goal be reached with the fewest negative side effects?

REFERENCES

Applegate, J. (1980). Time. In D. R. Cruickshank & Associates, *Teaching is tough* (pp. 257–302). Englewood Cliffs, NJ: Prentice-Hall.

Bainer, D. L. (1986). Perceived problems of elementary school teachers related to grade level, teaching experience, and student background. Unpublished doctoral dissertation, The Ohio State University, Columbus.

Cruickshank, D. (1969). *The inner-city simulation laboratory.* Chicago: Science Research Associates.

Cruickshank, D. R., & Associates. (1980). *Teaching is tough.* Englewood Cliffs, NJ: Prentice-Hall.

Haynes, N. M., Comer, J. P., & Hamilton-Lee, M. (1989). School climate enhancement through parent involvement. *Journal of School Psychology, 27,* 87–90.

Henderson, A. T. (1987). *The evidence continues to grow: Parent involvement improves student achievement.* Columbia, MD: National Committee for Citizens in Education.

Holland, J. (1973). *Making vocational choices: A theory of careers.* Englewood Cliffs, NJ: Prentice-Hall.

Holton, J. (1980). Student success. In D. R. Cruickshank & Associates, *Teaching is tough* (pp. 199–256). Englewood Cliffs, NJ: Prentice-Hall.

Mager, G. (1980). Parent relationships and home and community conditions. In D. R. Cruickshank & Associates, *Teaching is tough* (pp. 153–198). Englewood Cliffs, NJ: Prentice-Hall.

Myers, B. (1977). An empirical investigation of the relationship of teacher perceived problems to teacher personality variables and social-demographic variables. Unpublished doctoral dissertation, The Ohio State University, Columbus.

Myers, B. (1980). Relationships between classroom problems, personality, and place of work. In D. Cruickshank & Associates, *Teaching is tough* (pp. 303–321). Englewood Cliffs, NJ: Prentice-Hall.

Novak, C. (1980). Control. In D. R. Cruickshank & Associates, *Teaching is tough* (pp. 113–151). Englewood Cliffs, NJ: Prentice-Hall.

Rich, D. (1988). Bridging the parent gap in education reform. *Educational Horizons, 66,* 9–92.

Super, D. E. (1970). *Work values inventory.* Boston: Houghton Mifflin.

Tracey, K. (1980). Affiliation. In D. R. Cruickshank & Associates, *Teaching is tough* (pp. 75–111). Englewood Cliffs, NJ: Prentice-Hall.

Weinstein, C. S., & Mignano, A. J. (1997). *Elementary classroom management: Lessons from research and practice.* Second Edition. New York: McGraw-Hill.

Practice Teaching Manual

PART FOUR

Practice doesn't always make perfect, but it certainly helps. This manual provides an opportunity for you to gain much needed practice in three important areas. In Unit 1, Microteaching: Practicing Critical Teaching Skills, you can try out your ability to demonstrate the personal attributes and professional skills that are vital to teachers, as discussed in Chapters 10 and 11. In Unit 2, Reflective Teaching: Practicing Being a Thoughtful Practitioner, you have a chance to acquire and practice some of the qualities of reflective or thoughtful practitioners; you learned of these in Chapter 9. Finally, in Unit 3, Room 221: A Simulation: Solving Classroom Problems, you can take on the role of a teacher, encounter real-life classroom dramas, and consider how you would respond to each one.

To our knowledge, this is the first book to incorporate practice teaching experiences such as microteaching, Reflective Teaching, and simulation exercises. We are convinced that engaging in these techniques now will better prepare you for life in the classroom.

In Chapters 10 and 11 you learned that effective teachers possess certain distinguishing characteristics and abilities. This unit is designed to help you practice and improve your use of a few of these qualities and skills through microteaching.

Microteaching is scaled-down teaching. By that, we mean that instead of teaching a complete lesson to a complete class, you teach an abbreviated lesson to a small group of your classmates. An additional feature of microteaching is that your lessons are videotaped, thus allowing you to watch your own teaching performance. Using this approach, you can try out important teaching characteristics or abilities to find out how good you may be at them. For example, in Chapter 10 you learned that effective teachers display enthusiasm, and so in this unit you can develop and teach a short lesson in which you try to demonstrate this quality.

Overview of Microteaching

This unit is organized around four microteaching lessons intended to help you apply and refine your professional attributes and abilities. Each lesson is directed at a different aspect of your instructional performance. Microteaching Lesson One focuses on how well you convey the professional attributes of effective teachers. Microteaching Lesson Two helps you develop your ability to establish set. Microteaching Lesson Three helps you hone your questioning skills. And, finally, Microteaching Lesson Four emphasizes refining your ability to present information clearly.

MICROTEACHING FORMAT

Although each of the four activities is directed toward different skills or abilities, each will follow a similar format. You will (1) read about the activity, (2) review information about the specific skills in earlier chapters, (3) plan a short lesson using the guidelines in Chapter 5, (4) teach the lesson to a group of your classmates while being videotaped, (5) view the videotape in order to assess your performance, and (6) when time allows, replan or revise your lesson and reteach it to improve.

Before we begin with Microteaching Lesson One, it may be helpful to discuss guidelines for each phase of the activities.

Reading about the Activity   Each microteaching activity is described in this unit. It provides information about the skills to be developed, the length of the lesson, and the way in which the lesson will be evaluated. Reading this information will help you focus your planning and instructional efforts to gain the most from the activity.

Reviewing Relevant Information   Remember that these microteaching lessons are intended to help you practice and improve your use of the professional attributes and skills cited in Chapters 10 and 11. Before planning your microteaching lesson, you will be advised to review the sections of these chapters that describe in detail the skills you will be practicing. It will be important that you understand the skill or skills to be developed, the reasons they are important, and the specific instructional behaviors you can use. This information should be used to plan your lesson carefully to help you focus on the specific skills and to remind you to work to incorporate them into your lesson.

Planning the Lesson   When planning your microteaching lessons, you are encouraged to follow the principles and guidelines in Chapter 5 for daily lesson planning. For each lesson you should establish objectives and address each of the lesson plan components. Because the microteaching lessons are short (generally ranging from 4 to 12 minutes), your plan will not be terribly long. However, you should be certain to plan thoroughly for each lesson. This will not only improve your lesson performance but also give you an opportunity to practice your planning skills.

A common problem for teachers in microteaching lessons is that they try to teach a great deal more material than the time allows. In fact, at the end of her microteaching lesson a young English teacher whispered to a friend, "Decide what you think you can teach in the time you have, and then try to teach about one fifth of it!" Although this may be an exaggeration, you should probably attempt to teach only a portion of the concept or topic that first comes to mind. For example, it would be virtually impossible to effectively teach the entire scientific process in a 5-minute lesson. However, you could select one of the four steps in the process, perhaps on developing hypotheses, and teach a thorough and interesting lesson in 5 minutes. Don't try to teach too much.

Teaching the Lesson On the day your instructor establishes, you will teach your lesson to a group of your peers. Depending upon the arrangement the instructor prefers, this may range from a relatively small group (four or five students) to the entire class. The lesson will be videotaped to allow you to view your performance later. Remember to teach to your learners, not to the camera.

To help you learn to manage instructional time, each microteaching lesson will be timed. You will be required to conduct some form of valuable instruction for at least a minimum amount of time, and you will not be allowed to go beyond the established maximum time.

When it is your turn to teach, you will have a short amount of time to prepare the room and your materials. You can move the chairs or desks and use overhead projectors, handouts, or other materials. Then your instructor will make sure the video camera is operating and notify you to begin your lesson. When you have met the minimum length for the lesson, the instructor will give you a signal. Then, when you have reached the maximum allowed time, your instructor will have you stop your lesson. When you receive the signal for the minimum time limit, you might want to determine how much more of your lesson you can teach effectively in the time remaining. Often it is better to begin at this point to draw the lesson to an end and achieve closure rather than attempt to hurry through the rest of your planned lesson.

Viewing Your Videotaped Lesson After you have finished teaching your lesson, you will have the opportunity to view the videotape of your performance. Your instructor may choose to have you do this alone or with a small group of your peers, or in some instances both. It is wise to watch your lesson at least twice. The first time, simply allow yourself to form a general impression of the quality of your performance and to jot down some notes. Then watch the lesson again, this time using checklists or observation forms that allow you to focus on your use of specific desirable behaviors. Then in each activity, you will identify particular aspects of your performance that you should improve, and you will develop specific suggestions for how you might do so.

Reteaching the Lesson If time allows, your instructor may offer you the opportunity to reteach your lesson to improve your performance. If you are offered this opportunity, you are encouraged to take advantage of it even if your first lesson was satisfactory. Practicing the skills and evaluating how well you use them will help you become even more comfortable and confident.

Microteaching Lesson One: Conveying Positive Personal Attributes

RATIONALE AND OVERVIEW

As previously noted, Microteaching Lesson One gives you the chance to see what you look like as a teacher. Although we all have self-perceptions of what we probably look like when we're teaching, often our actions and words differ from what we imagine. Thus, one of the purposes of this first short lesson is simply to allow you the chance to plan and teach a lesson and then watch yourself on videotape. A more specific purpose is to allow you to compare your teaching "persona" with that of effective teachers. You may remember from Chapter 10 that effective teachers have motivating personalities, are professional, and convey optimism and an orientation toward success. Before you plan your first microteaching lesson, it would be wise to review the personal attributes and characteristics discussed in Chapter 10.

Planning the Lesson Microteaching Lesson One is to be at least 4 and not more than 5 minutes in length. You may teach your lesson on any topic you wish, but you should select a topic or concept that you can genuinely teach to your classmates. In other words, you should not pretend to teach them a concept that most of them are likely to know. As noted earlier, many teachers make the mistake in this first lesson of trying to teach too much in the time allowed. Select a very small concept or subconcept that you can teach thoroughly in 4 to 5 minutes. Develop an objective for your lesson, and follow the format for planning suggested in Chapter 5.

Teaching the Lesson Your instructor will tell you when to begin your lesson, when you have reached the minimum time limit, and when you must stop teaching. You should try to follow your instructional plan—but be flexible. When students don't seem to understand, don't keep pressing on just to "get through the content."

Viewing Your Videotaped Lesson After you have finished teaching your lesson, sit down alone or with some classmates and watch your videotaped lesson. It is probably a good idea to watch the tape twice. Watch it once without stopping, and consider your perceptions of the professional personality you conveyed. After you have watched the lesson, stop the tape and make some notes. If you are watching with classmates, ask them to give you their perceptions. Try to avoid focusing on your hair or clothes, and focus instead on

TABLE U1.1 Observation Form for Microteaching Lesson One: Conveying Professional Attributes

For each behavior listed below, rate the quality of the teacher's performance.

Behavior	Quality Rating			
	Excellent	Good	Fair	Poor
1. The teacher conveyed enthusiasm.	4	3	2	1
2. The teacher used humor effectively and conveyed warmth.	4	3	2	1
3. The teacher seemed credible and worthy of trust.	4	3	2	1
4. The teacher conveyed high expectations for him/herself and for learners.	4	3	2	1
5. The teacher was encouraging and supportive of learners.	4	3	2	1
6. The teacher was professional and businesslike.	4	3	2	1
7. The teacher adapted the lesson when time or learner misunderstanding required it.	4	3	2	1
8. The teacher appeared knowledgeable of the topic, of learners, and of pedagogy.	4	3	2	1

Specific suggestions for improvement:

how confident, personable, optimistic, and professional you seem to be. Then rewind the tape and prepare to view your performance again using the Observation Form for Microteaching Lesson One to guide your observation (Table U1.1).

Reteaching the Lesson If time permits, your instructor may allow you to teach another 4- to 5-minute lesson to help you become more comfortable teaching in front of the video camera. If you have the opportunity to do so, you will find that future microteaching lessons seem less intimidating, and you can focus your attention on your professional skills rather than on your nervousness.

Microteaching Lesson Two: Establishing Set

RATIONALE AND OVERVIEW

Microteaching Lesson One focused on your professional attributes and characteristics. Lesson Two now emphasizes your use of professional skills. Specifically, Microteaching Lesson Two focuses on your ability to effectively establish set in a short lesson. Remember from Chapter 11 that effective teachers establish three kinds of set to provide a context for the lesson or lessons they are about to teach. In this short lesson, your goal is to identify one of the three types of set you wish to establish and then to do so in a short lesson.

Before going on, you should review the suggestions in Chapter 11 regarding establishing set.

Planning the Lesson Your Microteaching Lesson Two must be at least 8 minutes and not more than 10 minutes in length. As before, you should build your lesson around the guidelines in Chapter 5. However, because Microteaching Lesson Two focuses only on establishing set, you do not need to teach an entire lesson. Consider the information in Chapter 11, and then determine a topic that you want to introduce as well as which of the three types of set you will use to do so. Since you may select any topic you wish, be creative and attempt to identify a topic that you can introduce in a meaningful, interesting way in the time allowed.

Teaching the Lesson You will conduct Microteaching Lesson Two in much the same way as your earlier microteaching lesson. You will have some time to organize your materials; then your instructor will notify you to begin, signal you when you have taught at least 8 minutes, and stop you when you reach the 10-minute limit.

Viewing Your Videotaped Lesson As before, you should view your videotaped lesson at least twice. The first time, make general notes about the way you established set and compare your perceptions with those of your classmates or peer learners. Then, use the Observation Form for Microteaching Lesson Two to evaluate

Part I

Circle the number of each of the following behaviors the teacher used in establishing set.

1. The teacher reviewed material from previous lesson(s).
2. The teacher asked a curiosity-provoking question at the beginning of the lesson.
3. The teacher provided an overview of the major points of the lesson.
4. The teacher demonstrated the major concepts or ideas of the lesson.
5. The teacher provided and explained a visual schema depicting the relationships of various aspects or concepts of the lesson.
6. The teacher provided a problem to engage students in processing the concepts to be learned.
7. The teacher pointed out the relevance of the lesson to students' lives and interests.
8. The teacher piqued students' interest or curiosity using a unique or novel question, problem, or scenario.
9. The teacher conveyed interest, enthusiasm, and curiosity about the topic.
10. The teacher informed students of the objectives or goals of the lesson and their responsibilities.

Part II

Rate how well you believe the teacher was able to do each of the following, and use the space below to explain your ratings.

Behavior	Quality Rating			
	Excellent	**Good**	**Fair**	**Poor**
1. The teacher captured students' attention.	4	3	2	1
2. The teacher provided a framework for the lesson.	4	3	2	1
3. The teacher related new information to what students had learned previously.	4	3	2	1
4. The teacher determined students' entry-level knowledge.	4	3	2	1

Specific suggestions for improvement:

your performance (Table U1.2). Then, based upon your general notes and ratings on the observation instrument, make a few specific suggestions for improving the way you will establish set in future lessons. Be certain to be specific about how and what you will do to improve.

Reteaching the Lesson   The opportunity to reteach your lesson is probably more important in Microteaching Lessons Two, Three, and Four than in Lesson One. These later activities are focused on professional skills that you can improve relatively easily. Thus, the more opportunities you have to practice them, evaluate your performance, and refine your skill, the more effectively you will be able to use them in the future.

Microteaching Lesson Three: Using Questions

RATIONALE AND OVERVIEW

In this activity, you will plan for, use, and evaluate your use of questions in a short lesson. Effective teachers conduct highly interactive lessons and use a variety of questions to keep students engaged, promote higher-order thinking, monitor students' understanding, and introduce variety—among other things. Your ability to use questions effectively is an important but complex skill. Before planning your microteaching lesson, review the discussion of questioning skills in Chapter 11.

Planning the Lesson   Lesson Three is to be between 8 and 10 minutes. In this lesson, you should attempt to include all lesson parts. Thus, address all lesson phases suggested in Chapter 5. Because this lesson is to focus your attention on using questions skillfully, you should not plan a lesson that will require you to present a great deal of information to your learners. Instead, select a topic that allows you to help your learners gain understanding by asking them questions. For example, you might wish to select a controversial issue that you wish your learners to examine critically. You could build your lesson around questions that would help learners see all sides of the issue, understand various points of view, and appreciate the complexity of the issue. In this type of lesson, you would use questions to guide your learners. Remember as you do your planning to include questions you can use during the lesson closure to help learners draw conclusions about the discussion.

TABLE U1.3 Observation Form for Microteaching Lesson Three: Using Questions

For each behavior below, indicate the quality of the teacher's performance.

Behavior	Quality Rating			
	Excellent	Good	Fair	Poor
1. The teacher asked a question early in the lesson to get students involved.	4	3	2	1
2. The teacher phrased questions clearly.	4	3	2	1
3. The teacher avoided repeating questions unless students didn't understand.	4	3	2	1
4. The teacher used adequate wait time after asking questions.	4	3	2	1
5. The teacher frequently asked appropriate questions.	4	3	2	1
6. The teacher called on all students to respond to questions, not just volunteers.	4	3	2	1
7. The teacher included questions at higher cognitive levels.	4	3	2	1
8. The teacher followed up students' responses appropriately.	4	3	2	1
9. The teacher's questions were clearly directed toward helping learners reach the objectives of the lesson.	4	3	2	1
10. Overall, the teacher used questions effectively.	4	3	2	1

Specific suggestions for improvement:

Teaching the Lesson Microteaching Lesson Three will be conducted just as Lessons Two was. You will have a few minutes to organize the room and your materials, and then your instructor will notify you to begin. When you have taught at least 8 minutes, the instructor will give you a signal and then tell you to stop when you reach 10 minutes.

Viewing Your Videotaped Lesson As you view your videotaped lesson the first time, focus on how well you used a variety of questions to reach your objective. Did you use many questions? Did the questions seem to guide learners, or did they seem random and unconnected? When you asked questions, did you use silence and effective nonverbal behavior to encourage learners to participate? Generally, how do you feel about your use of questioning as you watch the tape? After this first viewing, use the Observation Form for Microteaching Lesson Three to guide your second viewing (Table U1.3). Focus on specific things you did well and on specific aspects of your skill you want to improve; then establish a plan for improving your questioning skills.

Reteaching the Lesson Using questions effectively is a difficult but important professional skill. Beginning teachers generally are uncomfortable using questions

and prefer to teach in an expository and less interactive manner. However, we know that interactive teaching is more desirable. Because it is so difficult to become proficient and comfortable using questions, you are encouraged to take advantage of as many opportunities to reteach your lesson as you can. Each time you reteach, work to plan for and implement questions that integrate the suggestions you made for improving your weaknesses.

Microteaching Lesson Four: Providing Clear Instruction

RATIONALE AND OVERVIEW

In Microteaching Lesson One you focused on your professional attributes. In Lesson Two, you taught a lesson in which you attempted to establish set. And in Microteaching Lesson Three you focused on your use of questions. Now, in Microteaching Lesson Four, you will again attempt to teach a lesson that includes set induction, presentation of content, and closure—a complete lesson. However, in this lesson you will focus on your ability to provide instruction that is clear to learners.

Remember from Chapter 11 that instructional clarity may be one of the most important skills in helping students learn. The specific aspects of clarity can be organized into four categories related to various aspects of the lesson. To make your task more manageable, you will focus on only two of the four areas: (1) introducing and emphasizing content and (2) elaborating on important ideas or concepts. Before going on, return to Chapter 11 and review the discussion of instructional clarity.

Planning the Lesson   Microteaching Lesson Four is to be at least 8 minutes and not more than 10 minutes in length. Your primary goal during this exercise is to plan and teach a lesson in which you help learners come to understand clearly the major points of the lesson. The lesson should include all the aspects of a good lesson described in Chapter 5, and you should plan to maximize the reinforcement of major points by repeating them, writing them on the board, reviewing them, and so on. Thus, in planning your lesson, you must identify the two or three major ideas or points you want your learners to understand, organize them logically, develop explanations and examples of each point, determine questions you may use to ensure that students understand, and determine places in the lesson where you will review. You may also wish to highlight particular terms or points by writing them on the board for your learners.

Teaching the Lesson   Microteaching Lesson Four will be conducted very much like Lessons Two and Three. Your instructor will give you some time to organize yourself and your materials and then notify you to begin. When you have reached the 8-minute mark in the lesson, the instructor will signal you. At the end of 10 minutes he or she will ask you to stop. Remember that good lessons include a closure to help learners draw conclusions. When you know you are nearing the end of your allotted time, begin to draw the lesson to a close rather than present new content.

Viewing Your Videotaped Lesson   Instructional clarity is "in the eye of the beholder." That's why your learners are in the best position to help you determine whether you provided clear instruction. If at all possible, you should watch this videotaped lesson at least three times—two with your learners and once by yourself. During the first viewing, make notes about how clearly you identified and reinforced major points. Did you treat each major point as equally important? Were major points obvious and distinct from their explanations? Can your learners name the major points? Can they explain them? Generally, did the lesson seem to progress logically and clearly?

In the second viewing of the lesson, use the Observation Form for Microteaching Lesson Four with your learners to focus on your use of some of the specific clarity skills (Table U1.4). Then watch your lesson by yourself using your learners' comments and your own impressions to identify the strengths and weaknesses of your instructional clarity. Remember to identify specific aspects of your performance that you believe need to be improved and to suggest specific ways you will attempt to improve them in future lessons.

Reteaching the Lesson   Instructional clarity is a complex skill that requires you to consider and implement a variety of behaviors to help learners reach the instructional objectives. As a result, it is not uncommon for teachers to need several videotaped lessons focusing on their instructional clarity skills. If possible, reteach your lesson as many times as necessary to enable you to feel comfortable with your performance. When time allows and you have improved your original lesson, try teaching a new lesson to see if you are able to provide clear instruction with a different set of major ideas or points.

Additional Practice

Although this unit has included four microteaching lessons to help you improve your instructional behavior, good teachers are constantly working to improve their skills. In addition to doing the four microteaching lessons, you are encouraged to continue to practice honing your professional abilities. The following suggestions will help you do so.

EXPANDED MICROLESSONS

One of the things you can do to continue developing your professional skills is to expand the microteaching format to include longer lessons and more or different professional skills. For example, a reasonable next step would be to teach a slightly longer lesson, perhaps 15 to 20 minutes, in which you attempt to establish set, provide clear instruction, and use questions effectively. Or you might try teaching several short videotaped lessons in which you work to provide desirable feedback and reinforcement, monitor students' understanding, or use different instructional alternatives. You could develop your own observation instruments for these lessons using the guidelines for each skill included in Chapter 11.

VIDEOTAPING YOUR CLASSROOM TEACHING

Another way to continue your professional skill development is through constant assessment of your classroom behavior and interactions. Even if you feel quite competent in using the professional skills in short lessons to your peers, you may not be so proficient when faced with a classroom of thirty school-age students. By using

Part I

In the space below, enumerate the major points of the teacher's lesson and provide a brief explanation of each.

Part II

Rate the quality of the teacher's performance of each behavior listed below.

Behavior	Quality Rating			
	Excellent	**Good**	**Fair**	**Poor**
1. The teacher organized and presented the lesson in a logical manner.	4	3	2	1
2. The teacher identified important points.	4	3	2	1
3. The teacher wrote important points on the board or a chart.	4	3	2	1
4. The teacher repeated important points for emphasis.	4	3	2	1
5. The teacher included summaries and reviews within the lesson.	4	3	2	1
6. The teacher clearly explained important points.	4	3	2	1
7. The teacher presented examples to reinforce each major point.	4	3	2	1
8. The teacher pointed out similarities and differences between things.	4	3	2	1
9. The teacher explained unfamiliar words when necessary.	4	3	2	1
10. The teacher used pauses to reinforce important points or to allow learners to ask questions.	4	3	2	1

Specific suggestions for improvement:

guided observation and analysis, you can use your classroom teaching experiences as advanced forms of microteaching. First, you can videotape the lessons you teach during your field experiences. Merely set up the camera in the back of the room, turn it on before you begin your lesson, and turn it off when you are done. Then, carefully view your natural classroom lesson just as you did your microteaching lessons. This type of formal self-analysis will be extremely useful in helping you understand your classroom behavior.

You should also attempt to record some of your actual teaching even after you have finished student teaching and have your own classroom. Even skilled, experienced teachers are surprised at their classroom behavior when they see themselves on videotape. They find that they no longer are as effective in using their professional skills as they once were. Most schools have easy-to-use video cameras that teachers can borrow. Every so often, set up the camera in the back of the room for a couple of lessons, and then watch yourself critically. You will be surprised at how some of your professional skills have improved with classroom experience while others have grown less effective. One of the authors videotapes at least one lesson each term—and each time is humbled by the experience. Nevertheless, seeing ourselves on videotape helps us all become more aware of both our strengths and weaknesses.

Teaching is an experience filled with excitement, surprises, frustrations, and delight. By now, you are a step closer to entering this adventure.

Think back over your teacher preparation program thus far. Chances are your instructors have used a variety of experiences to ease you into the act of teaching. What were some of those experiences? Perhaps you have read and discussed biographies about the daily lives of teachers, viewed films or television documentaries about teaching and learning, and observed and analyzed teachers in their classrooms. The next step is to engage you in the act of teaching. Reflective Teaching (Cruickshank, 1991) is a program that allows you to practice the complete act of teaching. It requires you to plan a lesson and to implement those plans. Further, it allows you to find out how well your students learned and how satisfied they were with your teaching. Finally, it provides you with an opportunity to reflect on teaching and learning in order to extend your professional wisdom.

As suggested by the title, Reflective Teaching enables you to practice being a thoughtful or reflective practitioner. In Chapter 9 we pointed out that reflective practitioners are more thoughtful and wise about teaching. This is because they routinely and consciously examine their teaching behaviors, practices, and effectiveness. Their minds are a flurry of questions: Why am I doing what I am doing? What are the consequences of my teaching? How could I have done that differently? How can I improve? As a result of this self-analysis, a reflective practitioner is the ultimate student of teaching.

What Is Reflective Teaching?

Reflective Teaching is a contrived teaching experience carried out on campus rather than in an actual classroom setting. The experience provides you with the opportunity to practice the act of teaching, to evaluate its success, and to gain insights into teaching and learning that should enable you to be even more effective in future teaching episodes.

Although you and a group of friends can independently engage in Reflective Teaching, the program is generally part of a university course. The class is divided into groups of four to six persons. For each Reflective Teaching session, one person from each group is designated as the teacher and provided with the Reflective Teaching Lesson (RTL), which all teachers will use during the next session. Each designated teacher prepares the lesson independently, considering the best way to achieve the stated objective and to maximize learners' achievement and satisfaction. After instructing, the designated teachers evaluate their lessons by measuring students' learning and satisfaction. Finally, they analyze and reflect on teaching and learning in their small groups and then in an instructor-led discussion engaging the entire class.

As you can see, Reflective Teaching engages you in all four phases of teaching: planning, implementing those plans, evaluating, and reflecting on teaching.

Using Reflective Teaching

Each Reflective Teaching Lesson (RTL) contains a teaching objective, the resources you will need to meet that objective, and a description of ways to measure the learning and satisfaction of your learners. While some RTLs deal with professional education (for example, Clear Teacher Task), other RTLs address a variety of topics. The RTLs included in this chapter represent all three instructional domains (cognitive, psychomotor, and affective) and varied levels of learning within those domains. Further, each RTL focuses on a teacher behavior widely used in classroom situations. For example, in the Origami Task, you practice demonstration skills by teaching your students to fold a paper butterfly.

In order to emphasize evaluation and reflection, the lessons are brief—usually 10 to 15 minutes long. Your Reflective Teaching session, then, should take about 50 minutes:

- Teaching: 10–15 minutes
- Evaluation: 5 minutes
- Small-group discussion: 15 minutes
- Whole-class discussion: 15 minutes

Although a total of 41 RTLs are available, six are included in this chapter to help you practice becoming a reflective teacher.

Roles during Reflective Teaching

During a Reflective Teaching session, you will have a variety of responsibilities. These will vary depending on whether you are the designated teacher or a learner.

DESIGNATED TEACHER

When you are the designated teacher, your primary responsibility is to teach an RTL to a small group of your peers. Specifically, you will need to prepare a lesson that will enable your learners to achieve the lesson objective and to gain satisfaction from your teaching. More importantly, you will prepare for and lead your group in reflecting on the teaching and learning that occurred during the lesson.

Although all designated teachers present the same lesson during a Reflective Teaching session, you may teach the lesson using any method you choose. Use Learner Satisfaction Forms to access Student Satisfaction (see pp. 452 & 453). Your goal, after all, is to select a teaching strategy that you think will maximize students' learning and satisfaction. You must also ensure that all the materials you need for instruction are on hand when you teach. While you should provide materials related to teaching, your university instructor will provide copies of the test used to evaluate students' learning, scoring boxes, and the Learner Satisfaction Forms used to assess student satisfaction. If you need audiovisual equipment or other resources, communicate those needs to your instructor in advance. After all, planning ahead is part of the teaching process!

On the day of the Reflective Teaching session, arrive early to set up your teaching stations and "classroom." Will you seat your students in rows or a circle? How will you display your visual aids? Will you stand or remain seated while teaching? These are all instructional decisions you will need to make as the designated teacher.

When the learners arrive and all the teachers are ready to begin, the university instructor will signal you to begin teaching. Your RTL will specify how long your lesson should be. While you are teaching, the instructor may observe all or a part of your lesson. When the allocated instructional time has expired, the instructor must promptly stop all lessons and provide you with posttests, scoring boxes, and Learner Satisfaction Forms.

By reviewing these forms, you receive immediate feedback that may help you frame reflection and discussion questions. Then turn your attention to leading a discussion with your small group of peers. The questions you pose should focus the group's attention on the *processes* of teaching and learning, rather than on the content of the lesson. During this 15-minute reflective session, use discussion questions such as these:

- As the designated teacher, what knowledge, skills, or attitudes did you need to develop in your learners?
- How did you choose the teaching method to accomplish the lesson's objective? What factors influenced your choice of how to teach the lesson (for example, content of the lesson, availability of materials, the setting, your experience as a learner, your learning style, and time available for instruction)?
- How well did your teaching method work? Did your lesson go as planned?
- According to the posttests and Learner Satisfaction Forms, how well did your learners learn? How satisfied were they?
- How did the learners feel about their experience? What helped or hindered their learning? What suggestions do they have for improving the experience?
- What specifically did each participant discover about teaching and learning?
- What did you learn about teaching and learning and about yourself as a teacher as a result of this experience?

You may notice that some of these questions address the designated teacher; others are aimed at the learners or addressed to all members of the group. By carefully selecting questions that engage all participants in reflection, you can lead a discussion that will provide you with insights about your teaching.

LEARNER

When you are not assigned to act as a designated teacher, your role will be to receive instruction. It is important for you to be cooperative and available and to be on time. Above all, be yourself; role playing is not usually helpful to the designated teacher or to your learning experience.

When you arrive at class for the Reflective Teaching session, go directly to an assigned teaching station. After the lesson, you will need to complete two evaluations. A posttest will assess how much you learned during the lesson, and the Learner Satisfaction Form will measure how satisfied you were with the lesson. It is most helpful to the designated teacher if you provide honest feedback about how you felt and what contributed to or inhibited your learning and satisfaction.

Following the evaluation, the designated teacher will lead a 15-minute discussion. During the discussion, you should help the designated teacher think openly, honestly, and deeply about the teaching-learning experience. This will provide everyone in your small group with a better understanding of effective teaching.

Following the small group discussion, the entire class will engage in a debriefing led by the university instructor to further inquire into the teaching and learning processes. Your willingness and ability to interact during these reflective sessions will indicate your progress toward becoming a serious student of teaching.

Reflective Teaching Lessons

Following are six sample Reflective Teaching Lessons.* The Clear Teacher Task and Magic Squares Task pro-

*These six sample lessons are reproduced with permission from Phi Delta Kappa.

vide learning experiences in the cognitive domain and enable you to practice teaching behaviors such as designating, describing, and demonstrating. The Bowline Task and Origami Task provide experiences in the psychomotor domain and focus on demonstration. Finally, in the Time Task and the Honesty Task, you attempt to get students to "change their minds" about people, events, and the content learned. These two tasks are in the affective domain.

REFERENCES

Cruickshank, D. R. (1991). *Reflective teaching*. Bloomington, IN: Phi Delta Kappa.

THE CLEAR TEACHER TASK

Read each section carefully.

Description of Your Reflective Teaching Task

You are one of several participants chosen to teach this brief lesson to a small group of your peers. The exercise is intended to provide an opportunity for you to experience teaching and then to reflect on the shared teaching and learning. Plan to teach the lesson in such a way that you believe both learning and satisfaction will result.

Your lesson will be taught on _____

INTRODUCTION TO THE LESSON

Teachers sometimes designate and describe—that is, they denote things directly and specifically for learners, and they may tell something of the characteristics or qualities of the things denoted. The following are examples of designating and describing behavior:

1. An elementary teacher designates the planets in the solar system and describes the topographic and atmospheric conditions of each.

2. A social studies teacher designates the various routes fugitive slaves took in their flight to freedom using the Underground Railroad and then describes the perils each route seemed to hold.

3. A music teacher designates the notes of a chord and describes how to play them.

Following is an objective that requires you to designate items to a small group of your peers and then to elaborate on or describe them. The task was selected because your success in accomplishing it probably will not depend on your knowledge of some academic subject or on previous experience you may have had.

YOUR OBJECTIVE

Your goal is to get as many of your learners as possible to list the behaviors that distinguish teachers who are clear from those who are not. You will have a maximum of 15 minutes to accomplish that goal.

MATERIALS

1. Resources: *Behaviors of Clear Teachers* (attached)
2. Test (provided by your instructor)
3. Scoring box (provided by your instructor)
4. Learner Satisfaction Forms (provided by your instructor)

SPECIAL CONDITIONS AND LIMITATIONS

None

ENDING THE LESSON

When the instructor notifies you that time is up or when your learners are ready to take the test, (you may finish in less than 15 minutes), obtain copies of the test, scoring box, and Learner Satisfaction Form.

Give the learners the test. When the learners have finished the test (allow no more than five minutes), read them the correct answers so they can score their own tests, or collect and correct the tests yourself if you like. Enter the learners' individual test scores in the scoring box.

Next, pass out the Learner Satisfaction Forms, and encourage learners to give you maximum feedback. Return the tests and collect the Learner Satisfaction Forms.

Begin to work through the questions for small group discussion with your learners.

The idea for this RTL was contributed by Donald R. Cruickshank, The Ohio State University, Ohio.

Behaviors of Clear Teachers

According to a series of studies conducted at The Ohio State University, teacher behaviors that comprise clear teaching are numerous and identifiable. If it is necessary or desirable for teachers to be clear, then teachers must know these behaviors and use them in practice. Although there seem to be about 30 in all, several behaviors seem to best discriminate between teachers whose pupils say they are clear and teachers whose pupils say they are unclear. A clear teacher:

1. teaches at a pace appropriate to the topic and to learners.
2. teaches step-by-step.
3. explains things simply, that is, gives explanations we understand.
4. tries to find out if we don't understand.
5. stays with the topic until we understand.
6. repeats things we don't understand.
7. describes work to be done and how to do it.
8. asks if we know what to do and how to do it.
9. explains things, then shows an example.

Name _____

List as many behaviors as you can that distinguish clear from unclear teachers.

1.

2.

3.

4.

5.

6.

7.

8.

9.

Directions   Give learners 1 point for each of the attributes of clear teachers. A perfect score is 9.

LEARNER'S NAME	PERFORMANCE Score (0–9)
1	
2	
3	
4	
5	
6	
GROUP AVERAGE SCORE Add all scores and divide by number of learners.	

THE MAGIC SQUARES TASK

Read each section carefully.

Description of Your Reflective Teaching Task

You are one of several participants chosen to teach this brief lesson to a small group of your peers. The exercise is intended to provide an opportunity for you to experience teaching and then to reflect on the shared teaching and learning. Plan to teach the lesson in such a way that you believe both learning and satisfaction will result.

Your lesson will be taught on _____

INTRODUCTION TO THE LESSON

Teachers describe—that is, they tell about something. Teachers also demonstrate—that is, they show how to do something. The following are examples of describing and demonstrating behavior.

1. An elementary teacher describes and demonstrates how to perform division.
2. A chemistry teacher describes and demonstrates how to prepare a solution.
3. An auto mechanics teacher describes and demonstrates how to change a tire.
4. A physical education teacher describes and demonstrates how to do a forward roll.

Following is an objective that requires you to describe and demonstrate something to a small group of your peers. The task was selected because your success in accomplishing it probably will not depend on your knowledge of some academic subject or on previous experience you might have had.

YOUR OBJECTIVE

Your goal is to get as many of your learners as possible to be able to correctly construct a magic square where the number of cells on each side equals seven. You will have 15 minutes to accomplish your objective.

MATERIALS

1. Resources: *An Amusement for Centuries* (attached)
2. Test (provided by your instructor)
3. Answer sheet and scoring box (provided by your instructor)
4. Learner Satisfaction Forms (provided by your instructor)

SPECIAL CONDITIONS AND LIMITATIONS

None

ENDING THE LESSON

Notify the instructor when your learners are ready to take the test. (You may finish early.) Obtain copies of the test, scoring box, and Learner Satisfaction Form.

Give your learners the test, and when they have finished (no more than 5 minutes), read them the correct answers so that they can correct their own tests. Use the criteria given with the scoring box for scoring.

Next, pass out the Learner Satisfaction Forms. While the learners are completing them, collect the tests and record the scores in the scoring box. Return the tests and collect the Learner Satisfaction Forms.

Begin to work through the questions for small group discussion with your learners.

The idea for this RTL was contributed by Jerry Mager, Syracuse University, New York.

AN AMUSEMENT FOR CENTURIES

A magic square is one in which the columns, rows, and diagonals all add to the same number. For example, in this square they all add to 15:

```
15                          15
      ┌────┬────┬────┐
      │ 8  │ 1  │ 6  │ 15
      ├────┼────┼────┤
      │ 3  │ 5  │ 7  │ 15
      ├────┼────┼────┤
      │ 4  │ 9  │ 2  │ 15
      └────┴────┴────┘
15    15   15   15     15
```

The formation of magic squares has been an amusement for centuries. These boxes were sometimes said to possess magical properties; one particular square was inscribed on a silver plate and carried as a protection against the plague.

You can construct magic squares by trial and error, but the task is very time-consuming. Thanks to a rule De La Loubere discovered in 1693, it is possible to complete odd-numbered squares with ease. There are formulas for even-numbered squares, but they will not concern us at this stage. De La Loubere's rule may be stated as follows:

a) Place the numeral 1 in the middle cell of the top row.

b) Next place the successive numbers moving upwards diagonally to the right. If you have already reached the top row, move to the bottom row as if it were above the top row.

```
┌────┬────┬────┐
│    │ 1  │    │
├────┼────┼────┤
│    │    │    │
├────┼────┼────┤
│    │    │ 2  │
└────┴────┴────┘
```

Thus 2 goes to the bottom right-hand corner.

c) If you have reached the right-hand column, move to the left-hand column as if it were to the right of the right-hand column.

	1	
3		
		2

Thus 3 goes to the middle left-hand cell.

d) If, when moving diagonally, you find another number filling a cell, then move to the cell immediately below.

	1	
3		
4		2

Thus 4 goes below the 3.
5 would then go up diagonally to the right from the 4, and 6 up and to the right from 5.

e) When you reach the top right corner cell, place the number directly below.

	1	6
3	5	7
4		2

Thus 7 goes below the 6.

Now you have reached the right column again, so the 8 goes in the top left column as if it were to the right of the right-hand column.

8	1	6
3	5	7
4	9	2

This reaches the top line, so the 9 goes in the middle of the bottom row as if it were above the top row.

The following diagram summarizes the rules:
    In general, move diagonally up and to the right.

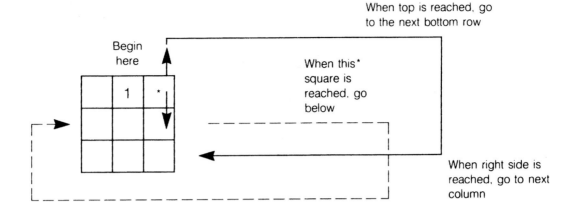

When any cell already has a number go directly below.

Let us now apply the rule to a 5-cell square.

<table>
<tr><td>65</td><td></td><td></td><td></td><td></td><td>65</td></tr>
</table>

17	24	1	8	15	65
23	5	7	14	16	65
4	6	13	20	22	65
10	12	19	21	3	65
11	18	25	2	9	65

65   65 65 65 65 65   65

All rows, columns, and diagonals add to 65.

Name _____

The square below has an odd number of cells on each side. Use the rules you have learned to construct a magic square.

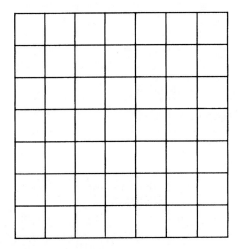

30	39	48	1	10	19	28
38	47	7	9	18	27	29
46	6	8	17	26	35	37
5	14	16	25	34	36	45
13	15	24	33	42	44	4
21	23	32	41	43	3	12
22	31	40	49	2	11	20

SCORING BOX

Directions   Give each learner 1 point for each number in the correct box. A perfect test score would be 49.

LEARNER'S NAME	PERFORMANCE Score
1	
2	
3	
4	
5	
6	
GROUP AVERAGE SCORE Add learner's scores and divide by number of learners.	

Read each section carefully.

Description of Your Reflective Teaching Task

You are one of several participants chosen to teach this brief lesson to a small group of your peers. The exercise is intended to provide an opportunity for you to experience teaching and then to reflect on the shared teaching and learning. Plan to teach the lesson in such a way that you believe both learning and satisfaction will result.

Your lesson will be taught on _____

INTRODUCTION TO THE LESSON

Teachers demonstrate—that is, they show learners how to do something. The following are examples of demonstrating behavior:

1. A science teacher demonstrates how to light a Bunsen burner.
2. A physical education teacher demonstrates a takedown in wrestling.
3. An English teacher demonstrates how to punctuate independent clauses.
4. A scoutmaster demonstrates how to use a compass and a map to find one's position in the woods.

Following is an objective that requires you to demonstrate something to a small group of your peers. The task was selected because your success in accomplishing it probably will not depend on your knowledge of some academic subject or on previous experience you may have had.

YOUR OBJECTIVE

Your goal is to get as many of your learners as possible to be able to tie a bowline knot. You will have 10 minutes to accomplish your objective.

MATERIALS

1. Resources: *The Bowline Knot* (attached)
2. One 2-foot length of 1/4" clothesline for each learner (provided by you)
3. Learner Satisfaction Forms (provided by your instructor)
4. Scoring box (attached)

SPECIAL CONDITIONS AND LIMITATIONS

None

ENDING THE LESSON

Notify the instructor when you think all your learners can demonstrate how to tie a bowline knot. (You may finish early.) Obtain copies of the Learner Satisfaction Form.

Test each learner one at a time and record the scores in the scoring box. Allow 5 minutes for testing. Only one test is allowed for each learner. Use the criteria given with the scoring box for scoring.

Next, pass out the Learner Satisfaction Forms and collect them when they are completed.

Begin to work through the questions for small group discussion with your learners.

The idea for this RTL was contributed by John Holton, Appoquinimink School District, Delaware.

THE BOWLINE KNOT

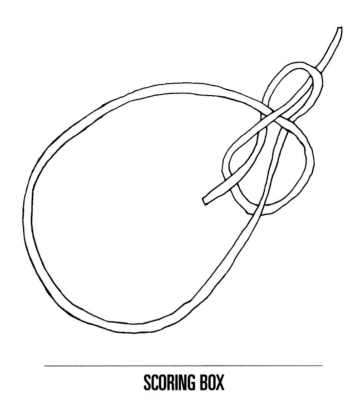

SCORING BOX

Directions Give each learner 1 point if the knot is tied without error and 0 points if any error is made.

LEARNER'S NAME	PERFORMANCE Score (0–1)
1	
2	
3	
4	
5	
6	
TOTAL (add)	

THE ORIGAMI TASK

Read each section carefully.

Description of Your Reflective Teaching Task

You are one of several participants chosen to teach this brief lesson to a small group of your peers. The exercise is intended to provide an opportunity for you to experience teaching and then to reflect on the shared teaching and learning. Plan to teach the lesson in such a way that you believe both learning and satisfaction will result.

Your lesson will be taught on _____

INTRODUCTION TO THE LESSON

Teachers describe—that is, they tell about something. Teachers also demonstrate—that is, they show how to do something. The following are examples of describing and demonstrating behavior:

1. A health education teacher describes and demonstrates how to give mouth-to-mouth resuscitation.
2. A physics teacher describes and demonstrates the phenomenon of centrifugal force.
3. A social studies teacher describes and then engages the class in a demonstration of how a bill becomes a law.
4. A home economics teacher describes and demonstrates the proper way to bathe an infant.

Following is an objective that requires you to describe and demonstrate something to a small group of your peers. The task was selected because your success in accomplishing it probably will not depend on your knowledge of some academic subject or on previous experience you may have had.

YOUR OBJECTIVE

Your goal is to get as many of your learners as possible to make a butterfly from paper using the techniques of origami. You will have 15 minutes to accomplish that goal.

MATERIALS

1. Resources: *The Japanese Art of Paper Folding* (attached)
2. Lightweight square paper for folding—enough for you and your learners (provided by you)
3. Scoring box (provided by your instructor)
4. Learner Satisfaction Form (provided by your instructor)

SPECIAL CONDITIONS AND LIMITATIONS

You may not touch or fold a learner's paper. After teaching the technique, test the learners by having them each fold a butterfly without *any* help from you.

ENDING THE LESSON

Notify the instructor when your learners are ready to take the test. (Your group may finish the task in less than the allotted time.) Obtain copies of the scoring box and Learner Satisfaction Form. Test each learner individually by having them fold a butterfly. Evaluate your learners' butterflies using the criteria given with the scoring box.

Next, pass out the Learner Satisfaction Forms. While the learners are completing them, record the ratings of the butterflies in the scoring box. Collect the Learner Satisfaction Forms.

Begin to work through the questions for small group discussion with your learners.

The idea for this RTL was contributed by Jerry Mager, Syracuse University, New York.

THE JAPANESE ART OF PAPER FOLDING

The Butterfly

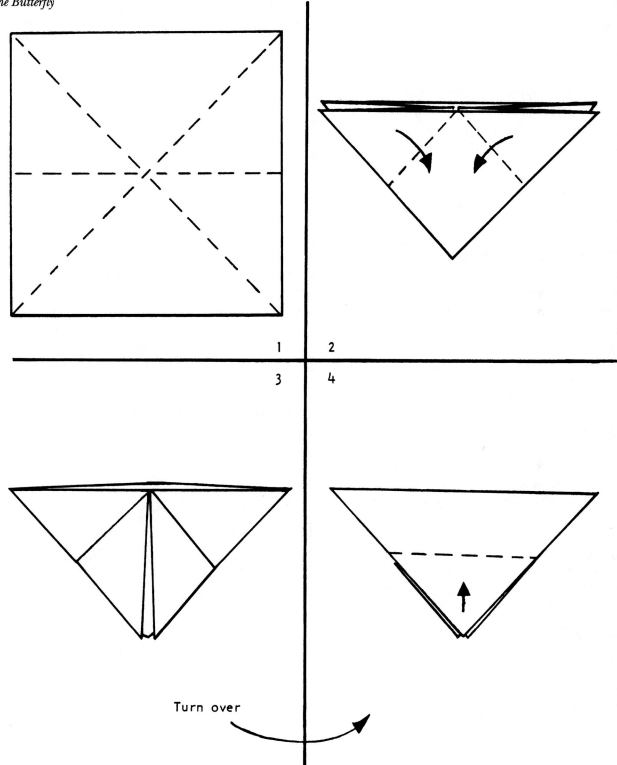

1   2

3   4

Turn over

5   6

7   8

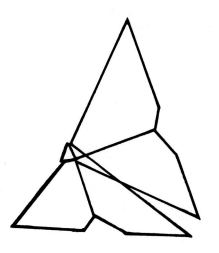

THE BUTTERFLY

THE ORIGAMI TASK: Scoring Box

Directions   Give each learner's butterfly:
  3 points if excellent,
  2 points if satisfactory, and
  1 point if unsatisfactory.

LEARNER'S NAME	RATING
1	
2	
3	
4	
5	
6	
AVERAGE SCORE (divide the total rating score by the number of learners)	

Read each section carefully.

Description of Your Reflective Teaching Task

You are one of several participants chosen to teach this brief lesson to a small group of your peers. The exercise is intended to provide an opportunity for you to experience teaching and then to reflect on the shared teaching and learning. Plan to teach the lesson in such a way that you believe both learning and satisfaction will result.

Your lesson will be taught on _____

INTRODUCTION TO THE LESSON

Teachers foster attitude change—that is, they attempt to get students to change their minds about people, events, content to be learned, and so forth. The following are examples of how teachers can foster attitude change:

1. A social studies teacher engages the class in a discussion of how persons of various national origins contribute to present-day American culture.
2. A foreign language teacher shows the class how learning a foreign language will be helpful in their everyday life.
3. A home economics teacher encourages boys to consider assuming responsibility for tasks at home.

Following is an objective that requires you to foster attitude change with a small group of your peers. The task was selected because your success in accomplishing it probably will not depend on your knowledge of some academic subject or on previous experience you may have had.

YOUR OBJECTIVE

Your goal is to get as many of your learners as possible to change their attitude toward the Western notion of time. Specifically, you should try to get your learners to disagree with the following statements, among others:

- Time is money.
- Time waits for no one.

- A stitch in time saves nine.
- Time is of the essence.

You will have 15 minutes to accomplish your goal.

MATERIALS

1. Pretest (attached)
2. Posttest (attached)
3. Scoring box (attached)
4. Learner Satisfaction Forms (provided by your instructor)

SPECIAL CONDITIONS AND LIMITATIONS

Before you begin teaching, obtain a copy of the pretest for each of your learners. Distribute the pretest and have learners respond to it. Collect the pretests before you start.

ENDING THE LESSON

Notify the instructor when your learners are ready to take the posttest. (You may finish early.) Obtain copies of the posttest and the Learner Satisfaction Form.

Give your learners the posttest, and when they are finished (allow no more than two minutes), return their pretests and ask them to indicate any changes they may have made from pre- to posttest.

Next, pass out the Learner Satisfaction Forms, and while the learners complete them, collect the pre- and posttests and record the changes in the scoring box. Return the pre- and posttests and collect the Learner Satisfaction Forms.

Begin to work through the questions for small group discussion with your learners.

The idea for this RTL was contributed by Donald R. Cruickshank, The Ohio State University, Ohio.

Name _____

Following are statements about time. Rate each on the basis of whether you agree or disagree with it by placing a checkmark (✓) in one column after each statement. The checkmark must be in a box and not on a line.

STATEMENTS	Strongly Agree	Agree	Disagree	Strongly Disagree
1 Time is money.				
2 Time waits for no one.				
3 A stitch in time saves nine.				
4 Time is of the essence.				

Give yourself:

    0 points for each item checked in the Strongly Agree column,

    1 point for each item checked in the Agree column,

    2 points for each item checked in the Disagree column, and

    3 points for each item checked in the Strongly Disagree column.

Total individual pretest score = _____

Name _____

Part A

Following are statements about time. Rate each on the basis of whether you agree or disagree with it by placing a checkmark (✓) in one column after each statement. The checkmark must be in a box and not on a line.

STATEMENTS	Strongly Agree	Agree	Disagree	Strongly Disagree
1 Time is money.				
2 Time waits for no one.				
3 A stitch in time saves nine.				
4 Time is of the essence.				

Part B

Do you think this Reflective Teaching experience has modified your attitude toward time somewhat? (*check one box*)

☐ YES ☐ NO

Part C

Give yourself:
  0 points for each item checked in the Strongly Agree column,
  1 point for each item checked in the Agree column,
  2 points for each item checked in the Disagree column, and
  3 points for each item checked in the Strongly Disagree column.

Total individual posttest score = _____

Part D

Total individual posttest score minus total individual pretest score = _____

This represents the amount of individual change. (You may have a negative number.)

When learners have completed the posttest, total the change scores (Part D, posttest) and record below.

Total learners' change	
Number of students with no change (zero change score)	
Number of students with change toward goal (postive change score)	
Number of students with change opposite goal (negative change score)	

From Part B

How many of your learners felt this experience modified their attitudes toward time? _____

THE HONESTY TASK

Read each section carefully.

Description of Your Reflective Teaching Task

You are one of several participants chosen to teach this brief lesson to a small group of your peers. The exercise is intended to provide an opportunity for you to experience teaching and then to reflect on the shared teaching and learning. Plan to teach the lesson in such a way that you believe both learning and satisfaction will result.

Your lesson will be taught on _____

INTRODUCTION TO THE LESSON

Teachers foster attitude change—that is, they attempt to get students to "change their minds" about people, events, content to be learned, and so forth. The following are examples of how teachers can foster attitude change:

1. Teachers in Montreal, Canada, a community whose history reveals a French-English schism, try to get students to respect and tolerate cultural differences.
2. Teachers try to change low-achieving pupils' attitudes toward learning so that they will have greater school success.
3. An English teacher tries to foster positive attitudes toward reading.

Following is an objective that requires you to foster attitude change with a small group of your peers. The task was selected because your success in accomplishing it probably will not depend on your knowledge of some academic subject or on previous experience you may have had.

YOUR OBJECTIVE

Your goal is to get as many of your learners as possible to change their attitude toward their notion of honesty. Specifically, you should try to get your learners to disagree with the following statements, among others.

- Honesty is the best policy.
- No legacy is so rich as honesty.

- He is wise who is honest.
- Truth will win out.

You will have 15 minutes to accomplish your goal.

MATERIALS

1. Pretest (attached)
2. Posttest (attached)
3. Scoring box (attached)
4. Learner Satisfaction Forms (provided by college instructor)

SPECIAL CONDITIONS AND LIMITATIONS

Before you begin teaching, obtain a copy of the pretest for each of your learners. Distribute the pretest and have learners respond to it. Collect the pretests before you start teaching.

ENDING THE LESSON

Notify the instructor when your learners are ready to take the posttest. (You may finish early.) Obtain copies of the posttest and the Learner Satisfaction Form.

Give your learners the posttest, and when they are finished (allow no more than two minutes), return their pretests and ask them to indicate any changes which they may have made from pre- to posttest.

Next, pass out the Learner Satisfaction Forms, and while they are being completed, collect the pre- and posttests and record the changes in the scoring box. Return the pre- and posttests and collect the Learner Satisfaction Forms.

Begin to work through the questions for small group discussion with your learners.

The idea for this RTL was contributed by Donald R. Cruickshank, The Ohio State University, Ohio.

Name _____

Following are statements about honesty. Rate each on the basis of whether you agree or disagree with it by placing a checkmark (✓) in one column after each statement. The checkmark must be in a box and not on a line.

STATEMENTS	Strongly Agree	Agree	Disagree	Strongly Disagree
1 Honesty is the best policy.				
2 No legacy is so rich as honesty.				
3 He is wise who is honest.				
4 Truth will win out.				

Give yourself:

0 points for each item checked in the Strongly Agree column,
1 point for each item checked in the Agree column,
2 points for each item checked in the Disagree column, and
3 points for each item checked in the Strongly Disagree column.

Total individual pretest score = _____

Name _____

Part A

Following are statements about honesty. Rate each on the basis of whether you agree or disagree with it by placing a checkmark (✓) in one column after each statement. The checkmark must be in a box and not on a line.

STATEMENTS	Strongly Agree	Agree	Disagree	Strongly Disagree
1 Honesty is the best policy.				
2 No legacy is so rich as honesty.				
3 He is wise who is honest.				
4 Truth will win out.				

Part B

Do you think this Reflective Teaching experience has modified your attitude toward honesty somewhat? (*check one box*)

☐ YES   ☐ NO

Part C

Give yourself:
   0 points for each item checked in the Strongly Agree column,
   1 point for each item checked in the Agree column,
   2 points for each item checked in the Disagree column, and
   3 points for each item checked in the Strongly Disagree column.

Total individual posttest score = _____

Part D

Total individual posttest score minus total individual pretest score = _____

This represents the amount of individual change. (You may have a negative number.)

When learners have completed the posttest, total the change scores (Part D, posttest) and record below.

Total learners' change	
Number of students with no change (zero change score)	
Number of students with change toward goal (postive change score)	
Number of students with change opposite goal (negative change score)	

From Part B

How many of your learners felt this experience modified their attitudes toward time? _____

Name of Designated Teacher _____

1. During the lesson, how satisfied were you as a learner? In arriving at a rating, consider the teaching methods used and how well they met your needs.

4	3	2	1
Very Satisfied	Mostly Satisfied	Somewhat Dissatisfied	Very Dissatisfied

2. What did your teacher do that contributed to your satisfaction?

3. What could your teacher have done to increase your satisfaction?

Name of Designated Teacher _____

1. During the lesson, how satisfied were you as a learner? In arriving at a rating, consider the teaching methods used and how well they met your needs.

4	3	2	1
Very Satisfied	Mostly Satisfied	Somewhat Dissatisfied	Very Dissatisfied

2. What did your teacher do that contributed to your satisfaction?

3. What could your teacher have done to increase your satisfaction?

One thing is certain, teaching is never dull! That is because each day you face different intellectually and emotionally challenging situations. We thought you might both enjoy and benefit from encountering a few of the more bothersome and frequently occurring situations that teachers report. That's why we have created Room 221: A Simulation: Solving Classroom Problems. This unit contains fourteen incidents that happen to you as a new teacher at Lincoln Park Middle School. Similar incidents occur in elementary and high schools.

The simulation begins as you visit your new school and chat with Pat Taylor, the principal. It continues as you work through all or a selection of the incidents that follow. These incidents, by the way, relate directly to various chapters in this book that deal with student diversity, learning, teaching, assessment, and so forth. They also represent the five major areas of teachers' concerns you learned about in Chapter 13: affiliation, control, parent relationships, student success, and time. The simulation provides a good opportunity to see how well you can apply what you have learned. Have fun—and good luck!

Meet the Principal

My name is Pat Taylor, and I'm principal of Lincoln Park Middle School. I'm so glad you could come in a few days before school starts. This way, you'll have a chance to become familiar with the school and the cumulative record information available for your students.

Let me tell you a few things about our community and school. As you know, we are a suburb of Capital City. Really, the city just grew to us. At one time, we were separated by farms and orchards. We're not what you would call an affluent suburb. Our income level is about average for the state, but it is a little bit lower than most nearby communities. Most of our families have blue-collar jobs, although a number own small businesses, and a few fathers and mothers are professionals.

Seventy percent of our students live with both biological parents, fifteen percent live with their mothers, and four percent with their fathers. The others live with one parent and a stepparent, with other relatives, or in foster homes. A very few live in a residential care facility for court-referred children. Most people think of this as a community of hard-working people who have high aspirations for their children. They tend to expect more than we are able to deliver. But that's all right. It's good to be challenged!

The 750 students in our grade-five-through-eight school score near average on most of the national standardized achievement tests, although they do better in reading than in mathematics. Average daily attendance is high, between 96 and 98 percent, so we must be doing something right. We think it's instruction. Our goal is to make classes so exciting that kids want to be here. Of course, attendance and tardiness are things we work at constantly. We also work at making kids proud of the school, keeping it neat and clean. I would describe Lincoln Park as orderly without being rigid, quiet without being permissive, and focused on the business of learning. In my mind we are the best school not only in the district but in the county. The kids know what is expected of them. And they do the best they can. They do their work, and they treat the school right. Generally, they're cooperative, happy, and proud they go to Lincoln Park.

You probably would like to know a little about your colleagues. There are thirty-nine teachers in Lincoln Park. Thirty are female, nine are male; four are black, or, if you prefer, African American, one is Hispanic, and another, Korean. The majority have been prepared as elementary teachers. Not many middle school teachers are prepared as such, but in our experience, these teachers do really well. In addition, we have an assistant principal, Dale Seymour; a guidance counselor, Merriam Roget; four teachers for exceptional children; a librarian; a home-school coordinator; and a nurse.

Our program reflects newer ideas in middle-level education, including such concepts as team teaching, detracking, and cooperative work. By team teaching, we mean that some teachers from different subject areas plan and sometimes teach together. For example, last year the social studies, English, music, and art teachers planned and jointly taught a unit on Colonial America. By detracking, we are moving toward more cooperative working teams, each consisting of diverse students. We also believe in invitational learning. Perhaps you've read about it in one of your textbooks. I don't want you to think that these are the answers to all education problems, but right now our faculty believes we are moving in the right direction.

One thing the teachers don't particularly like is that Lincoln Park is separated into four separate "houses." Because of the separation, some of them feel isolated from others they know and like to be with. We have several different "house" teaching arrangements. In the Orange House, which you are in, the classes all are self-contained; that is, one teacher is pretty much in charge of a group of students for the whole day. Most of our new teachers like to start this way and then move into something more challenging. Other "houses" feature team teaching, multiage grading, and block scheduling. That's when, instead of having about eight 50-minute class periods, you have three 2-hour classes every day.

Our parents are pretty satisfied with Lincoln Park School. We did a survey last year, and 87 percent said that we are meeting the children's educational needs well or extremely well. Ninety percent agree that the teachers expect the students to do their best and behave well. We understand that students are vulnerable and sensitive and that they should not be embarrassed. They should be respected.

We collect food and clothing for the needy and occasionally raise money for a worthy community cause. The teachers want students to have a strong sense of community involvement and charity toward others.

The Lincoln Park parents like the idea of having a middle school that is a mixture of both elementary and secondary grades. They see it as starting secondary school earlier but in a warm, protected environment. The students here like to think of themselves as young adults, too old for elementary school.

That's enough for now. I'll let you get on with the things you came in here to do. Dale and I will be around. Give us a nod if you need help.*

Fourteen Classroom Incidents

INCIDENT 1: SLEEPLESS IN ROOM 221

For the past hour, your students have been working in small groups on a project they seem to enjoy. However, as you monitor the activity, you notice that Ashley Smith has been somewhat lackadaisical. She has said nothing, and her head is down, resting on her arms. You make a mental note to talk with her later.

At the end of the group activity, you ask the students to return to their seats. As they move about the room, you hear loud laughter in one area. Sharon is repeating, "Wake up, Ashley—Ashley, wake up! You're

in my seat." As you approach, Ashley has a dazed look and she rubs her eyes.

Later you talk to Ashley about sleeping in class. She tells you that both her parents work a second shift and that she takes care of her younger siblings until they go to bed. Then she watches late-night television because she doesn't like to go to sleep until her parents are home.

You know Ashley can ill afford to miss any class work. She has barely passing grades and has been absent and tardy a number of times. How can you help?

Cumulative Record Information Ashley Smith lives with her mother, stepfather, and four younger school-age siblings in a blended family. Her parents work the afternoon-evening shift in a manufacturing plant. Except for weekends, the children are on their own, with Ashley as their primary supervisor. All the children have absence and tardiness problems. Ashley seems to have average academic ability, although her school achievement has been marginal. She has a slight hearing loss in both ears and has difficulty maintaining personal hygiene. Generally, her peers have little to do with her. She does not seem to have any close friends.

INCIDENT 2: ANGELO FIGHTS BACK

Angelo is a beautiful boy with dark, wavy hair, large brown eyes, and an olive complexion. The girls in class and throughout the school are very attracted to him—probably for his good looks, charm, and talent. He is also an accomplished guitarist, singer, and dancer. Angelo's appeal to the girls annoys the boys. To worsen matters, Angelo is disinterested in sports and other "masculine" activities.

This year Angelo has been the subject of considerable taunting. Occasionally, he has been pushed around. Today, when school began, a group of girls related that Angelo was beaten up on the way to school. Within 15 minutes, Angelo and his older brother enter the classroom, and the older brother shouts at one of the students, "Leave Angelo alone or else." What should you do?

Cumulative Record Information Angelo Carpanian lives with both parents and an older brother and sister. His ethnic background is Gypsy, and his family is part of an extended family living on the edge of the school community. The Carpanians own a used-car business and also operate games and rides at county fairs. They speak their own language and, in public, speak that language with their children. The Carpanians appear happy and reasonably prosperous. Angelo and his siblings have not had an easy time in school. They nor-

The description of Lincoln Park School and community was partly suggested by Lipsitz, J. (1984). *Successful schools for young adolescents* (pp. 27–58). New Brunswick, NJ, and London: Transaction Books.

mally are not permitted to mix freely with the other children, and after school they help their parents.

The girls like Angelo. He is a very handsome, thoughtful boy. He also is quite fun-loving when in their company. He plays guitar and dances.

Angelo's achievement throughout the grades has been very marginal. Mostly, he seems to have been eased upward through the grades. All his teachers agree that he is fun-loving but find him trying as a learner.

INCIDENT 3: SCHOOL IS BORING, BORING!

You really like Tom. He is good natured, laid back, has lots of friends, and never causes a problem. A perfect child? No! Tom doesn't like to learn. You find this strange for a boy who is on time and in school every day.

In school, he putters along, almost keeping up with the task at hand, but when it comes to homework or studying for exams, Tom is almost never ready. You have met with his mother on many occasions. She wants desperately to work with you and has taken all your suggestions including monitoring his efforts and withholding television until work is completed. This proves difficult because she isn't always certain what Tom must actually do; he is unclear, and she is not able to sit with Tom by the hour.

After months of this, you finally get Tom to do more than shrug his shoulders and smile when you ask what's wrong. Today he told you, "School is just plain boring." How do you react?

Cumulative Record Information   Thomas Lindgren lives with his mother, stepfather, and two younger sisters from his mother's second marriage. Tom's natural father left when he was an infant, and Tom has not seen or heard from him. Mrs. Lindgren has tried to find Tom's father in order to obtain child support. Tom has above-average ability according to standardized test results. However, his school achievement is marginal, with grades fluctuating in all subjects. Teachers describe him as an outwardly happy, friendly youngster who needs constant prodding to stay on task both with schoolwork and other responsibilities.

INCIDENT 4: MARNA, MARNA!

You had always dreaded having a student in the class who is regularly disruptive. Unfortunately, she has arrived. Marna is an attention grabber. You name it, she does it: won't stay put, calls out in class, talks constantly with those nearby, pokes others with her pen, takes things without permission, drops books, hums, won't take turns, and so on. You thought it was cruel when other teachers told you they wished one of their students—Marna—would move out of the district! Now

you are embarrassed to realize that you are beginning to feel this way, too. The students are alternately annoyed and pleased by Marna: When her actions disrupt *them*, they get angry. When her antics disrupt *you*, they laugh. You think you are becoming paranoid, but you know that your relationship with the class is generally very good. What do you do?

Cumulative Record Information   Marna Wright lives with her parents. She is an attractive girl with above-average academic ability. Throughout school, she has been cited as exhibiting immature social behavior; as early as grade 1, she has been referred to the school psychologist. The psychological reports are more descriptive than useful. They describe Marna as an only child born after her parents had been married 17 years. Both parents are very strict, and Marna presents no problem at home. When the school has contacted Marna's parents, they are chagrined to learn of her school behavior and vow to talk to her. At the same time, they have made clear that this seems to be a school problem and, to that extent, is beyond their control. On one occasion, they raised questions about the competency of Marna's teacher. Pat Taylor, your principal, has had lots of talks with Marna and feels she will eventually grow up.

INCIDENT 5: TEACHERS ARE SUPPOSED TO TEACH!

The class is working quietly on independent study assignments, and you are moving among the students monitoring their efforts, when one of Mrs. Armstrong's students enters the room announcing "Mrs. Armstrong ran out of chalk. Can she borrow some?" This interruption is the second already today and was sufficient to get the students off-task and buzzing.

A few minutes later another student appears at the door and hands you a note from Pat Taylor, the principal. "Please have all students take a recess between 10:00 and 10:30. We have a plumbing problem, and the water will be shut off after 10:30. Thanks."

At noon, you peruse the office bulletin board announcements and are reminded that student health screening will begin tomorrow, student progress cards are to have written comments this marking period, quarterly attendance forms are due, and your assignment for helping with the School Fair is to run the popcorn booth with one of the parents.

You stand there in almost a catatonic state thinking, when will I have time to plan and teach?

INCIDENT 6: HOW CAN I DO THAT?

You have been led to believe that to be a good teacher you must do three things: plan, teach, and assess students' learning. At least that's what you were taught in professional education courses. However, each of these activities takes lots of time. Where does it come from?

Of course, you must teach, and to be very good at it, you must plan. So, understandably, you devote almost all of your time and energy to these tasks. At the same time, you are feeling unprofessional because your assessment activities seem limited to making up and scoring tests. What you don't do very much is "informal assessment" such as systematic observation, use of checklists and rating scales, and collecting and evaluating the everyday work students do. You ask yourself— where will I get the time to do that?

INCIDENT 7: AM I GOOD ENOUGH?

You love teaching. Even before you decided to become a teacher, you thought a lot about the future and about the different ways you could help other people. Teaching seemed a pretty clear choice since you always liked school and enjoyed learning. However, it is becoming increasingly clear to you that some students do not share your attraction to school and learning. Some, like Tom Lindgren, find it boring and say so publicly, which doesn't help. Others are more passive and just doodle their time away, doing only what is required and giving one another sour looks—if they do anything at all. You are reminded of some popular movies and books about teachers who were great. How could you be more like them? Maybe that would make students enjoy learning more.

INCIDENT 8: TEACHING EVERY ONE

If all the students in the class were alike, it would be so much easier to teach. Unfortunately (or fortunately), they are not. The students of most concern to you are those who can't keep up. Andre Harrison is one. Today he sheepishly hands you the following note.

> Dear Teacher:
> Please excuse Andre from completing his homework. He worked very hard from the time he had supper until he went to bed. He even missed his favorite TV show. As you know, Andre is not a good reader, but he does try very hard. I know the homework wasn't too difficult, so in no way are we blaming you. We would appreciate any kind of help you can give our son.
> Yours truly,
>
> *Mrs. Alberta Harrison*

How can you individualize instruction in order to help more students learn?

INCIDENT 9: CRIME AND PUNISHMENT

One thing you hate to do is to punish students. To you, it is an admission that you haven't done something right—that you may have failed. Nevertheless, sometimes punishment is required. Pat Taylor, the principal of Lincoln Park Middle School, feels it is time to review the school's policy on discipline and punishment. All teachers have been asked to begin by writing a one-page response to the following questions:

1. Under what circumstances are discipline and punishment warranted?
2. What kinds of discipline and punishment should be allowed in our school?

What will you write?

INCIDENT 10: ATTENTION!

You are convinced that movies, MTV, computer software, and the like so dazzle students that it is difficult for teachers to compete for their attention. Certainly, from a student's point of view, school must look pretty bland and colorless—the same thing in the same way day after day. You have decided to make a list of ways to better capture and hold students' interest. What will you put on your list?

INCIDENT 11: PARENTS TO THE RESCUE

The older, more experienced teachers at Lincoln Park Middle School talk constantly of the "good old days." Frankly, you get a little tired of it, but there is probably truth in some of what they say. In fact, the entire staff is bothered by the seeming lack of parental support for school. On many occasions you have heard stories of parents who blame teachers for students' misbehavior, low grades, dislike of school, and so forth. When a child gets in trouble, more than likely the parents will find fault with the school and the teacher. Some teachers excuse this, pointing out that more parents are working longer hours, experiencing rough economic conditions, and having difficulty maintaining satisfying marriages. Accordingly, it is very difficult to get parents to help out when needed.

As a novice teacher, you want to withhold judgment. However, you do want to gain parent support. What can you do to get it?

INCIDENT 12: GETTING TO THE BOTTOM OF THINGS

Assessing students is anything but fun. It takes lots of time to do it well: hundreds of hours evaluating papers and tests, and then more time to figure out the grades for report cards. This marking period was no different, so you felt pretty good when you entered the last mark on the last report card yesterday before leaving school. Looking over your shoulder on the way out the door, you regarded the stack of cards on your desk as a major accomplishment.

Today, the day the report cards were to be distributed, they were nowhere to be found. Later, Don Parsons, a school custodian, entered the room with the cards in his rubber-gloved hand. "I found these in the urinal," he noted in a quiet voice. Several nearby students tittered. Looking back on the incident, you ask yourself—how could anyone do such a thing? What should you do?

INCIDENT 13: CATCH-22

Several of your students work pretty hard, but to little avail. They just don't get it. Although they listen and attend to each assignment, their work is often minimal or incorrect. Your heart goes out to these kids, and you are caught in a catch-22. If you give them passing grades, you are deceiving both them and yourself. If you fail them, they will likely give up. You say to yourself, there must be a solution. You decide to send home midterm failure notices. The next morning one

child's mother confronts you in the hall and demands, "Are you prejudiced against my son?" How would you react?

INCIDENT 14: SO MUCH FOR PROFESSIONALISM

You believe that teachers are professionals. It has been disheartening for you to hear and see teachers criticizing one another, making personal remarks about their students, gossiping, complaining about the principal, joking about parents, and taking sick days when they aren't sick. You vow never to go into the faculty lounge again. But you can't do that. What can you do?

ONE MORE INCIDENT: WHAT TO DO?

Recall a teacher dilemma you have witnessed. Write it down and share it with your peers.

Glossary

The following terms include selected boldfaced words and concepts defined in the text as well as some words and concepts used but not defined in the text.

academic games Instructional alternative where learners compete with each other one-to-one or team-to-team to determine which individual or group is superior at a given academic task (including spelldowns, anagrams, and so forth).

academic instruction time Actual amount of time the teacher is conducting instruction.

academic learning time (ALT) Amount of academic instruction time during which students are actively and successfully engaged in learning.

accountability The idea that teachers should be held responsible for what and how much students learn.

achievement need The need to do difficult tasks, including academic work, as well and efficiently as possible and to overcome obstacles.

achievement tests Tests that measure what a student knows in a subject area (for example, mathematics) compared to what other, like students know.

acquisition need The need to acquire knowledge or skill.

action research Process of conducting school-based research to improve teaching and learning.

action zone The triangular area, defined by imaginary lines across the front and down the middle of the classroom, where most student-teacher interaction occurs.

active listening When a teacher permits or encourages a learner to provide information or express some feeling and then paraphrases what the learner has said.

active teaching Instructional method containing five instructional phases: the opening, development, independent work, homework, and review.

activity reinforcers Special privileges given to students when they behave appropriately in order to increase the likelihood that they will repeat the behavior.

activity routines Classroom routines established to minimize problems related to such things as the location of materials and acceptable behaviors.

advance organizer A tool that prepares learners for new information to follow (for example, a video clip, an anecdote, or an illustration).

affective domain The area of learning that deals with students' feelings, interests, attitudes, appreciation; focuses on the attitudinal, emotional, and valuing goals for learners. Five subdivisions of this domain (arranged hierarchically from simple to complex) are receiving or attending, responding, valuing, organization, and characterization.

affiliation need The need to form associations and friendships with others.

allocated time Amount of mandated time intended or scheduled for academic activities.

alternative responses Part of a series of multiple-choice questions that offer possible solutions to the stem.

American Agenda Report of the Forty-first President of the United States regarding poverty and the underclass.

analysis The process of breaking down material into component parts so the material can be understood.

anecdotal comments Brief, teacher-written descriptions about students, usually found in school records.

anticipatory set An introductory activity that will capture students' attention, help them see the purpose and value of what they are to learn, and relate what they are to learn to what students already know.

applied behavioral analysis (ABA) Based on principles of operant conditioning. Teachers reward or reinforce learners when they do the right thing.

aptitude tests Tests that measure a student's general potential to learn. They provide information about students' comparative ability to deal with abstractions and to solve problems. Some aptitude tests measure the potential to learn in specific fields such as music, while others predict how well one would do generally in college.

assessment Process of collecting, synthesizing, and interpreting information to aid in decision making.

at-risk students Students most likely to experience school failure. Profiles of such students indicate that recurring at-risk factors include living with a single parent, being at home alone for long periods of time, having parent(s) with low levels of education or income, having low English language facility, and/or having a sibling who is a school dropout.

attention deficiency disorder (ADD) Disorder which prevents certain children from maintaining their attention on learning tasks.

autonomy need The need to strive for independence and freedom.

baseline Information about how often a specified student presently performs a desired behavior. Used in applied behavioral analysis.

behavior disorders Conduct disorder, anxiety-withdrawal disorder, and immaturity.

behavior modification Systematic attempt to change behavior by using rewards or adversive stimuli that are linked to those behaviors.

behavioral learning theory School of thought that attempts to explain why we behave as we do. Behaviorists are interested in finding out how external or environmental stimuli cause behavior and how behavior can be changed by modifying what happens in a learner's environment.

behaviorists Advocates of behavioral learning theory.

block plans Daily plans that clearly show the scope and sequence of a learning unit as well as general objectives, learning activities, evaluation, and resources.

brainstorming Instructional alternative where learners are asked to withhold judgment or criticism while they produce a very large number of ideas for something such as how to resolve a problem.

case study Written document that pieces together all kinds of information to obtain a more complete and articulated picture of a student.

centers of interest Classroom displays used to interest learners in themes or topics.

Chapter 1 compensatory education Federally funded program which among other things provides monies to improve student performance in reading and math.

child abuse A problem affecting many children at some time during childhood. Classifications include emotional/verbal, sexual, or physical abuse and neglect.

Children's Defense Fund Organization that advocates on behalf of America's children. Engages in research, public education, monitoring of federal agencies, litigation, child health, adolescent pregnancy prevention, child mental health, and so forth.

clarity The quality of presenting information that is clear or understandable to learners.

classical conditioning Learning that occurs when we already have an established connection (contiguity) between a stimulus and a response, and then a new stimulus is paired with the original stimulus long enough to evoke the same response when the original stimulus is absent.

classroom management Using the provisions and procedures needed to create and maintain an environment in which teaching and learning can occur.

climate Sociopsychological dimensions of the classroom including the emotional tone and the comfort level students feel with the teacher, with learning tasks, and with one another as a social group.

cognitive development Piaget suggests cognitive/intellectual development evolves through four stages: sensorimotor, preoperational, concrete operational, and formal operational. Most developmental theorists agree that all children proceed through all stages but at different rates.

cognitive domain Area of educational objectives that contains objectives related to intellectual tasks such as recalling, comprehending, applying, analyzing, synthesizing, and evaluating information.

cognitive learning theory School of thought that attempts to explain what goes on in the brain when we are learning; focuses on information processing (how we take in, store, and retrieve information) and meaningful learning (how to organize, structure, and teach information so that it might be best used).

cognitive style The consistent ways an individual responds to a wide range of perceptual learning tasks.

cognitivists Advocates of the cognitive learning theory.

cognizance need The need to explore, read, and seek knowledge.

colloquium Instructional alternative where a guest or guests are invited to class to be interviewed about their interests or activities.

completion item Type of test item which requires students to supply missing words in a statement or a short phrase that answers a question posed in a stem.

computer-assisted instruction (CAI) The use of computers to present programmed instruction or to assist learners with specific learning tasks. Most programs require learners to complete drills and practice exercises.

conceptual tempo Style of learning based on usage of time; one's conceptual tempo falls between impulsive and reflective.

concrete operational stage Piaget's third stage of intellectual development (approximately 7 to 11 years of age). Children become capable of logical thought and learn to solve specific problems and think logically about concrete experiences.

conflict resolution A method used in Teacher Effectiveness Training to encourage teachers to establish open and honest communication in the classroom in order to resolve problems.

construction need The need to organize and build.

constructivism An approach that asserts that for learners to gain deep understanding, they must actively come to know (construct) concepts for themselves.

contiguity Simple stimulus-response pairing or connection. When one stimulus is regularly associated with another, a response (S-R connection) is established. If two events occur together repeatedly they will eventually become associated, so that even if only one of the events occurs, the response will occur with it.

contracts Written agreements students and teachers enter into which describe the academic work the student is to accomplish at a particular level in a particular period of time.

contrariness need The need to act differently from others, to be novel or unconventional.

control need Teacher's need to have others behave well or appropriately.

convergent thinking Style that predisposes people to think in conventional, typical ways by encouraging them to look for a single, local answer to a given problem. Contrasts with divergent thinking.

cooperative learning Instructional procedures whereby learners work together in small groups and are usually rewarded for their collective accomplishments.

created response items Test questions which require students to develop or create a response in their own words.

criterion-referenced scores Student raw scores that are compared to a specific preestablished standard or criterion.

cue A verbal or visual signal that helps learners notice what they need to learn.

cumulative record A personal record kept for each school enrollee that contains personal information, home and family data, record of school attendance, school grades, standardized test scores, and teacher anecdotal comments.

day care programs Programs that provide child care services for children too young to attend school. Originally begun as a service to working parents, programs have expanded rapidly. Many have incorporated a child development and/or education program.

debates Formal discussions in which a few students present and contest varying points of view with regard to an issue.

deference need The need to conform and follow the lead of others; the need to admire others.

demonstrations Form of presentation whereby the teacher or learners show

how something works or operates or how to do a particular task.

development Orderly changes that occur in a person over time from conception to death. Includes physical, emotional, or cognitive changes across time.

developmental stages Erikson's comprehensive theory of emotional and social development suggests that there are eight critical stages, each leading to a positive or negative outcome—trust vs. mistrust, autonomy vs. shame and doubt, initiative vs. guilt, industry vs. inferiority, identity vs. role confusion, intimacy vs. isolation, generativity vs. stagnation, and integrity vs. despair.

dialogue journal A journal recording a running conversation that expresses thoughts, questions, and problems related to the roles, responsibilities, and practices of teaching.

direct teaching or instruction (expository teaching) An approach in which teachers control instruction by presenting information, giving directions to the class, and using criticism; associated with teacher-centered, teacher-controlled classrooms; an instructional procedure for teaching content in the most efficient, straightforward way.

discipline Actions teachers or others in the school take in response to a student who disobeys a reasonable classroom rule.

discovery learning Learning that occurs when students derive their own meaning from experiences and experiments.

discussion Occurs when students, or students and a teacher, converse back and forth to share information, ideas, or opinions, or to resolve a problem.

divergent thinking Style that predisposes a person to think in independent, flexible, and imaginative ways; often equated with creativity. Divergent thinkers can come up with different ideas for accomplishing a task or solving a problem. Contrasts with convergent thinking.

dominance need The need to lead, direct, organize, and control others.

drive The need or desire to gain something from or see some advantage in the learning experience.

dyslexia Reading impairment; often the result of genetic defect or brain injury.

economically disadvantaged children Children whose parents fall below a governmentally determined poverty line. Estimated to include 13 million children, 500,000 of whom are homeless.

Education for all Handicapped Children Act (Public Law 94-142) Law requiring that students with handicaps be placed in the least restrictive, or most normal school environment they can succeed in.

educationally disadvantaged children Children who do not perform well academically, who are more often identified as retarded, who drop out of school at a higher rate, and who are more likely to enter school with experiential defects. Such children tend to live in communities and states that spend less on education and have fewer well-paid teachers.

efficacy Having a sense of control over one's circumstances.

emotional intelligence (EQ) The ability to get along with others.

established structure The class rules and routines that effective teachers establish and enforce.

establishing set What teachers do at the beginning of a lesson to provide a context for the lesson and the instruction.

evaluation Process of making a qualitative judgment based on collected measurement data.

evaluative set The knowledge that a teacher establishes regarding what students already know about a topic.

exceptionality The special physical, social, emotional, or mental needs or gifts certain children have. Exceptional children may be considered either handicapped or gifted. Both types of children may be less than successful students unless certain adaptions are made for them.

executive planning routines Classroom routines that help a teacher to manage personal time and to fulfill the many roles of teaching, such as completing paperwork and clerical chores, grading papers, and planning.

exhibition need The need to attract a certain amount of attention to oneself; the need to amuse and excite others.

explicit instruction Teaching method whereby teachers review and check homework, present new content/skill,

guide students' practice, provide feedback and correctives, move to independent practice, and conduct regular reviews.

exposition need The need to receive attention, praise, and commendation by giving others information.

expository lesson A lesson in which the teacher presents facts, ideas, and explanations.

expository teaching (direct instruction) Occurs when teachers present information and direction to students. Teacher-centered, goal-oriented, structured approach to teaching.

extended-response items Test questions that do not place any restrictions on student responses, thus allowing greater creativity and flexibility of response.

extinction The elimination of minor misbehavior by ignoring it (as long as it is not dangerous or distracting to other students).

failure avoidance need The need to avoid embarrassment, shame, ridicule, or failure.

feedback Information teachers provide to inform students of their progress and to help them learn to monitor themselves and improve their own learning.

field dependent Cognitive style of a person who sees the larger picture but not its specifics or details. Field-dependent learners "see the forest" rather than the individual trees.

field independent Cognitive style of a person who sees the specifics or details of something but not the larger picture. Field-independent learners "see the individual trees" rather than the forest.

field observation Observations made or work carried on in a natural setting. Also referred to as fieldwork or field trips.

follow-up Phase of the questioning process where the teacher reacts to the student's response to a question.

formal interview A structured, face-to-face meeting with the explicit purpose of obtaining specific information about the interviewee's experiences, views, likes, and so forth.

formal observation Carefully planned observational efforts to obtain specific information about a target student or students.

formal operational stage Piaget's fourth stage of intellectual development, beginning at about age 11. At this level, children are more able to deal in abstractions or perform activities mentally.

formative assessment Ongoing student assessment conducted during the course of instruction.

gender roles Male/female roles learned early in life. The current tendency is to hope children acquire a gender role that combines traits traditionally thought unique to each gender.

generativity The ability to have and nurture children and/or be involved with future generations. Productivity and creativity are essential features.

Gifted and Talented Act (Public Law 95-561) Provides federal funding for gifted education.

gifted and talented children Children who possess outstanding abilities or potential in the areas of general intellectual capacity, specific academic aptitude, creative or productive thinking, leadership ability, visual or performing arts, and psychomotor ability.

grade equivalent scores Scores that describe the pupil's level of performance in comparison to pupils in a particular grade.

group alerting The process of keeping the students' attention and of holding them accountable for their behavior and learning.

handicapped or challenged children Students with special needs. May be mentally or physically challenged, emotionally disturbed, learning disabled, or have communication or behavior problems.

Head Start program Preschool program intended to counteract negative environmental effects for economically disadvantaged 3- and 4-year-old children.

higher-level cognitive skills The intellectual ability to analyze, synthesize, and evaluate information.

humanistic learning theory School of thought emphasizing the development of the learner as a psychologically healthy person. Advocates of this theory desire to make children feel better about themselves and be more accepting of others.

hyperactivity Behavior disorder characterized by abnormal amounts of movement, inattentiveness, and restlessness.

identity The organization of the individual's drives, abilities, beliefs, and history into a consistent self-image.

impulsive learning/thinking style Cognitive style of responding quickly but often inaccurately. Persons with this learning style tend to act without serious forethought and to do poorly in school tasks requiring analysis of details. (Not everyone who works fast is impulsive, however). Contrasts with reflective learning style.

independent study Any school-related assignment done more or less alone by students.

indirect teaching or instruction (learner centered instruction) Occurs when teachers provide students with experiences or information and then ask students for their observations and conclusions. Contrasts with direct instruction or expository teaching.

Individualized Educational Program (IEP) A learning program that teachers, parents, a qualified school official, and perhaps the student help develop for a student with special learning needs. It sets forth goals, services, and teaching strategies for that student. IEPs are mandated by the Education for All Handicapped Children Act.

individualized instruction Instruction that attempts to tailor teaching and learning to a learner's unique strengths and needs.

industry The discovery of pleasure in perseverance and productivity.

informal interview A face-to-face meeting that is more like casual conversation, allowing talk to flow naturally and spontaneously in more or less any direction.

informal observation Casual, unplanned observation of a student(s).

information processing Efforts to understand how we take in and store new information and how we retrieve it when it is needed.

initiative Pursuing activity for its own sake.

inquiry-oriented teaching The highly individual process of reflecting on one's teaching in order to make rational, deliberate decisions about teaching and learning.

instructional alternative Any teaching approach that can be used to facilitate student learning and satisfaction.

instructional clarity A quality of effective instruction that helps students come to a thorough and accurate understanding of the material. (See **clarity**.)

instructional objective Statement of concepts, attitudes, or skills that students are expected to achieve by the end of some period of instruction.

instructional planning Process by which someone (usually a teacher) decides how best to select and organize a learning experience to maximize both teacher and student achievement and satisfaction.

instructional routines Routines or procedures teachers regularly follow when they teach such as the formats for giving directions, monitoring student work, and questioning students.

intervention A reinforcement given to students every time they perform a desired behavior in order to encourage them to behave appropriately more often. Used in applied behavioral analysis.

intimacy Openness and commitment to others in meaningful and deep relationships.

inviolacy need The need to maintain one's self-respect.

invitational learning Occurs when teachers communicate to learners that they are "responsible, able, and valuable" people.

inviting classroom An appealing, positive place that provides a sense of physical and emotional safety for both students and the teacher.

Inviting School Success A program developed to get teachers to communicate to learners that they are "responsible, able, and valuable" people.

laboratory experiences Scaled-down teaching experiences carried out on campus, often with a small group of peers, rather than in an actual classroom setting.

latchkey children Children between about 6 and 13 years of age who do not have adult supervision for some part of the day.

latchkey programs Before- and after-school programs for children who otherwise would be without adult supervision.

learning module A self-contained package of individualized learning activities that guides students to know or to be able to do something.

learning style A consistent pattern of behavior and performance an individual uses to approach learning experiences. Includes how a person learns best; the person's learning personality; and the learner's tendency to use different sensory modes to understand experiences and to learn (visual, auditory, kinesthetic).

least restrictive environment A school setting that is as normal as possible given a child's special problems and needs. Often involves placing a child with disabilities into a regular classroom for all or part of the day. Mandated by the Education for All Handicapped Children Act.

long-term memory Seemingly limitless and permanent storage system where we keep information for a long time. Retrieval of long-term memory information is most effective when the information has been related to something we already know.

management routines Classroom routines used to organize the classroom and direct student behavior; nonacademic routines.

mandated time Formal time scheduled for school or academic activities.

mastery learning Allows students to study academic material at their own pace until they learn it. All students might be expected to reach a certain level of proficiency, and they are given time and corrective instruction until they master the material.

matching items Test questions that ask students to match items in one column with related items in another.

meaningful learning Occurs when information is effectively organized, structured, and taught so as to maximize its usefulness.

measurement Process of gathering objective, usually quantitative, information or data about student performance.

momentum The flow of activities and the pace of teaching and learning maintained in a classroom.

moral development A progressive increase in the capability for moral reasoning. Piaget suggests that moral development/reasoning evolves through two levels: morality of constraint and morality of cooperation.

moral education Akin to character education, values education, and citizenship education. Moral education is intended to help learners develop more responsible behavior both in school and out.

morality of constraint The first of two levels in Piaget's stages of moral reasoning. At this stage, children regard rules as sacred and unchangeable, and punishment as inflexible.

morality of cooperation Piaget's second stage of moral reasoning. At this stage, individuals regard rules as flexible, believe there can be exceptions to them, and believe that punishment must take into account the circumstances surrounding the misbehavior.

multiethnic education Educational practices that encourage learners to revere their roots and culture, as well as the cultures of others.

multiple-choice items Test questions that each consist of a stem which presents a problem or asks a question, followed by several alternative responses. Students are expected to select the alternative that offers the best solution to the problem or best answers the question presented in the stem.

negative reinforcement Encouraging desirable behaviors by removing or omitting an undesirable or aversive stimulus.

nonnegative affect A manner teachers have that ensures that learners feel psychologically safe and secure.

norm-referenced scores Raw scores of an individual student compared to those of other students who took the test; indicate how well a student's achievement compares with that of other students in the class, school, district, state, or nation.

normal curve Bell-shaped graph depicting the frequency with which particular scores are expected.

norming group The class-, school-, district-, statewide-, or national group of students standard scores are compared to.

nurturance need The need to help and nourish others.

observational learning Also called social learning. Occurs when learners learn by watching; in order for observational learning to be effective, learners must attend to someone's behavior, retain what they observed the "model" do, imitate or reproduce the behavior they saw, and experience reinforcement or satisfaction as a consequence.

operant conditioning Learning facilitated through reinforcement. Behaviors are strengthened or weakened depending upon the reinforcement or punishment received.

Operation Jump Start Program in which children receive an educational boost by starting their school year two weeks earlier than their classmates. As many as one-third of the nation's elementary schools participate. During this interval, teachers work with fewer than fifteen children at risk and their parents.

oral reports Instructional alternative whereby individuals or groups of learners are given or choose topics and present the researched topic to the rest of the class.

orderliness need The need to arrange, organize, and build.

orientation set A new instructional activity that engages students' attention.

overcorrection The compulsory practice of appropriate behavior as a result of undesirable behavior.

overlapping Teacher's ability to attend to more than one classroom activity or episode at a time.

parent relationships and home conditions need Teachers' need to maintain constructive relationships with parents and to be aware of the impact of home conditions on school success.

pedagogy The art and science of teaching; instruction in teaching methods.

percentile rank (PR) score Indicates what percentage of people taking the test scored at or below a given score.

perceptual modality preferences Learner's tendency to use different sensory modes to understand experiences and to learn (visual, auditory, kinesthetic). (See **learning style**.)

performance differences The way students vary with regard to school performance. Some students do well at most things, others do poorly at most things, but most students demonstrate an unevenness within a range of school activity.

physical environment Those aspects of the classroom that are concrete, easily identifiable, and exist independent of the people who inhabit the classroom.

physically challenged or impaired Having orthopedic handicaps, epilepsy, cerebral palsy, or other physical challenges.

play need The need to seek diversion, change, and relaxation.

positive expectations The desire effective teachers show for the academic progress and success of each student.

positive reinforcement Giving students praise, rewards, or a positive reaction when they choose to behave appropriately.

precision teaching Overlearning through continued practice.

preoperational, prelogical stage Piaget's second stage of intellectual development, lasting from approximately 2 to 7 years of age. Young learners at this stage develop knowledge from personal experience, explore and manipulate concrete objects, and learn the three Rs and other basic knowledge and skills. In this stage youngsters also begin to use symbols to represent ideas.

presentation Informative talk a more knowledgeable person makes to less knowledgeable persons.

proactive management Classroom management that focuses on preventing problems from arising in the classroom by eliciting student cooperation and involving students in educationally relevant activities.

probing Asking additional questions of the responding student to help expand or raise the level of the student's response.

problem Goal-response interference.

problem solving Requires learners to consider how they would attain a goal. A major goal of education is to assist learners in becoming better problem solvers. Different types of problems include well-structured problems (subject-matter-related) and ill-structured problems (life-related).

process approach An approach to instructional planning which results in a general rather than precise plan.

product approach An approach to instructional planning which results in a precise rather than a general plan.

programmed instruction (PI) Instruction whereby the material to be learned is usually presented in small parts (called frames) so students can teach themselves. Learners respond to the information; if their responses are correct, they receive positive reinforcement and the next step or frame is presented.

project method Form of individualization that allows learners to choose and work on projects and activities.

protocols Original records of some important event which learners study to try to understand the event or its consequences.

proximity Amount of space between teacher and students. Proximity can influence students' behavior and keep them alert.

psychological environment The social and emotional climate of the classroom, including the emotional tone and how students feel about the teacher, learning tasks, and one another as a social group.

psychomotor domain The area of learning that deals with students' physical abilities and skills. It includes behaviors such as handwriting, typing or keyboarding, swimming, sculpting, and so forth. According to Simpson, there are seven divisions of this domain: perception, set, guided response, mechanism, complex or overt response, adaptation, and origination.

psychosocial development Erikson's theory of development that describes the relationship between the individual's needs and the social environment. Suggests that adult personal and social characteristics are a result of the life stages in which individuals resolve various dichotomies (for example, trust vs. mistrust, autonomy vs. shame, industry vs. inferiority).

Public Law 93-247 A law defining abuse and neglect as "physical or mental injury, sexual abuse, negligent treatment, or maltreatment of a child under 18 by a person who is responsible for the child's welfare under circumstances which indicate that the child's health or welfare is harmed or threatened thereby."

Public Law 94-142 (Education of All Handicapped Children Act) Law requiring that students with handicaps be placed in the least restrictive (most normal) environment.

Public Law 95-561 (Gifted and Talented Act) Provides federal funding for gifted education.

punishment Something undesirable, painful, or discomforting that is applied to a student as a result of misbehavior and that is intended to weaken the probability that the inappropriate behavior will recur.

reactive management Classroom management that focuses on reacting to students' misbehavior.

reception learning Takes place when teachers present students with carefully organized and structured new information.

reciprocal teaching Occurs when the teaching function is slowly and systematically given over to students.

recitation Students are given information to study independently and then recite what they have learned when the teacher questions them.

recognition need The need to obtain positive attention; the need to be praised and recognized.

redirecting When teachers ask another student to answer the same question.

reflection Learning from experience through the ongoing process of critically examining and refining teaching practice. And, takes place by considering the personal, education, social, and ethical aspects of schooling.

reflective learning style Cognitive style of responding slowly, carefully, and accurately. (However, not all slow responders give accurate responses.) Contrasts with impulsive learning style.

reflective teaching A laboratory experience in a supportive environment that allows one to teach a lesson which serves as a basis for subsequent analysis and introspection.

reinforcement A principle of learning that recognizes that learners are more likely to do things when they feel good about doing them usually by receiving some reward or recognition.

reinforcement menu A list of reinforcers that are effective with a particular student or group of students.

reinforcement theory The idea that a teacher can influence student behavior by rewarding desirable behaviors and ignoring or discouraging undesirable behaviors.

reliability The quality of providing consistent measurement results over time; a measure of how well a test evaluates what it is meant to evaluate from one situation to the next.

reliability coefficients Statistical indications of the reliability of tests; range from .00 to 1.00, with zero representing no reliability and 1.00 indicating perfect reliability.

remediation Help for students who did not master the material the first time.

rephrasing When teachers restate the same question in different terms to help a student understand it.

research-based direct teaching or instruction The sequence of events followed by teachers who are more effective in bringing about student learning.

resilient children Children who are able to overcome negative circumstances and achieve successes.

restricted response items Created response test questions that set explicit parameters students are to respond within.

role confusion Having an inconsistent image of self with respect to one's drives, abilities, beliefs, and history.

role playing An activity in which learners take on the role of another person to see what it would be like to be that person.

routines Established procedures whose main function is to control and coordinate movement and events in the classroom.

rubric A matrix or table of indicators characteristic of particular levels of student performance; used to evaluate student work, usually projects or performances.

rules Authoritative directions for conduct which create an environment conducive to learning.

scheduling Changing the frequency of reinforcement based on students' behavior.

score band Range of scores that includes the student's actual score (usually at the middle of the band) and indicates how far above or below that score the student might have performed on a different day.

selected response items Test questions that require students to select or choose a correct response from a list of possible answers.

self-esteem Feelings of personal worth.

self-fulfilling prophecy When a person gets what he or she expects or achieves at the level he or she expects to reach.

self-referenced grading system When grades are determined by comparing a student's current performance with past performances. The grade is based upon improvement.

sensorimotor stage The first of Piaget's four stages of intellectual development, lasting from approximately 0 to 2 years of age. During this stage, the intellect develops primarily through the use of senses and motor activity.

set The context for the lesson and instruction to follow.

set induction Planning an introductory activity that will capture students' attention, help them see the purpose and value of what is to be learned, and relate what they are to learn to that which they already know.

short-term memory Severely limited storage system that holds only a small amount of information for merely seconds. Also referred to as working memory.

similance need The need to agree, believe, emulate, and imitate.

simulation games Specially designed competitive games that mirror some aspect of life.

simulations Experiences intended to give the appearance or have the effect of some situation in order to provide "firsthand experience" with how that situation works.

smoothness Moving students through a lesson with few interruptions.

social learning theory Also called observational learning. Its chief theorist, Bandura, states that for observational learning to be effective, learners must attend to someone's behavior, retain what they observed the "model" do, imitate or reproduce the behavior they saw, and experience reinforcement or satisfaction as a consequence.

social reinforcers Positive messages, either verbal or nonverbal, given to a student who behaves appropriately so as to increase the likelihood that the behavior will be repeated.

socioeconomic status (SES) Sociological term used to describe variations in wealth, background, and prestige of individuals in society.

sociogram Diagrammatic representation of the social relationships that exist within a group at a particular point in time; shows frequency of nomination; attractions.

sociometry Technique used to obtain information about the social acceptability of individuals within a group.

speech impairment The inability to produce effective speech because of difficulties in articulation, stuttering, or voicing.

standard deviation Indication of how widely the scores vary from the mean; small standard deviation indicates that scores do not differ greatly, most being very near the mean; large standard deviation indicates much variation in the scores.

standard scores Norm-referenced scores which report a student's performance in relation to the mean and standard deviation of the norming group.

standardized tests Tests that have controlled, consistent administration, scoring, and interpretation procedures. These tests allow a given student's score on a specific test to be compared with scores made by a very large number of similar students who have taken the same test.

standardized test score Score which shows how one student's performance compares to others.

stanine scores A nine-value scale that reports standardized test results; 5 is the midpoint or mean and each standard deviation is 2. Stanine scores are more easily interpreted than z scores and T scores because stanine scores are less precise.

stem The part of the multiple-choice question that presents a problem or asks a question.

student cooperation and accountability In direct instruction, holding students accountable for their academic work and for assisting each other and sharing materials.

student success need The need of teachers to help learners succeed both academically and socially.

succorance need The need to seek help from others.

summative assessment Assessment conducted after instruction is completed; used to make final judgments about a student's learning and to summarize a student's achievement or progress.

sustained expectations Teacher-held expectations that do not accurately reflect the student's ability. These expectations come about because some teachers stubbornly refuse to adjust their initially inaccurate expectations of students.

synthesis The ability to put component parts together in a new and different way.

T score Score scaled to the normal curve which uses 50 as the midpoint (mean) and sets each standard deviation at 10 points; all scores are positive; eliminates negative numbers and decimal places.

tangible reinforcers Concrete objects given to a student who behaves appropriately to increase the likelihood that the behavior will be repeated.

task orientation Characteristic of direct instruction that places the primary emphasis on academic learning.

teacher centrality Characteristic of direct instruction whereby teachers exert strong instructional direction and control.

Teacher Effectiveness Training (TET) Program developed to encourage teachers to establish open and honest communication in the classroom using such techniques as active listening and conflict resolution.

team teaching When teachers collaborate and jointly teach a group of students.

test blueprint Matrix that depicts the relationship between instructional objectives or topics covered, cognitive levels, and items on a test; used as a guide to developing teacher-made tests.

test sophistication The degree to which a student is comfortable and knowledgeable about how to complete tests efficiently.

theory of multiple intelligence A theory that suggests that intelligence includes many different kinds of skills and abilities.

time need The need to have sufficient time to do what needs to be done.

time on task Time when students are actively engaged in academic tasks.

time-out Removing the student from the situation and from attention and rewards in order to reduce unwanted student behavior.

transition set Information that helps students understand how new material relates to what they learned previously.

transitions Points in an instructional interaction when the context changes in some way, for example, when moving from one activity to another.

tutoring Form of individualization whereby either a teacher or a fellow student provides a learner or small group of learners with special help.

unit plan A plan for learning a major section or topic within a course. Usually learned over a period of weeks and limited to one topical area.

valence and challenge arousal Ability to engender students with curiosity and enthusiasm and get them involved in independent work.

validity The degree to which a test measures what it was intended to measure.

values clarification Methods whereby learners (1) identify how they feel or what they believe about something; (2) value that feeling or belief; and (3) if valued, act on it.

variety and challenge The ability to identify and assign independent study assignments that are different enough to be interesting and challenging enough to maintain attention.

visually impaired Having poor vision or considered educationally blind.

wait time The pause between teacher question and student response and the pause between student response and teacher reaction.

withitness The ability of a teacher to communicate to students that he or she is aware of student behavior throughout the classroom at all times, even when the teacher is not nearby or looking directly at the students.

z score Most basic type of standard score; mean is 0 and each standard deviation is 1. The larger the z score, the more the raw score differs from the mean; z scores are reported to two place values.

Visual Credits

p. 5 Ford Button, *Recess Time: The Best Cartoons from the Kappan,* Kristin Herzog (ed.), Phi Delta Kappa, Bloomington, IN, 1983, p. 79.

p. 17 Chuck Morman, *The Student Body: Great Cartoons from the Kappan,* Carol Bucheri, Terri Hampton, and Victoria Voelker (eds.), Phi Delta Kappa, Bloomington, IN, 1991, p. 81.

p. 23 Sidney Harris, *Scholarship: More Great Cartoons from the Kappan,* Kristin Herzog and Mary Miller (eds.), Phi Delta Kappa, Bloomington, IN, 1985, p. 24.

p. 57 Martha Campbell, *Scholarship: More Great Cartoons from the Kappan,* Kristin Herzog and Mary Miller (eds.), Phi Delta Kappa, Bloomington, IN, 1985, p. 90.

p. 58 Martha Campbell, *Recess Time: The Best Cartoons from the Kappan,* Kristin Herzog (ed.), Phi Delta Kappa, Bloomington, IN, 1983, p. 29.

p. 59 Martha Campbell, *Recess Time: The Best Cartoons from the Kappan,* Kristin Herzog (ed.), Phi Delta Kappa, Bloomington, IN, 1983, p. 18.

p. 70 Ford Button, *Recess Time: The Best Cartoons from the Kappan,* Kristin Herzog (ed.), Phi Delta Kappa, Bloomington, IN, 1983, p. 74.

p. 82 Randy Glasbergen, *The Student Body: Great Cartoons from the Kappan,* Carol Bucheri, Terri Hampton, and Victoria Voelker (eds.), Phi Delta Kappa, Bloomington, IN, 1991, p. 57.

p. 90 Dave Carpenter, *The Student Body: Great Cartoons from the Kappan,* Carol Bucheri, Terri Hampton, and Victoria Voelker (eds.), Phi Delta Kappa, Bloomington, IN, 1991, p. 78.

p. 128 Frank Cotham, *Recess Time: The Best Cartoons from the Kappan,* Kristin Herzog (ed.), Phi Delta Kappa, Bloomington, IN, 1983, p. 68.

p. 130 Glen Dines, *Recess Time: The Best Cartoons from the Kappan,* Kristin Herzog (ed.), Phi Delta Kappa, Bloomington, IN, 1983, p. 69.

p. 164 Kathy Cruickshank Grossart

p. 173 Kathy Cruickshank Grossart

p. 181 Kathy Cruickshank Grossart

p. 182 Glen Dines, *Recess Time: The Best Cartoons from the Kappan,* Kristin Herzog (ed.), Phi Delta Kappa, Bloomington, IN, 1983, p. 58.

p. 184 Frank Hauser, Jr., *The Student Body: Great Cartoons from the Kappan,* Carol Bucheri, Terri Hampton, and Victoria Voelker (eds.), Phi Delta Kappa, Bloomington, IN, 1991, p. 3.

p. 193 Fred Thomas, *The Student Body: Great Cartoons from the Kappan,* Carol Bucheri, Terri Hampton, and Victoria Voelker (eds.), Phi Delta Kappa, Bloomington, IN, 1991, p. 105.

p. 192 Frank Cotham, *Recess Time: The Best Cartoons from the Kappan,* Kristin Herzog (ed.), Phi Delta Kappa, Bloomington, IN, 1983, p. 55.

p. 206 Kathy Cruickshank Grossart

p. 216 Kathy Cruickshank Grossart

p. 218 Fred Thomas, (1995, December). PHI DELTA KAPPAN, Vol 4, No. 1, page 315.

p. 225 Bo Brown, (1995, Setember), PHI DELTA KAPPAN, Vol. 77, No. 1, page 61.

p. 225 Kathy Cruickshank Grossart

p. 235 Kathy Cruickshank Grossart

p. 255 Fred Thomas, *The Student Body: Great Cartoons from the Kappan,* Carol Bucheri, Terri Hampton, and Victoria Voelker (eds.), Phi Delta Kappa, Bloomington, IN, 1991, p. 55.

p. 260 Dave Carpenter, *The Student Body: Great Cartoons from the Kappan,* Carol Bucheri, Terri Hampton, and Victoria Voelker (eds.), Phi Delta Kappa, Bloomington, IN, 1991, p. 64.

p. 266 Bo Brown, *The Student Body: Great Cartoons from the Kappan,* Carol Bucheri, Terri Hampton, and Victoria Voelker (eds.), Phi Delta Kappa, Bloomington, IN, 1991, p. 36.

p. 275 Randy Glasbergen, *The Student Body: Great Cartoons from the Kappan,* Carol Bucheri, Terri Hampton, and Victoria Voelker (eds.), Phi Delta Kappa, Bloomington, IN, 1991, p. 22.

p. 280 Art Bouthillier, *The Student Body: Great Cartoons from the Kappan,* Carol Bucheri, Terri Hampton, and Victoria Voelker (eds.), Phi Delta Kappa, Bloomington, IN, 1991, p. 53.

p. 313 Francis H. Brummer, *The Student Body: Great Cartoons from the Kappan,* Carol Bucheri, Terri Hampton, and Victoria Voelker (eds.), Phi Delta Kappa, Bloomington, IN, 1991, p. 104.

p. 316 Art Bouthillier, *The Student Body: Great Cartoons from the Kappan,* Carol Bucheri, Terri Hampton, and Victoria Voelker (eds.), Phi Delta Kappa, Bloomington, IN, 1991, p. 115.

p. 322 Art Bouthillier, *The Student Body: Great Cartoons from the Kappan,* Carol Bucheri, Terri Hampton, and Victoria Voelker (eds.), Phi Delta Kappa, Bloomington, IN, 1991, p. 85.

p. 332 James Estes, *The Student Body: Great Cartoons from the Kappan,* Carol Bucheri, Terri Hampton, and Victoria Voelker (eds.), Phi Delta Kappa, Bloomington, IN, 1991, p. 12.

p. 334 Martha Campbell, *The Student Body: Great Cartoons from the Kappan,* Carol Bucheri, Terri Hampton, and Victoria Voelker (eds.), Phi Delta Kappa, Bloomington, IN, 1991, p. 9.

p. 343 Frank Cotham, *The Student Body: Great Cartoons from the Kappan,* Carol Bucheri, Terri Hampton, and Victoria Voelker (eds.), Phi Delta Kappa, Bloomington, IN, 1991, p. 68.

p. 383 George Abbott, *The Kappan,* vol. 74, no. 2, October 1992, p. 171.

Visual Credits

Name Index

Van Ments, M., 174, 179
Vaughan, P., 364
Viadero, D., 72
Voekl, K. E., 11

Wahlstrom, M., 260
Walberg, H. J., 21, 44, 71, 72, 73, 186,
    242, 308, 310, 314, 316, 320, 329,
    333, 336, 341, 349, 351, 363, 364,
    366, 368
Waldop, J., 17
Walker, D., 295, 296
Wallace, J., 299
Wallis, C., 43, 44
Walters, R. H., 388
Wang, M. C., 28, 310, 316, 329, 341, 363,
    366, 368
Ward, S. H., 385
Ware, J., 331
Watson, B., 63
Watson, D. G., 190
Watson, K., 179
Watson, M., 207

Waxman, H., 330
Webb, N. W., 215
Weil, M. L., 216, 218, 222, 224, 225
Weinfeld, F., 308
Weinstein, C. S., 364, 365, 366, 405
Weinstein, R., 314
Weisman, J., 25
Weissberg, R., 42
Weldman, C., 372, 375
Wellington, B., 295, 298
Wenglinsky, H., 11
Werner, E. E., 21, 27, 28
Wheldall, K., 364
White, K. A., 366
White, M. A., 385
White, R., 363
Whitmore, J. K., 21, 39
Wiggins, G., 259
Wilcox, R. T., 62
Wilen, W., 165, 338
Wiley, D., 333
Williams, C. R., 240
Williams, E. J., 297, 301, 346
Williams, R., 331

Willis, S., 35, 132, 258
Wilson, S. M., 293
Winfield, L. F., 28
Wingert, P., 25
Witkin, H. A., 40
Wittebols, J. H., 11
Wittrock, M. C., 55, 223, 350, 351
Wolfgang, C. H., 361, 372, 383, 384, 387
Wood, A., 308
Woolfolk, A. E., 40, 380, 381
Worsham, M. E., 374
Wynn, R., 35

Yinger, R. J., 153, 372, 373
York, R., 308

Zahorik, J. A., 8, 349
Zeichner, K. M., 296
Zheng, J., 81
Zimiles, H., 29
Zins, J., 42
Zlotnick, M., 321

Subject Index

enthusiasm of, 310
establishing set, 330–331
expectations for success, 314–316
feedback to students, 349–350
flexibility/adaptability of, 320–321
and instructional clarity, 345–348
instructional time, use of, 333–338
knowledge of subject matter, 321
monitoring of students, 348–349
questions, use of, 338–345
reinforcement of student behaviors, 350–351
research on, 307–309
supportiveness/encouragement of students, 316–318
variety in teaching, 331–333
warmth and humor, 310–312
Efficacy, meaning of, 33
Emotional intelligence, 42
Encouragement, of effective teachers, 316–318
Enthusiasm
characteristics of, 311
and effective teacher, 310
Equality of Educational Opportunity study, 308
Erikson's stages, psychosocial development, 36
Evaluation, student judgments, 135, 140
Evaluative set, 330
Exceptional children, 38–39
challenged children, 38–39
gifted children, 39
Executive planning routines, 374
Experience level, influences on teacher, 4–5
Experience units, 145
Explicit teaching, 225–226
Expository lesson, 59
Expository teaching, 167
versus discovery learning, 216
meaning of, 7
Extended response test items, 265–266
Extinction, 384

Family
changes/trends related to, 19
influence on schooling, 20–22
Feedback, 349–350
effective feedback, aspects of, 350
purpose of, 349
Field trips, 192
Field-dependence/field-independence, learner characteristics, 40
Fieldwork, 192
Fixed percentage system, 281
Flexibility
of effective teachers, 320–321
and lesson planning, 152
Flexible distribution system, 281–282

Formal curriculum, 133–134
Formal interviews, 86
Formal observation, 85
Formal operational stage, 37
Formative assessment, 257

Gender differences, 35–36
cognitive abilities, 35
communication/language, 36
and teacher feedback, 36
Gender, of teacher, 4
Gender roles, learning of, 35
Gifted and Talented Act of 1978, 39
Gifted students, 39
characteristics of, 39
Grade equivalent (GE) scores, 83, 263
Grading, 279–285
and comparisons of students, 281–282
components of grades, 280
criterion-referenced grading, 282
norm-referenced grading, 281–282
self-referenced grading, 282–283
standards used, 280–283
teacher anxiety about, 279
Group alerting, classroom management, 377–378
Guided response, 136, 140

Handicapped students. *See* Challenged students
Handouts, 167
Head Start, 33
Home of student, condition of, 405–406
Homeless children, 33
Human relationships programs, 34
Humanistic theory, 65–68
basic principles in, 66–67
humanistic teaching approaches, 67–68
Humor, and effective teacher, 310–312
Hurried children, 28–29

Impulsive students, 40–41
Inclusion, 38
Independent study, 181–189, 192
characteristics of, 183
closure, 186
context of, 183
criteria for good leaders/good study, 186
definition of, 181
delivery, 185
effective, criteria for, 187
preparation, 185
pros/cons of, 187–188
purposes of, 181–182
role of teacher, 183
teacher abilities related to, 184
time for use, 188–189

Indirect teaching, meaning of, 7
Individual Education Program (IEP), 38–39, 128, 234, 242
Individualized discussion, 192
Individualized instruction, 234–243
characteristics of, 235
computer-assisted instruction (CAI), 238
contracts in, 237
criteria for good program, 240
Dalton plan, 237
definition of, 234–235
distance education, 239
individually guided education (IGE), 238
individually prescribed instruction (IPI), 238
instructional goals, 235
learning activities, 235
programmed instruction (PI), 238
Project Method, 239
pros/cons of, 240–242
purpose of, 235
research findings on, 242
resource materials in, 236
and student mastery level, 236
teacher role in, 240
time factors, 236
time for use, 242
tutoring, 238–239
Winnetka plan, 237–238
Individually guided education (IGE), 238
Individually prescribed instruction (IPI), 238
Individuals with Disabilities Education Act (Public Law 101-476), 128, 234, 242
Influences on teachers
class size, 10–11
classroom environment, 11
materials/equipment, 11
objectives, 11
personal characteristics, 3–6
schooling experiences of teacher, 6–8
teaching theories, 12–13
time limits, 11
Informal interviews, 86
Information about students
case studies, 90–91
cumulative records, 82–84
evaluation of, 91–94
from interviews with students, 85–86
from observation of students, 84–85
parents/guardians as sources, 89–90
questionnaires, 86–87
sociometry, 87–89
Information observation, 85
Information processing theory, 56–59
attention, 57
memory, 56–59
Inquiry-oriented teaching, reflective practice as, 295

Observational assessment, 274–277
  checklists in, 275–276
  rating scales in, 276–277
  requirements of, 274–275
  rubrics, 277–278
Observational learning, 69–70
Operant conditioning, 69
Operation Jump Start, 27
Oral reports, 192
Organization, 136, 140
Orientation set, 330
Origination, 137
Overcorrection, 385–386
Overlapping, classroom management,
    376–377

Parent involvement, 404–407
  home conditions, teacher effect on,
      405–406
  importance of, 22
  learning about students from, 89–90
Pedagogical preparation, influences on
    teachers, 8–9
Pencil-and-paper tests, 264–274
  administration of, 273–274
  completion items, 271–272
  created response items, 264–267
  extended response items, 265–266
  matching items, 269–270
  multiple-choice tests, 268–269
  restricted response items, 265
  selected response items, 264, 267–272
  test blueprint, 272–273
  true-false items, 270
  validity/reliability, 272
Percentile rank (PR), 262–263
Personality needs, types of, 169–170
Personality of teacher, 5–6
  See also Effective teachers
Piaget's theory
  cognitive development, 37
  moral development, 37–38
Plan books, 128
Population (American)
  age distribution, 18
  changes, implications for teachers, 18
  diversity of, 18
  geographic distribution of, 18
  growth of, 17–18
Portfolio assessment, 277–279
Positive expectations, 225
Positive reinforcement, 378
Poverty, 33–34
  advocacy groups for children, 33
  homeless children, 33
  prevalence of, 24, 33
  risk factors for children, 21, 24, 400
  teaching interventions for children,
      33–34

Precision teaching, 72
Preoperational, prelogical stage, 37
Presentations, 163–171, 192
  characteristics of, 164
  closure, 168–169
  concept presentation, 167
  definition of, 164
  delivery, 166–167, 169
  effective presentation, criteria for, 171
  good presenters, characteristics of,
      165, 169
  handouts, 167
  and personality needs, 169–170
  preparation for, 165–166, 169
  pros/cons of, 168, 170
  purpose of, 164
  as reception learning, 163
  time for lectures, 171
  and visual aids, 166
Probing, questioning students, 343–344
Problem solving by students, 64–65, 192
  teaching strategies, 65
Problem solving by teachers, 410–413
  and positive attitude, 413
  problem-solving approach (PSA),
      411–412
Problems
  definition of, 399
  sources of, 400–401
  types of, 64
Problems of teachers
  affiliation, 401–402
  control, 403–404
  prevention of, 410
  relationships with parents, 404–407
  student success problems, 407–408
  and teacher personality, 409–410
  time constraints, 408–409
Problem-solving approach (PSA), 411–412
  stages/steps in, 411–412
Process approach, instructional
    planning, 130
Process questions, 340
Product approach, instructional
    planning, 130
Programmed instruction (PI), 71,
    193, 238
Project 2061, 133
Project method, 193, 239
Protocols, 193
Proximity, classroom management,
    377–378
Psychological environment, of classroom,
    363–370
Psychomotor domain, levels of,
    136–137, 140
Psychomotor outcome, 12
Psyhosocial development, 36–37
  Erikson's stages, 36
  facilitation of, 36–37

Punishment, 387–388
  criticisms of, 387
  definition of, 387
  guidelines for use, 387–388, 404

Questioning students, 338–345
  benefits of, 338
  effective questions, elements of, 338–340
  follow-up on responses, 342–345
  and presentations, 168
  probing, 343–344
  redirecting, 344
  rephrasing, 345
  tips for, 340
  types of questions, 339–340
  wait time and answer, 341–342
Questionnaires, 86–87
  types of questions, 86–87

Rating scales, in observational assessment,
    276–277
Reception learning, 59–60, 163
  characteristics of, 60
  versus discovery learning, 216
  principles of, 59–60
Reciprocal teaching, 60–61
  characteristics of, 60–61
Recitation, 193
  compared to discussions, 172
Redirecting, questioning students, 344
Reflection of teacher
  action research, 300
  benefits of, 296–298
  characteristics of, 294–295
  dialogue journals for, 299
  discussions in, 299–300
  as inquiry-oriented teaching, 295
  laboratory experiences, 300–301
  meaning of, 293
  See also Reflective Teaching program
Reflective students, 40
Reflective Teaching program, 301
Reinforcement, 350–351, 378–381
  activity reinforcers, 379
  criticism of use, 381
  effectiveness of, 351
  forms of, 332–333, 351
  guidelines for use, 378–379
  and lesson planning, 152
  positive reinforcement, 378
  purpose of, 350
  reinforcement menu, 380
  schedules of reinforcement, 380–381
  social reinforcers, 379
  tangible reinforcers, 379–380
  tips for use, 351
Reliability coefficients, 257
Reliability of test, 256–257, 272